HOLMAN
BIBLE
Concordance

3,000 Key Words from the KJV Bible
with References to the Passages
Where They Occur

HOLMAN BIBLE PUBLISHERS
NASHVILLE

U. S. Library of Congress Cataloging in Publication Data

Hooper, Jerry L.
   Holman Bible concordance.

   Includes index.
   1. Bible—Concordances, English. I. Title.
BS425.H63   220.2   79-186
ISBN-0-87981-093-9 (pbk.)

CONCORDANCE
TO THE HOLY SCRIPTURES

A handy listing of the chief words of the King James Version text of the Bible in the order of their appearance in the Old and New Testaments. The approximately 3,000 entries appear in boldface type on separate lines, followed by explanations of their meaning. Below this appear the principal references of each entry with book, chapter and verse and identifying phrase. When various forms of a given word are included the abbreviated word is followed by a suffix. Thus, under **abhor** the word abhorred appears as **a-ed**.

Abase—*humble, bring low, humiliate*
  Ezek. 21:26, **a** him that is high
  Dan. 4:37, walk in pride . . . able to **a**
  Matt. 23:12, whosoever exalteth . . . **a-th**
  Phil. 4:12, I know . . . how to be **a-ed**
Abated—*subsided, lessened*
  Gen. 8:3, the waters were **a**
  Lev. 27:18, **a** from thy estimation
  Deut. 34:7, nor his natural force **a**
  Judg. 8:3, their anger was **a** toward him
Abba—*(Aramaic for father)*
  Mark 14:36, and he said, **A**, Father
  Rom. 8:15, whereby we cry, **A**, Father
  Gal. 4:6, crying, **A**, Father
Abhor—*hate, despise*
  Ex. 5:21, made our savour to be **a-ed**
  Deut. 7:26, shalt utterly **a** it
  Job 19:19, my inward friends **a-ed** me
  Ps. 78:59, greatly **a-ed** Israel
  119:163, I hate and **a** lying
  Prov. 24:24, nations shall **a** him
  Is. 7:16, land that thou **a-est**
  49:7, whom the nation **a-eth**
  Ezek. 16:25, made thy beauty to be **a-ed**

Amos 6:8, I **a** the excellency of Jacob
  Rom. 12:9, **a** that which is evil
Abide—*continue steadfastly, await*
  Ex. 16:29, **a** ye every man in his place
  Num. 31:19, **a** without the camp seven
  Ruth 2:8, **a** here fast by my maidens
  1 Sam. 5:7, ark . . . shall not **a** with us
  22:23, **A** thou with me, fear not
  Ps. 15:1, shall **a** in thy tabernacle
  91:1, shall **a** under the shadow
  Prov. 15:31, reproof . . . **a-eth** among the
  Eccles. 1:4, the earth **a-eth** forever
  Jer. 49:18, no man shall **a** there
  Hos. 3:3, Thou shalt **a** for me many days
  Joel 2:11, day of the Lord . . . who can **a**
  Mal. 3:2, **a** the day of his coming
  Luke 2:8, shepherds **a-ing** in the field
  19:5, I must **a** at thy house
  24:29, **a** with us
  John 3:36, wrath of God **a-eth** on him
  5:38, ye have not his word **a-ing**
  8:35, the Son **a-eth** forever
  14:16, Comforter, that he may **a**
  15:4, **A** in me, and I in you

1

Abide *(Continued)*
  1 Cor. 3:14, if any man's work **a**
    7:18, they **a** even as I
    13:13, **a**-eth faith, hope, charity
  1 Pet. 1:23, liveth and **a**-eth forever
Ability—*power, strength*
  Ezra 2:69, gave after their **a**
  Dan. 1:4, had **a** in them to stand
  Matt. 25:15, according to his several **a**
  Acts 11:29, man according to his **a**
  1 Pet. 4:11, of the **a** which God giveth
Abjects—*outcasts*
  Ps. 35:15, **a** gathered . . . together
Able—*fit, qualified, competent*
  Gen. 13:6, land was not **a** to bear
  Deut. 16:17, man shall give as he is **a**
  Josh. 23:9, no man hath been **a** to stand
  1 Sam. 6:20, who is **a** to stand before
  1 Kin. 3:9, who is **a** to judge
  2 Chr. 2:6, who is **a** to build
  Job 41:10, who . . . is **a** to stand before
  Prov. 27:4, **a** to stand before envy
  Matt. 3:9, God is **a** of these stones
    9:28, believe ye that I am **a**
    10:28, which is **a** to destroy
    20:22, **a** to drink of the cup
  Luke 12:26, not **a** to do . . . least
    14:31, be **a** with ten thousand
  John 10:29, no man is **a** to pluck them
  Acts 6:10, not **a** to resist the wisdom
  Rom. 8:39, **a** to separate us from love
  1 Cor. 10:13, above that ye are **a**
  2 Cor. 3:6, made us **a** ministers
  Eph. 3:18, **a** to comprehend
  Phil. 3:21, **a** even to subdue all
  2 Tim. 2:2, **a** to teach others also
  James 4:12, **a** to save and to destroy
  Jude 24, **a** to keep you from falling
  Rev. 5:3, **a** to open the book
    6:17, who shall be **a** to stand
Aboard—*on a ship*
  Acts 21:2, we went **a**, and set forth
Abode—*place of residence*
  Gen. 49:24, his bow **a** in strength
  Ex. 24:16, glory of the Lord **a**
  Deut. 9:9, **a** in the mount forty days
  Judg. 21:2, **a** there till even before God
  2 Kin. 19:27, But I know thy **a**
  Luke 1:56, Mary **a** with her
  John 1:32, it **a** upon him
    39, and **a** with him that day
    8:44, **a** not in the truth
    14:23, make our **a** with him
  Acts 18:3, he **a** with them

Abolished—*did away with, put an end to*
  Ezek. 6:6, your works may be **a**
  2 Cor. 3:13, end of that which is **a**
  Eph. 2:15, **a** in his flesh the enmity
  2 Tim. 1:10, who hath **a** death
Abominable—*loathesome, detestable*
  Deut. 14:3, not eat any **a** thing
  Job 15:16, How much more **a** . . . is man
  Ps. 14:1, have done **a** works
    53:1, done **a** iniquity
  Is. 14:19, cast out . . . like an **a** branch
    65:4, which eat . . . of **a** things
  Jer. 44:4, this **a** thing that I hate
  Mic. 6:10, scant measure that is **a**
  1 Pet. 4:3, walked in . . . **a** idolatries
  Rev. 21:8, fearful . . . **a** . . . murderers
Abomination—*something to be loathed*
  Gen. 46:34, shepherd is an **a**
  Ex. 8:26, the **a** of the Egyptians
  Lev. 18:26, not commit any of these **a**-s
  Deut. 7:26, bring an **a** into thine house
    29:17, their **a**-s, and their idols
  1 Sam. 13:4, Israel also was had in **a**
  Ps. 88:8, hast made me an **a**
  Prov. 3:32, froward is **a** to the Lord
    8:7, wickedness is an **a**
  Is. 66:17, swine's flesh, and the **a**
  Jer. 4:1, put away thine **a**-s
  Ezek. 33:29, because of all their **a**-s
  Dan. 12:11, **a** that maketh desolate
  Luke 16:15, is **a** in the sight of God
  Rev. 17:5, mother of harlots and **a**-s
Abound—*to have in abundance*
  Prov. 28:20, faithful man shall **a**
  Rom. 15:13, that ye may **a** in hope
  1 Cor. 15:58, **a**-ing in the work of the
  2 Cor. 1:5, sufferings of Christ **a** in us
  Phil. 4:12, abased, and . . . how to **a**
  1 Thess. 4:1, **a** more and more
Above—*overhead, higher, heaven*
  Gen. 3:14, cursed **a** all cattle
  Ex. 20:4, that is in heaven **a**
  Ps. 8:1, glory **a** the heavens
  Matt. 10:24, disciple is not **a** his
  John 3:31, cometh from **a** is **a** all
    8:23, I am from **a**
  Eph. 4:6, God and Father . . . **a** all
  Phil. 2:9, **a** name . . . **a** every name
  Col. 3:1, seek those things which are **a**
  2 Thess. 2:4, **a** all that is called God
  James 1:17, every perfect gift is from **a**
Absent—*not present, away*
  Gen. 31:49, we are **a** one from another
  1 Cor. 5:3, **a** in body, but present

2

2 Cor. 5:6, a from the Lord
2 Cor. 5:8, a from the body
    10:1, a am bold toward you
Abstain—*cease or refrain from*
Acts 15:20, a from pollutions
1 Thess. 5:22, a from all appearance
1 Tim. 4:3, a from meats
1 Pet. 2:11, a from fleshly lusts
Abundance—*plenty, great quantity*
Deut. 28:47, for the a of all things
1 Kin. 18:41, sound of a of rain
Neh. 9:25, fruit trees in a
Ps. 52:7, trusted in the a of his riches
    72:7, and a of peace so long
Eccles. 5:10, a with increase
    12, a of the rich will not
Ezek. 16:49, and a of idleness
Matt. 12:34, out of the a of the heart
    13:12, he shall have more a
Mark 12:44, did cast in of their a
Luke 12:15, life consisteth not in the a
Rom. 5:17, receive a of grace
2 Cor. 12:7, the a of the revelations
Rev. 18:3, the a of her delicacies
Abundant—*affording plentiful supply*
Ex. 34:6, a in goodness and truth
Job 36:28, drop and distil upon man a-ly
2 Cor. 7:15, affection is more a
Accept—*approve*
Deut. 33:11, a the work of his hands
Job 13:8, will ye a his person
Prov. 18:5, not good to a the wicked
Luke 4:24, no prophet is a-ed
Rom. 15:31, be a-ed of the saints
2 Cor. 5:9, we may be a-ed of him
    6:2, now is the a-ed time
1 Tim. 1:15, worthy of all a-ation
Acceptable—*fit to be received*
Ps. 69:13, an a time
Is. 61:2, proclaim the a year
Eph. 5:10, proving what is a
Phil. 4:18, a sacrifice a
1 Tim. 2:3, this is good and a
Access—*approach, admittance*
Rom. 5:2, we have a by faith
Eph. 2:18, we both have a by one Spirit
    3:12, we have boldness and a
Accomplished—*achieved, realized*
Prov. 13:19, the desire a is sweet
Is. 40:2, her warfare is a
Luke 1:23, of his ministration were a
    12:50, straitened till it be a

John 19:28, all things are now a
1 Pet. 5:9, afflictions are a
Accord—*harmony, agreement*
Josh. 9:2, to fight . . . with one a
Acts 1:14, continued with one a
    8:6, with one a gave heed
Phil. 2:2, being of one a, of one mind
According—*agreeably to, just as*
Gen. 30:34, be a to thy word
Ex. 12:25, a as he hath promised
Job 34:11; Jer. 17:10, a to his ways
Matt. 16:27; Rom. 2:6, a to his works
John 7:24, a to the appearance
    18:31, judge him a to your law
Rom. 8:28, called a to his purpose
    12:6, differing a to the grace
    16:25, a to my gospel·
2 Cor. 8:12, a to that a man hath
Gal. 3:29, a to the promise
Accursed—*doomed to, deserving*
Josh. 6:18, keep yourselves from the a
Is. 65:20, the sinner . . . shall be a
Rom. 9:3, myself were a from Christ
1 Cor. 12:3, no man . . . calleth Jesus a
Gal. 1:8, let him be a
Accusation—*charge of misconduct*
Matt. 27:37, over his head his a
Luke 19:8, any man by false a
John 18:29, What a bring ye against
2 Pet. 2:11; Jude 9, railing a
Accuse—*charge with error or crime*
Prov. 30:10, A not a servant
Matt. 27:12, a-d of the chief priests
John 5:45, I will a you to the Father
Acts 22:30, was a-d of the Jews
Titus 1:6, children not a-d of riot
Acknowledge—*admit, confess*
Ps. 32:5, I a-d my sin
    51:3, I a my transgressions
Prov. 3:6, In all thy ways a him
Jer. 14:20, We a, O Lord, our wickedness
2 Cor. 1:13, a even to the end
1 John 2:33, he that a-th the Son
Acquaint—*become familiar*
Job 22:21, a now thyself with him
Ps. 139:3, a-ed with all my ways
Acquaintance—*intimate, friend*
Job 19:13, mine a are . . . estranged
Ps. 31:11, a fear to mine a
    55:13, my guide, and mine a
Luke 2:44, their kinfolk and a
Acquit—*clear, declare innocent*
Job 10:14, not a me from mine iniquity
Nah. 1:3, not at all a the wicked

3

Acre—*an indefinite area of land*
1 Sam. 14:14, an half a of land
Is. 5:10, ten a-s of vineyard
Actions—*deeds, works*
1 Sam. 2:3, by him a are weighed
Adamant—*diamond hard*
Ezek. 3:9, a harder than flint
Zech. 7:12, hearts as an a stone
Add—*enlarge, increase*
Gen. 30:24, a to me another son
Deut. 4:2, not a unto the word
1 Kin. 12:11, a to your yoke
Ps. 69:27, a iniquity unto their
Is. 30:1, a sin to sin
Matt. 6:27, can a one cubit
Luke 12:31, shall be a-ed unto you
Gal. 3:15, no man disannulleth, or a-eth
2 Pet. 1:5, a to your faith virtue
Rev. 22:18, any man . . . a unto these
Adder—*a poisonous snake*
Gen. 49:17, an a in the path
Ps. 58:4, are like the deaf a
91:13, tread upon the lion and a
Prov. 23:32, stingeth like an a
Adjure—*solemnly charge, command*
1 Sam. 14:24, Saul had a-ed the people
1 Kin. 22:16, many times shall I a thee
Matt. 26:63, I a thee by the living God
Mark 5:7, I a thee . . . torment me not
Acts 19:13, We a you by Jesus
Administered—*managed, directed*
2 Cor. 8:19, 20, which is a by us to the
Administration—*management*
1 Cor. 12:5, are differences of a-s
2 Cor. 9:12, For the a of this service
Admiration—*approval, wonder*
Jude 16, having men's persons in a
Rev. 17:6, wondered with great a
Admonish—*caution, warn*
Eccles. 12:12, by these, my son, be a-ed
Acts 27:9, Paul a-ed them
Rom. 15:14, a one another
Col. 3:16, a-ing one another in psalms
2 Thess. 3:15, a him as a brother
Heb. 8:5, Moses was a-ed of God
Admonition—*gentle reproof*
1 Cor. 10:11, written for our a
Eph. 6:4, in the nurture and a
Titus 3:10, first and second a reject
Adoption—*acceptance, choice*
Rom. 8:15, received the spirit of a
23, waiting for the a
9:4, pertaineth the a

Gal. 4:5, receive the a of sons
Eph. 1:5, predestinated as unto the a
Adorn—*beautify, decorate*
Is. 61:10, as a bride a-eth herself
Luke 21:5, a-ed with goodly stones
1 Tim. 2:9, women a themselves in
1 Pet. 3:3, a-ing . . . outward a-ing
Rev. 21:2, bride a-ed for her husband
Adulterer—*an impure person*
Lev. 20:10, a . . . surely be put to death
Ps. 50:18, partaker with a-s
Heb. 13:4, a-s God will judge
James 4:4, a-s and adulteresses
Adultery—*impurity, unchastity*
Ex. 20:14, Thou shalt not commit a
Deut. 5:18, Neither . . . commit a
Matt. 5:28, committed a with her
Luke 18:20, Do not commit a
James 2:11, Do not commit a
2 Pet. 2:14, Having eyes full of a
Advanced—*moved forward*
1 Sam. 12:6, a Moses and Aaron
Esther 5:11, a him above the princes
Advantage—*benefit, mastery*
Luke 9:25, what is a man a-d
Rom. 3:1, a then hath the Jew
2 Cor. 2:11, Satan should get an a
Adversary—*opponent, enemy*
Ex. 23:22, an a unto thine a-ies
1 Kin. 11:14, Lord stirred up an a
Is. 50:8, who is mine a
Matt. 5:25, Agree with thine a
Luke 18:3, avenge me of mine a
1 Cor. 16:9, and there are many a-ies
Phil. 1:28, terrified by your a-ies
Heb. 10:27, shall devour the a-ies
1 Pet. 5:8, because your a the devil
Adversity—*distress, affliction*
2 Sam. 4:9, my soul out of all a
Prov. 17:17, brother is born for a
24:10, faint in the day of a
Is. 30:20, give you the bread of a
Heb. 13:3, them which suffer a
Advertise—*inform, make known*
Num. 24:14, a thee what this people
Ruth 4:4, And I thought to a thee
Advice—*recommendation, counsel*
Judg. 19:30, consider of it, take a
1 Sam. 25:33, blessed be thy a
2 Chr. 10:9, What a give ye
Prov. 20:18, with good a make war
2 Cor. 8:10, herein I give my a

4

Advise—*give counsel*
　1 Kin. 12:6, How do ye a
　Prov. 13:10, the well a-d is wisdom
　Acts 27:12, more part a-d to depart
Advocate—*intercessor*
　1 John 2:1, a with the father, Jesus
Afar—*at a great distance*
　Gen. 22:4, saw the place a off
　Jer. 23:23, and not a God a off
　Matt. 26:58, Peter followed him a off
　Eph. 2:17, peace to you which were a off
Affairs—*concerns, business*
　Ps. 112:5, he will guide his a
　Eph. 6:22, ye might know our a
　2 Tim. 2:4, entangleth . . . with the a
Affect—*influence*
　Lam. 3:51, Mine eye a-eth mine heart
　Acts 14:2, made their minds evil a-ed
　Gal. 4:18, zealously a-ed always
Affection—*attachment, fondness*
　Rom. 1:26, gave them up unto vile a-s
　　　31, without natural a
　　　12:10, kindly a-ed one to another
　Col. 3:2, Set your a on things above
　　　5, inordinate a
　1 Thess. 2:8, a-ately desirous of you
　2 Tim. 3:3, Without natural a
Affinity—*relationship*
　1 Kin. 3:1, Solomon made a with Pharaoh
　2 Chr. 18:1, joined a with Ahab
　Ezra 9:14, join in a with the people
Affirm—*declare positively*
　Acts 25:19, whom Paul a-ed to be alive
　1 Tim. 1:7, nor whereof they a
　Titus 3:8, will that thou a constantly
Afflict—*to trouble, distress, hurt*
　Gen. 15:13, a them four hundred years
　Num. 11:11, wherefore hast thou a-ed
　1 Kin. 11:39, a the seed of David
　Ps. 55:19, God shall hear, and a them
　　　82:3, justice to the a-ed and needy
　Prov. 15:15, days of the a-ed are evil
　Is. 63:9, in . . . affliction he was a-ed
　Lam. 3:33, doth not a willingly
　Nah. 1:12, I will a thee no more
　1 Tim. 5:10, have relived the a-ed
　James 5:13, is any among you a-ed
Affliction—*distress, adversity, pain*
　Gen. 29:32, hath looked upon my a
　　　31:42, God hath seen mine a
　　　41:52, in the land of my a
　Deut. 16:3, even the bread of a
　2 Chr. 20:9, cry unto thee in our a
　　　33:12, when he was in a

Job 5:6, a cometh not forth of the dust
　　10:15, see thou mine a
　　30:16, days of a have taken hold
　　36:15, delivereth the poor in his a
Ps. 25:18, Look upon mine a
Is. 30:20, water of a, ye shall not
　　48:10, in the furnace of a
Jer. 16:19, my refuge in the day of a
Mark 4:17, a . . . ariseth for the word's
Acts 20:23, bonds and a-s abide me
2 Cor. 2:4, out of much a . . . I wrote
　　8:2, in a great trial of a
Phil. 1:16, to add a to my bonds
James 1:27, fatherless . . . in their a
Afraid—*fearful, alarmed*
　Gen. 3:10, a because I was naked
　Ex. 3:6, a to look upon God
　Lev. 26:6, none shall make you a
　Josh. 11:6, be not a because of them
　Judg. 7:3, whosoever is fearful and a
　Job 3:25, which I was a of is come
　　　9:28, I am a of all my sorrows
　　　19:29, Be ye a of the sword
　Ps. 27:1, of whom shall I be a
　　　91:5, a for the terror by night
　　　112:7, not be a of evil tidings
　Prov. 31:21, not a of the snow
　Is. 51:12, be a of a man that shall die
　Jer. 2:12, be horribly a
　Matt. 14:27; John 6:20, be not a
　Mark 5:36, Be not a, only believe
　Mark 9:32, and were a to ask him
　Luke 12:4, a of them that kill the body
　Gal. 4:11, I am a of you
　2 Pet. 2:10, are not a to speak evil
Afresh—*once more, anew*
　Heb. 6:6, crucify . . . Son of God a
Afterward—*at a later time*
　Gen. 38:30, And a came out his brother
　Ex. 11:1, a-s he will let you go
　Matt. 21:29, but a he repented
　Mark 16:4, a he appeared unto the
　John 13:36, thou shalt follow me a-s
　1 Cor. 15:46, a that which is spiritual
Against—*facing, opposite to*
　Gen. 4:8, Cain rose up a Abel
　　　16:12, hand will be a every man
　Lev. 20:3, set my face a that man
　Job 16:4, heap up words a you
　Matt. 12:30, not with me is a me
　Luke 4:11, thy foot a a stone
　Acts 9:5, to kick a the pricks
　　　19:38, matter a any man

Against (*Continued*)
Rom. 8:7, carnal mind is enmity a God
Gal. 5:23, a such there is no law
1 Pet. 3:12, a them that do evil
Rev. 2:4, somewhat a thee
Aged—*old*
Job 12:20, understanding of the a
15:10, grayheaded, and very a men
32:9, neither do the a understand
Jer. 6:11, a with him . . . full of days
Titus 2:2, 3, a men be sober . . . a women
Philem. 9, such an one as Paul the a
Ages—*long periods, eras*
Eph. 2:7, That in the a to come
3:5, in other a was not made
21, all a, world without end
Col. 1:26, hid from a and from
Agony—*intense suffering, torment*
Luke 22:44, being in an a he prayed
Agree—*consent, approve*
Amos 3:3 except they be a-d
Matt. 5:25, A with thine adversary
18:19, if two of you shall a
20:13, a with me for a penny
Acts 15:15, to this a the words of
1 John 5:8, and these three a in one
Agreement—*concurrence, conformity*
Is. 28:15, with hell are we at a
36:16, Make an a with me by
2 Cor. 6:16, what a hath the temple
Aileth—*pained, or uneasy*
Gen. 21:17, What a thee, Hagar
1 Sam. 11:5, What a the people
Air—*the atmosphere*
Gen. 1:26, 28, fowl of the a
Deut. 4:17, fowl that flieth in the a
2 Sam. 21:10, birds of the a
Job 41:16, no a can come between
Prov. 30:19, way of an eagle in the a
1 Cor. 9:26, as one that beateth the a
14:9, ye shall speak into the a
Eph. 2:2, prince of the power of the a
1 Thess. 4:17, meet the Lord in the a
Alarm—*call to arms*
Num. 10:5, 6, 7, 9, When ye blow an a
Jer. 4:19, the a of war
Joel 2:1, sound an a in my holy
Alas—*exclamation of sorrow, or worry*
Judg. 6:22, Gideon said, A, O Lord God
11:35, A, my daughter! thou hast
2 Kin. 6:5, A, master . . . was borrowed
Amos 5:16, the highways, A! a!
Rev. 18:10, 16, 19, A, a that great city

Alien—*a foreigner*
Ex. 18:3, a in a strange land
Deut. 14:21, mayest sell it unto an a
Job 19:15, I am an a in their sight
Ps. 69:8, a unto my mother's children
Lam. 5:2, our houses to a-s
Eph. 2:12, a-s from the commonwealth
Heb. 11:34, armies of the a-s
Alienated—*estranged, separated*
Ezek. 23:17, her mind was a from them
Eph. 4:18, a from the life of God
Col. 1:21, that were sometimes a
Alive—*having life, attentive*
Gen. 7:23, Noah only remained a
43:7, Is your father yet a
Num. 16:33, went down a into the pit
Deut. 32:39, I kill, and I make a
2 Kin. 5:7, to kill and to make a
Ezek. 13:18, save the souls a
Luke 15:24, son was dead, and is a
Acts 1:3, shewed himself a
Rom. 6:13, those that are a from dead
1 Cor. 15:22, Christ . . . all be made a
Rev. 1:18, I am a for evermore
Allegory—*a figurative statement*
Gal. 4:24, which things are an a
Alleluia—*praise to Jehovah*
Rev. 19:1, 3, 4, 6, saying (Amen), a
Allure—*tempt, to entice*
Hos. 2:14, I will a her
2 Pet. 2:18, they a through the lusts
Almighty—*God, as possessing all power*
Gen. 17:1, I am the A God
Ex. 6:3, by the name of God A
Job 11:7, find out the A unto perfection
29:5, when the A was yet with me
37:23, A, we cannot find him out
Ps. 91:1, shadow of the A
Rev. 4:8, Holy, holy, holy, Lord God A
11:17, Lord God A, which art
Alms—*relief of the poor, charity*
Matt. 6:1, do not your a before men
4, thine a may be in secret
Luke 12:33, Sell . . . and give a
Acts 10:2, which gave much a
24:17, bring a to my nation
Alone—*solitary, single, apart*
Gen. 2:18, Not good that man . . . be a
Job 7:16, let me a
Matt. 4:4, man shall not live by bread a
Mark 14:6, Let her a
Luke 9:18, as he was a praying
John 8:16, I am not a

Altar—*table of sacrifice*
Gen. 8:20, Noah builded an **a**
Ex. 17:15, Moses built an **a**
Lev. 6:9, the fire of the **a**
Judg. 6:24, Gideon built an **a**
Ps. 43:4, then will I go unto the **a**
Ezek. 6:4, your **a**-s shall be desolate
Matt. 5:23, bring thy gift to the **a**
    23:19, the gift, or the **a**
Rev. 9:13, four horns of the golden **a**
Alway, Always—*at all times*
Gen. 6:3, my spirit shall not **a** strive
Deut. 14:23, fear the Lord thy God **a**
Matt. 28:20, lo, I am with you **a**
Mark 14:7, me ye have not **a**
Phil 4:4, rejoice in the Lord **a**
Am—*exist, to be*
Ex. 3:14, I **A** that I **A**
Matt. 18:20, there **a** I in the midst
1 Cor. 15:10, I **a** what I **a**
Gal. 4:12, be as I **a**
Amazed—*bewildered, confused*
Is. 13:8, **a** one at another
Matt. 19:25, disciples . . . exceedingly **a**
Mark 2:12, **a** and glorified God
    14:33, he . . . began to be sore **a**
Luke 9:43, **a** at the mighty power of God
Acts 3:10, wonder and **a**-ment
Amen—*so be it, verily, truly*
Num. 5:22, and the woman shall say, **A a**
Ps. 41:13; 72:19; 89:52, **A** and **A**
Matt. 6:13, the glory, for ever, **A**
Rev. 3:14, These things saith the **A**
Ancient—*of great age, long standing*
Deut. 33:15, of the **a** mountains
1 Chr. 4:22, and these are **a** things
Job 12:12, With the **a** is wisdom
Dan. 7:9, 13, 22, **A** of days
Angel—*a heavenly messenger*
Gen. 24:7, send his **a** before thee
Ps. 78:25, Man did eat **a**-s' food
Is. 63:9, **a** of his presence
Luke 20:36, equal unto the **a**-s
    22:43, an **a** . . . strengthening him
John 20:12, two **a**-s in white sitting
Acts 6:15, as . . . the face of an **a**
    23:8, no resurrection, neither **a**
2 Cor. 11:14, into an **a** of light
Col. 2:18, and worshipping of **a**-s
Heb. 13:2, entertained **a**-s unawares
2 Pet. 2:4, God spared not the **a**-s
Rev. 2:1, 8, 12, **a** of the church
    9:11, **a** of the bottomless pit

Anger—*violent emotion, rage*
Gen. 49:7, Cursed be their **a**
Ex. 32:19, Moses' **a** waxed hot
Deut. 13:17, fierceness of his **a**
Neh. 9:17; Prov. 15:18, slow to **a**
Ps. 30:5, **a** endureth but a moment
    37:8, cease from **a**
Is. 5:25, **a** of the Lord kindled
Col. 3:21, provoke not . . . children to **a**
Angry—*provoked, wrathful*
Gen. 18:30, let not the Lord be **a**
Ps. 7:11, God is **a** with the wicked
Prov. 14:17, he that is soon **a**
    22:24, friendship with an **a** man
    29:22, **a** man stirreth up strife
Jonah 4:4, Doest thou well to be **a**
Matt. 5:22, is **a** with his brother
Eph 4:26, Be ye **a**, and sin not
Titus 1:7, not soon **a**
Anguish—*agony, torment, distress*
Ex. 6:9, **a** of spirit, and for
Is. 30:6, land of trouble and **a**
Jer. 6:24, **a** hath taken hold of us
Rom. 2:9, tribulation and **a** on every
2 Cor. 2:4, out of much . . . **a** of heart
Anoint—*to pour oil upon, to consecrate*
Ex. 28:41, **a** them, and consecrate them
Ps. 23:5, thou **a**-est my head with oil
    105:15, touch not mine **a**-ed
Matt. 6:17, fastest, **a** thine head
Mark 14:8, come aforehand to **a** my body
    16:1, they might come and **a** him
Luke 7:46, this woman hath **a**-ed my feet
Acts 10:38, God **a**-ed Jesus of Nazareth
2 Cor. 1:21, hath **a**-ed us is God
Rev. 3:18, **a** thine eyes with eye-salve
Answer—*a response*
Deut. 27:15, **a** and say, Amen
Ps. 65:5, wilt thou **a**
Prov. 15:1, **a** soft **a** turneth away
    24:26, lips that giveth a right **a**
    26:4, 5, **A** not a fool. A a fool
Eccles. 10:19, money **a**-eth all things
Mic. 3:7, for there is no **a** of God
Matt. 26:62, **A** thou nothing
Luke 2:47, astonished at his . . . **a**-s
    21:14, meditate . . . what ye shall **a**
John 19:9, Jesus gave him no **a**
Col. 4:6, how ye ought to **a** every man
1 Pet. 3:15, ready always to give an **a**
    3:21, the **a** of a good conscience
Ant—*a small insect*
Prov. 6:6, Go to the **a**, thou sluggard
    30:25, The **a**-s are a people

Antichrist—*power opposing Christ*
1 John 2:18, 22, a shall come. He is a
    4:3, this is that spirit of a
2 John 7, a deceiver and an a
Apostle—*chief disciples of Christ*
Matt. 10:2, names of the twelve a-s are
Luke 11:49, send them prophets and a-s
Rom. 1:1, called to be an a
    11:13, a of the Gentiles
1 Cor. 15:9, not meet to be called an a
2 Cor. 12:11, very chiefest a-s
Gal. 1:19, other of the a-s saw I none
    2:8, a-ship of the circumcision
Eph. 4:11, he gave some, a-s
1 Tim. 2:7; 2 Tim. 1:11, and an a
Apparel—*clothing*
2 Sam. 12:20, and changed his a
Esther 8:15, a of blue and white
Is. 63:1, glorious in his a
Ezek. 27:24, chests of rich a
1 Tim. 2:9, in modest a
James 2:2, gold ring, in goodly a
1 Pet. 3:3, of putting on of a
Appetite—*natural desire*
Job 38:39, the a of the young lions
Prov 23:2, if thou be a man given to a
Eccles. 6:7, the a is not filled
Is. 29:8, his soul hath a
Apple—*a fruit*
Deut. 32:10; Ps. 17:8, a of his eye
Prov. 25:11, a-s of gold in pictures
Song 2:3, a tree among the trees
    5, comfort me with a-s
Appoint—*to fix or establish*
Gen. 30:28, A me thy wages
Num. 3:10, thou shalt a Aaron
Job 14:13, wouldest a me a set time
Ps. 79:11, those that a-ed to die
Is. 26:1, salvation will God a
Jer. 49:19, who will a me the time
Luke 22:29, I a unto you a kingdom
1 Thess. 5:9, hath not a-ed us to wrath
Heb. 9:27, a-ed unto men once to die
Approach—*draw near to*
Lev. 18:14, 19, thou shalt not a
Luke 12:33, where no thief a-eth
1 Tim. 6:16, which no man can a
Approved—*commended or sanctioned*
Acts 2:22, a man a of God
Rom. 14:18, acceptable . . . a of men
    16:10, a in Christ
2 Tim. 2:15, shew thyself a

Aprons—*protections for clothing*
Gen. 3:7, and made themselves a
Acts 19:12, handkerchiefs or a
Archangel—*angel of the highest order*
1 Thess. 4:16, with the voice of the a
Jude 9, Michael the a, when contending
Arise—*to ascend, to stand up*
Gen. 31:13, a, get thee out from this
Deut. 9:12, A, get thee down
Ps. 3:7, A, O Lord; save me, O my God
Song 2:13, A, my love
Luke 15:18, will a and go to my father
Acts 22:16, a, and be baptized
Eph. 5:14, a from the dead, and Christ
2 Pet. 1:19, the day star a in your
Ark—*chest, a floating vessel*
Gen. 6:14, an a of gopher wood
Ex. 2:3, took for him an a of bulrushes
    37:1, made the a of shittim wood
Matt. 24:38, Noe entered into the a
Heb. 9:4, the a of the covenant
Rev. 11:19, the a of his testament
Arm—*the fore limb*
Ex. 6:6, with a stretched out a
Deut. 33:27, the everlasting a-s
Job 26:2, a that hath no strength
Ps. 37:17, a-s of the wicked . . . broken
    98:1, a hath gotten him the victory
Song 8:6, a seal upon thine a
Mark 10:16, took them up in his a-s
Arm—*to equip with weapons*
Gen. 14:14, a-ed his trained servants
Num. 31:3, A some of yourselves
Luke 11:21, a strong man a-ed
1 Pet. 4:1, a yourselves likewise
Armour—*defensive arms used in battle*
1 Sam. 31:9, stripped off his a
Luke 11:22, a wherein he trusted
Rom. 13:12, put on the a of light
2 Cor. 6:7, by the a of righteousness
Eph. 6:11, 13, the whole a of God
Array—*to clothe, to arrange in order*
Judg. 20:20, put themselves in a
Job 40:10, a thyself with glory
Matt. 6:29, Solomon . . . not a-ed like
1 Tim. 2:9, not with . . . costly a
Rev. 7:13, What are these . . . a-ed in
Arrogancy—*haughtiness, pride*
Prov. 8:13, pride, and a, and the evil
Is. 13:11, a of the proud to cease
Jer. 48:29, his a, and his pride
Arrow—*shaft shot from a bow*
1 Sam. 20:36, shot an a beyond him

Job 6:4, **a**-s of the Almighty
    41:28, **a** cannot make him flee
Ps. 45:5, **a**-s are sharp in the heart
Jer. 9:8, Their tongue is as an **a**
Lam. 3:12, as a mark for the **a**
Art—*skill, or systematic learning*
Ex. 30:25, the **a** of the apothecary
Acts 17:29, stone, graven by **a**
    19:19, which used curious **a**-s
Ascend—*go up*
Ps. 24:3, who shall **a** into the hill of
    139:8, If I **a** up into heaven
John 3:13, no man hath **a**-ed
    6:62, see the son of man **a** up
    20:17, I **a** unto my Father
Rom. 10:6, Who shall **a** into heaven
Ashamed—*confused by guilt*
Gen. 2:25, and were not **a**
Ps. 25:2, let me not be **a**
Is. 24:23, and the sun **a**
Mark 8:38, shall the Son of man be **a**
Rom. 1:16, not **a** of the gospel
2 Tim. 1:8, not . . . **a** of the testimony
Heb. 11:16, not **a** to be called their
1 Pet. 4:16, let him not be **a**
1 John 2:28, not be **a** before him
Ashes—*remains of burned material*
Gen. 18:27, am but dust and **a**
Lev. 6:11, carry forth the **a**
2 Sam. 13:19, put **a** on her head
1 Kin. 13:3, the **a** that are upon it
Esther 4:1, put on sackcloth with **a**
Job 2:8, sat down among the **a**
    42:6, repent in dust and **a**
Ps. 102:9, eaten **a** like bread
Jer. 6:26, wallow thyself in **a**
Luke 10:13, in sackcloth and **a**
Aside—*to one side or the other*
Num. 22:23, the ass turned **a**
1 Sam. 8:3, turned **a** after lucre
Ps. 40:4, turn **a** to lies
1 Pet. 2:1, laying **a** all malice
Ask—*request, petition*
Judg. 18:5, **A** counsel . . . of God
1 Kin. 3:5, **A** what I shall give thee
Ps. 2:8, **A** of me, and I shall give thee
Is. 7:11, **A** thee a sign of the Lord
Jer. 6:16, **a** for the old paths
Zech. 10:1, **A** ye of the Lord rain
Matt. 5:42, Give to him that **a**-eth
    7:7, **A** and it shall be given you
    21:22, whatsoever ye shall **a**
Mark 10:38 Ye know not what ye **a**

Luke 11:11, If a son shall **a** bread
1 Cor. 10:25, **a**-ing no question
James 1:5, lack wisdom, let him **a**
Asleep—*slumber, also death*
Judg. 4:21, for he was fast **a**
Matt. 26:40, 43, and findeth them **a**
Mark 4:38, hinder part of the ship, **a**
    14:40, found them **a** again
Acts 7:60, he had said this, he fell **a**
1 Cor. 15:6, but some are fallen **a**
1 Thess. 4:13, 15, them which are **a**
Ass—*donkey, burro*
Num. 22:30, am not I thine **a**
Prov. 26:3, a bridle for the **a**
Jer. 22:19, with the burial of an **a**
Zech. 9:9; Matt. 21:5, riding upon an **a**
Matt. 21:2, ye shall find an **a** tied
2 Pet. 2:16, **a** speaking with man's
Assay—*to try, or attempt*
Deut. 4:34, hath God **a**-ed to go and
Job 4:2, If we **a** to commune with thee
Acts 9:26, Saul . . . **a**-ed to join himself
Assemble—*come together*
2 Sam. 20:4, **A** me the men of Judah
Ezek. 11:17, **a** you out of the countries
Hos. 7:14, **a** themselves for corn
Matt. 26:3, **a**-ed . . . the chief priests
Acts 15:25, **a**-ed with one accord
Assembly—*a gathering*
Lev. 23:36, it is a solemn **a**
Ps. 86:14, **a**-ies of violent men
    111:1, **a** of the upright
Acts 19:39, determined in a lawful **a**
Heb. 12:23, To the general **a** and church
Assurance—*certainty, firmness of mind*
Is. 32:17, quietness and **a** for ever
Acts 17:31, hath given **a** unto all men
Col. 2:2, full **a** of understanding
Heb. 6:11, full **a** of hope unto the end
    10:22, full **a** of faith, having our
Astonied—*to be silent, astonished*
Job 17:8, upright men shall be **a**
Ezek. 4:17, and be **a** one with another
Dan. 4:19, Daniel . . . **a** for one hour
Astonished—*amazed, surprised*
Lev. 26:32, enemies . . . shall be **a**
Job 21:5, Mark me, and be **a**
Jer. 2:12, Be **a**, O ye heavens
Dan. 8:27, **a** at the vision
Matt. 7:28, were **a** at his doctrine
    10:26, **a** out of measure
Luke 24:22, women . . . made us **a**

Astonishment—*bewilderment*
Ps. 60:3, drink the wine of **a**
Jer. 8:21, **a** hath taken hold on me
   25:18, an **a**, an hissing
Mark 5:42, astonished with a great **a**
Astray—*out of the right way*
Ps. 119:176, gone **a** like a lost sheep
Prov. 7:25, go not **a** in her paths
Is. 53:6, All we like sheep have gone **a**
Matt. 18:13, and nine . . . went not **a**
1 Pet. 2:25, as sheep going **a**
Atonement—*ransom, reconciliation*
Ex. 30:15 make **a** for your souls
Lev. 23:27; 25:9, a day of **a**
2 Sam. 21:3, wherewith shall I make . . . **a**
Rom. 5:11, we have now received the **a**
Attain—*achieve, reach*
Prov. 1:5, man of understanding shall **a**
Hos. 8:5, they **a** to innocency
Rom. 9:30, have a-ed to righteousness
Phil. 3:11, **a** unto the resurrection
Attend—*heed, listen*
Ps. 17:1; 55:2, **a** unto my cry
Prov. 4:1, **a** to know understanding
1 Cor. 7:35, that ye may **a** upon the Lord
1 Tim. 4:13, give a-ance to reading
Author—*creator, originator*
1 Cor. 14:33, not the **a** of confusion
Heb. 5:9, the **a** of eternal salvation
   12:2, **a** and finisher of our faith
Authority—*rightful power, dominion*
Prov. 29:2, righteous are in **a**
Matt. 7:29, taught them as one having **a**
   8:9, For I am a man under **a**
   21:23, By what **a** doest thou these
Luke 9:1, gave them power and **a**
   19:17, have thou **a** over ten cities
   20:8, by what **a** I do these things
John 5:27, given him **a** to execute
1 Cor. 15:24, all rule and all **a**
1 Tim. 2:12, to usurp **a** over the man
Titus 2:15, rebuke with all **a**
Availeth—*to profit, aid*
Esther 5:13, all this **a** me nothing
Gal. 5:6, neither circumcision **a** any
James 5:16, prayer of a righteous man **a**
Avenge—*to exact satisfaction for*
Lev. 19:18, Thou shalt not **a**
1 Sam. 24:12, the Lord **a** me of thee
2 Sam. 22:48, It is God that a-th me
Ps. 18:47, It is God that a-th me
Jer. 5:9, 29, shall not my soul be **a-d**
Luke 18:3, **A** me of mine adversary

Rom. 12:19, **a** not yourselves
Rev. 18:20, God hath **a** you on her
Avoid—*elude, evade, escape from*
Prov. 4:15, **A** it, pass not by it
Rom. 16:17, which ye have learned; and **a**
1 Cor. 7:2, **a** fornication
1 Tim. 6:20, a-ing profane . . . babblings
2 Tim. 2:23, **a** unleavened questions
Awake—*rouse from sleep or inaction*
Judg. 5:12, **A**, **a**, Deborah; **a**, **a**
Ps. 17:15, shall be satisfied, when I **a**
   139:18, when I **a**, I am still with
Is. 51:9, **A**, **a**, put on strength
John 11:11, that I may **a** him out of
Rom. 13:11, high time to **a** out of sleep
1 Cor. 15:34, **A** to righteousness
Eph. 5:14, **A** thou that sleepest
Awe—*reverential fear*
Ps. 4:4, Stand in **a**, and sin not
   33:8, of the world stand in **a**
   119:161, standeth in **a** of thy word
Axe—*a cutting tool*
1 Sam. 13:20, sharpen every man his
   . . . **a**
1 Kin. 6:7, neither hammer nor **a** nor any
2 Kin. 6:5, **a** head fell into the water
Ps. 74:6, with a-s and hammers
Jer. 51:20, Thou art my battle **a**
Luke 3:9, the **a** is laid unto the root

B

Babbler—*idle talker, teller of secrets*
Eccles. 10:11, and a **b** is no better
Acts 17:18, what will this **b** say
Babbling—*idle talk*
Prov. 23:29, who hath **b**
1 Tim. 6:20, profane and vain **b-s**
2 Tim. 2:16, shun profane and vain **b-s**
Babe—*a very young child*
Ex. 2:6, behold, the **b** wept
Ps. 8:2, out of the mouth of **b-s**
Matt. 11:25, revealed them unto **b-s**
Luke 1:41, 44, the **b** leaped in her womb
1 Pet. 2:2, As newborn **b-s**
Back—*hinder part, to the rear*
Gen. 19:26, his wife looked **b**
Josh. 8:26, Joshua drew not his hand **b**
2 Sam. 2:23, can I bring him **b** again
Prov. 19:29, stripes for the **b** of fools
Is. 50:6, I gave my **b** to the smiters
Matt. 28:2, rolled **b** the stone

Luke 9:62, no man . . . looking **b** is fit
Heb. 10:38, if any man draw **b**
Backbite—*slander, speak evil of*
Prov. 25:23, a **b**-ing tongue
Rom. 1:30, **B**-rs, haters of God
2 Cor. 12:20, strifes, **b**-ings
Backslide—*abandon one's faith*
Prov. 14:14, the **b**-r in heart shall be
Jer. 3:14, Turn, O **b**-ing children
14:7, our **b**-ings are many
31:22, O thou **b**-ing daughter
Hos. 14:4, I will heal their **b**-ing
Backward—*in the reverse direction*
Gen. 49:17, his rider shall fall **b**
1 Sam. 4:18, fell from off the seat **b**
2 Kin. 20:10, shadow return **b** ten
Is. 59:14, judgment is turned away **b**
Bad—*evil, corrupt*
Lev. 27:10, good for a **b**, or a **b** for a
1 Kin. 3:9, discern between good and **b**
Matt. 13:48, but cast the **b** away
22:10, found, both **b** and good
2 Cor. 5:10, whether it be good or **b**
Bag—*purse, bundle*
Deut. 25:13, shalt not have in thy **b**
1 Sam. 17:49, put his hand in his **b**
Job 14:17, is sealed up in a **b**
Is. 46:6, lavish gold out of the **b**
Hag. 1:6, to put it into a **b**
Luke 12:33, **b**-s which wax not old
John 12:6, was a thief, and had the **b**
13:29, because Judas had the **b**
Bake—*cook in the oven*
Gen. 19:3, did **b** unleavened bread
Lev. 24:5, fine flour, and **b** twelve cakes
26:26, ten women shall **b** your bread
Num. 11:8, and **b**-d it in pans
1 Kin. 19:6, a cake **b**-n on the coals
Baker—*one who bakes*
Gen. 40:1, 20, 22, the chief **b**
1 Sam. 8:13, cooks, and to be **b**-s
Jer. 37:21, bread out of the **b**-s' street
Hos. 7:4, as an oven heated by the **b**
Balance—*scales for weighing*
Lev. 19:36, Just **b**-s, just weights
Job 31:6, weighed in an even **b**
Prov. 11:1; 20:23, a false **b**
Is. 40:15, the small dust of the **b**
Mic. 6:11, pure with the wicked **b**-s
Rev. 6:5, a pair of **b**-s in his hand
Bald—*lacking of hair*
2 Kin. 2:23, Go up, thou **b** head
Is. 3:24, of well set hair **b**-ness
22:12, call . . . to **b**-ness

Mic. 1:16, Make thee **b**, and poll thee
Balm—*fragrant ointment*
Gen. 43:11, little **b** and a little honey
Jer. 8:22, Is there no **b** in Gilead
Ezek. 27:17, honey, and oil, and **b**
Band—*group of men, or soldiers*
John 18:3, 12, received a **b** of men
Acts 10:1, **b** called the Italian **b**
23:12, the Jews **b**-ed together
27:1, a centurion of Augustus' **b**
Bands—*fillets, straps, or swaddles*
Judg. 15:14, his **b** loosed from off
Ps. 2:3, break their **b** asunder
Is. 58:6, loose the **b** of wickedness
Luke 8:29, he brake the **b**
Acts 16:26, every one's **b** were loosed
Col. 2:19, the body by joints and **b**
Banner—*a standard, a flag*
Ps. 60:4, given a **b** to them that fear
Song 6:4, terrible as an army with **b**-s
Is. 13:2, lift ye up a **b** upon the high
Banquet—*a sumptuous feast*
Esther 5:4, 6, came to the **b** . . . of wine
Job 41:6, the companions make a **b**
Song 2:4, brought me to the **b**-ing house
1 Pet. 4:3, **b**-ings, and . . . idolatries
Baptism—*sanctifying by water*
Matt. 21:25, The **b** of John
Mark 1:4, **b** of repentance
Rom. 6:4, buried with him by **b**
Eph 4:5, one Lord, one faith, one **b**
1 Pet. 3:21, **b** doth now also save
Baptize—*administer baptism*
Matt. 3:11; Mark 1:8; Luke 3:16,
b you with water . . . **b**
with the Holy Ghost
John 1:25, Why **b**-st thou then, if
33, **b**-th with the Holy Ghost
3:26, the same **b**-th, and all men
1 Cor. 1:17, Christ sent me not to **b**
Baptized—*sanctified by water*
Matt. 3:13, to be **b** of him
20:22, baptism that I am **b** with
Mark 1:8, have **b** you with water
10:39, withal shall ye be **b**
Luke 3:21, all the people were **b**
John 4:2, Jesus himself **b** not
10:40, where John at first **b**
Acts 1:5, **b** with the Holy Ghost
2:38, **b** every one of you
8:36, hinder me to be **b**
18:8, believed, and were **b**
Rom. 6:3, **b** into Jesus Christ

Baptized (*Continued*)
1 Cor. 1:13, **b** in the name of Paul
10:2, **b** unto Moses
12:13, one Spirit are we all **b**
15:29, are **b** for the dead
Gal. 3:27, **b** into Christ
Bare—*uncovered*
Is. 32:11, strip you, and make you **b**
47:2, make **b** the leg, uncover
Ezek. 16:7, 22, thou wast naked and **b**
Barn—*a storehouse*
2 Kin. 6:27, out of the **b**-floor
Job 39:12, gather it into thy **b**
Prov. 3:10, thy **b**-s be filled
Hag. 2:19, seed yet in the **b**
Matt. 6:26, reap, nor gather into **b**-s
Luke 12:18, pull down my **b**-s
Barrel—*storage vessel*
1 Kin. 17:12, handful of meal in a **b**
18:33, fill four **b**-s with water
Barren—*unproductive, fruitless*
Gen. 11:30, Sarai was **b**
29:31, Rachel was **b**
Ex. 23:26, cast their young, nor be **b**
1 Sam. 2:5, the **b** hath born seven
Ps. 107:34, a fruitful land into **b**-ness
Luke 23:9, Blessed are the **b**
2 Pet. 1:8, neither be **b** nor unfruitful
Base—*low in position or worth*
2 Sam. 6:22, be **b** in mine own sight
Job 30:8, children of **b** men
Is. 3:5, **b** against the honourable
Mal. 2:9, made you contemptible and **b**
Acts 17:5, lewd fellows of **b**-r sort
1 Cor. 1:28, **b** things of the world
Basket—*a woven vessel*
Jer. 24:2, **b** had very naughty figs
Amos 8:1, 2, **b** of summer fruit
Matt. 14:20, remained twelve **b**-s full
Acts 9:25, let him down . . . in a **b**
2 Cor. 11:33, **b** was I let down
Bastard—*illegitimate, or irregular*
Deut. 23:2, a **b** shall not enter into
Zech. 9:6, and a **b** shall dwell in
Heb. 12:8, then are ye **b**-s, and not
Bat—*obstruction of wood or metal*
Ex. 26:26, make **b**-s of shittim wood
Deut. 3:5, walls, gates, and **b**-s
Neh. 7:3, shut the doors, and **b** them
Job 40:18, bones are like **b**-s of iron
Ps. 107:16, cut the **b**-s of iron in
Battle—*armed conflict*
1 Sam. 17:47, the **b** is the Lord's
1 Chr. 5:20, they cried to God in the **b**

Job 39:25, he smelleth the **b**
Ps. 18:39, strength unto the **b**
24:8, Lord mighty in **b**
55:18, my soul in peace from the **b**
Eccles. 9:11, nor the **b** to the strong
Jer. 50:22, sound of **b** is in the land
Rev. 9:9, horses running to **b**
Beam—*a heavy piece of timber*
1 Sam. 17:7, spear was like a weaver's **b**
2 Kin. 6:5, one was felling a **b**
Song 1:17, the **b**-s of our house
Matt. 7:5, cast out the **b** out of
Bear—*a wild animal*
2 Kin. 2:24, two she **b**-s out of the wood
Prov. 17:12, **b** robbed of her whelps
Is. 11:7, cow and the **b** shall feed
Rev. 13:2, feet were as the feet of a **b**
Bear—*carry, support*
Gen. 4:13, greater than I can **b**
Ex. 20:16, shalt not **b** false witness
Ps. 91:12, **b** thee up in their hands
Prov. 18:14, wounded spirit who can **b**
Matt. 27:32, compelled to **b** his cross
Mark 10:19, Do not **b** false witness
John 1:7, to **b** witness of the Light
5:31, **b** witness of myself
15:4, branch cannot **b** fruit
8, **b** much fruit; so shall ye
27, ye also shall **b** witness
Acts 9:15, **b** my name before the Gentiles
Rom. 15:1, **b** the infirmities of the weak
1 Cor. 13:7, B-eth all things
Gal. 6:2, **B** ye one another's burdens
Heb. 9:28, **b** the sins of many
Beard—*hair growing on the face*
1 Sam. 17:35, caught him by his **b**
2 Sam. 20:9, Joab took Amasa by the **b**
Ps. 133:2, even Aaron's **b**
Jer. 48:37, bald, and every **b** clipped
Beast—*a dumb animal*
Job 18:3, are we counted as **b**-s
Ps. 73:22, I was as a **b**
Prov. 12:10, regardeth the life of his **b**
Eccles. 3:19, preeminence above a **b**
Luke 10:34, set him on his own **b**
1 Cor. 15:32, I have fought with **b**-s at
Beat—*to strike repeatedly*
Ex. 25:18, of **b**-en work shalt thou
27:20, pure olive oil **b**-en for the
Ps. 18:42, I **b** them small as the dust
Prov. 23:13, **b**-est him with the rod
Is. 2:4, shall **b** . . . into plowshares

1 Cor. 9:26, as one that **b**-eth the air
2 Cor. 11:25, Thrice . . . **b**-en with rods
Beautiful—*pleasing to the sight or mind*
 1 Sam 16:12, withal of a **b** countenance
 2 Sam. 11:2, **b** to look upon
 Eccles. 3:11, hath made every thing **b**
 Song 7:1, **b** are thy feet
 Is. 52:7, How **b** upon the mountains
 Matt. 23:27, indeed appear **b** outward
 Acts 3:10, alms at the **B** gate
 Rom. 10:15, How **b** are the feet of them
Beauty—*that which is pleasing*
 1 Chr. 16:29, worship the Lord in the **b**
 Job 40:10, with glory and **b**
 Ps. 29:2, in the **b** of holiness
 Prov. 20:29, **b** of old men . . . gray head
 Zech. 11:7, 10, my staff, ever **b**
Became, Become—*befit, be suitable to*
 2 Sam. 7:24, thou, Lord, art **b** their God
 Prov. 17:7, speech **b**-th not a fool
 Matt. 18:3, ye . . . **b** as little children
 Mark 9:3, his raiment **b** shining
 Rom. 1:22, they **b** fools
 1 Cor. 13:1, **b** as sounding brass
  11, when I **b** a man
 2 Cor. 5:17, all things are **b** new
 Heb. 5:9, **b** the author of . . . salvation
Bed—*a place to rest on*
 Deut. 3:11, **b**-stead was . . . of iron
 1 Chr. 5:1, defiled his father's **b**
 Ps. 63:6, remember thee upon my **b**
 Prov. 7:17, perfumed my **b**
 Is. 28:20, **b** is shorter than a man
 Ezek. 23:17, into the **b** of love
 Matt. 9:6, take up thy **b**
 Mark 4:21, candle . . . under a **b**
 Luke 11:7, children are with me in **b**
  17:34, two men in one **b**
 Acts 9:33, had kept his **b** eight years
 Heb. 13:4, and the **b** undefiled
 Rev. 2:22, cast her into a **b**
Bees—*the common honeybees*
 Judg. 14:8, swarm of **b**
 Ps. 118:12, compassed me about like **b**
Beg—*ask for, entreat*
 Prov. 20:4, shall he **b** in the harvest
 Matt. 27:58, to Pilate and **b**-ed the body
 Luke 16:3, I cannot dig; to **b** I am
Began, Begin—*start, come into existence*
 Gen. 4:26, then **b** men to call upon
 Ezek. 9:6, and **b** at my sanctuary
 Matt. 20:8, the labourers . . . **b**-ing from
  26:37, he . . . **b** to be sorrowful
 Luke 1:70, since the world **b**

Beginning—*inception, outset*
 Gen. 1:1, In the **b** God created
 Job 8:7, thy **b** was small
 Ps. 111:10, fear of the Lord is the **b**
 Eccles. 7:8, the end . . . than the **b**
 Mark 1:1, The **b** of the gospel
 John 1:1, **b** was the Word
 Rev. 21:6, the **b** and the end
Begotten—*generated*
 Ps. 2:7, this day have I **b** thee
 Acts 13:33, my Son . . . have I **b** thee
 John 1:18, the only **b** Son
 1 Pet. 1:3, **b** . . . unto a lively hope
Beguile—*deceive*
 Gen. 3:13, The serpent **b**-d me
  29:25, hast thou **b**-d me
 2 Cor. 11:3, serpent **b**-d Eve
 Col. 2:4, lest any man should **b** you
 2 Pet. 2:14, **b**-ing unstable souls
Behalf—*benefit, interest*
 Job 36:2, to speak on God's **b**
 Rom. 16:19, I am glad . . . on your **b**
 1 Cor. 1:4, thank my God . . . on your **b**
 Phil. 1:29, is given in the **b** of Christ
Behave—*manage, conduct*
 1 Sam. 18:5, **b**-d himself wisely
 Ps. 101:2, I will **b** myself wisely
 1 Cor. 13:5, Doth not **b** itself unseemly
 1 Tim. 3:15, how thou oughtest to **b**
Beheaded—*cut off the head*
 Matt. 14:10, **b** John in the prison
 Mark 6:16, It is John, whom I **b**
Behind—*in back of*
 Is. 38:17, cast all my sins **b** thy back
 Matt. 16:23, Get thee **b** me, Satan
 Col. 1:24, fill up that which is **b**
Behold—*look at, see*
 Gen. 3:22, **B**, the man is become as
 Ps. 46:8, **b** the works of the Lord
 Matt. 21:5, **B**, thy King cometh
 Luke 24:39, **B** my hands and my feet
 John 1:29, **B** the Lamb of God
  17:24, that they may **b** my glory
 2 Cor. 3:18, **b**-ing as in a glass the
Believe—*exercise belief or faith*
 Gen. 15:6, he **b**-d in the Lord
 2 Chr. 20:20, **b** in the Lord
 Matt. 8:13, as thou hast **b**-d, so be it
  9:28, **B** ye that I am able
  21:22, in prayer, **b**-ing
 Mark 9:24, Lord, I **b**; help thou mine
  15:32, we may see and **b**

Believe (*Continued*)
John 3:18, that **b**-th on him is not
9:35, **b** on the Son of God
11:25, he that **b**-th in me
14:1, ye **b** in God, **b** also in me
16:31, Do ye now **b**
Rom. 4:24, **b** on . . . that raised up Jesus
6:8, we **b** that we shall also live
10:16, who hath **b**-d our report
15:13, with all joy . . . **b**-ing
1 Cor. 13:7, Beareth all things, **b**-th
Gal. 2:16, even we have **b**-d in Jesus
1 Thess. 4:14, if we **b** that Jesus died
Heb. 4:3, which have **b**-d do enter
James 2:23, Abraham **b**-d God
1 John 5:1, Whosoever **b**-th that Jesus
10, **b**-th on the Son of God
Belly—*the lower body*
Gen. 3:14, upon thy **b** shalt thou go
Judg. 3:21, thrust it into his **b**
Job 15:2, fill his **b** with the east wind
Prov. 18:20, **b** shall be satisfied
Ezek. 3:3, cause thy **b** to eat
Jonah 1:17, Jonah was in the **b** of the
Luke 15:16, fain have filled his **b** with
John 7:38, **b** shall flow rivers
Rom. 16:18, serve . . . their own **b**
Phil. 3:19, whose God is their **b**
Titus 1:12, evil beasts, slow **b**-s
Rev. 10:9, make thy **b** bitter
Belong—*be a part of, apply to*
Gen. 40:8, interpretations **b** to God
Deut. 29:29, things **b** unto the Lord
32:35, To me **b**-eth vengeance
Ps. 3:8, Salvation **b**-eth unto the Lord
Prov. 24:23, **b** to the wise
Dan 9:9, To . . . God **b** mercies
Mark 9:41, ye **b** to Christ
Heb. 10:30, Vengeance **b**-eth unto me
Beloved—*one dearly loved, adored*
Deut. 33:12, The **b** of the Lord shall
Ps. 127:2, he giveth his **b** sleep
Is. 5:1, a song of my **b**
Matt. 3:17, This is my **b** Son
12:18, my **b**, in whom my soul
Rom. 12:19, Dearly **b**, avenge not
1 Cor. 4:14, as my **b** sons
Col. 3:12, elect of God, holy and **b**
Bend—*move from a straight line*
Ps. 11:2, the wicked **b** their bow
Is. 60:14, shall come **b**-ing unto thee
Jer. 9:3, they **b** their tongues
Ezek. 17:7, this vine did **b** her roots

Beneath—*in a lower place*
Ex. 20:4, above, or . . . in earth **b**
Deut. 5:8, or that is in the waters **b**
Prov. 15:24, depart from hell **b**
John 8:23, Ye are from **b**; I am . . . above
Benefit—*act of kindness*
Ps. 68:19, daily loadeth us with **b**-s
103:2, and forget not all his **b**-s
2 Cor. 1:15, ye might have a second **b**
1 Tim. 6:2, partakers of the **b**
Bereave—*strip, take away from*
Gen. 42:36, Me have ye **b**-d of my
Eccles. 4:8, I labour and **b** my soul
Lam. 1:20, abroad the sword **b**-th
Beseech—*implore*
Ex. 33:18, I **b** thee show me thy glory
Mal. 1:9, **b** God that he will be
Matt. 8:5, centurion, **b**-ing him
Luke 8:28, **b** thee, torment me not
Rom. 12:1, **b** you brethren . . . mercies
Eph. 4:1, **b** you that ye walk worthy
Besought—*implored*
Ex. 32:11, And Moses **b** the Lord his God
Deut. 3:23, I **b** the Lord at that time
1 Kin. 13:6, the man of God **b** the Lord
Matt. 8:31, the devils **b** him, saying
Acts 21:12, **b** him not to go up to
2 Cor. 12:8, I **b** the Lord thrice
1 Tim. 1:3, As I **b** thee to abide
Best—*highest, utmost*
Gen. 47:6, in the **b** of the land
2 Sam. 18:4, What seemeth you **b** I will
Ps. 39:5, man at his **b** state . . . vanity
Luke 15:22, Bring forth the **b** robe
1 Cor. 12:31, covet . . . the **b** gifts
Bestow—*grant to, give*
Luke 12:17, where to **b** my fruits
John 4:38, whereon ye **b**-ed no labour
1 Cor. 13:3, though I **b** all my goods
1 John 3:1, manner of love . . . hath **b**-ed
Betimes—*in good season, early*
Gen. 26:31, they rose up **b**
Job 8:5, seek unto God **b**
Prov. 13:24, chasteneth him **b**
Betray—*to prove faithless*
1 Chr. 12:17, to **b** me to mine enemies
Matt. 26:21, one of you shall **b** me
27:4, **b**-ed the innocent blood
Mark 13:12, brother shall **b** the brother
John 18:2, Judas also, which **b**-ed him
1 Cor. 11:23, night in which he was **b**-ed
Betroth—*to contract to marry*
Deut. 28:30, shalt **b** a wife
Hos. 2:19, 20, **b** thee unto me

Better—*preferable, better*
1 Sam. 15:22, obey is **b** than sacrifice
Ps. 118:8, 9, **b** to trust in the Lord
Prov. 8:11, wisdom is **b** than rubies
    17:1, **B** is a dry morsel
Eccles. 7:1, A good name is **b** than
Song 1:2, love is **b** than wine
Matt. 6:26, Are ye not much **b** then
    18:8, **b** for thee to enter into life
Mark 9:42, **b** for him that a millstone
Luke 5:39, The old is **b**
1 Cor. 7:9, **b** to marry
Heb. 8:6, a **b** covenant . . . **b** promises
    11:35, a **b** resurrection
Bewail—*grieve for, lament*
Judg. 11:37, and **b** my virginity
Luke 8:52, all wept, and **b**-ed her
2 Cor. 12:21, **b** many which have sinned
Beware—*be cautious, on guard*
Ex. 23:21, **B** of him, and obey
Deut. 6:12, **b** lest thou forget the Lord
Matt. 7:15, **B** of false prophets
    10:17, But **b** of men
Mark 8:15, **b** of the leaven
    12:38, **B** of the scribes
Luke 12:15, **b** of covetousness
Phil. 3:2, **B** of dogs, **b** of evil workers
Col. 2:8, **B** lest any man spoil you
Bewitched—*charmed, enchanted*
Acts 8:9, **b** the people of Samaria
Gal. 3:1, who hath **b** you
Bewrayeth—*reveals, discloses*
Prov. 29:24, heareth cursing, and **b**
Matt. 26:73, thy speech **b** thee
Beyond—*past, further away*
Num. 22:18, cannot go **b** the word
1 Sam. 20:22, the arrows are **b** thee
Jer. 25:22, isles . . . **b** the sea
1 Thess. 4:6, no man go **b** and defraud
Bid—*offer, propose*
Matt. 14:28, **b** me come unto thee
    22:3, call them that were **b**-den
    9, **b** to the marriage
Luke 9:61, let me first go **b** them
1 Cor. 10:27, that believe not **b** you
2 John 10, neither **b** him God speed
Bier—*frame on which the dead are carried*
2 Sam. 3:31, David . . . followed the **b**
Luke 7:14, he came and touched the **b**
Bill—*declaration in writing*
Deut. 24:1, 3, a **b** of divorcement
Mark 10:4, write a **b** of divorcement
Luke 16:6, Take thy **b** . . . and write

Bind—*fasten, restrain*
Gen. 37:7, **b**-ing sheaves in the field
Num. 30:2, oath to **b** his soul
Job 28:11, **b**-eth the floods
Prov. 3:3, **b** them about thy neck
Matt. 16:19, whatsoever . . . **b** on earth
    18:18, **b** on earth shall be bound
Mark 5:3, no man could **b** him
Bird—*winged creature*
Gen. 7:14, every **b** of every sort
Deut. 14:11, all clean **b**-s ye shall eat
Job 41:5, play . . . as with a **b**
Ps. 124:7, **b** out of the snare of the
Song 2:2, time of the singing of **b**-s
Is. 16:2, **b** cast out of the nest
Hos. 9:11, shall fly away like a **b**
Amos 3:5, **b** fall in a snare
Matt. 8:20, **b**-s of the air have nests
Birth—*coming into life*
Job 3:16, untimely **b** I had not been
Eccles. 7:1, than the day of one's **b**
Luke 1:14, many shall rejoice at his **b**
John 9:1, blind from his **b**
Birthright—*rights of the first born*
Gen. 25:31, Sell me this day thy **b**
    43:33, first born according to his **b**
1 Chr. 5:2, the **b** was Joseph's
Heb. 12:16, for . . . meat sold his **b**
Bishop—*spiritual overseer*
1 Tim. 3:2, **b** then must be blameless
1 Pet. 2:25, Shepherd and **B** of your
Bit—*part of a bridle; set the teeth into*
Ps. 32:9, mouth . . . held in with **b**
Amos 5:19, a serpent **b** him
James 3:3, put **b**-s in the horses' mouths
Bite—*seize with the teeth*
Gen. 49:17, that **b**-th the horse heels
Eccles. 10:8, a serpent shall **b** him
Jer. 8:17, and they shall **b** you
Mic. 3:5, **b** with their teeth, any cry
Gal. 5:15, **b** and devour one another
Bitter—*harsh, having a biting taste*
Ex. 12:8, **b** herbs they shall eat
Job 13:26, thou writest **b** things
Prov. 5:4, **b** as wormwood
Is. 5:20, **b** for sweet . . . sweet for **b**
    22:4, I will weep **b**-ly
Matt. 26:15, went out and wept **b**-ly
James 3:14, envying and strife
Bitterness—*anguish, impiety*
1 Sam. 15:32, **b** of death is past
Job 10:1, in the **b** of my soul
Rom. 3:14, mouth is full of . . . **b**

15

Bitterness (*Continued*)
Eph. 4:31, all **b**, and wrath, and anger
Heb. 12:15, lest any root of **b**
Black—*the darkest color*
Job 30:30, My skin is **b** upon me
Song 1:5, I am **b**, but comely
Matt. 5:36, not make one hair . . . **b**
Rev. 6:5, I beheld . . . a **b** horse
12, **b** as sackcloth
Blame—*find fault with, reproach*
Gen. 43:9, bear the **b** for ever
2 Cor. 6:3, the ministry be not **b-d**
8:20, no man should **b** us
Eph. 1:4, be holy and without **b**
Blameless—*sinless, without fault*
Gen. 44:10, ye shall be **b**
Luke 1:6, ordinances of the Lord **b**
1 Cor. 1:8, **b** in the day of our Lord
1 Thess. 5:23, soul and body . . . **b**
Titus 1:7, a bishop must be **b**
2 Pet. 3:14, without spot, and **b**
Blaspheme—*to speak with irreverence*
Lev. 24:16, **b**-th the name of the Lord
Ezek. 20:27, your fathers have **b-d** me
Matt. 9:3, This man **b**-th
Mark 3:29, **b** against the Holy Ghost
Luke 22:65, other things **b**-ously spake
Acts 6:11, heard him speak **b**-ous words
Rev. 16:9, **b** the name of God
Blasphemy—*irreverence, indignity to God*
Matt. 12:31, All manner of sin and **b**
15:19, out of the heart . . . **b**-ies
26:65, ye have heard his **b**
Mark 7:22, evil eye, **b**, pride
Col. 3:8, wrath, malice, **b**
Blast—*sound, damage by wind*
Gen. 41:6, seven thin ears and **b**-ed
Ex. 15:8, with the **b** of thy nostrils
Job 4:9, By the **b** of God
Is. 37:27, **b**-ed before it be grown up
Amos 4:9, smitten you with **b**-ing
Blemish—*defect, or fault*
Ex. 12:5, lamb shall be without **b**
2 Sam. 14:25, there was no **b** in you
Eph. 5:27, should be holy and without **b**
1 Pet. 1:19, a lamb without **b**
2 Pet. 2:13, spots they are and **b**-es
Bless—*grant divine favor to*
Gen. 1:22, And God **b**-ed them
12:2, I will **b** thee and make thy
28:3, God Almighty **b** thee
2 Sam. 7:29, please thee to **b** the house
Ps. 29:11, **b** his people with peace
103:1, **B** the Lord, O my soul

Matt. 5:44, **b** them that curse you
Mark 14:22, Jesus took bread and **b**-ed
1 Cor. 10:16, cup of **b**-ing which we **b**
James 3:9, Therewith **b** we God
Blessed—*consecrated, highly favored*
Job 1:21, **b** be the name of the Lord
Prov. 31:28, children . . . call her **b**
Matt. 5:3-11, **B** are the (they)
Luke 1:48, generations shall call me **b**
John 12:13, **B** is the King
Titus 2:13, Looking for that **b** hope
Rev. 14:13, **B** are the dead
Blessing—*divine favor*
Gen. 12:2, thou shalt be a **b**
27:36, taken away my **b**
Deut. 11:26, set before you . . . a **b**
Prov. 10:6, **B**-s are upon the head of
Ezek. 34:26, showers of **b**
Mal. 3:10, pour you out a **b**
Eph. 1:3, spiritual **b**-s in heavenly
1 Pet. 3:9, ye should inherit a **b**
Blind—*to darken, deprive of sight*
Deut. 16:19, doth **b** the eyes of the wise
Job 29:15, I was eyes to the **b**
John 12:40, He hath **b**-ed their eyes
Rom. 2:19, a guide to the **b**
2 Cor. 3:14, their minds were **b**-ed
1 John 2:11, darkness hath **b**-ed his eyes
Blindness—*state of being blind*
2 Kin. 6:18, Smite this people . . . with **b**
Rom. 11:25, **b** in part is happened
Eph. 4:18, the **b** of their heart
Blood—*life giving body fluid*
Gen. 4:10, voice of thy brother's **b**
9:6, sheddeth man's **b** . . . his **b**
49:11, in the **b** of grapes
Ps. 51:14, Deliver me from **b**-guiltiness
55:23, **b**-y and deceitful men
Prov. 29:10, **b**-thirsty hate the upright
Is. 1:15, your hands are full of **b**
49:26, drunken with their own **b**
Matt. 16:17, flesh and **b** hath not
26:28, my **b** . . . new testament
27:4, betrayed the innocent **b**
John 6:55, my **b** is drink indeed
Acts 17:26, made of one **b** all nations
20:28, purchased with his own **b**
Rom. 3:25, through faith in his **b**
5:9, being now justified by his **b**
1 Cor. 15:50, and **b** cannot inherit
Eph. 1:7, redemption through his **b**
1 John 1:7, **b** of Jesus Christ
1 John 5:6, but by water and **b**
Rev. 7:14, white in the **b** of the Lamb

Blossom—*come into flower*
Num. 17:8, rod of Aaron . . . bloomed **b-s**
Is. 35:1, desert shall . . . **b** as the rose
Hab. 3:17, the fig tree shall not **b**
Blot—*to erase, remove*
Ex. 32:33, **b** out of my book
Ps. 51:1, **b** out my transgressions
Is. 43:25, I am he that **b**-eth out
Jer. 18:23, **b** out their sin
Col. 2:14, **B**-ing out the handwriting
Blow—*to move, as air*
Ex. 15:10, Thou didst **b** with thy wind
Num. 10:9, ye shall **b** an alarm
Ps. 39:10, consumed by the **b**
Is. 40:7, spirit of the Lord **b**-eth upon
54:16, smith that **b**-eth the coals
Zech. 9:14, God shall **b** the trumpet
John 3:8, wind **b**-eth where it listeth
Boast—*self-praise, bragging*
2 Chr. 25:19, lifteth thee up to **b**
Ps. 44:8, In God we **b**
Prov. 27:1, **B** not thyself of tomorrow
Is. 10:15, Shall the ax **b** itself
2 Tim. 3:2, of their own selves . . . **b**-ers
James 4:16, ye rejoice in your **b**-ings
Boat—*a water craft*
2 Sam. 19:18, went over a ferry **b**
John 6:22, his disciples into the **b**
Acts 27:30, they had let down the **b**
Bodies—*physical beings of men*
Neh. 9:37, dominion over our **b**
Job 13:12, your **b** to **b** of clay
Jer. 31:40, valley of the dead **b**
Rom. 1:24, dishonour their own **b**
8:11, quicken your mortal **b**
12:1, present your **b** a living
Heb. 10:22, **b** washed with pure
Rev. 11:9, see their dead **b** three
Body—*the physical person*
Job 19:26, worms destroy this **b**
Lam. 4:7, more ruddy in **b**
Matt. 6:22, light of the **b** is the eye
10:28, destroy both soul and **b**
26:26, Take, eat; this is my **b**
27:58, begged the **b** of Jesus
Luke 12:4, them that kill the **b**
22:19, This is my **b**
John 2:21, spake of the temple of his **b**
Rom. 8:10, **b** is dead because of sin
23, redemption of our **b**
1 Cor. 6:20, glorify God in your **b**
9:27, I keep under my **b**
13:3, I give my **b** to be burned
15:44, natural **b** . . . spiritual **b**

2 Cor. 5:8, be absent from the **b**
Gal. 6:17, bear in my **b** the marks
Eph. 4:4, There is one **b**
Phil. 1:20, magnified in my **b**
3:21, change our vile **b**
Col. 1:18, he is the head of the **b**
3:15, ye are called in one **b**
1 Pet. 2:24, bare our sins in his own **b**
Bold—*daring, courageous*
Prov. 28:1, righteous are **b** as a lion
2 Cor. 11:21, whereinsoever any is **b**
Eph. 3:12, In whom we have **b**-ness
6:19, open my mouth **b**-ly
Heb. 4:16, Let us therefore come **b**-ly
1 John 4:17, may have **b**-ness in the day
Bond—*a uniting tie, a shackle*
Eph. 4:3, Spirit in the **b** of peace
1 Cor. 12:13, we be **b** or free
Gal. 3:28, there is neither **b** nor free
Phil. 1:13, that my **b**-s in Christ are
Col. 3:14, is the **b** of perfectness
Heb. 13:3, Remember . . . that are in **b**-s
Rev. 13:16, rich and poor, free and **b**
Bondage—*restraint, servitude*
Ex. 13:3, out of the house of **b**
John 8:33, were never in **b** to any man
Rom. 8:15, not received the spirit of **b**
2 Cor. 11:20, if a man bring you into **b**
Gal. 5:1, entangled . . . with the yoke of **b**
Bone—*parts of the skeleton of the body*
Gen. 2:23, This is now **b** of my **b**-s
Judg. 9:2, your **b** and your flesh
Job 10:11, fenced me with **b**-s
19:20, **b** cleaveth to my skin
Ps. 6:2, heal me; for my **b**-s are vexed
Prov. 15:30, report maketh the **b**-s fat
25:15, soft tongue breaketh the **b**
Ezek. 37:1, valley . . . was full of **b**-s
Matt. 23:27, full of dead men's **b**-s
Luke 24:39, hath not flesh and **b**-s
John 19:36, A **b** of him . . . not be broken
Book—*collection of written material*
Ex. 17:14, for a memorial in a **b**
Job 19:23, printed in a **b**
Ps. 69:28, blotted out of the **b**
Eccles. 12:12, making many **b**-s . . . no end
Is. 34:16, out of the **b** of the Lord
Ezek. 2:9, lo, a roll of a **b** was therein
Mal. 3:16, a **b** of remembrance
Luke 4:17, when he had opened the **b**
20:42, in the **b** of Psalms

Book (*Continued*)
John 21:25, world . . . not contain the **b**-s
Phil. 4:3; Rev. 3:5; 22:19, **b** of life
Rev. 22:19, away from the words of the **b**
Booth—*a rough shelter*
Lev. 23:42, Ye shall dwell in **b**-s
Ionah 4:5, there made him a **b**, and sat
Born—*brought into life*
Gen 15:3, 10, one **b** in my house
Ex. 21:4, **b** him sons or daughters
Job 14:1, Man that is **b** . . . of few days
Prov. 17:17, brother is **b** for adversity
Is. 9:6, unto us a child is **b**
Matt. 2:1, Jesus was **b** in Bethlehem
John 3:3, Except a man be **b** again
Acts 22:28, But I was free **b**
Gal. 4:29, **b** after the flesh
1 Pet. 1:23, **b** again, not of corruptible
Borne—*supported, conveyed*
Job 34:31, I have **b** chastisement
Is. 53:4, Surely he hath **b** our griefs
Matt. 23:4, burdens and grievous to be **b**
3 John 6, **b** witness of thy charity
Borrow—*receive as a loan*
Deut. 15:6, thou shalt lend . . . not **b**
Ps. 37:21, wicked **b**-eth, and payeth not
Prov. 22:7, **b**-er is servant to the
Matt. 5:42, him that would **b** of thee
Bosom—*the human breast*
Ex. 4:6, thine hand into thy **b**
Num. 11:12, Carry them in thy **b**
Deut. 13:6, wife of thy **b**
1 Kin. 3:20, and laid it in her **b**
Prov. 17:23, taketh a gift out of the **b**
Is. 40:11, carry them in his **b**
Luke 6:38, shall men give into your **b**
    16:22, angels into Abraham's **b**
John 13:23, leaning on Jesus' **b**
Both—*two, a pair*
Gen. 3:7, eyes of them **b** were opened
Matt. 15:14, blind, **b** shall fall into
Luke 7:42, forgave them **b**
Acts 1:1, **b** to do and teach
Eph. 2:14, peace, who hath made **b** one
Bottle—*hollow vessel, of skin or clay*
Gen. 21:14, bread, and a **b** of water
Judg. 4:19, she opened a **b** of milk
1 Sam. 1:24, and a **b** of wine
Job. 32:19, ready to burst like new **b**-s
Matt. 9:17, put new wine into old **b**-s
Bottomless—*unfathomable*
Rev. 9:1, given the key of the **b** pit
    20:3, cast him into the **b** pit

Bough—*branch of a tree*
Gen. 49:22, Joseph is a fruitful **b**
2 Sam. 18:9, thick **b**-s of a great oak
Is. 17:6, top of the uppermost **b**
Ezek. 31:6, made their nests in his **b**-s
Bought—*purchased*
Gen. 17:12, **b** with money of any
    33:19, **b** a parcel of a field
1 Kin. 16:24, **b** the hill Samaria
1 Cor. 6:20, For ye are **b** with a price
2 Pet. 2:1, the Lord that **b** them
Bound—*made fast, restrained*
Job 36:8, they be **b** in fetters
Matt. 16:19, bind on earth . . . **b** in
heaven
Luke 10:34, and **b** up his wounds
John 11:44, **b** about with a napkin
Heb. 13:3, in bonds as **b** with them
Bountiful—*free in giving, generous*
Ps. 13:6, he hath dealt **b**-ly
2 Cor. 9:6, soweth **b**-ly . . . reap also **b**-ly
    9:11, enriched . . . to all **b**-ness
Bow—*any thing bent*
Gen. 9:13, I do set my **b** in the cloud
2 Sam. 1:18, teach . . . the use of the **b**
Job 20:24, the **b** of steel
Hos. 1:5, I will break the **b** of Israel
Bow—*to bend the head, knee, or body*
Ex. 20:5, Thou shalt not **b** down thyself
Ps. 57:6, my soul is **b**-ed down
Is. 45:23, unto me every knee shall **b**
John 19:30, **b**-ed his head, and gave up
Eph. 3:14, I **b** my knees unto the Father
Phil. 2:10, every knee should **b**
Bowels—*intestines, or the seat of pity*
Gen. 43:30, his **b** did yearn
Job 30:27, My **b** boiled
Acts 1:18, all his **b** gushed out
Phil. 1:8, in the **b** of Jesus Christ
Col. 3:12, **b** of mercies, kindness
1 John 3:17, **b** of compassion
Box—*a receptacle, or case*
2 Kin. 9:1, take this **b** of oil
Matt. 26:7, alabaster **b** of . . . ointment
Boy—*male child*
Gen. 25:27, the **b**-s grew
Joel 3:3, given a **b** for an harlot
Zech. 8:5, streets . . . full of **b**-s
Bracelets—*ornamental bands*
Gen. 24:22, two **b** for her hands
    38:18, Thy signet, and thy **b**
Num. 31:50, gold, chains, and **b**
Ezek. 16:11, put **b** upon thy hands

Brake—*to burst asunder*
Judg. 7:19, and **b** the pitchers
    9:53, all to **b** his skull
Matt. 14:19, blessed, and **b**, and gave
Luke 5:6, and their net **b**
John 19:32, and **b** the legs of the first
Bramble—*thorny shrub*
Judg. 9:14, all the trees unto the **b**
Is. 34:13, nettles and **b**-s in fortresses
Luke 6:44, not of a **b** bush gather they
John 15:6, cast forth as a **b**
Branch—*limb of a tree*
Job 15:32, his **b** shall not be green
Prov. 11:28, shall flourish as a **b**
Is. 4:2, day shall the **b** of the Lord
John 15:2, every **b** that beareth fruit
Brand—*torch*
Judg. 15:5, set the **b**-s on fire
Zech. 3:2, is not this a **b** plucked out
Brass—*probably copper, sometimes bronze*
Gen. 4:22, artificer in **b** and iron
Num. 21:9, Moses made a serpent of **b**
Deut. 33:25, shoes shall be iron and **b**
1 Sam. 17:5, helmet of **b** upon his head
1 Kin. 7:14, Tyre, a worker in **b**
Ps. 107:16, broken the gates of **b**
Matt. 10:9, gold, nor silver, nor **b**
1 Cor. 13:1, become as sounding **b**
Rev. 1:15, feet like unto fine **b**
Brawler—*quarrelsome person*
Prov. 21:9, a **b**-ing woman
1 Tim. 3:3, patient, not a **b**
Titus 3:2, evil of no man, to be no **b**-s
Bray—*loud harsh cry of an ass*
Job 6:5, Doth the wild ass **b**
    30:7, Among the bushes they **b**-ed
Prov. 27:22, Though thou shouldest **b**
Breach—*gap or opening*
Lev. 24:20, **B** for **b**, eye for eye
Ps. 60:2, heal the **b**-s thereof
    106:23, stood before him in the **b**
Is. 58:12, repairer of the **b**
Bread—*food, sustenance*
Gen. 3:19, sweat of thy face . . . eat **b**
    18:5, fetch a morsel of **b**
Deut. 8:3; Matt. 4:4, live by **b** alone
    16:8, shalt eat unleavened **b**
1 Kin. 17:6, brought him **b** and flesh
Ps. 102:9, eaten ashes like **b**
Prov. 9:17, **b** eaten in secret
    31:27, eateth not the **b** of idleness
Eccles. 11:1, Cast thy **b** upon the waters
Is. 55:2, money for that which is not **b**

Matt. 4:3, that these stones be made **b**
    6:11, give us . . . our daily **b**
Mark 7:27, to take, the children's **b**
Luke 11:11, if a son shall ask **b**
Break—*part, burst asunder*
Ex. 22:6, If fire **b** out, and catch in
Ps. 2:9, **b** them with a rod of iron
    89:31, if they **b** my statutes
Song 2:17, Until the day **b**
Is. 42:3, bruised reed shall he not **b**
    44:23, **b** forth into singing
Jer. 4:3, **B** up your fallow ground
Matt. 12:20, reed shall he not **b**
Breath—*air inhaled and exhaled*
Gen. 2:7, his nostrils the **b** of life
    6:17, wherein is the **b** of life
Job 33:4, **b** of the Almighty . . . life
Acts 17:25, he giveth to all life and **b**
Breathe—*respiration*
Ps. 27:12, and such as **b** out cruelty
John 20:22, he **b**-d on them
Acts 9:1, and Saul, yet **b**-ing out
Breeches—*underclothing*
Ex. 28:42, **b** to cover their nakedness
Lev. 6:10, shall put on his . . . linen **b**
Ezek. 44:18, shall have linen **b** upon
Brethren—*plural of brother*
Gen. 29:4, My **b**, whence be ye
Job 6:15, My **b** have dealt deceitfully
Ps. 133:1, **b** to dwell together
Hos. 2:1, Say ye unto your **b**
Matt. 5:47, if ye salute your **b** only
    12:46, mother . . . **b** stood without
    23:8, and all ye are **b**
    25:40, of the least of these my **b**
Mark 12:20, there were seven **b**
Luke 18:29, no man that hath left . . . **b**
Acts 7:2, Men, **b**, and fathers
1 Tim. 4:6, put the **b** in remembrance
1 Pet. 1:22, unfeigned love of the **b**
1 John 3:14, because we love the **b**
Bribes—*corruptive presents*
1 Sam. 8:3, took **b**, and perverted
Ps. 26:10, right hand is full of **b**
Brick—*baked clay blocks or tiles*
Gen. 11:3, make **b**, and burn them
Ex. 5:7, no more straw to make **b**
Is. 9:10, the **b**-s are fallen
    65:3, incense upon altars of **b**
Bride—*woman to be, or newly married*
Is. 61:10, as a **b** adorneth
    62:5, rejoiceth over the **b**
John 3:29, He that hath the **b**
Rev. 22:17, Spirit and the **b** say, Come

Bridechamber—*the bride's abode*
Matt. 9:15, children of the **b** mourn
Mark 2:19, children of **b** fast while
Luke 5:34, make children of **b** fast
Bridegroom—*man to be, or newly married*
Is. 61:10, as a **b** decketh himself
Jer. 7:34, the voice of the **b**
Matt. 9:15, long as the **b** is with them
25:1, went forth to meet the **b**
John 3:29, hath the bride is the **b**
Bridle—*part of a harness*
2 Kin. 19:28, put . . . my **b** in thy lips
Ps. 32:9, must be held in with . . . **b**
39:1, I will keep my mouth with a **b**
Bridle—*restrain, govern*
James 1:26, and **b**-th not his tongue
3:2, able also to **b** the whole body
Brier—*thorn, nettle*
Is. 5:6, there shall come up **b**-s
55:13, instead of the **b** shall come
Heb. 6:8, thorns and **b**-s is rejected
Bright—*shining, radiant*
Job 37:11, he scattereth his **b** cloud
Jer. 51:11, make **b** the arrows
Ezek. 32:8, all the **b** lights of heaven
Luke 11:36, **b** shining of a candle
Acts 10:30, man stood before me in **b**
Rev. 22:16, the **b** and morning star
Brimstone—*sulphur*
Gen. 19:24, Sodom and . . . Gomorrah **b**
Is. 30:33, like a stream of **b**
Ezek. 38:22, hail stones, fire and **b**
Luke 17:29, rained fire and **b**
Rev. 19:20, lake of fire burning with **b**
Bring—*to carry, fetch*
Gen. 1:11, earth **b** forth grass
Deut. 7:1, shall **b** thee into the land
Job 33:30, **b** back his soul
Eccles. 12:4, God shall **b** every work
Is. 65:9, **b** forth a seed out of
Mal. 3:10, **b** ye all the tithes
Matt. 1:21, she shall **b** forth a son
Luke 2:10, behold I **b** you good tidings
John 12:24, **b**-eth forth much fruit
1 Pet. 3:18, that he might **b** unto God
Brink—*edge, brim, margin*
Gen. 41:3, kine upon the **b** of the river
Ex. 2:3, flags by the river's **b**
Josh. 3:8, when ye are come to the **b**
Broad—*wide, extensive*
Job, 36:16, strait into a **b** place
Ps. 119:96, commandment is exceeding **b**
Matt. 7:13, **b** is the way, that leadeth

Broidered—*ornamented with needlework*
Ex. 28:4, and a **b** coat
Ezek. 16:10, 13, clothed . . . with **b** work
Broken—*violently separated*
Judg. 16:9, a thread of tow is **b**
Ps. 34:18, them that are of a **b** heart
Prov. 25:19, like a **b** tooth
Matt. 15:37, they took up of the **b** meat
John 19:36, bone of him shall not be **b**
1 Cor. 11:24, body, which is **b** for you
Eph. 2:14, **b** down the middle wall
Brook—*small stream, a creek*
Deut. 8:7, a land of **b**-s of water
Ps. 42:1, panteth after the water **b**-s
Prov. 18:4, wisdom as a flowing **b**
John 18:1, his disciples over the **b**
Broth—*thin soup*
Judg. 6:19, and he put the **b** in a pot
Is. 65:4, **b** of abominable things
Brother—*a male relative, or associate*
Ps. 50:20, speakest against thy **b**
Prov. 17:17, **b** is born for adversity
18:24, sticketh closer than a **b**
Eccles. 4:8, neither child nor **b**
Matt. 5:22, whosoever is . . . with his **b**
12:50, same is my **b**, and sister
1 Cor. 8:13, lest I make my **b** to offend
Gal. 1:19, James the Lord's **b**
1 John 2:9, He that . . . hateth his **b**
Brotherly—*fraternal, kindly*
Rom. 12:10, one to another with **b** love
Heb. 13:1, let **b** love continue
2 Pet. 1:7, godliness **b** kindness
Brow—*eyebrow, edge of steep place*
Is. 48:4, and thy **b** brass
Luke 4:29, led him unto the **b** of the hill
Bruise—*to injure, to break*
Gen. 3:15, **b** thy head, and thou shalt **b**
Jer. 30:12, Thy **b** is incurable
Matt. 12:20, **b**-d reed shall he not
Luke 4:18, at liberty them that are **b**-d
Rom. 16:20, **b** Satan under your feet
Brutish—*beastly*
Ps. 92:6, **b** man knoweth not
Prov. 12:1, he that hateth reproof is **b**
Jer. 10:8, they are altogether **b**
51:17, Every man is **b**
Buckler—*shield*
2 Sam. 22:31, he is a **b** to them
Ps. 18:2, my **b**, and the horn of salvation
91:4, his truth . . . thy shield and **b**
Bud—*blossom, germinate*
Num. 17:8, rod . . . brought forth **b**-s

Job 38:27, the **b** of the tender herb
Is. 55:10, maketh it bring forth and **b**
Hos. 8:7, the **b** shall yield no meal
Heb. 9:4, Aaron's rod that **b**-ed
Buffet—*to slap, strike, beat*
Matt. 26:67, spit in his face, and **b**-ed
1 Cor. 4:11, are naked, and are **b**-ed
2 Cor. 12:7, messenger of Satan to **b** me
1 Pet. 2:20, when ye be **b**-ed for faults
Build—*erect, construct*
Gen. 11:4, let us **b** us a city
Num. 23:1, **B** me here seven altars
1 Sam. 2:35, will **b** him a sure house
1 Chr. 17:4, shalt not **b** me an house
Job 20:19, house which he **b**-ed not
Ps. 127:1, Except the Lord **b** the
Jer. 29:5, **B** ye houses, and dwell
Matt. 16:18, this rock will I **b** my
Acts 20:32, to **b** you up
Builders—*those who construct*
2 Kin. 22:6, Unto carpenters, and **b**
Ps. 118:22, stone . . . the **b** refused
Matt. 21:42, stone . . . the **b** rejected
Acts 4:11, set at naught of you **b**
Building—*an edifice, or its erection*
1 Kin. 6:38, seven years in **b** it
1 Cor. 3:9, ye are God's **b**
2 Cor. 5:1, we have a **b** of God
Eph. 2:21, the **b** fitly framed together
Bulrush—*marsh-growing plant*
Ex. 2:3, took for him an ark of **b**-es
Is. 18:2, vessels of **b**-es upon the
58:5, bow down his head as a **b**
Bulwarks—*fortresses, protection*
Deut. 20:20, that shalt build **b**
Ps. 48:13, Mark ye well her **b**
Is. 26:1, appoint for walls and **b**
Bundle—*package*
Gen. 42:35, every man's **b** of money
1 Sam. 25:29, bound in the **b** of life
Matt. 13:30, bind them in **b**-s to burn
Burden—*a weight*
2 Sam. 15:33, be a **b** unto me
2 Kin. 9:25, Lord laid this **b** upon him
Job 7:20, I am a **b** to myself
Ps. 55:22, Cast thy **b** upon the Lord
Jer. 23:34, The **b** of the Lord
Zech. 9:1, The **b** of the word of the
Matt. 11:30, my **b** is light
20:12, borne the **b** and heat of
Gal. 6:5, man shall bear his own **b**
Burdensome—*weighty, oppressive*
2 Cor. 11:9, kept myself from being **b**
12:13, 14, was not **b** to you

1 Thess. 2:6, might have been **b**
Burial—*internment*
Eccles. 6:3, that ye have no **b**
Jer. 22:19, buried with the **b** of an ass
Matt. 26:12, she did it for my **b**
Buried—*interred*
Gen. 15:15, **b** in a good old age
Ruth 1:17, and there will I be **b**
Eccles. 8:10, so I saw the wicked **b**
Acts 2:29, he is both dead and **b**
Rom. 6:4, we are **b** with him
Col. 2:12, **B** with him in baptism
Burn—*consume with fire*
Gen. 11:3, make brick, and **b** them
Ex. 3:2, behold, the bush **b**-ed with fire
Deut. 5:23, mountain did **b** with fire
Matt. 13:30, bind . . . bundles to **b** them
Luke 12:35, and your lights **b**-ing
Rom. 1:27, **b**-ed in their lust
1 Cor. 13:3, I give my body to be **b**-ed
Burst—*explode, break*
Job 32:19, ready to **b** like new bottles
Prov. 3:10, shall **b** out with new wine
Nah. 1:13, **b** thy bonds in sunder
Mark 2:22, new wine doth **b** the bottles
Bury—*to inter*
Gen. 49:29, **b** me with my fathers
Ps. 79:3, there was none to **b** them
Luke 9:60, Let the dead **b** their dead
John 19:40, manner of the Jews is to **b**
Bush—*small tree*
Ex. 3:2, the **b** burned with fire
Song 5:11, his locks are **b**-y
Mark 12:26, in the **b** God spake unto
Acts 7:30, in a flame of fire in a **b**
Bushel—*dry measure*
Matt. 5:15, candle . . . under a **b**
Mark 4:21, put under a **b**, or a bed
Luke 11:33, neither under a **b**
Business—*employment, occupation*
Deut. 24:5, be charged with any **b**
Judg. 18:7, had no **b** with any man
Ps. 107:23, that do **b** in great waters
Prov. 22:29, man diligent in his **b**
Luke 2:49, must be about my Father's **b**
Acts 6:3, may appoint over his **b**
Rom. 12:11, not slothful in **b**
1 Thess. 4:11, study . . . to do your own **b**
Busybody—*a meddling person*
2 Thess. 3:11, but are **b**-ies
1 Tim. 5:13, tattlers also, and **b**-ies
1 Pet. 4:15, a **b** in other men's matters

Butler—*cupbearer, manservant*
  Gen. 40:1, **b** of the king of Egypt
    41:9, spake the chief **b**
Butter—*curdled milk, or curds*
  Judg. 5:25, **b** in a lordly dish
  Deut. 32:14, **B** of kine, and milk of
  Ps. 55:21, words . . . smoother than **b**
  Prov. 30:33, of milk bringeth forth **b**
  Is. 7:15, **B** and honey shall he eat
Buy—*acquire by purchase*
  Gen. 43:2, **b** us a little food
  Prov. 23:23, **B** the truth, and sell it not
  Jer. 32:7, **B** thee my field
  Matt. 13:44, selleth all . . . and **b**-eth
  John 13:29, **B** those things that we have
  James 4:13, **b** and sell, and get gain
  Rev. 3:18, **b** of me gold tried
    13:17, no man might **b** or sell
Buyer—*purchaser*
  Prov. 20:14, it is naught, saith the **b**
  Is. 24:2, as with the **b** so with seller
  Ezek. 7:12, Let not the **b** rejoice
By and by—*soon, later*
  Matt. 13:21, **b** he is offended
  Mark 6:25, give me **b** in a charger
  Luke 17:7, will say unto him **b**
Byword—*a common saying*
  Deut. 28:37, an astonishment . . . a **b**
  1 Kin. 9:7, and a **b** among all people
  Job 30:9, their song, yea, I am their **b**

C

Cage—*inclosure, confinement*
  Jer. 5:27, as a **c** is full of birds
  Rev. 18:2, a **c** of every unclean . . . bird
Cake—*a small loaf, or mass*
  Gen. 18:6, make **c**-s upon the hearth
  1 Kin. 17:13, make me . . . little **c** first
Calamity—*a great misfortune*
  2 Sam. 22:19; Ps. 18:18, day of my **c**
  Ps. 57:1, until these **c**-s be overpast
  Prov. 19:13, foolish son is the **c**
    27:10, in the day of the **c**
Calf—*young of the bovine*
  Gen. 18:7, fetch a **c** tender and
  Is. 11:6, **c** and the young lion
  Luke 15:23, bring hither the fatted **c**
  Heb. 9:12, blood of goats and **c**-ves
  Rev. 4:7, second beast like a **c**
Call—*speak loudly, designate, invoke*
  Gen. 4:26, men to **c** upon the name

  Deut. 4:26, **c** heaven and earth to
  Ruth 1:20, **C** me not Naomi, **c** me Mara
  I Kin. 17:18, **c** my sin to remembrance
  Ps. 4:1, Hear me when I **c**
    18:3, I will **c** upon the Lord
  Is. 5:20, **c** evil good, and good evil
    7:14, **c** his name Immanuel
  Jer. 3:9, shalt **c** me, My father
  Matt. 9:13, not come to **c** the righteous
  Luke 6:46, why **c** ye me, Lord, Lord
  John 13:13, Ye **c** me Master and Lord
  Acts 10:15, that **c** not thou common
  1 Pet. 1:17, if ye **c** on the Father
Calling—*vocation*
  Rom. 11:29, gifts and **c** of God
  1 Cor. 7:20, abide in the same **c**
  2 Tim. 1:9, called us with an holy **c**
  Heb. 3:1, partakers of the heavenly **c**
  2 Pet. 1:10, make your **c** and election
Calm—*quiet, tranquil*
  Ps. 107:29, maketh the storm a **c**
  Jonah 1:11, that the sea may be **c**
  Matt. 8:26, there was a great **c**
Camel—*a large animal*
  Gen. 24:64, she lighted off the **c**
  Matt. 19:24, easier for a **c** to go through
    23:24, at a gnat, and swallow a **c**
  Mark 1:6, clothed with **c**'s hair
Camp—*a collection of shelters, to lodge*
  Ex. 14:19, angel . . . went before the **c**
  Deut. 23:14, God walketh in . . . thy **c**
  Is. 29:3, I will **c** against thee
  Jer. 50:29, **c** against it round about
  Nah. 3:17, which **c** in the hedges
  Rev. 20:9, compassed the **c** of the saints
Candle—*that which gives light*
  Job 18:6, his **c** shall be put out
  Ps. 18:28, thou wilt light my **c**
  Prov. 20:27, of man is the **c** of the Lord
  Zeph. 1:12, search Jerusalem with **c**-s
  Matt. 5:15, light a **c** and put it under
  Rev. 22:5, they need no **c** neither light
Candlestick—*candle holder*
  Ex. 25:31, shalt make a **c** of pure gold
  1 King. 7:49, the **c**-s of pure gold
  2 Kin. 4:10, table, and a stool, and a **c**
  Luke 8:16, setteth it on a **c**
Canker—*gangrene*
  2 Tim. 2:17, will eat as doth a **c**
  James 5:3, your gold and silver is **c**-ed
Captive—*one made prisoner, or subjugated*
  Ps. 68:18, led captivity **c**

Jer. 13:17, flock is carried away c
Luke 4:18, preach deliverance to the c's
Eph. 4:8, he led captivity c
2 Tim. 3:6, lead c silly women
Captivity—*slavery, imprisonment*
Job 42:10, Lord turned the c of Job
Is. 46:2, themselves are gone into c
Rom. 7:23, bringing me into c to the law
Eph. 4:8, he led c captive
2 Cor. 10:5, bringing into c . . . thought
Carcase—*dead body*
Gen. 15:11, fowls came upon the c-s
Judg. 14:8, turned aside to see the c
Is. 14:19, a c trodden under feet
Matt. 24:28, wheresoever the c is
Care—*anxiety, concern*
Ps. 142:4, no man c-d for my soul
Matt. 13:22, the c of this world
Mark 4:38, Master, c-st thou not
Luke 8:14, choked with c-s and riches
10:34, to an inn, and took c of him
John 12:6, not that he c-d for the poor
1 Cor. 9:9, Doth God take c for oxen
12:25, the same c one for another
1 Tim. 3:5, take c of the church
1 Pet. 5:7, Casting all your c upon him
Careful—*watchful, giving good heed*
Jer. 17:8, be c in the year of drought
Luke 10:41, thou art c and troubled
1 Cor. 7:32, have you without c-ness
Phil. 4:6, Be c for nothing
Careless—*thoughtless, negligent*
Judg. 18:7, dwelt c after the manner
Is. 32:8, hear my voice, ye c daughters
Ezek. 39:6, them that dwell c-ly
Carnal—*pertaining to the body, animal*
Rom. 8:6, to be c-ly minded is death
1 Cor. 9:11, shall reap your c things
2 Cor. 10:4, weapons . . . are not c
Carpenter—*a wood worker*
2 Sam. 5:11, c-s, and masons
2 Kin. 22:6, Unto c-s, and builders
Is. 44:13, c stretched out his rule
Zech. 1:20, Lord shewed me four c-s
Matt. 13:55, not this the c's son
Mark 6:3, Is not this the c the son of
Carriage—*vehicle*
1 Sam. 17:22, David left his c
Is. 46:1, your c-s were heavy loaden
Acts 21:15, we took up our c-s
Carry—*convey, transport*
Is. 40:11, and c them in his bosom
53:4, griefs, and c-ed our sorrows

Luke 10:4, C neither purse, nor scrip
16:22, was c-ed by the angels into
Heb. 13:9, Be not c-ed about with divers
Cart—*wagon, dray, chariot*
1 Sam. 6:7-14, laid the ark upon the c
Is. 5:18, draw sin . . . with a c rope
28:27, 28, neither is a c wheel
Case—*situation, condition*
Ps. 144:15, people, that is in such a c
Matt. 5:20, ye shall in no c enter
19:10, If the c of the man be so
Cassia—*kind of cinnamon*
Ex. 30:24, of c five hundred shekels
Ps. 45:8, thy garments smell of . . . c
Ezek. 27:19, c . . . in thy market
Cast—*throw, fling or hurl*
Gen. 21:10, C out this bondwoman
37:20, c him into some pit
Ps. 51:11, C me not away from thy
Eccles. 11:1, C thy bread upon the
Matt. 7:5, first c out the beam
Luke 19:35, c their garments upon the
John 6:37, I will in no wise c out
Rom. 13:12, c off the works of darkness
1 Pet. 5:7, C-ing all your care upon him
Castle—*citadel, fortress*
1 Chr. 11:5, 7, David took the c of Zion
Acts 21:34, to be carried into the c
22:24, be brought into the c
Catch—*lay hold on, seize*
Ps. 10:9, lieth in wait to c the poor
Mark 12:13, to c him in his words
Luke 5:10, henceforth thou shalt c men
John 10:12, wolf c-eth them
Caterpillar—*wormlike larva*
2 Chr. 6:28, if there be locusts or c-s
Is. 33:4, like gathering of the c
Joel 2:25, locust hath eaten . . . and the c
Cattle—*all domesticated animals*
Ex. 12:29, smote all the firstborn of c
20:10, thy maid servant, nor thy c
Ps. 50:10, the c upon a thousand hills
104:14, the grass to grow for the c
Caught—*taken, seized, entangled*
Gen. 22:13, ram c in a thicket
Jer. 50:24, thou art found, and also c
John 21:3, that night they c nothing
Josh. 18:10, Joshua c lots for them
Judg. 15:4, c three hundred foxes
1 Kin. 7:15, c two pillars of brass
Matt. 7:5, c out the beam . . . mote
2 Cor. 12:4, he was c up into paradise

23

Caul—*fatty membrane*
Ex. 29:13, c that is above the liver
Lev. 3:4, 10, 15, c above the liver
Hos. 13:8, rend the c of their heart
Cause—*sake, interest, to make*
Gen. 7:4, I will c it to rain
Ps. 67:1, c his face to shine upon us
Prov. 3:30, Strive not . . . without c
Matt. 5:22, angry . . . without a c
19:5, this c shall a man leave
Luke 23:22, I have found no c of death
John 15:25, hated me without a c
Rom. 16:17, mark them . . . c divisions
Col. 4:16, c that it be read also
1 Tim. 1:16, for this c I obtained mercy
1 Pet. 4:6, for this c was the gospel
Cave—*hollow place in the earth*
1 Kin. 18:4, hid them by fifty in a c
John 11:8, It was a c . . . stone lay upon
Heb. 11:38, and in dens and c-s
Cease—*to come to an end, to pass away*
Gen. 8:22, summer and winter . . . not c
Deut. 15:11, poor shall never c
Ps. 37:8, C from anger
46:9, He maketh wars to c
Prov. 23:4, c from thine own wisdom
Luke 7:45, not c-d to kiss my feet
1 Cor. 13:8, be tongues, they shall c
1 Thess. 5:17, Pray without c-ing
Cedar—*tree, chiefly of pine family*
1 Kin. 5:6, c trees out of Lebanon
6:15, boards of c
Job 40:17, moveth his tail like a c
Ps. 92:12, grow like a c in Lebanon
Ceiled—*covered*
2 Chr. 3:5, house he c with fir tree
Jer. 22:14, it is c with cedar
Hag. 1:4, dwell in your c houses
Celebrate—*commemorate, observe*
Lev. 23:32, shall ye c your sabbath
Is. 38:18, death can not c thee
Celestial—*heavenly, angelic*
1 Cor. 15:40, there are also c bodies
Censer—*incense burner*
Lev. 16:12, take a c full of . . . coals
Ezek. 8:11, every man his c in his hand
Heb. 9:4, the golden c and ark
Rev. 8:3, 5, angel took the c and filled
Certain—*fixed, sure*
Ex. 3:12, C-ly I will be with thee
16:4, gather a c rate every day
Josh. 23:13, Know for a c-ty that the
Luke 1:5, c priest named Zacharias

1 Cor. 4:11, have no c dwelling place
Heb. 10:27, c fearful looking for of
Certify—*verify, testify, attest*
2 Sam. 15:28, word from you to c me
Ezra 4:16, We c the king that
Gal. 1:11, But I c you, brethren
Chaff—*husks of grain*
Ps. 1:4, the c which the wind driveth
Is. 5:24, the flame consumeth the c
Matt. 3:12, burn up the c with
Chain—*connected links, a bond, or fetter*
Judg. 8:26, c-s . . . about their camel's
1 Kin. 6:21, partition by the c-s of gold
Mark 5:3, bind him, no, not with c-s
Acts 12:7, c-s fell off from his hands
Jude 6, reserved in everlasting c-s
Rev. 20:1, pit and a great c in his
Chalcedony—*light colored quartz*
Rev. 21:19, the third, a c
Challengeth—*dareth, defyeth*
Ex. 22:9, which another c to be his
Chamber—*a room*
Gen. 43:30, entered into his c
Judg. 3:24, covereth his feet . . . summer c
2 Kin. 4:10, Let us make a little c
Ps. 19:5, bridegroom . . . out of his c
Matt. 24:26, he is in the secret c-s
Chambering—*lewdness*
Rom. 13:13, not in c and wantonness
Chamberlain—*royal attendant, or steward*
2 Kin. 23:11, Nathanmelech the c
Esther 1:10, seven c-s that served
Acts 12:20, Blastus the king's c
Champion—*defender, protector, advocate*
1 Sam. 17:4, there went out a c
23, the c the Philistine
Chance—*fortune, fate*
Deut. 22:6, bird's nest c to be before
Eccles. 9:11, time and c happeneth
Luke 10:31, by c there came down
1 Cor. 15:37, it may c of wheat
Change—*variation, alteration, to shift*
Gen. 35:2, c your garments
Job 14:14, will I wait, till my c come
17:12, they c the night into day
Prov. 24:21, meddle not . . . given to c
Jer. 13:23, the Ethiopian c his skin
Dan. 2:21, c-th the times and
Mal. 3:6, I am the Lord, I c not
Rom. 1:25, c-d the truth of God
1 Cor. 15:51, but we shall all be c-d
Phil. 3:21, Who shall c our vile body

Chant—*to sing monotonously*
Amos 6:5, c to the sound of the viol
Chapel—*a small church*
Amos 7:13, it is the king's c
Chapmen—*peddlers, hawkers*
2 Chr. 9:14, that which c and merchants
Chapt—*dried, cracked*
Jer. 14:4, ground is c ... no rain
Charge—*responsibility, to command*
Lev. 8:35, keep the c of the Lord
Job 1:22, sinned not, nor c-d God
Ps. 91:11, give his angels c over
Matt. 4:6, He shall give his angels c
Mark 5:43, he c-d them straitly
Luke 5:14, c-d him to tell no man
Acts 7:60, lay not this sin to their c
1 Cor. 9:18, gospel of Christ without c
1 Tim. 5:21, I c thee before God
Chargeable—*liable*
2 Cor. 11:9, I was c to no man
1 Thess. 2:9, would be c to none of you
Chariot—*a two wheeled vehicle*
Gen. 46:29, Joseph made ready his c
2 Kin. 2:11, appeared a c of fire
Ps. 20:7, some trust in c-s
46:9, burneth the c in the fire
104:3, who maketh the clouds his c
Acts 8:28, sitting in his c read Esaias
Charity—*brotherly love and benevolence*
1 Cor. 13:1, and have not c
14:1, Follow after c
Col. 3:14, all these things put on c
1 Tim. 1:5, the commandment is c out of
2 Tim. 2:22, righteousness, faith, c
1 Pet. 4:8, c shall cover the multitude
2 Pet. 1:7 and to brotherly kindness c
3 John 6, borne witness of thy c
Charmer—*a magician, enchanter*
Deut. 18:11, or a c or consulter
Ps. 58:5, not hearken to voice of c-s
Chase—*pursue, hunt*
Lev. 26:7, ye shall c your enemies
Deut. 32:30, How ... one c a thousand
Job 20:8, he shall be c-d away
Ps. 35:5, Angel of the Lord c them
Chaste—*pure, modest, undefiled*
2 Cor. 11:2, present you as a c virgin
Titus 2:5, be discreet, c
1 Pet. 3:2, your c conversation
Chasten—*to correct by punishment*
Deut. 8:5, as a man c-eth his son
Ps. 38:1, c me in thy hot displeasure
94:12, man whom thou c-est
Prov. 19:18, C thy son while there is

1 Cor. 11:32, we are c-ed of the Lord
Heb. 12:6, the Lord loveth he c-eth
Chastise—*punish*
Lev. 26:28, will c you seven times
1 Kin. 12:11, c-d you with whips
Luke 23:16, I will therefore c him
Heb. 12:8, if ye be without c-ment
Chatter—*jabber, prate*
Is. 38:14, so did I c
Cheek—*side of face, jowls*
Job 16:10, smitten me upon the c
Is. 50:6, gave ... my c-s to them
Joel 1:6, he hath the c teeth
Matt. 5:39, smite thee on thy right c
Cheer—*good spirits, restrained joy*
Deut. 24:5, shall c up his wife
Judg. 9:13, which c-eth God and man
Prov. 15:13, c-ful countenance
Matt. 9:2, Son, be of good c; thy sins
14:27, Be of good c; it is I
John 16:33, of good c; I have overcome
Acts 23:11, Be of good c, Paul
2 Cor. 9:7, God loveth a c-ful giver
Cheese—*milk-curd food*
1 Sam. 17:18, carry these ten c-s
2 Sam. 17:29, and c of kine
Job 10:10, curdled me like c
Chickens—*young of birds*
Matt. 23:37, as a hen gathereth her c
Chide—*scold, reprove, censure*
Ex. 17:2, people did c with Moses
Judg. 8:1, they did c with him sharply
Ps. 103:9, He will not always c
Chief—*best, greatest, leader*
1 Sam. 9:22, sit in the c-est place
Matt. 20:27, whosoever will be c among
Mark 10:44, the c-est shall be servant
Luke 22:26, he that is c doth serve
2 Cor. 11:5, whit behind the very c-est
1 Tim. 1:15, of whom I am c
Child—*young person of either sex*
Gen. 21:8, the c grew
Prov. 22:6, Train up a c in the way
23:13, not correction from the c
Eccles. 4:8, neither c nor brother
Is. 9:6, unto us a c is born
11:6, a little c shall lead them
Jer. 31:20, Is he a pleasant c
Matt. 18:2, Jesus called a little c
1 Cor. 13:11, I was a c, I spake as a c
2 Tim. 3:15, from a c thou hast known
Children—*young people, associates*
Gen. 3:16, sorrow ... bring forth c

Children (*Continued*)
1 Sam. 16:11, Are here all thy c
Job 5:4, His c are far from safety
Ps. 103:13, as a father pitieth his c
Prov. 17:6, C's c are the crown of old
    31:28, her c . . . call her blessed
Is. 30:9, lying c that will not hear
    49:21, I have lost my c
Jer. 31:15, Rachel weeping for her c
Ezek. 18:2, c's teeth are set on edge
Matt. 18:3, and become as little c
    19:14, Suffer little c . . . to come
John 12:36, may be the c of light
1 John 2:1, My little c these things
Rev. 2:23, kill her c with death

Choice—*preference, select*
Gen. 23:6, the c of our sepulchres
1 Sam. 9:2, Saul, a c young man
2 Sam. 10:9, chose all the c men
Acts 15:7, God made c among us

Choke—*strangle, suffocate, stifle*
Matt. 13:22, riches, c the word
Mark 4:19, lusts of things . . . c the word
Luke 8:14, and are c-d with cares

Choose—*select, prefer*
Ex. 17:9, C us out men
Deut. 7:6, Lord . . . hath c-n thee
Josh. 24:15, c you this day whom ye
Ps. 119:30, have c-n the way of truth
Is. 7:15, and c the good
Matt. 12:18, servant, whom I have c-n
Heb. 11:25, C-ing rather to suffer
1 Pet. 2:9, ye are a c-n generation

Christ—*title of Jesus as the Messiah*
Matt. 16:16, Thou are the C, the Son
Luke 24:46, it behoved C to suffer
John 1:41, found the Messias . . . C
Acts 2:36, Jesus . . . both Lord and C
Rom. 1:16, not ashamed of the gospel of
    C
1 Cor. 1:23, we preach C crucified
Phil. 1:21, For me to live is C
Col. 3:4, C, who is our life
1 Thess. 4:16, the dead in C shall rise
2 Thess. 2:2, the day of C is at hand
    3:5, patient waiting for C
2 John 9, not in the doctrine of C

Christian—*follower of Christ*
Acts 11:26, called C-s first in
    26:28, persuadest me to be a C
1 Pet. 4:16, any man suffer as a C

Church—*a body of believers*
Matt. 16:18, upon this rock . . . my c
    18:17, tell it unto the c

Acts 15:4, received of the c
1 Cor. 11:18, come together in the c
    14:35, for women to speak in c
2 Cor. 11:8, I robbed other c-es
Eph. 5:23, Christ is the head of the c
1 Tim. 3:5, shall he take care of the c
Heb. 12:23, general assembly and c

Churl—*a rough, ill-bred man*
1 Sam. 25:3, the man was c-ish and evil
Is. 32:5, 7, the c said to be bountiful

Cinnamon—*aromatic bark or spice*
Prov. 7:17, perfumed my bed with . . . c
Song 4:14, Saffron; calamus and c
Rev. 18:13, and c and odours

Circuit—*district, route*
1 Sam. 7:16, year to year in c to Bethel
Job 22:14, he walketh in the c of heaven
Ps. 19:6, his c unto the ends of it
Eccles. 1:6, according to his c-s

Circumcise—*cut off the foreskin*
Gen. 17:10, every man child . . . be c-d
Deut. 30:6, Lord . . . will c thine heart
Luke 1:59, eighth day they came to c
Phil. 3:5, C-d the eighth day
Col. 2:11, In whom also ye are c-d

Circumspect—*cautious, prudent, vigilant*
Ex. 23:13, in all things . . . be c
Eph. 5:15, walk c-ly, not as fools

Cistern—*reservoir, tank*
Prov. 5:15, waters out of thine own c
Eccles. 12:6, wheel broken at the c
Jer. 2:13, hewed them out c-s

Citizen—*inhabitant, civilian*
Luke 15:15, joined himself to a c
Acts 21:39, a c of no mean city
Eph. 2:19, fellow-c-s with the saints

City—*a large town*
Gen. 4:17, builded a c . . . name of the c
    11:4, build us a c and a tower
Ps. 46:4, make glad the c of God
    127:1, except the Lord keep the c
Eccles. 9:14, a little c and few men
Is. 1:26, The c of righteousness
    19:18, The c of destruction
Matt. 21:10, all the c was moved
Luke 9:5, When ye go out of that c
John 19:41, beheld the c and wept
Acts 7:58, cast him out of the c
Heb. 12:22, the c of the living God
Rev. 21:2, I John saw the holy c

Clad—*clothe*
1 Kin 11:29, c himself . . . a new garment
Is. 59:17, was c with zeal as a cloak

26

Clamor—*noise, din*
Prov. 9:13, foolish woman is c-ous
Eph. 4:31, anger, and c . . . be put away
Clap—*strike the palms together*
Job 27:23, Men shall c their hands
Ps. 47:1, O c your hands, all ye people
    98:8, Let the floods c their hands
Is. 55:12, trees of the field shall c
Claws—*talons*
Deut. 14:6, the cleft into two c
Dan. 4:33, nails like birds c
Zech. 11:16, tear their c in pieces
Clay—*soft, plastic earth*
1 Kin. 7:46, cast them, in the c ground
Job 4:19, that dwell in houses of c
    33:6, I also am formed out of the c
Is. 64:8, the c and thou our potter
Jer. 18:6, c in the potter's hand
Dan. 2:33, part of iron and part of c
John 9:6, spat . . . made c . . . anointed
Rom. 9:21, potter power over the c
Clean—*free from dirt or defilement*
2 Kin. 5:12, may I not wash . . . and be c
Ps. 19:9, The fear of the Lord is c
    24:4, He that hath c hands
    51:10, Create in me a c heart
Is. 1:16, Wash you, make you c
Matt. 8:3, I will, be thou c
    23:25, make c the . . . cup
John 13:10, washed . . . is c every whit
Cleanse—*render free from dirt, pollution*
Ps. 19:12, c thou me from secret faults
Matt. 8:3, his leprosy was c-d
    23:26, c first that which is within
Luke 4:27, none . . . c-d, saving Naaman
Acts 10:15, 11:9, What God hath c-d
2 Cor. 7:1, c . . . from all filthiness
James 4:8, C your hands, ye sinners
1 John 1:7, blood of Jesus . . . c-th
Clear—*to free from, to cleanse*
Gen. 44:16, how shall we c ourselves
Num. 14:18, no means c-ing the guilty
2 Sam. 23:4, by c shining after rain
Ps. 51:4, be c when thou judgest
Song 6:10, as the moon, c as the sun
Matt. 7:5, then shalt thou see c-ly
Rom. 1:20, invisible things . . . c-ly seen
Rev. 22:1, water of life, c as crystal
Cleave—*remain faithful, cut asunder*
Gen. 2:24, shall c unto his wife
Josh. 23:8, c unto the Lord your God
Job 38:38, the clods c fast together
Ps. 102:5, my bones c to my skin

Hab. 3:9, didst c the earth with rivers
Matt. 19:5, c to his wife; and they
Rom. 12:9, c to that which is good
Clefts—*cracks, divisions, crevices*
Song 2:14, art in the c of the rock
Is. 2:21, go into the c of the rocks
Jer. 49:16, dwellest in the c of the rock
Clemency—*mercy, mildness, leniency*
Acts 24:4, hear us of thy c
Climbed—*ascended, scaled, arose*
1 Sam. 14:13, c up upon his hands
Luke 19:4, and c up into a sycamore
John 10:1, but c-eth up some other way
Clods—*lump of earth*
Job 7:5, flesh clothed with c of dust
    21:33, the c of the valley
Is. 28:24, break the c of his ground
Hos. 10:11, Jacob shall break his c
Cloke—*loose outer garment*
Is. 59:17, clad with zeal as a c
Matt. 5:40, let him have thy c also
1 Thess. 2:5, nor a c of covetousness
2 Tim. 4:13, c that I left at Troas
1 Pet. 2:16, c of maliciousness
Close—*come together, shut fast*
Num. 16:33, the earth c-d upon them
Prov. 18:24, c-r than a brother
Luke 9:36, They kept it c and told no
Acts 28:27, eyes have they c-d
Closet—*a small room for privacy*
Joel 2:16, and the bride out of her c
Matt. 6:6, prayest, enter into thy c
Luke 12:3, spoken in the ear in c-s
Cloth—*fabric*
1 Sam. 19:13, covered it with a c
    21:9, in a c behind the ephod
Matt. 9:16, of new c unto an old garment
Clothe—*to cover with a garment*
Job 10:11, c-d me with skin and flesh
Ps. 65:13, pastures are c-d with flocks
    93:1, he is c-d with majesty
Matt. 6:30, God so c the grass
    25:36, Naked, and ye c-d me
Mark 15:17, c-d him with purple
Luke 7:25, A man c-d in soft raiment
    12:28, God so c the grass
Rev. 3:5, shall be c-d in white
Clothes—*coverings for the body*
Ex. 19:10, let them wash their c
Deut. 29:5, your c are not waxen old
Mark 5:28, If I may but touch his c
    14:63, high priest rent his c
Luke 2:7, wrapped him in swaddling c
John 11:44, bound . . . with grave c

Clothing—*garments*
Job 22:6, stripped the naked of their c
24:10, go naked without c
Is. 3:7, neither bread nor c
Jer. 10:9, blue and purple is their c
Matt. 7:15, come to you in sheep's c
Mark 12:38, love to go in long c
Acts 10:30, man . . . before me in bright c
James 2:3, him that weareth the gay c
Cloud—*visible water particles*
Gen. 9:13, I do set my bow in the c
Ex. 13:21, by day in a pillar of a c
14:24, pillar of fire and of the c
24:15, c covered the mount
Ps. 36:5, reacheth unto the c-s
105:39, a c for a covering
Matt. 24:30, Son of . . . coming in the c-s
Mark 9:7, a voice came out of the c
Luke 12:54, see a c rise out of the west
21:27, in a c with power . . . glory
Acts 1:9, c received him out of their
1 Thess. 4:17, caught up . . . in the c-s
Jude 12, c-s they are without water
Rev. 1:7, behold he cometh with c-s
Cloudy—*overcast, hazy*
Ex. 33:9, the c pillar descended
Ps. 99:7, spake unto them in the c pillar
Ezek. 30:3, day of the Lord a c day
Clout—*rag, shred*
Josh. 9:5, shoes and c-ed upon their feet
Jer. 38:11, took . . . old cast c-s . . . rags
Cloven—*cleft, split, parted*
Lev. 11:3, c-footed, and cheweth the cud
7, 26, c-footed nor cheweth cud
Deut. 14:7, them that divide the c hoof
Acts 2:3, c tongues like as of fire
Cluster—*bunch, group*
Num. 13:23, branch with one c of grapes
Is. 65:8, new wine found in the c
Mic. 7:1, there is no c to eat
Rev. 14:18, gather the c-s of the vine
Coal—*a burning ember, blackness*
Prov. 6:28, hot c-s and . . . not be burned
25:22, heap c-s of fire upon his
Is. 6:6, a live c in his hand
Lam. 4:8, visage is blacker than a c
John 18:18, who had made a fire of c-s
21:9, fire of c-s there, and fish
Rom. 12:20, heap c-s of fire on his head
Coast—*boundary, sea shore*
Deut. 3:17, Jordan, and the c thereof
1 Chr. 4:10, and enlarge my c

Mark 5:17, to depart out of their c-s
Acts 27:2, to sail by the c-s of Asia
Coat—*an outer garment*
Gen. 3:21, Lord God make c-s of skins
37:3, made . . . c of many colours
Lev. 16:4, put on the holy linen c
Matt. 5:40, any . . . take away thy c
Luke 9:3, neither have two c-s apiece
John 21:7, girt his fisher's c unto him
Cock—*rooster*
Matt. 26:34, 75, before the c crow
Mark 13:35, at the c-crowing or in the
Cockatrice—*venomous serpent*
Is. 11:8, child's hand on c den
14:29, Serpent's root come forth a c
59:5, they hatch c' eggs
Jer. 8:17, will send . . . c-s, among you
Cockle—*a noxious weed*
Job 31:40, and c instead of barley
Coffer—*chest, strong box*
1 Sam. 6:8, 11, 15, the c laid on cart
Coffin—*casket, burial case*
Gen. 50:26, Joseph put in c in Egypt
Cold—*low temperature, absence of heat*
Gen. 8:22, c and heat, and summer
Job 24:7, no covering in the c
37:9, c out of the north
Prov. 25:13, c of snow in the time of
25, c waters to a thirsty soul
Matt. 10:42, a cup of c water
24:12, love of many . . . wax c
John 18:18, fire of coals; for it was c
2 Cor. 11:27, in fastings often, in c
Rev. 3:15, thou are neither c nor hot
Collection—*contributions, donations*
2 Chr. 24:6, bring the Lord c that Moses
1 Cor. 16:1, c for the saints
Colour—*hue, tint*
Num. 11:7, as the c of bdellium
Prov. 23:31, giveth his c in the cup
Is. 54:11, lay thy stones with fair c-s
Rev. 17:3, upon a scarlet c-ed beast
Colt—*young male equine animal*
Job 11:12, man . . . like a wild ass's c
Zech. 9:9, upon a c the foal of an ass
Matt. 21:2, an ass tied, and a c
John 12:15, king cometh . . . on an ass's c
Come—*approach, draw near*
Gen. 6:18, thou shalt c into the ark
Ps. 95:6, O c let us worship
Zech. 9:9, thy King c-th unto thee
Matt. 6:10, thy kingdom c
11:28, C unto me, all ye that

Mark 10:14, little children to c unto
Luke 21:27, see Son of man c-ing
John 17:1, Father, the hour is c
Rev. 22:20, I c quickly . . . Even so c
Comely—*pleasing, good looking*
1 Sam. 16:18, and a c person
Ps. 33:1, praise is c for the upright
Song 1:5, I am black, but c
Is. 53:2, he hath no form nor c-ness
1 Cor. 11:13, is it c that a woman pray
Comfort—*assistance, encouragement*
Gen. 5:29, This same shall c us
18:5, c ye your hearts
Job 29:25, one that c-eth the mourners
Ps. 23:4, thy rod . . . staff they c me
77:2, my soul refused to be c-ed
Song 2:5, c me with apples
Is. 54:11, afflicted . . . and not c-ed
61:2, to c all that mourn
Lam. 1:21, there is none to c me
Matt. 5:4, that mourn . . . shall be c-ed
9:22, Daughter, be of good c
Luke 16:25, now he is c-ed, thou art
Acts 9:31, in the c of the Holy Ghost
Rom. 15:4, c of the scriptures
2 Cor. 1:3, and the God of all c
7:4, I am filled with c
13, we were c-ed in your c
Phil. 2:1, if any c of love
1 Thess. 4:18, c one another
2 Thess. 2:17, C your hearts
Comforter—*guide and helper*
Job 16:2, miserable c-s are ye all
Eccles. 4:1, they had no c
Ps. 69:20, looked . . . for c-s
Nah. 3:7, whence shall I seek c-s
John 14:16, shall give you another C
Comfortless—*forlorn, cheerless*
John 14:18, I will not leave you c
Coming—*drawing near*
2 Sam. 3:25, going out and thy c in
Mal. 3:2, abide the day of his c
Matt. 24:30, see the Son of man c
26:64, c in the clouds of heaven
Luke 19:23, at my c I might have
John 5:25, hour is c and now is
1 Cor. 1:7, for the c of our Lord
James 5:8, c of the Lord draweth nigh
2 Pet. 3:4, promise of his c
Command—*order with authority*
Gen. 18:19, c his children and his
Ps. 33:9, he c-ed, and it stood fast
Luke 8:25, he c-eth even the winds
9:54, c fire . . . from heaven

John 15:14, if ye do whatsoever I c you
Acts 17:30, c-eth all men every where
1 Tim. 4:11, These things c and teach
Commandment—*order given by authority*
Ex. 20:6, love me, and keep my c-s
34:28, tables . . . the ten c-s
Ps. 19:8, c of the Lord is pure
Prov. 6:20, son, keep thy father's c
Eccles. 12:13, Fear God, and keep his c-s
Matt. 5:19, one of these least c-s
22:36, which is great c
40, two c-s hang all the law
John 14:15, If ye love me, keep my c-s
15:10, If ye keep my c-s
1 Tim. 1:5, end of the c is charity
Commend—*praise, intrust*
Prov. 12:8, man . . . c-ed according to
Eccles. 8:15, then I c-ed mirth
Luke 16:8, Lord c-ed the unjust steward
23:46, Father, into thy hands I c
Acts 20:32, I c you to God
Rom. 5:8, God c-eth his love toward us
1 Cor. 8:8, meat c-eth us not to God
2 Cor. 3:1, letters of c-ation from you
Commit—*give in trust*
Ex. 20:14, not c adultery
Ps. 31:5, Into thine hand I c my spirit
37:5, C thy way unto the Lord
Prov. 16:3, C thy works unto the Lord
Luke 12:48, to whom men . . . c-ed much
18:20, Do not c adultery
John 5:22, hath c-ed all judgment
8:34, Whosoever c-eth sin
1 John 3:8, He that c-eth sin is of the
Common—*general, profane*
Lev. 4:27, if . . . c people sin
Num. 16:29, these men die the c death
Eccles. 6:1, There is an evil . . . it is c
Jer. 26:23, graves of the c people
Matt. 28:15, saying is c-ly reported
Mark 12:37, the c people heard him
Acts 2:44, and had all things c
10:15, that call not thou c
1 Cor. 5:1, It is reported c-ly
Tit. 1:4, after the c faith
Jude 3, write unto you of the c salvation
Commotion—*tumult, riot, disturbance*
Jer. 10:22, great c out of the north
Luke 21:9, shall hear of wars and c-s
Communed—*took counsel together*
Eccles. 1:16, c with mine own heart
Luke 6:11, c one with another
24:15, while they c together

Communicate—*convey, make known*
Gal. 6:6, c unto him that teacheth
1 Tim. 6:18, willing to c
Heb. 13:16, do good and to c forget not
Communication—*intercourse, association*
Matt. 5:37, c be, Yea, Yea
Luke 24:17, What manner of c-s
1 Cor. 15:33, evil c-s corrupt good
Eph. 4:29, Let no corrupt c proceed
Communion—*share, fellowship*
1 Cor. 10:16, c of the blood of Christ
2 Cor. 6:14, and what c hath light
13:14, c of the Holy Ghost
Compact—*closely packed*
Ps. 122:3, city that is c together
Eph. 4:16, joined together and c-ed
Companion—*comrade, associate*
Job 30:29, and a c to owls
Prov. 13:20, c of fools shall be
Phil. 2:25, c in labour
Company—*companions*
Ps. 55:14, unto the house of God in c
Mark 6:39, all sit down by c's
Luke 23:27, followed him a great c
2 Thess. 3:14, have no c with him
Heb. 12:22, an innumerable c of angels
Compare—*liken to*
Prov. 3:15, not to be c-d unto her
Lam. 4:2, c-able to fine gold
Rom. 8:18, not . . . c-ed with the glory
1 Cor. 2:13, c-ing spiritual things
Comparison—*act of comparing*
Judg. 8:2, have I done now in c of you
Hag. 2:3, in c of it as nothing
Mark 4:30, what c shall we compare it
Compass—*circular course, make a circuit*
Num. 34:5, the border shall fetch a c
Judg. 6:4, c the city seven times
2 Kin. 3:9, fetched a c of seven days'
Job 16:13, His archers c me round about
Ps. 18:5, sorrows of hell c-ed me about
Is. 44:13, marketh it out with the c
Matt. 23:15, ye c sea and land to make
Luke 19:43, c thee round, and keep thee
Compassion—*pity, sympathy*
Ex. 2:6, she had c on him
Ps. 86:15, a God full of c
111:4, gracious and full of c
Matt. 9:36, he was moved with c on them
15:32, I have c on the multitude
Luke 15:20, his father . . . had c
Rom. 9:15, have c on whom I will have c

Heb. 5:2, have c on the ignorant
1 Pet. 3:8, having c one of another
Compel—*to force, oblige*
Matt. 5:41, c thee to go a mile
27:32, they c-ed to bear his cross
Luke 14:23, c them to come in, that my
Complain—*grumble, deplore, bewail*
1 Sam. 1:16, abundance of my c-t
Job 7:11, c in the bitterness of my
Ps. 144:14, no c-ing in our streets
Jude 16, These are murmurers, c-ers
Complete—*entire, perfect, whole*
Lev. 23:15, seven sabbaths shall be c
Col. 2:10, ye are c in him
4:12, and c in all the will of God
Comprehend—*understand, include*
Job 37:5, things . . . which we cannot c
Is. 40:12, c-ed the dust of the earth
John 1:5, darkness c-ed it not
Rom. 13:9, briefly c-ed in this saying
Conceal—*hide, secrete, cover*
Gen. 37:26, brother, and c his blood
Job 6:10, have not c-ed the words
Ps. 40:10, not c-ed thy lovingkindness
Prov. 12:23, prudent man c-eth
Jer. 50:2, publish and c not
Conceit—*vanity, pride*
Prov. 18:11, an high wall in his own c
26:5, fool wise in his own c
Rom. 11:25, be wise in your own c-s
Conceive—*initiation of life, to imagine*
Num. 11:12, Have I c all this people
Job 15:35, They c mischief
Ps. 51:5, in sin did my mother c me
Is. 7:14, virgin shall c and bear
Acts 5:4, why hast thou c-d this thing
James 1:15, when lust hath c-d
Concerning—*relating or belonging to*
Matt. 4:6, his angels charge c thee
Luke 24:44, in the psalms, c me
Rom. 1:3, C his Son Jesus Christ
11:28, As c the gospel, they are
1 Cor. 12:1, now c spiritual gifts
Phil. 3:6, C zeal, persecuting the church
1 Pet. 4:12, c the fiery trial
Concision—*a faction, schism*
Phil. 3:2, beware of the c
Conclude—*decide, settle, terminate*
Rom. 3:28, we c that a man is justified
11:32, God hath c-ed them
Gal. 3:22, scripture hath c-d all
Conclusion—*end, decision*
Eccles. 12:13, c of the whole matter

Concord—*harmony, union, agreement*
2 Cor. 6:15, what c hath Christ with
Concourse—*assemblage, congregation*
Prov. 1:21, crieth in chief place of c
Acts 19:40, give an account of this c
Concupiscence—*lust, evil desire*
Rom. 7:8, wrought . . . all manner of c
Col. 3:5, evil c and covetousness
1 Thess. 4:5, Not in the lust of c
Condemn—*pronounce to be wrong*
Job 9:20, own mouth shall c me
Prov. 12:2, wicked devices will he c
Is. 50:9, who is he that shall c
Mark 10:33, they shall c him to death
Luke 6:37, c not . . . shall not be c-ed
John 3:17, God sent not his Son . . . to c
Rom. 2:1, thou c-est thyself
Titus 2:8, speech, that cannot be c-ed
1 John 3:20, For if our heart c us
Condemnation—*censure, blame*
Luke 23:40, thou art in the same c
John 3:19, this is the c, that light is
Rom. 8:1, no c to them which are in
James 3:1, shall receive the greater c
  5:12, lest ye fall into c
Condescend—*to stoop, submit*
Rom. 12:16, but c to men of low estate
Conduct—*guidance, behavior*
2 Sam. 19:15, to c the king over Jordan
Acts 17:15, they that c-ed Paul
1 Cor. 16:11, but c him forth in peace
Conduit—*a channel, tube, pipe*
2 Kin. 18:17, stood by c of upper pool
  20:20, made a pool, and a c
Is. 7:3, the c of the upper pool
  36:2, c of upper pool in highway
Confection—*a preparation, sweetmeats*
Ex. 30:35, c after the art of the
1 Sam. 8:13, daughters to be c-aries
Confederate—*united, an accomplice*
Gen. 14:13, these were c with Abram
Ps. 83:5, they are c against thee
Is. 7:2, Syria is c with Ephraim
Conferred—*counselled, conversed*
Acts 4:15, they c among themselves
  25:12, Festus c with the council
Gal. 1:16, I c not with flesh and blood
Confess—*to acknowledge, to put faith in*
Ps. 32:5, I will c my transgressions
Matt. 10:32, c me before men, him will
Mark 1:5, baptized . . . c-ing their sins
John 1:20, c-ed, and denied not; but c-ed
Acts 23:8, Pharisees c both

Rom. 10:9, thou shalt c with thy mouth
  14:11, every tongue shall c
James 5:16, C your faults one to
1 John 1:9, If we c our sins, he is
Confession—*acknowledgment, admission*
Josh. 71:9, and make c unto him
Rom. 10:10, with the mouth c is made
1 Tim. 6:13, Jesus . . . witnessed a good c
Confidence—*trust, assurance, hope*
Ps. 118:8, than to put c in man
Prov. 3:26, the Lord shall be thy c
Eph. 3:12, with c by the faith
Phil. 3:3, and have no c in the flesh
Heb. 3:6, if we hold fast the c
Confident—*assured beyond doubt*
Ps. 27:3, in this will I be c
Prov. 14:16, the fool rageth, and is c
2 Cor. 5:6, we are always c knowing
Phil. 1:6, Being c of this very thing
Confirm—*to establish*
Is. 35:3, and c the feeble knees
Mark 16:20, c-ing the word with signs
Rom. 15:8, to c the promises made unto
1 Cor. 1:8, also c you unto the end
Confirmation—*corroboration, ratification*
Phil. 1:7, defence and c of the gospel
Heb. 6:16, an oath for c is to them
Confiscation—*seizure, appropriation*
Ezra 7:26, to banishment, or c of goods
Conflict—*combat, contest, battle*
Phil. 1:30, same c which ye saw in me
Col. 2:1, ye knew what great c I have
Conform—*agree, comply, accede*
Rom. 8:29, to be c-ed to the image
  12:2, be not c-ed to this world
Phil. 3:10, made c-able unto his death
Confound—*confuse*
Gen. 11:7, c their language
Ps. 22:5, trusted . . . and were not c-ed
Is. 24:23, the moon shall be c-ed
Acts 2:6, came together, and were c-ed
1 Pet. 2:6, shall not be c-ed
Confusion—*turmoil*
Lev. 18:23, it is c
Job 10:15, I am full of c
Ps. 71:1, let me never be put to c
Is. 45:16, go to c together
Jer. 3:25, our c covereth us
1 Cor. 14:33, God is not the author of c
James 3:16, c and every evil work
Congregation—*as assembly*
Ex. 12:3, Speak ye unto all the c
Job 15:34, c of hypocrites shall be

Congregation (*Continued*)
Ps. 1:5, in the c of the righteous
26:5, c of evil doers
74:19, the c of thy poor
82:1, in the c of the mighty
149:1, c of saints
Acts 13:43, when the c was broken up
Conquer—*overpower, master, subdue*
Rom. 8:37, more than c-ors through him
Rev. 6:2, went forth c-ing and to c
Conscience—*inner voice, or moral sense*
John 8:9, convicted by their own c
Acts 23:1, I have lived in all good c
24:16, a c void of offence
Rom. 2:15, their c also bearing witness
13:5, wrath . . . for c sake
1 Cor. 8:7, their c being weak
1 Tim. 3:9, faith in a pure c
4:2, c seared with a hot iron
Heb. 9:14, purge your c from dead works
10:22, hearts sprinkled from evil c
1 Pet. 3:16, Having a good c
Consecrate—*set apart to God's service*
Ex. 32:29, C yourselves to day to the
Heb. 7:28, Son . . . c-d for evermore
10:20, way, which he hath c-d
Consent—*to yield, accord*
Prov. 1:10, entice thee, c thou not
Luke 14:18, with one c began to make
23:51, not c-ed to the counsel
Acts 8:1, Saul was c-ing unto his death
1 Tim. 6:3, c not to wholesome words
Consider—*ponder, study, meditate*
Deut. 32:29, c their latter end
Ps. 41:1, blessed is he that c-eth poor
77:5, c-ed the days of old
Prov. 6:6, c her ways, and be wise
Eccles. 7:14, in the day of adversity c
Jer. 2:10, and c diligently
Matt. 6:28, C the lilies of the field
7:3, c-est not the beam that is in
Luke 12:24, C the ravens: for they
Gal. 6:1, c-ing thyself, lest thou also
Heb. 10:24, let us c one another
Consist—*be composed, inhere*
Luke 12:15, man's life c-eth not
Col. 1:17, by him all things c
Consolation—*comfort, solace*
Job 15:11, Are the c-s of God small
Luke 6:24, ye have received your c
Acts 4:36, the son of c
Rom. 15:5, the God of patience and c
2 Cor. 1:6, for your c and salvation
Phil. 2:1, if there be . . . any c in Christ

2 Thess. 2:16, given us everlasting c
Heb. 6:18, might have a strong c
Conspiracy—*plot, intrigue*
2 Sam. 15:12, and the c was strong
Acts 23:13, forty which made this c
Constant—*faithful, true, steadfast*
1 Chr. 28:7, c to do my commandments
Prov. 21:28, that heareth speaketh c-ly
Constrain—*urge, compel, drive*
Job 32:28, spirit within me c-eth me
2 Kin. 4:8, she c-ed him to eat bread
Luke 24:29, but they c-ed him
2 Cor. 5:14, Love of Christ c-eth us
1 Pet. 5:2, not by c-t, but willingly
Consult—*consider, deliberate, confer*
Ps. 62:4, only c to cast him down
1 Kin. 12:6, 8, king Rehoboam c-ed
Matt. 26:4, c-ed that they . . . take Jesus
Luke 14:31, c-eth whether he be able
John 12:10, chief priests c-ed
Consume—*destroy, waste away*
Gen. 41:30, famine shall c the land
Ex. 3:2, the bush was not c-ed
Deut. 4:24, God is a c-ing fire
5:25, this great fire will c us
Ps. 39:11, makest his beauty to c away
49:14, beauty shall c in the grave
90:7, we are c-d by thine anger
Zech. 14:12, their tongue shall c away
Luke 9:54, c them, even as Elias did
Gal. 5:15, heed that ye be not c-d
2 Thess. 2:8, shall c with the spirit
Consumption—*waste, destruction, decay*
Lev. 26:16, appoint over you terror, c
Deut. 28:22, shall smite thee with a c
Is. 10:22, the c decreed shall overflow
Contain—*hold, keep, embody, retain*
1 Kin. 8:27, heavens cannot c
Rom. 2:14, the things c-ed in the law
1 Cor. 7:9, cannot c, let them marry
1 Pet. 2:6, it is c-ed in the scripture
Contemn—*despise, scorn, disdain*
Ps. 10:13, doth the wicked c God
107:11, c-ed counsel of the most high
Ezek. 21:10, it c-eth the rod of my son
Contempt—*derision, mockery, disdain*
Job 12:21, poureth c upon princes
Prov. 18:3, then cometh also c
Dan. 12:2, to shame and everlasting c
2 Cor. 10:10, and his speech c-ible
Contend—*strive, struggle*
Job 40:2, that c-eth with the almighty

Is. 49:25, will c with him that c-eth
50:8, who will c with me
57:16, I will not c forever
Jude 3, earnestly c for the faith
9, when c-ing with the devil
Content—*satisfied*
Gen. 37:27, his brethren were c
Mark 15:15, Pilate . . . to c the people
Luke 3:14, be c with your wages
Phil. 4:11, I have learned . . . to be c
1 Tim. 6:6, godliness with c-ment is
Heb. 13:5, be c with such things as ye
Contention—*struggle, strife*
Prov. 13:10, by pride cometh c
18:6, A fool's lips enter into c
1 Cor. 1:11, there are c-s among you
Phil. 1:16, The one preach Christ of c
Titus 3:9, foolish questions . . . and c-s
Contentious—*quarrelsome, disagreeable*
Prov. 21:19, a c and an angry woman
Rom. 2:8, them that are c do not obey
1 Cor. 11:6, if any man seem to be c
Continual—*perpetual, unbroken, constant*
Prov. 15:15, merry heart hath c feast
19:13, a wife are a c dropping
Luke 18:5, lest by her c coming
Rom. 9:2, great heaviness and c sorrow
Continually—*constantly, without ceasing*
1 Chr. 16:11, seek his face c
Ps. 34:1, his praise shall c be in my
Prov. 6:21, Bind them c upon thine heart
Acts 6:4, give ourselves c to prayer
Heb. 7:3, abideth a priest c
Continue—*to abide, persist*
Job 14:2, as a shadow, and c-th not
Luke 6:12, c-d all night in prayer
John 2:12, c-d there not many days
8:31, If ye c in my word, then
15:9, c ye in my love
Acts 13:43, c in the grace of God
Rom. 2:7, patient c-ance in well doing
Gal. 2:5, the gospel might c with you
Col. 4:2, C in prayer, and watch in the
Heb. 13:1, Let brotherly love c
Contradiction—*opposition, denial*
Heb. 7:7, without all c less is blessed
12:3, endured such c of sinners
Contrariwise—*on the contrary, perversely*
2 Cor. 2:7, that c ye ought rather
Gal. 2:7, but c when they saw
1 Pet. 3:9, not evil but c blessing
Contrary—*adverse, opposed*
Lev. 26:21, if ye walk c unto me
Matt. 14:24, for the wind was c

Rom. 11:24, graffed c to nature
16:17, c to the doctrine
Gal. 5:17, c the one to the other
1 Thess. 2:15, and are c to all men
1 Tim. 1:10, c to sound doctrine
Contribution—*gift, donation, tax*
Rom. 15:26, certain c for poor saints
Contrite—*repentant, sorrowful*
Ps. 34:18, saveth such of c spirit
51:17, broken and a c heart
Is. 66:2, poor and of a c spirit
Controversy—*debate, disagreement*
Deut. 25:1, if there be a c between men
2 Sam. 15:2, when any man that had a c
Jer. 25:31, a c with the nations
Mic. 6:2, the Lord hath a c with people
Convenient—*fit, suitable*
Prov. 30:8, feed me with food c
Jer. 40:4, seemeth good and c
Mark 6:21, when a c day was come
14:11, how he might c-ly betray
Acts 24:25, when I have a c season
Eph. 5:4, nor jesting, which are not c
Conversant—*acquainted, versed*
Josh. 8:35, strangers that were c
1 Sam. 25:15, we were c with them
Conversation—*intercourse, behavior*
Ps. 50:23, ordereth his c aright
Gal. 1:13, have heard of my c
Eph. 4:22, concerning the former c
Phil. 1:27, c be as it becometh
Heb. 13:5, c be without covetousness
James 3:13, show out of a good c
1 Pet. 1:15, holy in all manner of c
2:12, Having your c honest
2 Pet. 2:7, the filthy c of the wicked
Conversion—*regeneration*
Acts 15:3, declaring the c of Gentiles
Convert—*to change, to turn*
Ps. 19:7, perfect, c-ing the soul
Matt. 18:3, Except ye be c-ed
Acts 3:19, Repent . . . and be c-ed
James 5:20, he which c-eth the sinner
Convicted—*persuaded, convinced*
John 8:9, c by their own conscience
Convince—*to persuade by argument*
Job 32:12, none of you that c-d Job
John 8:46, which of you c-th me of sin
Titus 1:9, to c the gainsayers
Convocation—*an assembly, convention*
Ex. 12:16, there shall be an holy c
Num. 28:25, 26, ye shall have an holy c

Cook—*one who prepares food*
1 Sam. 8:13, daughters . . . to be c-s
9:23, 24, Samuel said unto the c
Cool—*lacking in warmth*
Gen. 3:8, walking . . . in the c of the day
Luke 16:24, and c my tongue
Copper—*a reddish malleable metal*
Ezra 8:27, two vessels of fine c
2 Tim. 4:14, Alexander the c-smith
Copy—*facsimile, duplicate*
Deut. 17:18, write him a c of this law
Josh. 8:32, wrote there . . . a c of the law
Prov. 25:1, proverbs Hezekiah c-ed out
Corban—*a gift*
Mark 7:11, if any man shall say, It is C
Cord—*string, or small rope*
Job 36:8, holden in c-s of affliction
41:1, or his tongue with a c
Prov. 5:22, with the c-s of his sins
Eccles. 12:6, the silver c be loosed
Is. 5:18, draw iniquity with c-s of
Mic. 2:5, cast a c by lot
John 2:15, made a scourge of small c-s
Corn—*all types of grain*
Gen. 41:5, seven ears of c came up
Lev. 2:14, green ears of c
2 Sam. 17:19, spread ground c thereon
2 Kin. 4:42, full ears of c in the husk
Matt. 12:1, began to pluck the ears of c
Mark 4:28, after that the full c in the
John 12:24, Except a c of wheat fall
Corner—*meeting point of two lines*
Job 38:6, who laid the c stone thereof
Ps. 118:22, the head stone of the c
Prov. 7:12, in wait at every c
Is. 28:16, precious c stone
Matt. 21:42, become the head of the c
Acts 10:11, knit at the four c-s
Eph. 2:20, Christ . . . being the chief c
Rev. 7:1, on the four c of the earth
Cornet—*a wind musical instrument*
2 Sam. 6:5, on timbrels, and on c-s
1 Chr. 15:28, with sound of the c
Dan. 3:5, sound of the c flute, harp
Corpse—*a dead body*
2 Kin. 19:35, they were all dead c-s
Nah. 3:3, stumble upon their c-s
Mark 6:29, his c and laid it in a tomb
Correct—*to chasten, to improve*
Job 5:17, the man whom God c-eth
Prov. 3:12, the Lord loveth he c-eth
29:17, C thy son, and he shall give
Jer. 10:24, c me, but with judgment
2 Tim. 3:16, profitable . . . for c-ion

Corrupt—*change from good to bad*
Gen. 6:11, The earth also was c
Ps. 14:1, They are c they have done
Prov. 25:26, and a c spring
Matt. 6:19, where moth and rust doth c
7:17, a c tree bringeth forth
1 Cor. 15:33, evil communications c
2 Cor. 7:2, we have c-ed no man
Eph. 4:22, put off . . . old man, which is c
2 Tim. 3:8, men of c minds
James 5:2, Your riches are c-ed
Corrupters—*defilers, debasers*
Is. 1:4, children that are c
Jer. 6:28, they are all c
Corruptible—*wicked, sinful*
Rom. 1:23, made like to c man
1 Cor. 9:25, do it to obtain a c crown
15:53, 54, this c must put on
1 Pet. 1:23, not of c seed
Corruption—*defilement*
Lev. 22:25, their c is in them
Job 17:14, c Thou art my father
Ps. 16:10; Acts 2:27, Holy One to see c
Rom. 8:21, delivered from bondage of c
1 Cor. 15:42, It is sown in c
Gal. 6:8, shall of the flesh reap c
2 Pet. 1:4, the c that is in the world
2:19, are the servants of c
Cost, liness, ly—*expense, expensive*
2 Sam. 24:24, which doth c me nothing
1 Kin. 5:17, c-ly stones, and hewed
John 12:3, spikenard, very c-ly
1 Tim. 2:9, or pearls, or c-ly array
Rev. 18:19, by reason of her **c-liness**
Cottage—*small house, bungalow*
Is. 1:8, left as a c in a vineyard
24:20, shall be removed like a c
Zeph. 2:6, shall be . . . c-s for shepherds
Couch—*bed, litter, crouch*
Gen. 49:4, he went up to my c
9, he c-ed as a lion
Job 38:40, When they c in their dens
Ps. 6:6, water with c with my tears
Luke 5:19, Let him down . . . with his c
Acts 5:15, laid them on beds and c-s
Coulter—*cutter on a plow*
1 Sam. 13:20, 21, his share, and his c
Council—*assembly, congress, meeting*
Matt. 5:22, shall be in danger of the c
10:17, deliver you up to the c-s
Acts 5:27, set them before the c
6:12, and brought him to the c
Counsel—*advice, plan, scheme*
Ex. 18:19, I will give thee c

Ps. 1:1, walketh not in the c of
33:11, c of the Lord standeth
55:14, took sweet c together
73:24, guide me with thy c
Prov. 11:14, Where no c is, thy people
19:20, Hear c and receive
Eccles. 8:2, I c thee to keep
Is. 28:29, wonderful in c
Jer. 23:18, stood in the c of the Lord
Matt. 22:15, took c . . . might entangle
Luke 7:30, reject the c of God
Acts 9:23, the Jews took c to kill him
1 Cor. 4:5, the c-s of the hearts
Eph. 1:11, after the c of his own will
Heb. 6:17, immutability of his c
Rev. 3:18, I c thee to buy of me gold
Counseller, or—*an adviser*
Prov. 11:14, in the multitude of c-s
Is. 9:6, shall be called Wonderful, C
Mic. 4:9, is thy c perished
Mark 15:43, an honourable c
Luke 23:50, man named Joseph, a c
Rom. 11:34, or who hath been his c
Count—*reckon*
Job 18:3, are we c-ed as beasts
Ps. 44:22, c-ed as sheep for the
Prov. 17:28, his peace, is c-ed wise
Eccles. 7:27, c-ing one by one
Luke 14:28, and c-eth the cost, whether
Phil. 3:8, I c all things but loss
2 Pet. 3:9, as some men c slackness
James 5:11, e them happy which endure
Countenance—*expression of the face*
Gen. 4:6, why is thy c fallen
Num. 6:26, The Lord lift up his c
1 Sam. 16:12, of a beautiful c, and
2 Sam. 14:27, a woman of a fair c
Ps. 4:6; 44:3; 89:15, light of thy c
Prov. 15:13, heart maketh a cheerful c
Song 2:14, thy c is comely
Dan. 1:15, their c-s appeared fairer
Matt. 6:16, the hypocrites, of a sad c
28:3, His c was like lightning
Rev. 1:16, c was as the sun shineth
Country—*tract of land, a region*
Gen. 12:1, Get thee out of thy c
Prov. 25:25, good news from a far c
Is. 8:9, give ear, all ye of far c-ies
Matt. 2:12, departed into their own c
21:33, 25:14, went into a far c
Luke 2:8, were in the same c shepherds
15:13, his journey into a far c
John 4:44, no honours in his own c

Countrymen—*fellow-citizens, compatriots*
2 Cor. 11:26, in perils by mine own c
1 Thess. 2:14, suffered of your own c
Couple—*pair, join*
Ex. 26:6, c the curtains together
Judg. 19:3, having . . . a c of asses
2 Sam. 13:6, make me a c of cakes
Is. 21:7, saw a chariot with c horsemen
1 Pet. 3:2, conversation c-d with fear
Courage—*fearlessness, bravery, valor*
Josh. 1:7, be thou strong and very c-ous
Deut. 31:6, be strong and of a good c
Ps. 27:14, be of good c
Is. 41:6, every one said . . . be of good c
Course—*direction traveled, order, turn*
Judg. 5:20, stars in their c-s fought
1 Chr. 23:6, divided them into c-s
Ezra 3:11, they sang together by c
Acts 20:24, might finish my c with joy
2 Tim. 4:7, I have finished my c
James 3:6, setteth on fire the c of
Court—*an inclosed space, a palace*
Ex. 27:9, thou shalt make the c
Ps. 84:10, a day in thy c-s is better
135:2, in the c-s of the house
Courteous—*polite, obliging, affable*
Acts 27:3, Julius c-ly entreated Paul
28:7, lodged us three days c-ly
1 Pet. 3:8, be pitiful, be c
Cousin—*relative, kinsman*
Luke 1:36, behold thy c Elizabeth
58, her neighbors and her c-s
Covenant—*a mutual agreement*
Gen. 6:18, will I establish my c
Num. 10:33, ark of the c of the Lord
2 Kin. 23:2, the book of the c
Job 31:1, I made a c with mine eyes
Ps. 25:10, unto such as keep his c
103:18, To such as keep his c
Acts 3:25, c which God made with our
Gal. 4:24, these are the two c-s
Heb. 8:6, mediator of a better c
13:20, blood of the everlasting c
Cover—*to overspread, hide from sight*
Gen. 20:16, a c-ing of the eyes
Job 36:32, clouds he c-eth the light
Ps. 32:1, forgiven, whose sin is c-ed
91:4, c thee with his feathers
Prov. 10:12, but love c-eth all sins
Is. 6:2, with twain he c his face
Matt. 10:26, nothing c-ed, that shall
Luke 23:30, to the hills, C us

Cover (*Continued*)
1 Cor. 11:4, having his head c-ed
1 Pet. 4:8, charity shall c the
Covering—*concealment, protection*
Gen. 20:16, he is to thee a c
2 Sam. 17:19, c over the well's mouth
Ps. 105:39, he spread a cloud for a c
Is. 50:3, make sackcloth their c
1 Cor. 11:15, her hair is given for c
Covert—*a covering, protection*
Job 38:40, in the c to lie in wait
Ps. 61:4, trust in the c of thy wings
Is. 4:6, for a c from storm and rain
16:4, be thou a c to them
32:2, a c from the tempest
Covet—*to long for, desire*
Ex. 20:17, Thou shalt not c
Prov. 21:26, c-eth greedily all the day
Mic. 2:2, c fields, and take them
Acts 20:33, have c-ed no man's silver
Rom. 13:9, thou shalt not c
1 Cor. 12:31, c earnestly the best
1 Tim. 6:10, while some c-ed after
Covetous—*avaricious, greedy*
Ps. 10:3, and blesseth the c
1 Cor. 5:10, not altogether with the . . . c
Eph. 5:5, nor c man, who is an idolater
2 Tim. 3:2, lovers of their own selves, c
Covetousness—*greediness*
Ps. 119:36, Incline my heart . . . not to c
Mark 7:22, Thefts, c, wickedness
Luke 12:15, Take heed, and beware of c
1 Thess. 2:5, a cloak of c
Heb. 13:5, conversation be without c
Cow—*bovine, heifer*
Lev. 22:28, Whether it be c or ewe
Job 21:10, c calveth, and casteth not
Is. 11:7, the c and the bear shall feed
Craft—*art, skill, cunning, deceit*
Job 15:5, the tongue of the c-y
Dan. 8:25, shall cause c to prosper in
Mark 14:1, sought . . . take him by c
Acts 18:3, he was of the same c
19:25, this c we have our wealth
2 Cor. 12:16, being c-y, I caught you
Craftiness—*deceit*
Job 5:13, wise in their own c
Luke 20:23, he perceived their c
2 Cor. 4:2, not walking in c
Craftsmen—*tradesmen, articifers*
2 Kin. 24:14, all the c and smiths
Hos. 13:2, all of it the work of the c
Acts 19:24, brought . . . gain unto the c

Crag—*steep rugged rock*
Job 39:28, upon the c of the rock
Crane—*tall wading bird, heron*
Is. 38:14, like a c or swallow
Jer. 8:7, turtle and the c . . . observe
Crashing—*shattering, breaking*
Zeph. 1:10, a great c from the hills
Crave—*seek, long for, beseech, implore*
Prov. 16:26, his mouth c-th it of him
Mark 15:43, Joseph . . . c-d body of Jesus
Create—*to bring into being, produce*
Gen. 1:1, c-d the heaven and the earth
Ps. 51:10, C in me a clean heart
Is. 43:1, the Lord that c-ed thee
45:12, made the earth . . . c-ed man
57:19, I c the fruits of the lips
65:17, c new heavens . . . new earth
Mal. 2:10, hath not one God c-d us
Mark 13:19, God c-d unto this time
Eph. 2:10, c-d in Christ Jesus
3:9, c-d all things by Jesus
4:24, God is c-d in righteousness
Col. 1:16, by him were all things c-d
Creation—*act of creating, originating*
Mark 10:6, beginning of the c God made
13:19, c which God created
2 Pet. 3:4, from the beginning of the c
Creator—*the Lord God*
Eccles. 12:1, remember now thy c
Is. 40:28, C of the ends of the earth
Rom. 1:25, the creature more than the C
1 Pet. 4:19, as unto a faithful C
Creature—*a being with life*
Gen. 1:21, every living c that moveth
Mark 16:15, preach the gospel to every c
2 Cor. 5:17, he is a new c: old things
1 Tim. 4:4, for every c of God is good
James 1:18, firstfruits of his c-s
Creditor—*lender, seller*
Deut. 15:2, every c that lendeth
Is. 50:1, which of my c-s is it
Luke 7:41, certain c . . . had two debtors
Creep—*move stealthily*
Gen. 1:26, c-ing thing that c-eth
Ps. 104:20, beasts . . . c forth
148:10, c-ing things, and flying
Acts 10:12, wild beasts, and c-ing things
2 Tim. 3:6, which c into houses
Crew—*crowed*
Matt. 26:74, immediately the cock c
Mark 14:68, the porch; and the cock c
Luke 22:60, while he yet spake, the cock c
Crib—*feeding place, manger*
Job 39:9, abide by thy c

Prov. 14:4, no oxen . . . c is clean
Is. 1:3, the ass his master's c
Crime—*iniquity, transgression, vice*
Job 31:11, this is an heinous c
Ezek. 7:23, land is full of bloody c-s
Acts 25:27, signify the c-s laid against
Crimson—*red, scarlet*
2 Chr. 2:7, in purple, and c, and blue
Is. 1:18, like c they shall be as wool
Jer. 4:30, clothest thyself with c
Cripple—*lame*
Acts 14:8, c from his mother's womb
Crooked—*distorted from right*
Deut. 32:5, perverse and c generation
Ps. 125:5, turn aside unto their c ways
Eccles. 1:15, c cannot be made straight
Luke 3:5, the c shall be made straight
Phil. 2:15, c and perverse nation
Crop—*craw, clip, snip off*
Lev. 1:16, shall pluck away his c
Ezek. 17:22, will c off from the top
Cross—*symbol of Christianity*
Matt. 10:38, that taketh not his c
27:40, come down from the c
John 19:17, he bearing his c went forth
25, stood by the c of Jesus
1 Cor. 1:17, lest the c of Christ should
1 Cor. 1:18, preaching of the c is to
Gal. 6:14, save in the c of our Lord
Eph. 2:16, in one body by the c
Phil. 2:8, even the death of the c
3:18, enemies of the c of Christ
Col. 1:20, peace . . . blood of his c
Heb. 12:2, endured the c, despising
Crouch—*bend, stoop, squat*
1 Sam. 2:36, shall come and c to him
Ps. 10:10, he c-eth, and humbleth
Crow—*loud shrill sound of cock*
Matt. 26:34, 75, before the cock c
Luke 22:34, cock shall not c this day
Crown—*ornamental fillet, to adorn*
Gen. 49:26, on the c of the head
Ps. 8:5, c-ed him with glory
21:3, settest a c of pure gold
65:11, Thou c-est the year with
103:4, c-eth thee with loving
Prov. 12:4, virtuous woman is a c
14:18, are c-ed with knowledge
24, c of the wise is their
16:31, hoary head is a c of glory
17:6, children's children are the c
1 Cor. 9:25, to obtain a corruptible c
2 Tim. 4:8, a c of righteousness
Heb. 2:9, see Jesus . . . c-ed with glory

Crucify—*to fasten to a cross*
Matt. 20:19, mock . . . scourge . . . c him
26:2, betrayed to be c-ed
27:22, Let him be c-ed
35, they c-ed him
28:5, Jesus, which was c-ed
Mark 13:15, cried out again, C him
1 Cor. 1:13, was Paul c-ed for you
23, we preach Christ c-ed
2 Cor. 13:4, c-ed through weakness
Gal. 2:20, I am c-ed with Christ
6:14, world is c-ed unto me
Heb. 6:6, c to themselves the Son of
Cruel, ty—*hard-hearted, inhumanity*
Gen. 49:5, instruments of c-ty
Ps. 27:12, such as breathe out c-ty
Prov. 11:17, he that is c troubleth
27:4, Wrath is c, and anger is
Song 8:6, jealousy is c as the grave
Ezek. 34:4, with c-ty have ye ruled
Crumbs—*fragments*
Matt. 15:27, dogs eat of the c
Mark 7:28, eat of the children's c
Cruse—*small vessel holding liquid*
1 Sam. 26:16, c of water from Saul's
1 Kin. 14:3, c of honey, and go to him
19:6, a c of water at his head
2 Kin. 2:20, Bring me a new c
Crush—*press, squeeze, smash*
Lev. 22:24, shall not offer . . . c-ed
Job 5:4, they are c-ed in the gate
39:15, that the foot may c them
Amos 4:1, oppress the poor, c the needy
Cry—*clamor, tumult, to pray*
Gen. 4:10, thy brother's blood c-eth
18:21, according to the c of it
Lev. 13:45, shall c, Unclean, Unclean
Ps. 9:12, the c of the humble
17:1, O Lord, attend unto my c
27:7, Hear, O Lord, when I c with my
130:1, Out of the depths have I c-ed
Prov. 8:1, Doth not wisdom c
Is. 42:2, shall not c . . . nor cause his
14, c like a travailing woman
Matt. 3:3, one c-ing in the wilderness
25:6, at midnight . . . a c
Mark 15:8, multitude c-ing aloud began
Mark 15:37, c-ed with a loud voice
Rev. 21:4, neither sorrow, nor c-ing
Crystal—*transparent quartz*
Job 28:17, gold and the c cannot equal
Ezek. 1:22, the colour of terrible c

Crystal (*Continued*)
Rev. 4:6, sea of glass like unto **c**
   21:11, jasper stone, clear as **c**
Cubit—*measure of about* 18 *inches*
Gen. 6:15, length of the ark . . . 300 **c-s**
Deut. 3:11, after the **c** of a man
Esther 5:14, gallows . . . fifty **c-s** high
Ezek. 43:13, **c** and a hand breadth
Matt. 6:27, add one **c** unto his stature
Cucumbers—*garden vegetable*
Num. 11:5, the fish . . . **c** and the melons
Is. 1:8, lodge in a garden of **c**
Cud—*rechewed food*
Lev. 11:3, and cheweth the **c**
Deut. 14:6, cheweth the **c** among
Cumber—*hindrance, trouble*
Luke 10:40, Martha was **c**-ed about
   13:7, why **c**-eth it the ground
Cummin—*aromatic seed plant*
Matt. 23:33, of mint and anise and **c**
Cunning—*skillful, wise*
Gen. 25:27, Esau was a **c** hunter
1 Sam. 16:16, man, who is a **c** player
Ps. 137:5, let . . . hand forget her **c**
Song. 7:1, hands of a **c** workman
Is. 3:3, the **c** artificer
Jer. 9:17, send for **c** women
Eph. 4:14, carried . . . by . . . **c** craftiness
2 Pet. 1:16, not followed **c**-ly devised
Cup—*a vessel used to drink from*
Ps. 23:5, my **c** runneth over
   116:13, I will take the **c**
Prov. 23:31, his colour in the **c**
Matt. 10:42, **c** of cold water only
   20:22, able to drink of the **c**
   23:35, the outside of the **c**
   26:27, took the **c**, and gave thanks
   39, let this **c** pass from me
Mark 7:4, washing of **c-s** and pots
Luke 22:20, **c** is the new testament
John 18:11, the **c** which my Father
1 Cor. 10:16, The **c** of blessing
   21, the **c** of devils
Cupbearer—*court attendant, butler*
1 Kin. 10:5, his ministers . . . his **c-s**
2 Chr. 9:4, their apparel; his **c-s**
Neh. 1:11, for I was the King's **c**
Curdled—*coagulated, congealed*
Job 10:10, and **c** me like cheese
Cure—*remedy, to heal*
Luke 7:21, same hour he **c**-d many
   13:32, do **c-s** to day and to morrow
Curious—*inquisitive, meddling*
Ex. 28:8, **c** girdle of the ephod

Ps. 139:15, **c**-ly wrought
Acts 19:19, many of them . . . used **c** arts
Curse—*imprecate evil, to swear*
Gen. 3:14, **c**-d above all cattle
   12:3, **c** him that **c**-th thee
   27:12, shall bring a **c** upon me
Lev. 19:14, shalt not **c** the deaf
Mal. 4:6, smite the earth with a **c**
Matt. 25:41, Depart from me, ye **c**-d
Mark 14:71, began to **c** and to swear
Luke 6:28, Bless them that **c** you
Acts 23:12, bound themselves under a **c**
Rom. 3:14, whose mouth is full of **c**-ing
   12:14, bless, and **c** not
Gal. 3:13, hath redeemed us from the **c**
James 3:9, therewith **c** we men
Curtain—*a hanging screen*
Ex. 26:1, ten **c-s** of fine twined linen
Is. 40:22, the heavens as a **c**
Song 1:5, as the **c-s** of Solomon
Custody—*safe keeping, charge*
Num. 3:36, under the **c** and charge
Esther 2:3, 8, 14, unto the **c** of He'ge
Custom—*habitual practice, a tax*
Gen. 31:35, **c** of women is upon me
Judg. 11:39, it was a **c** in Israel
Ezra 4:13, toll, tribute, and **c**
Matt. 9:9, sitting at the receipt of **c**
Luke 4:16, as his **c** was
John 18:39, a **c**, that I should release
Acts 28:17, **c-s** of our fathers
Rom. 13:7, **c** to whom **c**
1 Cor. 11:16, we have no such **c**
Cut—*to slash or gash*
Ex. 9:15, shalt be **c** off from the earth
Judg. 1:6, **c** of his thumbs . . . toes
Ps. 12:3, shall **c** off all flattering
   90:6, in the evening it is **c** down
Prov. 10:31, froward tongue shall be **c**
Is. 45:2, **c** in sunder the bars of iron
Jer. 7:29, **C** off thine hair
Matt. 5:30, hand offend thee, **c** it off
   21:8, others **c** down branches
   24:51, shall **c** him asunder
Mark 5:5, crying, and **c**-ing himself
   14:47, **c** off his ear
Acts 7:54, they were **c** to the heart
Rom. 11:22, thou also shalt be **c** off
Cymbal—*clashing plate*
Ps. 150:5, upon the high sounding **c-s**
1 Cor. 13:1, sounding brass . . . tinkling **c**

D

Daily—*happening each successive day*
Ex. 5:13, Fulfill your . . . **d** tasks
2 Kin. 25:30, a **d** rate for every day
Matt. 6:11, this day our **d** bread
Luke 9:23, take up his cross **d**
    11:3, day by day our **d** bread
1 Cor. 15:31, I die **d**
Heb. 3:13, exhort one another **d**
James 2:15, destitute of **d** food
Dainty—*delicate, nice, fastidious*
Ps. 141:4, not eat of their **d**-es
Prov. 23:6, desire thou his **d** meats
Rev. 18:14, things which were **d**
Dale—*valley, vale*
Gen. 14:17, which is the king's **d**
2 Sam. 18:18, which is in the king's **d**
Dam—*female parent of quadrupeds*
Ex. 22:30, seven days . . . with his **d**
Lev. 22:27, be seven days under the **d**
Deut. 22:6, not take the **d** with the young
Damage—*injury, harm, hurt*
Prov. 26:6, and drinketh **d**
Acts 27:10, with hurt and much **d**
2 Cor. 7:9, receive **d** by us in nothing.
Damnable—*deserving condemnation*
2 Pet. 2:1, shall bring in **d** heresies
Damnation—*everlasting punishment*
Matt. 23:14, receive the greater **d**
    33, escape the **d** of hell
John 5:29, unto the resurrection of **d**
Rom. 13:2, shall receive to themselves **d**
1 Cor. 11:29, drinketh **d** to himself
2 Pet. 2:3, their **d** slumbereth not
Damned—*condemned to punishment*
Mark 16:16, believeth shall not be **d**
Rom. 14:23, he that doubteth is **d**
2 Thess. 2:12, they all might be **d**
Damsel—*a young girl*
Gen. 24:14, the **d** to whom I shall say
Matt. 14:11, head . . . given to the **d**
Mark 5:39, the **d** is not dead
John 18:17, the **d** that kept the door
Acts 12:13, **d** came . . . named Rhoda
    16:16, certain **d** possessed with a
Dance—*move nimbly to music*
Job 21:11, and their children **d**
Ps. 149:3, Praise his name in the **d**
    150:4, with the timbrel and **d**
Eccles. 3:4, time to mourn . . . time to **d**
Lam. 5:15, **d** is turned into mourning

Matt. 11:17; Luke 7:32, ye have not **d-d**
Mark 6:22, came in, and **d-d**, and pleased
Luke 15:25, he heard musick and **d**-ing
Danger—*peril, jeopardy, hazard*
Matt. 5:22, be in **d** of the judgment
Mark 3:29, in **d** of eternal damnation
Acts 19:27, our craft is in **d** to be set
Dare—*undertake, challenge*
Rom. 5:7, some would even **d** to die
    15:18, I will not **d** to speak
1 Cor. 6:1, **D** any of you, having a matter
2 Cor. 10:12, **d** not make ourselves
Dark—*black, obscure, gloomy*
Ex. 10:15, that the land was **d**-ened
Job 12:25, They grope in the **d**
    24:16, In the **d** they dig
    38:2, that **d**-eneth counsel by words
Ps. 49:4; Prov. 1:6, **d** sayings
Is. 5:30, light is **d**-ened in the windows
Matt. 24:29, sun shall be **d**-ened
Luke 23:45, sun was **d**-ened, and the vail
John 20:1, early, when it was yet **d**
Rom. 1:21, foolish heart was **d**-ened
Eph 4:18, understanding **d**-ened
2 Pet. 1:19, shineth in a **d** place
Darkness—*blackness, blindness*
Gen. 1:2, **d** was upon the face
Deut. 5:22, thick **d** with a great voice
    28:29, the blind gropeth in **d**
2 Sam. 22:10, **d** was under his feet
Eccles. 2:13, far as light excelleth **d**
    14, the fool walketh in **d**
Is. 5:20, **d** for light . . . light for **d**
Matt. 6:23, Luke 11:34, body . . . full of **d**
    10:27, What I tell you in **d**
Luke 1:79, light to them that sit in **d**
    23:44, **d** over all the earth
John 1:5, **d** comprehended it not
    3:19, loved **d** rather than light
Acts 26:18, turn them from **d** to light
Rom. 13:12, cast off the works of **d**
1 Cor. 4:5, hidden things of **d**
2 Cor. 4:6, light to shine out of **d**
Col. 1:13, from the power of **d**
Heb. 12:18, unto blackness, and **d**
1 Pet. 2:9, out of **d** into . . . light
2 Pet. 2:4, into chains of **d**
1 John 1:5, in him is no **d** at all
    2:8, because the **d** is past
    11, **d** hath blinded his eyes
Rev. 16:10, kingdom was full of **d**
Dart—*short pointed weapon*
2 Sam. 18:14, took three **d**-s in his

DART

Dart (*Continued*)
Job 41:29, **D**-s are counted as stubble
Prov. 7:23, **d** strike through his liver
Eph. 6:16, fiery **d**-s of the wicked
Heb. 12:20, thrust through with a **d**
Dash—*shatter, crush, throw*
Ps. 2:9; Hos. 13:16, **d** them in pieces
91:12; Matt. 4:6, **d** thy foot
Ps. 137:9, **d**-eth thy little ones
Daughter—*a female descendant*
Gen. 24:23, 47, Whose **d** art thou
Josh. 17:3, had no sons, but **d**-s
Ps. 45:9, kings' **d**-s were among
144:12, **d**-s may be as corner stones
Eccles. 12:4, the **d**-s of musick
Matt. 9:22, **D**, be of good comfort
15:28, her **d** was made whole
21:5, Tell ye the **d** of Sion
Luke 8:42, **d**, about twelve years of age
23:28, **D**-s of Jerusalem, weep not
Heb. 11:24, son of Pharoah's **d**
Day—*24 hours, period, era, time*
Gen. 1:5, God called the light **D**
41:9, remember my faults this **d**
Ex. 20:8, sabbath **d**, to keep it holy
2 Kin. 7:9, this **d** is a **d** of good
Job 3:3, Let the **d** perish
Ps. 2:7, this **d** have I begotten thee
84:10, a **d** in thy courts
Prov. 3:2, 16, length of **d**-s
4:18, more unto the perfect **d**
27:1, what a **d** may bring forth
Song 2:17; 4:6, Until the **d** break
Is. 2:2, Come to pass in the last **d**-s
13:6, **d** of the Lord is at hand
Mic. 4:1, last **d**-s, shall come to pass
Zeph. 1:15, That **d** is a **d** of wrath
Matt. 7:22, Many will say . . . in that **d**
25:13, neither the **d** nor the hour
Luke 21:34, that **d** come . . . unawares
24:46, from the dead the third **d**
John 11:9, not twelve hours in the **d**
16:23, in that **d** ye shall ask me
19:42, the Jews' preparation **d**
Acts 2:17, in the last **d**-s, saith God
Rom. 2:5, against the **d** of wrath
13:12, night is far spent . . . **d** is at
1 Cor. 1:8, blameless in the **d** of our
3:13, the **d** shall declare it
2 Cor. 6:2, in the **d** of salvation have I
Eph. 6:13, withstand in the evil **d**
Phil. 1:6, until the **d** of Jesus Christ
3:5, Circumcised the eighth **d**
Heb. 13:8, Christ . . . to **d**, and for ever

2 Pet. 3:8, one **d** . . . as a thousand years
Rev. 1:10, Spirit on the Lord's **d**
Dayspring—*dawn*
Job 38:12, the **d** to know his place
Luke 1:78, the **d** from on high
Day star—*morning star*
2 Pet. 1:19, the **d** arise in your hearts
Daytime—*hours of daylight*
Job 5:14, meet with darkness in the **d**
Ps. 22:2, I cry in the **d**
42:8, loving kindness in the **d**
Is. 4:6, a shadow in the **d**
Dead—*destitute of life, deceased*
Gen. 23:3, stood up before his **d**
Lev. 19:28, cuttings . . . for the **d**
Josh. 1:2, Moses my servant is **d**
1 Sam. 24:14, after a **d** dog
Ps. 31:12, forgotten as a **d** man
88:5, Free among the **d**
115:7, **d** praise not the Lord
Prov. 21:16, congregation of the **d**
Eccles. 4:2, the **d** which are already **d**
9:5, **d** know not anything
Jer. 22:10, Weep ye not for the **d**
Ezek. 24:17, make no mourning for the **d**
Matt. 8:22, let the **d** bury their **d**
9:24, maid is not **d**, but sleepeth
22:32, not the God of the **d**
Luke 16:31, though one rose from the **d**
John 5:25, the **d** shall hear the voice
6:49, did eat manna . . . and are **d**
11:44, he that was **d** came forth
Acts 10:42, Judge of quick and **d**
Rom. 6:4, Christ was raised up from the **d**
1 Cor. 15:12, he rose from the **d**
35, How are the **d** raised up
1 Tim. 5:6, is **d** while she liveth
2 Tim. 4:1, judge the quick and the **d**
Heb. 11:4, he, being **d**, yet speaketh
James 2:17, if it hath not works, is **d**
20, faith without works is **d**
Rev. 1:5, first begotten of the **d**
14:13, Blessed are the **d**
20:13, the sea gave up the **d**
Deadly—*fatal*
1 Sam. 5:11, was a **d** destruction
Ps. 17:9, from my **d** enemies
Mark 16:18, if they drink any **d** thing
James 3:8, tongue . . . full of **d** poison
Rev. 13:3, his **d** wound was healed
Deaf—*deprived of hearing*
Ex. 4:11, who maketh the dumb, or **d**
Lev. 19:14, Thou shalt not curse the **d**

40

Ps. 38:13, But I, as a **d** man
Mic. 7:16, ears shall be **d**
Matt. 11:5, lepers are cleansed . . . **d** hear
Mark 7:37, maketh both the **d** to hear
Deal—*treat with*
Gen. 24:49, if ye will **d** kindly
Ruth 1:8, the Lord **d** kindly with you
Ps. 116:7, Lord hath **d**-t bountifully
Prov. 12:22, they that **d** truly are his
Luke 1:25, hath the Lord **d**-t with me
    2:48, why hast thou thus **d**-t with
John 4:9, Jews have no **d**-ings with
Acts 7:19, The same **d**-t subtilly
Rom. 12:3, according as God hath **d**-t to
Heb. 12:7, God **d**-eth with you as . . .
    sons
Dear—*precious, beloved*
Jer. 12:7, the **d**-ly beloved of my soul
    31:20, Is Ephraim my **d** son
Luke 7:2, centurion's servant, who was **d**
Acts 20:24, neither count I my life **d**
Rom. 12:19, **d**-ly beloved, avenge not
Eph. 5:1, followers of God as **d**
Col. 1:7, our **d** fellow servant
    13, into the kingdom of his **d** Son
1 Thess. 2:8, because ye were **d** unto us
2 Tim. 1:2, my **d**-ly beloved son
1 Pet. 2:11, **D**-ly beloved, I beseech you
Dearth—*scarcity*
Gen. 41:54, seven years of **d** began
2 Chr. 6:28, there be **d** in the land
Neh. 5:3, buy corn, because of the **d**
Acts 7:11, came a **d** over all the land
Death—*cessation of life*
Gen. 27:2, know not the day of my **d**
Num. 16:29, these . . . die the common **d**
    23:10, die the **d** of the righteous
Ruth 1:17, but **d** part thee and me
1 Sam. 20:3, a step between me and **d**
1 Kin. 2:26, thou are worthy of **d**
Job 3:21, long for **d** . . . cometh not
    38:17, gates of **d** been opened
Ps. 13:3, lest I sleep the sleep of **d**
    23:4, valley of the shadow of **d**
    89:48, what man . . . shall not see **d**
    107:10, darkness and . . . shadow of **d**
    116:3, sorrows of **d** compassed me
Prov. 8:36, all . . . that hate me love **d**
Song 8:6, love is strong as **d**
Is. 25:8, swallow up **d** in victory
Jer. 8:3, **d** . . . chosen rather than life
    21:8, of life, and the way of **d**
Ezek. 18:32; 33:11, no pleasure in the **d**

Matt. 15:4, let him die the **d**
Luke 1:79, and in the shadow of **d**
John 4:47, he was at the point of **d**
    5:24, is passed from **d** unto life
Acts 2:24, loosed the pains of **d**
Rom. 8:6, to be carnally minded is **d**
    38, neither **d**, nor life
1 Cor. 15:21, since by man came **d**
    54, **D** is swallowed up
    55, O **d**, where is thy sting
Phil. 1:20, whether . . . by life, or by **d**
2 Tim. 1:10, Christ, who . . . abolished **d**
Heb. 2:9, taste of **d** for every man
James 5:20, save a soul from **d**
1 John 3:14, passed from **d** unto life
    5:16, there is a sin unto **d**
Rev. 21:4, there shall be no more **d**
Debate—*contend*
Prov. 25:9, **D** thy cause with thy
Is. 58:4, fast for strife and **d**
Rom. 1:29, envy, murder, **d**, deceit
2 Cor. 12:20, there be **d**-s, envyings
Debt—*obligation owed another*
1 Sam. 22:2, everyone that was in **d**
2 Kin. 4:7, sell the oil, and pay thy **d**
Matt. 6:12, forgive us our **d**-s
    18:27, and forgave him the **d**
Rom. 4:4, reckoned of grace, but of **d**
Debtor—*one who owes a debt*
Matt. 6:12, as we forgive our **d**-s
Luke 7:41, creditor which had two **d**-s
Rom. 1-14, I am **d** both to the Greeks
    8:12, we are **d**-s, not to the flesh
Gal. 5:3, he is a **d** to do the whole law
Decease—*death, dead*
Is. 26:14, they are **d**-d
Matt. 22:25, married a wife, **d**-d
Luke 9:31, spake of his **d**
2 Pet. 1:15, may be able after my **d**
Deceit—*deception, fraud*
Job 15:35, their belly prepareth **d**
    31:5, my foot hath hasteth to **d**
Ps. 101:7, He that worketh **d** shall not
Prov. 14:8, the folly of fools is **d**
    20:17, Bread of **d** is sweet
Is. 53:9, neither . . . **d** in his mouth
Jer. 5:27, their houses full of **d**
Rom. 1:29, full of envy . . . **d**
Col. 2:8, philosophy and vain **d**
1 Thess. 2:3, exhortation was not of **d**
Deceitful—*insincere*
Gen. 34:13, answered . . . **d**-ly
Ps. 52:4, O thou **d** tongue

Deceitful (*Continued*)
Prov. 14:25, **d** witness speaketh lies
Jer. 17:9, heart is **d** above all things
Matt. 13:22, the **d**-ness of riches
2 Cor. 4:2, handling the . . . of God **d**-ly
    11:13, false apostles, **d** workers
Heb. 3:13, through the **d**-ness of sin
Deceive—*cheat, mislead*
Gen. 31:7, your father hath **d**-d me
Deut. 11:16, your heart be not **d**-d
Lev. 6:2, hath **d**-d his neighbour
1 Sam. 19:17, Why hast thou **d**-d me so
Matt. 24:4, Take heed that no . . . **d** you
    27:63, remember . . . **d**-r said
1 Cor. 3:18, Let no man **d** himself
2 Tim. 3:13, **d**-ing, and being **d**-d
James 1:22, **d**-ing your own selves
1 John 1:8, no sin, we **d** ourselves
Deck—*array, overspread*
Job 40:10, **D** thyself now with majesty
Prov. 7:16, have **d**-ed my bed with
Is. 61:10, a bridegroom **d**-eth himself
Jer. 10:4, **d** it with silver . . . gold
Rev. 17:4, **d**-ed with gold and
Declare—*publish, proclaim*
Gen. 41:24, none that could **d** it
Ex. 9:16, that my name may be **d**-d
Deut. 1:5, began Moses to **d** this law
1 Chr. 16:24, **D** his glory . . . heathen
Job 38:4, **d**, if thou hast understanding
Ps. 2:7, I will **d** the decree
    19:1, heavens **d** the glory of God
Is. 42:9, new things do I **d**
Matt. 13:66, **D** unto us the parable
John 1:18, begotten Son . . . hath **d**-d
Acts 13:32, we **d** unto you glad tidings
    17:23, him **d** I unto you
1 Cor. 15:1, I **d** unto you the gospel
Heb. 2:12, I will **d** thy name
Decree—*order, regulation*
Job 28:26, made a **d** for the rain
Prov. 8:15, kings reign, and princes **d**
Is. 10:1, Woe . . . that **d** unrighteous **d**-s
Jer. 5:22, sea by a perpetual **d**
Dan. 3:10, Thou, O king, hast made a **d**
Luke 2:1, went out a **d** from Caesar
Acts 17:7, contrary to the **d**-s of Caesar
1 Cor. 7:37, hath so **d**-d in his heart
Dedicate—*set apart, consecrate*
Num. 7:11, for the **d**-ing of the altar
Deut. 20:5, What man . . . hath not **d**-d it
1 Kin. 8:63, children of Israel **d**-d
1 Chr. 26:27, spoils. . . did they **d**

Ezra 6:16, **d**-ion of this house of God
Heb. 9:18, **d**-d without blood
Deed—*an act, a thing done*
Gen. 20:9, thou hast done **d**-s unto me
1 Sam. 25:34, For in very **d**, as the Lord
Luke 11:48, allow the **d**-s of your fathers
    24:19, a prophet mighty in **d**
John 3:19, their **d**-s were evil
Acts 7:22, mighty in words and in **d**-s
Rom. 8:13, mortify the **d**-s of the body
Col. 3:17, ye do in word or **d**
1 John 3:18, in **d** and in truth
Deep—*profound, great depth*
Gen. 1:2, darkness was upon . . . the **d**
    2:21, God caused a **d** sleep to
Job 12:22, He discovereth **d** things
Ps. 69:2, I am come into **d** waters
    92:5, thy thoughts are very **d**
Prov. 8:28, the fountains of the **d**
Luke 5:4, Launch out into the **d**
John 4:11, and the well is **d**
Rom. 10:7, shall descend into the **d**
2 Cor. 8:2, their **d** poverty abounded
Defence—*protection, answer, or plea*
Job 22:25, Almighty shall be thy **d**
Ps. 7:10, My **d** is of God
    59:17, God is my **d**
Eccles. 7:12, wisdom is a **d**
Acts 22:1, hear ye my **d**
Phil. 1:17, for the **d** of the gospel
Defer—*to put off*
Gen. 34:19, **d**-ed not to do the thing
Prov. 13:12, Hope **d**-ed maketh the heart
Eccles. 5:4, **d** not to pay it
Is. 48:9, will I **d** mine anger
Defile—*soil, make foul or impure*
Lev. 18:24, **D** not ye . . . in any of these
Is. 59:3, hands are **d**-ed with blood
Ezek. 9:7, **D** the house
Matt. 15:20, things which **d** a man
Mark 7:2, eat bread with **d**-d . . . hands
John 18:28, lest they should be **d**-d
1 Cor. 3:17, any man **d** the temple of God
    8:7, conscience . . . is **d**-d
1 Tim. 1:10, **d** themselves with mankind
Heb. 12:15, thereby many be **d**-d
James 3:6, it **d**-th the whole body
Rev. 3:4, have not **d**-d their garments
Defraud—*cheat*
Lev. 19:13, shalt not **d** thy neighbour
Mark 10:19, **D** not, Honour thy father
2 Cor. 7:2, we have **d**-ed no man
1 Thess. 4:6, go beyond and **d** his

Delay—*put off, postpone*
Ex. 22:29, Thou shalt not **d** to offer
    32:1, Moses **d**-ed to come down
Ps. 119:60, make haste, and **d** not
Matt. 24:48, My lord **d**-eth his coming
Delicate—*not coarse, gentle, dainties*
Deut. 28:54, tender . . . and very **d**
1 Sam. 15:32, Agag came unto him **d**-ly
Jer. 6:2, comely and **d** woman
    51:34, filled his belly with my **d**-s
Delight—*pleasure, to give joy*
Num. 14:8, If the Lord **d** in us
Deut. 10:15, Lord had a **d** in thy fathers
Job 27:10, **d** himself in the almighty
Ps. 1:2, his **d** is in the law
    37:4, **D** thy self also in the Lord
    40:8, I **d** to do thy will
    51:16, **d**-est not in burnt offering
Prov. 12:22, that deal truly are his **d**
Is. 58:13, call the sabbath a **d**
Mic. 7:18, because he **d**-eth in mercy
Rom. 7:22, For I **d** in the law of God
Deliver—*release, set free*
Gen. 32:11, **D** me . . . from the hand
Ps. 18:2, The Lord is . . . my **d**-er
    22:20, **D** my soul from the sword
    25:20, O keep my soul, and **d** me
    55:18, He . . . **d**-ed my soul in peace
    70:1, Make haste, O God, to **d** me
Prov. 23:14, **d** his soul from hell
Matt. 6:13, into temptation, but **d** us
    20:19, shall **d** him to the Gentiles
Luke 4:17, **d**-ed unto him the book of
John 19:11, he that **d**-ed me unto thee
Rom. 4:25, was **d**-ed for our offences
Col. 1:13, hath **d**-ed us from the power
Jude 3, faith . . . **d**-ed unto the saints
Deliverance—*a setting free*
Gen. 45:7, to save . . . by a great **d**
2 Kin. 13:17, The arrow of the Lord's **d**
Ps. 32:7, with the songs of **d**
Luke 4:18, preach **d** to the captives
Heb. 11:35, tortured, not accepting **d**
Den—*a lair, a cave*
Job 37:8, the beasts go into **d**-s
Ps. 10:9, as a lion in his **d**
Jer. 7:11, **d** of robbers in your eyes
Dan. 6:7, cast into the **d** of lions
Matt. 21:13, made it a **d** of thieves
Heb. 11:38, **d**-s and caves of the earth
Deny—*to refuse, make a negative answer*
Gen. 18:15, Sarah **d**-ed . . . I laughed not
Josh. 24:27, lest ye **d** your God

Matt. 10:33, whosoever shall **d** me
    16:24, let him **d** himself
Mark 14:30, thou shalt **d** me thrice
John 1:20, he confessed, and **d**-ed not
1 Tim. 5:8, he hath **d**-ed the faith
Titus 2:12, **d**-ing ungodliness
2 Tim. 2:12, **d** him, he also will **d** us
2 Peter 2:1, **d**-ing the Lord that bought
1 John 2:22, he that **d**-eth that Jesus
Jude 4, **d**-ing the only Lord God
Rev. 2:13, hast not **d**-ed my faith
Depart—*leave, go elsewhere*
Gen. 12:4, Abram **d**-ed, as the Lord had
Job 21:14, say unto God, **D** from us
Ps. 34:14, **D** from evil, and do good
Matt. 2:12, **d**-ed into their own country
Luke 2:29, thou thy servant **d** in peace
    5:8, **D** from me; for I am a sinful
    10:30, wounded him, and **d**-ed
1 Cor. 7:10, the wife **d** from her husband
2 Tim. 4:6, time of my **d**-ure is at hand
Heb. 3:12, in **d**-ing from the living God
Depth—*profoundness, lower parts*
Ex. 15:5, **d**-s have covered them
Job 28:14, **d** saith, It is not in me
Ps. 33:7, layeth up the **d** in storehouses
    77:16, **d**-s also were troubled
    130:1, Out of the **d**-s have I cried
Prov. 9:18, are in the **d**-s of hell
Is. 7:11, in the **d**, or in the height
Matt. 18:6, drowned in the **d** of the sea
Mark 4:5, had no **d** of earth
Rom. 8:39, Nor height, nor **d**, nor any
    11:33, O the **d** of the riches
Eph. 3:18, breadth, and length, and **d**
Rev. 2:24, known the **d**-s of Satan
Derision—*mockery, scorn*
Job 30:1, have me in **d**
Ps. 2:4, Lord shall have them in **d**
    59:8, all the heathen in **d**
Lam. 3:14, I was a **d** to all my people
Ezek. 36:4, became a prey and **d** to
Descend—*move downward*
Ex. 19:18, Lord **d**-ed upon it in fire
    33:9, cloudy pillar **d**-ed, and stood
    34:5, Lord **d**-ed in the cloud
Matt. 3:16, Spirit of God **d**-ing like
    7:25, rain **d**-ed . . . floods came
Mark 15:32, Let Christ the king . . . **d**
Rom. 10:7, Who shall **d** into the deep
Eph. 4:10, He that **d**-ed is the same
1 Thess. 4:16, Lord himself shall **d**
James 3:15, This wisdom **d**-eth not

43

DESCENT

Descent—*the going down*
Luke 18:37, **d** of the mount of Olives
Heb. 7:3, 6, without **d** . . . whose **d**
Desert—*a wilderness*
Ex. 3:1, backside of the **d**
Job 24:5, wild asses in the **d**
Ps. 102:6, like an owl of the **d**
Is. 13:21, wild beasts of the **d**
40:3, straight in the **d** a highway
43:19, rivers in the **d**
Mark 6:31, Come ye . . . into a **d** place
John 6:31, did eat manna in the **d**
Desire—*natural longing*
Gen. 3:6, tree to be **d-d** to make
16, **d** shall be to thy husband
Deut. 14:26, whatsoever thy soul **d-th**
Judg. 8:24, would **d** a request of you
2 Chr. 15:15, sought him with . . . whole **d**
Job 36:20, **D** not the night
Ps. 19:10, More to be **d-d** . . . than gold
112:10, **d** of the wicked shall
140:8, Grant not . . . **d-s** of the wicked
145:16, satisfiest the **d** of every
Prov. 11:23, **d** of the righteous is only
13:19, **d** accomplished is sweet
21:10, soul of the wicked **d-th** evil
Ezek. 24:21, the **d** of your eyes
Hag. 2:7, **d** of all nations shall come
Matt. 13:17, have **d-d** to see those
16:1, **d-d** him that he would
Mark 9:35, If any man **d** to be first
11:24, things . . . ye **d**, when ye
pray
Luke 10:24, prophets . . . have **d-d** to see
Acts 13:7, **d-d** to hear the word of God
2 Cor. 5:2, earnestly **d-ing** to be
7:7, he told us your earnest **d**
Eph. 3:13, I **d** that ye faint not
Col. 1:9, **d** that ye might be filled
1 Tim. 3:1, he **d-th** a good work
Heb. 11:16, now they **d** a better country
1 Pet. 2:2, newborn babes, **d** the sincere
Desirous—*eagerly wishing*
Luke 23:8, was **d** to see him of a long
Gal. 5:26, be **d** of vain glory
1 Thess. 2:8, affectionately **d** of you
Desolate—*deserted, gloomy*
Ex. 23:29, lest the land become **d**
Lev. 26:22, your highways shall be **d**
Ps. 25:16, mercy upon me; for I am **d**
143:4, my heart within me is **d**
Jer. 2:12, be ye very **d**
Ezek. 6:6, your altars . . . made **d**
35:3, I will make thee most **d**

Matt. 23:38, house is left unto you **d**
Acts 1:20, his habitation be **d**
Gal. 4:27, **d** hath many more children
Desolation—*laid waste, ruined*
Lev. 26:31, your sanctuaries unto **d**
Josh. 8:28, a **d** unto this day
Ps. 46:8, what **d-s** he hath made
Prov. 1:27, fear cometh as **d**
Is. 47:11, **d** . . . come upon thee suddenly
Zeph. 1:15, a day of wasteness and **d**
Matt. 24:15, the abomination of **d**
Despise—*look down upon*
Gen. 25:34, Esau **d-d** his birthright
Lev. 26:15, shall **d** my statutes
2 Sam. 6:16, she **d-d** him in her heart
Job 19:18, young children **d-d** me
Ps. 106:24, **d-d** the pleasant land
Prov. 1:7, **d** wisdom . . . instruction
15:5, fool **d-th** his father's
Jer. 4:30, thy lovers will **d** thee
Matt. 6:24, hold to the one, and **d** the
18:10, **d** not one of these little
Luke 10:16, he that **d-th** you **d-th** me
Acts 13:41, Behold, ye **d-rs**, and wonder
1 Cor. 11:22, **d** ye the church of God
1 Tim. 4:12, Let no man **d** thy youth
1 Thess. 4:8, that **d-th**, **d-th** not man
Heb. 12:2, the cross, **d-ing** the shame
James 2:6, But ye have **d-d** the poor
Destitute—*needy, forsaken*
Gen. 24:27, not left **d** my master
Ps. 102:17, regard the prayer of the **d**
141:8, leave not my soul **d**
1 Tim. 6:5, minds . . . **d** of the truth
Heb. 11:37, being **d**, afflicted
James 2:15, naked, and **d** of daily food
Destroy—*tear down, ruin*
Gen. 6:13, I will **d** them with the earth
18:23, thou also **d** the righteous
Deut. 4:31, not forsake thee, neither **d**
Job 6:9, please God to **d** me
Matt. 2:13, the young child to **d** him
5:17, not that I am come to **d**
10:28, **d** both soul and body
26:61, I am able to **d** the temple
Mark 1:24, art thou come to **d** us
14:58, I will **d** this temple that
Luke 17:27, flood came and **d-ed** them
John 2:19, **D** this temple, and in
John 10:10, and to kill, and to **d**
1 Cor. 1:19, **d** the wisdom of the wise
6:13, God shall **d** both it . . . them
Gal. 2:18, again the things which I **d-ed**

44

Destruction—*downfall, havoc, ruin*
Job 26:6, **d** hath no covering
Ps. 90:3, Thou turnest man to **d**
   91:6, **d** that wasteth at noon day
   103:4, redeemeth thy life from **d**
Prov. 16:18, Pride goeth before **d**
   18:7, A fool's mouth is his **d**
   27:20, Hell and **d** are never full
Matt. 7:13, Broad is way . . . to **d**
Rom. 3:16, **D** . . . in their ways
   9:22, vessels of wrath fitted to **d**
2 Thess. 1:9, punished with everlasting **d**
1 Tim. 6:9, which drown men in **d**
2 Pet. 2:1, bring upon themselves . . . **d**
Determine—*shape, settle, end*
Ex. 21:22, pay as the judges **d**
1 Sam. 20:7, be sure that evil is **d-d**
2 Chr. 2:1, Solomon **d-d** to build
Luke 22:22, Son . . . goeth, as it was **d-d**
Acts 11:29, **d-d** to send relief unto
   19:39, be **d-d** in a lawful assembly
1 Cor. 2:2, I **d-d** not to know any thing
Device—*project, scheme*
2 Chr. 2:14, to find out every **d**
Ps. 140:8, further not his wicked **d**
Prov. 1:31, filled with their own **d-s**
   19:21, many **d-s** in a man's heart
Jer. 18:12, will walk after our . . . **d-s**
Acts 17:29, graven by art and man's **d**
2 Cor. 2:11, are not ignorant of his **d-s**
Devil—*an evil spirit, a wicked person*
Lev. 17:7, offer . . . sacrifices unto **d-s**
Ps. 106:37, sons . . . daughters unto **d-s**
Matt. 4:1, to be tempted of the **d**
   24, those . . . possessed with **d-s**
   9:32, dumb . . . possessed with a **d**
Luke 7:33, ye say, He hath a **d**
John 6:70, one of you is a **d**
   7:20, Thou hast a **d**
Acts 13:10, thou child of the **d**
1 Cor. 10:20, they sacrifice to **d-s**
Eph. 6:11, against the wiles of the **d**
2 Tim. 2:26, out of the snare of the **d**
James 2:19, **d-s** also believe . . . tremble
   4:7, Resist the **d**, and he will flee
Rev. 12:9, old serpent, called the **D**
Devise—*form a scheme, or plan*
Ex. 31:4, To **d** cunning works
Ps. 36:4, He **d-th** mischief upon his bed
   52:2, Thy tongue **d-th** mischiefs
Prov. 24:8, He that **d-th** to do evil
2 Pet. 1:16, cunningly **d-d** fables

Devour—*eat greedily, consume*
Gen. 37:20, evil beast hath **d-ed** him
   41:7, seven thin ears **d-ed** the seven
Deut. 32:42, my sword shall **d** flesh
2 Chr. 7:13, command the locusts to **d**
Prov. 30:14, **d** the poor from off the
Is. 1:20, shall be **d-ed** with the sword
   30:27, his tongue as a **d-ing** fire
Amos 7:4, it **d-ed** the great deep
Luke 8:5, fowls of the air **d-ed** it
2 Cor. 11:20, if a man **d** you
Gal. 5:15, bite and **d** one another
1 Pet. 5:8, seeking whom he may **d**
Devout—*devoted to God*
Luke 2:25, Simeon . . . was just and **d**
Acts 2:5, **d** men, out of every nation
   22:12, a **d** man according to the
Dew—*condensed moisture*
Gen. 27:28, give . . . of the **d** of heaven
Deut. 32:2, speech shall distill as the **d**
Judg. 6:37, **d** be on the fleece only
2 Sam. 1:21, let there be no **d**
Ps. 110:3, hast the **d** of thy youth
Prov. 19:12, is as **d** upon the grass
Song 5:2, my head is filled with **d**
Is. 18:4, a cloud of **d** in the heat
Dan. 4:15, wet with the **d** of heaven
Hos. 6:4, your goodness is as . . . early **d**
Diadem—*a badge of regal power*
Job 29:14, as a robe and a **d**
Is. 28:5, a **d** of beauty
Ezek. 21:26, Remove the **d**
Dial—*a sun dial*
2 Kin. 20:11, down in the **d** of Ahaz
Is. 38:8, in the sun **d** of Ahaz
Diamond—*precious stone*
Ex. 28:18, a sapphire, and a **d**
Jer. 17:1, written . . . point of a **d**
Ezek. 28:13, **d**, the beryl, the onyx
Die—*cease from life, perish*
Gen. 2:17, eatest . . . thou shalt surely **d**
   6:17, everything . . . shall **d**
   30:1, Give me children, or else I **d**
Num. 23:10, Let me **d** the death of
Ruth 1:17, Where thou **d-st**, will I **d**
Job 14:14, If a man **d**, shall he live
   29:18, I shall **d** in my nest
Ps. 104:29, **d**, and return to their dust
   118:17, I shall not **d**, but live
Prov. 10:21, fools **d** for want of wisdom
Eccles. 3:2, to be born . . . time to **d**
Is. 22:13, eat . . . tomorrow we shall **d**
   51:12, afraid of a man that shall **d**
Jer. 34:5, Thou shalt **d** in peace

Die (*Continued*)
Ezek. 18:4, soul that sinneth, it shall **d**
Jonah 4:8, better . . . to **d** than to live
Matt. 15:4, curseth . . . mother, let him **d**
Mark 14:31, If I should **d** with thee
John 11:26, believeth . . . shall never **d**
    50, one man . . . **d** for the people
1 Cor. 15:3, Christ **d-d** for our sins
    22, For as in Adam all **d**
1 Thess. 4:14, believe that Jesus **d-d**

Differ—*to vary, be unlike*
Ex. 11:7, doth put a **d**-ence between
Acts 15:9, no **d**-ence between us
Rom 10:12, no **d**-ence between the Jew
    12:6, **d**-ing according to the grace
1 Cor. 4:7, thee to **d** from another
    12:5, **d**-ences of administration
    15:41, **d**-eth from another star

Dig—*shovel, do servile work*
Gen. 21:30, witness . . . that I have **d**-ed
Deut. 8:9, thou mayest **d** brass
Ps. 119:85, proud have **d**-ed pits for me
Prov. 16:27, ungodly man **d**-eth up evil
Amos 9:2, Though they **d** into hell
Luke 6:48, built an house, and **d**-ed
    13:8, till I shall **d** about it
    16:3, cannot **d** . . . beg I am ashamed

Diligence—*careful attention*
Luke 12:58, give **d** that thou mayest
2 Tim. 4:9, Do thy **d** to come shortly
2 Pet. 1:5, giving all **d**, add to your

Diligent—*painstaking*
Deut. 4:9, keep thy soul **d**-ly
Prov. 10:4, hand of the **d** maketh rich
Is. 21:7, he hearkened **d**-ly
Matt. 2:8, search **d**-ly for the young
Luke 15:8, seek **d**-ly till she find it
2 Cor. 8:22, have oftentimes proved **d**

Dim—*impaired*
Gen. 27:1, old, and his eyes were **d**
Deut. 34:7, his eye was not **d**
Lam. 4:1, How is the gold become **d**

Diminish—*lessen*
Lev. 25:16, shalt **d** the price of it.
Jer. 26:2, **d** not a word
Ezek. 16:27, **d**-ed thine ordinary food
Rom. 11:12, **d**-ing of them the riches

Dinner—*the principal meal*
Prov. 15:17, Better is a **d** of herbs
Matt. 22:4, I have prepared my **d**
Luke 11:38, not first washed before **d**

Dip—*to immerse, to wet*
Gen. 37:31, **d**-ed the coat in the blood

Deut. 33:24, **d** his foot in oil
Lev. 4:6, priest shall **d** his finger in
Matt. 26:23, He that **d**-eth his hand
Luke 16:24, **d** the tip of his finger in
John 13:26, had **d**-ed the sop
Rev. 19:13, a vesture **d**-ed in blood

Direct—*point, aim, immediate*
Num. 19:4, sprinkle . . . **d**-ly before
Ps. 5:3, morning will I **d** my prayer
Prov. 3:6, he shall **d** thy paths
Is. 40:13, **d**-ed the Spirit of the Lord
Ezek. 42:12, way **d**-ly before the wall
1 Thess. 3:11, Christ, **d** our way
2 Thess. 3:5, Lord **d** your hearts into

Disannul—*to render void*
Job 40:8, Wilt thou also **d** my judgment
Is. 28:18, covenant with death . . . **d**-ed
Gal. 3:15, no man **d**-eth, or addeth
Heb. 7:18, a **d**-ing of the commandment

Discern—*perceive, recognize*
2 Sam. 14:17, to **d** good and bad
    19:35, can I **d** between good and
Ezra 3:13, not **d** the noise of . . . joy
Eccles. 8:5, a wise man's heart **d**-eth
Matt. 16:3, ye can **d** the face of the sky
1 Cor. 2:14, they are spiritually **d**-ed
    11:29, not **d**-ing the Lord's body
Heb. 4:12, is a **d**-er of the thoughts
    5:14, to **d** both good and evil

Discharge—*unloading, release*
1 Kin. 5:9, to be **d**-d there
Eccles. 8:8, no **d** in that war

Disciple—*a learner, a follower*
Is. 8:16, seal the law among my **d**-s
Matt. 9:14, came to him the **d**-s of John
    10:1, called . . . his twelve **d**-s
    24, **d** is not above his master
    12:1, his **d**-s were an hungered
    19:13, the **d**-s rebuked them
    21:1, then sent Jesus two **d**-s
    26:26, gave it to the **d**-s
Luke 11:1, as John also taught his **d**-s
John 13:35, know that ye are my **d**-s
    19:26, **d** standing by, . . . he loved
    20:19, the **d**-s were assembled
    21:4, **d**-s knew not . . . it was Jesus
Acts 6:7, number of the **d**-s multiplied
    14:22, the souls of the **d**-s

Discomfited—*scattered, routed*
Num. 14:45, smote them, and **d** them
Judg. 4:15, Lord **d** Sisera
Is. 31:8, his young men shall be **d**

Discourage—*dishearten, depress*
Num. 32:7, **d** ye the heart of the

Deut. 1:21, fear not, neither be **d-d**
Is. 42:4, shall not fail nor be **d-d**
Discover—*lay open to view*
1 Sam. 14:8, we will **d** ourselves unto
2 Sam. 22:16, foundations . . . were **d-ed**
Prov. 25:9, **d** not a secret to another
Is. 57:8, **d-ed** thyself to another
Lam. 2:14, have not **d-ed** thine iniquity
Mic. 1:6, **d** the foundations thereof
Acts 27:39, they **d-ed** a certain creek
Discreet—*cautious, careful*
Gen. 41:33, a man **d** and wise
39, none so **d** and wise
Mark 12:34, he answered **d-ly**
Titus 2:5, To be **d**, chaste, keepers at
Discretion—*care, prudence, caution*
Ps. 112:5, guide his affairs with **d**
Prov. 1:4, subtilty . . . knowledge and **d**
2:11, **D** shall preserve thee
11:22, fair woman . . . without **d**
Is. 28:26, instruct him to **d**
Disease—*illness, sickness*
Ex. 15:26, will put none of these **d-s**
1 Kin. 15:23, old age he was **d-d** in
2 Kin. 15:26, will put none of these **d-s**
Job 30:18, great force of my **d**
Ps. 41:8, an evil **d** . . . cleaveth fast
103:3, who healeth all thy **d-s**
Eccles. 6:2, it is an evil **d**
Matt. 4:23, all manner of **d** among
14:35, all that were **d-d**
Mark 1:34, healed . . . sick of divers **d-s**
Luke 9:1, authority . . . to cure **d-s**
John 6:2, on them that were **d-d**
Disguise—*conceal, mask, hide*
1 Kin. 14:2, Arise . . . and **d** thyself
22:30, I will **d** myself
Job 24:15, and **d-th** his face
Dish—*shallow concave vessel*
Ex. 37:16, his **d-s** . . . spoons . . . bowls
Judg. 5:25, butter in a lordly **d**
2 Kin. 21:13, as a man wipeth a **d**
Mark 14:20, dippeth with me in the **d**
Dishonest—*wanting in honesty*
Ezek. 22:27, to get **d** gain
2 Cor. 4:2, the hidden things of **d-y**
Dishonour—*shames, reproach*
Ps. 35:26, clothed with shame and **d**
Prov. 6:33, wound and **d** shall he get
Mic. 7:6, the son **d-eth** the father
Rom. 1:24, to **d** their own bodies
1 Cor. 11:4, his head covered, **d-eth**
15:43, It is sown in **d**
2 Tim. 2:20, to honour, and some to **d**

Dismayed—*terrified, frightened*
Deut. 31:8, fear not, neither be **d**
2 Kin. 19:26, **d** and confounded
Is. 41:10, be not **d** . . . I am thy God
Jer. 10:2, **d** at the signs of heaven
Ezek. 3:9, neither be **d** at their looks
Disobedience—*neglect or refusal to obey*
Rom. 5:19, by one man's **d**
2 Cor. 10:6, revenge all **d**
Eph. 2:2, in the children of **d**
Disobedient—*refractory*
Luke 1:17, turn . . . **d** to the wisdom of
Rom. 1:30, **d** to parents
Titus 3:3, were sometimes foolish, **d**
1 Pet. 2:7, unto them which be **d**
Disorderly—*not in order, confusedly*
2 Thess. 3:6, brother that walked **d**
11, which walk among you **d**
Disperse—*scatter*
1 Sam. 14:34, **D** yourselves among
Prov. 15:7, lips of the wise **d** knowledge
Jer. 25:34, days of your . . . **d-ions**
Ezek. 12:15, **d** them in the countries
John 7:35, will he go unto the **d-d**
2 Cor. 9:9, As . . . written, He hath **d-d**
Displease—*annoy, give offense*
Gen. 38:10, which he did **d-d** the Lord
2 Sam. 11:25, Let not this . . . **d** thee
Ps. 60:1, thou hast been **d-d**
Zech. 1:2, Lord hath been sore **d-d**
Matt. 21:15, they were sore **d-d**
Mark 10:14, Jesus . . . was much **d-d**
Dispute—*argue with*
Job 23:7, the righteous might **d**
Mark 9:33, What was it . . . ye **d-d** among
Phil. 2:14, do . . . things without . . . **d-ings**
1 Cor. 1:20, the **d-r** of this world
1 Tim. 6:5, Perverse **d-ings** of men
Disquieted—*vexed, agitated*
1 Sam. 28:15, why hast thou **d** me
Ps. 39:6, they are **d** in vain
42:5, why art thou **d** in me
Prov. 31:21, the earth is **d**
Dissemble—*conceal, cloak*
Josh. 7:11, stolen, and **d-d** also
Jer. 42:20, ye **d-d** in your hearts
Prov. 26:4, I go in with **d-rs**
24, **d-th** with his lips
Dissolve—*break up, clear up*
Job 30:22, and **d-st** my substance
Ps. 75:3, all the inhabitants . . . are **d-d**

Dissolve (*Continued*)
Dan. 5:12, and **d**-ing of doubts
2 Pet. 3:11, all these things . . . be **d**-d
Distaff—*staff used in spinning*
Prov. 31:19, her hands hold the **d**
Distil—*fall in drops*
Deut. 32:2, shall **d** as the dew
Job 36:28, drop and **d** upon man
Distress—*pain, misery, worry*
Gen. 35:3, in the day of my **d**
Deut. 2:9, **D** not the Moabites
28:53, enemies shall **d** thee
Ps. 25:17, bring thou me out of my **d**-es
Prov. 1:27, when **d** and anguish cometh
Is. 25:4, strength to the needy in his **d**
29:2, Yet I will **d** Ariel
Lam. 1:20, for I am in **d**
Zeph. 1:17, I will bring **d** upon men
Luke 21:23, there shall be great **d**
1 Cor. 7:26, good for the present **d**
1 Thess. 3:7, and **d** by your faith
Distribute—*allot, share, divide*
Job 21:17, God **d**-th sorrows
Luke 18:22, **d** unto the poor
John 6:11, **d**-d to the disciples
Rom. 12:13, **D**-ing to the necessity
1 Cor. 7:17, God hath **d**-d to every
2 Cor. 9:13, for your liberal **d**-ion
Ditch—*earthen conduit for water*
2 Kin. 3:16, valley full of **d**-es
Prov. 23:27, whore in a deep **d**
Matt. 15:14, both shall fall into the **d**
Divers—*different in kind*
Deut. 22:9, not sow . . . with **d** seeds
11, garment of **d** sorts
25:13, shalt not have . . . **d** weights
2 Sam. 13:18, garment of **d** colours
Matt. 4:24, taken with **d** diseases
24:7, earthquakes, in **d** places
1 Cor. 12:4, **d**-ities of gifts
2 Tim. 3:6, led away with **d** lusts
Heb. 1:1, at sundry times . . . **d** manner
James 1:2, fall into **d** temptations
Divide—*separate, part*
Gen. 1:4, God **d**-d the light from
Josh. 13:7, **d** this land for an
1 Kin. 3:25, **D** the living child in two
Prov. 16:19, **d** the spoil with the proud
Is. 53:12, will I **d** him a portion
Dan. 2:41, the kingdom shall be **d**-d
Matt. 25:32, shepherd **d**-th his sheep
Luke 11:17, Every kingdom **d**-d against
15:12, he **d**-d unto them his living
2 Tim. 2:15, **d**-ing the word of truth

Divination—*augury, prediction*
Num. 22:7, with the rewards of **d**
Jer. 14:14, a false vision and **d**
Ezek. 13:6, vanity and lying **d**
Acts 16:16, with a spirit of **d**
Divine—*godlike, heavenly, foretell*
Ezek. 13:9, and that **d** lies
Mic. 3:11, prophets . . . **d** for money
Zech. 10:2, the **d**-rs have seen a lie
Heb. 9:1, ordinances of **d** service
2 Pet. 1:4, partakers of the **d** nature
Division—*separation, parting*
Ex. 8:23, I will put a **d** between
John 7:43, there was a **d** among
Rom. 16:17, cause **d**-s and offenses
1 Cor. 1:10, that there be no **d**-s
3:3, among . . . envying . . .
and **d**-s
Divorce—*dissolution of a marriage*
Lev. 21:14, widow, or a **d**-d woman
Deut. 24:1, 3, a bill of **d**-ment
Jer. 3:8, given her a bill of **d**
Matt. 5:31, 32, writing of **d**-ment
Do—*bring about or complete*
Gen. 11:6, this they begin to **d**
30:31, thou wilt **d** this thing
Ex. 20:9, Six days . . . labor, and **d** all
1 Kin. 2:6, **D** . . . according to thy
wisdom
Ps. 1:3, whatsoever he **d**-eth shall
34:14, Depart from evil, and **d** good
Prov. 2:14, Who rejoice to **d** evil
24:29, I will **d** so to him as he
Eccles. 3:14, whatsoever God **d**-eth, it
Matt. 5:44, **d** good to them that hate
6:1, **d** not your alms before men
12:50, whosoever . . . **d** the will of
23:3, **d** not ye after their works
John 2:5, Whatsoever he saith . . . **d** it
5:30, of mine own self **d** nothing
7:17, If any man will **d** his will
15:5, without me ye can **d** nothing
Acts 16:30, what must I **d** to be saved
Rom. 13:3, **d** that which is good
1 Cor. 9:23, **d** for the gospel's sake
11:24, this **d** in remembrance of
Gal. 6:10, let us **d** good unto all men
Phil. 2:13, both to will and to **d**
2 Tim. 4:5, **d** the work of an evangelist
Heb. 10:7, Lo, I come . . . to **d** thy will
1 Pet. 3:11, eschew evil, and **d** good
1 John 1:6, we lie, and **d** not the truth

Doctor—*learned man*
Luke 2:46, in the midst of the **d**-s
  5:17, Pharisees and **d**-s of the law
Acts 5:34, Gamaliel, a **d** of the law
Doctrine—*teaching, instruction*
Deut. 32:2, My **d** shall drop as the rain
Job 11:4, My **d** is pure
Prov. 4:2, I give you good **d**
Mark 1:22, astonished at his **d**
John 7:16, My **d** is not mine, but his
Acts 2:42, in the apostles' **d**
Rom. 16:17, contrary to the **d** which ye
Col. 2:22, commandments and **d**-s of
Eph. 4:14, every wind of **d**
1 Tim. 4:6, of faith and good **d**
2 Tim. 3:10, thou hast . . . known my **d**
Titus 1:9, able by sound **d**
Heb. 6:2, Of the **d** of baptisms
Rev. 2:24, as many as have not this **d**
Doer—*one who performs or executes*
Gen. 39:22, he was the **d** of it
2 Kin. 22:5, the **d**-s of the work
Ps. 101:8, cut off all wicked **d**-s
Rom. 2:13, the **d**-s of the law shall be
James 1:22, be ye **d**-s of the word
  4:11, not a **d** of the law
Dog—*an animal, low, worthless person*
1 Sam. 17:43, Am I a **d**, that thou comest
2 Sam. 3:8, Am I a **d**'s head
Ps. 22:16, For **d**-s have compassed me
  59:6, make a noise like a **d**
Eccles. 9:4, living **d** is better than
Is. 56:10, they are all dumb **d**-s
Luke 16:21, the **d**-s came and licked
Phil. 3:2, Beware of **d**-s, beware of evil
Rev. 22:15, For without are **d**-s
Doing—*accomplishing*
Ps. 66:5, terrible in his **d** toward
Prov. 20:11, child is known by his **d**-s
Is. 1:16, put away the evil of your **d**-s
Matt. 21:42, is the Lord's **d**, and it is
Acts 10:38, went about **d** good
Rom. 2:7, patient continuance in well **d**
2 Cor. 8:11, perform the **d** of it
Gal. 6:9, not be weary in well **d**
Eph. 6:6, **d** the will of God from
2 Thess. 3:13, not weary in well **d**
1 Pet. 2:15, that with well **d** ye may
  3:17, suffer . . . well **d** . . . evil **d**
Dominion—*authority*
Gen. 1:26, them have **d** over the fish
  37:8, shalt thou . . . have **d** over us
Job 25:2, **D** and fear are with him

Ps. 8:6, Thou madest him to have **d**
  49:14, upright shall have **d** over
  103:22, in all places of his **d**
Is. 26:13, lords beside thee have had **d**
Zech. 9:10, his **d** shall be from sea
Rom. 6:9, death hath no more **d** over
2 Cor. 1:24, have **d** over your faith
Col. 1:16, or **d**-s, or principalities
1 Pet. 4:11, to whom be praise and **d**
Rev. 1:6, be glory and **d** for ever
Done—*engaged in, completed*
Gen. 20:9, deeds . . . ought not to be **d**
Ex. 31:15, Six days may work be **d**
Matt. 1:22, Now all this was **d**, that
  6:10, kingdom come. Thy . . . be **d**
  18:19, be **d** for them of my Father
2 Cor. 3:7, glory was to be **d** away
Door—*entrance way*
Gen. 4:7, sin lieth at the **d**
  6:16, **d** of the ark shalt thou set
  18:1, sat in the tent **d**
Ex. 12:7, on the upper **d** post
  24, Lord will pass over the **d**
Judg. 4:20, Stand in the **d** of the tent
2 Sam. 11:9, Uriah slept at the **d**
Job 31:9, laid wait at my neighbour's **d**
Ps. 84:10, had rather be a **d** keeper in
  141:3, keep the **d** of my lips
Prov. 26:14, **d** turneth upon his hinges
Matt. 6:6, thou hast shut thy **d**, pray
  25:10, went to buy . . . **d** was shut
  27:60, rolled a great stone to the **d**
John 10:9, I am the **d**
  18:16, Peter stood at the **d**
1 Cor. 16:9, a great **d** and effectual
James 5:9, judge standeth before the **d**
Rev. 3:8, set before thee an open **d**
  4:1, a **d** was opened in heaven
Double—*two-fold, divided in two*
Gen. 43:12, take **d** money in your hand
2 Kin. 2:9, **d** portion of thy spirit
Ps. 12:2, with a **d** heart
Is. 40:2, **d** for all her sins
1 Tim. 5:17, be counted worthy of **d**
James 1:8 **d** minded man is unstable
Doubt—*be undecided, indecision*
Gen. 37:33, without **d** rent in pieces
Job 12:2, No **d** but ye are the people
Ps. 126:6, shall **d**-less come again
Is. 63:16, **d**-less thou art our Father
Matt. 14:31, wherefore didst thou **d**
  21:21, ye have faith, and **d** not
  28:17, but some **d**-ed

Doubt (*Continued*)
Luke 11:20, no **d** the kingdom of God
 12:29, neither be ye of **d**-ful mind
John 13:22, disciples looked . . . **d**-ing
Acts 10:20, go with them, **d**-ing nothing
Rom. 14:23, that **d**-eth is damned
1 Cor. 9:2, yet **d**-less I am to you
1 Tim. 2:8, holy hands, without . . . **d**-ing
Dove—*a pigeon*
Gen. 8:8, he sent forth a **d** from
Ps. 55:6, O that I had wings like a **d**
Song 1:15, thou hast **d**'s eyes
Is. 38:14, I did mourn as a **d**
Matt. 3:16, Spirit . . . descending like a **d**
 10:16, serpents . . . harmless as **d**-s
John 1:32, from heaven like a **d**
Down—*toward a lower point*
Gen. 12:10, went **d** into Egypt
2 Sam. 3:35, till the sun be **d**
2 Chr. 32:30, brought it straight **d**
Ps. 23:2, lie **d** in green pastures
Eccles. 3:21, beast that goeth **d**-ward
Matt. 4:6, Son of God, cast . . . **d**
 8:32, herd . . . ran violently **d**
John 8:6, Jesus stooped **d**
Dragon—*fabulous monster*
Deut. 32:33, Their wine . . . poison of **d**-s
Job 30:29, I am a brother to **d**-s
Ps. 91:13, young lion and the **d** shalt
 148:7, Praise the Lord . . . ye **d**-s
Is. 51:9, cut Rahab, and wounded the **d**
Jer. 9:11, Jerusalem . . . a den of **d**-s
Rev. 20:2, the **d**, that old serpent
Drank—*swallowed liquid*
Gen. 9:21, and he **d** of the wine
1 Kin. 17:6, and he **d** of the brook
Dan. 1:5, of the wine which he **d**
Mark 14:23, and they all **d** of it
Luke 17:27, They did eat, they **d**
John 4:12, Jacob, which . . . **d** thereof
1 Cor. 10:4, **d** of that spiritual Rock
Draw—*pull up or toward*
Gen. 24:13, come out to **d** water
Judg. 3:22, not **d** the dagger out
Ps. 69:18; 73:28, **D** nigh unto my soul
Prov. 20:5, man of understanding will **d**
Is. 12:3, **d** water out of the wells of
Jer. 31:3, lovingkindness have I **d**-n
Luke 21:28, your redemption **d**-eth nigh
John 4:11, nothing to **d** with
 12:32, lifted up . . . will **d** all men
Acts 11:10, **d**-n up again into heaven
Heb. 10:22, Let us **d** near with a true
 38, if any man **d** back

James 2:6, **d** you before the judgment
 4:8, **D** nigh to God . . . he will **d**
Dread—*great fear*
Gen. 28:17, How **d**-ful is this place
Deut. 1:29, **D** not, neither be afraid
Job 15:21, A **d**-ful sound is in his ears
Is. 8:13, let him be your **d**
Mal. 4:5, the great and **d**-ful day
Dream—*thoughts during sleep*
Gen. 20:3, God came . . . in a **d**
 28:12, he **d**-ed . . . behold a ladder
 37:19, Behold, this **d**-er cometh
Judg. 7:13, I **d**-ed a **d**, and lo, a cake
Job 20:8, fly away as a **d**
Ps. 73:20, As a **d** when one awaketh
 126:1, we were like them that **d**
Is. 29:7, **d** of a night vision
Dan. 1:17, understanding in all . . . **d**-s
Joel 2:28, your old men shall **d d**-s
Matt. 1:20, appeared unto him in a **d**
 2:12, warned of God in a **d**
 27:19, suffered . . . things . . . in a **d**
Acts 2:17, your old men shall **d d**-s
Jude 8, these filthy **d**-ers defile
Dress—*clothe, prepare*
Gen. 2:15, garden of Eden to **d** it
Ex. 30:7, when he **d**-eth the lamps
Lev. 7:9, that is **d**-ed in the frying pan
Deut. 28:39, plant . . . and **d** them
Heb. 6:7, for them by whom it is **d**-ed
Drew—*pulled along*
Gen. 47:29, time **d** nigh that Israel
Ex. 2:10, I **d** him out of the water
Josh. 8:26, Joshua **d** not his hand back
Ruth 4:8, he **d** off his shoe
Zeph. 3:2, she **d** not near to her God
Matt. 21:34, time of the fruit **d** near
 26:51, **d** his sword, and struck
Luke 24:15, Jesus himself **d** near
Acts 5:37, and **d** away much people
Dried—*freed from moisture*
Gen. 8:7, waters were **d** up
Lev. 2:14, corn **d** by the fire
Job 18:16, His roots shall be **d** up
Ps. 22:15, My strength is **d** up
 69:3, crying: my throat is **d**
Jer. 23:10, pleasant places . . . are **d** up
Ezek. 17:24, **d** up the green tree
Zech. 11:17, arm shall be clean **d** up
Mark 11:20, the fig tree **d** up
Drink—*swallow liquid*
Gen. 35:14, poured a **d** offering
Lev. 10:9, Do not **d** wine or strong **d**

Num. 6:3, He . . . shall **d** no vinegar
Job 6:4, poison . . . **d**-eth up my spirit
   21:20, shall **d** of the wrath of
Ps. 16:4, their **d** offerings of blood
   80:5, givest them tears to **d**
Prov. 5:15, **D** waters . . . of . . . own
   cistern
   20:1, Wine is mocker, strong **d**
Eccles. 9:7, **d** . . . wine with a merry heart
Is. 22:13, let us eat and **d**; for tomorrow
   24:9, strong **d** shall be bitter
Joel 1:5, howl, all ye **d**-ers of wine
Matt. 11:18, neither eating nor **d**-ing
   25:35, thirsty, and ye gave me **d**
   26:27, **D** ye all of it
   27:34, gave him vinegar to **d**
John 6:55, my blood is **d** indeed
   18:11, cup . . . shall I not **d** it
Rom. 12:20, if he thirst, give him **d**
1 Cor. 10:4, all **d** the same spiritual **d**
   21, Ye cannot **d** the cup of
   11:25, as oft as ye **d** it
Heb. 6:7, earth which **d**-eth in the rain
Drive—*move furiously*
Gen. 4:14, thou hast **d**-n me out
2 Kin. 9:20, **d**-ing is . . . **d**-ing of Jehu
Job 18:11, Terrors . . . shall **d** him to his
Ps. 1:4, which the wind **d**-eth away
   40:14, let them be **d**-n backward
   114:3, Jordan was **d**-n back
Prov. 25:23, north wind **d**-th away rain
Mark 1:12, Spirit **d**-th him into the
John 2:15, **d** them all out of the temple
Dromedaries—*riding camels*
1 Kin. 4:28, for the horses and **d**
Esther 8:10, camels, and young **d**
Drop—*descend, sphere of fluid*
Deut. 32:2, doctrine shall **d** as the rain
Job 36:27, small the **d**-s of water
Ps 65:11, thy paths **d** fatness
Prov. 27:15, **d**-ing in a very rainy day
Eccles. 10:18, the house **d**-eth through
Song 4:11, **d** as the honeycomb
Is 40:15, nations are as a **d**
   45:8, **D** down, ye heavens
Luke 22:44, great **d**-s of blood falling
Drown—*sink, overwhelm*
Ex. 15:4, captains . . . **d**-ed in the Red Sea
Song 8:7, neither can the floods **d** it
Matt. 18:6, **d**-ed in the depth of the sea
1 Tim. 6:9, which **d** men in destruction
Drunk—*consumed liquid, intoxicated*
Lev. 11:34, all drink that may be **d**

Deut. 32:42, mine arrows **d** with blood
Is. 29:9, **d**-en, but not with wine
   63:6, make them **d** in my fury
Luke 5:39, having **d** old wine
John 2:10, when men have well **d**, then
Eph. 5:18, be not **d** with wine
1 Thess. 5:7, are **d**-en in the night
Drunkard—*a toper, a sot*
Deut. 21:20, he is a glutton, and a **d**
Ps. 69:12, was the song of the **d**-s
Joel 1:5, Awake, ye **d**-s, and weep
1 Cor. 5:11, idolater, or a railer, or a **d**
Drunkenness—*intoxication*
Deut. 29:19, to add **d** to thirst
Luke 21:34, overcharged with . . . **d**
Rom. 13:13, walk . . . not in rioting and **d**
Gal 5:21, **d**, revellings, and such like
Dry—*devoid of moisture*
Gen. 1:9, let the **d** land appear
Ps. 63:1, in a **d** and thirsty land
Prov 17:1, Better is a **d** morsel
Is. 53:2, as a root out of a **d** ground
Jer. 4:11, **d** wind of the high places
Ezek. 37:4, O ye **d** bones, hear the word
Matt. 12:43, walketh through **d** places
Mark 11:20, saw the fig tree **d**-ed up
Luke 23:31, what shall be done in the **d**
Due—*owed, fit, appropriate*
Lev. 10:13, it is thy **d** . . . thy sons' **d**
   26:4, give you rain in **d** season
Ps. 104:27, their meat in **d** season
Prov. 15:23, word spoken in **d** season
Matt 18:34, should pay all that was **d**
Luke 23:41, **d** reward of our deeds
1 Cor. 15:8, born out of **d** time
Gal. 6:9, in **d** season we shall reap
1 Tim. 2:6, to be testified in **d** time
Dumb—*without voice or understanding*
Ex. 4:11, who maketh the **d**; or deaf
Ps. 39:2, I was **d** with silence
Matt. 9:32, brought to him a **d** man
Mark 7:37, deaf to hear . . . **d** to speak
Luke 1:20, thou shalt be **d**, and not able
1 Cor. 12:2, carried away unto these **d**
2 Pet. 2:16, **d** ass speaking with man's
Dung—*animal excrement*
Ex. 29:14, and his skin, and his **d**
1 Sam. 2:8, beggar from the **d**-hill
Luke 13:8, dig about it, and **d** it
   14:35, fit for the land nor . . . **d**-hill
Phil. 3:8, count them but **d**
Dungeon—*underground prison*
Gen. 41:40, hastily out of the **d**

51

DUNGEON

Dungeon (*Continued*)
Jer. 38:6, cast him into the **d**
Lam. 3:53, cut off my life in the **d**
Durst—*did dare*
Mark 12:34, no man . . . **d** ask him
Acts 5:13, rest **d** no man join
Jude 9, **d** not bring against him
Dust—*fine, dry particles of earth*
Gen. 2:7, Lord God formed man of the **d**
3:14, **d** shalt thou eat all the days
19, **d** thou art . . . unto **d** shalt
13:16, as the **d** of the earth
1 Sam. 2:8, raiseth . . . poor out of the **d**
Job 30:19, I am become like **d** and ashes
34:15, man shall turn again unto **d**
42:6, I . . . repent in **d** and ashes
Ps. 30:9, Shall the **d** praise thee
72:9, enemies shall lick the **d**
103:14, remembereth that we are **d**
Is. 26:19, sing, ye that dwell in **d**
40:15, small **d** of the balance
65:25, **d** shall be the serpent's meat
Dan. 12:2, many . . . that sleep in the **d**
Matt. 10:14, shake off the **d** of your feet
Luke 10:11, the very **d** of your city
Acts 22:23, threw **d** into the air
Rev. 18:19, cast **d** on their heads
Duty—*rightful obligation*
Ex. 21:10, her **d** of marriage
Ezra 3:4, **d** of every day required
Eccles. 12:13, the whole **d** of man
Luke 17:10, which was our **d** to do
Rom. 15:27, their **d** is also to minister
Dwell—*live, abide*
Gen. 4:20, father of such as **d** in tents
Lev. 19:34, stranger that **d**-eth with
Deut. 12:11, cause his name to **d** there
1 Chr. 17:1, I **d** in an house of cedars
Ps. 5:4, neither shall evil **d** with thee
15:1, who shall **d** in thy holy hill
23:6, **d** in the house of the Lord
24:1, world, and they that **d** therein
91:1, He that **d**-eth . . . secret place
Prov. 21:9, better to **d** in a corner
Is. 57:15, **d** in the high and holy place
Matt. 12:45, they enter in and **d** there
Luke 21:35, **d** on the face of . . . earth
John 1:38, where **d**-est thou
1 Cor. 4:11, have no certain **d**-ing place
Eph. 3:17, Christ may **d** in your hearts
Col. 1:19, in him should all fulness **d**
1 Tim. 6:16, **d**-ing in the light which no
2 Tim. 1:5, **d**-t first in thy

2 Pet. 2:8, righteousness man **d**-ing among
1 John 3:17, how **d**-eth the love of God
4:12, God **d**-eth in us

E

Each—*every one of several*
Gen. 15:10, laid **e** piece one against
Luke 13:15, doth not **e** one of you on
Phil. 2:3, let **e** esteem other better
Eagle—*king of birds*
Ex. 19:4, bare you on **e**-s' wings
Deut. 28:49, swift as the **e** flieth
32:11, **e** stirring up here nest
Ps. 103:5, youth is renewed like the **e's**
Prov. 30:19, way of an **e** in the air
Lam. 4:19, swifter than the **e**-s
Ezek. 10:14, the face of an **e**
Obad. 4, exalt thyself as the **e**
Matt. 24:28, there . . . **e**-s be gathered
Rev. 4:7, beast was like a flying **e**
Ear—*organ of hearing*
Gen. 20:8, told all . . . in their **e**-s
Job 12:11, Doth not the **e** try words
33:16, he openeth the **e**-s of men
42:5, by the hearing of the **e**
Ps. 31:2, Bow down thine **e** to me
44:1, We have heard with our **e**-s
94:9, He that planted the **e**
115:6, have **e**-s, but . . . hear not
Prov. 18:15, **e** . . . seeketh knowledge
20:12, hearing **e** . . . seeing eye
25:12, upon an obedient **e**
Is. 55:3, Incline your **e**, and come unto
Matt. 10:27, what ye hear in the **e**, that
11:15, He that hath **e**-s to hear
26:51, smote off his **e**
Mark 7:33, put his fingers into his **e**-s
1 Cor. 2:9, Eye . . . not seen, nor **e** heard
12:16, if the **e** shall say
2 Tim. 4:3, having itching **e**-s
Rev. 2:7, He that hath an **e**, let him
Ear—*spike or head of grain*
Gen. 41:5, seven **e**-s of corn
Ex. 9:31, the barley was in the **e**
Lev. 2:14, green **e**-s of corn dried
Job 24:24, as the tops of the **e**-s of corn
Matt 12:1, to pluck the **e**-s of corn
Mark 4:28, the full corn in the **e**
Ear—*to plough, serve*
Gen. 45:6, neither be **e**-ing nor harvest
Ex. 34:21, in **e**-ing time and in harvest

Deut. 21:4, neither e-ed nor sewn
1 Sam. 8:12, set them to e his ground
Is. 30:24, young asses that e the ground
Ear—*to listen*
Ex. 15:26, give e to his commandments
Deut. 32:1, Give e, O ye heavens
Job 32:11, I gave e to your reasons
Ps. 17:1, give e unto my prayer
78:1, Give e, O my people
80:1, Give e, O shepherd of Israel
Prov. 17:4, liar giveth e to a naughty
Is. 1:2, Hear, O heavens, and give e
8:9, give e, all ye of far countries
Earring—*an ornament*
Gen. 24:22, golden e of half a shekel
Prov. 25:12, an e of gold
Ezek. 16:12, I put . . . e-s in thin ears
Hos. 2:13, decked herself with . . . e-s
Early—*soon, betimes*
Gen. 19:27, Abraham gat up e
1 Sam. 29:10, as soon as ye be up e in
Ps. 46:5, God . . . help her . . . right e
57:8, I myself will awake e
Mark 16:9, when Jesus was risen e
John 20:1, cometh Mary Magdalene e
James 5:7, receive the e and latter rain
Earnest—*serious*
Luke 22:44, in . . . he prayed . . . e-ly
56, e-ly looked upon him
Rom. 8:19, e expectation of the creature
2 Cor. 1:22, given the e of the Spirit
5:2, e-ly desiring to be clothed
Eph. 1:14, the e of our inheritance
Heb. 2:1, ought to give the more e heed
James 5:17, and he prayed e-ly
Earth—*the world in which we live, soil*
Gen. 1:1, God created the heaven . . . e
12:3, families of the e be blessed
Ex. 9:14, none like me in all the e
20:11, Lord made heaven and e
Lev. 6:28, e-en vessel
Deut. 32:1, hear, O, e the words of my
Josh. 2:11, heaven above . . . e beneath
1 Sam. 2:10, Lord shall judge . . . the e
14:15, the e quaked
1 Kin. 18:1, send rain upon the e
2 Kin. 5:15, no God in all the e
Job 5:10, Who giveth rain upon the e
8:9, our days upon e are a shadow
12:15 they overturn the e
16:18, O e, cover not thou my
blood
19:25, latter day upon the e

24:4, poor of the e hide
themselves
38:4, laid the foundations of
the e
39:14, leaveth her eggs in the e
Ps. 2:2, kings of the e set themselves
12:6, in a furnace of e
8:1, 9, excellent is thy name in . . . e
24:1, The e is the Lord's
25:13, seed shall inherit the e
37:11, meek shall inherit the e
46:2, though the e be removed
47:2, great King over all the e
65:9, Thou visitest the e, and
72:6, as showers that water the e
85:11, Truth . . . spring out of the e
98:3, ends of the e have seen
Prov. 2:22, wicked . . . cut off from the e
10:30, wicked . . . not inhabit the e
30:21, the e is disquieted
Eccles. 12:7, dust return to the e
Song 2:12, flowers appear on the e
Is. 1:2, give ear, O e
24:1, Lord maketh the e empty
34:1, let the e hear
49:6, salvation unto the end of the e
55:9, heavens are higher than the e
60:2, darkness shall cover the e
61:11, the e bringeth forth her bud
66:1, the e is my footstool
Jer. 19:1, get a potter's e-en bottle
22:29, O e, e, e, hear the word
23:24, Do not I fill heaven and e
50:23, whole e cut asunder
Joel 3:16, heavens . . . e shall shake
Jonah 2:6, e with her bars was
Mic. 7:2, man is perished out of the e
17, move . . . like worms of the e
Nah. 1:5, e is burned at his presence
Hab. 2:20, let the e keep silence
Mal. 4:6, smite the e with a curse
Matt. 5:5, meek . . . shall inherit the e
6:10, thy will be done in e, as in
19, treasures upon e
10:34, come to send peace on e
11:25, Lord of heaven and e
24:35, Heaven and e shall pass
25:25, hid thy talent in the e
27:51, and the e did quake
28:18, power is given . . . me
in . . . e
Mark 4:5, because it had no depth of e

Earth (*Continued*)
Luke 2:14, on e peace, good will
    12:49, come to send fire on the e
    18:8, shall he find faith on the e
    23:44, darkness over all the e
John 3:12, If I have told you e-ly
    12:32, be lifted up from the e
    17:4, glorified thee on the e
Rom. 10:18, sound went into all the e
1 Cor. 15:47, the first man is of the e, e-y
2 Cor. 4:7, treasure in e-en vessels
    5:1, know that if our e-ly house
Eph. 6:3, mayest live long on the e
Phil. 3:19, who mind e-ly things
Col. 3:2, not on things on the e
2 Tim. 2:20, also of wood and of e
Heb. 11:13, pilgrims on the e
    12:26, voice then shook the e
James 3:15, not from above, but is e-ly
    5:5, lived in pleasure on the e
    18, e brought forth her fruit
2 Pet. 3:5, e standing out of the water
1 John 5:8, three . . . witness in e
Rev. 1:5, prince of the kings of the e
    21:1, a new heaven and a new e
Earthquake—*concussion of the earth*
1 Kin. 19:11, and after the wind an e
Is. 29:6, with e, and great noise
Amos 1:1, two years before the e
Matt. 24:7, shall be famines . . . and e-s
    28:2, behold, there was a great e
Rev. 8:5, lightnings, and an e
Ease—*freedom from care*
Ex. 18:22, so shall it be e-ier
Deut. 23:13, e thyself abroad
2 Chr. 10:9, E somewhat the yoke that
Job 7:13, my couch . . . e my complaint
    16:12, I was at e, but he hath
    21:23, dieth . . . being wholly at e
Ps. 25:13, His soul shall dwell at e
Is. 1:24, I will e me of mine adversaries
    32:9, 11, ye women that are at e
Jer. 46:27, be in rest and at e
Ezek. 23:42, multitude being at e
Amos 6:1, Woe to them . . . at e in Zion
Matt. 9:5, whether is e-ier, to say
    19:24, It is e-ier for a camel to
Luke 12:19, take thine e, eat, drink
    16:17, e-ier for heaven and earth
2 Cor. 8:13, that other men be e-d
East—*toward the sunrise*
Gen. 2:14, toward the e of Assyria
    3:24, e of the garden of Eden
    41:6, blasted with the e wind

Ex. 10:13, Lord brought an e wind
    14:21, by a strong e wind
Num. 3:38, tabernacle toward the e
Judg. 6:3, the children of the e
1 Kin. 4:30, wisdom . . . children of the e
Job 1:3, greatest of all the men of the e
    15:2, belly with the e wind
    27:21, e wind carrieth him away
Ps. 48:7, the ships . . . with an e wind
    103:12, far as the e is from the west
Is. 41:2, righteous man from the e
    46:11, ravenous bird from the e
Matt. 2:1, came wise men from the e
    8:11, many shall come from the e
    24:27, lightning . . . out of the e
Rev. 7:2, angel ascending from the e
    21:13, On the e three gates
Easter—*Passover so called*
Acts 12:4, after E to bring him forth
Eat—*consume food*
Gen. 2:16, tree . . . thou mayest freely e
    3:1, shall not e of every tree
    9:4, blood . . . shall ye not e
Ex. 2:20, call him, that he may e bread
    12:4, man according to his e-ing
Lev. 6:16, with unleavened . . . e-en
    21:22, e the bread of his God
Num. 18:10, every male shall e it
Deut. 8:9, land wherein thou shalt e
Judg. 14:14, Out of the e-er came forth
2 Chr. 30:18, yet did they e the passover
Job 5:5, Whose . . . the hungry e-eth
    6:6, Can . . . unsavoury be e-en
Ps. 22:26, meek . . . e and be satisfied
    78:25, man did e angels' food
Ps. 102:9, I have e-en ashes like bread
    128:2, e the labour of thine hands
Prov. 13:25, e-eth to the satisfying
    23:7, E and drink, saith he to
    27:18, keepeth the fig tree shall e
    31:27, e-eth not the bread of
Eccles. 5:12, e little or much
Is. 3:14, ye have e-en up the vineyard
    7:15, Butter and honey shall he e
    11:7, e straw like the ox
    22:13, e and drink; for tomorrow
    55:1, come ye, buy, and e
Matt. 12:1, pluck the ears . . . to e
    14:16, give ye them to e
    15:27, the dogs e of the crumbs
    26:26, Take, e; this is my body
Mark 5:43, something . . . given her to e
    7:5, e bread with unwashen

Luke 14:15, e bread . . . kingdom of God
  15:23, let us e, and be merry
John 4:32, I have meat to e
  6:31, Our fathers did e manna in
Acts 10:13, Rise, Peter; kill, and e
Rom. 14:2, e all things . . . e-eth herbs
1 Cor. 10:3, e the same spiritual meat
2 Tim. 2:17, e as doth a canker
Heb. 13:10, they have no right to e
James 5:3, e your flesh as it were fire
Rev. 2:7, to e of the tree of life
Edge—*border, that which cuts*
Gen. 34:26, with the e of the sword
Ex. 13:20, in the e of the wilderness
Judg. 3:16, dagger which had two e-s
Ps. 89:43, turned the e of his sword
Eccles. 10:10, he do not whet the e
Jer. 31:29, children's teeth . . . set on e
Luke 21:24, fall by the e of the sword
Edify—*instruct, improve*
Acts 9:31, churches rest . . . were e-ed
Rom. 14:19, wherewith . . . e another
1 Cor. 10:23, but all things e not
Eph. 4:12, e-ing of the body of Christ
1 Tim. 1:4, rather than godly e-ing
Effect—*power to produce results*
Num. 30:8, make her vow . . . of none e
Ps. 33:10, maketh the devices . . . of
  none e
Is. 32:17, the e of righteousness
Jer. 48:30, lies shall not e it
Mark 7:13, making the word . . . of
  none e
Rom. 3:3, faith of God without e
Gal. 5:4, Christ is become of no e
Effectual—*adequate, efficient*
1 Cor. 16:9, great door and e is opened
Gal. 2:8, he that wrought e-ly in Peter
Eph. 3:7, by the e working of his power
1 Thess. 2:13, which e-ly worketh
James 5:16, The e fervent prayer of
Egg—*ovum of animals*
Job 6:6, any taste in the white of an e
  39:14, leaveth her e-s in the earth
Is. 10:14, gathereth e-s that are left
Jer. 17:11, partridge sitteth on e-s
Luke 11:12, Or if he shall ask an e
Either—*each of two or more*
Gen. 31:24, speak not . . . e good or bad
Lev. 10:1, took e of them his censer
Deut. 17:3, e the sun, or moon, or any
Eccles. 9:1, no man knoweth e love or
Matt. 6:24, for e he will hate the one
  12:33, E make the tree good

Luke 6:42, E how canst thou say to
  16:13, for e he will hate
John 19:18, two other with him, on e
1 Cor. 14:6, speak . . . e by revelation
Elders—*seniors in dignity and experience*
Ex. 24:9, seventy of the e of Israel
1 Sam. 15:30, honour me . . . before the e
Ps. 107:32, assembly of the e
Prov. 31:23, when he . . . among the e
Matt. 15:2, tradition of the e
Acts 14:23, e in every church
1 Tim 5:17, Let the e that rule well
Heb. 11:2, the e obtained a good report
James 5:14, call for the e of the church
Rev. 4:4, four and twenty e sitting
Elect—*chosen, selected*
Is. 45:4, Israel mine e
Matt. 24:22, for the e's sake
Luke 18:7, God avenge his own e
Titus 1:1, to the faith of God's e
1 Pet. 2:6, a chief corner stone, e
2 John 1, The elder unto the e lady
Election—*a selecting*
Rom. 9:11, purpose of . . . according to e
  11:5, e of grace
1 Thess. 1:4, your e of God
2 Pet. 1:10, your calling and e sure
Eleven—*ten and one*
Gen. 37:9, moon and the e stars
Matt. 28:16, e disciples went away
  33, e gathered together
Acts 1:26, numbered with the e
  2:14, Peter . . . with the e
Embrace—*hug, clasp in the arms*
Gen. 29:13, and e-d him, and kissed him
2 Kin. 4:16, thou shalt e a son
Job 24:8, e the rock for want of
Prov. 5:20, e the bosom of a stranger
Eccles. 3:5, time to e . . . from e-ing
  8:3, right hand should e me
Heb. 11:13, persuaded of them, and e-d
Emerald—*a jewel*
Ex. 28:18, second row . . . an e
Ezek. 27:16, in thy fairs with e-s
Rev. 4:3, sight like unto an e
  21:19, the fourth, an e
Emerods—*tumors, piles*
Deut. 28:27, e, and with the scab
1 Sam. 5:6, smote them with e
Empty—*devoid of contents*
Gen. 24:20, and e-ied her pitcher
  41:27, the seven e ears blasted
Ex. 23:15, none . . . appear before me e

55

Empty (*Continued*)
Deut. 15:13, not let him go away **e**
Neh. 5:13, be he shaken out, and e-ied
Job 22:9, Thou hast sent widows away **e**
Is. 29:8, he awaketh, and his soul is **e**
    34:11, and the stones of e-iness
Jer. 51:34, hath made me an **e** vessel
Nah. 2:2, the e-iers have e-ied them
Encamp—*settle temporarily*
Ex. 13:20, took their journey . . . and e-ed
Job 19:21, **e** round about my tabernacle
Ps. 27:3, host should **e** against me
    34:7, angel of the Lord e-eth round
Zech. 9:8, I will **e** about mine house
End—*final point, termination*
Gen. 6:13, the **e** of all flesh is come
Ex. 23:16, in the **e** of the year, when
Num. 23:10, let my last **e** be like his
Deut. 8:16, do thee good at thy latter **e**
Job 8:7, yet thy latter **e**
    16:3, Shall vain words have an **e**
    26:10, day and night come to an **e**
    42:12, the latter **e** of Job
Ps. 37:37, the **e** of that man is peace
    39:4, Lord, make me to know mine **e**
    102:27, thy years shall have no **e**
    119:96, an **e** of all perfection
Prov. 14:12, the **e** thereof are the ways
Eccles. 3:11, from the beginning to the **e**
    4:8, no **e** of all his labour
    16, no **e** of all the people
    7:2, that is the **e** of all men
    8, Better is the **e** of a thing
    12:12, making . . . books . . . no **e**
Is. 9:7, peace there shall be no **e**
Jer. 5:31, what will ye do in the **e**
    8:20, the summer is e-ed
Lam. 1:9, remembereth not her last **e**
    4:18, for our **e** is come
Hab. 2:3, at the **e** it shall speak
Matt. 13:39, harvest is the **e** . . . world
    24:6, but the **e** is not yet
    14, then shall the **e** come
    26:58, Peter . . . sat . . . to see the **e**
    28:20, I am with you . . . unto the **e**
Luke 1:33, kingdom there shall be no **e**
    21:9, **e** is not by and by
John 13:1, he loved them unto the **e**
    18:37, To this **e** was I born
Phil. 3:19, Whose **e** is destruction
1 Tim. 1:5, the **e** of the commandment
Heb. 6:8, whose **e** is to be burned
    16, and **e** of all strife
James 5:11, have seen the **e** of the Lord

1 Pet. 1:9, Receiving the **e** of your
    4:7, the **e** of all things is at
2 Pet. 2:20, the latter **e** is worse
Rev. 2:26, keepeth my works unto the **e**
    21:6; 22:13, beginning and the **e**
Endure—*to last, to remain*
Gen. 33:14, the children be able to **e**
Ex. 18:23, shalt be able to **e**
Esther 8:6, can I **e** to see the evil
Job 8:15, hold it fast, but . . . not **e**
    31:23, his highness I could not **e**
Ps. 9:7, Lord shall **e** for ever
    72:5, as long as the sun and moon **e**
    17, His name shall **e** for ever
    100:5, truth e-th to all generations
    135:13, name, O Lord, e-th for ever
Prov. 27:24, **e** to every generation
Ezek. 22:14, Can thine heart **e**
Matt. 24:13, But he that shall **e**
John 6:27, meat which e-th unto . . . life
Rom. 9:22, e-d with . . . longsuffering
1 Cor. 13:7, hopeth . . . e-th all things
Heb. 12:7, If ye **e** chastening
2 Tim. 2:3, therefore **e** hardness
James 1:12, Blessed is the man that e-th
1 Pet. 1:25, word of the Lord e-th for
    2:19, a man for conscience . . . **e**
Enemy—*opponent, foe, adversary*
Ex. 23:22, an **e** unto thine e-ies
Judg. 5:31, let all thine e-ies perish
1 Sam. 24:19, For if a man find his **e**
1 Kin. 21:20, thou found me, O mine **e**
Ps. 8:2, still the **e** and the avenger
    23:5, in the presence of mine e-ies
    38:19, But mine e-ies are lively
    72:9, his e-ies shall lick the dust
    119:98, made me . . . than mine e-ies
    127:5, speak with the e-ies
    139:22, I count them mine e-ies
Prov. 16:7, even his e-ies to be at peace
    24:17, Rejoice not when thine **e**
    27:6, kisses of an **e** are deceitful
Is. 9:11, Lord . . . join his e-ies together
Jer. 15:11, will cause the **e** to entreat
Mic. 7:6, e-ies . . . men of his . . . house
Matt. 5:43, thou shalt . . . hate thine **e**
Matt. 5:44, I say . . . Love your e-ies
Acts 13:10, thou **e** of all righteousness
Rom. 5:10, e-ies, we were reconciled
Gal. 4:16, Am I therefore become your **e**
Phil. 3:18, are the e-ies of the cross
2 Thess. 3:15, count him not as an **e**

Enough—*sufficient*
Gen. 33:9, 11, I have e, my brother
Ex. 36:5, bring much more than e
Josh. 17:6, The hill is not e for us
Is. 56:11, dogs which can never have e
Hos. 4:10, shall eat, and not have e
Mal. 3:10, not be room e to receive it
Matt. 10:25, it is e for the disciple
25:9, lest there be not e for us
Luke 22:38, said unto them, It is e

Enquire—*ask after*
Gen. 25:22, went to e of the Lord
Ex. 18:15, come unto me to e of God
1 Sam. 17:56, E thou whose son
Ps. 78:34, e-d early after God
Prov. 20:25, after vows to make e-y
Ezek. 14:3, should I be e-d of at all
Matt. 2:7, Herod . . . e-d . . . diligently
Luke 22:23, to e among themselves
Acts 19:39, but if ye e any thing
1 Pet. 1:10, the prophets have e-d

Entangle—*confuse, involve*
Ex. 14:3, They are e-d in the land
Matt. 22:15, took counsel how . . . e him
Gal. 5:1, be not e-d again with the yoke
2 Tim. 2:4, No man that warreth e-th
2 Pet. 2:20, they are again e-d

Enter—*go or pass into*
Gen. 7:13, selfsame day e-ed Noah
Ps. 100:4, E into his gates with
Prov. 4:14, E not into the path . . . wicked
18:6, lips e into contention
Is. 2:10, E into the rock, and hide thee
Ezek. 2:2, the spirit e-ed into me
Dan. 11:24, He shall e peaceably
Matt. 6:6, when thou prayest, e unto
7:13, E ye in at the strait gate
18:3, not e into the kingdom
25:21, e . . . joy of thy Lord
26:41, e not into temptation
Luke 7:6, I am not . . . that thou . . . e
13:24, Strive to e in at the strait
22:3, then e-d Satan into Judas
24:26, to e into his glory
John 10:1, that e-eth not by the door
Acts 8:3, e-ing every house
Rom. 5:12, as by one man sin e-ed into
Heb. 3:11, shall not e into my rest
9:12, e-ed in once into holy place

Entice—*allure, attract*
Ex. 22:16, a man e a maid
Prov. 1:10, if sinners e thee
16:29, e-th his neighbour
1 Cor. 2:4, not with e-ing words

Col. 2:4, beguile you with e-ing words
James 1:14, drawn away . . . and e-d
Envy—*malicious grudging*
Gen. 30:1, Rachel e-ied her sister
Job 5:2, and e slayeth the silly one
Ps. 37:1, neither be thou e-ious
73:3, I was e-ious at the foolish
Prov. 3:31, E thou not the oppressor
23:17, Let not . . . heart e sinners
Eccles. 4:4, for this a man is e-ied
Ezek. 35:11, according to thine e
Matt. 27:18, for e they had delivered
Acts 7:9, patriarchs, moved with e
13:45, Jews . . . were filled with e
Rom. 1:29, full of e, murder, debate
13:13, not in strife and e-ing
2 Cor. 12:20, lest there be . . . e-ings
Gal. 5:26, e-ing one another
Phil. 1:15, preach Christ even of e
1 Tim. 6:4, whereof cometh e, strife
Titus 3:3, living in malice and e
James 3:14, bitter e-ing and strife

Epistle—*a letter*
Acts 15:30, they delivered the e
Rom. 16:22, Tertius, who wrote this e
1 Thess. 5:27, e to be read unto all
2 Thess. 2:15, by word, or our e
2 Pet. 3:1, second e . . . I now write

Equal—*agreeing in quantity or quality*
Job 28:17, gold . . . crystal cannot e
Ps. 17:2, the things that are e
Prov. 26:7, legs of the lame . . . not e
Ezek. 18:25, way of the Lord is not e
Matt. 20:12, hast made them e unto us
Luke 20:36, e unto the angels
John 5:18, making himself e with God
2 Cor. 8:14, there may be e-ity
Phil. 2:6, not robbery to be e with God
Col. 4:1, that which is just and e

Equity—*right, justice*
Ps. 98:9, judge . . . people with e
99:4, dost establish e
Prov. 2:9, Then . . . understand . . . e
Eccles. 2:21, knowledge, and in e
Is. 11:4, reprove with e for the meek
Mic. 3:9, pervert all e
Mal. 2:6, walked with me in peace and e

Err—*wander, miss the point, or truth*
Lev. 5:18, ignorance wherein he e-ed
1 Sam. 26:21, the fool, and have e-ed
Ps. 95:10, people that do e in their
Prov. 10:17, refuseth reproof e-eth
Is. 35:8, though fools, shall not e

Err (*Continued*)
Matt. 22:29, Ye do **e**, not knowing the
Mark 12:24, Do ye not therefore **e**
Heb. 3:10, They do . . . **e** in their heart
James 1:16, Do not **e**, my beloved
Error—*wandering, violation of truth*
2 Sam. 6:7, smote him for his **e**
Ps. 19:12, Who can understand his **e-s**
Is. 32:6, iniquity . . . to utter **e** against
Jer. 10:15, and the work of **e-s**
Matt. 27:64, the last **e** shall be worse
James 5:20, sinner from the **e** of his
1 John 4:6, spirit of truth, and . . . of **e**
Jude 11, the **e** of Balaam
Escape—*flee from danger*
Gen. 14:13, came one that had **e-d**
19:17, **E** for thy life; look not
Josh. 8:22, let none . . . remain or **e**
Ezra 9:14, no remnant nor **e-ing**
Job 19:20, **e-d** with the skin of my teeth
Prov. 19:5, speaketh lies shall not **e**
Eccles. 7:26, whoso pleaseth God shall **e**
Is. 20:6, how shall we **e**
Matt. 23:33, can ye **e** the damnation
Luke 21:36, be accounted worthy to **e**
John 10:39, but he **e-d** out of their
Rom. 2:3, shalt **e** the judgment of God
1 Cor. 10:13, make a way to **e**
2 Pet. 1:4, having **e-d** the corruption
Espoused—*to take as a wife, wedded to*
2 Sam. 3:14, which I **e** to me
Matt. 1:18, his mother Mary was **e**
Luke 1:27, a virgin **e** to a man
2:5, Mary his **e** wife
2 Cor. 11:2, **e** you to one husband
Establish—*make stable or firm*
Gen. 6:18, I **e** my covenant
Deut. 28:9, **e** thee an holy people
Ps. 89:2, faithfulness shalt thou **e**
93:2, Thy throne is **e-ed** of old
Prov. 20:18, Every purpose is **e-ed** by
Is. 9:7, **e** it with judgment . . . justice
49:8, to **e** the earth
Jer. 10:12, he hath **e-ed** the world
Dan. 6:8, O king, **e** the decree
Matt. 18:16, every word may be **e-ed**
Acts 16:5, churches **e** in the faith
Rom. 3:31, yea, we **e** the law
Heb. 13:9, the heart be **e-ed** with grace
2 Pet. 1:12, **e-ed** in the present truth
Estate—*settled condition*
Ps. 136:23, in our low **e**
Eccles. 1:16, I am come to great **e**
3:18, **e** of the sons of men

Rom. 12:16, to men of low **e**
Col. 4:8, he might know your **e**
Jude 6, kept not their first **e**
Esteem—*value highly*
Deut. 32:15, lightly **e-ed** the Rock of
1 Sam. 18:23, poor man . . . lightly **e-ed**
Job 36:19, Will he **e** thy riches
41:27, He **e-eth** irons as straw
Is. 29:16, be **e-ed** as the potter's clay
53:3, despised, and we **e-ed** him not
Luke 16:15, highly **e-ed** among men
Phil. 2:3, each **e** other better than
1 Thess. 5:13, to **e** them very highly
Heb. 11:26, **E-ing** the reproach of Christ
Eternal—*always existing*
Deut. 33:27, the **e** God is thy refuge
Is. 60:15, make thee an **e** excellency
Matt. 25:46, the righteous into life **e**
Mark 3:29, is in danger of **e** damnation
10:30, world to come **e** life
John 3:15, not perish, but have **e** life
4:36, gathereth fruit unto life **e**
6:54, eateth my flesh . . . hath **e**
10:28, I give unto them **e** life
17:3, this is life **e**
Acts 13:48, were ordained to **e** life
Rom. 6:23, the gift of God is **e** life
2 Cor. 4:17, **e** weight of glory
Eph. 3:11, According to the **e** purpose
1 Tim. 6:12, lay hold on **e** life
Titus 1:2, In hope of **e** life
Heb. 5:9, the author of **e** salvation
6:2, dead, and of **e** judgment
9:12, **e** redemption
1 Pet. 5:10, called us unto his **e** glory
Jude 7, the vengeance of **e** fire
Evangelist—*bringer of glad tidings*
Acts 21:8, Philip the **e**
Eph. 4:11, prophets; and some, **e-s**
2 Tim. 4:5, work of an **e**
Evening—*the close of the day*
Gen. 1:5, 8, 13, 19, 23, 31, **e** . . . morning
Judg. 19:9, day draweth toward **e**
Ps. 90:6, in the **e** it is cut down
104:23, to his labour until the **e**
Eccles. 11:6, in the **e** withhold not thine
Is. 17:14, behold at **e-tide** trouble
Jer. 6:4, shadows of the **e** are stretched
Dan. 8:26, vision of the **e**
Matt. 14:15, it was **e**, his disciples
16:2, When it is **e**
Mark 11:11, the **e-tide** was come
Luke 24:29, it is toward **e**, and day

John 20:19, the same day at e, being
Acts 28:23, from morning till e
Ever—*at any time, continually*
Gen. 3:22, take . . . eat . . . live for e
    13:15, to thy seed for e
Ex. 3:15, this is my name for e
    12:17, by an ordinance for e
Job 19:24, graven . . . in the rock for e
Ps. 10:16, The Lord is King for e
    19:9, feat . . . enduring for e
    22:26, heart shall live for e
    23:6, in the house of the Lord for e
    44:23, cast us not off for e
    48:8, God will establish it for e
    51:3, my sin is e before me
    72:17, His name shall endure for e
    132:14, This is my rest for e
Prov. 27:24, riches are not for e
Eccles. 1:4, earth abideth for e
Matt. 6:13, power, and the glory, for e
Luke 15:31, Son, thou are e with me
John 8:35, but the Son abideth e
    14:16, he may . . . with you for e
Rom. 16:27, through Jesus Christ for e
Phil. 4:20, Father be glory for e and e
1 Thess. 5:15, e follow . . . which is good
Heb. 7:25, e liveth to make intercession
1 Pet. 1:23,, liveth and abideth for e
Everlasting—*eternal, continuing*
Gen. 9:16, remember the e covenant
    49:26, utmost bound of the e hills
Ps. 24:7, be ye lift up, ye e doors
    90:2, from e to e, thou are God
    119:142, Thy . . . e righteousness
    145:13, Thy kingdom . . . e kingdom
Is. 9:6, e Father, The Prince of Peace
Hab. 3:6, the e mountains . . . scattered
Matt. 18:8, to be cast into e fire
    19:29, shall inherit e life
    25:46, e punishment
John 3:16, not perish, but have e life
Rom. 16:26, of the e God
2 Thess. 1:9, with e destruction
1 Tim. 6:16, be honour and power e
Heb. 13:20, blood of the e covenant
Jude 6, he hath reserved in e chains
Rev. 14:6, having the e gospel to preach
Evermore—*always, forever*
Deut. 28:29, spoiled e
2 Sam. 22:51, to his seed for e
Ps. 16:11, there are pleasures for e
    105:4, seek his face e
    121:8, time forth, and even for e

John 6:34, Lord, e give us this bread
1 Thess. 5:16, Rejoice e
Rev. 1:18, I am alive for e . . . Amen
Every—*all considered separately*
Gen. 4:14, e one that findeth me shall
Job 12:10, soul of e living thing
Prov. 20:6, proclaim e one . . . goodness
    30:5, E word of God is pure
Is. 53:6, have turned e one to his own
Jer. 10:14, E man is brutish
Matt. 7:8, e one that asketh, receiveth
    12:36, e idle word that men shall
    18:16, e word may be established
    20:9, they received e man a penny
Mark 13:34, to e man his work
Luke 2:3, taxed, e one into his own city
    3:5, E valley shall be filled
John 1:9, lighteth e man that cometh
    3:8, e one that is born . . . Spirit
    15:2, E branch . . . that beareth not
    19:23, to e soldier a part
Rom. 13:1, e soul be subject unto
1 Cor. 4:17, teach e where in e church
1 Cor. 11:3, head of e man is Christ
Eph. 4:7, unto e one of us . . . grace
Phil. 2:9, name which is above e name
Col. 1:10, fruitful in e good work
Heb. 12:1, let us lay aside e weight
James 1:17, E good gift and e perfect
1 John 4:1, believe not e spirit
Evil—*that which is not good*
Gen. 2:9, tree . . . of good and e
Ex. 32:14, Lord repented of the e which
Deut. 22:14, bring up an e name upon
    24:7, put e away from among
1 Sam. 25:21, requited me e for good
2 Kin. 6:33, this e is of the Lord
Job 30:26, looked for good, then e came
    35:12, pride of e man
Ps. 34:13, Keep thy tongue from e
    37:27, Depart from e
    51:4, done this e in thy sight
    91:10, There shall no e befall thee
    97:10, love the Lord, hate e
    121:7, preserve thee from all e
Prov. 3:7, fear the Lord . . . depart from e
    13:21, E pursueth sinners
    16:27, ungodly man diggeth up e
Eccles. 2:21, is vanity and a great e
Is 1:16, put away the e of your doings
    7:15, he may know to refuse the e
    59:7, Their feet run to e

EVIL

Evil (*Continued*)
Matt. 5:11, say all manner of **e** against
6:13, but deliver us from **e**
12:34, how can ye, being **e**
27:23, Why, what **e** hath he done
Luke 11:34, when thine eye is **e**
John 18:23, If I have spoken **e**, bear
Rom. 12:17, Recompense . . . man **e** for **e**
14:16, good be **e** spoken of
1 Cor. 13:5, thinketh no **e**
Phil. 3:2, Beware of dogs . . . **e** workers
1 Thess. 5:15, render **e** for **e**
1 Tim. 6:10, money . . . root of all **e**
Titus 1:12, **e** beasts, slow bellies
1 Pet. 3:9, Not rendering **e** for **e**
3 John 11, follow not that which is **e**
Ewe—*female sheep*
Gen. 21:29, these seven **e** lambs
2 Sam. 12:3, one little **e** lamb
Ps. 78:71, **e**-s great with young
Exact—*require by force*
Neh. 5:7, Ye **e** usury, every one
Job 11:6, God **e**-eth of thee less
Is. 58:3, and **e** all your labours
Luke 3:13, **E** no more than that
Exalt—*raise high, lift up*
Ex. 15:2, father's God, and I will **e** him
Ps. 34:3, let us **e** his name together
99:5, **E** ye the Lord our God
Prov. 14:34, Righteousness **e**-eth
Matt. 11:23, which art **e**-ed unto heaven
Luke 1:52, and **e**-ed them of low degree
Acts 5:31, Him hath God **e**-ed
2 Cor. 11:20, if a man **e** himself
Phil. 2:9, God . . . hath highly **e**-ed him
James 1:9, rejoice in that he is **e**-ed
1 Pet. 5:6, that he may **e** you in due
Examine—*search into, explore*
Ps. 26:2, **E** me, O Lord
Luke 23:14, having **e**-d him before you
Acts 22:24, be **e**-d by scourging
Example—*specimen, or model*
Matt. 1:19, make her a publick **e**
John 13:15, I have given you an **e**
1 Tim. 4:12, an **e** of the believers
James 5:10, for an **e** of suffering
1 Pet. 2:21, leaving us an **e**
Exceeding—*in a very great degree*
Gen. 15:1, thy **e** great reward
Num. 14:7, is an **e** good land
1 Sam. 2:3, Talk no more so **e** proudly
1 Kin. 4:29, gave Solomon wisdom . . . **e**
Ps. 123:3, **e**-ly filled with contempt
Eccles. 7:24, far off, and **e** deep

Matt. 2:10, rejoiced with **e** great joy
26:38, My soul is **e** sorrowful
Mark 9:3, shining, **e** white as snow
Rom. 7:3, become **e** sinful
2 Cor. 7:4, **e** joyful in . . . tribulation
Gal. 1:14, being more **e**-ly zealous
Eph. 2:7, the **e** riches of his grace
1 Thess. 3:10, praying **e**-ly
2 Thess. 1:3, your faith groweth **e**-ly
2 Pet. 1:4, **e** great and precious
Jude 24, faultless . . . with **e** joy
Excellency—*worth, superiority*
Deut. 33:26, in his **e** on the sky
Eccles. 7:12, but the **e** of knowledge is
Is. 35:2, see . . . **e** of our God
1 Cor. 2:1, came not with **e** of speech
2 Cor. 4:7, **e** of the power may be of God
Phil. 3:8, **e** of the knowledge of Christ
Excellent—*surpassing others*
Job 37:23, he is **e** in power . . . judgment
Ps. 8:1, how **e** is thy name . . . the earth
36:7, How **e** is thy loving kindness
148:13, his name alone is **e**
Prov. 17:7, **E** speech becometh not a
Is. 12:5, for he hath done **e** things
Hab. 1:4, obtained a more **e** name than
Except—*unless*
Gen. 32:26, not let thee go, **e** thou
Ps. 127:1, **E** the Lord build the house
Matt. 18:3, **E** ye be converted, and
24:22, **e** those days . . . shortened
John 3:2, miracles . . . **e** God be with him
5, **E** a man be born of water
4:48, **E** ye see signs and wonders
6:53, **E** ye eat the flesh of the Son
Rom. 10:15, how . . . preach, **e** they be
1 Cor. 15:36, not quickened, **e** it die
2 Tim. 2:5, **e** he strive lawfully
Excess—*overmuch, intemperate*
Matt. 23:25, full of extortion and **e**
Eph. 5:18, wine, wherein is **e**
1 Pet. 4:3, 4, **e** of wine . . . **e** of riot
Execute—*carry out, finish*
Ex. 12:12, I will **e** judgment
Num. 8:11, **e** the service of the Lord
1 Kin. 6:12, and **e** my judgments
2 Kin. 10:30, **e**-ing that which is right
Mark 6:27, the king sent an **e**-ioner
John 5:27, authority to **e** judgment also
Exercise—*set in action*
Ps. 131:1, neither do I **e** myself in
Jer. 9:24, Lord which **e** loving kindness
Matt. 20:25, Gentiles **e** dominion
1 Tim. 4:7, **e** thyself . . . unto godliness

60

Heb. 5:14, e-ed to discern . . . good and
2 Pet. 2:14, e-d with covetous practices
Exhort—*urge by argument*
Luke 3:18, other things in his e-ation
Acts 13:15, any word of e-ation for
Rom. 12:8, he that e-th, on e-ation
1 Tim. 6:2, These things teach and e
2 Tim. 4:2, e with all long suffering
Titus 1:9, may be able . . . to e
2:15, speak, and e, and rebuke
Heb. 3:13, e one another daily
10:25, e-ing one another: and
Expectation—*act of looking forward*
Ps. 9:18, the e of the poor . . . not perish
62:5, my e is from him
Prov. 10:28, e of the wicked shall perish
Luke 3:15, as the people were in e
Rom. 8:19, earnest e of the creature
Expedient—*advantageous*
John 16:7, e for you that I go
18:14, e that one man . . . die
1 Cor. 6:12, all things are not e
Experience—*knowledge acquired*
Gen. 30:27, e that the Lord hath
Eccles. 1:16, great e of wisdom
Rom. 5:4, patience, e; and e, hope
Expert—*having knowledge or skill*
1 Chr. 12:33, e in war
Jer. 50:9, of a mighty e man
Acts 26:3, e in all customs
Expired—*gone past*
1 Sam. 18:26, days were not e
2 Sam. 11:1, after the year was e
Acts 7:30, when forty years were e
Expound—*open to view or understanding*
Judg. 14:19, which e the riddle
Mark 4:34, he e all things
Acts 18:26, e unto him the way of God
Express—*declare, indicate*
Num. 1:17, e-ed by their names
1 Tim. 4:1, Spirit speaketh e-ly
Heb. 1:3, e image of his person
Eye—*organ of sight*
Gen. 3:5, your e-s shall be opened
Ex. 21:24, E for e, tooth for tooth
Deut. 7:16, e shall have no pity
32:10, as the apple of his e
2 Kin. 6:17, I pray thee, open his e-s
Job 11:20, e-s of the wicked shall fail
16:20, mine e poureth out tears
17:7, Mine e also is dim by reason
24:15, No e shall see me
28:21, it is hid from the e-s

Ps. 6:7, Mine e is consumed because
13:3, lighten mine e-s, lest I
17:8, as the apple of the e
19:8, Lord . . . enlightening the e-s
32:8, will guide thee with mine e
34:15, e-s of the Lord are upon
36:1, no fear of God before his e-s
119:37, Turn away mine e-s from
121:1, I will lift up mine e-s unto
145:15, e-s of all wait upon thee
Prov. 3:7, Be not wise in thine own e-s
10:10, He that winketh with the e
22:9, that hath a bountiful e
Eccles. 6:9, Better . . . sight of the e-s
Is. 35:5, e-s of the blind . . . be opened
52:8, they shall see e to e
Jer. 9:1, mine e-s a fountain of tears
Lam. 2:11, Mine e-s do fail with tears
Ezek. 12:2, e-s to see, and see not
Hab. 1:13, Thou are of purer e
Matt. 5:29, if thy right e offend thee
7:3, mote . . . in thy brother's e
9:29, Then touched he their e-s
13:16, blessed are your e-s
20:15, Is thine e evil, because
24:31, their e-s were opened
Mark 10:25, through the e of a needle
Luke 2:30, e-s have seen thy salvation
16:23, in hell he lift up his e-s
John 4:35, Lift up your e-s
9:6, anointed the e-s of the blind
11:41, Jesus lifted up his e-s
1 Cor. 2:9, E hath not seen, nor ear
1 Cor. 15:52, in the twinkling of an e
Gal 3:1, before whose e-s Jesus Christ
Eph. 1:18, e-s of your understanding
1 Pet. 3:12, For the e-s of the Lord
2 Pet. 2:14, Having e-s full of adultery
Rev. 1:7, and every e shall see him
21:4, wipe away all tears from . . .
e-s

F

Fables—*fictitious story, common talk*
1 Tim. 1:4, Neither give heed to f
4:7, profane and old wives' f
Titus 1:14, giving heed to Jewish f
2 Pet. 1:16, cunningly devised f

Face—*front of the head*
Gen. 1:2, darkness was upon the f of
    3:19, In the sweat of thy f shalt
    7:18, ark went upon the f of
    17:3, Abram fell on his f
    32:30, for I have seen God f to f
Ex. 33:11, Lord spake unto Moses f to f
    23, my f shall not be seen
Num. 6:25, The Lord make his f shine
Deut. 1:17, not be afraid of the f of man
2 Kin. 14:8, look one another in the f
Ezra 9:6, blush to lift up my f to thee
Job 33:26, he shall see his f with joy
    38:30, f of the deep is frozen
Ps. 13:1, how long . . . hide thy f from me
    24:6, generation . . . that seek thy f
    34:16, f of the Lord is against
    67:1, cause his f to shine upon us
    83:16, fill their f-s with shame
    84:9, look upon the f of thine
Prov. 27:19, f answereth to f
Eccles. 8:1, man's wisdom maketh his f
Is. 25:8, wipe away tears from . . . f-s
    50:6, I hid not my f from shame
Jer. 5:3, f-s harder than a rock
Matt. 26:67, Then did they spit in his f
Luke 1:76, thou shalt go before the f of
    22:64, they struck him on the f
    24:5, bowed down their f-s
John 11:44, his f was bound about with
2 Cor. 3:18, with open f beholding
1 Pet. 3:12, f of the Lord is against
Fade—*grow weak, disappear*
2 Sam. 22:46, Strangers shall f away
Is. 28:1, beauty is a f-ing flower
    64:6, we all do f as a leaf
Jer. 8:13, and the leaf shall f
James 1:11, shall the rich man f away
1 Pet. 1:4, inheritance . . . f-th not away
Fail—*fall short, be lacking*
Gen. 42:28, their heart f-ed them
    47:15, for the money f-eth
Deut. 31:6, he will not f thee, nor
1 Sam. 17:32, Let no man's heart f
1 Kin. 8:25, not f thee a man
    17:14, neither . . . cruse of oil f
Job 11:20, eyes of the wicked shall f
    14:11, As the waters f from the sea
    19:14, My kinsfolk have f-ed
Ps. 38:10, my strength f-eth me
    77:8, his promise f for evermore
Prov. 22:8, rod of his anger shall f
Eccles. 10:3, wisdom f-eth him
Hab. 3:17, labour of the olive shall f

Luke 21:26, Men's hearts f-ing them for
    22:32, that thy faith f not
1 Cor. 13:8, Charity never f-eth
Heb. 12:15, lest any man f of the grace
Faint—*become weak*
Gen. 45:26, Jacob's heart f-ed
Deut. 20:3, let not your hearts f
Ps. 27:13, f-ed, unless I had believed
    84:2, My soul longeth . . . even f-eth
    119:81, My soul f-eth for thy
Prov. 24:10, f in the day of adversity
Is. 1:5, and the whole heart f
    10:18, when a standardbearer f-eth
    40:28, ends of the earth, f-eth not
    29, He giveth power to the f
    30, Even the youths shall f
    31, they shall walk, and not f
    44:12, drinketh no water, and is f
Jonah 2:7, my soul f-ed within
Matt. 15:32, lest they f in the way
Luke 18:1, always to pray, and not to f
Gal. 6:9, we shall reap, if we f not
Eph. 3:13, desire that ye f not
Fair—*unblemished, pure, handsome*
Gen. 6:2, daughters of men . . . were f
    12:11, thou art a f woman
Judg. 15:2, is not her . . . sister f-er
Ps. 45:2, Thou art f-er than the
Prov. 26:25, speaketh f, believe him not
Song 1:8, O thou f-est among women
Jer. 11:16, A green olive tree, f
    46:20, a very f heifer
Matt. 16:2, say, It will be f weather
Acts 27:8, The f havens
Gal. 6:12, as desire to make a f shew
Faith—*belief in God and the Scriptures*
Deut. 32:20, children in whom is no f
Hab. 2:4, the just shall live by his f
Matt. 6:30, clothe you, O ye of little f
    9:2, Jesus seeing their f said
    15:28, O woman, great is thy f
    17:20, f as a grain of mustard
    23:23, law, judgment, mercy . . . f
Mark 4:40, how is it that ye have no f
    11:22, saith . . . Have f in God
Luke 7:50, Thy f hath saved thee
    8:25, Where is your f
    17:5, Increase your f
    18:8, shall he find f on the earth
    22:32, that thy f fail not
Acts 6:5, full of f and of the Holy Ghost
    14:27, opened the door of f
    15:9, purifying their hearts by f
    20:21, f toward our Lord Jesus

Rom. 3:3, unbelief make the **f** of God
    4:14, **f** is made void
    5:1, being justified by **f**, we have
    10:17, **f** cometh by hearing
1 Cor. 13:2, though I have all **f**, so
    15:14, your **f** is also vain
    16:13, stand fast in the **f**
2 Cor. 13:5, whether ye be in the **f**
Gal. 2:16, by the **f** of Jesus Christ
    5:5, hope of righteousness by **f**
    22, gentleness, goodness, **f**
Eph. 2:8, by grace . . . saved through **f**
    4:5, One Lord, one **f**, one baptism
    6:16, taking the shield of **f**
Phil. 1:25, furtherance and joy of **f**
Col. 2:5, stedfastness of your **f** in
1 Thess. 1:3, Remembering . . . work of **f**
    5:8, breastplate of **f** and love
2 Thess. 1:3, that your **f** groweth
1 Tim. 1:2, my own son in the **f**
    3:9, mystery of the **f** in a pure
    4:1, some shall depart from the **f**
    5:12, cast off their first **f**
2 Tim. 4:7, I have kept the **f**
Titus 1:13, be sound in the **f**
    2:2, sound in **f**, in charity
Heb. 10:22, in full assurance of **f**
    11:1, **f** is the substance of
    12:2, author and finisher of our **f**
James 1:3, trying of your **f** worketh
    2:1, have not the **f** of our Lord
1 Pet. 1:5, through **f** unto salvation
2 Pet. 1:5, add to your **f** virtue
Jude 20, your most holy **f**
Rev. 2:13, and hast not denied my **f**

Faithful—*trusty, honest, upright*
Num. 12:7, Moses . . . **f** in all mine house
Deut. 7:9, he is God, the **f** God
1 Sam. 2:35, will raise me up a **f** priest
2 Kin. 12:15, for they dealt **f**-ly
Neh. 9:8, foundest his heart **f**
Ps. 31:23, the Lord preserveth the **f**
    89:1, make known thy **f**-ness to all
    101:6, Mine eyes . . . be upon the **f**
    119:86, All thy commandments are **f**
    143:1, in thy **f**-ness answer me
Prov. 13:17, a **f** ambassador is health
    14:5, A **f** witness will not lie
    20:6, **f** man who can find
    27:6, **F** are the wounds of a friend
Is. 1:21, How is the **f** city become
    11:5, **f**-ness the girdle of his reins
Jer. 23:28, let him speak my word **f**-ly

Matt. 24:45, a **f** and wise servant
    25:23, good and **f** servant
1 Cor. 1:9, God is **f**, by whom ye were
Eph. 1:1, to the **f** in Christ Jesus
1 Thess. 5:24, **F** is he that calleth
1 Tim. 1:12, for that he counted me **f**
    4:9, This is a **f** saying
2 Tim. 2:2, same commit thou to **f** men
Titus 1:6, having **f** children
Heb. 10:23, for he is **f** that promised
1 Pet. 4:19, as unto a **f** Creator
Rev. 1:5, Christ, who is the **f** witness
    2:10, be thou **f** unto death, and
    19:11, was called **F** and True

Fall—*drop down, sink into sin, ruin*
Gen. 45:24, See that ye **f** not out by the
1 Sam. 3:19, let none of his words **f**
Job 4:13, deep sleep **f**-eth on men
Ps. 5:10, **f** by their own counsels
    16:6, are **f**-en . . . in pleasant places
    37:24, Though he **f** . . . not be utterly
Prov. 10:8, 10, a prating fool shall **f**
    16:18, haughty spirit before a **f**
    24:16, just man **f**-eth seven times
Eccles. 4:10, him . . . alone when he **f**-eth
    11:3, where the tree **f**-eth, there
Is. 34:4, leaf **f**-eth off from the vine
    40:30, young men shall utterly **f**
Ezek. 24:6, let no lot **f** upon it
Dan. 3:5, ye **f** down and worship
    11:26, shall **f** down slain
Mic. 7:8, when I **f**, I shall rise
Matt. 7:27, and great was the **f** of it
    10:29, shall not **f** on the ground
    12:11, **f** into the pit on the
    15:14, both shall **f** into the ditch
Luke 2:34, set for the **f** and rising
    8:13, in time of temptation **f** away
Rom. 11:12, the **f** of them be the riches
    14:4, master he standeth or **f**-eth
    13, **f** in his brother's way
1 Cor. 10:12, take heed lest he **f**
    15:6, 18, are **f**-en asleep
Gal. 5:4, ye are **f**-en from grace
1 Tim. 3:6, he **f** into the condemnation
1 Tim. 3:7, lest he **f** into reproach
    6:9, rich **f** into temptation
Heb. 4:11, lest any man **f** . . . example
    6:6, If they shall **f** away, to renew
    10:31, **f** into the hands of . . . God
James 1:2, ye **f** into divers temptations
2 Pet. 1:10, ye shall never **f**
    3:17, **f** from . . . own stedfastness

FALSE

False—*untruthful, dishonest*
Ex. 20:16, shalt not bear **f** witness
23:1, shalt not raise a **f** report
7, far from a **f** matter
Ps. 119:104, 128, I hate every **f** way
120:3, thou **f** tongue
Prov. 6:19; 12:17; 14:5; 19:5, **f** witness
11:1, A **f** balance is abomination
17:4, heed to **f** lips
Zech. 10:2, diviners . . . told **f** dreams
Matt. 19:18, not bear **f** witness
24:24, **f** Christs, and **f** prophets
Mark 13:22, For **f** Christs
Luke 19:8, taken . . . by **f** accusation
2 Tim. 3:3, trucebreakers, **f** accusers
Falsehood—*want of truth*
2 Sam. 18:13, I should have wrought **f**
Ps. 144:8, is a right hand of **f**
Is. 57:4, are ye not . . . a seed of **f**
Jer. 13:25, forgotten me . . . trusted in **f**
Hos. 7:1, for they commit **f**
Mic. 2:11, walking in the spirit and **f**
Falsely—*not truly, treacherously*
Gen. 21:33, that thou wilt not deal **f**
Lev. 6:3, and sweareth **f**
Deut. 19:18, hath testified **f** against
Jer. 5:31, the prophets prophesy **f**
Matt. 5:11, say . . . evil against you **f**
Luke 3:14, accuse any **f**
1 Tim. 6:20, oppositions of science **f**
Fame—*renown*
Num. 14:15, heard the **f** of thee
Josh. 6:27, his **f** was noised
1 Kin. 10:1, the **f** of Solomon
Is. 66:19, have not heard my **f**
Matt. 14:1, heard of the **f** of Jesus
Mark 1:28, his **f** spread abroad
Familiar—*well known, closely acquainted*
Lev. 19:31, that have **f** spirits
1 Sam. 28:7, **f** spirit at En-dor
Job 19:14, **f** friends have forgotten
Ps. 41:9, mine own **f** friend
Jer. 20:10, all my **f**-s watched
Family—*a household*
Gen. 10:5, every one . . . after their **f**-s
12:3, in thee shall all **f**-s of
Deut. 29:18, man, or woman, or **f**
Judg. 6:15, behold, my **f** is poor
Job 31:34, contempt of **f**-s terrify me
Ps. 107:41, maketh him **f**-s like a
Jer. 3:14, and two of a **f**
31:1, God of all the **f**-s of Israel
Eph. 3:15, Of . . . the whole **f** in heaven

Famine—*scarcity of food*
Gen. 12:10, there was a **f** in the land
41:27, shall be seven years of **f**
42:19, corn for the **f** of your houses
1 Chr. 21:12, three years' **f**
Job 5:20, In **f** he shall redeem thee
Ps. 33:19, to keep them alive in **f**
Is. 14:30, I will kill thy root with **f**
Jer. 14:12, consume them . . . by the **f**
Amos 8:11, not a **f** of bread, nor a
Matt. 24:7, there shall be **f**-s, and
Luke 15:14, a mighty **f** in that land
Rom. 8:35, **f**, or nakedness, or peril
Famish—*starve, die of hunger*
Gen. 41:55, land of Egypt was **f**-ed
Prov. 10:3, suffer the soul . . . to **f**
Zeph. 2:11, will **f** all the gods
Famous—*well known*
Num. 16:2, **f** in the congregation
1 Chr. 5:24, men of valour, **f** men
Fan—*a wind instrument*
Is. 30:24, shovel and with the **f**
41:16, Thou shalt **f** them
Matt. 3:12, Whose **f** is in his hand
Far—*distant, remote*
Gen. 18:25, That be **f** from thee to do
Ex. 23:7, **f** from a false matter
Deut. 13:7, nigh . . . or **f** off from thee
Jos. 9:6, We be come from a **f** country
2 Sam. 20:20, F be it, **f** be it from
Ps. 22:11, Be not **f** from me
97:9, thou are exalted **f** above all
103:12, As **f** as the east is from
119:155, Salvation is **f** from the
Prov. 4:24, perverse lips put **f** from
15:29, Lord is **f** from the wicked
27:10, than a brother **f** off
Is. 60:4, thy sons shall come from **f**
Jer. 49:30, Flee, get you **f** off, dwell
Ezek. 11:15, Get you **f** from the Lord
Matt. 15:8, their heart is **f** from me
Mark 6:35, the day was now **f** spent
12:34, art not **f** from the kingdom
Luke 15:13, journey into a **f** country
22:51, Suffer ye thus **f**
John 21:8, they were not **f** from land
Acts 17:27, though he be not **f** from
Rom. 13:12, night is **f** spent, the day
2 Cor. 4:17, a **f** more exceeding
Eph. 1:21, F above all principality
Phil. 1:23, Christ; which is **f** better
Fare—*live, price of passage*
1 Sam. 17:18, how thy brethren **f**

64

Jonah 1:3, paid the f thereof
Acts 15:29, F ye well
18:21, bade them f-well
2 Cor. 13:11, Finally, brethren, f-well
Farthing—*coin worth about one penny*
Matt. 5:26, paid the uttermost f
10:29, two sparrows sold for a f
Mark 12:42, two mites . . . make a f
Fashion—*mold, shape, form*
Ex. 37:19, after the f of almonds
Job 10:8, thine hands have . . . f-ed me
31:15, did not one f us in the womb
Ps. 33:15, He f-eth their hearts alike
Is. 44:12, f-eth it with hammers
45:9, clay say to him that f-eth it
Mark 2:12, We never saw it on this f
Luke 9:29, the f of his countenance
1 Cor. 7:31, f of this world passeth
Phil. 2:8, being found in f as a man
1 Pet. 1:14, not f-ing yourselves
Fast—*abstain from food, secure*
Judg. 4:21, f asleep and weary
Ps. 33:9, he commanded, and it stood f
38:2, thine arrows stick f
65:6, setteth f the mountains
Prov. 4:13, f hold of instruction
Is. 58:3, we f-ed . . . and thou seest not
4, ye f for strife and debate
5, wilt thou call this a f
6, is not this the f that I have
Joel 1:14, Sanctify ye a f, call a
Zech. 7:5, did ye at all f unto me
Matt. 4:2, had f-ed forty days
6:16, when ye f, be not, as the
Matt. 6:18, appear not unto men to f
Mark 2:18, Pharisees f . . . disciples f not
19, children . . . bridechamber f
Luke 18:12, I f twice in the week
Acts 13:3, had f-ed and prayed
Fasting—*going without food*
Esther 4:3, mourning . . . the Jews . . . f
Ps. 35:13, I humbled my soul with f
109:24, knees are weak through f
Joel 2:12, Turn ye . . . to me . . . with f
Matt. 15:32, will not send them away f
17:21, goeth not out but by . . . f
Luke 2:37, served God with f-s and
2 Cor. 6:5, in watchings, in f-s
Fat—*oily matter, richness*
Gen. 45:18, shall eat the f of the land
49:20, his bread shall be f
Judg. 3:17, Eglon was a very f man
Neh. 8:10, eat the f, and drink the
9:25, a f land, and . . . became f

Ps. 17:10, inclosed in their own f
92:14, shall be f and flourishing
119:70, heart is as f as grease
Prov. 11:25, liberal soul . . . made f
13:4, diligent shall be made f
15:30, report maketh the bones f
Is. 5:17, waste places of the f ones
6:10, the heart of this people f
25:6, a feast of f things
30:23, shall be f and plenteous
Luke 15:23, bring hither the f-ted calf
Father—*male parent*
Gen. 2:24, leave his f and his mother
4:20, f of such as dwell in tents
9:23, saw not their f-'s nakedness
17:4, shalt be a f of many nations
43:7, Is your f yet alive
48:17, held up his f-'s hand
Ex. 20:12, Honour thy f and thy mother
21:15, he that smiteth his f, or
Deut. 5:9, the iniquity of the f-s
1 Sam. 17:34, servant kept his f-'s sheep
2 Sam. 7:12, shalt sleep with thy f-s
Job 17:14, Thou art my f
29:16, I was a f to the poor
38:38, Hath the rain a f
Ps. 22:4, Our f-s trusted in thee
68:5, A f of the fatherless, and
89:26, Thou art my f, my God
103:13, Like as a f pitieth his
Prov. 1:8, hear the instruction of thy f
6:20, keep thy f-'s commandment
10:1, wise son maketh a glad f
17:6, glory of children are . . . f-s
Is. 9:6, The everlasting F, the Prince
63:16, Doubtless thou art our F
Jer. 3:19, Thou shalt call me, My f
Mal. 2:10, Have we not all one f
Matt. 5:16, glorify your F . . . in heaven
6:9, F which art in heaven
7:21, that doeth the will of my f
11:25, I thank thee, O F, Lord of
26, Even so, F: for so it seemed
27, delivered unto me of my F
27, knoweth the Son, but the F
27, neither knoweth . . . the F
26:29, with . . . my F-'s kingdom
28:19, baptizing . . . name of the F
Mark 8:38, cometh in the glory of his F
14:36, he said, Abba, F
Luke 2:49, be about my F-'s business
10:21, I thank thee, O F
11:2, Our F which art in heaven
15:18, arise and go to my f

Father (*Continued*)
Luke 23:34, said Jesus, F, forgive them
46, F, . . . hands I commend
24:49, I send the promise of my F
John 2:16, make not my F-'s house an
5:17, My F worketh hitherto, and
10:15, even so know I the F
14:2, In my F-'s house are many
17:1, F, the hour is come; glorify
1 Cor. 4:15, yet have ye not many f-s
2 Cor. 1:3, F of mercies . . . God of all
Eph. 3:14, I bow my knees unto the F
6:4, f-s, provoke not your children
Phil. 2:11, to the glory of God the F
Heb. 1:5, I will be to him a F
3:9, when your f-s tempted me
1 Peter 1:3, Blessed be the God and F
2 Peter 1:17, received from God the F
1 John 2:13, because ye . . . known the F
2 John 4, a commandment from the F
Jude 1, are sanctified by God the F
Rev. 1:6, priests unto God and his F
Fatherless—*orphans*
Ex. 22:22, not afflict any widow, or f
Ps. 10:14, thou art the helper of the f
68:5, A father of the f
Hos. 14:3, in thee the f findeth mercy
James 1:27, To visit the f and widows
Fatness—*abundance*
Gen. 27:28, and the f of the earth
Deut. 32:15, thou art covered with f
Ps. 36:8, satisfied with the f of thy
65:11, and thy paths drop f
Rom. 11:17, root and f of the olive tree
Fault—*defect, blemish, want*
Gen. 41:9, I do remember my f-s
Ex. 5:16, the f is in thine own people
1 Sam. 29:3, I have found no f in him
Ps. 19:12, from secret f-s
Matt. 18:15, tell him his f between
Luke 23:4, I find no f in this man
1 Cor. 6:7, is utterly a f among you
Heb. 8:7, first covenant had been f-less
James 5:16, Confess your f-s one to
Jude 24, to present you f-less
Rev. 14:5, without f before the throne
Favour—*kind regard, support*
Gen. 18:3, I have found f in thy sight
29:17, Rachel was . . . well f-ed
41:3, seven other kine . . . ill f-ed
Ruth 2:13, find f in thy sight
Esther 2:15, Esther obtained f in the

Job 10:12, granted me life and f
Ps. 112:5, man sheweth f, and lendeth
Prov. 3:4, So shalt thou find f
Jer. 16:13, will not shew you f
Lam. 4:16, they f-ed not the elders
Luke 1:28, thou that are highly f-ed
30, thou hast found f with God
2:52, in f with God and man
Acts 7:46, Who found f before God
Fear—*anxiety, dread*
Gen. 9:2, f of you and the dread
15:1, F not, Abram. I am thy
26:24, f not, for I am with thee
Ex. 14:31, the people f-ed the Lord
Lev. 25:17, but thou shalt f thy God
Deut. 6:13, shalt f the Lord thy God
25:18, and he f-ed not God
31:8, f not, neither be dismayed
Josh. 4:14, f-ed Moses, all the days
22:25, cease from f-ing the Lord
Job 1:9, Job f God for naught
Ps. 19:9, The f of the Lord is clean
Ps. 23:4, I will f no evil: for thou
25:12, what man . . . f-eth the Lord
27:1, whom shall I f
76:8, earth f-ed, and was still
96:4, be f-ed above all gods
112:1, Blessed is the man that f-eth
Prov. 1:7, f of the Lord . . . beginning
14:16, A wise man f-eth
24:21, f thou the Lord
Eccles. 12:13, F God, and keep his
Song 3:8, of f in the night
Is. 59:19, they f the name of the Lord
Jer. 5:24, Let us now f the Lord
Matt. 8:26, Why are ye f-ful, O ye
14:5, he f-ed the multitude
28:5, F not ye: for I know
Luke 1:30, F not, Mary: for thou hast
2:10, F not . . . behold, I bring you
12:32, F not, little flock
20:19, and they f-ed the people
21:11, f-ful sights and great signs
23:40, Dost not thou f God
John 12:15, F not, daughter of Sion
Acts 5:26, for they f-ed the people, lest
9:31, walking in the f of the Lord
13:26, whosoever . . . f-eth God
2 Tim. 1:7, given us the spirit of f
1 John 4:18, There is no f in love
Rev. 21:8, The f-ful, an unbelieving
Feast—*festival, eat sumptuously*
Gen. 19:3, made them a f, and did bake

Lev. 23:2, the f-s of the Lord
Deut. 16:16, the f of unleavened bread
2 Chr. 7:8, kept the f seven days
Job 1:4, sons went and f-ed
Eccles. 10:19, f is made for laughter
Is. 1:14, appointed f-s my soul
25:6, f of wines on the lees
Amos 8:10, turn your f-s into mourning
Luke 20:46, the chief rooms at f-s
John 6:4, a f of the Jews, was nigh
Acts 18:21, by all means keep this f
Jude 12, spots in your f-s of charity
Feathers—*plumage of birds*
Lev. 1:16, pluck . . . his crop with his f
Ps. 68:13, her f with yellow gold
91:4, shall cover thee with his f
Dan. 4:33, hairs . . . grown like eagles' f
Fed—*gave food to*
Gen. 41:2, fatfleshed; and they f in a
Ex. 16:32, f you in the wilderness
Ps. 37:3, verily thou shalt be f
Jer. 5:8, They were as f horses in the
Ezek. 34:8, and f not my flock
Dan. 5:21, f him with grass like oxen
Luke 16:21, desiring to be f with the
1 Cor. 3:2, I have f you with milk
Feeble—*weak, wanting strength*
Gen. 30:42, But when the cattle were f
Neh. 4:2, What do these f Jews
Job 4:4, strengthened the f knees
Ps. 38:8, I am f and sore broken
Prov. 30:26, conies are but a f folk
Is. 35:3, confirm the f knees
Jer. 47:3, children for f-ness of hands
Ezek. 7:17, All hands shall be f, and
Zech. 12:8, he that is f among them
1 Cor. 12:22, which seem to be more f
1 Thess. 5:14, comfort the f-minded
Heb. 12:12, hang down, and the f knees
Feed—*give food to, nourish*
Gen. 25:30, F me, I pray thee, with
Ex. 22:5, shall f in another man's field
1 Sam. 17:15, to f his father's sheep
2 Sam. 5:2, shalt f my people Israel
1 Kin. 17:4, commanded the ravens to f
1 Chr. 11:2, Thou shalt f my people
Job 24:20, worm shall f sweetly on him
Ps. 28:9, f them also, and lift them up
49:14, death shall f on them
Prov. 10:21 lips of the righteous f
30:8, f me with food convenient
Is. 40:11, f his flock like a shepherd
49:26, I will f them that oppress

Jer. 3:15, f you with knowledge
23:15, f them with wormwood
Lam. 4:5, They that did f delicately
Ezek. 34:10, cease from f-ing the flock
15, I will f my flock, and
Dan. 11:26, that f of the portion of
Zeph. 3:13, shall f and lie down
Matt. 6:26, your heavenly Father f-eth
Mark 5:11, a great herd of swine f-ing
Luke 8:32, swine f-ing on the mountain
John 21:15, saith unto him, F my lambs
Acts 20:28, f the church of God
Rom. 12:20, thine enemy hunger, f him
1 Cor. 13:3, my goods to f the poor
1 Peter 5:2, F the flock of God which
Feel—*to sense by touch, sensibility*
Gen. 27:21, that I may f thee
Judg. 16:26, that I may f the pillars
Job 20:20, shall not f quietness
Ps. 58:9, your pots can f the thorns
Eccles. 8:5, commandment shall f no
Eph. 4:19, being past f-ing have given
Heb. 4:15, be touched with the f-ing
Feet—*lower end of the legs*
Gen. 18:4, wash your f, and rest
49:33, up his f into the bed
Ex. 12:11, your shoes on your f, and
25:26, that are on the four f
Lev. 8:24, great toes of their right f
11:21, legs above their f
Deut. 11:24, the soles of your f shall
Judg. 3:24, he covereth his f in his
19:21, washed their f, and did
Ruth 3:8, behold, a woman lay at his f
1 Sam. 25:24, And fell at his f
2 Sam. 22:37, so that my f did not slip
1 Kin. 15:23, he was diseased in his f
2 Chr. 16:12, was diseased in his f
Job 29:15, and f was I to the lame
30:12, they push away my f
33:11, putteth my f in the stocks
Ps. 8:6, put all things under his f
22:16, pierced my hands and my f
31:18, my f in a large room
40:2, and set my f upon a rock
66:9, not our f to be moved
115:7, f . . . but they walk not
119:105, a lamp unto my f
122:2, f shall stand within thy
Prov. 1:16, their f run to evil
29:5, spreadeth a net for his f
Song 5:3, I have washed my f

Feet (*Continued*)
Is. 3:16, a tinkling with their **f**
    37:25, sole of my **f** have I dried
    59:7, Their **f** run to evil
Jer. 13:16, your **f** stumble upon the
    18:22, hid snares for my **f**
    38:22, **f** are sunk in the mire
Ezek. 1:7, their **f** were straight **f**
Matt. 18:8, two hands or two **f**
Mark 7:25, and came and fell at his **f**
Luke 7:38, stood at his **f** behind him
    44, washed my **f** with tears
    8:35, sitting at the **f** of Jesus
Luke 10:39, also sat at Jesus' **f**
    24:39, Behold my hands and my **f**
    40, shewed . . . hands and his **f**
John 11:2, wiped his **f** with her hair
    12:3, anointed the **f** of Jesus
    13:5, wash the disciples' **f**
    14, wash one another's **f**
Rom. 3:15, **f** are swift to shed blood
    10:15, beautiful are the **f** of
Rev. 1:15, his **f** like unto fine brass
    13:2, **f** were as the **f** of a bear
    22:8, before the **f** of the angel
Feign—*pretend*
1 Sam. 21:13, **f**-ed himself mad
2 Sam. 14:2, **f** thyself to be a mourner
1 Kin. 14:5, **f** . . . to be another woman
    6, why **f**-est thou thyself to be
Ps. 17:1, goeth not out of **f**-ed lips
Luke 20:20, spies, which should **f**
2 Pet. 2:3, with **f**-ed words make
Fell—*dropped, or cause to drop*
Gen. 4:5, and his countenance **f**
    15:12, deep sleep **f** upon Abram
    17:3, and Abram **f** on his face
    33:4, **f** on his neck, and kissed
Ex. 32:28, there **f** of the people that
Lev. 9:24, and **f** on their faces
Num. 11:9, the dew **f** upon the camp
    9, the manna **f** upon it
    14:5, Moses and Aaron **f** on their
Deut. 9:18, I **f** down before the Lord
Josh. 5:14, Joshua **f** on his face
Judg. 5:27, there he **f** down dead
    13:20, **f** on their faces to the
Ruth 2:10, Then she **f** on her face
1 Sam. 4:18, **f** from off the seat
    31:4, Saul took a sword, and **f**
2 Sam. 21:22, **f** by the hand of David
1 Kin. 2:32, **f** upon two men more
    18:7, knew him, and **f** on his
    38, the fire of the Lord **f**

2 Kin. 1:2, Ahaziah **f** down through a
    3:19, shall **f** every good tree
    4:37, went in, and **f** at his
    6:5, axe head **f** into the water
1 Chr. 10:4, Saul took a sword, and **f**
    5, **f** likewise on the sword
2 Chr. 17:10, fear of the Lord **f**
Ps. 27:2, enemies . . . stumbled and **f**
Jer. 46:16, one **f** upon another
Ezek. 11:13, **f** I down upon my face
    39:23, **f** they all by the sword
Dan. 3:7, **f** down and worshipped the
    4:31, **f** a voice from heaven
    8:17, afraid, and **f** upon my
Matt. 13:4, some seeds **f** by the way side
    5, Some **f** upon stony places
    7, And some **f** among thorns
    8, other **f** into good ground
Luke 5:8, he **f** down at Jesus' knees
    8:6, And some **f** upon a rock; and
    23, they sailed he **f** asleep
    10:30, and **f** among thieves
Acts 5:5, **f** down, and gave up the ghost
    10, Then **f** she down straightway
    7:60, said this, he **f** asleep
    9:4, **f** to the earth, and heard a
    18, **f** from his eyes . . . scales
    10:25, **f** down at his feet
    11:15, Holy Ghost **f** on them
    12:7, chains **f** off from his hands
    19:17, fear **f** on them all
    20:37, **f** on Paul's neck, and
Heb. 11:30, walls of Jericho **f** down
Rev. 5:14, **f** down and worshipped him
    7:11, **f** before the throne
    16:19, cities of the nations **f**
    19:4, the four beasts **f** down
    10, I **f** at his feet to worship
Fellow—*companion*
Judg. 7:13, told a dream unto his **f**
1 Sam. 21:15, shall this **f** come into my
    29:4, Make this **f** return, that
1 Kin. 22:27, Put this **f** in the prison
Eccles. 4:10, one will lift up his **f**
Is. 44:11, his **f**-s shall be ashamed
Matt. 11:16, calling unto their **f**-s
    12:24, **f** doth not cast out devils
Luke 23:2, found this **f** perverting
John 9:29, as for this **f**, we know not
Acts 17:5, certain lewd **f**-s
    18:13, This **f** persuadeth men
Fellowship—*association*
Ps. 94:20, iniquity have **f** with thee

1 Cor. 10:20, should have **f** with devils
2 Cor. 6:14, **f** hath righteousness
Gal. 2:9, the right hand of **f**
Eph. 3:9, the **f** of the mystery
    5:11, **f** with the unfruitful
1 John 1:3, ye also may have **f** with us
    3, our **f** is with the Father
    7, **f** one with another
Felt—*sensed by touch*
Gen. 27:22, **f** him, and said, The voice
Ex. 10:21, darkness which may be **f**
Prov. 23:35, I **f** it not: when shall
Mark 5:29, **f** . . . that she was healed
Acts 28:5, into the fire, and **f** no harm
Female—*one of the feminine gender*
Gen. 1:27, male and **f** created he
    6:19, they shall be male and **f**
Lev. 3:1, whether it be a male or **f**
    5:6, a **f** from the flock, a lamb
Num. 5:3, male and **f** shall ye put
Deut. 4:16, likeness of male or **f**
Matt. 19:4, made them male and **f**
Mark 10:6, God made them male and **f**
Gal. 3:28, neither male nor **f**
Fenced—*enclosed, walled*
Num. 32:17, dwell in the **f** cities
Deut. 3:5, cities were **f** with high
Josh. 10:20, entered into **f** cities
1 Sam. 6:18, **f** cities, and . . . villages
2 Kin. 3:19, shall smite every **f** city
Job 10:11, **f** me with bones and sinews
Jer. 5:17, impoverish thy **f** cities
Ferry—*a boat for crossing a stream*
2 Sam. 19:18, there went over a **f** boat
Fervent—*glowing, zealous*
Acts 18:25, being **f** in the spirit
Rom. 12:11, **f** in spirit; serving
2 Cor. 7:7, your **f** mind toward me
Col. 4:12, labouring **f**-ly for you
James 5:16, effectual **f** prayer of a
1 Pet. 4:8, have **f** charity among
2 Pet. 3:10, melt with the **f** heat
Fetch—*to bring, get*
Gen. 18:4, a little water . . . be **f**-ed
Ex. 2:5, she sent her maid to **f** it
Num. 20:10, **f** you water out of this rock
Josh. 15:3, and **f**-ed a compass
Judg. 11:5, went to **f** Jephthah
1 Sam. 4:3, **f** the ark of the covenant
    16:11, Send and **f** him
2 Sam. 5:23, **f** a compass behind them
1 Kin. 17:10, **F** me . . . a little water
Neh. 8:15, **f** olive branches, and pine

Is. 56:12, I will **f** wine
Jer. 25:23, they **f**-ed forth Urijah
    36:21, sent Jehudi to **f** the roll
Acts 28:13, thence we **f**-ed a compass
Fetters—*shackles, bindings*
Judg. 16:21, bound him with **f**
2 Sam. 3:34, nor thy feet put into **f**
Job 36:8, if they be bound in **f**
Ps. 105:18, feet they hurt with **f**
Mark 5:4, bound with **f** and chains
    4, the **f** broken in pieces
Fever—*increase in bodily heat*
Deut. 28:22, consumption, and . . . **f**
Matt. 8:14, wife's mother . . . sick of a **f**
    15, and the **f** left her
Luke 4:38, was taken with a great **f**
John 4:52, seventh hour the **f** left
Acts 28:8, lay sick of a **f** and of a
Few—*limited in number, not many*
Gen. 24:55, abide with us a **f** days
    29:20, seemed . . . but a **f** days
    34:30, I being **f** in number, they
    47:9, **f** and evil have the days
Lev. 25:52, remain but **f** years
Num. 13:18, strong or weak, **f** or many
    26:56, between many and **f**
    35:8, but from them that have **f**
Deut. 4:27, be left **f** in number
    33:6, let not his men be **f**
Josh. 7:3, for they are but **f**
1 Sam. 14:6, save by many or by **f**
1 Chr. 16:19, When ye were but **f**
2 Chr. 29:34, priests were too **f**
Neh. 2:12, I and some **f** men with me
Job 10:20, Are not my days **f**
Ps. 105:12, When they were but a **f** men
    109:8, Let his days be **f**
Eccles. 5:2, let thy words be **f**
    9:14, a little city and **f** men
Is. 10:19, trees . . . shall be **f**
Ezek. 12:16, I will leave a **f** men
Matt. 9:37, but the labourers are **f**
    20:16, but **f** chosen
    25:21, faithful over a **f**
Mark 8:7, had a **f** small fishes
Luke 12:48, beaten with **f** stripes
    13:23, are there **f** that be saved
Acts, 17:4, chief women not a **f**
Heb. 13:22, letter unto you in **f** words
1 Pet. 3:20, **f**, that is, eight
Rev. 2:14, a **f** things against thee
Fidelity—*faithfulness, loyalty*
Titus 2:10, but shewing all good **f**

Field—*open grass land*
Gen. 2:5, every plant of the **f**
20, every beast of the **f**
23:20, the **f**, and the cave that is
25:29, Esau came from the **f**
Ex. 9:19, all that thou hast in the **f**
22, every herb of the **f**
10:15, or in the herb of the **f**
23:11, beasts of the **f** shall eat
Lev. 19:9, reap the corners of thy **f**
19, thy **f** with mingled seed
Num. 23:14, brought him into the **f**
Deut. 7:22, lest the beasts of the **f**
11:15, send grass in thy **f-s**
20:19, tree of the **f** is man's
Judg. 9:43, laid wait in the **f**
Ruth 2:3, gleaned in the **f** after the
8, not to glean in another **f**
1 Sam. 20:24, hid himself in the **f**
30:11, an Egyptian in the **f**
2 Sam. 14:6, two strove . . . in the **f**
1 Kin. 11:29, two were alone in the **f**
Job 5:23, beasts of the **f** . . . at peace
Ps. 96:12, Let the **f** be joyful
Prov. 24:30, the **f** of the slothful
31:16, She considereth a **f**
Jer. 4:17, As keepers of a **f**
26:18, be plowed like a **f**
32:44, shall buy **f-s** for money
Lam. 4:9, want of the fruits of the **f**
Ezek. 17:5, in a fruitful **f**
Dan. 4:15, tender grass of the **f**
Hos. 2:12, beasts of the **f** shall eat
Joel 1:20, beasts of the **f** cry also
Matt. 6:28, the lilies of the **f**
13:38, The **f** is the world
27:10, gave them . . . potter's **f**
Luke 2:8, shepherds abiding in the **f**
15:15, sent him into his **f-s**
17:36, Two men shall be in the **f**
John 4:35, look on the **f-s**
Acts 1:18, purchased a **f** with the reward
- 19, is to say, The **f** of blood
James 5:4, have reaped down your **f-s**
Fierce—*furious, violent*
Gen. 49:7, anger, for it was **f**
Ex. 32:12, Turn from thy **f** wrath
Num. 25:4, **f** anger of the Lord
Deut. 13:17, the **f-ness** of his anger
2 Chr. 28:11, **f** wrath of the Lord
Job 10:16, huntest me as a **f** lion
41:10, None is so **f**
Ps. 88:16, Thy **f** wrath goeth over me

Is. 19:4, **f** king shall rule over
33:19, not see a **f** people
Matt. 8:28, exceeding **f**, so that no
2 Tim. 3:3, accusers, incontinent, **f**
James 3:4, ships . . . driven of **f** winds
Rev. 19:15, **f-ness** and . . . of Almighty
Fiery—*burning, hot*
Num. 21:6, Lord sent **f** serpents among
Ps. 21:9, as a **f** oven
Dan. 3:6, midst of a burning **f** furnace
7:9, throne was like the **f** flame
Eph. 6:16, the **f** darts of the wicked
Heb. 10:27, and **f** indignation
1 Pet. 4:12, concerning the **f** trial
Fifteen—*ten and five*
Gen. 5:10, eight hundred and **f** years
Judg. 8:10, about **f** thousand men
Hos. 3:2, to me for **f** pieces of silver
Acts 7:14, threescore and **f** souls
Gal. 1:18, abode with him **f** days
Fifth—*one more than the fourth*
Gen. 1:23, morning were the **f** day
Lev. 5:16, shall add the **f** part
2 Sam. 2:23, under the **f** rib
Neh. 6:5, **f** time with an open letter
Jer. 1:3, Jerusalem captive in the **f**
Rev. 6:9, he had opened the **f** seal
Fifty—*five times ten*
Gen. 6:15, the breadth of it **f** cubits
Ex. 18:21, rulers of **f-ies**
26:5, **F** loops shalt thou make in
Lev. 23:16, sabbath . . . number **f** days
25:10, hallow the **f-eth** year
Esther 5:14, gallows be made of **f** cubits
Luke 9:14, sit down by **f-ies**
John 8:57, Thou art not yet **f** years old
Acts 13:20, four hundred and **f** years
Fig—*a fruit*
Gen. 3:7, they sewed **f** leaves together
Deut. 8:8, and vines, and **f** trees
Judg. 9:11, But the **f** tree said
Matt. 7:16, or **f-s** of thistles
Matt. 21:19, the **f** tree withered away
Mark 11:13, a **f** tree afar off having
13:28, a parable of the **f** tree
Luke 6:44, men do not gather **f-s**
John 1:48, wast under the **f** tree
James 3:12, Can the **f** tree, my brethren
Rev. 6:13, **f** tree casteth her untimely
Fight—*strive, struggle against*
Ex. 14:14, The Lord shall **f** for you
Josh. 9:2, to **f** with Joshua and with
1 Sam. 8:20, and **f** our battles

2 Chr. 26:11, host of f-ing men
Neh. 4:20, God shall f for us
Ps. 35:1, f against them that f against
144:1, and my fingers to f
1 Tim. 6:12, F the good f of faith
James 4:2, ye f and war
Rev. 2:16, f against them with the sword
Figure—*likeness*
Deut. 4:6, similitude of any f
Is. 44:13, after the f of a man
1 Cor. 4:6, I have in a f
Heb. 9:24, are the f-s of the true
1 Pet. 3:21, f whereunto even baptism
Fill—*put or pour into*
Gen. 1:22, f the waters in the seas
42:25, commanded to f their
Job 41:7, f his skin with barbed
Ps. 83:16, F their faces with shame
Prov. 7:18, let us take our f of love
Is. 8:8, f the breadth of thy land
Jer. 23:24, f heaven and earth
Rev. 18:6, filled f to her double
Fillet—*a band, a circlet*
Ex. 27:10, f-s shall be of silver
38:10, their f-s were of silver
Jer. 52:21, f of twelve cubits
filth—*corruption, nastiness*
2 Chr. 29:5, f-iness out of the holy
Job 15:16, abominable and f-y is man
Is. 4:4, Lord . . . washed away the f
28:8, full of vomit and f-iness
64:6, are as f-y rags
Nah. 3:6, cast abominable f
2 Cor. 7:1, cleanse . . . from all f-iness
Col. 3:8, f-y communication out of
Titus 1:11, for f-y lucre's sake
James 1:21, lay apart all f-iness
1 Pet. 3:21, putting away of the f
Finally—*lastly*
2 Cor. 13:11, F, brethren, farewell
Eph. 6:10, F, my brethren, pray for
2 Thess. 3:1, F, brethren pray for
1 Pet. 3:8, F, be ye all of one
Find—*meet with, or light upon*
Gen. 18:26, If I f in Sodom fifty
28, If I f there forty and five
32:5, f grace in thy sight
Num. 32:33, your sin will f you out
Deut. 4:29, thou shalt f him, if thou
Ruth 1:9, that ye may f rest, each of
2:13, Let me f favour
2 Sam. 15:25, I shall f favour in the
Job 11:7, searching f out God

Prov. 1:13, We shall f all precious
3:4, f favour . . . understanding
8:35, f-eth me f-eth life
18:22, f-eth a wife f-eth a good
Song 5:8, if ye f my beloved
Matt. 7:7, seek, and ye shall f
10:39, that f-eth his life shall
11:29, f rest unto your souls
21:2, ye shall f an ass tied
Mark 11:2, ye shall f a colt tied
13:36, he f you sleeping
14:37, f-eth them sleeping
Luke 2:12, shall f the babe wrapped
11:9, seek, and ye shall f
15:8, seek . . . till she f it
23:4, I f no fault in this man
John 10:9, go in and out, and f pasture
18:38, f in him no fault at all
Acts 7:46, to f a tabernacle for the
23:9, We f no evil in this man
Rom. 11:33, his ways past f-ing out
2 Cor. 9:4, f you unprepared
Rev. 18:14, shalt f them no more
Fine—*excellent, not coarse*
Gen. 41:42, arrayed him in . . . f linen
Ex. 25:4, scarlet, and f linen, and
Ps. 19:10, than much f gold: sweeter
81:16, the f-st of the wheat
Prov. 31:24, She maketh f linen, and
Mark 15:46, And he bought f linen
Luke 16:19, in purple and f linen
Rev. 19:14, clothed in f linen, white
Finger—*an extremity of the hand*
Ex. 8:19, This is the f of God
Lev. 4:6, dip his f in the blood
Deut. 9:10, written with the f of God
2 Sam. 21:20, had on every hand six
1 Kin. 12:10, little f shall be thicker
1 Chr. 20:6, f-s and toes were four
Prov. 6:13, he teacheth with his f-s
Jer. 52:21, thickness . . . was four f-s
Mark 7:33, put his f-s into his ears
Luke 11:20, the f of God cast out
16:24, tip of his f in water
John 8:6, his f wrote on the ground
20:25, f into the print of the
27, Reach hither thy f
Finish—*complete*
Gen. 2:1, heavens . . . earth were f-ed
Ex. 40:33, So Moses f-ed the work
2 Chr. 7:11, Solomon f-ed the house
John 4:34, and to f his work
17:4, I have f-ed the work
19:30, he said, It is f-ed

Finish (*Continued*)
Acts 20:24, I might **f** my course with
Rom. 9:28, **f** the work, and cut it short
Heb. 12:2, the author and **f**-er
James 1:15, sin, when it is **f**-ed
Fir—*an evergreen tree*
2 Sam. 6:5, instruments made of **f** wood
1 Kin. 6:15, house with planks of **f**
Ps. 104:17, the **f** trees are her house
Ezek. 27:5, ship boards of **f** trees
Fire—*combustion, excessive warmth*
Gen. 19:24, **f** from the Lord out of
22:6, he took the **f** in his hand
Ex. 3:2, flame, of **f** out of . . . a bush
9:24, **f** mingled with the hail
13:21, by night in a pillar of **f**
Num. 3:4, offered strange **f**
Deut. 9:3, consuming **f** he shall destroy
1 Kin. 18:38, the **f** of the Lord fell
Neh. 9:12, the night by a pillar of **f**
Job 18:5, spark of his **f** shall not
Ps. 46:9, burneth the chariot in the **f**
105:39, and **f** to give light
Is. 66:15, the Lord will come with **f**
Jer. 23:29, my word like as a **f**
Dan. 3:25, walking in the midst of the **f**
10:6, his eyes as lamps of **f**
Mark 9:47, be cast into hell **f**
Luke 3:17, burn with **f** inquenchable
12:49, come to send **f** on the earth.
Acts 2:3, cloven tongues like as of **f**
Acts 7:30, Lord in a flame of **f**
Rom. 12:20, coals of **f** on his head
1 Cor. 3:13, shall be revealed by **f**
Jude 7, the vengenance of eternal **f**
Rev. 3:18, gold tried in the **f**
21:8, with **f** and brimstone
Firm—*solid, fixed*
Josh. 3:17, the covenant . . . stood **f**
Job 41:24, heart is as **f** as a stone
Ps. 73:4, but their strength is **f**
Dan. 6:7, and to make a **f** decree
Heb. 3:6, hope **f** unto the end
Firmament—*sky or heavens*
Gen. 1:6, there be a **f** in the midst
Ps. 19:1, the **f** sheweth his handywork
Ezek. 1:25, a voice from the **f**
First—*prime, foremost*
Gen. 1:5, morning were the **f** day
38:28, This came out **f**
Prov. 18:17, **f** in his own cause
Hos. 2:7, return to my **f** husband

Matt. 6:33, seek ye **f** the kingdom of
7:5, **f** cast out the beam out of
19:30, **f** shall be last
22:38, **f** and great commandment
28:1, the **f** day of the week
Mark 3:27, will **f** bind the strong man
12:28, the **f** commandment
1 John 4:19, because he **f** loved us
Jude 6, kept not their **f** estate
Rev. 1:17, I am the **f** and the last
2:4, thou hast left thy **f** love
22:13, end, the **f** and the last
Firstborn—*eldest, elect*
Gen. 10:15, Canaan begat Sidon his **f**
19:37, **f** bare a son
27:19, I am Esau thy **f**: I have
Ex. 11:5, the **f** in the land of Egypt
Matt. 1:25, brought forth her **f** son
Luke 2:7, she brought forth her **f** son
Heb. 12:23, church of the **f**
Firstfruits—*earliest fruits or results*
Ex. 23:16, the **f** of thy labours
Deut. 26:10, the **f** of the land
Prov. 3:9, **f** of all thine increase
Rom. 8:23, **f** of the Spirit
James 1:18, **f** of his creatures
Rev. 14:4, **f** unto God and to the Lamb
Fish—*water animals*
Gen. 1:26, dominion over the **f** of the
Num. 11:5, remember the **f**, which we
2 Chr. 33:14, entering in at the **f** gate
Is. 50:2, their **f** stinketh, because
Jonah 1:17, had prepared a great **f**
Matt. 14:17, loaves, and two **f**-es
Luke 5:6, great multitude of **f**-es
11:11, or if he ask a **f**
John 21:10, the **f** which ye have now
Fishers—*one who fishes, catches*
Is. 19:8, **f** also shall mourn
Jer. 16:16, I will send for many **f**
Matt. 4:19, make you **f** of men
Mark 1:17, to become **f** of men
John 21:7, girt his **f**-'s coat
Fit—*qualified, suitable*
Lev. 16:21, by the hand of a **f** man
1 Chr. 7:11, soldiers, **f** to go out
12:8, **f** for the battle
Prov. 24:27, make it **f** for thyself in
Luke 9:62, **f** for the kingdom of God
Acts 22:22, it is not **f** that he should
Col. 3:18, it is **f** in the Lord
Rom. 9:22, **f**-ed to destruction
Eph. 4:16, whole body **f**-ly joined

Fitches—*a type of grain*
Is. 28:25, cast abroad the **f**, and
    27, the **f** are not threshed
Ezek. 4:9, lentiles . . . millet . . . **f**
Five—*four and one*
Gen. 5:6, an hundred and **f** years
Ex. 22:1, restore **f** oxen for an ox
Lev. 26:8, **f** of you shall chase an
1 Sam. 17:40, **f** smooth stones out of
2 Chr. 4:2, **f** cubits the height
Esther 9:6, destroyed **f** hundred men
Is. 30:17, at the rebuke of **f**
Matt. 14:17, **f** loaves, and two fishes
    25:2, **f** . . . wise . . . **f** . . . foolish
    20, deliveredst . . . **f** talents
2 Cor. 11:24, **f** times . . . forty stripes
Rev. 17:10, **f** are fallen, and one is
Fixed—*set, established*
Ps. 57:7, My heart is **f**, O God, my
    112:7, his heart is **f**, trusting in
Luke 16:26, there is a great gulf **f**
Flag—*rank growing water plant*
Ex. 2:3, laid it in the **f**-s by the
Job 8:11, can the **f** grow without
Is. 19:6, reeds and **f**-s shall wither
Flagon—*narrow mouthed vessel*
2 Sam. 6:19, flesh, and a **f** of wine
Song 2:5, Stay me with **f**-s
Is. 22:24, the vessels of **f**-s
Hos. 3:1, love **f**-s of wine
Flame—*a blaze*
Gen. 3:24, **f**-ing sword which turned
Ex. 3:2, appeared unto him in a **f**
Judg. 13:20, Lord ascended in the **f**
Ps. 106:18, **f** burned up the wicked
Song 8:6, hath a most vehement **f**
Is. 4:5, of a **f**-ing fire by night
    5:24, the **f** consumeth the chaff
    10:17, his Holy One for a **f**
Ezek. 20:47, the **f**-ing **f** shall
Joel 2:5, noise of a **f** of fire
Acts 7:30, in a **f** of fire in a bush
2 Thess. 1:8, **f**-ing fire taking
Rev. 19:12, eyes were as a **f** of fire
Flat—*level, plain*
Lev. 21:18, or he that hath a **f** nose
Num. 22:31, bowed down . . . and fell **f**
Josh. 6:5, city shall fall down **f**
    20, the wall fell down **f**
Flatter—*praise insincerely*
Job 17:5, he that speaketh **f**-y
    32:21, **f**-ing titles
Ps. 5:9, **f** with their tongue

Prov. 6:24, from the **f**-y of the tongue
    7:21, **f**-ing of her lips she
1 Thess. 2:5, used we **f**-ing words
Flax—*the linen plant*
Ex. 9:31, **f** and the barley was smitten
Judg. 15:14, arms became of **f**
Ezek. 40:3, with a line of **f** in his
Matt. 12:20, smoking **f** shall he not
Flea—*a wingless insect*
1 Sam. 24:14, dead dog, after a **f**
    26:20, come out to seek a **f**
Fled—*ran away from*
Gen. 14:10, remained **f** to the mountain
    31:21, he **f** with all that he had
    39:18, garment with me, and **f**
Is. 22:3, all thy rulers are **f**
Matt. 26:56, forsook him, and **f**
Mark 14:52, and **f** from them naked
    16:8, **f** from the sepulchre
Luke 8:34, they **f**, and went and told
Rev. 20:11, earth and the heaven **f**
Flee—*to hasten away*
Gen. 16:8, **f** from the face of my
Lev. 26:17, **f** when none pursueth
Ps. 11:1, **F** as a bird to your
    139:7, I **f** from thy presence
Prov. 28:1, wicked **f** when no man
Is. 30:16, **f** upon horses
Matt. 2:13, **f** into Egypt, and be thou
    3:7, **f** from the wrath to
1 Tim. 6:11, man of God, **f** these things
2 Tim. 2:22, **F** also youthful lusts
Rev. 9:6, death shall **f** from them
Fleece—*sheep's wool*
Deut. 18:4, of the **f** of thy sheep
Judg. 6:37, a **f** of wool in the floor
Job 31:20, were not warmed with the **f**
Flesh—*animals, mankind, muscles, tissue*
Gen. 2:23, and **f** of my **f**
    24, They shall be one **f**
    7:21, **f** died that moved upon
    37:27, our brother and our **f**
Ex. 16:3, by the **f** pots . . . and did eat
Num. 16:22, spirits of all **f**
Deut. 12:20, I will eat **f**
Job 19:26, in my **f** shall I see God
    41:23, The flakes of his **f**
Ps. 16:9, my **f** also shall rest in hope
    84:2, **f** crieth out for the living
    136:25, food to all **f**
Eccles. 12:12, is a weariness of the **f**
Is. 40:6, All **f** is grass
Dan. 1:15, fairer and fatter in **f**

Flesh (*Continued*)
Matt. 16:17, **f** and blood hath not
26:41, but the **f** is weak
Mark 13:20, no **f** should be saved
Luke 24:39, spirit hath not **f** and
John 1:14, the Word was made **f**
3:6, born of the **f** is **f**
Rom. 8:1, who walk not after the **f**
9:8, children of the **f**
Gal. 4:13, through infirmity of the **f**
6:8, **f** shall of the **f** reap
Eph. 2:3, the desires of the **f**
5:31, two shall be one **f**
6:12, wrestle not against **f**
1 Pet. 2:11, abstain from **f**-ly lusts
Jude 23, garment spotted by the **f**
Rev. 19:21, fowls . . . filled with their **f**
Flies—*common insects*
Ex. 8:21, send swarms of **f** upon thee
Ps. 78:45, divers sorts of **f** among
Eccles. 10:1, **f** cause the ointment
Flight—*hasty departure*
Lev. 26:8, put ten thousand to **f**
Is. 52:12, haste, nor go by **f**
Amos 2:14, **f** shall perish from the
Matt. 24:20, **f** be not in winter
Heb. 11:34, turned to **f** the armies of
Flint—*a tough, hard stone*
Deut. 8:15, out of the rock of **f**
32:13, oil out of the **f**-y rock
Ps. 114:8, **f** into a fountain of
Is. 5:28, counted like **f**
Ezek. 3:9, adamant harder than **f**
Flock—*company of people, multitudes*
Gen. 4:4, the firstlings of his **f** and
29:2, three **f**-s of sheep lying
30:31, again feed and keep thy **f**
38, **f**-s came to drink
Ex. 2:16, to water their father's **f**
10:9, our **f**-s and with our herds
Judg. 5:16, bleatings of the **f**-s
1 Sam. 17:34, took a lamb out of the **f**
2 Chr. 32:28, and cotes for **f**-s
Ps. 77:20, leddest thy people like a **f**
Prov. 27:23, state of thy **f**-s
Is. 40:11, feed his **f** like a shepherd
Jer. 23:2, scattered my **f**, and driven
Ezek. 45:15, one lamb out of the **f**
Amos 6:4, eat the lambs out of the **f**
Hab. 3:17, the **f** shall be cut off from
Matt. 26:31, sheep of the **f** shall be
Luke 2:8, watch over their **f** by night
12:32, Fear not, little **f**
1 Pet. 5:2, **f** of God which is among

Flood—*great flow of water*
Gen. 6:17, I, do bring a **f** of waters
7:17, **f** was forty days upon the
9:15, no more become a **f**
Ex. 15:8, **f**-s stood upright as an
Josh. 24:2, other side of the **f**
Ps. 24:2, established it upon the **f**-s
66:6, went through the **f** on foot
Jer. 46:8, Egypt riseth up like a **f**
Dan 9:26, end . . . shall be with a **f**
Matt. 7:25, **f**-s came, and the winds
Luke 17:27, **f** came, and destroyed them
Floor—*a place for threshing grain*
Gen. 50:11, mourning in the **f** of Atad
Ruth 3:3, get thee down to the **f**
1 Kin. 6:30, the **f** . . . he overlaid
7:7, from one side of the **f**
Joel 2:24, **f**-s . . . full of wheat
Matt. 3:12, will throughly purge his **f**
Flour—*finely ground grain*
Ex. 29:2, wheaten **f** shalt thou make
Lev. 2:1, offering . . . of fine **f**
2 Sam. 13:8, she took **f**, and kneaded
Ezek. 16:13, eat fine **f**, and honey
Rev. 18:13, fine **f**, and wheat, and
Flourish—*increase, thrive*
Ps. 72:7, shall the righteous **f**
92:7, workers of iniquity do **f**
14, be fat and **f**-ing
103:15, as a flower . . . so he **f**-eth
Prov. 11:28, shall **f** as a branch
Eccles. 12:5, the almond tree shall **f**
Is. 17:11, make thy seed to **f**
Ezek. 17:24, made the dry tree to **f**
Phil. 4:10, your care of me hath **f**-ed
Flow—*to move, run, proceed*
Ex. 3:8, land **f**-ing with milk and
Josh. 4:18, **f**-ed over all his banks
Job 20:28, goods shall **f** away in the
Ps. 147:18, and the waters **f**
Jer. 31:12, **f** together to the goodness
Joel 3:18, hills shall **f** with milk
John 7:38, shall **f** rivers of living
Flower—*a blossom, choicest part*
Job 14:2, cometh forth like a **f**
2 Chr. 4:5, a cup, with **f**-s of lilies
1 Sam. 2:33, die in the **f** of their
Ps. 103:15, as a **f** of the field, so he
Song 2:12, the **f**-s appear
Is. 28:1, beauty is a fading **f**
1 Cor. 7:36, pass the **f** of her age
1 Pet. 1:24, **f** thereof falleth away
Fly—*move through the air*
Gen. 1:20, fowl that may **f** above the

Job 5:7, as the sparks **f** upward
    20:8, **f** away as a dream
Ps. 18:10, he did **f** upon the wings
Prov. 23:5, **f** away as an eagle toward
Is. 14:29, a fiery **f**-ing serpent
Rev. 8:13, **f**-ing through the midst
    12:14, might **f** into the wilderness
    19:17, fowls that **f** in the midst
Foes—*adversaries*
1 Chr. 21:12, destroyed before thy **f**
Ps. 27:2, mine enemies and my **f**
    89:23, beat down his **f**
Acts 2:35, I make thy **f** thy footstool
Fold—*a shelter for sheep, to lap over*
Num. 32:24, **f**-s for your sheep; and do
Ps. 50:9, he goats out of thy **f**-s
Prov. 6:10, little **f**-ing of the hands
Eccles. 4:5, fool **f**-eth his hands
Is. 13:20, shepherds make their **f**
John 10:16, which are not of this **f**
    16, one **f**, and one shepherd
Heb. 1:12, shalt thou **f** them up
Folk—*people in general*
Prov. 30:26, conies . . . a feeble **f**
Jer. 51:58, and the **f** in the fire
Mark 6:5, hands upon a few sick **f**
John 5:3, multitude of impotent **f**
Acts 5:16, bringing sick **f**-s
Follow—*go or come after*
Gen. 24:5, not be willing to **f** me unto
    44:4, Up, **f** after the men
Ex. 11:8, all the people that **f** thee
    21:22, yet no mischief **f**
Deut. 18:22, if the thing **f** not
Judg. 3:28, said unto them, F after me
Ruth 1:16, return from **f**-ing after
1 Sam. 12:14, **f**-ing the Lord your God
2 Sam. 1:6, **f**-ed hard after
Ps. 23:6, goodness . . . mercy . . . **f** me
    63:8, soul **f**-eth hard after thee
    119:150, **f** after mischief
Prov. 21:21, **f**-eth after righteousness
Is. 5:11, they may **f** strong drink
Matt. 4:19, he saith unto them, F me
    20, left their nets, and **f**-ed
    8:19, **f** thee whithersoever thou
    12:15, great multitude **f**-ed him
    16:24, take up his cross, and **f**
    19:21, and come and **f** me
Mark 5:37, suffered no man to **f** him
    14:54, Peter **f**-ed him afar off
Luke 22:10, **f** him into the house
    39, disciples also **f**-ed him

John 10:27, I know them, and they **f** me
    18:15, Peter **f**-ed Jesus
Eph. 5:1, Be ye . . . **f**-ers of God
1 Thess. 2:14, **f**-ers of the churches
Heb. 12:14, F peace with all men
1 Pet. 3:13, **f**-ers of that which is good
3 John 11, **f** not that which is evil
Rev. 14:4, are they which **f** the Lamb
    13, their works do **f** them
Folly—*want of sense, sin*
Gen. 34:7, he had wrought **f** in Israel
Judg. 19:23, do not this **f**
Prov. 14:18, The simple inherit **f**
    15:21, F is joy to him
Is. 9:17, every mouth speaketh **f**
Jer. 23:13, seen **f** in the prophets
Food—*victuals, something that nourishes*
Gen. 2:9, and good for **f**
    3:6, the tree was good for **f**
    43:2, buy us a little **f**
Lev. 3:11, the **f** of the offering made
Deut. 10:18, giving him **f** and raiment
Job 38:41, for the raven his **f**
Ps. 78:25, Man did eat angels' **f**
    136:25, Who giveth **f** to all flesh
Prov. 6:8, her **f** in the harvest
    30:8, feed me with **f** convenient
1 Tim. 6:8, having **f** . . . content
James 2:15, destitute of daily **f**
Fool—*simpleton*
1 Sam. 26:21, I have played the **f**
2 Sam. 3:33, Died Abner as a **f** dieth
Ps. 14:1, The **f** hath said in his heart
Prov. 1:7, **f**-s despise . . . instruction
    15:5, **f** despiseth his father's
    24:7, Wisdom is too high for a **f**
    26:3, a rod for the **f**-'s back
    29:11, A **f** uttereth all his mind
Eccles. 10:14, A **f** also is full of words
Hos. 9:7, the prophet is a **f**
Matt. 5:22, shall say, Thou **f**
    23:17, Ye **f**-s and blind
Luke 24:25, O **f**-s, and slow of heart
Rom. 1:22, wise, they became **f**-s
1 Cor. 3:18, let him become a **f**
    4:10, **f**-s for Christ's sake
Eph. 5:15, walk . . . not as **f**-s
Foolish—*silly, unwise*
Gen. 31:28, hast now done **f**-ly
Deut. 32:6, **f** people and unwise
Job 1:22, nor charged God **f**-ly
    5:3, seen the **f** taking root
Ps. 5:5, **f** shall not stand in thy
    75:4, Deal not **f**-ly

Foolish (*Continued*)
Prov. 14:17, soon angry dealeth f-ly
 24, f-ness of fools is folly
 15:2, mouth . . . poureth . . . f-ness
 24:9, thought of f-ness is sin
Lam. 2:14, seen vain and f things
Matt. 25:8, f said unto the wise
2 Cor. 11:21, I speak f-ly
1 Pet. 2:15, ignorance of f men

Foot—*lowest part of the leg*
Gen. 8:9, rest for the sole of her f
 41:44, lift his hand or f
Deut. 33:24, let him dip his f in oil
2 Sam. 21:20, every f six toes
1 Chr. 20:6, and six on each f
Ps. 26:12, f standeth . . . even place
 91:12, dash thy f against
 121:3, suffer thy f to be moved
Prov. 3:23, thy f shall not stumble
 25:19, a f out of joint
Matt. 22:13, Bind him hand and f
Luke 4:11, dash thy f against
Rev. 10:2, right f upon the sea

Footmen—*footsoldiers, runners*
Num. 11:21, six hundred thousand f
2 Sam. 8:4, twenty thousand f
Jer. 12:5, thou hast run with the f

Footstool—*rest for the feet*
1 Chr. 28:2, for the f of our God
Ps. 99:5, and worship at his f
 110:1, enemies thy f
 132:7, we will worship at his f
Is. 66:1, earth is my f
Mark 12:36, thine enemies thy f
James 2:3, or sit here under my f

Forasmuch—*since, seeing that*
Gen. 41:39, F as God hath shewed thee
Deut. 12:12, f as he hath no part nor
Jer. 10:6, F as there is none like unto
Matt. 18:25, But f as he had not to pay
1 Cor. 11:7, f as he is the image and
Heb. 2:14, F then as the children are
1 Pet. 4:1, F then as Christ hath

Forbad—*commanded against*
Deut. 2:37, the Lord our God f us
Matt. 3:14, John f him, saying, I have
Mark 9:38, f him, because he followeth
2 Pet. 2:16, f the madness of the

Forbear—*to do without*
Ex. 23:5, and wouldest f to help him
Prov. 24:11, If thou f to deliver them
 25:15, by long f-ing is a prince
Jer. 20:9, I was weary with f-ing, and

Ezek. 24:17, F to cry, make no mourning
Rom. 3:25, through the f-ance of God
1 Cor. 9:6, power to f working
2 Cor. 12:6, I f, lest any man should
Eph. 4:2, f-ing one another in love
Col. 3:13, F-ing one another, and
1 Thess. 3:1, when we could no longer f

Forbid—*prohibit*
Gen. 44:7, God f that thy servants
1 Sam. 20:2, he said unto him, God f
Matt. 19:14, f them not, to come unto
Mark 9:39, But Jesus said, F him not
Luke 18:16, f them not: for of such
 23:2, f-ing to give tribute to
Acts 10:47, Can any man f water, that
1 Cor. 14:39, and f not to speak with
1 Tim. 4:3, F-ing to marry, and

Force—*strength, vigor*
Gen. 31:31, wouldest take by f thy
Deut. 34:7, his natural f abated
1 Sam. 2:16, I will take it by f
2 Sam. 13:12, do not f me
Job 30:18, the great f of my disease
 36:19, nor all the f-s of strength
 40:16, f is in the navel of the
Jer. 18:21, blood by the f of the sword
Dan. 11:10, a multitude of great f-s
Matt. 11:12, the violent take it by f
Heb. 9:17, is of f after men are

Forehead—*brow*
Ex. 28:38, shall be upon Aaron's f
Lev. 13:42, bald head, or his bald f
1 Sam. 17:49, stone sunk into his f
Jer. 3:3, thou hadst a whore's f
Ezek. 3:8, strong against their f-s
 9:4, mark upon the f-s of the men
 16:12, I put a jewel on thy f
Rev. 9:4, the seal of God in their f-s
 17:5, upon her f was a name

Foreigner—*one of another nation*
Ex. 12:45, f and a hired servant
Deut. 15:3, f thou mayest exact
Obad. 11, f-s entered into his gates
Eph. 2:19, no more strangers and f-s

Forepart—*front*
Ex. 28:27, toward the f thereof, over
Ezek. 42:7, court on the f of thee
Acts 27:41, the f stuck fast, and

Forest—*woodland*
1 Sam. 22:5, into the f of Hareth
1 Kin. 7:2, house of the f of Lebanon
2 Chr. 27:4, the f-s he built castles
Ps. 50:10, every beast of the f is

Is. 10:18, consume the glory of his **f**
44:14, among the trees of the **f**
56:9, all ye beasts in the **f**
Jer. 5:6, lion out of the **f** shall
21:14, kindle a fire in the **f**
Ezek. 15:2, among the trees of the **f**
Amos 3:4, Will a lion roar in the **f**
Forgave—*pardoned*
Ps. 78:38, **f** their iniquity, and
99:8, a God that **f**-st them
Matt. 18:27, and **f** him the debt
Luke 7:42, he frankly **f** them both
43, to whom he **f** most
Forget—*lose remembrance of*
Gen. 27:45, he **f** that which thou hast
41:51, me **f** all my toil
Deut. 4:9, lest thou **f** the things which
6:12, lest thou **f** the Lord
Ps. 9:17, all the nations that **f** God
13:1, How long wilt thou **f** me
74:23, **F** not the voice of thine
88:12, land of **f**-fulness
119:176, I . . . **f** thy commandments
Prov. 3:1, My son, **f** not my law; but
4:5, get understanding: **f** it not
31:5, they drink, and **f** the law
Is. 54:4, **f** the shame of thy youth
Jer. 2:32, maid **f** her ornaments
23:27, cause my people to **f** my
Heb. 6:10, **f** your work and labour of
13:2, **f**-ful to entertain strangers
16, to communicate **f** not
James 1:24, **f**-teth what manner of man
Forgive—*pardon*
Gen. 50:17, **f** the trespass of the
Ex. 32:32, Wilt, **f** their sin
Num. 30:5, the Lord shall **f** her
Ps. 25:18, and **f** all my sins
86:5, good and ready to **f**
Jer. 18:23, **f** not their iniquity
Matt. 6:12, **f** us our debts, as we **f**
9:5, Thy sins be **f**-n thee
6, on earth to **f** sins
Mark 2:7, who can **f** sins but God only
11:26, if ye do not **f**
Luke 6:37, **f**, and ye shall be **f**-n
7:47, sins . . . many, are **f**-n
23:34, Jesus, Father, **f** them
2 Cor. 2:10, ye **f** any thing, I **f** also
Eph. 4:32, **f**-ing one another
Col. 2:13, **f**-n you all trespasses
1 John 1:9, just to **f** us our sins
Forgiveness—*pardon, remission*
Ps. 130:4, there is **f** with thee

Mark 3:29, Holy Ghost hath never **f**
Acts 13:38, preached unto you the **f**
26:18, may receive **f** of sins
Eph. 1:7, **f** of sins, according to
Col. 1:14, even the **f** of sins
Forgotten—*ceased to have in mind*
Gen. 41:30, plenty . . . **f** in the land
Deut. 32:18, **f** God that formed thee
Job 19:14, friends have **f** me
28:4, the waters **f** of the foot
Ps. 9:18, needy . . . not always be **f**
31:12, I am **f** as a dead man
77:9, God **f** to be gracious
Jer. 2:32, my people have **f** me
Lam. 2:6, caused . . . sabbaths to be **f**
Ezek. 23:35, thou hast **f** me
Matt. 16:5, had **f** to take bread
Luke 12:6, is **f** before God
Form—*shape, fashion*
Gen. 1:2, the earth was without **f**
2:7, God **f**-ed man of the dust
2 Sam. 14:20, this **f** of speech
Job 33:6, **f**-ed out of the clay
Ps. 95:5, hands **f**-ed the dry land
Prov. 26:10, that **f**-ed all things
Is. 45:7, I **f** the light, and create
53:2, no **f** nor comeliness
Amos 4:13, that **f**-eth the mountains
7:1, he **f**-ed grasshoppers
Mark 16:12, appeared in another **f**
Gal. 4:19, until Christ be **f**-ed in you
1 Tim. 2:13, Adam . . . **f**-ed, then Eve
Former—*previous*
Gen. 40:13, after the **f** manner
Deut. 24:4, Her **f** husband, which
Ruth 4:7, This was the manner in **f** time
Ps. 79:8, not against us **f** iniquities
Is. 42:9, **f** things are come to pass
46:9, Remember the **f** things of old
65:16, **f** troubles are forgotten
Jer. 10:16, he is the **f** of all things
Ezek. 16:55, return to their **f** estate
Acts 1:1, The **f** treatise have I made
1 Pet. 1:14, according to the **f** lusts
Rev. 21:4, **f** things are passed away
Fornication—*criminal intercourse*
Is. 23:17, shall commit **f** with all
Matt. 15:19, murders, adulteries, **f**-s
19:9, except it be for **f**
John 8:41, We be not born of **f**
1 Cor. 6:18, Flee **f** . . . **f** sinneth
1 Thess. 4:3, should abstain from **f**

Fornication (*Continued*)
Rev. 2:20, to commit f, and to eat
17:2, the wine of her f
Forsake—*desert, abandon*
Deut. 4:31, he will not f thee
Josh. 1:5, not fail thee, nor f thee
2 Chr. 15:2, if ye f him, he will f
Ezra 9:9, God hath not f-n us
Job 6:14, f-th the fear of the
Ps. 22:1, God, why hast thou f-n me
27:9, leave me not, neither f
10, father and my mother f me
38:21, F me not, O God
Prov. 1:8, f not the law of thy mother
2:17, f-th the guide of her youth
3:3, not mercy and truth f
9:6, F the foolish, and live
Is. 55:7, Let the wicked f his way
Jer. 5:7, thy children have f-n me
Ezek. 9:9, Lord hath f-n the earth
20:8, f the idols of Egypt
Matt. 19:27, f-n all, and followed
27:46, God, why hast thou f-n me
Mark 15:34, God, why hast thou f-n me
2 Cor. 4:9, Persecuted, but not f-n
Heb. 13:5, never leave thee, nor f
2 Pet. 2:15, have f-n the right
Forsook—*deserted*
Deut. 32:15, then he f God which made
1 Kin. 12:8, he f the counsel
2 Chr. 12:1, f the law of the Lord
Matt. 26:56, disciples f him, and fled
Mark 1:18, f their nets, and followed
Luke 5:11, they f all, and followed
2 Tim. 4:16, but all men f me
Heb. 11:27, By faith he f Egypt
Fort—*a defense work*
2 Sam. 5:9, David dwelt in the f, and
Is. 25:12, fortress of the high f of
Jer. 52:4, built f-s against it
Ezek. 4:2, build a f against it, and
33:27, f-s and in the caves
Dan. 11:19, turn his face toward the f
Forth—*forward, abroad*
Gen. 1:11, the earth bring f grass
12, the earth brought f grass
3:16, shalt bring f children
8:7, he sent f a raven, which
8, he sent f a dove from him
18, Noah went f, and his sons
19:10, the men put f their hand
24:45, Rebekah came f with her

Ex. 3:10, mayest bring f my people
11, bring f the children of
7:5, stretch f mine hand
Judg. 20:25, Benjamin went f against
1 Sam. 30:21, went f to meet David
2 Sam. 19:7, therefore arise, go f
Ps. 1:3, bringeth f his fruit in his
51:15, my mouth shall shew f thy
57:3, God shall send f his mercy
Ps. 90:2, mountains were brought f
92:2, shew f thy lovingkindness
104:14, he may bring f food
Prov. 31:20, she reacheth f her hands
Song 3:11, Go f, O ye daughters
Is. 14:7, they break f into singing
37:36, angel of the Lord went f
43:21, shall shew f my praise
Jer. 32:21, brought f thy people
52:7, went f out of the city
Ezek. 1:13, out of the fire went f
Dan. 2:13, decree went f that the wise
Hos. 10:1, bringeth f fruit unto
Matt. 1:21, she shall bring f a son
12:13, Stretch f thine hand
13:3, Behold, a sower went f to
Mark 1:41, put f his hand ... touched
7:26, he would cast f the devil
John 1:43, Jesus would go f into
Acts 1:26, they gave f their lots
26:25, speak f ... truth
Forthwith—*immediately*
Matt. 26:49, f he came to Jesus, and
Mark 5:13, f Jesus gave them leave
John 19:34, f came there out blood and
Acts 9:18, he received sight f
21:30, and f the doors were shut
Fortify—*protect*
2 Chr. 11:11, f-ied the strong holds
Neh. 3:8, f-ied Jerusalem ... the broad
4:2, Jews? will they f themselves
Jer. 51:53, should f the height of her
Nah. 3:14, f thy strongholds
Fortress—*a stronghold*
2 Sam. 22:2, my rock, and my f
Ps. 18:2, rock, and my f, and my
91:2, my refuge and my f
Is. 34:13, brambles in the f-es
Jer. 6:27, a tower and a f among my
Forty—*four times ten*
Gen. 7:4, the earth f days and f nights
17, f days upon the earth
Ex. 16:35, Israel did eat manna f years
34:28, f days and f nights
Num. 33:38, died there, in the f-ieth

FORTY

Ps. 95:10, F years long was I grieved
Matt. 4:2, f days and f nights
Mark 1:13, in the wilderness f days
2 Cor. 11:24, f stripes save one
Forward—*onward, ahead*
Gen. 26:13, waxed great, and went f
1 Sam. 10:3, Then shalt thou go on f
2 Kin. 20:9, shadow go f ten degrees
Job 23:8, I go f, but he is not there
Jer. 7:24, went backward, and not f
Ezek. 1:9, every one straight f
Acts 19:33, the Jews putting him f
2 Cor. 8:8, the f-ness of others
3 John 6, bring f on their journey
Fought—*contended, strove*
Num. 21:1, then he f against Israel
Judg. 5:20, They f from heaven
2 Chr. 20:29, the Lord f against
1 Cor. 15:32, I have f with beasts
2 Tim. 4:7, I have f a good fight
Rev. 12:7, angels f . . . dragon f
Foul—*dirty, loathsome, not fair*
Job 16:16, My face is f with weeping
Ezek. 32:2, and f-edst their rivers
34:19, that which ye have f-ed
Matt. 16:3, will be f weather to day
Mark 9:25, he rebuked the f spirit
Rev. 18:2, hold of every f spirit
Found—*discovered, established*
Gen. 2:20, there was not f an help meet
6:8, Noah f grace in the eyes of
Ex. 22:7, if the thief be f
Lev. 6:3, have f that which was lost
Deut. 17:2, If there be f among you
Judg. 14:18, not f out of my riddle
Ruth 2:10, Why have I f grace in thine
Job 28:12, where shall wisdom be f
Ps. 84:3, the sparrow hath f an house
Prov. 25:16, Hast thou f honey? eat
30:6, thou be f a liar
Eccles. 7:29, this only have I f
Song 3:1, sought him, but I f him not
Is. 51:3, joy and gladness shall be f
Jer. 15:16, Thy words were f, and I did
Dan. 5:27, balances, and art f wanting
6:11, and f Daniel praying
Mal. 2:6, iniquity was not f in his
Matt. 8:10, not f so great faith
27:32, f a man of Cyrene, Simon
Mark 11:4, and f the colt tied
14:40, he f them asleep again
Luke 2:46, they f him in the temple
15:6, I have f my sheep
24:2, f the stone rolled away

John 1:41, We have f the Messias
Acts 13:22, I have f David the son of
1 Cor. 15:15, we are f false witnesses
Phil. 2:8, being f in fashion
Rev. 18:24, in her was f the blood of
Foundation—*groundwork*
Ex. 9:18, f thereof even until now
2 Sam. 22:8, f-s of heaven moved
Job 4:19, whose f is in the dust, which
Ps. 87:1, His f is in the holy mountains
104:5, laid the f-s of the earth
Prov. 10:25, is an everlasting f
Is. 28:16, corner stone, a sure f
Matt. 13:35, from the f of the world
Luke 6:48, and laid the f on a rock
Rom. 15:20, upon another man's f
2 Tim. 2:19, the f of God standeth sure
Heb. 1:10, hast laid the f of the earth
6:1, the f of repentance
Founded—*established*
Ps. 24:2, he hath f it upon the seas
Prov. 3:19, by wisdom hath f the earth
Amos 9:6, f his troop in the earth
Matt. 7:25, for it was f upon a rock
Fountain—*a spring of water*
Gen. 7:11, f-s of the great deep
16:7, found her by a f of water
Ps. 36:9, with thee is the f of life
Prov. 5:16, Let thy f-s be dispersed
14:27, fear of the Lord is a f
Eccles. 12:6, be broken at the f
Mark 5:29, f of her blood was dried up
James 3:12, no f both yield salt
Rev. 7:17, living f-s of water
21:6, athirst of the f of the water
Four—*three and one*
Gen. 2:10, and became into f heads
Ex. 25:12, cast f rings of gold
Lev. 11:20, creep, going upon all f
2 Kin. 7:3, there were f leprous men
Is. 11:12, the f corners of the earth
Matt. 15:38, f thousand men, beside
Mark 13:27, from the f winds
Luke 19:8, I restore him f-fold
John 11:39, been dead f days
Fourscore—*eighty*
Gen. 16:16, Abram was f and six years
Ex. 7:7, And Moses was f years old
Luke 2:37, widow of about f and four
Foursquare—*four sided with equal angles*
Ex. 27:1, the altar shall be f
Rev. 21:16, And the city lieth f
Fourteen—*ten and four*
Gen. 31:41, served thee f years

Fourteen (*Continued*)
2 Chr. 13:21, and married f wives
  30:15, passover on the f-th day
Is. 36:1, f-th year of king Hezekiah
Matt. 1:17, Abraham to David are f
2 Cor. 12:2, above f years ago
Acts 27:27, when the f-th night was
Fourth—*one more than the third*
Gen. 1:19, morning were the f day
Ex. 20:5, the third and f generation
Judg. 19:5, came to pass on the f day
Matt. 14:25, f watch of the night
Rev. 6:7, the voice of the f beast
Fowl—*a winged creature*
Gen. 1:20, f that may fly above the
  6:7, thing, and the f-s of the air
Lev. 20:25, unclean f-s and clean
1 Kin. 4:23, fallowdeer and fatted f
Ps. 8:8, f of the air, and the fish
  148:10, creeping . . . and flying f
Jer. 9:10, the f of the heavens and the
Hos. 9:8, a share of a f
Matt. 6:26, Behold, the f-s of the air
Rev. 19:17, saying to all the f-s
Fox—*a crafty animal*
Judg. 15:4, caught three hundred f-es
Neh. 4:3, if a f go up, he shall
Song 2:15, the f-es, the little f-es
Ezek. 13:4, like the f-es in the deserts
Matt. 8:20, The f-es have holes, and
Luke 13:32, Go ye, and tell that f
Fragments—*broken pieces*
Matt. 14:20, took up of the f that
Mark 6:43, twelve baskets full of the f
John 6:12, Gather up the f that remain
Frame—*shape, arranged*
Judg. 12:6, could not f to pronounce it
Ps. 94:20, f-th mischief by a law
Jer. 18:11, I f evil against you, and
Hos. 5:4, They will not f their doings
Eph. 2:21, all the building fitly f-d
Heb. 11:3, worlds were f-d by the word
Frankincense—*a fragrant incense*
Ex. 30:34, sweet spices with pure f
1 Chr. 9:29, the oil, and the f, and
Song 4:6, to the hill of f
Matt. 2:11, gold, and f, and myrrh
Free—*not under control, at liberty*
Gen. 2:16, garden . . . mayest f-ly eat
Ex. 21:11, go out f without money
Ps. 51:12, with thy f spirit
Is. 58:6, let the oppressed go f
Matt. 10:8, f-ly . . . received, f-ly give
  17:26, Then are the children f

John, 8:32, truth shall make you f
Acts 22:28, sum obtained I this f-dom
Rom. 6:7, he that is dead is f-d
  22, now being made f from sin
  8:2, f from the law
Gal. 5:1, Christ hath made us f
Eph. 6:8, he be bond or f
Rev. 19:18, all men, both f and bond
Freewill—*without restraint*
Lev. 22:18, all his f offerings
Ezra 7:16, f offering of the people
Ps. 119:108, f offerings of my mouth
Fresh—*new, lately produced*
Num. 11:8, was as the taste of f oil
Job 33:25, flesh shall be f-er than
Ps. 92:10, be anointed with f oil
James 3:12, yield salt water and f
Fret—*tease, irritate*
Lev. 13:51, plague is a f-ting leprosy
1 Sam. 1:6, for to make her f
Prov. 19:3, his heart f-teth against
  24:19, F not thyself because of
Friend—*an associate*
Gen. 38:12, he and his f Hirah
Ex. 33:11, a man speaketh unto his f
Judg. 14:20, he had used as his f
Ruth 2:13, thou hast spoken f-ly unto
Job 16:20, My f-s scorn me
Ps. 38:11, My lovers . . . f-s stand aloof
Prov. 14:20, the rich hath many f-s
  17:17, A f loveth at all times
  18:24, a f that sticketh closer
Hos. 3:1, beloved of her f
Matt. 11:19, f of publicans
  20:13, F, I do thee no wrong
John 15:13, lay down his life for his f-s
James 4:4, know ye not that the f-ship
Frogs—*amphibious animals*
Ex. 8:2, smite all thy borders with f
Ps. 78:45, and f, which destroyed them
  105:30, land brought forth f
Rev. 16:13, unclean spirits like f
Frost—*frozen dew*
Gen. 31:40, consumed me, and the f by
Ex. 16:14, small as the hoar f
Job 37:10, breath of God f is given
Ps. 78:47, their sycamore trees with f
Jer. 36:30, in the night to the f
Froward—*petulant, obstinate*
Deut. 32:20, are a very f generation
2 Sam. 22:27, f thou wilt shew thyself
Ps. 101:4, f heart shall depart from

Prov. 10:31, f tongue shall be cut out
    21:8, way of man is f
Is. 57:17, he went on f-ly in the way
1 Pet. 2:18, but also the f
Fruit—*produce, increase*
Gen. 1:11, f tree yielding f after
    3:6, took of the f thereof, and
Ex. 21:22, her f depart from her
Lev. 25:19, land shall yield her f
    27:30, f of the tree, is the Lord's
Deut. 28:53, f of thine own body
Ps. 1:3, bringeth forth his f in his
    92:14, bring forth f in old age
Prov. 11:30, f of the righteous
Song 4:16, and eat his pleasant f-s
Is. 5:1, in a very f-ful hill
Jer. 6:19, even the f of their thoughts
Matt. 7:16, know them by their f-s
John 4:36, f unto life eternal
Rom. 7:4, bring forth f unto God
Col. 1:10, f-ful in every good work
James 3:17, full of mercy and good f-s
Frustrate—*to defeat, baffle*
Ezra 4:5, to f their purpose, all the
Is. 44:25, f-th the tokens of the liars
Gal. 2:21, do not f the grace of God
Fuel—*a source of heat*
Is. 9:5, be with burning and f of fire
    19, shall be as the f of the fire
Ezek. 15:4, cast into the fire for f
    21:32, shalt be for f to the fire
Fugitive—*outlaw, deserter*
Gen. 4:12, f and a vagabond shalt thou
Judg. 12:4, Ye . . . are f-s of Ephraim
2 Kin. 25:11, the f-s that fell away
Is. 15:5, f-s shall flee unto Zoar
Ezek. 17:21, f-s with all his bands
Fulfil—*make complete, bring to pass*
Gen. 29:27, F her week
Ex. 5:13, F your works, your daily
2 Chr. 36:21, f the word of the Lord
Ps. 20:5, Lord f all thy petitions
    148:8, stormy wind f-ing his word
Matt. 1:22, done that it might be f-ed
    5:17, not come to destroy, but to f
Luke 22:16, it be f-ed in the kingdom
Gal. 6:2, f the law of Christ
Col. 1:25, you, to f the word of God
Rev. 20:3, thousand years . . . f-ed
Full—*filled up, complete, sated*
Gen. 25:8, old man, and f of years
    35:29, old and f of days
1 Chr. 21:24, buy it for the f price

Job 10:15, I am f of confusion
Ps. 33:5, Earth is f of the goodness of
    73:10, waters of a f cup
Is. 11:9, shall be f of the knowledge
Mic. 3:8, f of power by the spirit
Matt. 14:20, remained twelve baskets f
    23:27, f of dead men's bones
Luke 4:1, being f of the Holy Ghost
    11:34, body also is f of light
John 1:14, f of grace and truth
Acts 2:13, men are f of new wine
1 Cor. 4:8, ye are f, now ye are rich
    10:26, Lord's, and the f-ness
1 John 1:4, that your joy may be f
Rev. 14:18, her grapes are f-y ripe
Fuller—*a cloth bleacher and finisher*
2 Kin. 18:17, highway of the f-'s field
Mal. 3:2, and like f-'s soap
Mark 9:3, no f . . . can white them
Furious—*raging, violent*
2 Kin. 9:20, for he driveth f-ly
Prov. 29:22, and a f man aboundeth
Ezek. 23:25, shall deal f-ly with
Dan. 2:12, king was angry and very f
Nah. 1:2, Lord revengeth, and is f
Furlongs—*eighth parts of a mile*
Luke 24:13, about threescore f
John 11:18, about fifteen f off
Rev. 14:20, thousand and six hundred f
Furnace—*a device for burning fuel*
Gen. 15:17, smoking f, and a burning
Ps. 12:6, silver tried in a f
Is. 31:9, and his f in Jerusalem
Dan. 3:15, midst of a burning fiery f
Matt. 13:42, into a f of fire
Rev. 1:15, as they burned in a f
Furnish—*supply with, equip*
Deut. 15:14, f him liberally out of
Ps. 78:19, God f a table in the
Prov. 9:2, hath also f-ed her table
Is. 65:11, f the drink offering unto
Matt. 22:10, f-ed with guests
Mark 14:15, large upper room f-ed and
2 Tim. 3:17, f-ed unto all good works
Furniture—*equipment*
Gen. 31:34, the camel's f
Ex. 31:7, all the f of the tabernacle
    8, the table and his f, and the
Nah. 2:9, of all the pleasant f
Furrows—*a plow trench*
Job 31:38, the f likewise . . . complain
Ps. 65:10, settlest the f thereof
    129:3, they made long their f
Ezek. 17:10, wither in the f where it

Further—*to a greater distance*
Num. 22:26, angel of the Lord went **f**
Job 38:11, Hitherto . . . come, but no **f**
Ps. 140:8, **f** not his wicked device
Matt. 26:65, what **f** need have we
Luke 24:28, though he . . . have gone **f**
Acts 24:4, I be not **f** tedious
Phil. 1:12, unto the **f**-ance of the gospel
Heb. 12:9, **F**-more we have had fathers

Fury—*violence, wrath, rage*
Gen. 27:44, thy brother's **f** turn
Is. 27:4, **F** is not in me
Jer. 4:4, my **f** come forth like fire
6:11, full of the **f** of the Lord
30:23, Lord goeth forth with **f**
Ezek. 5:13, cause my **f** to rest upon
19:12, plucked up in **f**
Mic. 5:15, anger and **f** upon the heathen

G

Gain—*attain, grow rich*
Judg. 5:19, they took no **g** of money
Prov. 3:14, **g** thereof than fine gold
Is. 33:15, the **g** of oppressions
Ezek. 22:12, hast greedily **g**-ed of
27, to get dishonest **g**
Dan. 11:39, divide the land for **g**
Matt. 16:26, shall **g** the whole world
18:15, hast **g**-ed thy brother
Luke 9:25, **g** the whole world, and lose
Acts 16:19, hope of their **g**-s was gone
19:24, brought no small **g** unto
1 Cor. 9:20, that I might **g** the Jews
2 Cor. 12:17, Did I make a **g** of you
1 Tim. 6:5, supposing . . . **g** is godliness
James 4:13, sell, and get **g**

Gall—*a bitter bodily fluid, rancor*
Deut. 29:18, beareth **g** and wormwood
Job 20:14, it is the **g** of asps
Ps. 69:21, gave me also **g** for my meat
Jer. 8:14, water of **g** to drink
Lam. 3:19, the wormwood and the **g**
Amos 6:12, turned judgment into **g**
Matt. 27:34, vinegar . . . mingled with **g**
Acts 8:23, in the **g** of bitterness

Gallery—*a corridor, or balcony*
Song 7:5, king is held in the **g**-ies
Ezek. 41:15, the **g**-ies thereof on the
42:3, **g** against **g** in three stories

Galley—*a vessel rowed with oars*
Is. 33:21, shall go no **g** with oars

Gallows—*a form for executions*
Esther 5:14, **g** be made of fifty cubits
7:10, hanged Haman on the **g**
9:25, his sons . . . hanged on the **g**

Garden—*cultivated ground*
Gen. 2:8, the Lord God planted a **g**
3:8, God walking in the **g**
10, I heard thy voice in the **g**
Deut. 11:10, as a **g** of herbs
Song 6:11, down into the **g** of nuts
Is. 1:8, a lodge in a **g** of cucumbers
58:11, be like a watered **g**
Lam. 2:6, as if it were of a **g**
Joel 2:3, land is as the **g** of Eden
John 18:1, where was a **g**
26, Did not I see thee in the **g**
19:41, in the **g** a new sepulchre
20:15, supposing him to be the **g**-er

Garment—*an article of clothing*
Gen. 25:25, all over like an hairy **g**
38:14, put her widow's **g**-s off
39:12, she caught him by his **g**
Ex. 28:2, make holy **g**-s for Aaron
Deut. 22:11, **g** of divers sorts
Josh. 9:5, and old **g**-s upon them
Ps. 22:18, part my **g**-s among them
Ps. 102:26, wax old like a **g**
Is. 59:17, the **g**-s of vengeance
Dan. 7:9, whose **g** was white as snow
Joel 2:13, heart and not your **g**-s
Matt. 9:20, touched the hem of his **g**
22:11, had not on a wedding **g**
Mark 16:5, young man . . . a long white **g**
Luke 24:4, two men . . . in shining **g**-s
Acts 12:8, Cast thy **g** about thee
Heb. 1:11, wax old as doth as **g**
Rev. 1:13, a **g** down to the foot

Garner—*a grain storehouse*
Ps. 144:13, That our **g**-s may be full
Joel 1:17, the **g**-s are laid desolate
Matt. 3:12, wheat into the **g**

Garnish—*decorate, adorn*
Job 26:13, he hath **g**-ed the heavens
Matt. 23:29, and **g** the sepulchres of
Luke 11:25, findeth it swept and **g**-ed
Rev. 21:19, wall of the city were **g**-ed

Garrison—*a fortified place*
1 Sam. 10:5, the **g** of the Philistines
14:12, men of the **g** answered
1 Chr. 18:13, he put **g**-s in Edom
Ezek. 26:11, thy strong **g**-s shall go
2 Cor. 11:32, kept the city . . . with a **g**

Gate—*door, place of vantage*
Gen. 22:17, thy seed . . . possess the g of
   28:17, this is the g of heaven
Ex. 20:10, stranger . . . within thy g-s
Judg. 16:3, took the doors of the g
Ps. 24:7, Lift up your heads, O ye g-s
   100:4, Enter into his g-s with
Is. 38:10, go to the g-s of the grave
Matt. 7:13, Enter ye in at the strait g
   16:18, g-s of hell shall not
Acts 12:14, Peter stood before the g
Gather—*collect or bring together*
Gen. 1:10, g-ing . . . of the waters
   31:46, Jacob said . . . G stones
   41:35, let them g all the food
Ps. 26:9, G not my soul with
   33:7, g-eth the waters of the sea
Is. 40:11, g the lambs with his arm
   66:18, g all nations and tongues
John 4:36, g-eth fruit unto life
   6:12, G up the fragments
2 Thess. 2:1, g-ing together unto him
Rev. 14:19, g-ed the vine of the earth
Gave—*bestowed, delivered up*
Gen. 2:20, Adam g names to all cattle
   3:12, she g me of the tree
   25:17, he g up the ghost
Neh. 9:15, g-st them bread from heaven
Job 1:21, Lord g . . . Lord hath taken
Ps. 21:4, He asked life . . . thou g-st
   68:11, Lord g the word: great was
   69:21, g me also gall for my meat
   21, they g me vinegar to drink
   77:1, and he g ear unto me
Eccles 12:7, return unto God who g it
Is. 50:6, I g my back to the smiters
Matt. 10:1, g them power . . . unclean
   15:36, g thanks, and brake them
   26:48, betrayed him g them a sign
Mark 8:6, and g thanks, and brake
Luke 7:44, g-st me no water for my feet
   23:24, Pilate g sentence
John 3:16, g his only begotten son
   13:26, sop, he g it to Judas
   19:30, bowed . . . and g up the ghost
Acts 12:23, he g not God the glory
Rom. 1:28, g them over to a reprobate
1 Cor. 3:6, but God g the increase
Eph. 1:22, g him to be the head over
1 Tim. 2:6, Who g himself a ransom
Gender—*breed*
Lev. 19:19, shalt not let thy cattle g
Job 38:29, frost . . . who hath g-ed it

Gal. 4:24, g-eth to bondage, which is
2 Tim. 2:23, they do g strifes
General—*all or chief part, a leader*
2 Sam. 17:11, Israel be g-ly gathered
1 Chr. 27:34, g of the King's army
Heb. 12:23, the g assembly and church
Generation—*all people living at one time*
Gen. 2:4, are the g-s of the heavens
Deut. 1:35, not one . . . of this evil g
Ps. 90:1, dwelling place in all g-s
   100:5, truth endureth to all g-s
Matt. 3:7, O g of vipers, who hath
   24:34, This g shall not pass
Luke 1:48, all g-s shall call me blessed
   21:32, g shall not pass away
1 Pet. 2:9, a chosen g, a royal
Gentile—*one not a Jew*
Is. 66:19, my glory among the G-s
Luke 2:32, light to lighten the G-s
Acts 14:2, Jews stirred up the G-s
Rom. 2:9, Jew first . . . also of the G
   11:11, salvation . . . unto the G-s
1 Cor. 12:13, we be Jews or G-s
Rev. 11:2, it is given unto the G-s
Gentle—*mild, meek*
Ps. 18:35, thy g-ness hath . . . me great
2 Cor. 10:1, g-ness of Christ
1 Thess. 2:7, But we were g among you
2 Tim. 2:24, but be g unto all men
Titus 3:2, no brawlers, but g
1 Pet. 2:18, not only to the good and g
Get—*obtain, betake*
Gen. 12:1, G thee out of thy country
   34:4, G me this damsel to wife
Deut. 8:18, power to g wealth
   17:8, g thee up into the place
Judg. 14:2, g her for me to wife
2 Sam. 20:6, g him fenced cities
Prov. 4:5, G wisdom, g understanding
   7, thy g-ing g understanding
   18:15, prudent g-eth knowledge
Eccles. 3:6, time to g, and a time to
Is. 30:11, G you out of the way
Jer. 48:44, g-eth up out of the pit
Matt. 4:10, G thee hence, Satan: for
   16:23, G thee behind me
Acts 7:3, G thee out of thy country
James 4:13, buy and sell, and g gain
Ghost—*Spirit, soul of man*
Gen. 25:8, Then Abraham gave up the g
Job 3:11, Why did I not give up the g
Matt. 1:18, with child of the Holy G
   27:50, cried . . . yielded up the g
   28:19, Son, and of the Holy G

Ghost (*Continued*)
Mark 1:8, baptize you with the Holy **G**
Luke 1:15, be filled with the Holy **G**
Acts 2:4, all filled with the Holy **G**
2 Cor 13:14, communion of the Holy **G**
Giant—*large man*
Gen. 6:4, g-s in the earth in those days
Deut. 3:13, called the land of g-s
1 Chr. 20:6, was the son of the g
Job 16:14, runneth upon me like a g
Gift—*present, endowment*
Gen. 25:6, Abraham gave g-s, and sent
Ex. 23:8, no g: for the g blindeth
Ps. 68:18, hast received g-s for men
Prov. 18:16, A man's g maketh room for
Prov. 21:14, A g in secret pacifieth
Is. 1:23, every one loveth g-s, and
Matt. 2:11, presented unto him g-s
    5:23, bring thy g to the altar
John 4:10, thou knewest the g of God
Acts 2:38, the g of the Holy Ghost
Rom. 6:23, g of God is eternal life
James 1:17, good g and every perfect g
Gird—*clothe, equip, put on*
Ex. 29:5, g him with the . . . girdle
Job 38:3, G up now thy loins
Ps. 45:3, G thy sword upon thy
Is. 3:24, a g-ing of sackcloth
Jer. 6:26, g thee with sackcloth
Ezek. 16:10, g-ed thee about with fine
John 13:5, towel wherewith he was g-ed
    21:18, young, thou g-edst thyself
Girdle—*a belt, or sash*
Ex. 28:8, the curious g of the ephod
    40, make . . . g-s, and bonnets
    29:9, shalt gird them with g-s
2 Kin. 1:8, girt with a g of leather
Ps. 109:19, g wherewith he is girded
Is. 3:24, instead of a g a rent
Jer. 13:1, Go and get thee a linen g
Matt. 3:4, leathern g about his loins
Rev. 1:13, paps with a golden g
Girl—*female child*
Joel 3:3, and sold a g for wine
Zech. 8:5, boys and g-s playing
Girt—*donned, bound about*
2 Kin. 1:8, g with a girdle of leather
John 21:7, g his fishers' coat unto him
Eph. 6:14, loins g about with truth
Rev. 1:13, g about the paps . . . golden
Give—*bestow, yield, forego*
Gen. 1:29, have g-n you every . . . seed

Ex. 20:12, land . . . Lord thy God g-th
Num. 6:26, upon thee, and g thee peace
Ps. 29:11, Lord will g strength unto
    80:11, G ear, O Shepherd
    145:15, g-st them their meat
Is. 9:6, unto us as a son is g-n
Matt. 6:11, G us this day our daily
    10:8, freely g
    16:19, g unto thee the keys
    26:9, and g to the poor
    28:18, All power is g-n unto me
Mark 12:15, Shall we g, or . . . not g
Luke 1:77, g knowledge of salvation
    6:38, G, and it shall be g-n
    11:9, Ask, and it shall be g-n
    22:19, my body . . . g-n for you
John 6:11, when he had g-n thanks
    10:11, good shepherd g-th his life
    14:27, my peace I g unto you
Acts 20:35, more blessed to g than to
Rom. 12:20, if he thirst, g him drink
    14:6, for he g-th God thanks
1 Cor. 3:10, grace of God which is g-n
2 Cor. 12:7, was g-n to me a thorn in
Eph. 4:27, Neither g place to the devil
    5:20, G-ing thanks always
James 4:6, g-th grace unto the humble
1 John 5:11, hath g-n to us eternal life
Glad—*joyful, happy*
Ex. 4:14, he will be g in his heart
Num. 10:10, in the day of your g-ness
Deut. 28:47, and with g-ness of heart
1 Chr. 16:31, Let the heavens be g
Ps. 16:9, my heart is g, and my glory
    32:11, Be g in the Lord
    100:2, Serve the Lord with g-ness
    122:1, was g when they said unto me
Prov. 10:1, wise son maketh a g father
Is. 16:10, And g-ness is taken away
Matt. 5:12, Rejoice, and be exceeding g
Luke 1:14, shalt have joy and g-ness
    19, shew thee these g tidings
    8:1, g tidings of the kingdom
Acts 2:46, g-ness and singleness of heart
2 Cor. 11:19, For ye suffer fools g-ly
Glass—*a clear substance, a mirror*
Job 37:18, as a molten looking g
Is. 3:23, g-es, and the fine linen
1 Cor. 13:12, through a g darkly
James 1:23, his natural face in a g
Rev. 4:6, was a sea of g like unto
Glean—*to gather what is left*
Lev. 19:10, not g thy vineyard

Ruth 2:8, Go not to **g** in another field
15, **g** even among the sheaves
17, she **g**-ed in the field
Is. !7:6, **g**-ing grapes shall be left
Jer. 49:9, leave some **g**-ing grapes
Glitter—*gleam, glisten*
Deut. 32:41, If I whet my **g**-ing sword
Job 20:25, **g**-ing sword cometh out
Ezek. 21:10, furbished that it may **g**
Nah. 3:3, sword and the **g**-ing spear
Glorify—*praise, exalt*
Ps. 50:23, offereth praise **g**-eth me
86:12, **g** thy name for evermore
Is. 66:5, Let the Lord be **g**-ied
Matt. 5:16, **g** your Father . . . in heaven
John 12:28, Father, **g** thy name
13:31, is the Son of man **g**-ied
16:14, He shall **g** me
17:1, **g** thy Son . . . **g** thee
Acts 13:48, **g**-ied the word of the Lord
1 Cor. 6:20, **g** God in your body
Heb. 5:5, Christ **g**-ied not himself
Glorious—*noble, exalted*
Ex. 15:1, he hath triumphed **g**-ly
Neh. 9:5, blessed be thy **g** name
Ps. 87:3, **G** things are spoken of thee
Is. 49:5, **g** in the eyes of the Lord
2 Cor. 4:4, **g** gospel of Christ
Phil. 3:21, like . . . his **g** body
1 Tim. 1:11, the **g** gospel of the blessed
Glory—*nobility, magnificence*
Gen. 31:1, hath he gotten all this **g**
Ex. 16:7, see the **g** of the Lord
33:18, shew me thy **g**
1 Chr. 16:24, his **g** among the heathen
29:11, the power, and the **g**
Job 19:9, stripped me of my **g**
29:20, My **g** was fresh in me
Ps. 8:1, thy **g** above the heavens
24:7, King of **g** shall come in
105:3, **G** ye in his holy name
Prov. 16:31, hoary head . . . crown of **g**
Is. 6:3, earth is full of his **g**
35:2, shall see the **g** of the Lord
66:19, my **g** among the Gentiles
Jer. 13:16, Give **g** to the Lord
Ezek. 10:4, the **g** of the Lord went up
Hos. 4:7, change their **g** into shame
Matt. 6:29, Solomon in all his **g** was
Luke 2:9, **g** of the Lord shone round
14, **G** to God in the highest
17:18, returned to give **g** to God

John 8:50, I seek not mine own **g**
Rom. 2:7, seek for **g** and honour
3:23, come short of the **g** of God
1 Cor. 5:6, Your **g**-ing is not good
Gal. 5:25, not be desirous of vain **g**
Heb. 2:7, crownedst . . . **g** and honour
Gnash—*strike together*
Ps. 35:16, **g**-ed . . . with their teeth
37:12, **g**-eth . . . with his teeth
112:10, he shall **g** with his teeth
Lam. 2:16, hiss and **g** the teeth
Matt. 8:12, weeping and **g**-ing of teeth
Mark 9:18, foameth, and **g**-eth with his
Gnat—*a tiny insect*
Matt. 23:24, which strain at a **g**
Gnaw—*bite off little by little*
Zeph. 3:3, they **g** not the bones till
Rev. 16:10, they **g**-ed their tongues
Go—*move, depart*
Gen. 3:14, thy belly shalt thou **g**
Ex. 5:1, Let my people **g**, that they
33:14, My presence shall **g** with
Lev. 11:21, **g**-eth upon all four
Judg. 18:2, **G**, search the land: who
20:31, **g**-eth up to the house of
Ruth 1:16, thou **g**-est, I will **g**
2 Kin. 2:23, **G** up, thou bald head
Ps. 122:1, Let us **g** into the house of
Prov. 4:14, **g** not in the way of evil
6:6, **G** to the ant, thou sluggard
Eccles. 9:7, **G** thy way, eat thy bread
Matt. 2:8, **G** and search diligently
28:19, **G** ye therefore, and teach
Mark 16:15, **G** ye into all the world
Luke 22:8, **G** and prepare . . . passover
John 9:7, **G**, wash in the pool
14:2, I **g** to prepare a place for
5, know not whither thou **g**-est
Heb. 6:1, let us **g** on unto perfection
Goad—*a pointed instrument*
Judg. 3:31, hundred men with an ox **g**
1 Sam. 13:21, and to sharpen the **g**-s
Eccles. 12:11, words of the wise . . . **g**-s
Goat—*a horned animal*
Ex. 26:7, curtains of **g**-s' hair
Lev. 3:12, if his offering be a **g**
Num. 15:27, he shall bring a she **g** of
1 Sam. 19:13, a pillow of **g**-s' hair
Dan. 8:5, the **g** had a notable horn
Matt. 25:32, sheep from the **g**-s
Heb. 9:13, blood of bulls and of **g**-s

God—*the Supreme Being*
Gen. 1:1, **G** created the heaven and
    2, Spirit of **G** moved upon
    3, **G** said, Let there be light
    27, **G** created man in his own
    2:3, **G** blessed the seventh day
    17:1, I am the Almighty **G**
    31:50, **G** is witness betwixt me
Ex. 3:15, and the **G** of Jacob
    20:2, I am the Lord thy **G**, which
    5, Lord thy **G** am a jealous **G**
Lev. 25:17, but thou shalt fear thy **G**
Deut. 6:5, love the Lord thy **G**
    10:7, your **G**, is **G** of **g-s**
    20:18, against the Lord your **G**
    33:27, eternal **G** is thy refuge
Ruth 1:16, and thy **G** my **G**
2 Sam. 16:16, **G** save the King
    22:3, **G** of my rock; in him will
    32, who is **G**, save the Lord
1 Kin. 2:23, **G** do so to me, and more
    18:21, if the Lord be **G**, follow
2 Kin. 5:7, Am I **G**, to kill and make
1 Chr. 13:10, there he died before **G**
Job 40:9, Hast thou an arm like **G**
Ps. 7:1, **G**, in thee do I put my trust
    14:1, heart, There is no **G**
    16:1, Preserve me, O **G**
    46:1, **G** is our refuge and strength
Ps. 46:5, **G** is in the midst of her; she
    49:7, give to **G** a ranson for him
    67:1, **G** be merciful unto us, and
    6, **G**, even our own **G**, shall
    70:1, Make haste, O **G**, to deliver
    86:10, thou art **G** alone
    145:1, I will extol thee, my **G**, O
Prov. 30:5, Every word of **G** is pure
Eccles. 5:2, **G** is in heaven
Is. 44:8, Is there a **G** beside me
    53:4, stricken, smitten of **G**, and
Jer. 23:23, a **G** at hand . . . **G** afar off
Ezek. 37:27, I will be their **G**, and
Dan. 2:47, your **G** is a **G** of **g-s**
Hos. 11:9, for I am **G**, and not man
Matt. 2:12, warned of **G** in a dream
    3:16, he saw the Spirit of **G**
    4:3, If thou be the Son of **G**
    5:9, called the children of **G**
    22:37, shalt love the Lord thy **G**
    27:46, My **G**, my **G**, why hast
    54, this was the Son of **G**
Mark 10:9, **G** hath joined together
    11:22, Have faith in **G**
    16:10, sat on the right hand of **G**

Luke 2:14, Glory to **G** in the highest
    12:28, **G** so clothed the grass
    18:16, such is the kingdom of **G**
    23:40, Dost not thou fear **G**
John 3:16, **G** so loved the world, that
    17, **G** sent not his Son into the
    4:24, **G** is a Spirit
    14:1, believe in **G**, believe also
    20:17, to my **G**, and your **G**
Acts 10:40, Him **G** raised up the third
    12:22, the voice of a **g**
    17:24, **G** that made the world and
Rom. 1:25, truth of **G** into a lie
    8:14, they are the sons of **G**
1 Cor. 15:57, thanks be to **G**, which
2 Cor. 3:3, Spirit of the living **G**
Gal. 5:21, inherit the kingdom of **G**
    6:7, **G** is not mocked
Eph. 1:3, Blessed be the **G** and Father
    4:6, One **G** and Father of all
Phil. 4:7, peace of **G** which passeth
Col. 1:15, image of the invisible **G**
Titus 2:11, grace of **G** that bringeth
Heb. 12:29, **G** is a consuming fire
1 Pet. 4:10, manifold grace of **G**
2 Pet. 1:21, holy men of **G** spake
1 John 3:20, **G** is greater than our
    4:12, No man hath seen **G**
2 John 10, neither bid him **G** speed
Rev. 7:17, **G** shall wipe away all tears
    11:17, O Lord **G** Almighty
    17:17, words of **G** . . . fulfilled
Goddess—*a female deity*
1 Kin. 11:5, went after Ashtoreth the **g**
Acts 19:27, temple of the great **g**
    37, blasphemers of your **g**
Godhead—*the Divine*
Acts 17:29, the **G** is like unto gold
Rom. 1:20, his eternal power and **G**
Col. 2:9, fulness of the **G** bodily
Godliness—*pious actions*
1 Tim. 2:2, in all **g** and honesty
    3:16, great is the mystery of **g**
    4:8, but **g** is profitable
    6:6, **g** with contentment
2 Tim. 3:5, having a form of **g**
2 Pet. 1:7, to **g** brotherly kindness
Godly—*pious, reverencing God*
Ps. 12:1, for the **g** man ceaseth
2 Cor. 1:12, simplicity and **g** sincerity
    7:10, **g** sorrow worketh
Heb. 12:28, with reverence and **g** fear
2 Pet. 2:9, deliver the **g** out of

Gods—*idols*
Gen. 3:5, shall be as g knowing good
Ex. 20:3, have no other g before me
Judg. 5:8, They chose new g
Is. 37:12, g of the nations delivered
Jer. 22:9, and worshipped other g
Dan. 2:47, your God is a God of g
Gal. 4:8, by nature are no g

Going—*moving, departure*
Gen. 15:12, when the sun was g down
Job 1:7, g to and fro in the earth
Ps. 121:8, shall preserve thy g out
Mic. 5:2, whose g-s forth have been
Matt. 26:46, Rise, let us be g
Mark 10:32, way g up to Jerusalem
Luke 14:31, g to make war against
1 Pet. 2:25, as sheep g astray
Jude 7, g after strange flesh

Gold—*a precious metal*
Gen. 2:12, g of that land is good
Ex. 3:22, and jewels of g
Job 31:24, If I have made g my hope
Ps. 19:10, yea, than much fine g
72:15, of the g of Sheba
Prov. 16:16, better . . . get wisdom than g
25:11, apples of g in pictures
Lam. 4:1, How is the g become dim
Zech. 9:3, fine g as the mire
Matt. 10:9, neither g, nor silver, nor
Acts 3:6, Silver and g have I none
20:33, coveted no man's silver, or g
James 2:2, man with a g ring
5:3, g and silver is cankered
1 Pet. 1:7, more precious than of g
Rev. 3:18, buy of me g tried in the

Golden—*made of gold*
Gen. 24:22, g earring of half a shekel
Lev. 8:9, did he put the g plate
1 Sam. 6:18, the g mice, according to
Dan. 3:5, a worship the g image
Rev. 1:12, I saw seven g candlesticks
21:15, g reed to measure the city

Goldsmith—*worker in gold*
Neh. 3:31, Malchiah the g's son
32, the g-s and the merchants
Is. 40:19, and the g spreadeth it over
46:6, and hire a g; and he

Gone—*departed*
Gen. 31:30, thou wouldest needs be g
Ex. 16:14, dew that lay was g up
Deut. 23:23, which is g out of thy lips
Ps. 19:4, line is g out through
42:4, I had g with the multitude
109:23, g like the shadow

Prov. 7:19, he is g a long journey
Song 2:11, rain is over and g
Is. 1:4, are g away backward
16:8, are g over the sea
Lam. 1:3, Judah is g into captivity
Matt. 25:8, our lamps are g out
Mark 5:30, virtue had g out of him
2 Pet. 2:15, and are g astray

Good—*commendable, virtuous*
Gen. 1:4, the light, that it was g
15:15, buried in a g old age
50:20, God meant it unto g
Lev. 27:10, a g for a bad
Deut. 31:6, strong and of a g courage
Job 7:7, eye shall no more see g
Ps. 106:1, give thanks . . . for he is g
136:1, for he is g . . . his mercy
Prov. 22:1, g name . . . to be chosen
25:25, g news from a far country
Is. 39:8, G is the word of the Lord
Jer. 24:3, Figs; the g figs, very g
33:11, Lord is g; for his mercy
Amos 5:14, Seek g, and not evil
Matt. 3:10, bringeth not forth g fruit
9:2, be of g cheer; thy sins be
13:45, seeking g-ly pearls
19:16, G Master, what
25:23, g and faithful servant
Mark 9:50, Salt is g, but if the salt
Luke 6:27, do g to them which hate
10:42, hath chosen that g part
18:19, Why callest thou me g
John 10:14, I am the g shepherd
Acts 23:1, lived in all g conscience
Rom. 2:10, every man that worketh g
12:21, overcome evil with g
16:18, by g words and fair
Gal. 6:10, do g unto all
Phil. 4:8, things are of g report
2 Thess. 2:16, g hope through grace
1 Tim. 6:12, Fight the g fight of faith
James 1:17, Every g gift and every
1 Pet. 3:11, eschew evil, and do g

Goodman—*master of a house*
Prov. 7:19, For the g is not at home
Matt. 24:43, if the g of the house had

Goodness—*excellence, virtue*
Ex. 33:19, my g pass before thee
2 Chr. 6:41, saints rejoice in g
Ps. 23:6, g and mercy shall follow
25:7, remember . . . for thy g' sake
31:19, how great is thy g, which
Prov. 20:6, every one his own g
Zech. 9:17, For how great is his g

Goodness (*Continued*)
Rom. 11:22, g and severity of God
Gal. 5:22, gentleness, g, faith
2 Thess. 1:11, good pleasure of his **g**
Goods—*personal property*
Gen. 14:21, take the g to thyself
24:10, g of his master were in
Neh. 9:25, houses full of all g
Job. 26:28, his g shall flow away
Ezek. 38:12, have gotten cattle and g
Matt. 12:29, and spoil his g
24:47, ruler over all his g
Luke 12:19, hast much g laid up
19:8, half of my g I give to the
Rev. 3:17, rich, and increased with g
Gorgeous—*showy, impressive*
Ezek. 23:12, clothed most g-ly
Luke 7:25, which are g-ly apparelled
23:11, arrayed him in a g robe
Gospel—*glad tidings*
Matt. 4:23, the g of the Kingdom
11:5, have the g preached
Mark 16:15, preach the g to every
Luke 4:18, preach the g to the poor
Rom. 1:16, I am not ashamed of the g
10:16, not all obeyed the g
15:29, blessing of the g of Christ
2 Cor. 10:14, preaching the g of Christ
11:4, or another g
Gal. 1:7, pervert the g of Christ
Eph. 1:13, g of your salvation
6:15, the g of peace
Phil. 1:5, fellowship in the g
Col. 1:23, from the hope of the g
1 Pet. 4:17, that obey not the g
Rev. 14:6, the everlasting g
Government—*authority*
Is. 9:6, g . . . be upon his shoulder
22:21, thy g into his hand
1 Cor. 12:28, g-s, diversities of tongues
2 Pet. 2:10, and despise g
Governor—*chief ruler*
Gen. 42:6, Joseph was the g over
Judg. 5:9, heart is toward the g-s of
Ps. 22:28, the g among the nations
Jer. 20:1, chief g . . . house of the Lord
Matt. 2:6, come a G, that shall rule
27:11, Jesus stood before the g
Acts 7:10, he made him g over Egypt
James 3:4, withersoever the g listeth
Grace—*kindness, favor, divine mercy*
Gen. 6:8, Noah found g in the eyes of
Ex. 33:12, also found g in my sight
Esther 2:17, she obtained g and favour

Ps. 45:2, g is poured into thy lips
Luke 2:40, the g of God was upon him
John 1:16, received, and g for g
Rom. 1:5, by whom we have received g
5:2, this g wherein we stand
16:20, The g of our Lord Jesus
2 Cor. 9:8, make all g abound
12:9, My g is sufficient
1 Thess. 1:1, G be upon you, and peace
2 Thess. 2:16, good hope through g
Phil. 25, g of our Lord Jesus Christ
Heb. 4:16, the throne of g
James 4:6, giveth g unto the humble
2 Pet. 3:18, grow in g, and in the
Gracious—*abounding in mercy and love*
Gen. 43:29, God be g unto thee, my son
Ex. 33:19, g to whom I will be g
Neh. 9:31, art a g and merciful God
Ps. 77:9, God forgotten to be g
111:4, Lord is g and full of
112:4, is g and full of compassion
119:29, grant me thy law g-ly
Amos 5:15, Lord God of hosts will be g
Luke 4:22, wondered at the g words
1 Pet. 2:3, tasted that the Lord is g
Graff—*transplant in the flesh*
Rom. 11:23, God is able to g them in
24, g-ed contrary to nature
Grain—*fruit of cereal grasses*
Amos 9:9, shall not the least g fall
Matt. 13:31, to a g of mustard seed
1 Cor. 15:37, wheat, or . . . other g
Grandmother—*a parent's mother*
2 Tim. 1:5, dwelt first in thy g Lois
Grant—*confer, convey*
Lev. 25:24, g a redemption for the
Job. 10:12, Thou hast g-ed my life
Ps. 85:7, and g us thy salvation
Prov. 10:24, of the righteous . . . g-ed
Matt. 20:21, G that . . . my two sons
Mark 10:37, G unto us that we may sit
Rev. 3:21, overcometh will I g to sit
19:8, g-ed that she should
Grape—*fruit of the vine*
Num. 6:3, eat moist g-s, or dried
Deut. 32:14, pure blood of the g
Song 2:15, our vines have tender g-s
Is. 18:5, the sour g is ripening
Jer. 31:29, have eaten a sour g
Matt. 7:16, men gather g-s of thorns
Luke 6:44, bramble . . . gather they g-s
Grass—*herbage, pasture*
Gen. 1:11, the earth bring forth g

88

Num. 22:4, ox licketh up the **g**
2 Sam. 23:4, **g** springing out of the
2 King. 19:26, **g** on the house tops
Ps. 102:11, and I am withered like **g**
103:15, man, his days are as **g**
Prov. 27:25, tender **g** sheweth itself
Is. 15:6, the **g** faileth
37:27, **g** on the housetops
40:6, All flesh is **g**
7, The **g** withereth, the flower
Dan. 5:21, fed him with **g** like oxen
Matt. 6:30, God so clothe the **g** of the
1 Pet. 1:24, all flesh is as **g**, and
Grasshopper—*a jumping insect*
Lev. 11:22, and the **g** after his kind
Num. 13:33, in our own sight as **g-s**
Judg. 6:5, as **g-s** for multitude
Job. 39:20, make him afraid as a **g**
Is. 40:22, inhabitants . . . are as **g-s**
Grave—*place of burial, death*
Gen. 35:20, set a pillar upon her **g**
2 Sam. 3:32, wept at the **g** of Abner
Job 17:13, the **g** is mine house
Ps. 30:3, brought . . . soul from the **g**
49:15, from the power of the **g**
Song 8:6, jealousy is cruel as the **g**
Ezek. 37:12, I will open your **g-s**
Nah. 1:14, make thy **g** . . . thou art vile
Matt. 27:52, and the **g-s** were opened
John 11:17, lain in the **g** four days
12:17, Lazarus out of his **g**
1 Cor. 15:55, **g**, where is thy victory
Rev. 11:9, bodies to be put in **g-s**
Graven—*carved*
Ex. 20:4, make unto thee any **g** image
32:16, of God, **g** upon the tables
Lev. 26:1, you no idols nor **g** image
Ps. 97:7, they that serve **g** images
Jer. 50:38, the land of **g** images
Acts 17:29, stones, **g** by art
Gray—*whitened by age*
Gen. 42:38, down my **g** hairs with sorrow
Deut. 32:25, with the man of **g** hairs
Hos. 7:9, **g** hairs are here and there
Grayheaded—*hoary*
1 Sam. 12:2, I am old and **g**
Job. 15:10, **g** and very aged men
Ps. 71:18, also when I am old and **g**
Great—*large, big, expanded*
Gen. 1:16, two **g** lights . . . **g-er** light
12:2, will make of thee a **g** nation
15:1, thy exceeding **g** reward
Ex. 18:11, **g-er** than all gods
32:30, Ye have sinned a **g** sin

Deut. 1:17, small as well as the **g**
Judg. 1:6, cut off . . . thumbs . . . **g** toes
2 Sam. 5:10, David went on, and grew **g**
19:32, for he was a very **g** man
1 Chr. 16:25, For **g** is the Lord
Job 31:25, because my wealth was **g**
Ps. 48:1, **G** is the Lord, and greatly
57:10, mercy is **g** unto the heavens
Prov. 15:16, **g** treasure and trouble
Zeph. 1:14, The **g** day of the Lord is **near**
Mal. 4:5, the **g** and dreadful day
Matt. 2:10, rejoiced with exceeding **g**
4:16, darkness saw **g** light
5:12, **g** is your reward in heaven
7:27, **g** was the fall of it
11:11, not risen a **g-er** than John
15:28, **g** is thy faith
28:2, there was a **g** earthquake
Mark 14:43, with him a **g** multitude
Luke 2:5, wife, being **g** with child
10, good tidings of **g** joy
5:6, a **g** multitude of fishes
6:23, your reward is **g** in heaven
Luke 22:44, **g** drops of blood
John 5:20, **g-er** works than these
15:13, **G-er** love hath no man
Acts 11:5, a **g** sheet, let down
1 Cor. 13:13, **g-est** of these is charity
2 Cor. 3:12, use **g** plainness of speech
1 Tim. 6:6, contentment is **g** gain
Rev. 8:10, fell a **g** star from heaven
15:3, **G** and marvelous are thy
21:3, I heard a **g** voice out of
Greatly—*much, in a large manner*
Gen. 3:16, **g** multiply thy sorrow
Num. 14:39, the people mourned **g**
1 Sam. 28:5, his heart **g** trembled
Ps. 28:7, my heart **g** rejoiceth
89:7, God is **g** to be feared
Is. 42:17, they shall be **g** ashamed
Jer. 9:19, we are **g** confounded
Zech. 9:9, Rejoice **g**, O daughter
Matt. 12:27, ye therefore do **g** err
John 3:29, rejoiceth **g** because of the
Phil 4:10, I rejoiced in the Lord **g**
Greatness—*immensity*
Neh. 13:22, according to the **g** of thy
1 Chr. 29:11, Thine, O Lord, is the **g**
Ps. 150:2, his excellent **g**
Is. 63:1, the **g** of his strength
Jer. 13:22, the **g** of thine iniquity
Dan. 4:22, for thy **g** is grown
Eph. 1:19, **g** of his power to us-ward

89

Greedy—*avaricious*
Ps. 17:12, a lion that is g of his prey
Prov. 15:27, He that is g of gain
Is. 56:11, they are g dogs
1 Tim. 3:8, not g of filthy lucre
Greek—*person or thing of or from Greece*
Luke 23:38, G, and Latin, and Hebrew
Acts 16:1, but his father was a G
    21:37, Canst thou speak G
Gal. 3:28, neither Jew nor G
Rev. 9:11, in the G tongue
Green—*color blended of yellow and blue*
Gen. 1:30, every g herb for meat
Lev. 23:14, parched corn, nor g ears
Job 8:16, He is g before the sun
Ps. 23:2, to lie down in g pastures
    37:25, like a g bay tree
Jer. 17:2, g trees upon the high hills
Ezek. 17:24, have dried up the g tree
Luke 23:31, do these things in a g tree
Greet—*salute*
Matt. 23:7, And g-ings in the markets
Rom. 16:5, Likewise g the church that
1 Cor. 16:20, All the brethren g you
2 Tim. 4:21, Eubulus g-eth thee
1 Pet. 5:14, G ye one another with a
Grew—*became, increased*
Gen. 21:8, the child g, and was
Ex. 1:12, more they multiplied and g
1 Sam. 2:21, Samuel g before the Lord
2 Sam. 5:10, David went on and g great
Mark 4:7, thorns g up, and choked it
Luke 2:40, And the child g
Acts 12:24, word of God g and multiplied
    19:20, mightily g the word of God
Grief—*sorrow*
Gen. 26:35, Which were a g of mine
Job 2:13, that his g was very great
Ps. 31:10, my life is spent with g
Prov. 17:25, foolish son is a g to his
Is. 17:11, a heap in the day of g
    53:4, hath borne our g-s
Jer. 45:3, hath added g to my sorrow
Heb. 13:17, with joy, and not with g
Grieve—*to sorrow, be in pain*
Gen. 6:6, it g-d him at his heart
    45:5, be not g-d, nor angry with
Ps. 78:40, and g him in the desert
    95:10, Forty years long was I g-d
Amos 6:6, are not g-d for the affliction
Mark 3:5, g-d for the hardness of their
John 21:17, Peter was g-d because he

2 Cor. 2:5, he hath not g-d me, but in
Eph. 4:30, G not the holy Spirit of God
Heb. 3:10, I was g-d with that generation
Grievous—*painful, offensive*
Gen. 12:10, famine was g in the land
Ex. 8:24, a g swarm of flies
Ps. 10:5, His ways are always g
Prov. 15:1, g words stir up anger
Matt. 15:22, g-ly vexed with a devil
Acts 25:7, g complaints against Paul
Grind—*reduce to small particles*
Judg. 16:21, he did g in the prison
Eccles. 12:3, the g-ers cease
    4, sound of the g-ing is low
Is. 3:15, g the faces of the poor
    47:2, Take the millstones, and g
Matt. 21:44, it will g him to powder
    24:41, women . . . g-ing at the mill
Groan—*low sound of pain*
Ex. 2:24, God heard their g-ing
Job 24:12, Men g from out of the city
Ezek. 30:24, he shall g before him with
Joel 1:18, How do the beasts g
John 11:33, g-ed in the spirit, and
Acts 7:34, I have heard their g-ing
Rom. 8:22, g-eth and travaileth
    26, g-ings which cannot be
2 Cor. 5:2, in this we g, earnestly
Grope—*feel one's way*
Deut. 28:29, thou shalt g at noonday
Job 12:25, They g in the dark
Is. 59:10, We g for the wall
Ground—*soil, earth*
Gen. 2:5, was not a man to till the g
    7, man of the dust of the g
    9, out of the g made the Lord
    4:2, a tiller of the g
    8:21, will not again curse the g
Deut. 28:56, her foot upon the g
Josh. 3:17, stood firm on dry g
1 Sam. 3:19, his words fall to the g
2 Sam. 14:22, Joab fell to the g
Job 5:6, trouble spring out of the g
Ps. 89:44, his throne down to the g
Is. 3:26, desolate . . . sit upon the g
    29:4, spirit, out of the g
Jer. 4:3, Break up your fallow g
    14:4, Because the g is chapt
Lam. 2:21, lie on the g in the streets
Hos. 10:12, break up your fallow g
Matt. 13:8, other fell into good g
Mark 4:5, And some fell on stony g
Luke 14:18, have bought a piece of g
    19:44, lay thee even with the g

John 8:6, his finger wrote on the **g**
9:6, he spat on the **g**
Acts 7:33, thou standest is holy **g**
Eph. 3:17, rooted and **g**-ed in love
Grove—*group of trees*
Gen. 21:33, Abraham planted a **g**
Ex. 34:13, and cut down their **g**-s
1 Kin. 15:13, made an idol in a **g**
2 Kin. 17:10, **g**-s in every high hill
2 Chr. 19:3, hast taken away the **g**-s
33:19, set up **g**-s and graven
Mic. 5:14, will pluck up thy **g**-s
Grow—*increase*
Gen. 48:16, **g** into a multitude
Ex. 10:5, every tree which **g**-eth for
Judg. 16:22, hair . . . began to **g**
19:9, day **g**-eth to an end
2 Kin. 19:29, things as **g** of themselves
Ps. 90:5, like grass which **g**-eth up
147:8, who maketh grass to **g** upon
Is. 11:1, Branch shall **g** out of his
Hos. 14:5, he shall **g** as the lily
Mal. 4:2, **g** up as calves of the stall
Matt. 6:28, lilies . . . how they **g**
Eph. 4:15, **g** up into him in all things
1 Pet. 2:2, that ye may **g** thereby
2 Pet. 3:18, **g** in grace, and in the
Grown—*increased*
Ex. 2:11, when Moses was **g**, that he
Lev. 13:37, black hair **g** up therein
Deut. 32:15, waxen fat, thou art **g** thick
2 Sam. 10:5, until your beards be **g**
2 Kin. 4:18, And when the child was **g**
Prov. 24:31, all **g** over with thorns
Jer. 50:11, **g** fat as the heifer at
Grudge—*treat spitefully*
Lev. 19:18, any **g** against the children
2 Cor. 9:7, not **g**-ingly, or of
James 5:9, **G** not one against another
1 Peter 4:9, to another without **g**-ing
Guard—*defense, protection*
Gen. 40:4, **g** charged Joseph with them
1 Chr. 11:25, set him over his **g**
Jer. 39:9, captain of the **g** carried
Ezek. 38:7, be thou a **g** unto them
Acts 28:16, the captain of the **g**
Guests—*visitors*
1 Kin. 1:41, Adonijah and all the **g**
Prov. 9:18, her **g** are in the depths of
Matt. 22:10, furnished with **g**
Guide—*lead, or a leader*
Job 38:32, canst thou **g** Arcturus

Ps. 25:9, meek will he **g** in judgment
32:8, I will **g** thee with mine eye
48:14, our **g** even unto death
112:5, **g** his affairs with discretion
Prov. 23:19, **g** thine heart in the way
Is. 58:11, And the Lord shall **g** thee
Mic. 7:5, ye not confidence in a **g**
Matt. 23:16, unto you, ye blind **g**-s
Luke 1:79, **g** our feet . . . way of peace
Acts 8:31, except some man should **g** me
Rom. 2:19, art a **g** of the blind
1 Tim. 5:14, bear children, **g** the house
Guile—*craft, treachery*
Ex. 21:14, to slay him with **g**
Ps. 32:2, whose spirit there is no **g**
34:13, thy lips from speaking **g**
John 1:47, in whom is no **g**
2 Cor. 12:16, I caught you with **g**
1 Pet. 2:1, all malice, and all **g**
22, neither was **g** found in
3:10, lips that speak no **g**
Rev. 14:5, their mouth was found no **g**
Guiltless—*innocent*
Ex. 20:7, Lord will not hold him **g**
Num. 5:31, the man be **g** from iniquity
32:22, be **g** before the Lord
2 Sam. 3:28, I and my kingdom are **g**
1 Kin. 2:9, hold him not **g**
Matt. 12:7, not have condemned the **g**
Guilty—*morally delinquent*
Gen. 42:21, **g** concerning our brother
Lev. 6:4, he hath sinned, and is **g**
Num. 35:31, murderer, which is **g** of
Ezek. 22:4, become **g** in thy blood
Matt. 26:66, He is **g** of death
Rom. 3:19, become **g** before God
1 Cor. 11:27, **g** of the body and blood
James 2:10, one point, he is **g** of all
Gush—*issue violently*
Ps. 78:20, that the waters **g**-ed out
Is. 48:21, rock . . . waters **g**-ed out
Jer. 9:18, eyelids **g** out with waters
Acts 1:18, all his bowels **g** out

H

Habitation—*dwelling place*
Gen. 49:5, cruelty . . . in their **h**-s
Ex. 15:2, I will prepare him an **h**
Deut. 26:15, Look down from thy holy **h**
Job 5:3, suddenly I cursed his **h**
Ps. 71:3, Be thou my strong **h**
Prov. 3:33, blesseth the **h** of the just
Is. 34:13, be an **h** of dragons

HABITATION

Habitation (*Continued*)
Jer. 21:13, enter into our **h**-s
Hab. 3:11, moon stood still in their **h**
Luke 16:9, into everlasting **h**-s
Acts 1:20, Let his **h** be desolate
Rev. 18:2, is become the **h** of devils
Had—*held in possession, obtained, caused*
Gen. 1:31, every thing that he **h** made
12:1, the Lord **h** said unto Abram
33:10, I **h** seen the face of God
Ex. 2:6, And she **h** compassion on him
13:17, Pharaoh **h** let the people go
39:43, **h** done it as the Lord **h**
Deut. 9:16, **h** made you a molten calf
Josh. 14:15, the land **h** rest from war
Judg. 1:19, they **h** chariots of iron
8:30, for he **h** many wives
Ruth 3:7, when Boaz **h** eaten and drunk
2 Sam. 18:33, would God I **h** died for
1 Kin. 4:26, Solomon **h** forty thousand
10:4, queen of Sheba **h** seen all
11:3, he **h** seven hundred wives
2 Chr. 14:6, Lord **h** given him rest
Ezra 10:44, **h** taken strange wives
Esther 2:7, she **h** neither father nor
Ps. 27:13, I **h** fainted, unless I **h**
55:6, that I **h** wings like a dove
Ezek. 1:5, **h** the likeness of a man
Dan. 7:1, Daniel **h** a dream and visions
Matt. 1:25, she **h** brought forth her
4:2, when he **h** fasted forty days
19:1, **h** finished these sayings
20:34, **h** compassion on them
Mark 5:25, **h** an issue of blood twelve
8:7, they **h** a few small fishes
14:23, when he **h** given thanks
15:24, when they **h** crucified him
Luke 2:43, they **h** fulfilled the days
8:42, for he **h** one only daughter
10:39, she **h** a sister called Mary
23:46, Jesus **h** cried with a loud
John 2:15, when he **h** made a scourge
12:9, he **h** raised from the dead
13:12, he **h** washed their feet
26, when he **h** dipped the sop
20:18, that she **h** seen the Lord
Acts 13:3, when they **h** fasted and
16:10, he **h** seen the vision
25:6, he **h** tarried among them
1 Cor. 11:24, when he **h** given thanks
James 2:21, he **h** offered Isaac his
Rev. 21:12, and **h** twelve gates
Hail—*frozen rain drops, a salutation*
Ex. 9:18, rain a very grievous **h**

Job 38:22, the treasures of the **h**
Ps. 78:47, destroyed their vines with **h**
105:32, gave them **h** for rain
148:8, Fire, and **h**; snow, and
Ezek. 38:22, **h**-stones, fire . . . brimstone
Matt. 26:49, said, **H**, master; and kissed
28:9, saying, All **h**
Mark 15:18, **H**, King of the Jews!
Rev. 8:7, **h** and fire mingled with
16:21, **h** . . . weight of a talent
Hair—*covering of the skin*
Gen. 25:25, like an **h**-y garment
27:11, Esau . . . is a **h**-y man
42:38, bring down my gray **h**-s
Ex. 26:7, curtains of goats' **h**
Lev. 13:10, turned the **h** white
1 Sam. 14:45, not one **h** of his head
2 Sam. 14:26, weighed the **h** of his
Is. 46:4, even to hoar **h**-s will I
Dan. 3:27, nor was an **h** . . . singed
4:33, **h**-s were grown like eagles'
Matt. 5:36, one **h** white or black
10:30, **h**-s . . . are all numbered
Mark 1:6, clothed with camel's **h**
John 11:2, wiped his feet with her **h**
1 Cor. 11:14, if a man have long **h**
1 Pet. 3:3, plaiting the **h**
Half—*one of two equal parts, a part*
Gen. 24:22, earring of **h** a shekel
Ex. 24:6, Moses took **h** of the blood
1 Sam. 14:14, were an **h** acre of land
2 Sam. 10:4, shaved off the one **h** of
1 Kin. 10:7, the **h** was not told me
13:8, give me **h** thine house
Ps. 55:23, not live out **h** their days
Dan. 12:7, time, times, and an **h**
Luke 10:30, leaving him **h** dead
Rev. 12:14, times, and **h** a time
Hallowed—*consecrated*
Ex. 20:11, sabbath day, and **h** it
Lev. 12:4, she shall touch no **h** thing
1 Sam. 21:6, priest gave him **h** bread
Matt. 6:9, heaven, **H** be thy name
Halt—*stop, lame*
Gen. 32:31, **h**-ed upon his thigh
1 Kin. 18:21, **h** ye between two opinions
Ps. 38:17, I am ready to **h**, and my
Matt. 18:8, better . . . enter into life **h**
Luke 14:21, maimed, and the **h**, and the
John 5:3, blind, **h**, withered
Hammer—*an instrument for beating*
Judg. 4:21, took an **h** in her hand
5:26, with the **h** she smote

92

1 Kin. 6:7, **h** nor axe nor any tool
Is. 44:12, fashioneth it with **h-s**
Jer. 50:23, **h** of the whole earth
Hand—*end of the arm, side, act*
Gen. 13:9, left **h** . . . right **h**
16:12, every man's **h** against him
24:2, thy **h** under my thigh
27:22, **h-s** are the **h-s** of Esau
43:12, double money in your **h**
Ex. 17:12, Moses' **h-s** were heavy
21:24, **h** for **h**, foot for foot
33:22, cover thee with my **h**
Num. 11:23, Lord's **h** waxed short
Deut. 15:8, open thine **h** wide
1 Sam. 5:11, **h** of God was very heavy
16:23, harp, and . . . with his **h**
19:5, put his life in his **h**
26:18, evil is in mine **h**
27:1, escape out of his **h**
1 Kin. 18:44, cloud . . . like a man's **h**
2 Kin. 19:18, work of men's **h-s**
1 Chr. 12:2, both the right **h** . . . left
Job 2:6, Behold, he is in thine **h**
27:23, clap their **h-s** at him
31:27, mouth hath kissed my **h**
Ps. 16:8, he is at my right **h**
22:16, pierced my **h-s** . . . feet
24:4, clean **h-s**, and a pure
26:10, right **h** is full of bribes
31:5, Into thine **h** I commit
Prov. 3:16, left **h** riches and honour
10:4, dealeth with a slack **h**
11:21, Though **h** join in **h**
24:33, little folding of the **h-s**
Eccles. 9:10, thy **h** findeth to do
11:6, withhold not thine **h**
Song 2:6, right **h** doth embrace me
Is. 1:12, required this at your **h**
6:6, having a live coal in his **h**
19:4, into the **h** of a cruel lord
40:12, waters in the hollow of his **h**
Ezek. 10:2, thine **h** with coals of fire
37:1, **h** of the Lord was upon me
Dan. 4:35, none can stay his **h**
Mic. 7:3, do evil with both **h-s**
Hab. 3:4, horns coming out of his **h**
Matt. 3:2, kingdom of heaven is at **h**
5:30, right **h** offend thee
6:3, let not thy left **h** know
12:13, Stretch forth thine **h**
18:8, thy **h** or thy foot offend
22:44, Sit thou on my right **h**

Mark 16:19, sat on the right **h** of God
Luke 9:62, put his **h** to the plow
John 20:27, reach hither thy **h**
1 Cor. 12:21, eye cannot say unto the **h**
2 Cor. 5:1, house not made with **h-s**
Gal. 6:11, written . . . with mine own **h**
1 Thess. 4:11, work with your own **h-s**
2 Thess. 3:17, Paul with mine own **h**
1 Tim. 2:8, lifting up holy **h-s**
Heb. 1:13, Sit on my right **h**
12:12, the **h-s** which hang down
Rev. 1:3, for the time is at **h**
Handful—*a small quantity*
Gen. 41:47, earth brought forth by **h-s**
1 Kin. 17:12, **h** of meal in a barrel
Ps. 72:16, shall be an **h** of corn
Eccles. 4:6, Better . . . **h** with quietness
Jer. 9:22, **h** after the harvestman
Handle—*touch, feel, use the hands*
Gen. 4:21, all such as **h** the harp
Judg. 5:14, **h** the pen of the writer
Col. 2:21, touch not; taste not; **h** not
Handmaid—*female attendant*
Gen. 16:1, an **h**, an Egyptian
Ex. 23:12, the son of thy **h**
Ruth 3:9, I am Ruth thine **h**
Ps. 86:16, save the son of thine **h**
Luke 1:38, Behold the **h** of the Lord
Hang—*suspend*
Gen. 40:19, **h** thee on a tree
Deut. 21:22, and thou **h** him on a tree
28:66, thy life shall **h** in doubt
Esther 7:10, so they **h-ed** Haman
Job 26:7, **h-eth** the earth upon nothing
Ps. 137:2, **h** our harps upon the willows
Matt. 18:6, millstone were **h-ed** about
27:5, departed, and went and **h-ed**
Acts 5:30, ye slew and **h-ed** on a tree
Happen—*occur*
Prov. 12:21, no evil **h** to the just
Is. 41:22, shew us what shall **h**
Jer. 44:23, this evil is **h-ed** unto you
Mark 10:32, what things should **h**
Luke 24:14, things which had **h-ed**
1 Cor. 10:11, things **h-ed** unto them for
1 Pet. 4:12, strange thing **h-ed** unto
Happy—*care free, content, joyous*
Gen. 30:13, Leah said, H am I
Job 5:17, **h** is the man whom God
Ps. 144:15, H is that people
Prov. 3:13, H is the man that findeth
Mal. 3:15, now we call the proud **h**
John 13:17, **h** are ye if you do them

Happy (*Continued*)
1 Cor. 7:40, **h**-ier if she so abide
James 5:11, count them **h** which endure
Hard—*difficult, trying*
Gen. 18:14, any thing too **h** for the Lord
Ex. 18:26, **h** causes they brought
Deut. 15:18, shall not seem **h** unto thee
1 Kin. 10:1, prove him with **h** question
2 Kin. 2:10, hast asked a **h** thing
2 Chr. 9:1, Solomon with **h** questions
Job 41:24, **h** as a piece of . . . millstone
Ps. 63:8, soul followeth **h** after thee
Prov. 13:15, way of transgressors is **h**
Jer. 32:27, any thing too **h** for me
Ezek. 3:5, and of an **h** language
Matt. 25:24, thou art an **h** man
John 6:60, This is an **h** saying
Acts 9:5, **h** for thee to kick against
Heb. 5:11, say, and **h** to be uttered
2 Pet. 3:16, things **h** to be understood
Harden—*strengthen, stiffen*
Ex. 4:21, but I will **h** his heart
Deut. 15:7, shalt not **h** thine heart
Job 6:10, **h** myself in sorrow
Ps. 95:8, **H** not your heart
Prov. 21:29, wicked man **h**-eth his face
Mark 6:52, for their heart was **h**-ed
John 12:40, blinded their eyes, and **h**-ed
Acts 19:9, But when divers were **h**-ed
Hardness—*solidity, asperity*
Job 38:38, dust groweth into **h**
Mark 3:5, grieved for the **h** of their
16:14, unbelief and **h** of heart
Rom. 2:5, **h** and impenitent heart
2 Tim. 2:3, endure **h**, as a good
Harm—*injury, hurt, damage*
1 Sam. 26:21, no more do thee **h**
2 Kin. 4:41, no **h** in the pot
Ps. 105:15, do my prophets no **h**
Matt. 10:16, **h**-less as doves
Acts 27:21, gained this **h** and loss
Phil. 2:15, may be blameless and **h**-less
Heb. 7:26, holy, **h**-less, undefiled
1 Pet. 3:13, who is he that will **h** you
Harp—*a stringed instrument*
Gen. 4:21, handle the **h** and organ
1 Sam. 10:5, pipe, and a **h**, before them
16:16, a cunning player on an **h**
1 Chr. 25:3, prophesied with a **h**
Job 30:31, **h** . . . turned to mourning
Ps. 33:2, Praise the Lord with **h**
137:2, hanged our **h**-s upon the
150:3, with the psaltery and **h**
Rev. 14:2, harping with their **h**-s

Harrow—*tool for breaking up soil*
2 Sam. 12:31, saws, and under **h**-s of iron
1 Chr. 20:3, **h**-s of iron, and with axes
Job 39:10, will he **h** the valleys
Harvest—*gathering of crops*
Gen. 8:22, seedtime and **h** . . . not cease
45:6, neither be earing nor **h**
Ex. 23:16, feast of **h**, the firstfruits
Deut. 24:19, thou cuttest down thine **h**
Judg. 15:1, in the time of wheat **h**
Ruth 1:22, beginning of barley **h**
1 Sam. 12:17, Is it not wheat **h** to day
Prov. 6:8, gathereth her food in the **h**
10:5, he that sleepeth in **h**
25:13, cold of snow . . . time of **h**
26:1, as rain in **h**, so honour
Is. 18:4, cloud of dew . . . heat of **h**
Jer. 8:20, **h** is past, the summer is
Joel 3:13, for the **h** is ripe
Matt. 9:37, **h** truly is plenteous
13:30, grow together until the **h**
Luke 10:2, The **h** truly is great
John 4:35, white ready to **h**
Rev. 14:15, **h** of the earth is ripe
Haste—*swiftness, dispatch*
Ex. 12:11, shall eat it in **h**
1 Sam. 20:38, Make speed, **h**, stay not
2 Sam. 4:4, she made **h** to flee
Prov. 28:20, that maketh **h** to be rich
Is. 59:7, **h** to shed innocent blood
Luke 19:5, Zacchaeus, make **h**, and
Hate—*ill will, dislike intensely*
Ex. 20:5, generation of them that **h**
Lev. 19:17, shalt not **h** thy brother
Deut. 19:11, any man **h** his neighbour
Ps. 97:10, love the Lord, **h** evil
119:163, I **h** and abhor lying
Prov. 1:22, and fools **h** knowledge
8:13, froward mouth, do I **h**
13:24, spareth his rod **h**-th his
15:10, that **h**-th reproof shall die
Eccles. 3:8, love, and a time to **h**
Is. 1:14, your . . . feasts my soul **h**-th
Amos 5:15, **H** the evil, and love the
Mic. 3:2, **h** the good, and love the evil
Matt. 5:44, good to them that **h** you
6:24, either he will **h** the one
24:10, and shall **h** one another
Luke 6:22, when men shall **h** you
John 7:7, **h** you; but me it **h**-th
14:26, **h** not his father, and mother
15:18, If the world **h** you

Eph. 5:29, ever yet h-d his own flesh
1 John 3:15, Whosoever h-th his brother
Hatred—*ill will, enmity*
Ps. 25:19, hate me with cruel h
    139:22, hate them with perfect h
Prov. 10:12, H stirreth up strifes
    15:17, a stalled ox and h
Eccles. 9:6, their love, and their h
Gal. 5:20, h, variance, emulations
Haughty—*proud, overbearing*
2 Sam. 22:28, eyes are upon the h
Ps. 131:1, my heart is not h
Prov. 16:18, h spirit before a fall
    21:24, Proud and h scorner
Is. 2:17, h-ness of men . . . made low
Mic. 2:3, neither shall ye go h-ly
Head—*upper or foremost part or place*
Gen. 3:15, it shall bruise thy h
Ex. 12:27, the people bowed the h
1 Sam. 1:11, no razor come upon his h
1 Kin. 2:6, let not his hoar h go down
2 Kin. 4:19, he said . . . My h, my h
    6:5, axe h fell into the water
Ps. 24:7, Lift up your h-s, O ye
    66:12, men to ride over our h-s
    118:22, h stone of the corner
Prov. 25:22, coals of fire upon his h
Eccles. 2:14, man's eyes are in his h
Is. 59:17, helmet of salvation upon . . . h
Jer. 18:16, and wag his h
Dan. 2:38, Thou art this h of gold
    7:6, the beast had also four h-s
Matt. 5:36, swear by thy h
    14:8, Give me . . . John Baptist's h
Matt. 27:39, wagging their h-s
Mark 12:10, the h of the corner
Luke 21:18, not an hair of your h
    28, look up, and lift up your h
John 13:9, also my hands and my h
Acts 1:18, falling h-long, he burst
    21:24, they may shave their h-s
1 Cor. 11:3, h of every man is Christ
Eph. 1:22, h over all things
    5:23, Christ is the h of the church
Col. 2:19, And not holding the H
2 Tim. 3:4, Traitors, h-y, highminded
1 Pet. 2:7, made the h of the corner
Rev. 1:14, h and his hairs are white
Heal—*cure, make sound*
Ex. 15:26, the Lord that h-eth thee
Num. 12:13, H her now, O God
Deut. 32:29, alive; I wound, and I h

2 Kin. 2:21, I have h-ed these waters
2 Chr. 7:14, and will h their land
Ps. 6:2, O Lord, h me; for my bones
    147:3, h-eth the broken in heart
Is. 53:5, his stripes we are h-ed
Jer. 3:22, will h your backslidings
    17:14, h me . . . I shall be h-ed
    30:13, no h-ing medicines
Hos. 14:4, I will h their backsliding
Matt 4:23, h-ing all manner of sickness
    10:8, H the sick
Mark 3:2, would h him on the sabbath
    15, have power to h sicknesses
Luke 4:18, to h the brokenhearted
    23, Physician, h thyself
    9:2, of God, and to h the sick
    11, h-ed them . . . need of h-ing
1 Cor. 12:9, gifts of h . . . same spirit
James 5:16, pray . . . that ye may be h-ed
Rev. 22:2, the h-ing of the nations
Health—*freedom from disease or pain*
Gen. 43:28, our father is in good h
2 Sam. 20:9, art thou in h, my brother
Ps. 42:11, the h of my countenance
Prov. 3:8, shall be h to thy navel
    13:17, faithful ambassador is h
Is. 58:8, thine h shall spring forth
Jer. 30:17, will restore h unto thee
Acts 27:34, this is for your h
3 John 2, prosper and be in h
Heap—*pile, mass, great number*
Gen. 31:46, stones, and made an h
Ex. 15:8, floods . . . upright as an h
Deut. 32:23, h mischiefs upon them
Josh. 3:13, shall stand upon an h
Job 16:4, I could h up words
    27:16, though he h up silver
Ps. 33:7, waters . . . together as an h
    39:6, he h-eth up riches
Prov. 25:22, h coals of fire upon
Is. 25:2, made of a city an h
Ezek. 24:10, H on wood, kindle the fire
Hab. 1:10, for they shall h dust
2 Tim. 4:3, h to themselves teachers
James 5:3, have h-ed treasure together
Hear—*listen to, receive sound*
Gen. 4:23, H my voice; ye wives
Ex. 20:19, Speak . . . and we will h
Lev. 5:1, h the voice of swearing
Deut. 6:4, H, O Israel: the Lord is
1 Sam. 15:14, lowing . . . oxen which I h
1 Kin. 8:30, h thou in heaven
2 Kin. 4:31, neither voice, nor h-ing

Hear (*Continued*)
Job 13:17, **H** diligently my speech
    27:9, Will God **h** his cry
Job 35:13, God will not **h** vanity
Ps. 4:1, **H** me when I call, O God
    65:2, thou that **h**-est prayer
    135:17, ears, but they **h** not
Prov. 20:12, **h**-ing ear . . . seeing eye
Eccles. 12:13, Let us **h** the conclusion
Is. 1:2 **H**, O heavens and give ear
    28:14, **h** the word of the Lord
Ezek. 37:4, dry bones, **h** the word
Amos 5:23, **h** the melody of thy viols
Matt. 10:27, **h** in the ear, that preach
    11:15, ears to **h**, let him **h**
    13:13, **h**-ing they **h** not
    15:10, **H** and understand
    17:5, I am well pleased; **h** ye him
    24:6, ye shall **h** of wars
Mark 4:24, Take heed what ye **h**
    7:37, maketh both the deaf to **h**
John 5:24, He that **h**-eth my word
    6:60, who can **h** it
    10:3, and the sheep **h** his voice
    12:47, any man **h** my words
Acts 7:37, like unto me; him . . . **h**
    17:32, We will **h** thee again
Rom. 10:17, faith cometh by **h**-ing
    11:8, ears that they should not **h**
Heb. 5:11, seeing ye are dull of **h**-ing
James 1:19, every man be swift to **h**
Rev. 3:20, if any man **h** my voice
Heard—*been told, attended*
Gen. 3:10, **h** thy voice in the garden
Job 15:8, Hast thou **h** the secret
    26:14, little a portion is **h** of him
Ps. 10:17, **h** the desire of the humble
    38:13, I, as a deaf man, **h** not
Song 2:12, voice of the turtle is **h**
Is. 65:19, voice of weeping . . . no more **h**
Jer. 31:15, voice was **h** in Ramah
Ezek. 1:24, **h** the noise of their wings
Matt. 6:7, **h** for their much speaking
Luke 1:13, thy prayer is **h**
Acts 4:4, which **h** the word believed
    19:10, dwelt in Asia **h** the word
1 Cor. 2:9, Eye . . . not seen, nor ear **h**
2 Cor. 12:4, **h** unspeakable words
Eph. 1:13, ye **h** the word of truth
Phil. 4:9, learned, and received, and **h**
Rev. 10:4, I **h** a voice from heaven
Hearken—*listen*
Ex. 18:19, **H** now unto my voice
Deut. 18:15, unto him ye shall **h**

Josh. 1:17, so will we **h** unto thee
Job. 37:14, **H** unto this, O Job
Ps. 103:20, **h**-ing unto the voice of
Prov. 23:22, **H** unto thy father
    29:12, if a ruler **h** to lies
Dan. 9:19, O Lord, **h** and do
Mark 4:3, **H**; Behold . . . out a sower
Acts 12:13, a damsel came to **h**
Heart—*seat of the affections*
Gen. 8:21, the imagination of man's **h**
Ex. 4:21, I will harden his **h**
    31:6, **h**-s of all that are wise **h**-ed
Num. 15:39, seek not after your own **h**
Deut. 28:65, a trembling **h**
Josh. 5:1, their **h** melted
Judg. 5:16, great searchings of **h**
    16:25, their **h**-s were merry
1 Sam. 10:9, God gave him another **h**
    13:14, a man after his own **h**
    16:7, the Lord looketh on the **h**
2 Sam. 6:16, she despised him in her **h**
1 Kin. 3:9, an understanding **h**
    15:3, his **h** was not perfect
1 Chr. 28:9, serve him with a perfect **h**
2 Chr. 17:6, his **h** was lifted up
Job 23:16, God maketh my **h** soft
    29:13, caused the widow's **h** to sing
    41:24, **h** is as firm as a stone
Ps. 4:7, put gladness in my **h**
    9:1, O Lord, with my whole **h**
    10:6, 11, 13, said in his **h**
    12:2, and with a double **h**
    15:2, speaketh the truth in his **h**
    17:3, Thou hast proved mine **h**
    19:14, the meditation of my **h**
    22:14, my **h** is like wax
    27:3, my **h** shall not fear
    38:10, My **h** panteth
    44:21, knoweth the secrets of the **h**
    51:10, Create in me a clean **h**
    17, broken and a contrite **h**
    111:1, praise . . . with my whole **h**
    119:11, word have I hid in mine **h**
Prov. 4:23, keep thy **h** . . . all diligence
    12:20, Deceit is in the **h**
    16:5, one that is proud in **h**
    17:22, merry **h** doeth good like
    23:7, thinketh in his **h**, so is he
    26, My son, give me thine **h**
    25:20, singeth songs to a heavy **h**
Eccles. 8:5, wise man's **h** discerneth
    11:9, let thy **h** cheer thee
Song. 8:6, as a seal upon thine **h**

Is. 35:4, say to them . . . of a fearful **h**
47:10, thou hast said in thine **h**
Jer. 11:20, triest the reins and the **h**
17:9, **h** is deceitful above all
10, I, the Lord, search the **h**
24:7, give them an **h** to know me
Ezek. 11:19, one **h** . . . stony **h** . . . **h** of flesh
18:31, make you a new **h**
21:7, every **h** shall melt
44:7, 9, uncircumcised in **h**
Dan. 4:16, a beat's **h** be given unto him
Joel 2:13, rend your **h**, and not your
Mal. 4:6, turn the **h** of the fathers
Matt. 5:8, Blessed are the pure in **h**
28, adultery . . . already in his **h**
6:21, treasure is . . . your **h** be
11:29, meek and lowly in **h**
12:34, abundance of the **h**
15:8, their **h** is far from me
19:8, the hardness of your **h**-s
Mark 12:30, love the Lord . . . all thy **h**
Luke 2:19, pondered them in her **h**
51, all these sayings in her **h**
24:25, slow of **h** to believe all
John 14:1, Let not your **h** be troubled
Acts 2:37, they were pricked in their **h**
7:54, they were cut to the **h**
Rom. 8:27, he that searcheth the **h**-s
10:10, with the **h** man believeth
2 Cor. 3:3, fleshy tables of the **h**
6:11, our **h** is enlarged
9:7, he purposeth in his **h**
Eph. 3:17, Christ may dwell in your **h**-s
5:19, making melody in your **h**
6:5, in singleness of your **h**
Phil. 4:7, keep your **h**-s and minds
Col. 3:22, but in singleness of **h**
2 Thess. 3:5, Lord direct your **h**-s into
Heb. 4:12, thoughts and intents of the **h**
10:22, draw near with a true **h**
James 1:26, deceiveth his own **h**
2 Pet. 1:19, day star arise in your **h**-s
Heat—*warmth*
Gen. 8:22, cold and **h**, and summer
Gen. 18:1, in the **h** of the day
Deut. 29:24, **h** of this great anger
1 Kin. 1:1, but he gat no **h**
Job 24:19, Drought and **h** consume
Eccles. 4:11, two lie together . . . have **h**
Is. 25:4, a shadow from the **h**
Hos. 7:4, oven **h**-ed by the baker
Matt. 20:12, burden and **h** of the day

2 Pet. 3:10, melt with fervent **h**
Rev. 16:9, scorched with great **h**
Heathen—*worshippers of false gods*
Lev. 26:33, scatter you among the **h**
Ps. 2:1, Why do the **h** rage
102:15, **h** shall fear . . . the Lord
Matt. 6:7, repetitions, as the **h** do
Acts 4:25, Why did the **h** rage
Gal. 1:16, preach him among the **h**
Heaven—*firmament, abode of God*
Gen. 1:1, God created the **h**
8, God called the firmament **H**
28:17, this is the gate of **h**
Ex. 20:22, talked with you from **h**
Deut. 33:13, precious things of **h**
1 Sam. 2:10, out of **h** shall he thunder
1 Kin. 8:27, the **h** and **h** of **h**-s . . . contain
2 Kin. 7:2, Lord would . . . windows in **h**
Job 11:8, It is as high as **h**
22:12, God in the height of **h**
14, walketh in the circuit of **h**
Ps. 19:1, **h**-s declare the glory of God
103:11, **h** is high above the earth
Eccles. 5:2, God is in **h**, and thou
Is. 14:12, art thou fallen from **h**
65:17, new **h**-s and a new earth
Jer. 7:18, cakes to the queen of **h**
23:24, Do I not fill **h** and earth
Ezek. 32:8, All the bright lights of **h**
Mal. 3:10, open you the windows of **h**
Matt. 5:3, theirs is the kingdom of **h**
12, great is your reward in **h**
6:9, Father which art in **h**
14, your **h**-ly Father will also
10:7, kingdom of **h** is at hand
16:19, keys . . . kingdom of **h**
Mark 13:31, **H** and earth shall pass
Luke 10:20, your names are written in **h**
15:18, have sinned against **h**
John 3:12, I tell you of **h**-ly things
13, Son of man which is in **h**
1 Cor. 15:47, second man is . . . from **h**
48, the **h**-ly . . . that are **h**-ly
2 Cor. 5:1, eternal in the **h**-s
12:2, caught up to the third **h**
Gal. 1:8, or an angel from **h**, preach
Eph. 6:9, Master also is in **h**
Phil. 3:20, our conversation is in **h**
Heb. 12:23, written in **h**
James 5:12, swear not, neither by **h**
18, and the **h** gave rain
Rev. 4:1, a door was opened in **h**
21:1, I saw a new **h**

Heavy—*weighty, burdensome, slow*
Ex. 17:12, Moses' hands were **h**
2 Chr. 10:10, father made our yoke **h**
    11, put a **h** yoke upon you
Ps. 38:4, burden . . . too **h** for me
    69:20, I am full of **h**-ness
Prov. 25:20, songs to an **h** heart
    27:3, a fool's wrath is **h**-ier
Is. 58:6, to undo the **h** burdens
Matt. 11:28, labour and are **h** laden
    23:4, they bind **h** burdens
    26:43, their eyes were **h**
Luke 9:32, were **h** with sleep
Hedge—*a fence of bushes, obstruction*
Job 1:10, made an **h** about him
Prov. 15:19, is as an **h** of thorns
Mic. 7:4, sharper than a thorn **h**
Luke 14:23, into the highways and **h**-s
Heed—*give attention*
Ps. 39:1, take **h** to my ways
Mark 13:5, Take **h** lest any man deceive
1 Tim. 1:4, give **h** to fables
Heb. 2:1, give the more earnest **h**
Heel—*hinder part of the foot*
Gen. 3:15, thou shalt bruise his **h**
    25:26, took hold on Esau's **h**
    49:17, that biteth the horse **h**
Ps. 41:9, lifted up his **h** against me
Height—*elevation, altitude*
Job 22:12, God in the **h** of heaven
Prov. 25:3, The heaven for **h**
Rom. 8:39, Nor **h**, nor depth
Rev. 21:16, breadth and the **h** . . . equal
Heir—*one who inherits*
Gen. 15:3, born in my house is mine **h**
Prov. 30:23, handmaid that is **h** to her
Jer. 49:1, Hath Israel no sons . . . no **h**
Matt. 21:38, This is the **h**; come
Rom. 8:17, then **h**-s; **h**-s of God
Gal. 4:7, **h** of God through Christ
James 2:5, and **h**-s of the kingdom
Held—*retained, restrained*
Gen. 24:21, wondering . . . **h** his peace
Esther 7:4, I had **h** my tongue
Dan. 12:7, he **h** up his right hand
Matt. 26:63, But Jesus **h** his peace
Hell—*place of the dead, or of punishment*
Deut. 32:22, burn unto the lowest **h**
2 Sam. 22:6, sorrows of **h** compassed
Job 26:6, **H** is naked before him
Ps. 16:10, not leave my soul in **h**
    86:13, my soul from the lowest **h**
    139:8, if I make my bed in **h**

Prov. 5:5, steps take hold on **h**
    27:20, **H** and destruction
Ezek. 32:21, speak to him out of . . . **h**
Amos 9:2, Though they dig into **h**
Jonah 2:2, out of the belly of **h**
Hab. 2:5, enlargeth his desire as **h**
Matt. 5:22, in danger of **h** fire
    10:28, destroy . . . body in **h**
    16:18, gates of **h** . . . not prevail
    23:15, more the child of **h**
Luke 16:23, in **h** he lift up his eyes
Acts 2:31, soul was not left in **h**
James 3:6, tongue . . . set on fire of **h**
2 Pet. 2:4, angels . . . cast them down to **h**
Rev. 1:18, have the keys of **h**
Helmet—*head armor*
1 Sam. 17:5, an **h** of brass upon his
Is. 59:17, an **h** of salvation
Eph. 6:17, take the **h** of salvation
Help—*aid, assistance*
Gen. 2:18, an **h** meet for him
2 Cor. 20:9, thou wilt hear and **h**
Job 6:13, Is not my **h** in me
Ps. 33:20, our **h** and our shield
    46:1, very present **h** in trouble
    121:1, hills . . . whence cometh my **h**
Is. 41:6, **h**-ed every one his neighbour
    13, Fear not; I will **h** thee
Matt. 15:25, Lord **h** me
Mark 9:24, **h** thou mine unbelief
2 Cor. 1:11, **h**-ing together by prayer
Heb. 4:16, grace to **h** in time of need
Helper—*one who aids*
Job 30:13, they have no **h**
Ps. 10:14, the **h** of the fatherless
    30:10, Lord, be thou my **h**
    54:4, God is mine **h**
Rom. 16:3, my **h**-s in Christ Jesus
Heb. 13:6, Lord is my **h**
Hence—*from this place*
Gen. 37:17, They are departed **h**
Ex. 13:19, carry my bones away **h**
Matt. 4:10, Get thee **h**, Satan
    23:39, shall not see me **h**-forth
    26:29, not drink **h**-forth of
John 15:55, **H**-forth I call you not
    20:15, if thou have borne him **h**
Rom. 6:6, **h**-forth we should not serve
Eph. 4:14, **h** be no more children
Herb—*plants*
Gen. 1:11, the **h** yielding seed
Deut. 11:10, as a garden of **h**-s
Ps. 37:2, and wither as the green **h**

Matt. 13:32, the greatest among **h**-s
Rom. 14:2, who is weak, eateth **h**-s
Herd—*a number of animals*
Gen. 13:5, Abram, had flocks, and **h**-s
Jonah 3:7, man nor beast, flock nor **h**
Hab. 3:17, be no **h** in the stalls
Matt. 8:30, an **h** of many swine
Heritage—*a possession*
Ex. 6:8, give it you for an **h**
Job 20:29, **h** appointed unto him by
Ps. 16:6, I have a goodly **h**
127:3, children . . . **h** of the Lord
1 Pet. 5:3, lords over God's **h**
Hid—*concealed, secreted*
Gen. 3:8, Adam and his wife **h**
Deut. 33:19, treasures **h** in the sand
Josh. 2:4, took the two men, and **h**
1 Sam. 20:24, David **h** himself in the
2 Sam. 17:9, he is **h** now in some pit
Job 38:30, waters are **h** as with a
Ps. 19:6, nothing **h** from the heat
69:5, sins are not **h** from thee
Is. 45:3, **h**-den riches of secret places
50:6, **h** not my face from shame
Matt. 13:44, treasure **h** in a field
25:25, **h** thy talent in the earth
4:22, For there is nothing **h**
John 8:59, Jesus **h** himself
1 Cor. 2:7, even the **h**-den wisdom
Col. 3:3, your life is **h** with Christ
Heb. 11:23, **h** three months of his
Hide—*to secrete*
Gen. 18:17, Shall I **h** from Abraham
Job 14:13, **h** me in the grave
20:12, **h** it under his tongue
Ps. 27:5, time of trouble . . . **h** me
9, **H** not thy face far from me
Is. 2:10, **h** thee in the dust
3:9, their sin . . . they **h** it not
Jer. 38:14, **h** nothing from me
James 5:20, **h** a multitude of sins
High—*elevated, arrogant*
Gen. 29:7, Lo, it is yet **h** day
Deut. 2:27, go along by the **h** way
2 Sam. 22:3, my **h** tower, and my refuge
Job 11:8, It is as **h** as heaven
22:12, the stars, how **h** they are
Ps. 49:2, low and **h**, rich and poor
62:9, men of **h** degree are a lie
91:14, I will set him on **h**
103:11, heaven is **h** above the
Prov. 24:7, Wisdom is too **h** for a fool
Is. 32:15, spirit be poured . . . from on **h**

Matt. 4:8, an exceeding **h** mountain
Mark 5:7, Son of the most **h** God
Mark 11:10, Hosanna in the **h**-est
Luke 1:78, dayspring from on **h**
2:14, Glory to God in the **h**-est
John 19:31, sabbath day was an **h** day
Rom. 12:16, Mind not **h** things
13:11, **h** time to awake
Phil. 3:14, prize of the **h** calling
Heb. 3:1, Apostle and **H** Priest
Hill—*elevated ground*
Gen. 49:26, of the everlasting **h**-s
Deut. 11:11, a land of **h**-s and valleys
Ps. 15:1, dwell in thy holy **h**
24:3, Who shall ascend into the **h**
50:10, cattle upon a thousand **h**-s
121:1, lift up mine eyes unto the **h**-s
Is. 5:1, vineyard in a very fruitful **h**
25, the **h**-s did tremble
Matt. 5:14, city that is set on an **h**
Luke 4:29, unto the brow of the **h**
23:30, and to the **h**-s, Cover us
Hinder—*check, retard, obstruct*
Gen. 24:56, **H** me not, seeing the Lord
Job 11:10, who can **h** him
Luke 11:52, them . . . entering in ye **h**-ed
1 Cor. 9:12, we should **h** the gospel
Gal. 5:7, who did **h** you that ye
1 Thess. 2:18, but Satan **h**-ed us
1 Pet. 3:7, your prayers be not **h**-ed
Hire—*wages, pay, to let or lease*
Gen. 30:18, God hath given me my **h**
Deut. 24:15, shalt give him his **h**
Is. 7:20, with a razor that is **h**-ed
Mic. 3:11, priests . . . teach for **h**
Zech. 8:10, no **h** for man . . . **h** for beast
Matt. 20:1, went . . . to **h** labourers
7, no man hath **h**-ed us
Luke 10:7, labourer is worthy of his **h**
15:19, as one of thy **h**-ed servants
Hitherto—*to this place, up to now*
Josh. 17:14, Lord hath blessed me **h**
1 Sam. 7:12, **H** hath the Lord helped us
John 5:17, My Father worketh **h**
1 Cor. 3:2, **h** ye were not able to bear
Hold—*retain, sustain, accept, judge*
Ex. 20:7, not **h** him guiltless
Judg. 18:19, **H** thy peace
Job 6:24, and I will **h** my tongue
27:6, righteousness I **h** fast
Ps. 119:117, **H** thou me up
Prov. 4:13, Take fast **h** of instruction
Is. 4:1, seven women . . . **h** of one man

Hold (*Continued*)
33:15, from h-ing of bribes
41:13, God will **h** thy right hand
Amos 6:10, H thy tongue
Matt. 6:24, he will **h** to the one
Mark 7:8, **h** the tradition of men
Phil. 2:16, H-ing forth the word of
29, **h** such in reputation
1 Thess. 5:21, **h** fast that which is good
1 Tim. 1:19, H-ing faith . . . conscience
6:12, lay **h** on eternal life
Titus 1:9, H-ing fast the faithful word
Hole—*cavity, opening*
2 Kin. 12:9, bored a **h** in the lid of it
Song 5:4, by the **h** of the door
Is. 11:8, play on the **h** of the asp
Ezek. 8:7, a **h** in
Hag. 1:6, put it into a bag with **h-s**
Matt. 8:20, foxes have **h-s**
Holiness—*freedom from sin, sacredness*
Ex. 15:11, like thee, glorious in **h**
28:36, H to the Lord
1 Chr. 16:29, in the beauty of **h**
Ps. 29:2, in the beauty of **h**
47:8, the throne of his **h**
93:5, **h** becometh thine house
Is. 35:8, be called The way of **h**
Jer. 31:23, and mountain of **h**
Rom. 6:22, have your fruit unto **h**
2 Cor. 7:1, perfecting **h** in the fear
1 Thess. 3:13, hearts unblameable in **h**
1 Tim. 2:15, faith . . . charity and **h**
Heb. 12:10, partakers of his **h**
Holy—*sacred, acceptable to God*
Ex. 3:5, the place . . . is **h** ground
20:8, sabbath day, to keep it **h**
Lev. 20:7, be ye **h**, for I am the Lord
Deut. 7:6, thou art an **h** people
1 Sam. 2:2, none **h** as the Lord
2 Kin. 4:9, this is an **h** man of God
1 Chr. 16:10, Glory ye in his **h** name
Ps. 11:4, Lord is in his **h** temple
16:10, suffer thine H One to see
99:9, worship at his **h** hill
145:21, bless his **h** name
Is. 6:3, H, **h**, **h**, is the Lord
Hab. 2:20, Lord is in his **h** temple
Matt. 7:6, give not that which is **h**
Mark 6:20, a just man and an **h**
Luke 1:49, **h** is his name
4:34, the H One of God
John 17:11, H Father, keep . . . thine own
Acts 2:27, thine H One

Rom. 12:1, a living sacrifice, **h**
16:16, with an **h** kiss
1 Cor. 3:17, the temple of God is **h**
7:34, **h** both in body and in spirit
Eph. 1:4, be **h** and without blame
Col. 1:22, **h** and unblameable
1 Tim. 2:8, lifting up **h** hands
2 Tim. 1:9, called us with an **h** calling
3:15, hast known the **h** scriptures
Holy Ghost—*God's Spirit, the Comforter*
Matt. 1:20, in her is of the H G
3:11, baptize you with the H G
12:31, blasphemy against the H G
Luke 3:22, H G descended in a bodily
4:1, full of the H G
12:12, H G shall teach you
John 14:26, Comforter . . . the H G
20:22, Receive ye the H G
Acts 2:4, all filled with the H G
38, the gift of the H G
7:51, do always resist the H G
10:38, the H G and with power
19:2, Have ye received the H G
Rom. 9:1, witness in the H G
1 Cor. 2:13, which the H G teacheth
Holy Spirit—*God's Spirit*
Luke 11:13, give the H S to them
Eph. 1:13, that **h** S of promise
4:30, grieve not the H S of God
1 Thess. 4:8, given unto his **h** S
Home—*dwelling, place of refuge*
Lev. 18:9, she be born at **h**
Deut. 24:5, be free at **h** one year
Ruth 1:21, brought me **h** again empty
1 Kin. 13:15, Come **h** with me, and eat
2 Chr. 25:19, abide now at **h**
Prov. 7:19, the goodman is not at **h**
Eccles. 12:5, goeth to his long **h**
Mark 5:19, Go **h** to thy friends, and tell
John 19:27, took her unto his own **h**
1 Cor. 11:34, hunger, let him eat at **h**
14:35, ask their husbands at **h**
2 Cor. 5:6, are at **h** in the body
1 Tim. 5:4, shew piety at **h**
Titus 2:5, discreet . . . keepers at **h**
Honest—*upright, truthful*
Luke 8:15, an **h** and good heart
Acts 6:3, seven men of **h** report
Rom. 12:17, **h** in the sight of all men
13:13, Let us walk **h-ly**, as in
2 Cor. 8:21, Providing for **h** things
13:7, do that which is **h**
Phil. 4:8, whatsoever things are **h**
1 Thess. 4:12, That we may walk **h-ly**

1 Tim. 2:2, in all godliness and **h**-y
Heb. 13:18, willing to live **h**-ly
Honour—*esteem, respect*
Ex. 20:12, H thy father and thy mother
Lev. 19:32, **h** the face of the old man
Num. 27:20, some of thine **h** upon him
1 Sam. 2:30, them that **h** me I will **h**
1 Kin. 3:13, not asked, both riches and **h**
1 Chr. 29:28, full of days, riches, and **h**
Ps. 96:6, H and majesty are before
Prov. 15:33, and before **h** is humility
Eccles. 6:2, riches, wealth, and **h**
Matt. 13:57, prophet is not without **h**
15:4, H thy father and mother
8, **h**-est me with their lips
John 5:23, all men should **h** the Son
44, receive **h** one of another
Rom. 2:10, glory, **h**, and peace
12:10, in **h** preferring one another
13:7, dues . . . **h** to whom **h**
1 Tim. 5:17, worthy of double **h**
6:16, **h** and power everlasting
1 Pet. 2:17, H all men . . . H the king
3:7, giving **h** unto the wife
Rev. 5:13, Blessing, and **h**, and glory
Honourable—*worthy of respect*
Gen. 34:19, more **h** than all the house
1 Sam. 9:6, he is an **h** man
Ps. 45:9, among thy **h** women
Is. 9:15, ancient and **h**, he is the
Nah. 3:10, cast lots for her **h** men
Mark 15:43, an **h** counsellor
Acts 13:50, devout and **h** women
Heb. 13:4, Marriage is **h** in all
Hope—*pleasing expectancy, desire*
Ruth 1:12, I have **h**
Job 7:6, days . . . spent without **h**
31:24, have made gold my **h**
Ps. 39:7, my **h** is in thee
71:5, thou art my **h**, O Lord
119:81, I **h** in thy word
Prov. 13:12, H deferred . . . heart sick
19:18, while there is **h**
26:12, more **h** of a fool
Eccles. 9:4, to all the living . . . **h**
Is. 57:10, There is no **h**
Luke 6:35, **h**-ing for nothing again
Acts 2:26, my flesh shall rest in **h**
23:6, **h** and resurrection . . . dead
28:20, **h** of Israel I am bound
Rom. 4:18, against **h** believed in **h**
5:5, **h** maketh not ashamed
8:24, **h** . . . seen is not **h**
12:12, Rejoicing in **h**

1 Cor. 13:7, **h**-eth all things
13, abideth faith, **h**, charity
2 Cor. 1:7, **h** of you is stedfast
Gal. 5:5, the **h** of righteousness
Eph. 4:4, are called in one **h** of your
Col. 1:23, away from the **h** of the gospel
27, the **h** of glory
1 Thess. 5:8, helmet, the **h** of salvation
2 Thess. 2:16, good **h** through grace
Titus 3:7, the **h** of eternal life
Heb. 6:19, **h** we have as an anchor
11:1, substance of things **h**-ed for
1 Pet. 1:3, begotten . . . a lively **h**
Horn—*an appendage, symbol of strength*
Gen. 22:13, ram caught . . . by his **h**
Josh. 6:5, long blast with the ram's **h**
2 Sam. 22:3, the **h** of my salvation
Dan. 7:7, and it had ten **h**-s
Hab. 3:4, **h**-s coming out of his hand
Rev. 5:6, seven **h**-s and seven eyes
Horrible—*dreadful, terrible*
Ps. 11:6, and an **h** tempest
40:2, up also out of an **h** pit
Jer. 5:30, wonderful and **h** thing
Hos. 6:10, I have seen an **h** thing
Horse—*a hoofed quadruped*
Gen. 49:17, biteth the **h** heels
1 Kin. 10:29, **h** for an hundred and
Job 39:19, given the **h** strength
Ps. 32:9, Be ye not as the **h** . . . mule
33:17, **h** is a vain thing for
Prov. 26:3, A whip for the **h**
Jer. 4:13, **h**-s are swifter than eagles
46:4, Harness the **h**
Hos. 14:3, we will not ride upon **h**-s
Hospitality—*entertainment of strangers*
Rom. 12:13; 1 Tim. 3:2, given to **h**
Titus 1:8, but a lover of **h**
1 Pet. 4:9, Use **h** one to another
Host—*great multitude, an entertainer*
Gen. 32:2, This is God's **h**
Deut. 4:19, even all the **h** of heaven
Josh. 5:15, captain of the Lord's **h**
1 Chr. 12:22, **h**, like the **h** of God
Ps. 24:10, Lord of **h**-s, he is the King
27:3, Though an **h** should encamp
Is. 48:2, Lord of **h**-s is his name
Luke 2:13, multitude of the heavenly **h**
10:35, and gave them to the **h**
Rom. 16:23, Gaius mine **h**
Hot—*having warmth, fiery*
Ex. 16:21, when the sun waxed **h**

101

Hot (*Continued*)
32:19, Moses' anger waxed **h**
Deut. 9:19, anger and **h** displeasure
2 Sam. 11:15, forefront of the **h**-est
Ps. 39:3, My heart was **h** within me
Prov. 6:28, Can one go upon **h** coals
1 Tim. 4:2, seared with a **h** iron
Rev. 3:15, art neither cold not **h**
Hour—*a division or point in time*
Dan. 3:6, the same **h** be cast
Matt. 8:13, healed in the self same **h**
20:12, have wrought but one **h**
24:36, day and **h** knoweth no man
26:40, not watch with me one **h**
Mark 13:32, day . . . **h** knoweth no man
15:34, ninth **h** Jesus cried
Luke 12:39, what **h** the thief would
John 5:25, the **h** is coming, and now
11:9, are there not twelve **h**-s
12:27, Father, save me from this **h**
17:1, Father, the **h** is come
Acts 3:1, at the **h** of prayer
Rev. 3:10, the **h** of temptation
House—*dwelling place, family group*
Gen. 15:3, one born in my **h** is mine
Ex. 20:2, out of the **h** of bondage
17, not covet thy neighbour's **h**
Deut. 8:12, hast built goodly **h**-s
22:8, thou buildest a new **h**
2 Kin. 20:1, Set thine **h** in order
Neh. 13:11, the **h** of God forsaken
Job 30:23, **h** appointed for all living
Ps. 23:6, dwell in the **h** of the Lord
55:14, walked into the **h** of God
84:3, sparrow hath found an **h**
93:5, holiness becometh thine **h**
102:7, a sparrow . . . on the **h** top
127:1, Except the Lord build the **h**
Prov. 9:1, Wisdom hath builded her **h**
24:3, wisdom is an **h** builded
Eccles. 7:2, **h** of mourning . . . **h** of
Is. 5:8, them that join **h** to **h**
6:4, **h** was filled with smoke
Matt. 7:25, winds . . . beat upon that **h**
10:12, come into an **h**, salute it
12:25, **h** divided against itself
21:13, **h** shall be called the **h**
23:38, your **h** is left . . . desolate
Mark 12:40, devour widows' **h**-s
Luke 10:7, Go not from **h** to **h**
11:17, a **h** divided against a **h**
John 14:2, Father's **h** are many mansions
Acts 2:46, breaking bread from **h** to **h**
7:49, what **h** will ye build me

Rom. 16:5, church that is in their **h**
2 Cor. 5:1, **h** not made with hands
2, **h** which is from heaven
1 Tim. 3:4, ruleth well his own **h**
15, behave . . . in the **h** of God
2 Tim. 3:6, sort . . . which creep into **h**-s
1 Pet. 2:5, built up a spiritual **h**
Household—*a family*
Gen. 18:19, children and his **h** after
Ex. 1:1, every man and his **h**
Prov. 31:27, looketh well to . . . her **h**
Matt. 10:36, man's foes . . . of his own **h**
13:52, a man that is an **h**-er
Gal. 6:10, them . . . of the **h** of faith
Eph. 2:19, and of the **h** of God
Humble—*depress, not high*
Ex. 10:3, refuse to **h** thyself
Deut. 8:2, **h** thee, and to prove thee
2 Chr. 34:27, **h** thyself before God
Ps. 35:13, **h**-d my soul with fasting
Prov. 6:3, go, **h** thyself, and make sure
Mic. 6:8, walk **h**-y with thy God
2 Cor. 12:21, my God will **h** me among
Col. 3:12, Put on . . . **h**-ness of mine
James 4:6, giveth grace unto the **h**
Hunger—*desire for food*
Deut. 8:3, suffered thee to **h**
28:48, in **h**, and in thirst
Prov. 19:15, idle soul shall suffer **h**
Is. 49:10, shall not **h** nor thirst
Matt. 5:6, Blessed are they which do **h**
25:35, I was an **h**-ed
Luke 15:17, and I perish with **h**
John 6:35, cometh to me shall never **h**
Rom. 12:20, if thine enemy **h**, feed
1 Cor. 11:34, if any man **h**
Hungry—*having a craving desire*
2 Sam. 17:29, The people is **h**, and weary
Job 22:7, withholden bread from the **h**
Ps. 50:12, If I were **h**
146:7, giveth food to the **h**
Prov. 25:21, If thine enemy be **h**
Is. 29:8, when an **h** man dreameth
Ezek. 18:7, given his bread to the **h**
1 Cor. 11:21, one is **h** and another is
Phil. 4:12, to be full and to be **h**
Hunt—*search for, follow after*
Gen. 10:9, mighty **h**-er before the Lord
27:5, field to **h** for venison
1 Sam. 26:20, doth **h** a partridge
Ps. 140:11, evil shall **h** the violent
Ezek. 13:18, **h** the souls of my people
Mic. 7:2, **h** every man his brother

Hurt—*cause pain, wound*
Gen. 4:23, a young man to my **h**
Ps. 15:4, sweareth to his own **h**
    105:18, feet they **h** with fetters
Is. 11:9, They shall not **h** nor destroy
Jer. 25:6, I will do you no **h**
Mark 16:18, deadly thing . . . not **h** them
Acts 27:10, with **h** and much damage
Rev. 6:6, **h** not the oil and the wine
Husband—*a man who has a wife*
Gen. 3:16, desire shall be to thy **h**
    29:32, now . . . my **h** will love me
    30:20, how will my **h** dwell with me
Ex. 4:25, a bloody **h** art thou
Prov. 12:4, woman is a crown to her **h**
Is. 54:5, thy Maker is thine **h**
Mark 10:12, shall put away her **h**
John 4:16, Go, call thy **h**
Rom. 7:2, 3, if her **h** be dead
1 Cor. 7:2, every woman . . . her own **h**
    3, **h** render unto the wife
2 Cor. 11:2, espoused you to one **h**
Eph. 5:23, **h** is the head of the wife
    25, **H**-s, love your wives
Rev. 21:2, bride adorned for her **h**
Hymn—*sacred song*
Matt. 26:30, sung an **h**, they went out
Eph. 5:19, psalms and **h**-s and
Hyprocrisy—*false appearances*
Is. 32:6, work iniquity, to practice **h**
Matt. 23:28, within ye are full of **h**
1 Tim. 4:2, Speaking lies in **h**
James 3:17, wisdom . . . without **h**
Hypocrite—*deceiver, cheat*
Job 8:13, **h**'s hope shall perish
    15:34, the congregation of **h**-s
Is. 9:17, for every one is an **h**
Matt. 7:5, Thou **h**, first cast out
    22:18, Why tempt ye me, ye **h**-s
    23:13, scribes and Pharisees, **h**-s
Luke 12:56, Ye **h**-s, ye can discern

I

Idle—*unemployed, vain*
Ex. 5:8, for they be **i**
    17, Ye are **i**, ye are **i**
Prov. 19:15, **i** soul shall suffer hunger
    31:27, eateth . . . bread of **i**-ness
Ezek. 16:49, abundance of **i**-ness
Matt. 12:36, every **i** word that men shall
    20:6, Why stand ye here . . . **i**

Luke 24:11, words seemed . . . as **i** tales
1 Tim. 5:13, not only **i**, but tattlers
Idol—*a false god*
Lev. 19:4, Turn ye not unto **i**-s
Is. 66:3, as if he blessed an **i**
Jer. 50:38, they are mad upon their **i**-s
Acts 15:20, abstain from . . . **i**-s
1 Cor. 10:7, Neither be **i**-aters
1 John 5:21, keep yourself from **i**-s
Ignorance—*want or neglect of knowledge*
Lev. 4:2, soul shall sin through **i**
    5:15, trespass, and sin through **i**
Acts 17:30, this **i** God winked at
Eph. 4:8, the **i** that is in them
1 Pet. 1:14, former lusts in your **i**
    2:15, silence the **i** of foolish
Ignorant—*unenlightened*
Is. 63:16, Abraham be **i** of us
Acts 4:13, unlearned and **i** men
    17:23, Whom . . . ye **i**-ly worship
Rom. 1:13, would not have you **i**
1 Cor. 14:38, man be **i**, let him be **i**
2 Cor. 2:11, not **i** of his devices
2 Pet. 3:8, not **i** of this one thing
Ill—*contrary to good*
Gen. 41:3, **i** favoured and leanfleshed
    43:6, dealt so **i** with me
Is. 3:11, it shall be **i** with him
Rom. 13:10, Love worketh no **i**
Image—*copy, likeness, idol*
Gen. 1:26, Let us make man in our **i**
    9:6, **i** of God made he man
Ex. 20:4, not make . . . any graven **i**
Job 4:16, **i** was before mine eyes
Matt. 22:20, **i** and superscription
1 Cor. 11:7, the **i** and glory of God
Col. 1:15, **i** of the invisible God
Imagination—*conceit, fancy*
Gen. 8:21, **i** of man's heart is evil
Deut. 31:21, for I know their **i**
Jer. 3:17, **i** of their evil heart
Rom. 1:21, become vain in their **i**-s
2 Cor. 10:5, Casting down **i**-s
Imagine—*fancy, scheme, devise*
Ps. 2:1, the people **i** a vain thing
    21:11, **i**-d a mischievous device
Zech. 7:10, **i** evil against his brother
Acts 4:25, people **i** vain things
Immediately—*at once*
Matt. 26:74, the cock crew
Mark 4:15, Satan cometh **i**
John 5:9, **i** the man was made whole

Immediately (*Continued*)
Acts 13:11, i there fell . . . a mist
Rev. 4:2, i I was in the spirit
Immortality—*unending existence*
1 Cor. 15:53, mortal must put on i
1 Tim. 6:16, Whom only hath i
2 Tim. 1:10, brought life and i to
Impossible—*unattainable*
Matt. 19:26, With men this is i
Luke 1:37, with God nothing shall be i
Heb. 6:18, it was i for God to lie
11:6, without faith it is i to
Impute—*ascribe, charge*
2 Sam. 19:19, Let not my lord i iniquity
Rom. 4:6, God i-eth righteousness
5:13, sin is not i-ed when there is
2 Cor. 5:19, not i-ing their trespasses
Incline—*lean or tend toward*
Josh. 24:23, i your heart unto the Lord
Ps. 119:36, I my heart unto thy
Prov. 2:18, her house i-eth unto death
Is. 37:17, I thine ear, O Lord
Incorruptible—*incapable of dissolution*
1 Cor. 9:25, corruptible . . . but we an i
15:52, dead shall be raised i
1 Pet. 1:4, To an inheritance i
Increase—*growth, amplify, expand*
Deut. 6:3, that ye may i mightily
14:22, tithe all the i
Job 31:12, root out all mine i
Ps. 62:10, riches i, set not your heart
67:6, the earth yield her i
Prov. 28:8, usury and unjust gain i-eth
Eccles. 1:18, i knowledge, i sorrow
Luke 2:52, Jesus i-ed in wisdom
1 Cor. 3:6, but God gave the i
2 Cor. 10:15, when your faith is i
Col. 1:10, i-ing in the knowledge of God
Indeed—*verily, truly*
Gen. 20:12, yet i she is my sister
Jos. 7:20, I I have sinned against the
2 Sam. 14:5, I am i a widow woman
1 Kin. 8:27, God i dwell on the earth
Matt. 3:11, I i baptize you with water
Luke 24:34, The Lord is risen i
John 6:55, For my flesh is meat i
8:36, ye shall be free i
Rom. 14:20, All things i are pure
1 Tim. 5:5, she that is a widow i
Indignation—*anger, ire, wrath*
Deut. 29:28, wrath, and in great i
Ps. 69:24, Pour out thine i upon them
Is. 30:27, his lips are full of i
Jer. 15:17, thou hast filled me with i

Nah. 1:6, who can stand before his i
Matt. 20:24, were moved with i
Luke 13:14, answered with i
Heb. 10:27, of judgment and fiery i
Infirmity—*weakness, failing*
Ps. 77:10, I said, This is my i
Matt. 8:17, himself took our i-es
Luke 13:12, art loosed from thine i
John 5:5, an i thirty and eight years
Rom. 15:1, bear the i-es of the weak
2 Cor. 12:9, I rather glory in mine i-es
Gal. 4:13, through i of the flesh
1 Tim. 5:23, and thine often i-es
Heb. 4:15, feeling of our i-es
Inhabitants—*permanent residents*
Gen. 34:30, stink among the i
Num. 13:32, eateth up the i thereof
Ruth 4:4, Buy it before the i
Ps. 49:1, give ear, all ye i
Joel 2:1, i of the land tremble
Inherit—*come into possession of*
Gen. 15:1, give thee this land to i it
Ex. 32:13, they shall i it for ever
Judg. 11:2, not i in our father's house
Ps. 37:11, meek shall i the earth
Prov. 3:35, The wise shall i glory
14:18, The simple i folly
Is. 54:3, shall i the Gentiles
Matt. 5:5, meek . . . shall i the earth
19:29, shall i everlasting life
25:34, i the Kingdom prepared
Luke 10:25, do to i eternal life
1 Cor. 6:9, shall not i the kingdom
15:50, corruption i in corruption
Rev. 21:7, overcometh shall i all things
Inheritance—*a gift or blessing*
Ex. 34:9, take us for thine i
Deut. 4:2, be unto him a people of i
Ps. 2:8, give . . . heathen for thine i
28:9, and bless thine i
94:14, neither will he forsake his i
Prov. 13:22, man leaveth an i to his
Eccles. 7:11, Wisdom is good with an i
Mark 12:7, the i shall be ours
Acts 7:5, he gave him none i
Eph. 1:11, In whom . . . we . . . obtained
an i
1 Pet. 1:4, an i incorruptible
Iniquity—*want of uprightness, sin*
Lev. 16:22, shall bear . . . all their i-es
Deut. 5:9, visiting the i of the fathers
32:4, a God . . . without i
Job 4:8, plow i, and sow wickedness
13:26, possess the i-es of my youth

Ps. 25:11, pardon mine i, for it is
   32:5, mine i have I not hid
   51:5, I was shapen in i and in sin
     9, blot out all mine i-es
Prov. 22:8, that soweth i shall reap
Is. 1:4, a people laden with i
   31:2, help of them that work i
   53:5, he was bruised for our i-es
Jer. 31:30, shall die for his own i
Ezek. 18:30, i shall not be your ruin
   33:8, shall die in his i
Matt. 24:12, because i shall abound
Luke 13:27, depart . . . all ye workers of i
1 Cor. 13:6, Rejoiceth not in i, but
Titus 2:14, redeem us from all i
James 3:6, tongue is . . . a world of i

Innocent—*harmless, guiltless*
Ex. 23:7, the i . . . slay thou not
Job 4:7, who ever perished, being i
   22:19, i laugh them to scorn
Prov. 6:17, hands that shed i blood
Is. 59:7, make haste to shed i blood
Matt. 27:4, have betrayed the i blood
   24, I am i of the blood of

Instruct—*teach, furnish with directions*
Deut. 4:36, that he might i thee
Neh. 9:20, thy good spirit to i them
Ps. 32:8, I will i thee and teach thee
Prov. 16:22, i-ion of fools is folly
Matt. 13:52, i-ed unto the kingdom of
Rom. 2:18, being i-ed out of the law
1 Cor. 4:15, ten thousand i-ers in Christ
2 Tim. 3:16, for i-ion in righteousness

Instrument—*tool, implement, means*
Num. 35:16, smite him . . . i of iron
Ps. 33:2, an i of ten strings
   150:4, stringed i-s and organs
Is. 41:15, a new sharp threshing i
Ezek. 33:32, and can play well on an i
Amos 6:5, invent . . . i-s of musick
Rom. 6:13, i-s of unrighteousness

Integrity—*moral soundness, honesty*
Gen. 20:5, i of my heart
Job 2:3, he holdeth fast his i
Ps. 26:1, have walked in mine i
Prov. 19:1, poor that walketh in his i
   20:7, just man walketh in his i

Intercession—*mediation*
Is. 53:12, i for the transgressors
Rom. 8:26, Spirit . . . maketh i for us
1 Tim. 2:1, prayers, i-s . . . thanks
Heb. 7:25, ever liveth to make i

Interpret—*to explain*
Gen. 41:8, understand a dream to i it
Prov. 1:6, a proverb, and the i-ation
John 1:42, which is by i-ation
1 Cor. 12:10, the i-ation of tongues
   14:27, and let one i
2 Pet. 1:20, of any private i

Intreat—*beg, supplicate*
Ex. 8:8, I the Lord, that he may
Ruth 1:16, I me not to leave thee
1 Kin. 13:6, I now the face of the Lord
Ps. 45:12, shall i thy favour
1 Tim. 5:1, i him as a father
James 3:17, and easy to be i-ed

Inward—*toward the center*
Job 19:19, All my i friends abhorred
   38:36, wisdom in the i parts
Jer. 31:33, put my law . . . i parts
Matt. 7:15, but i-ly . . . ravening wolves
2 Cor. 4:16, i man is renewed day by day

Iron—*a metal*
Gen. 4:22, artificer in brass or i
Deut. 3:11, a bedstead of i
   8:9, whose stones are i
   33:25, shoes . . . i and brass
Judg. 1:19, they had chariots of i
2 Kin. 6:6, the i did swim
Job 19:24, graven with an i pen
   40:18, bones are like bars of i
Ps. 2:9, break them with a rod of i
Prov. 27:17, I sharpeneth i
Jer. 11:4, from the i furnace
1 Tim. 4:2, seared with a hot i

Ivory—*animal tusks*
1 Kin. 10:18, made a great throne of i
Song 7:4, neck is as a tower of i
Amos 6:4, Lie upon beds of i

J

Jealous—*suspicious, envious*
Ex. 20:5, Lord thy God am a j God
   34:14, name is J, is a j God
Num. 5:14, spirit of j-y come upon
Josh. 24:19, holy God; he is a j God
1 Kin. 19:10, very j for the Lord
Prov. 6:34, j-y is the rage of a man
Song 8:6, j-y is cruel as the grave
Nah. 1:2, God is j
Rom. 10:19, provoke you to j-y by them
2 Cor. 11:2, j . . . with godly j-y

Join—*connect, unite*
Prov. 11:21, Though hand **j** in hand
Is. 5:8, woe, unto them that **j** house to
Matt. 19:6, what . . . God . . . **j**-ed
   together
1 Cor. 1:10, perfectly **j**-ed together
   6:17, he that is **j**-ed unto the Lord
Eph. 5:31, shall be **j**-ed unto his wife
Joint—*place of union of two things*
Gen. 32:25, Jacob's thigh was out of **j**
Ps. 22:14, my bones are out of **j**
Prov. 25:19, and a foot out of **j**
Rom. 8:17, and **j**-heirs with Christ
Journey—*trip, passage through life*
Gen. 33:12, Let us take our **j**
Josh. 9:11, Take victuals . . . for the **j**
Neh. 2:6, how long shall thy **j** be
Matt. 10:10, Nor scrip for your **j**
Mark 13:34, man taking a far **j**
Luke 9:3, Take nothing for your **j**
   15:13, his **j** into a far country
Acts 1:12, a sabbath day's **j**
   9:3, **j**-ed, he came near Damascus
Rom. 1:10, might have a prosperous **j**
2 Cor. 11:26, In **j**-ings, often, in perils
Joy—*gladness, bliss, delight*
1 Chr. 15:16, lifting up the voice with **j**
Ezra 3:12, shouted aloud for **j**
Job 29:13, widow's heart to sing for **j**
   33:26, shall see his face with **j**
Ps. 66:1, Make a **j**-ful noise unto
   126:5, sow in tears shall reap in **j**
Prov. 17:21, father of a fool hath no **j**
Eccles. 9:7, eat thy bread with **j**
Is. 52:9, Break forth into **j**
Joel 1:12, **j** is withered away
Matt. 25:21, enter thou into the **j** of
Luke 15:7, **j** shall be in heaven over
John 15:11, that your **j** might be full
Acts 20:24, finish my course with **j**
Rom. 14:17, and **j** in the Holy Ghost
Gal. 5:22, Spirit is love, **j**, peace
Phil. 2:2, Fulfill ye my **j**
1 Thess. 3:9, we **j** for your sakes
James 1:2, count it all **j** when ye fall
1 John 1:4, that your **j** may be full
Judge—*form an opinion, one who decides*
Gen. 16:5, Lord **j** between me and thee
   18:25, the **J** of all the earth
Matt. 7:1, **J** not . . . be not **j**-d
   2, judgment ye **j** . . . be **j**-d
John 7:24, **j** righteous judgments
   51, our law **j** any man
   12:47, came not to **j** the world

Acts 10:42, **J** of quick and dead
Heb. 12:23, God the **J** of all
   13:4, adulterers God will
Judgment—*a just decision*
Gen. 18:19, to do justice and **j**
Ex. 12:12, I will execute **j**
Lev. 18:4, Ye shall do my **j**-s
Deut. 1:17, the **j** is God's
   16:19, shalt not wrest **j**
Ezra 7:26, let **j** be executed speedily
Job 8:3, Doth God pervert **j**
Ps. 1:5, ungodly . . . not stand in the **j**
   19:9, **j**-s of the Lord are true
   119:66, Teach me good **j**
Prov. 21:3, To do justice and **j**
   28:5, Evil men understand not **j**
Jer. 10:24, correct me, but with **j**
Amos 5:24, let **j** run down as waters
Matt. 5:21, be in danger of the **j**
   7:2, what **j** ye judge
   27:19, set down on the **j** seat
John 5:30, judge: and my **j** is just
   18:33, Pilate entered . . . **j** hall
Acts 25:10, I stand at Caesar's **j** seat
Heb. 9:27, but after this the **j**
   10:27, fearful looking for of **j**
2 Pet. 3:7, against the day of **j**
1 John 4:17, boldness in the day of **j**
Jude 15, To execute **j** upon all
Rev. 19:2, true and righteous are his **j**-s
Just—*upright, honest*
Gen. 6:9, Noah was a **j** man
Lev. 19:36, **J** balances, **j** weights, a **j**
Job 9:2, how should man be **j** with
Ps. 7:9, establish the **j**
Prov. 4:18, path of the **j** . . . shining
   24:16, **j** man falleth seven times
Is. 26:7, way of the **j** is uprightness
Hab. 2:4, **j** shall live by his faith
Matt. 5:45, rain on the **j** and . . . unjust
   27:24, blood of this **j** person
Luke 15:7, ninety and nine **j** persons
   23:50, a good man, and a **j**
John 5:30, my judgment is **j**
Acts 7:52, the coming of the **J** One
Rom. 1:17, The **j** shall live by faith
Phil. 4:8, whatsoever things are **j**
Heb. 2:2, **j** recompence of reward
1 Pet. 3:18, suffered . . . **j** for the un**j**
1 John 1:9, **j** to forgive us our sins
Justice—*equity, right, fairness*
Gen. 18:19, do **j** and judgment

Job 8:3, doth the Almighty pervert **j**
Ps. 89:14, **J** and judgment are the
Is. 59:14, and **j** standeth afar off
Jer. 31:23, O habitation of **j**
Justify—*vindicate, absolve*
Job 9:20, If I **j** myself, mine own
25:4, can man be **j**-ed with God
Matt. 11:19, wisdom is **j**-ed of her
Luke 10:29, willing to **j** himself
Rom. 8:33, It is God that **j**-eth
Justly—*honestly, fairly*
Mic. 6:8, do **j**, and to love mercy
Luke 23:41, indeed **j**; for we receive
1 Thess. 2:10, holily . . . **j** . . .
unblameably

K

Keep—*retain, maintain, withhold*
Gen. 18:19, **K** the way of the Lord
Ex. 20:6, **k** my commandments
8, sabbath day, to **k** it holy
Num. 6:24, Lord bless thee . . . **k**
Deut. 5:15, to **k** the sabbath day
Ps. 17:8, **K** me as the apple of the
34:13, **K** thy tongue from evil
Prov. 4:23, **K** thy heart . . . diligence
6:20, **k** thy . . . commandment
Is. 41:1, **K** silence before me
Hab. 2:20, let all the earth **k** silence
Matt. 19:17, life, **k** the commandments
26:18, I will **k** the passover
Luke 8:15, having heard the word, **k** it
11:28, word of God, and **k** it
John 8:51, If a man **k** my saying
12:25, **k** it unto life eternal
14:23, he will **k** my words
17:15, **k** them from evil
1 Cor. 9:27, I **k** under my body
14:28, **k** silence in the church
Eph. 4:3, **k** the unity of the Spirit
Phil. 4:7, **k** your hearts and minds
1 Tim. 5:22, **k** thyself pure
6:20, **k** that which is committed
James 1:27, **k** himself unspotted
1 John 5:21, **k** yourselves from idols
Jude 21, **K** yourselves in the love of God
Keeper—*one who has the care of another*
Gen. 4:9, Am I my brother's **k**
Esther 2:3, **k** of the women
Ps. 121:15, The Lord is thy **k**

Acts 5:23, **k**-s standing without
Titus 2:5, discreet, chaste, **k**-s at home
Key—*that which serves to unlock*
Matt. 16:19, **k**-s of the kingdom
Luke 11:52, away the **k** of knowledge
Rev. 1:18, **k**-s of hell and of death
9:1, **k** of the bottomless pit
Kill—*slay, destroy*
Ex. 20:13, Thou shalt not **k**
Deut. 32:39, I **k**, and I make alive
2 Kin. 5:7, God, to **k** and to make alive
Job 5:2, wrath **k**-eth the foolish man
Matt. 5:21, Thou shalt not **k**
10:28, them which **k** the body
Luke 15:23, fatted calf, and **k** it
John 5:18, Jews sought . . . to **k** him
7:19, Why go ye about to **k** me
10:10, for to steal, and to **k**
Acts 10:13, Rise, Peter; **k**, and eat
Rom. 8:36, we are **k**-ed all the day
2 Cor. 3:6, letter **k**-eth . . . spirit
James 5:6, condemned and **k**-ed the just
Kind—*considerate, sort or breed*
Gen. 1:11, yielding fruit after his **k**
2 Chr. 10:7, If thou be **k** to this people
Matt. 17:21, this **k** goeth not out
1 Cor. 13:4, suffereth long, and is **k**
Eph. 4:32, be ye **k** one to another
Kindle—*ignite, arouse*
Gen. 30:2, Jacob's anger was **k**-ed
Ex. 35:3, shall **k** no fire
Prov. 26:21, contentious man to strife
Is. 50:11, sparks that ye have **k**-ed
James 3:5, matter a little fire **k**-eth
Kindness—*good will, generosity, grace*
Ruth 3:10, more **k** in the latter and
2 Sam. 2:6, will requite you this **k**
16:17, Is this thy **k** to thy friend
Ps. 117:2, his merciful **k** is great
Prov. 31:26, tongue is the law of **k**
2 Cor. 6:6, by **k**, by the Holy Ghost, by
Col. 3:12, **k**, humbleness . . . meekness
2 Pet. 1:7, to brotherly **k** charity
King—*a chief ruler*
Judg. 9:8, trees went . . . to anoint a **k**
17:6, there was no **k** in Israel
1 Sam. 8:5, make us a **k** to judge us
10:24, God save the **k**
Job 18:14, to the **k** of terrors
Ps. 5:2, my **K**, and my God
24:8, Who is this **k** of glory
Prov. 8:15, By me **k**-s reign
22:29, he shall stand before **k**-s

King (*Continued*)
Eccles. 10:20, Curse not the **k**
Is. 43:15, the creator of Israel, your **k**
Jer. 10:7, fear thee, O **K** of nations
Matt. 2:2, is born **K** of the Jews
    21:5, Behold, thy **K** cometh
    27:11, Art thou the **K** of the
Luke 23:2, he himself is Christ a **K**
John 12:15, thy **k** cometh
1 Tim. 6:15, **K** of kings, and Lord of
1 Pet. 2:17, Fear God. Honour the **K**
Kingdom—*domain, spiritual realm*
Ex. 19:6, be unto me a **k** of priests
1 Chr. 29:11, thine is the **k**, O Lord
Ps. 22:28, For the **k** is the Lord's
    145:13, Thy **k** is an everlasting **k**
Obad. 21, the **k** shall be the Lord's
Matt. 3:2, the **k** of heaven is at hand
    4:23, the gospel of the **k**
    6:10, Thy **k** come. Thy will be
    13:38, children of the **k**
    16:19, the keys of the **k**
    19:14, such is the **k** of heaven
    26:29, in my Father's **k**
Mark 12:34, not far from the **k** of God
Luke 6:20, for yours is the **k**
    12:32, to give you the **k**
    22:29, appoint unto you a **k**
John 3:3, cannot see the **k** of God
    18:36, My **k** is not of this world
Rom. 14:17, the **k** of God is not meat
Col. 1:13, the **k** of his dear Son
2 Tim. 4:18, unto his heavenly **k**
James 2:5, heirs of the **k** which he
Kiss—*salute with the lips*
Gen. 29:11, Jacob **k**-ed Rachel
2 Sam. 20:9, beard . . . right hand to **k**
    him
Song 1:2, **k** me with the **k**-es of his
Matt. 26:48, whomsoever I shall **k**
    49, Hail, Master; and **k**-ed him
Luke 7:45, not ceased to **k** my feet
    15:20, on his neck, and **k**-ed him
    22:48, Son of man with a **k**
Rom. 16:16, Salute . . . with an holy **k**
1 Pet. 5:14, with a **k** of charity
Knee—*joint midway of the leg*
Gen. 41:43, cried . . . Bow the **k**
Matt. 27:29, bowed the **k** before him
Rom. 14:11, every **k** shall bow to me
Phil. 2:10, Jesus every **k** should bow
Heb. 12:12, and the feeble **k**-s
Kneel—*rest upon the knees*
Gen. 24:11, made his camels to **k**

Ps. 95:6, let us **k** before the Lord
Luke 11:41, **k**-ed down, and prayed
Knew—*had knowledge of, perceived*
Gen. 28:16, this place; and I **k** it not
Ex. 1:8, which **k** not Joseph
Jer. 1:5, Before I formed thee . . . I **k** thee
Matt. 7:23, profess . . . I never **k** you
Luke 6:8, but he **k** their thoughts
John 4:10, **k**-est the gift of God
1 Cor. 1:21, by wisdom **k** not God
2 Cor. 5:21, sin for us, who **k** no sin
    12:2, **k** a man in Christ above
Rev. 19:12, name written, that no man **k**
Knock—*rap, strike*
Matt. 7:7, **k**, and it shall be opened
Luke 13:25, stand without, and to **k**
Acts 12:13, as Peter **k**-ed at the door
Rev. 3:20, I stand at the door, and **k**
Know—*understand, be acquainted with*
Gen. 3:22, to **k** good and evil
1 Sam. 3:7, Samuel . . . yet **k** the Lord
    17:28, I **k** thy pride
Job 10:7, **k**-est that I am not wicked
    13:18, **k** that I shall be justified
    19:25, **k** that my redeemer liveth
Ps. 1:6, **k**-eth . . . way of . . . righteous
    46:10, **k** that I am God
    56:9, this I **k**; for God is for me
Prov. 27:1, **k**-est not what a day may
Eccles. 9:5, living **k** . . . dead **k** not
Is. 7:15, **k** to refuse the evil
    59:8, way of peace they **k** not
Jer. 17:9, wicked: who can **k** it
Hos. 6:3, **k**, if we follow on to **k**
Matt. 6:3, left hand **k** what thy right
    7:11, **k** how to give good gifts
    20, by their fruits ye shall **k**
    9:30, See that no man **k** it
    12:33, tree is **k**-n by his fruit
    25:12, I **k** you not
Mark 1:24, **k** thee who thou art
    13:33, ye **k** not when the time is
Luke 10:22, man **k**-eth who the Son is
    19:42, If thou hadst **k**-n, even
    22:57, Woman, I **k** him not
John 8:32, **k** the truth, and the truth
    10:14, **k** my sheep, and am **k**-n
    14:7, If ye had **k**-n me
    21:17, **k**-est all things; thou **k**-est
Acts 1:7, not for you to **k** the times
    19:15, Jesus I **k**, and Paul I **k**
1 Cor. 13:9, we **k** in part . . . prophesy
    12, **k** in part . . . then shall I **k**

Eph. 3:19, to **k** the love of Christ
1 Thess. 3:5, I sent to **k** your faith
2 Tim. 3:15, **k-n** the holy scriptures
1 John 3:2, **k** that, when he shall appear
3 John 12, **k** that our record is true
Rev. 2:2, I **k** thy works
Knowledge—*wisdom, acquaintance*
Gen. 2:9, tree of **k** of good and evil
Deut. 1:39, no **k** between good and evil
1 Sam. 2:3, Lord is a God of **k**
2 Chr. 1:10, Give me now wisdom and **k**
Job 21:22, Shall any teach God **k**
Ps. 19:2, night unto night sheweth **k**
139:6, Such **k** is too wonderful
Prov. 1:7, is the beginning of **k**
10:14, Wise men lay up **k**
17:27, hath **k** spareth his words
Eccles. 1:18, **k** increaseth sorrow
Is. 11:9, full of the **k** of the Lord
28:9, Whom shall he teach **k**
Hos. 4:6, destroyed for lack of **k**
Luke 11:52, taken away the key of **k**
Acts 24:22, having more perfect **k**
Rom. 10:2, but not according to **k**
11:33, wisdom and **k** of God
1 Cor. 8:1, **K** puffeth up, but charity
13:8, **k**, it shall vanish away
15:34, have not the **k** of God
Eph. 3:19, love . . . which passeth **k**
Col. 2:3, treasures of wisdom and **k**
1 Tim. 2:4, unto the **k** of the truth
2 Pet. 1:5, 6, virtue **k**; And to **k**
3:18, grow in grace, and in the **k**

L

Labour—*work, toil, effort*
Gen. 31:42, and the **l** of my hands
Ex. 20:9, Six days shalt thou **l**
Job 9:29, why then **l** I in vain
Ps. 78:46, gave . . . **l** unto the locust
127:1, they **l** in vain that build it
128:2, eat the **l** of thine hands
Prov. 14:23, In all **l** there is profit
23:4, **L** not to be rich
Eccles. 2:22, hath man of all his **l**
4:9, good reward for their **l**
5:12, sleep of a **l**-ing man
Is. 22:4, **l** not to comfort me
Lam. 5:5, we **l**, and have no rest
Matt. 11:28, Come . . . all ye that **l**

John 6:27, **L** not for the meat which
Rom. 16:12, who **l** in the Lord
1 Cor. 15:10, I **l**-ed more abundantly
58, your **l** is not in vain
Gal. 4:11, bestowed . . . **l** in vain
Eph. 4:28, rather let him **l**, working
Phil. 1:22, the fruit of my **l**
1 Thess. 1:3, work of faith, and **l** of
Heb. 4:11, **l** therefore to enter into that
Lack—*be without, deficiency*
Deut. 8:9, shalt not **l** any thing
Prov. 6:32, woman **l**-eth understanding
28:27, giveth . . . poor shall not **l**
Matt. 19:20, what **l** I yet
Mark 10:21, one thing thou **l**-est
1 Thess. 4:12, may have **l** of nothing
James 1:5, If any of you **l** wisdom
Lady—*female head of a household*
Judg. 5:29, Her wise **l**-ies answered
Is. 47:5, The **l** of kingdoms
7, I shall be a **l** for ever
2 John 1, unto the elect **l**
Laid—*placed*
Ex. 2:3, she **l** it in the flags
1 Kin. 17:19, **l** him upon his own bed
Job 6:2, calamity **l** in the balances
38:6, **l** the corner stone thereof
Ps. 3:5, I **l** me down and slept
Nah. 3:7, Nineveh is **l** waste
Mark 6:5, **l** his hands upon a few sick
Luke 12:19, **l** up for many years
John 11:34, Where have ye **l** him
Acts 20:3, Jews **l** wait for him
2 Tim. 4:8, **l** up for me a crown
1 John 3:16, he **l** down his life
Lamb—*young sheep, unsophisticated*
Gen. 22:8, God will provide . . . a **l**
Is. 40:11, gather the **l**-s with his
53:7, as a **l** to the slaughter
65:25, wolf and the **l** shall feed
Hos. 4:16, as a **l** in a large place
Luke 10:3, send you forth as **l**-s
John 1:29, Behold the **L** of God
21:15, Feed my **l**-s
Acts 8:32, like a **l** dumb before
1 Pet. 1:19, a **l** without blemish
Lame—*disabled, crippled*
2 Sam. 9:13, **l** on both his feet
Job 29:15, feet was I to the **l**
Matt. 15:31, the **l** to walk
Lamp—*light producing device*
Gen. 15:17, burning **l** that passed
1 Sam. 3:3, **l** of God went out

Lamp (*Continued*)
2 Sam. 22:29, For thou art my l
Ps. 119:105, Thy word is a l unto
Dan. 10:6, eyes as l-s of fire
Matt. 25:8, for our l-s are gone out
Rev. 4:5, seven l-s of fire burning
Land—*surface of the earth*
Gen. 1:9, let the dry l appear
15:18, seed have I given this l
Ex. 1:7, the l was filled with them
Deut. 6:3, l . . . with milk and honey
8:8, l of wheat, and barley
1 Sam. 6:5, your mice that mar the l
Job 28:13, in the l of the living
Ps. 37:29, righteous. . . inherit the l
88:12, the l of forgetfulness
Is. 2:7, l is also full of horses
Matt. 2:6, Bethlehem in the l of Juda
27:45, darkness over all the l
Acts 4:37, Having l, sold it
Heb. 11:29, Red Sea as by dry l
Language—*human speech*
Gen. 11:1, whole earth was one l
Ps. 19:3, There is no speech or l
Ezek. 3:5, 6, speech and of a hard l
Acts 2:6, speak in his own l
Large—*abundant, ample, big*
Ex. 3:8, a good land and a l
Ps. 31:8, set my feet in a l room
Is 22:18, ball into a l country
Matt. 28:12, gave l money to the
Luke 22:12, a l upper room
Gal. 6:11, see how l a letter
Last—*final one or time*
Gen. 49:1, befall you in the l days
Num. 23:10, let my l end be like
Is. 44:6, first, and I am the l
Matt. 12:45, l state of that man
19:30, first . . . l, and the l . . . first
Luke 11:26, l state of that man
12:59, paid the very l mite
John 6:39, raise it . . . at the l day
1 Cor. 15:45, the l Adam was made a
52, of an eye, at the l trump
1 Pet. 1:5, revealed in the l time
Rev. 1:17, I am the first and the l
Laugh—*express pleasure or scorn*
Gen. 18:13, Wherefore did Sarah l
Job 8:21, fill thy mouth with l-ing
22:19, innocent l them to scorn
Prov. 14:13, Even in l-ter the heart
Eccles. 3:4, A time to weep, and . . . l
Matt. 9:24, They l-ed him to scorn

Luke 6:25, Woe unto you that l now
James, 4:9, let your l-ter be turned
Law—*rules of conduct*
Ex. 12:49, One l shall be to him
Josh. 1:8, This book of the l shall
2 Kin. 22:8, found the book of the l
Ps. 19:7, l of the Lord is perfect
94:20, frameth mischief by a l
Prov. 1:8, forsake not . . . l of thy mother
28:7, keepeth the l is a wise
29:18, keepeth the l, happy is he
Matt. 5:17, not . . . come to destroy the l
7:12, the l and the prophets
John 7:51, our l judge any man
19:7, a l, and by our l he ought
Rom. 2:14, having not the l, are a l
4:15, the l worketh wrath
13:10, Love . . . fulfilling of the l
1 Cor. 6:7, go to l one with another
Gal. 3:24, l was our schoolmaster
5:23, against such there is no l
6:2, so fulfill the l of Christ
Titus 3:9, avoid . . . strivings about the l
Heb. 7:19, l made nothing perfect
James 1:25, the perfect l of liberty
Lay—*rested upon*
Ex. 22:25, l upon him usury
Num. 12:11, l not the sin upon us
2 Sam. 4:5, who l on a bed at noon
Ps. 4:8, l me down in peace
Prov. 10:14, Wise men l up knowledge
Matt. 6:19, L not up . . . treasures
John 10:15, I l down my life
Acts 7:60, l not this sin to their
1 Tim. 6:19, L-ing up in store
Heb. 6:2, l-ing on of hands
1 Pet. 2:1, l-ing aside all malice
Lead—*guide, conduct*
Ex. 13:21, of a cloud, to l them
Deut. 32:12, Lord alone did l him
Ps. 23:2, l-eth me beside the still
27:11, l me in a plain path
25:5, L me in thy truth
Is. 11:6, a little child shall l them
40:11, gently l those that are with
Matt. 6:13, l us not into temptation
15:14, the blind l the blind
John 10:3, sheep by name, and l-eth
1 Tim. 2:2, may l a quiet . . . life
2 Tim. 3:6, l captive silly women
Learn—*acquire knowledge or skill*
Gen. 30:27, I have l-ed by experience
Deut. 31:13, l to fear the Lord
Prov. 1:5, hear, and will increase l-ing

110

Is. 1:17, L to do well
2:4, neither shall they l war
Matt. 11:29, l of me
Acts 26:24, much l-ing . . . make thee mad
Rom. 15:4, were written for our l-ing
Eph. 4:20, ye have so l-ed Christ
2 Tim. 3:7, Ever l-ing
Heb. 5:8, Yet l-ed he obedience
Least—*smallest*
Judg. 6:15, l in my father's house
2 Kin. 18:24, l of my master's servants
Matt. 5:19, of these l commandments
19, l in the kingdom of heaven
Luke 16:10, faithful in that which is l
1 Cor. 15:9, I am the l of the apostles
Leave—*depart, forsake, deposit*
Gen. 2:24, man l his father . . . mother
Ruth 1:16, Intreat me not to l thee
Job 9:27, l off my heaviness
Ps. 16:10, not l my soul in hell
49:10, l their wealth to others
Matt. 18:12, not l the ninety and nine
19:5, l father and mother
John 14:27, Peace I l with you
16:28, I l the world
1 Cor. 7:13, let her not l him
Heb. 13:5, I will never l thee, nor
Leaven—*something that causes ferment*
Ex. 12:19, no l found in your houses
Lev. 6:17, not be baked with l
Matt. 13:33, kingdom . . . is like unto l
16:6, beware of the l
Luke 13:21, It is like l
1 Cor. 5:6, a little l leaveneth
7, Purge out . . . the old l
Lend—*allow another the use of*
Deut. 15:6, shalt l unto many nations
23:19, not l upon usury
Prov. 22:7, is servant to the l-er
Luke 6:34, sinners also l to sinners
11:5, Friend, l me three loaves
Length—*distance from point to point*
Prov. 3:16, L of days is in her right
Ezek. 31:7, l of his branches
Eph. 3:18, the breadth, and l
Leopard—*wild, cat-like animal*
Is. 11:6, l shall lie down with the
Jer. 13:23, skin, or the l his spots
Hos. 13:7, as a l by the way
Rev. 13:2, was like unto a l
Leper—*one suffering from leprosy*
2 Chr. 26:21, Uzziah the king was a l

Matt. 8:2, came a l and worshipped
Mark 14:3, house of Simon the l
Less—*smaller in number or quantity*
Gen. 1:16, l-er light to rule the
Is. 40:17, counted . . . l than nothing
2 Cor. 12:15, the l I be loved
Eph. 3:8, I am l than the least
Liar—*an untruthful person*
Job 24:25, who will make me a l
John 8:55, be a l like unto you
Rom. 3:4, God be true . . . every man a l
1 John 5:10, God hath made him a l
Liberty—*freedom from restraint*
Lev. 25:10, proclaim l throughout
Ps. 119:45, And I will walk at l
Is. 61:1, proclaim l to the captives
Luke 4:18, set at l . . . bruised
Rom. 8:21, glorious l of the children
2 Cor. 3:17, of the Lord is, there is l
Gal. 2:4, to spy out our l
5:13, ye have been called unto l
James 1:25, into the perfect law of l
1 Pet. 2:16, using your l for a cloak
Lick—*stroke with the tongue*
1 Kin. 21:19, dogs l-ed the blood of
Ps. 72:9, enemies shall l the dust
Luke 16:21, dogs . . . l-ed his sores
Lie—*speak untruthfully, recline*
Deut. 19:11, l in wait for him
Job 34:6, Should I l against my right
Ps. 23:2, l down in green pastures
119:69, proud have forged a l
Eccles. 4:11, if two l together
Acts 5:3, Satan filled thine heart to l
Rom. 1:25, truth of God into a l
Col. 3:9, L not one to another
1 Tim. 4:2, speaking l-s in hypocrisy
Heb. 6:18, impossible for God to l
Life—*union of soul and body*
Gen. 2:7, nostrils the breath of l
Ex. 21:23, thou shalt give l for l
Deut. 30:19, set before you l and death
Josh. 2:14, Our l for yours
1 Sam. 25:29, bound in the bundle of l
Job 10:1, My soul is weary of my l
Ps. 16:11, shew me the path of l
36:9, with thee is the fountain of l
133:3, even l for evermore
Prov. 4:13, keep her, for she is thy l
8:35, whoso findeth me findeth l
Jer. 21:8, set before you the way of l
Dan. 12:2, awake, some to everlasting l
Matt. 6:25, take no thought for your l
10:39, loseth his l for my sake

Life (*Continued*)
16:25, save his l shall lose it
19:16, that I may have eternal l
20:28, his l a ransom for many
Mark 8:35, save his l shall lose it
10:17, may inherit eternal l
Luke 12:15, man's l consisteth not
23, the l is more than meat
18:30, to come l everlasting
John 4:36, fruit into l eternal
5:24, from death unto l
6:35, I am the bread of l
10:11, giveth his l for the sheep
11:25, the resurrection, and the l
12:25, He that loveth his l
14:6, way, the truth, and the l
15:13, lay down his l for his
17:3, this is l eternal
20:31, have l through his name
Acts 3:15, killed the Prince of l
Rom. 6:4, walk in newness of l
23, gift of God is eternal l
2 Cor. 3:6, but the spirit giveth l
Gal. 6:8, Spirit reap l everlasting
Phil. 2:16, Holding forth the word of l
4:3, names are in the book of l
Col. 3:4, Christ, who is our l
1 Tim. 2:2, a quiet and peaceable l
Titus 3:7, hope of eternal l
James 1:12, receive the crown of l
1 John 1:1, of the Word of l
5:12, that hath the Son hath l
Rev. 2:10, give thee a crown of l
13:8, not written in the book of l
Lift—*raise, elevate*
Gen. 13:14, L up now thine eyes
Ex. 14:16, l thou up thy rod
Num. 6:26, Lord l up his countenance
Job 38:34, Canst thou l up thy voice
Ps. 3:3, the l-er up of mine head
24:7, L up your heads, O ye gates
121:1, l up mine eyes unto the hills
134:2, L up your hands
Is. 2:4, not l up sword against
5:26, l up an ensign
13:2, L ye up a banner
Luke 18:13, l up so much as his eyes
John 3:14, Son of man be l-ed up
1 Tim. 3:6, being l-ed up with pride
James 4:10, and he shall l you up
Light—*opposite of darkness, felicity*
Gen. 1:3, Let there be l . . . was l
Ex. 10:23, had l in their dwellings

Job 18:5, l of the wicked . . . put out
38:19, the way where l dwelleth
Ps. 4:6, l of thy countenance upon
27:1, my l and my salvation
119:105, a l unto my path
Prov. 4:8, path . . . as shining l
Is. 2:5, let us walk in the l
5:20, darkness for l, and l for
8:20, there is no l in them
60:1, Arise, shine; for thy l is
Jer. 31:35, giveth the sun for a l by
Mic. 7:9, bring me forth to the l
Matt. 5:14, Ye are the l of the world
15, Neither do men l a candle
6:22, l of the body is the eye
11:30, my burden is l
Luke 2:32, l to lighten the Gentiles
16:8, wiser than the children of l
John 1:7, to bear witness of the l
9, That was the true L
8:12, I am the l of the world
12:35, Walk while ye have the l
1 Cor. 4:5, bring to l the hidden
2 Cor. 4:4, l of the glorious gospel
Eph. 5:8, walk as children of l
1 John 1:7, if we walk in the l, as he
Likeness—*similarity*
Gen. 1:26, in our image, after our l
Ex. 20:4, or any l of any thing that is
Deut. 4:16, l of male or female
Rom. 8:3, l of sinful flesh
Phil. 2:7, made in the l of men
Lily—*a flower*
Song 2:1, the l of the valleys
Hos. 14:5, he shall grow as the l
Matt. 6:28, Consider the l-es
Linen—*woven flax fibres*
Gen. 41:42, vestures of fine l
Prov. 31:24, She maketh fine l
Jer. 13:1, get thee a l girdle
John 20:5, saw the l clothes lying
Rev. 19:14, fine l, white and clean
Lion—*a wild cat-like beast*
Gen. 49:9, Judah is a l's whelp
1 Sam. 17:34, out of the paw of the l
1 Chr. 11:32, slew a l in a pit
Ps. 7:2, tear my soul like a l
57:4, My soul is among l-s
Prov. 28:1, are bold as a l
Eccles. 9:4, living dog . . . dead l
1 Pet. 5:8, the devil, as a roaring l
Rev. 9:8, as the teeth of l-s
Lips—*the mouth, organs of speech*
Ex. 6:12, of uncircumcised l

1 Sam. 1:13, only her l moved
2 Kin. 19:28, my bridle in thy l-s
Ps. 12:2, with flattering l and . . . double
    4, our l are our own
    17:1, goeth not out of feigned l
    31:18, lying l be put to silence
    51:15, open thou my l
Prov. 26:23, Burning l and a wicked
Is. 6:5, a man of unclean l
    28:11, with stammering l
Matt. 15:8, honoureth me with their l
Rom. 13:3, poison . . . under their l
1 Cor. 14:21, other tongues and other l
1 Pet. 3:10, l that they speak no guile
Little—*small, not great*
Gen. 18:4, Let a l water, I pray you
Judg. 4:19, a l water to drink
1 Sam. 2:19, mother made him a l coat
Ps. 8:5, l lower than the angels
    37:16, l that a righteous man
Prov. 6:10, l sleep, a l slumber, a l
    15:16, l with fear of the Lord
    16:8, Better is a l with
    30:24, four things . . . l upon thee
Eccles. 5:12, eat l or much
Song 2:15, the l foxes
Is. 11:6, l child shall lead them
    28:10, here a l, and there a l
Matt. 6:30, O ye of l faith
    18:3, become as l children
Luke 7:47, l is forgiven . . . loveth l
    12:32, Fear not, l flock
    18:16, Suffer l children to
John 7:33, Yet a l while am I with
1 Cor. 5:6, a l leaven leaveneth
Heb. 2:7, a l lower than the angels
James 3:5, tongue is a l member
Live—*to be alive, abide, be quickened*
Gen. 3:22, eat, and l forever
    42:18, This do, and l
    45:3, doth my father yet l
Deut. 8:3, not l by bread only
Job 7:16, I would not l always
    19:25, my redeemer l-eth
Ps. 119:175, Let my soul l
Is. 55:3, hear, and your soul shall l
Ezek. 5:11, as I l, saith the Lord
Hab. 2:4, just shall l by his faith
Matt. 4:4, not l by bread alone
Luke 10:28, this do, and thou shalt l
    20:38, for all l unto him
John 11:25, were dead, yet shall he l

Rom. 1:17, just shall l by faith
    8:12, to l after the flesh
    14:8, we l, we l unto the Lord
2 Cor. 5:15, not . . . l unto themselves
Gal. 2:20, with Christ: nevertheless I l
Phil. 1:21, to me to l is Christ
James 4:15, the Lord will, we shall l
Living—*active, vigorous, not dead*
Gen. 2:7, man became a l soul
Num. 16:48, the dead and the l
Deut. 5:26, voice of the l God
1 Kin. 3:25, divide the l child in two
Job 28:13, in the land of the l
Eccles. 7:2, l will lay it to his
Dan. 6:26, he is the l God
Matt. 16:16, Son of the l God
Mark 12:44, cast in . . . even all her l
John 4:10, have given thee l water
    6:51, I am the l bread
    7:38, rivers of l water
Rom. 12:1, bodies a l sacrifice
1 Cor. 15:45, Adam was made a l soul
2 Cor. 6:16, temple of the l God
Titus 3:3, l in malice and envy
Rev. 7:17, unto l fountains of waters
Loaves—*a lump of baked bread*
1 Sam. 10:3, carrying three l of bread
Matt. 14:17, five l, and two fishes
Mark 6:52, the miracle of the l
Locks—*strands of hair*
Judg. 16:13, weavest the seven l
Song 4:1, doves' eyes within thy l
Is. 47:2, uncover thy l
Ezek. 44:20, their l to grow long
Locust—*a long-winged insect*
Ex. 10:13, east wind brought the l-s
Lev. 11:22, ye may eat; the l
1 Kin. 8:37, blasting, mildew, l
Prov. 30:27, The l-s have no king
Nah. 3:17, many as the l-s
Matt. 3:4, his meat was l-s
Lodge—*live, abide, a house*
Num. 22:8, L here this night
Ruth 1:16, thou l-est, I will l
Is. 1:8, l in a garden of cucumbers
Luke 13:9, fowls . . . l-ed in the branches
Acts 10:6, l-eth with one Simon a
1 Tim. 5:10, if she have l-ed strangers
Loins—*region of the kidneys*
Ex. 12:11, with your l girded
2 Kin. 4:29, Gird up thy l
Matt. 3:4, girdle about his l
Luke 12:35, Let your l be girded

Loins (*Continued*)
Eph. 6:14, I girt about with truth
1 Pet. 1:13, gird up the l of your mind
Long—*extensive in time or space*
Ex. 2:3, could not l-er hide him
2 Sam. 3:1, there was l war between
Job 3:21, Which l for death
Ps. 84:2, soul l-eth, yea, even
Prov. 3:2, l life, and peace shall
Matt. 23:14, pretence make l prayer
1 Cor. 11:14, if a man have l hair
13:4, charity suffereth l
Eph. 6:3, live l on the earth
Rev. 6:10, How l, O Lord
Longsuffering—*very patient*
Num. 14:18, Lord is l, and of great
Ps. 86:15, l, and plenteous
2 Cor. 6:6, by l, by kindness
2 Tim. 4:2, all l and doctrine
2 Pet. 3:9, but is l to us-ward
Look—*direct the eyes, face, a glance*
Gen. 19:17, l not behind thee
Ex. 3:2, l-ed . . . the bush burned
6, afraid to l upon God
38:8, l-ingglasses of the women
2 Sam. 11:2, beautiful to l upon
Esther 1:11, she was fair to l on
Job 30:26, I l-ed for good . . . evil came
35:5, L unto the heavens
Ps. 84:9, l upon the face . . . anointed
Prov. 6:17, proud l, a lying tongue
23:31, L not thou upon the wine
Eccles. 12:3, l out of the windows
Song 1:6, L not upon me . . . I am black
Is. 17:7, a man l to his maker
22:4, L away from me
45:22, L unto me, and be ye saved
Matt. 11:3, do we l for another
14:19, l-ing up to heaven, he
Luke 2:38, that l-ed for redemption
9:62, to the plough, and l-ing back
John 4:35, l on the fields
7:52, Search, and l; for out of
Acts 3:4, said, L on us
6:3, l ye out . . . seven men
Phil. 2:4, L not every man on his own
3:20, we l for the Saviour
Heb. 10:27, fearful l-ing for of judgment
2 Pet. 3:13, l for new heavens
Rev. 14:1, I l-ed, and, lo, a Lamb
Loose—*set free*
Deut. 25:9, l his shoe from off his
Job 38:31, or l the bands of Orion
Ps. 116:16, thou hast l-ed my bonds

Eccles. 12:6, the silver cord be l-ed
Matt. 16:19, l on earth . . . l-ed in
Luke 19:30, colt . . . l him, and bring
Acts 2:24, l-ed the pains of death
1 Cor. 7:27, Art thou l-ed from a wife
Lord—*Supreme Being, one who has power*
Gen. 2:4, L God made the earth
4:1, gotten a man from the L
18:12, my l being old also
21:1, L visited Sarah
Deut. 4:35, that the L he is God
6:4, L our God is one L
10:17, L of l-s, a great God
Josh. 3:5, L will do wonders
Ruth 2:4, L be with you . . . L bless thee
1 Sam. 3:18, it is the L: let him do
2 Sam. 7:3, the L is with thee
Ps. 8:1, O L our L, how excellent
23:1, the L is my shepherd
100:3, Know ye that the L he is
110:1, said unto my L, Sit thou
123:3, Have mercy upon us, O L
Is. 60:14, the city of the L
Ezek. 13:9, know that I am the L God
Mal. 4:5, dreadful day of the L
Matt. 7:21, every one that saith . . . L, L
12:8, man is L . . . of the sabbath
22:4, If David then call him L
Mark 9:24, L, I believe; help thou mine
12:29, L our God is one L
Luke 4:18, Spirit of the L is upon me
6:46, why call ye me, L, L
22:33, L, I am ready to go
John 13:13, Ye call me Master and L
20:13, have taken away my L
28, My L and my God
Acts 2:36, crucified, both L and Christ
8:24, Pray ye to the L
Rom. 1:3, his Son Jesus Christ our L
10:9, confess . . . the L Jesus
2 Cor. 13:14, grace of the L Jesus
Eph. 4:5, One L, one faith, one
5:17, what the will of the L is
Phil. 2:11, confess that . . . Christ is L
Col. 3:24, for ye serve the L Christ
Heb. 12:5, the chastening of the L
Rev. 1:10, Spirit of the L's day
4:8, Holy, holy, holy, L God
22:20, Even so, come, L Jesus
Lose—*cease to have, fail to obtain*
Prov. 23:8, vomit up, and l thy sweet
Eccles. 3:6, time to get . . . time to l
Matt. 16:25, save his life shall l it
25, l his life for my sake

Mark 9:41, shall not l his reward
Lost—*not to be found, ruined*
Lev. 6:3, found that which was l
Ps. 119:176, astray like a l sheep
Ezek. 37:11, and our hope is l
Matt. 5:13, salt have l his savour
    18:11, save that which was l
Luke 15:24, he was l, and is found
John 6:12, remain, that nothing be l
2 Cor. 4:3, hid to them that are l
Lot—*without man's choice, circumstances*
Lev. 16:8, other l for the scapegoat
Num. 26:55, land shall be divided by l
Ps. 22:18, cast l-s upon my vesture
Prov. 1:14, Cast in thy l among us
Jonah 1:7, the l fell upon Jonah
Luke 17:32, Remember L's wife
John 19:24, not rend it, but cast l-s
Acts 1:26, the l fell upon Matthias
    8:21, neither part nor l in this
Love—*affection, reverence*
Gen. 29:20, the l he had to her
Ex. 20:6, thousands of them that l me
Lev. 19:18, l thy neighbour as thyself
Deut. 6:5, l the Lord thy God with all
2 Sam. 1:26, passing the l of women
Ps. 31:23, O l the Lord, all ye his
Prov. 3:12, Lord l-eth he correcteth
    8:17, I l them that l me
    10:12, l coacereth all sins
    12:1, l-eth instruction l-eth
    17:17, A friend l-eth at all
    20:13, L not sleep
Eccles. 3:8, A time to l, and a time
Amos 5:15, Hate the evil, and l the
Zech. 8:17, l no false oath
Matt. 5:44, L your enemies
    6:24, hate the one, and l the
    22:39, l thy neighbour as thy
    24:12, l of many shall wax cold
Luke 6:27, L your enemies
John 3:16, God so l-ed the world
    13:35, have l one to another
    15:13, greater l hath no man
Rom. 12:9, l be without dissimulation
2 Cor. 9:7, God l-eth a cheerful giver
Gal. 5:13, by l serve one another
Eph. 5:2, And walk in l, as Christ
Col. 3:19, Husbands, l your wives
1 Tim. 6:10, l of money is the root
Titus 2:4, l their husbands . . . children
Heb. 13:1, Let brotherly l continue

James 2:8, l thy neighbour as thy
1 John 4:7, let us l one another
Jude 21, Keep . . . in the l of God
Rev. 2:4, thou hast left thy first l
Low—*not high or elevated*
1 Sam. 2:7, bringeth l, and lifteth up
Job 5:11, set up . . . those that be l
    40:12, proud . . . and bring him l
Ps. 8:5, a little l-er than the angels
    86:13, my soul from the l-est hell
Matt. 11:29, I am meek and l-ly in
Rom. 12:16, condescend to men of l
Phil. 2:3, in l-liness of mind
Lowly—*humble, not high in rank*
Ps. 138:6, respect unto the l
Prov. 11:2, with the l is wisdom
Zech. 9:9, l, and riding upon an ass
Matt. 11:29, meek and l in heart
Lucre—*profit, riches*
1 Sam. 8:3, turned aside after l
1 Tim. 3:3, not greedy of filthy l
1 Pet. 5:2, not for filthy l
Lump—*a mass*
2 Kin. 20:7, Take a l of figs
Rom. 11:16, the l is also holy
1 Cor. 5:6, Leaveneth the whole l
    7, that ye may be a new l
Lust—*inordinate or sinful desire*
Deut. 12:15, whatsoever thy soul l-eth
Prov. 6:25, L not after her beauty
Matt. 5:28, looketh on a woman to l
Mark 4:19, l-s of other things
Rom. 13:14, fulfil the l-s thereof
1 John 2:16, l of the flesh . . . l of the
Jude 16, walking after their own l-s
Lying—*untruthful, falsifying*
1 Kin. 22:22, a l spirit
Ps. 119:163, I hate and abhor l
Prov. 6:17, proud look, a l tongue
    12:22, L lips are abomination
Eph. 4:25, putting away l
2 Thess. 2:9, signs and l wonders

M

Mad—*deranged, inflamed*
1 Sam. 21:13, feigned himself **m**
Eccles. 2:2, laughter, It is **m**
John 10:20, hath a devil, and is **m**
Acts 26:24, learning doth make thee **m**
Made—*fashioned, brought about*
Gen. 1:7, God **m** the firmament

115

Made (*Continued*)
  Ex. 4:11, Who hath **m** man's mouth
  Job 4:14, **m** all my bones to shake
    17:6, **m** me a byword
    31:24, **m** gold my hope
  Ps. 8:5, **m** him a little lower . . . angels
    119:73, Thy hands have **m** me
  Prov. 20:9, have **m** my heart clean
  Eccles. 7:29, God hath **m** man upright
  Matt. 9:22, faith hath **m** thee whole
  John 1:3, All things were **m** by him
    5:6, Wilt thou be **m** whole
  2 Cor. 5:21, **m** him to be sin for us
  Eph. 3:7, Whereof I was **m** a minister
  Heb. 6:4, **m** partakers of the Holy
Magnify—*enlarge, increase*
  Job 7:17, man . . . shouldest **m** him
  Ps. 34:3, O **m** the Lord with me
  Is. 42:21, he will **m** the law
  Luke 1:46, My soul doth **m** the Lord
  Rom. 11:13, I **m** mine office
  Phil. 1:20, Christ . . . **m**-ed in my body
  Acts 19:17, name of . . . Jesus was **m-ed**
Maid—*young, unmarried woman*
  Gen. 16:6, thy **m** is in thy hand
  Ex. 22:16, if a man entice a **m**
  Job 31:1, should I think upon a **m**
  Prov. 30:19, way of a man with a **m**
  Jer. 2:32, **m** forget her ornaments
  Luke 8:54, saying, **M** arise
Maiden—*a virgin*
  Judg. 19:24, here is my daughter a **m**
  Ruth 2:8, abide here fast by my **m-s**
  Job 41:5, bind him for thy **m**
  Ps. 148:12, Both young men, and **m-s**
Majesty—*exalted dignity, grandeur*
  Job 37:22, with God is terrible **m**
  Ps. 93:1, he is clothed with **m**
  Heb. 1:3, right hand of the **m**
  Jude 25, glory and **m**, dominion and
Make—*fashion, bring about*
  Gen. 1:26, Let us **m** man in our image
    2:18, **m** him an help meet for him
  Ex. 20:4, **m** unto thee any graven image
    25, **m** me an altar of stone
  2 Sam. 7:26, thy name be **m**-ed for ever
  Eccles. 12:12, **m**-ing many books . . . no
  Is. 45:7, I **m** peace, and create evil
  Matt. 3:3, **m** his paths straight
    4:19, **m** you fishers of men
  Luke 11:39, **m** clean the outside of
    19:5, Zacchaeus, **m** haste, and
  John 1:23, **M** straight the way of the

  Heb. 13:21, **M** you perfect in every
  2 Pet. 1:10, **m** your calling . . . sure
Maker—*the Creator*
  Job 4:17, more pure than his **m**
    35:10, Where is God my **m**
  Is. 17:7, day shall a man look to his **M**
    54:5, thy **M** is thine husband
  Heb. 11:10, builder and **m** is God
Male—*like a man*
  Gen. 5:2, **M** and female created he
    34:25, and slew all the **m-s**
  Deut. 4:16, likeness of **m** or female
  Matt. 19:4, made them **m** and female
  Gal. 3:28, neither **m** nor female
Malice—*enmity, ill will*
  1 Cor. 5:8, the leaven of **m**
  Eph. 4:31, from you, with all **m**
  Col. 3:8, anger, wrath, **m**
  1 Pet. 2:1, laying aside all **m**
Man—*the human being or race, a male*
  Gen. 1:26, Let us make **m**
    3:22, **m** is become as one of us
  Num. 12:3, **m** Moses was very meek
    23:19, God is not a **m**
  1 Sam. 16:17, Provide me now a **m**
  1 Kin. 2:2, and shew thyself a **m**
  2 Kin. 5:8, Elisha the **m** of God
  Job 5:7, Yet **m** is born unto trouble
    14:1, **M** that is born of a woman
    25:6, less **m**, that is a worm
    33:12, God is greater than **m**
  Ps. 1:1, Blessed is the **m** that walketh
    19:5, strong **m** to run a race
    37:37, Mark the perfect **m**
  Prov. 3:4, in the sight of God and **m**
  Eccles. 12:13, the whole duty of **m**
  Is. 2:22, Cease ye from **m**
  Matt. 4:4, **M** shall not live by bread
    6:24, No **m** can serve two
    8:20, Son of **m** hath not where to
    26:2, the Son of **m** is betrayed
  Mark 2:27, not **m** for the sabbath
    8:30, tell no **m** of him
    10:25, for a rich **m** to enter
  Luke 6:45, a good **m** . . . an evil **m**
    9:22, the Son of **m** must suffer
  John 1:6, a **m** sent from God
    3:4, How can a **m** be born when
    7:12, He is a good **m**
    19:5, Behold the **m**
    41, was never **m** yet laid
  Rom. 6:6, our old **m** is crucified
    13:8, Owe no **m** anything

1 Cor. 13:11, when I became a **m**
    15:21, by **m** came death
2 Cor. 12:2, I knew a **m** in Christ above
Gal. 6:4, every **m** prove his own work
Eph. 4:13, unto a perfect **m**
Col. 3:9, put off the old **m**
James 1:8, double minded **m** is unstable
1 John 2:1, if any **m** sin
Manifest—*open, clear*
John 9:3, works of God . . . made **m**
    17:6, **m**-ed thy name
Rom. 8:19, **m**-ation of the sons of God
    10:20, I was made **m**
Eph. 5:13, **m** by the light . . . **m** is light
Col. 1:26, but now is made **m**
1 Tim. 3:16, God was **m** in the flesh
Manifold—*various in kind or quality*
Neh. 9:26, according to thy **m** mercies
Ps. 104:24, how **m** are thy works
Eph. 3:10, **m** wisdom of God
1 Pet. 1:6, through **m** temptations
    4:10, stewards of the **m** grace
Manner—*custom, habit, measure*
Gen. 18:11, after the **m** of women
Matt. 5:11, say all **m** of evil against
    6:9, After this **m** . . . pray ye
John 19:40, **m** of the Jews is to bury
1 Cor. 15:33, corrupt good **m**-s
Gal. 3:15, speak after the **m** of men
Mantle—*a cloak, outer garment*
1 Kin. 19:19, cast his **m** upon him
Job 1:20, arose and rent his **m**
Many—*numerous, varied*
Gen. 17:4, father of **m** nations
    37:3, coat of **m** colours
Judg. 7:4, people are yet too **m**
1 Kin. 11:1, Solomon loved **m** strange
Job 13:23, **m** are my iniquities
Ps. 71:7, I am as a wonder unto **m**
Prov. 14:20, the rich hath **m** friends
Song 8:7, **M** waters cannot quench love
Jer. 14:7, our backslidings are **m**
Matt. 7:22, **M** will say to me in that
    22:14, **m** are called, but few
    24:12, love of **m** shall wax cold
Luke 7:47, Her sins, which are **m**
    21:8, **m** shall come in my name
John 14:2, are **m** mansions
Acts 2:43, **m** wonders and signs
Rom. 12:4, **m** members in one body
1 Cor. 11:30, **m** are weak . . . **m** sleep
James 3:1, be not **m** masters
Rev. 1:15, sound of **m** waters

Mar—*injure, damage, deface*
Lev. 19:27, **m** the corners . . . beard
Ruth 4:6, **m** mine own inheritance
1 Sam. 6:5, mice that **m** the land
Mark 2:22, and the bottles will be **m**-red
Mark—*a sign, impression, target*
Gen. 4:15, Lord set a **m** upon Cain
1 Sam. 20:20, though I shot at a **m**
Ps. 37:37, **M** the perfect man
Lam. 3:12, as a **m** for the arrow
Phil. 3:14, press toward the **m**
Rev. 14:9, his **m** in his forehead
    19:20, **m** of the beast
Marriage—*wedlock, matrimony*
Ex. 21:10, and her duty of **m**
Matt. 22:30, marry, nor are given in **m**
John 2:1, there was a **m** in Cana
Heb. 13:4, **M** is honourable in all
Rev. 19:7, **m** of the Lamb
Marry—*to join in wedlock*
Matt. 5:32, **m** her that is divorced
    19:9, **m** another, committeth
    10, it is not good to **m**
Mark 12:25, they neither **m**, nor are
Luke 20:34, children of this world **m**
1 Cor. 7:9, better to **m** than to burn
1 Tim. 5:11, that the younger women **m**
Marvel—*wonder, be surprised*
Ex. 34:10, I will do **m**-s
Matt. 8:10, Jesus heard it, he **m**-led
Mark 5:20, and all men did **m**
Luke 1:63, name is John . . . they **m**-ed all
John 3:7, not that I said unto thee
Marvellous—*exciting wonder*
Job 37:5, God thundereth **m**-ly
Ps. 17:7, **m** lovingkindness
    78:12, **M** things did he
John 9:30, herein is a **m** thing
1 Pet. 2:9, darkness into his **m** light
Rev. 15:3, Great and **m** are thy works
Master—*male person in authority*
Job 3:19, servant is free from his **m**
Jonah 1:6, So the ship **m** came to him
Matt. 6:24, No man can serve two **m**-s
    8:19, **M**, I will follow thee
    17:24, Doth not your **m** pay
    23:8, one is your **M**, even Christ
    26:25, **M**, is it I
Mark 5:35, why troublest thou the **M**
    9:5, **M**, it is good to be here
John 3:10, Art thou a **m** of Israel
    13:13, Ye call me **M** and Lord
1 Cor. 3:10, as a wise **m**-builder

Master (*Continued*)
Eph. 6:5, to them that are your **m**-s
2 Tim. 2:5, also strive for **m**-ies
James 3:1, be not many **m**-s
Mastery—*victory, triumph*
Ex. 32:18, voice of them that shout for **m**
1 Cor. 9:25, man that striveth for the **m**
2 Tim. 2:5, a man also strive for **m**-s
Matter—*subject of concern*
Gen. 30:15, Is it a small **m**
Ex. 23:7, Keep . . . far from a false **m**
Deut. 17:8, a **m** too hard for thee
Job 19:28, the root of the **m** is found
Prov. 16:20, handleth a **m** wisely
Eccles. 12:13, conclusion of the . . . **m**
Mark 1:45, blaze abroad the **m**
1 Cor. 6:2, to judge the smallest **m**-s
James 3:5, great a **m** a little fire
Mean—*common, low, have intention*
Josh. 4:21, What **m** these stones
Prov. 22:29, not stand before **m** men
Matt. 9:13, and learn what that **m**-eth
Acts 17:20, know . . . what these things **m**
21:39, citizen of no **m** city
1 Cor. 14:11, not the **m**-ing of the voice
Means—*agency or instrumentality*
Ex. 34:7, by no **m** clear the guilty
Matt. 5:26, shalt by no **m** come out
1 Cor. 8:9, lest by any **m** this liberty
Measure—*capacity, extent, to compute*
Gen. 18:6, three **m**-s of fine meal
Deut. 25:15, just **m** shalt thou have
2 Kin. 7:1, **m** of fine flour be sold for
Ps. 80:5, tears to drink in great **m**
Matt. 7:2, and with what **m** ye mete
13:33, hid in three **m**-s of meal
2 Cor. 11:23, in stripes above **m**
Eph. 4:7, to the **m** of the gift of Christ
Rev. 21:16, **m**-ed the city with the reed
Meat—*food, in general*
Gen. 1:29, it shall be for **m**
27:4, make me savoury **m**
Judg. 14:14, eater came forth **m**
Ps. 69:21, gave me also gall for my **m**
145:15, **m** in due season
Prov. 23:3, dainties . . . are deceitful **m**
Is. 65:25, dust . . . the serpent's **m**
Matt. 3:4, **m** was locusts and wild honey
6:25, the life more than **m**
25:35, and ye gave me **m**
Luke 12:42, portion of **m** in due season
Luke 24:41, have ye here any **m**
John 4:34, My **m** is to do the will of him
6:55, For my flesh is **m** indeed

Rom. 14:17, kingdom of God is not **m**
1 Cor. 6:13, **M**-s for the belly
Meddle—*impertinently interfere with*
2 Chr. 25:19, **m** to thine hurt
35:21, forbear . . . **m**-ing with God
Prov. 20:3, every fool will be **m**-ing
Mediator—*one who comes between others*
Gal. 3:19, in the hand of a **m**
20, is not a **m** of one, but God
1 Tim. 2:5, **m** between God and men
Heb. 8:6, **m** of a better covenant
12:24, Jesus the **m** of a new
Meditate—*contemplate, study*
Gen. 24:63, Isaac went out to **m**
Ps. 1:2, law doth he **m** day and night
19:14, **m**-ion of my heart
1 Tim. 4:15, **M** upon these things
Meek—*gentle, humble, mild tempered*
Num. 12:3, man Moses was very **m**
Ps. 37:11, **m** shall inherit the earth
147:6, Lord lifteth up the **m**
Is. 61:1, preach . . . unto the **m**
Matt. 5:5, Blessed are the **m**
11:29, for I am **m** and lowly
21:5, **m**, and sitting upon an ass
1 Cor. 4:21, in the spirit of **m**-ness
Gal. 5:23, **M**-ness, temperance
Eph. 4:2, With all lowliness and **m**-ness
1 Tim. 6:11, love, patience, **m**-ness
1 Pet. 3:4, a **m** and quiet spirit
Meet—*suitable, fit, proper*
Gen. 2:18, an help **m** for him
Matt. 3:8, fruits **m** for repentance
Col. 1:12, made us **m** to be partakers
Melody—*sweet and agreeable sounds*
Is. 23:16, make sweet **m**, sing many
51:3, and the voice of **m**
Eph. 5:19, making **m** in your heart
Melt—*liquify, soften*
Josh. 2:11, our hearts did **m**
Judg. 5:5, mountains **m**-ed from before
Ps. 46:6, uttered his voice . . . earth **m**-ed
97:5, hills **m** like wax
Is. 64:2, the **m**-ing fire burneth
Member—*any part of a whole*
Matt. 5:29, one of thy **m**-s . . . perish
1 Cor. 6:15, bodies are the **m**-s of Christ
12:12, the body . . . hath many **m**-s
14, body is not one **m**
James 3:5, the tongue is a little **m**
Memorial—*monument or remembrance*
Ex. 3:15, **m** unto all generations
17:14, Write this for a **m** in a book

Josh. 4:7, these stones shall be for a **m**
Ps 9:6, their **m** is perished
Matt. 26:13, told for a **m** of her
Acts 10:4, thine alms . . . for a **m**
Memory—*things remembered*
Ps. 109:15, cut off the **m** of them
Prov. 10:7, **m** of the just is blessed
Is. 26:14, made all their **m** to perish
1 Cor. 15:2, if ye keep in **m**
Men—*human being, particularly the males*
Gen. 6:1, **m** began to multiply
1 Sam. 4:9, quit yourselves like **m**
2 Chr. 6:18, in very deed dwell with **m**
Job 11:3, lies make **m** hold their peace
　　32:9, Great **m** are not always wise
Ps. 82:7, But ye shall die like **m**
　　116:11, All **m**
Is. 46:8, and shew yourselves **m**
Matt. 10:17, beware of **m**
Mark 1:17, you to become fishers of **m**
Luke 20:4, from heaven, or of **m**
Rom. 6:19, I speak after the manner of **m**
1 Thess. 2:4, not as pleasing **m**, but God
Jude 16, having **m**'s persons in
Mention—*notice of anything*
Ps. 71:16, make **m** of thy righteousness
Is. 63:7, **m** the lovingkindness of the
Rom. 1:9, **m** of you . . . in my prayers
Merchandise—*wares, goods*
Deut. 21:14, not make **m** of her
Prov. 3:14, better than the **m** of silver
Matt. 22:5, farm, another to his **m**
John 2:16, house an house of **m**
Rev. 18:12, **m** of gold, and silver, and
Merchant—*a trader*
Gen. 23:16, current money with the **m**
1 Kin. 10:28, **m-s** received the linen
Hos. 12:7, He is a **m**, the balances
Rev. 18:3, **m-s** of the earth are . . . rich
Merciful—*unwilling to punish*
Ex. 34:6, Lord God, **m** and gracious
2 Sam. 22:26, wilt shew thyself **m**
Ps. 67:1, God be **m** unto us, and bless
Prov. 11:17, The **m** man doeth good
Matt. 5:7, Blessed are the **m**
Luke 6:36, **m**, as your Father also is **m**
　　18:13, be **m** to me a sinner
Mercy—*forbearance to inflict harm*
Ex. 33:19, **m** on whom I will shew **m**
2 Sam. 24:14, for his **m-s** are great
Ezra 3:11, his **m** endureth for ever
Ps. 6:2, Have **m** upon me, O Lord
　　89:1, I will sing of thy **m-s**

Matt. 5:7, for they shall obtain **m**
Rom. 9:15, **m** on whom I will have **m**
　　12:1, by the **m-s** of God
Eph. 2:4, God, who is rich in **m**
Col. 3:12, bowels of **m-s**
James 5:11, pitiful, and of tender **m**
Merry—*happy, joyous*
Judg. 16:25, their hearts were **m**
Prov. 15:15, **m** heart hath a continual
　　17:22, **m** heart doeth good like a
Eccles. 8:15, eat . . . drink . . . be **m**
Luke 12:19, eat, drink, and be **m**
　　15:29, make **m** with my friends
James 5:13, Is any man **m**
Message—*a communication*
Judg. 3:20, I have a **m** from God unto
Hag. 1:13, in the Lord's **m**
Luke 19:14, sent a **m** after him
Messenger—*one who bears word*
2 Kin. 6:32, **m** cometh, shut the door
Matt. 11:10, my **m** before thy face
2 Cor. 12:7, the **m** of Satan
Middle—*center part*
Josh. 12:2, from the **m** of the river
Ezek. 1:16, wheel in the **m** of a wheel
Eph. 2:14, broken down the **m** wall
Midnight—*hour between eleven and one*
Ruth 3:8, it came to pass at **m**
Ps. 119:6, At **m** I will arise to give
Matt. 25:6, at **m** there was a cry made
Acts 16:25, at **m** Paul and Silas prayed
　　20:7, continued his speech until **m**
Midst—*central part or place*
Gen. 1:6, in the **m** of the waters
Prov. 30:19, ship in the **m** of the sea
Matt. 10:16, sheep in the **m** of wolves
　　18:20, there am I in the **m** of them
Luke 24:36, Jesus . . . stood in the **m** of
John 20:26, in the **m**, and said, Peace
Might—*force or power*
Gen. 49:3, my firstborn, my **m**
Deut. 6:5, thy soul, and with all thy **m**
Judg. 5:31, sun . . . goeth forth in his **m**
　　6:14, Go in this thy **m**
2 Sam. 6:14, David danced . . . all his **m**
Eccles. 9:10, do it with thy **m**
Is. 40:29, to them that have no **m**
Jer. 9:23, mighty man glory in his **m**
Zech. 4:6, Not by **m**, nor by power
Acts 19:20, **m-ily** grew the word of God
Eph. 1:21, principality, . . . power, and **m**
Col. 1:29, worketh in me **m-ily**
Mighty—*having great power, wonderful*
Gen. 10:9, **m** hunter before the Lord

Mighty (*Continued*)
Deut. 10:17, a great God, a **m**, and a
2 Sam. 1:19, how are the **m** fallen
Ps. 24:8, strong and **m**, **m** in battle
 89:13, Thou hast a **m** arm
Is. 63:1, **m** to save
Jer. 32:18, the Great, the **M** God
Mark 6:5, could there do no **m** work
Luke 9:43, the **m** power of God
 24:19, prophet **m** in deed and word
Acts 18:24, **m** in the scriptures
2 Cor. 13:3, but is **m** in you
Eph. 1:19, working of his **m** power
1 Pet. 5:6, the **m** hand of God
Milk—*nourishing white fluid*
Gen. 49:12, teeth white with **m**
Ex. 3:8, land flowing with **m** and honey
Judg. 4:19, she opened a bottle of **m**
Job 10:10, poured me out as **m**
Prov. 30:33, churning of **m** bringeth
1 Cor. 3:2, have fed you with **m**
Heb. 5:12, such as have need of **m**
1 Pet. 2:2, the sincere **m** of the word
Mind—*the intellect and spirit*
Lev. 24:12, **m** of the Lord
Ps. 31:12, as a dead man out of **m**
Prov. 29:11, fool uttereth all his **m**
Is. 46:8, bring it again to **m**
Hab. 1:11, Then shall his **m** change
Mark 5:15, and in his right **m**
Luke 12:29, neither be ye of doutbful **m**
Acts 28:6, changed their **m-s**
Rom. 1:28, over to a reprobate **m**
 8:7, carnal **m** is enmity against
 14:5, fully persuaded in his own **m**
1 Cor. 1:10, joined . . . in the same **m**
2 Cor. 8:12, there be first a willing **m**
 13:11, be of one **m**, live in
Phil. 2:2, one accord, of one **m**
 3, in lowliness of **m** let each
1 Tim. 6:5, men of corrupt **m-s**
James 1:8, A double **m-ed** man
1 Pet. 1:13, gird up the loins of your **m**
 3:8, be ye all of one **m**
Minister—*clergyman, attend, or assist*
Ezra 7:24, **m-s** of this house of God
Is. 61:6, call you the **M-s** of our God
Matt. 20:26, let him be your **m**
 28, to be **m-ed** unto, but to **m**
Luke 1:2, and **m-s** of the word
2 Cor. 3:6, **m-s** of the new testament
 11:23, Are they **m-s** of Christ
Eph. 3:7, Whereof I was made a **m**
1 Tim. 4:6, be a good **m** of Jesus

Ministry—*God's service*
Hos. 12:10, **m** of the prophets
Acts 6:4, to the **m** of the word
2 Cor. 5:18, **m** of reconciliation
Eph. 4:12, for the work of the **m**
Col. 4:17, Take heed to the **m**
2 Tim. 4:5, make full proof of thy **m**
Heb. 8:6, obtained a more excellent **m**
Miracle—*a supernatural happening*
Luke 23:8, hoped to have seen some **m**
John 2:11, beginning of **m-s** did Jesus
 10:41, John did no **m**
 11:47, this man doeth many **m-s**
Acts 15:12, **m-s** and wonders God
1 Cor. 12:10, another the working of **m-s**
Mischief—*harm, hurt, injury*
1 Kin. 20:7, see how this man seeketh **m**
Job 15:35, They conceive **m**
Ps. 52:2, Thy tongue deviseth **m-s**
Prov. 6:18, feet . . . swift in running to **m**
 24:16, wicked shall fall into **m**
Acts 13:10, all subtilty and all **m**
Misery—*distress, woe*
Job 3:20, light given to him . . . in **m**
Prov. 31:7, remember his **m** no more
Eccles. 8:6, **m** of man is great
Rom. 3:16, and **m** are in their ways
Mixed—*mingled, blended*
Prov. 23:30, that go to seek **m** wine
Is. 1:22, wine **m** with water
Dan. 2:41, iron **m** with miry clay
Heb. 4:2, not being **m** with faith
Mock—*mimic, taunt, deride*
2 Kin. 2:23, children . . . **m-ed** him
Prov. 14:9, Fools make a **m** at sin
 20:1, Wine is a **m-er**
Matt. 27:29, knee before him, and **m-ed**
Gal. 6:7, God is not **m-ed**
Moment—*minute portion of time*
Num. 16:21, consume them in a **m**
Job 21:13, in a **m** go down to the grave
 34:20, In a **m** shall they die
Ps. 30:5, his anger endureth but a **m**
Is. 26:20, hide thyself . . . for a little **m**
1 Cor. 15:52, **m**, in the twinkling of an
Money—*riches, portable wealth*
Gen. 43:12, double **m** in your hand
2 Kin. 5:26, Is it a time to receive **m**
Eccles. 7:12, **m** is a defence
 10:19, **m** answereth all things
Jer. 32:25, Buy thee the field for **m**
Matt. 21:12, tables of the **m-changers**
 22:19, shew me the tribute **m**

Mark 6:8, no **m** in their purse
Luke 19:23, my **m** into the bank
Acts 8:20, Thy **m** perish with thee
1 Tim. 6:10, love of **m** . . . root of all evil
Moon—*the earth's satellite*
Gen. 37:9, **m** and the eleven stars
Josh. 10:12, thou, **M**, in the valley of
1 Sam. 20:5, to morrow is the new **m**
Job 31:26, **m** walking in brightness
Ps. 136:9, **m** and stars to rule by night
Song 6:10, fair as the **m**
Is. 1:13, new **m**-s and sabbaths
   3:18, round tires like the **m**
Joel 2:31, and the **m** into blood
Matt. 24:29, **m** shall not give her
Luke 21:25, signs in the sun . . . **m**
Acts 2:20, and the **m** into blood
Morning—*time before noon*
Gen. 19:15, when the **m** arose
Ex. 8:20, Rise up early in the **m**
Deut. 28:67, would God it were **m**
Job 38:7, **m** stars sang together
Ps. 55:17, and **m**, and at noon
   139:9, take the wings of the **m**
Eccles. 11:6, In the **m** sow thy seed
Joel 2:2, **m** spread upon the mountains
Mark 16:2, in the **m**, the first day
Rev. 22:16, the bright and **m** star
Morrow—*the following day*
Prov. 27:1, Boast not thyself of to **m**
Is. 22:13, drink; for to we shall die
Matt. 6:34, Take . . . no thought for the **m**
James 4:14, not what shall be on the **m**
Morsel—*a little bit of food*
Gen. 18:5, fetch a **m** of bread
Ruth 2:14, dip thy **m** in the vinegar
Job 31:17, eaten my **m** myself alone
Prov. 17:1, Better is a dry **m**
Mortal—*a being subject to death*
Job 4:17, shall **m** man be more just
Rom. 6:12, reign in your **m** body
   8:11, quicken your **m** bodies
1 Cor. 15:53, **m** . . . put on immortality
2 Cor. 4:11, manifest in our **m** flesh
Mother—*female parent*
Gen. 2:24, man leave his father . . . **m**
   3:20, the **m** of all living
   17:16, she shall be a **m** of nations
Ex. 20:12, Honour thy father and thy **m**
Job 17:14, Thou art my **m**
Ezek. 16:44, the **m**, so is her daughter

Hos. 2:2, Plead with your **m**
Matt. 12:48, Who is my **m**? and who
   19:19, Honour thy . . . and thy **m**
John 19:27, the disciple, Behold thy **m**
Heb. 7:3, Without father, without **m**
Mourn—*to grieve for*
Gen. 37:35, down into the grave . . .**m**-ing
Is. 61:2, to comfort all that **m**
Matt. 5:4, Blessed are they that **m**
Luke 6:25, for ye shall **m** and weep
James 4:9, laughter be turned to **m**-ing
Mouth—*an opening*
Ex. 4:11, Who hath made man's **m**
Deut. 17:6, the **m** of two witnesses
Judg. 7:6, putting their hand to their **m**
Job 8:21, fill thy **m** with laughing
   15:6, own **m** condemneth thee
   29:10, cleaved to the roof of . . . **m**
Ps. 8:2, Out of the **m** of babes and
   19:14, Let the words of my **m**
   39:1, keep my **m** with a bridle
   55:21, words of his **m** were smoother
   71:15, My **m** shall shew forth
Prov. 4:24, put away . . . a froward **m**
   13:3, that keepeth his **m** keepeth
Eccles. 5:2, Be not rash with thy **m**
Matt. 13:35, open my **m** in parables
Luke 21:15, give you a **m** and wisdom
Acts 3:21, **m** of all his holy prophets
Titus 1:11, Whose **m**-s must be stopped
James 3:3, put bits in the horses' **m**-s
Move—*to change place or posture*
Gen. 1:2, Spirit of God **m**-d upon the
Ex. 11:7, not a dog **m** his tongue
1 Sam. 1:13, only her lips **m**-d
Jer. 4:24, all the hills **m**-d lightly
Matt. 9:36, **m**-d with compassion
Mark 1:41, Jesus, **m**-d with compassion
John 5:3, the **m**-ing of the water
Acts 17:28, in him we live, and **m**
2 Pet. 1:21, **m**-d by the Holy Ghost
Much—*great in quantity*
Num. 16:3, Ye take too **m** upon you
Prov. 25:27, not good to eat **m** honey
Eccles. 1:18, in **m** wisdom is **m** grief
Luke 7:47, for she loved **m**
   16:10, faithful also in **m**
Multiply—*increase*
Gen. 1:22, Be fruitful, and **m**
Ex. 32:13, I will **m** your seed
Dan. 4:1, Peace be **m**-ed unto you

Multiply (*Continued*)
2 Cor. 9:10, m your seed sown
Heb. 6:14, m-ing I will m thee
Multitude—*great gathering*
Gen. 16:10, not be numbered for m
Ex. 23:2, not follow a m to do evil
Deut. 1:10, as the stars of heaven for m
Job 32:7, m of years . . . teach wisdom
Ps. 51:1, m of thy tender mercies
Prov. 24:6, m of counsellors . . . safety
Matt. 14:15, send the m away
James 5:20, hide a m of sins
1 Pet. 4:8, cover a m of sins
Murder—*take the life of another*
Ps. 10:8, doth he m the innocent
Matt. 19:18, Thou shalt do no m
Rom. 1:29, full of envy, m, debate
Gal. 5:21, Envyings, m, drunkenness
Murderer—*a malicious killer*
Num. 35:16, m-s shall . . . be put to
death
John 8:44, a m from the beginning
Acts 28:4, this man is a m
1 Tim. 1:9, m-s of fathers . . . of
mothers
1 John 3:15, hateth his brother is a m
Murmur—*to grumble, complain*
Ex. 17:3, people m against Moses
Is. 29:24, that m-ed . . . learn doctrine
Luke 15:2, Pharisees and scribes m-ed
John 6:43, M not among yourselves
Phil. 2:4, Do all things without m-ings
Musick—*melodic and harmonic tones*
1 Sam. 18:6, with instruments of m
Eccles. 12:4, the daughters of m
Luke 15:25, he heard m and dancing
Muzzle—*bind up the mouth*
Deut. 25:4, not m the ox when he
1 Cor. 9:9, not m the mouth of the ox
1 Tim. 5:18, not m the ox
Myrrh—*an aromatic gum resin*
Gen. 43:11, spices, and m, and nuts
Ps. 45:8, garments smell of m
Song 5:13, sweet smelling m
Matt. 2:11, frankincense and m
John 19:39, mixture of m and aloes
Mystery—*something secret or unknown*
Matt. 13:11, m-es of the kingdom
1 Cor. 2:7, wisdom of God in a m
4:1, stewards of the m-s
13:2, and understand all m-s
Eph. 3:9, the fellowship of the m
6:19, the m of the gospel
1 Tim. 3:9, the m of the faith

N

Nail—*metal binder, finger protection*
Deut. 21:12, and pare her n-s
Judg. 4:21, took a n of the tent
Is. 22:23, as a n in a sure place
Dan. 4:3, his n-s like bird claws
John 20:25, hands the print of the n-s
Naked—*unclothed, defenseless*
Gen. 2:25, they were both n
Job 1:21, N came I out . . . and n . . .
return
26:6, Hell is n before him
Matt. 25:36, N, and ye clothed me
Heb. 4:13, all things are n
Name—*appellation, reputed character*
Gen. 3:20, called his wife's n Eve
Ex. 20:7, n of the Lord thy God in vain
Deut. 29:20, blot out his n
Neh. 9:10, So didst thou get thee a n
Job 1:21, blessed be the n of the Lord
Ps. 8:1, how excellent is thy n
18:49, sing praises unto thy n
72:17, His n shall endure for ever
102:15, fear the n of the Lord
111:9, holy and reverend is his n
Prov. 22:1, good n is rather to be chosen
30:9, n of my God in vain
Is. 42:8, the Lord: that is my n
48:2, Lord of hosts is his n
57:15, whose n is Holy
Matt. 6:9, Hallowed by thy n
10:22, for my n's sake
18:5, one such little child in my n
Mark 5:9, My n is Legion: for we are
Luke 21:8, many shall come in my n
John 15:16, ye shall ask . . . in my n
Acts 3:16, through faith in his n
4:12, none other n under heaven
Eph. 1:21, above . . . every n that is n-ed
Phil. 2:9, n which is above every n
4:3, whose n-s are in the book
3 John 14, Greet the friends by n
Nation—*people under one government*
Gen. 12:2, make of thee a great n
20:4, slay also a righteous n
Ex. 19:6, kingdom of priests . . . holy n
Ps. 33:12, Blessed . . . n whose God is
Prov. 14:34, Righteousness exalteth a n
Is. 2:4, n shall not lift up sword
18:2, a n scattered and peeled
52:15, shall he sprinkle many n-s

Matt. 24:7, **n** shall rise against **n**
    28:19, Go . . . and teach all **n-s**
John 11:50, that the whole **n** perish not
Acts 2:5, devout men, out of every **n**
Gal. 3:8, shall all **n-s** be blessed
Phil. 2:15, a crooked and perverse **n**
Rev. 5:9, and tongue, and people, and **n**
Natural—*fixed by nature's laws*
Deut. 34:7, nor his **n** force abated
Rom. 1:31, without **n** affection
1 Cor. 15:44, It is sown a **n** body
2 Tim. 3:3, Without **n** affection
2 Pet. 2:12, as **n** brute beasts
Nature—*the world of matter*
Rom. 1:26, that which is against **n**
1 Cor. 11:14, Doth not even **n** . . . teach
Heb. 2:16, on him the **n** of angels
2 Pet. 1:4, partakers of the divine **n**
Near—*close by*
Ex. 19:22, which come **n** to the Lord
Judg. 20:34, knew not that evil was **n**
Ps. 22:11, for trouble is **n**
Prov. 27:10, a neighbour that is **n**
Joel 3:14, day of the Lord is **n**
Mark 13:28, ye know that summer is **n**
Heb. 10:22, draw **n** with a true heart
Neck—*connection of the trunk and head*
Gen. 27:16, upon the smooth of his **n**
Ex. 13:13, thou shalt break his **n**
Deut. 28:48, yoke of iron upon thy **n**
Prov. 3:3, bind them about thy **n**
Matt. 18:6, millstone . . . about his **n**
Luke 15:20, fell on his **n**, and kissed
Need—*urgent want*
Matt. 6:8, what things ye have **n** of
    9:12, be whole **n** not a physician
    21:3, The Lord hath **n** of them
Luke 10:42, But one thing is **n**-ful
1 Cor. 12:21, hand, I have no **n** of thee
Phil. 4:19, God shall supply all your **n**
Heb. 4:16, help in time of **n**
1 John 3:17, seeth his brother have **n**
Rev. 3:17, have **n** of nothing
Needy—*in want*
Deut. 15:11, open thine hand . . . to thy **n**
Ps. 9:18, **n** . . . not always be forgotten
    40:17, But I am poor and **n**
    72:13, He shall spare the poor and **n**
Is. 14:30, **n** shall lie down in safety
Neighbour—*one who is near to another*
Lev. 19:18, thou shalt love thy **n** as
Prov. 3:29, Devise not evil against thy **n**
    27:10, better is a **n** that is near

Hab. 2:15, that giveth his **n** drink
Matt. 5:43, Thou shalt love thy **n**
Luke 10:29, And who is my **n**
Heb. 8:11, teach every man his **n**
Nest—*place where eggs are hatched*
Num. 24:21, puttest thy **n** in a rock
Deut. 32:11, eagle stirreth up her **n**
Jer. 49:16, thy **n** as high as the eagle
Obad. 4, set thy **n** among the stars
Matt. 8:20, birds of the air have **n-s**
Net—*a trap or snare*
Job 19:6, compassed me with his **n**
Ps. 57:6, prepared a **n** for my steps
Is. 51:20, as a wild bull in a **n**
Matt. 13:47, kingdom . . . is like unto a **n**
Never—*not at any time*
Lev. 6:13, fire . . . it shall **n** go out
Deut. 15:11, poor shall **n** cease out of
Job 3:16, infants which **n** saw light
Ps. 31:1, let me **n** be ashamed
Matt. 7:23, I **n** knew you
John 4:14, of the water . . . **n** thirst
    7:46, N man spake like this man
    8:51, shall **n** see death
    19:41, was **n** man yet laid
Heb. 13:5, I will **n** leave thee
New—*of recent origin*
Ps. 33:3, Sing unto him a **n** song
Eccles. 1:9, no **n** thing under the sun
Is. 65:17, **n** heavens and a **n** earth
Ezek. 11:19, put a **n** spirit within you
Matt. 26:28, blood of the **n** testament
John 13:34, A **n** commandment I give
2 Cor. 5:17, he is a **n** creature
Eph. 4:24, put on the **n** man
Rev. 21:1, **n** heaven . . . **n** earth
Nigh—*near, close*
Deut. 4:7, who hath God so **n**
Ps. 34:18, **n** unto them . . . of a broken
    145:18, **n** unto all them that call
Eph. 2:13, made **n** by the blood of Christ
James 4:8, Draw **n** to God . . . draw **n**
Night—*the dark hours, darkness*
Gen. 1:5, the darkness he called N
Ex. 13:21, by **n** in a pillar of fire
Josh. 1:8, meditate therein day and **n**
Job 17:12, change the **n** into day
Ps. 19:2, **n** unto **n** sheweth knowledge
    91:5, afraid for the terror by **n**
Is. 21:11, Watchman, what of the **n**
Luke 2:8, watch over their flock by **n**
John 9:4, the **n** cometh, when no man
Rom. 13:12, The **n** is far spent
1 Thess. 5:2, as a thief in the **n**

Noise—*sound of any kind*
Ex. 32:17, n of war in the camp
1 Kin. 1:41, n of the city being in an
Ps. 66:1, Make a joyful n unto God
Luke 1:65, sayings were n-d abroad
2 Pet. 3:10, pass away with a great n
Rev. 6:1, the n of thunder
Nothing—*not anything, of little value*
Job 6:21, now ye are n
26:7, hangeth the earth upon n
Ps. 49:17, he shall carry n away
Prov. 13:7, himself rich, yet hath n
Lam. 1:12, Is it n to you, all ye that
Mark 14:60, Answerest thou n
Luke 6:35, lend, hoping for n again
John 15:5, without me ye can do n
1 Cor. 4:4, I know n by myself
Gal. 6:3, be something, when he is n
Phil. 4:6, Be careful of n
James 1:4, perfect and entire, wanting n
Nourished—*supported, maintained*
1 Tim. 4:6, n up in the words of faith
James 5:5, ye have n your hearts
Number—*an aggregate of units, to reckon*
Gen. 15:5, stars, if thou be able to n
Num. 1:3, n them by their armies
2 Sam. 24:4, to n the people of Israel
Job 14:16, thou n-est my steps
Ps. 139:18, more in n than the sand
Matt. 10:30, hairs . . . are all n-ed
Mark 15:28, n-ed with the transgressors
Nurse—*an attendant*
Gen. 35:8, Deborah Rebekah's n
Ex. 2:7, a n of the Hebrew women
Num. 11:12, as a n-ing father
1 Thess. 2:7, as a n cherisheth her

O

Oak—*a tree*
2 Sam. 18:10, Absalom hanged in an o
Is. 1:30, an o whose leaf fadeth
Amos 2:9, he was strong as the o-s
Oath—*a solemn declaration or pledge*
Gen. 26:3, I will perform the o
Josh. 2:20, will be quit of thine o
Zech. 8:17, love no false o
Matt. 5:33, perform . . . thine o-s
Obedience—*act of obeying*
Rom. 16:26, for the o of faith

2 Cor. 10:5, to the o of Christ
Heb. 5:8, yet learned he o by the things
1 Pet. 1:2, unto o and sprinkling of the
Obedient—*dutiful, subject to authority*
Deut. 4:30, be o unto his voice
Prov. 25:12, wise reprover upon an o
Is. 1:19, If ye be willing and o
2 Cor. 2:9, whether ye be o in all things
Phil. 2:8, o unto death
Titus 2:5, o to their own husbands
1 Pet. 1:14, As o children
Obey—*yield submission to*
Ex. 19:5, if ye will o my voice
Deut. 11:27, if ye o the commandments
1 Sam. 15:22, o is better than sacrifice
Matt. 8:27, the winds and the sea o him
Acts 5:29, o God rather than men
36, as many as o-ed him
Eph. 6:1, Children, o your parents
Heb. 11:8, By faith Abraham . . . o-ed
13:17, O them that have the rule
Observe—*to heed, and obey*
Gen. 37:11, his father o-ed the saying
Prov. 23:26, let thine eyes o my ways
Eccles. 11:4, He that o-eth the wind
Matt. 28:20, Teaching them to o all
Mark 10:20, have I o-ed from my youth
Gal. 4:10, Ye o days, and months
Obtain—*get possession of*
Gen. 16:2, I may o children by her
Prov. 8:35, shall o favour of the Lord
Is. 35:10, o joy and gladness
1 Cor. 7:25, o mercy of the Lord
9:24, So run, that ye may o
1 Thess. 5:9, to o salvation by our Lord
Heb. 11:35, o a better resurrection
Occasion—*need, incident, use*
Judg. 9:33, do . . . as thou shalt find o
Jer. 2:24, in her o who can turn her
Rom. 14:13, o to fall in his brother's
Gal. 5:13, use not liberty for an o
1 Tim. 5:14, give none o to the adversary
Offence—*affront, injury, or sin*
Eccles. 10:4, yielding pacifieth . . . o-s
Is. 8:14, a rock of o to both
Matt. 16:23, Satan: thou art an o unto
18:7, Woe . . . because of o-s
Acts 24:16, conscience void of o
1 Cor. 10:32, Give none o
Gal. 5:11, o of the cross
Phil. 1:10, without o till the day of
1 Pet. 2:8, and a rock of o
Offend—*to displease, to commit sin*
Job 34:31, I will not o any more

Matt. 5:29, right eye o thee, pluck it
Mark 14:27, All shall be o-ed because
Luke 17:2, o one of these little
James 3:2, For in many things we o all
Offer—*to proffer, make sacrifice of*
Judg. 5:2, willingly o-ed themselves
Ps. 50:14, O unto God thanksgiving
Mal. 1:8, o the blind . . . o the lame
Matt. 5:24, come and o thy gift
Luke 6:29, check o also the other
1 Cor. 8:1, things o-ed unto idols
Phil. 2:17, I be o-ed upon the sacrifice
Heb. 9:14, o-ed himself without spot
Office—*duty, charge, or trust*
Ps. 109:8, and let another take his o
Rom. 12:4, members have not the same o
1 Tim. 3:1, desire the o of a bishop
10, use the o of a deacon
Heb. 7:5, o of the priesthood
Often—*frequently, repeated*
Prov. 29:1, being o reproved hardeneth
Luke 13:34, o would I have gathered
1 Cor. 11:26, For as o as ye eat this
1 Tim. 5:23, thine o infirmities
Oil—*unctuous combustible substance*
Ex. 25:6, O for the light
Job 29:6, rock poured me out rivers of o
Ps. 23:5, anoint my head with o
45:7, with the o of gladness
55:21, his words were softer than o
104:15, o to make his face to shine
Prov. 5:3, her mouth is smoother than o
Matt. 25:8, Give us of your o
Luke 10:34, pouring in o and wine
Rev. 6:6, hurt not the o and the wine
Ointment—*an unguent*
Job 41:31, the sea like a pot of o
Ps. 133:2, like precious o upon
Matt. 26:7, alabaster box . . . precious o
Luke 7:46, anointed my feet with o
John 12:5, Why was not this o sold
Old—*not new, young, or fresh*
Gen. 15:15, buried in a good o age
44:20, child of his o age
Deut. 29:5, shoe is not waxen o upon
Ruth 1:12, too o to have an husband
1 Sam. 12:2, o and greyheaded
Job 42:17, being o and full of days
Prov. 20:29, beauty of o men is the
Matt. 5:21, said by them of o time
9:16, new cloth unto an o
17, new wine into o bottles

John 3:4, man be born when he is o
Rom. 6:6, our o man is crucified
1 Cor. 5:7, Purge out . . . the o leaven
2 Cor. 3:14, reading of the o testament
5:17, o things are passed away
Col. 3:9, put off the o man
Rev. 12:9, o serpent, called the Devil
Once—*for one time, or at one time*
Gen. 18:32, will speak yet but this o
Is. 66:8, shall a nation be born at o
Rom. 6:10, he died unto sin o
Heb. 9:27, appointed . . . o to die
One—*a single unit, unity*
Deut. 6:4, Lord our God is o Lord
Job 33:23, o among a thousand
Matt. 19:5, they twain shall be o flesh
John 10:30, I and my Father are o
17:21, they all may be o
Eph. 4:4, o body . . . o Spirit . . . o hope
1 Tim. 2:5, o God, and o mediator
James 4:12, There is o lawgiver
Open—*not closed, free, to unclose*
Gen. 3:5, your eyes shall be o-ed
Ps. 5:9, throat is an o sepulchre
51:15, Lord, o thou my lips
Prov. 27:5, O rebuke is better than
Is. 26:2, O ye the gates
42:7, To o the blind eyes
Ezek. 16:63, never o thy mouth any
Matt. 7:7, knock, and it shall be o-ed
20:33, our eyes may be o-ed
Luke 13:25, Lord, Lord, o unto us
24:32, he o-ed to us the scriptures
John 1:51, ye shall see heaven o
Rev. 4:1, door was o-ed in heaven
5:2, Who is worthy to o the book
Oppress—*impose burdens upon*
Lev. 25:14, shall not o one another
Hos. 12:7, merchant . . . loveth to o
Acts 10:38, all that were o-ed of the
James 2:6, Do not rich men o you
Oppression—*cruelty, injustice*
Ps. 12:5, For the o of the poor
62:10, Trust not in o
Eccles. 7:7, o maketh a wise man mad
Ordain—*set apart, decree*
1 Chr. 17:9, o a place for my people
Ps. 8:3, stars, which thou hast o-ed
Mark 3:14, o-ed twelve, that they
John 15:16, chosen you, and o-ed you
1 Tim. 2:7, I am o-ed a preacher
Order—*regular arrangement*
Judg. 13:12, How shall we o the child

Order *(Continued)*
2 Kin. 20:1, Set thine house in **o**
Titus 1:5, set in **o** the things . . . wanting
Heb. 5:6, the **o** of Melchisedec
Ordinance—*rule established by authority*
Job 38:33, the **o**-s of heaven
Mal. 3:7, gone away from mine **o**-s
Rom. 13:2, resisteth the **o** of God
Eph. 2:15, commandments . . . in **o**-s
Col. 2:14, the handwriting of **o**-s
1 Pet. 2:13, Submit . . . to every **o** of man
Ought—*to be necessary, fit, becoming*
Matt. 23:23, these **o** ye to have done
Luke 24:26, **O** not Christ to have
John 4:20, where men **o** to worship
Acts 5:29, **o** to obey God rather than
Heb. 5:12, ye **o** to be teachers
James 3:10, things **o** not so to be
Out—*beyond limits*
Num. 32:23, your sin will find you **o**
Prov. 4:23, **o** of it are the issues
Matt. 12:34, **o** of the abundance of the
2 Tim. 4:2, in season, **o** of season
Outward—*external, exterior*
1 Sam. 16:7, on the **o** appearance
Rom. 2:28, **o** in the flesh
2 Cor. 4:16, our **o** man perish
Overcome—*conquer, get the better of*
Gen. 49:19, **o** him . . . **o** at the last
Jer. 23:9, man whom wine hath **o**
John 16:33, I have **o** the world
Rom. 12:21, Be not **o** of evil
1 John 2:13, ye have **o** the wicked one
Overtake—*catch up with*
Amos 9:10, evil shall not **o** . . . us
Gal. 6:1, man be **o**-n in a fault
1 Thess. 5:4, day . . . **o** you as a thief
Overthrow—*demolish, destroy, rout*
Ex. 23:24, shalt utterly **o** them
Prov. 18:5, **o** the righteousness in
Acts 5:39, of God, ye cannot **o** it
2 Tim. 2:18, **o** the faith of some
Overwhelm—*cover completely, crush, bury*
Job 6:27, ye **o** the fatherless
Ps. 61:2, my heart is **o**-ed
78:53, the sea **o**-ed their enemies
Owe—*be indebted to*
Matt. 18:28, Pay me that thou **o**-st
Rom. 13:8, **O** no man any thing
Philem. 19, **o**-st unto me even thine
Own—*belonging exclusively to*
1 Chr. 29:14, of thine **o** have we given
Prov. 14:10, heart knoweth his **o**

John 1:11, unto his **o** . . . **o** received him
10:3, calleth his **o** sheep by name
Acts 2:6, speak in his **o** language
1 Tim. 5:8, any provide not for his **o**
2 Pet. 3:3, walking after their **o** lusts
Ox—*bovine animal*
Job 6:5, loweth the **o** over his fodder
Prov. 7:22, **o** goeth to the slaughter
15:17, stalled **o** and hatred
1 Tim. 15:18, muzzle the **o** that treadeth

P

Pain—*suffering*
Ps. 25:18, mine affliction and my **p**
55:4, My heart is sore **p**-ed
116:3, **p**-s of hell gat hold upon
Acts 2:24, loosed the **p**-s of death
Rev. 21:4, neither . . . be any more **p**
Palace—*residence of a sovereign*
1 Chr. 29:1, the **p** is not for man
Luke 11:21, strong man . . . keepeth his **p**
Pardon—*forgive, absolve*
Ex. 23:21, not **p** your transgressions
2 Chr. 30:18, good Lord **p** every one
Neh. 9:17, art a God ready to **p**
Ps. 25:11, O Lord, **p** mine iniquity
Is. 55:7, he will abundantly **p**
Parents—*fathers and mothers*
Matt., 10:21, rise up against their **p**
Luke 2:41, his **p** went to Jerusalem
18:29, house, or **p**, or brethren
John 9:2, did sin, this man, or his **p**
Rom. 1:30, disobedient to **p**
2 Cor. 12:14, for the **p** . . . **p** for the
Eph. 6:1, Children, obey your **p**
2 Tim. 3:2, disobedient to **p**, unthankful
Part—*a portion, to divide*
Num. 18:20, **p** among them: I am thy **p**
Ps. 22:18, **p** my garments among them
Matt. 27:35, and **p**-ed his garments
Luke 10:42, Mary hath . . . that good **p**
11:39, inward **p** is full of ravening
John 13:8, hast no **p** with me
Acts 8:21, neither **p** nor lot
1 Cor. 13:9, know in **p** . . . prophesy in **p**
Partaker—*one having a part, or share*
Ps. 50:18, been **p** with adulterers
Matt. 23:30, not have been **p**-s with
1 Cor. 9:10, should be **p** of his hope
Eph. 5:7, Be not . . . **p**-s with them

Heb. 3:1, **p**-s of the heavenly calling
    14, made of **p**-s of Christ
    6:4, **p**-s of the Holy Ghost
2 Pet. 1:4, **p**-s of the divine nature
Pass—*to go by, beyond, over, or through*
Gen. 15:17, burning lamp that **p**-ed
Prov. 4:15, Avoid it, **p** not by it
Matt. 26:39, let this cup **p** from me
John 5:24, **p**-ed from death unto life
2 Cor. 5:17, old things are **p**-ed away
Rev. 21:1, first earth were **p**-ed away
Past—*former time, beyond*
Deut. 4:32, now of the days that are **p**
Song 2:11, the winter is **p**, the rain
Jer. 8:20, harvest is **p**, the summer is
Rom. 11:33, ways **p** finding out
Pastors—*shepherds, ministers*
Jer. 3:15, will give you **p**
    10:21, **p** are become brutish
    23:1, **p** that destroy . . . the sheep
Eph. 4:11, and some, **p** and teachers
Path—*way, track, or course*
Gen. 49:17, an adder in the **p**
Job 28:7, **p** which no fowl knoweth
Ps. 16:11, shew me the **p** of life
    27:11, lead me a plain **p**
    119:105, a light unto my **p**
Prov. 4:18, **p** of the just . . . shining
Matt. 3:3, make his **p**-s straight
Patience—*sufferance*
Matt. 18:26, Have **p** with me
Luke 21:19, In your **p** possess ye your
Rom. 5:3, tribulation worketh **p**
    15:4, **p** and comfort . . . scriptures
Col. 1:11, all **p** and longsuffering
2 Thess. 1:4, for your **p** and faith
James 1:4, **p** have her perfect work
    5:11, the **p** of Job
Patient—*long suffering*
Rom. 12:12, hope; **p** in tribulation
2 Thess. 3:5, **p** waiting for Christ
1 Tim. 3:3, **p** not a brawler
James 5:8, Be ye also **p**; stablish
Pay—*satisfy a debt, wages*
Ex. 22:7, thief . . . let him **p** double
Deut. 23:21, not slack to **p** it
Job 22:27, thou shalt **p** thy vows
Matt. 18:28, **P** me that thou owest
Peace—*freedom from turmoil*
Gen. 15:15, go to thy fathers in **p**
Lev. 26:6, I will give **p** in the land
Num. 6:26, countenance . . . give thee **p**
2 Kin. 9:17, let him say, Is it **p**
Job 13:13, Hold your **p**

Ps. 4:8, lay me down in **p**
    34:14, seek **p**, and pursue it
    37:37, end of that man is **p**
    119:165, Great **p** have they which
    147:14, maketh **p** in thy borders
Prov. 3:17, all her paths are **p**
    16:7, his enemies be at **p** with
Eccles. 3:8, time of war . . . time of **p**
Is. 9:6, Father, The Prince of **P**
    52:7, tidings, that publisheth **p**
    57:19, **P**, **p** to him that is far off
Jer. 6:14, **P**, **p**; when there is no **p**
Matt. 10:34, I came not to send **p**
Mark 9:50, have **p** one with another
Luke 1:79, guide our feet. . . way of **p**
    2:14, on earth **p**, good will toward
John 14:27, **P** I leave with you, my **p**
    20:19, saith . . . **P** be unto you
Acts 18:9, speak, and hold not thy **p**
Rom. 10:15, preach the gospel of **p**
    15:33, the God of **p** be with you
1 Cor. 7:15, God hath called us to **p**
Gal. 5:22, fruit of the Spirit is . . . **p**
Eph. 2:14, For he is our **p**
Phil. 4:7, **p** of God, which passeth
2 Thess. 3:16, Lord of **p** . . . give you **p**
Heb. 12:14, follow **p** with all men
James 2:16, Depart in **p**
1 Pet. 5:14, **P** be with you all
People—*human beings*
Ex. 6:7, take you to me for a **p**
Ruth 1:16, thy **p** shall be my **p**
Ps. 2:1, **p** imagine a vain thing
    100:3, we are his **p**, and the sheep
Prov. 11:14, no counsel is, the **p** fall
    29:18, no vision, the **p** perish
    30:25, ants are a **p** not strong
Matt. 1:21, save not **p** from their sins
Mark 7:6, **p** honoureth me with . . . lips
John 11:50, man should die for the **p**
Perceive—*note through the mind*
Deut. 29:4, given you an heart to **p**
Mark 2:8, Jesus **p**-d in his spirit
Luke 6:41, **p**-st not the beam that is
    8:46, I **p** that virtue is gone
John 12:19, **P** ye how ye prevail
Acts 10:34, **p** that God is no respecter
1 John 3:16, **p** we the love of God
Perdition—*future utter destruction*
John 17:12, the son of **p**
1 Tim. 6:9, drown men in . . . **p**
Rev. 17:8, bottomless pit, and go into **p**
Perfect—*without flaw, fault or blemish*
Deut. 32:4, He is the Rock, his work is **p**

PERFECT

Perfect (*Continued*)
Ps. 19:7, law of the Lord is **p**
Prov. 4:18, unto the **p** day
Matt. 5:48, Be ye therefore **p**
1 Cor. 13:10, when that which is **p** is
2 Cor. 12:9, strength . . . **p** in weakness
James 1:4, patience have her **p** work
      25, **p** law of liberty
1 John 4:17, our love made **p**
Perform—*carry through, fulfill*
Ps. 57:2, God that **p**-eth all things
Rom. 4:21, he was able also to **p**
2 Cor. 8:11, Now . . . **p** the doing of it
Phil. 1:6, **p** it until the day of Jesus
Perish—*to be destroyed*
Num. 17:12, we die, we **p**, we all **p**
2 Sam. 1:27, the weapons of war **p**-ed
Job 34:15, All flesh shall **p** together
Ps. 1:6, way of the ungodly shall **p**
Prov. 29:18, no vision, the people **p**
Matt. 8:25, Lord, save us: we **p**
      18:14, one . . . little ones should **p**
John 6:27, for the meat which **p**-eth
2 Pet. 3:9, not willing that any should **p**
Perpetual—*continuous, everlasting*
Ex. 31:16, for a **p** covenant
Ps. 9:6, come to a **p** end
Jer. 15:18, Why is my pain **p**
      51:39, sleep a **p** sleep
Hab. 3:6, the **p** hills did bow
Persecute—*to oppress, to harass*
Job 19:22, Why do ye **p** me as God
Ps. 7:1, save me from all them that **p** me
      143:3, enemy hath **p**-ed my soul
Matt. 5:11, men . . . revile you, and **p** you
      44, pray for them which . . . **p** you
John 15:20, if they have **p**-d me
Acts 9:4, Saul, why **p**-st thou me
1 Cor. 4:12, we bless; being **p**-d
2 Cor. 4:9, **P**-d, but not forsaken
Person—*the human being, the body*
Deut. 1:17, shall not respect **p**-s
Ps. 15:4, a vile **p** is contemned
      26:4, have not sat with vain **p**-s
Matt. 22:16, regardest not the **p** of men
Rom. 2:11, no respect of **p**-s with God
Jude 16, having men's **p**-s in admiration
Persuade—*convince, win over*
Prov. 25:15, a prince **p**-d
Matt. 28:14, we will **p** him, and
Acts 26:28, Almost thou **p**-st me
Rom. 14:14, am **p**-d by the Lord Jesus
Gal. 1:10, do I now **p** men, or God
Heb. 6:9, **p**-d better things of you

Perverse—*turned away from the right*
Deut. 32:5, **p** and crooked generation
Job 6:30, taste discern **p** things
Prov. 4:24, **p** lips put far from thee
      23:33, heart . . . utter **p** things
Acts 20:30, speaking **p** things
Phil. 2:15, a crooked and **p** nation
Pervert—*to turn from the right*
Deut. 16:19, **p** . . . words of . . . righteous
Job 8:3, Doth God **p** judgment
Luke 23:14, one that **p**-eth the people
Gal. 1:7, **p** the gospel of Christ
Petition—*prayer, supplication*
1 Sam. 1:17, God . . . grant thee thy **p**
1 Kin. 2:16, I ask one **p** of thee
Ps. 20:5, the Lord fulfill all thy **p**-s
Dan 6:7, shall ask a **p** of any God or
      13, maketh his **p** three times a
Physician—*a medical doctor*
Jer. 8:22, Gilead; is there no **p** there
Matt. 9:12, be whole need not a **p**
Luke 4:23, **P**, heal thyself
Col. 4:14, Luke, the beloved **p**
Pictures—*drawings, representations*
Num. 33:52, destroy all their **p**
Prov. 25:11, of gold in **p** of silver
Is. 2:16, upon all pleasant **p**
Piece—*a part or fragment*
1 Sam. 2:36, that I may eat a **p** of bread
2 Sam. 11:21, cast a **p** of a millstone
Zech. 11:12, for my price thirty **p**-s of
Matt. 9:16, **p** of new cloth
Luke, 24:42, a **p** of a broiled fish
Pierce—*thrust into, penetrate*
Ps. 22:16, they **p**-d my hands . . . feet
Prov. 12:18, the **p**-ings of a sword
Zech. 12:10, on me whom they have **p**
Luke 2:35, **p** through thy own soul
John 19:34, with a spear **p**-d his side
Pillar—*a column, an upright support*
Gen. 19:26, she became a **p** of salt
Job 26:11, The **p**-s of heaven tremble
Prov. 9:1, hewn out her seven **p**-s
Gal. 2:9, John, who seemed to be **p**-s
1 Tim. 3:15, **p** and ground of the truth
Pillow—*cushion for the head*
Gen 28:18, stone . . . for his **p**-s
1 Sam. 19:13, **p** of goats' hair for his
Mark 4:38, asleep on a **p**
Pipe—*wind instrument*
1 Sam. 10:5, tabret, and a **p**, and a harp
1 Kin. 1:40, people piped with **p**-s

128

1 Cor. 14:7, whether **p** or harp
Rev. 18:22, harpers . . . musicians . . . **p-rs**
Piped—*played upon the pipe*
1 Kin. 1:40, people **p** with pipes
Matt. 11:17, We have **p** unto you
1 Cor. 14:7, known what is **p** or harped
Pit—*hole in the ground, trap, the grave*
Gen. 14:10, Siddim was full of slime **p-s**
  37:20, cast him into some **p**
Ex. 21:33, shall open a **p** . . . dig a **p**
Job 33:18, his soul from the **p**
Pitcher—*a vessel for holding water*
Gen. 24:14, Let down thy **p**, I pray thee
Judg. 7:16, **p-s**, and lamps within the **p-s**
Eccles. 12:6, **p** be broken at the
Mark 14:13, man bearing a **p** of water
Pity—*sympathy in distress*
Deut. 7:16, eye shall have no **p**
Job 19:21, Have **p** upon me, have **p**
Ps. 103:13, father **p**-ieth his children
Prov. 19:17, hath **p** upon the poor
Matt. 18:33, I had **p** on thee
Place—*distinct spot or location, to put*
Gen. 1:9, waters . . . be gathered . . .
  one **p**
Ex. 3:5, **p** . . . thou standest is holy
Judg. 18:10, **p** where there is no want
Job 9:6, shaketh the earth out of her **p**
Ps. 24:3, who shall stand in his holy **p**
Prov. 15:3, eyes . . . Lord . . . in every **p**
Is. 49:20, **p** is too strait for me
Matt. 26:36, a **p** called Gethsemane
  27:33, Golgotha . . . **p** of a skull
  28:6, **p** where the Lord lay
Luke 4:17, **p** where it was written
  14:9, Give this man **p**
John 14:2, go to prepare a **p** for you
  18:2, Judas . . . knew the **p**
Rom. 12:19, rather give **p** unto wrath
Eph. 4:27, Neither give **p** to the devil
2 Pet. 1:19, light . . . in a dark **p**
Rev. 20:11, was found no **p** for them
Plague—*that which smites or troubles*
Gen. 12:17, Lord **p**-ed Pharaoh
Lev. 13:2, like the **p** of leprosy
Mark 5:29, she was healed of that **p**
Rev. 16:21, the **p** of the hail
  21:9, the seven last **p-s**
Plain—*flat, smooth, clear, level land*
Gen. 19:17, neither stay . . . all the **p**
Ps. 27:11, lead me in a **p** path
Prov. 15:19, way . . . righteous is made **p**
Is. 40:4, the rough places **p**

Hab. 2:2, make it **p** upon tables
Mark 7:35, and he spake **p**
Plainly—*clearly, distinctly*
Deut. 27:8, write all the word . . . **p**
Ezra 4:18, hath been **p** read
Is. 32:4, shall be ready to speak **p**
John 16:25, shew you **p** of the Father
Plant—*vegetable growth, to sow seed*
Gen. 2:8, God **p**-ed a garden eastward
Deut. 6:11, trees, which thou **p**-edst not
2 Kin. 19:29, **p** vineyards, and eat the
Job 14:9, boughs like a **p**
Ps. 1:3, tree **p**-ed by the rivers
  92:13, **p**-ed in the house of the
Eccles. 3:2, a time to **p**, and a time to
Is. 51:16, that I may **p** the heavens
  53:2, grow up . . . as a tender **p**
Matt. 15:13, **p** . . . Father hath not **p**-ed
Mark 12:1, certain man **p**-ed a vineyard
Luke 17:6, be thou **p**-ed in the sea
1 Cor. 3:6, I have **p**-ed, Apollos
Play—*frolic, sport, perform*
Ex. 32:6, and rose up to **p**
1 Sam. 16:17, man that can **p** well
2 Sam. 10:12, **p** the men for our people
Job 41:5, **p** with him as with a bird
Ps. 33:3, **p** skillfully with a loud
Is. 11:8, **p** on the hole of the asp
Plead—*to argue a cause*
Job 9:19, set me a time to **p**
Ps. 43:1, Judge me . . . and **p** my cause
Is. 1:17, **p** for the widow
Jer. 2:9, I will yet **p** with you
Pleasant—*agreeable, gratifying*
Gen. 2:9, every . . . **p** to the sight
2 Sam. 1:23, lovely and **p** in their lives
Ps. 16:6, lines are fallen . . . **p** places
  133:1, **p** it is for brethren to
Prov. 9:17, bread eaten in secret is **p**
  16:24, **P** words are as honeycomb
Song 4:16, and eat his **p** fruits
Ezek. 33:32, one that hath a **p** voice
Dan. 10:3, I ate no **p** bread
Please—*give or have pleasure in*
1 Kin. 3:10, the speech **p**-d the Lord
Prov. 16:7, man's ways **p** the Lord
Matt. 3:17, Son, in whom I am well **p**-d
John 8:29, those things that **p** him
Rom. 15:1, not to **p** ourselves
  3, Christ **p**-d not himself
1 Cor. 7:33, how he may **p** his wife
  34, how she may **p** her husband
  10:5, God was not well **p**-d
Heb. 13:16, sacrifices God is well **p**-d

Pleasure—*joy, gladness, gratification*
Gen. 18:12, waxed old shall I have **p**
Job 36:11, and their years in **p**-s
Ps. 16:11, there are **p**-s for evermore
51:18, Do good in thy good **p**
149:4, Lord taketh **p** in his people
Prov. 21:17, loveth **p** . . . be a poor man
Eccles. 5:4, he hath no **p** in fools
Is. 53:10, **p** of the Lord shall prosper
Luke 8:14, cares and riches and **p**-s
12:32, Father's good **p** to give
2 Cor. 12:10, take **p** in infirmities
Phil. 2:13, to do of his good **p**
Heb. 11:25, **p**-s of sin for a season
James 5:5, lived in **p** on the earth
Plenteous—*abundant, rich*
Gen. 41:34, seven **p** years
Ps. 86:5, **p** in mercy unto all
Prov. 21:5, diligent tend only to **p**
Is. 30:23, earth . . . shall be fat and **p**
Matt. 9:37, harvest truly is **p**
Plentiful—*abundant, fruitful*
Ps. 68:9, God, didst send a **p** rain
Jer. 2:7, into a **p** country
Luke 12:16, brought forth **p**-ly
Plenty—*abundance*
Gen. 41:29, seven years of great **p**
Prov. 3:10, thy barns be filled with **p**
Joel 2:26, And ye shall eat in **p**
Plow—*tool for breaking earth, its use*
Deut. 22:10, not **p** with an ox and an
Job 4:8, they that **p** iniquity
Prov. 20:4, sluggard will not **p**
Is. 2:4, their swords into **p**-shares
Joel 3:10, **p**-shares into swords
Luke 9:62, put his hand to the **p**
1 Cor. 9:10, **p** in hope
Pluck—*pull, draw, strip off*
Gen. 8:11, an olive leaf **p**-t off
Ex. 4:7, **p**-ed it out of his bosom
Ps. 25:15, **p** my feet out of the net
Prov. 14:1, foolish **p**-eth it down
Matt. 5:29, offend thee, **p** it out
Mark 2:23, to **p** the ears of corn
Luke 17:6, **p**-ed up by the root
John 10:28, **p** them out of my hand
Point—*sharpened end, indivisible part*
Jer. 17:1, with the **p** of a diamond
Mark 5:23, at the **p** of death
James 2:10, offend in one **p**
Poison—*that which taints or destroys*

Deut. 32:24, with the **p** of serpents
33, wine is the **p** of dragons
Ps. 140:3, adders' **p** is under their lips
Pomp—*display, ostentation*
Is. 14:11, Thy **p** is brought down to
Ezek. 32:12, spoil the **p** of Egypt
Ponder—*weigh in the mind*
Prov. 4:26, **P** the path of thy feet
5:6, **p** the path of life
Luke 2:19, **p**-ed them in her heart
Poor—*ill favored, needy, meek*
Ex. 23:6, wrest the judgment of thy **p**
1 Sam. 2:8, raiseth . . . **p** out of the dust
2 Sam. 12:4, took the **p** man's lamb
Job 5:16, so the **p** hath hope
29:16, was a father to the **p**
Ps. 40:17, I am **p** and needy, yet
69:33, the Lord heareth the **p**
Prov. 13:7, is that maketh himself **p**
22:22, Rob not the **p**, because
Is. 3:15, grind the faces of the **p**
Matt. 5:3, Blessed are the **p** in
26:11, ye have the **p** always
Mark 10:21, and give to the **p**
12:42, came a certain **p** widow
Luke 4:18, preach the gospel to the **p**
19:8, my goods I give to the **p**
1 Cor. 13:3, my goods to feed the **p**
2 Cor. 8:9, your sakes he became **p**
James 2:5, God chosen the **p** of this
Portion—*part, allotment, fate*
Gen. 31:14, any **p** or inheritance
Deut. 32:9, Lord's **p** is his people
2 Kin. 2:9, double **p** of thy spirit
2 Chr. 10:16, What **p** have we in David
Ps. 119:57, Thou art my **p**, O Lord
Eccles 11:2, Give a **p** to seven
Dan. 1:8, the **p** of the king's meat
Matt. 24:51, **p** with the hypocrites
Luke 15:12, **p** of goods that falleth
Possess—*occupy, control, own*
Gen. 24:60, thy seed **p** the gate
Job 7:3, made to **p** months of vanity
Matt. 4:24, **p**-ed with devils
Luke 18:12, tithes of all that I **p**
21:19, patience **p** ye your souls
2 Cor. 6:10, and yet **p**-ing all things
Possession—*property, wealth*
Gen. 17:8, for an everlasting **p**
34:10, and get you **p**-s therein
Ps. 44:3, land in **p** by their own sword
Prov. 28:10, have good things in **p**
Matt. 19:22, for he had great **p**-s
Acts 2:45, sold their **p**-s and goods

Possible—*capable of being or occurring*
Matt. 19:26, with God all things are **p**
26:39, **p**, let this cup pass
Luke 18:27, are **p** with God
Rom. 12:18, If it be **p**, as much as lieth
Pot—*metal of earthen vessel*
Ex. 16:3, when we sat by the flesh **p-s**
2 Kin. 4:40, there is death in the **p**
Job 41:31, deep to boil like a **p**
Jer. 1:13, I see a seething **p**
Mark 7:8, the washing of **p-s** and cups
Pour—*to cause to flow*
1 Sam. 1:15, **p**-ed out my soul
Job 10:10, **p**-ed me out as milk
29:6, rock **p**-ed me out rivers of oil
Is. 44:3, **p** water upon him . . . thirsty
Joel 2:28, **p** out my spirit . . . all flesh
Matt. 26:7, **p**-ed it on his head
John 2:15, **p**-ed out the changers'
Acts 10:45, **p**-ed out the gift . . . Holy
Rev. 16:2, **p**-ed out his vial
Poverty—*need, lack, indigence*
Prov. 20:13, lest thou come to **p**
23:21, glutton shall come to **p**
30:8, neither **p** nor riches
2 Cor. 8:9, through his **p** . . . be rich
Power—*ability, strength, agency*
Ex. 15:6, become glorious in **p**
Deut. 8:18, thee **p** to get wealth
2 Sam. 22:33, God is my strength and **p**
1 Chr. 29:11, the **p**, and the glory
Job 26:14, his **p** who can understand
Ps. 37:35, seen the wicked in great **p**
49:15, from the **p** of the grave
Prov. 3:27, **p** of thine hand to do it
Eccles. 8:8, **p** in the day of death
Is. 40:29, giveth **p** to the faint
Hab. 2:9, delivered from the **p** of evil
Matt. 6:13, kingdom, and the **p**, and
9:6, **p** on earth to forgive
28:18, all **p** is given unto me
Mark 9:1, kingdom of God come with **p**
13:26, in the clouds with great **p**
14:62, on the right hand of **p**
Luke 1:35, **p** of the Highest shall
4:6, All this **p** will I give thee
14, in the **p** of the spirit
5:24, Son of man hath **p**
10:19, **p** to tread on serpents
12:5, **p** to cast into hell
22:69, right hand the **p** of
John 1:12, **p** to become the sons of
10:18, **p** to lay it down . . . **p** to
17:2, **p** over all flesh

Acts 1:8, ye shall receive **p**, after
8:10, This man is the great **p** of
19, Give me also this **p**
Rom. 1:4, Son of God with **p**
16, **p** of God unto salvation
9:21, potter **p** over the clay
13:1, no **p** but of God
1 Cor. 1:24, Christ the **p** of God
5:4, **p** of our Lord Jesus Christ
9:18, I abuse not my **p**
Eph. 1:21, all principality, and **p**
2:2, prince of the **p** of the air
Col. 1:13, from the **p** of darkness
Heb. 1:3, by the word of his **p**
1 Pet. 3:22, **p-s** being made subject
Jude 25, majesty, dominion and **p**
Rev. 2:26, give **p** over the nations
Praise—*commendation, to applaud*
Ex. 15:11, fearful in **p-s**
Deut. 10:21, He is thy **p**
Judg. 5:2, **P** ye the Lord
Neh. 12:46, songs of **p**
Ps. 22:25, My **p** shall be of thee
89:5, the heavens shall **p** thy
Prov. 27:21, so is a man to his **p**
Is. 38:18, the grave cannot **p** thee
John 9:24, Give God the **p**
Rom. 2:29, whose **p** is not of men
2 Cor. 8:18, whose **p** is in the gospel
Phil. 4:8, if there be any **p**
Pray—*supplicate, entreat*
Gen. 20:7, he shall **p** for thee
1 Sam. 7:5, I will **p** for you unto
1 Sam. 12:23, sin . . . in ceasing to **p**
Job 21:15, what profit . . . if we **p**
Ps. 55:17, morning . . . noon, will I **p**
Is. 45:20, **p** unto a god . . . cannot save
Matt. 5:44, **p** for them . . . despitefully
6:6, **p** to thy Father . . . in secret
7, **p**, use not vain repetitions
14:23, mountain apart to **p**
26:41, Watch, and **p**, that ye enter
Mark 11:24, when ye **p**, believe
Luke 11:1, Lord, teach us to **p**
18:1, men ought always to **p**
22:40, **P** that ye enter not into
John 14:16, I will **p** the Father
1 Cor. 11:13, comely that a woman **p**
14:14, **p** in an unknown tongue
Col. 1:9, do not cease to **p** for you
1 Thess. 5:17, **P** without ceasing
James 5:13, afflicted? let him **p**
16, **p** one for another

131

Prayer—*words addressed to God*
1 Kin. 8:45, hear . . . in heaven their **p**
Neh. 11:17, thanksgiving in **p**
Ps. 4:1, hear my **p**
    55:1, Give ear to my **p**
Is. 56:7, called an house of **p**
Matt. 17:21, not out but by **p** and
    21:22, whatsoever . . . ask in **p**
Luke 6:12, continued all night in **p**
    19:46, My house . . . house of **p**
Acts 3:1, the hour of **p**
Rom. 1:9, mention of you . . . in my **p-s**
    12:12, continuing instant in **p**
1 Cor. 7:5, yourselves to fasting and **p**
Col. 4:2, Continue in **p**, and watch
1 Pet. 3:7, your **p-s** be not hindered

Preach—*to proclaim the gospel*
Is. 61:1, anointed me to **p** good tidings
Matt. 4:17, that time Jesus began to **p**
    11:5, poor . . . gospel **p-ed** to them
Mark 1:4, **p** the baptism of repentance
    39, **p-ed** in their synagogues
16:15, **p** the gospel to every
Luke 4:43, **p** the kingdom of God
Acts 5:42, teach and **p** Jesus Christ
    17:3, Jesus, whom I **p** unto you
1 Cor. 1:17, not to baptize, but to **p**
    23, We **p** Christ crucified
2 Cor. 4:5, For we **p** not ourselves
2 Tim. 4:2, **P** the word; be instant
1 Pet. 3:19, **p-ed** unto the spirits

Preacher—*expounder of religion*
Eccles. 1:1, The words of the **P**
Rom. 10:14, how . . . hear without a **p**
1 Tim. 2:7, I am ordained a **p**
2 Pet. 2:5, **p** of righteousness

Preaching—*public religious discourse*
Matt. 3:1, John . . . **p** in the wilderness
Acts 8:4, every where **p** the word
    20:9, Paul was long **p**, he sunk
Rom. 16:25, **p** of Jesus Christ
1 Cor. 1:18, **p** of the cross is to them
    15:14, then is our **p** vain

Precious—*costly, dear, esteemed*
1 Sam. 3:1, word of the Lord was **p**
Ps. 49:8, redemption of their soul is **p**
    116:15, **P** in the sight of the Lord
Prov. 3:15, more **p** than rubies
Is. 13:12, man more **p** than fine gold
Matt. 26:7, box of very **p** ointment
1 Pet. 1:7, more **p** than of gold that
    19, the **p** blood of Christ

Prepare—*make ready, fit, adapt*
1 Sam. 7:3, **p** your hearts unto the Lord
2 Chr. 16:14, **p-d** by the apothecaries'
Ps. 23:5, **p-st** a table before me
    57:6, **p-d** a net for my steps
Is. 40:3, **P** ye the way of the Lord
Jonah 1:17, **p-d** a great fish to swallow
Matt. 25:34, the kingdom **p-d** for you
John 14:2, I go to **p** a place for you
1 Cor. 2:9, **p-d** for them that love him

Presence—*personality mine*
Ex. 33:14, My **p** shall go with thee
Ps. 23:5, **p** of mine enemies
    95:2, before his **p** with thanksgiving
Is. 64:2, nations may tremble at thy **p**
Luke 13:26, eaten and drunk in thy **p**
Rev. 14:10, in the **p** of the Lamb

Present—*a gift, in attendance, to give*
Gen. 43:11, carry down the man a **p**
1 Sam. 17:16, **p-ed** himself forty days
Ps. 46:1, a very **p** help in trouble
Luke 2:22, to **p** him to the Lord
John 14:25, being yet **p** with you
Rom. 12:1, **p** your bodies a living
1 Cor. 5:3, but **p** in spirit
Col. 1:22, **p** you holy and unblameable
2 Tim. 4:10, loved this **p** world
Jude 24, **p** you faultless before the

Presently—*soon, shortly*
Prov. 12:16, fool's wrath is **p** known
Matt. 21:19, **p** the fig tree withered

Preserve—*save from injury, protect*
Deut. 6:24, he might **p** us alive
Job 7:20, O thou **p-r** of men
Ps. 16:1, **P** me, O God; for in thee
    86:2, **P** my soul; for I am holy
Prov. 2:11, Discretion shall **p** thee
    14:3, lips of the wise shall **p**
Luke 17:33, lose his life shall **p** it
1 Thess. 5:23, **p-d** blameless unto the

Press—*crowd*
Mark 2:4, come nigh unto him for the **p**
    5:27, in the **p** behind, and touched
Luke 6:38, good measure, **p-ed** down
Phil. 3:14, I **p** toward the mark

Prevail—*overcome*
Gen. 7:20, did the waters **p**
1 Sam. 2:9, by strength shall no man **p**
Ps. 65:3, Iniquities **p** against me
Jer. 20:7, stronger than I, and hast **p-ed**
Matt. 16:18, of hell shall not **p**

Prevent—*forestall, hinder, go before*
Job 3:12, Why did the knees **p** me

Matt. 17:25, Jesus p-ed him
1 Thess. 4:15p them which are asleep
Prey—*spoil, booty, plunder*
Ps. 76:4, than the mountains of **p**
Is. 10:2, widows may be their **p**
Jer. 28:2, shall have his life for a **p**
Ezek. 22:25, lion ravening the **p**
Price—*value, worth*
Lev. 25:16, increase . . . diminish the **p**
Deut. 23:18, the **p** of a dog
Prov. 31:10, her **p** is far above rubies
Is. 55:1, without money and without **p**
Zech. 11:12, **p** thirty pieces of silver
Matt. 13:46, one pearl of great **p**
Acts 5:2, kept back part of the **p**
1 Cor. 6:20, For ye are bought with a **p**
Pride—*conceit, disdain*
1 Sam. 17:28, I know thy **p**
Prov. 8:13, **p**, and arrogancy, and the
13:10, by **p** cometh contention
16:18, **P** . . . before destruction
Mark 7:22, blasphemy, **p**, foolishness
1 John 2:16, and the **p** of life
Priest—*a minister*
Gen. 14:18, **p** of the most high God
Ex. 19:6, shall be . . . a kingdom of **p**-s
1 Sam. 2:35, raise me up a faithful **p**
2 Chr. 15:3, without a teaching **p**
Ps. 110:4, **p** . . . order of Melchizedek
Is. 24:2, with the people, so with the **p**
Ezek. 44:21, Neither . . . any **p** drink wine
Matt. 8:4, shew thyself to the **p**
Heb. 2:17, faithful high **p**
3:1, High **P** of our profession
5:6, **p** for ever after the order of
Prince—*royalty, sons of royalty*
Ex. 2:14, a **p** and a judge over us
2 Sam. 3:38, **p** and a great man fallen
Is. 9:6, **P** of Peace
Matt. 9:34, the **p** of the devils
John 12:31, the **p** of this world
Acts 3:15, killed the **P** of life
5:31, to be a **P** and a Saviour
Eph. 2:2, **p** of the power of the air
Principality—*sovereignty, supreme power*
Rom. 8:38, nor **p**-s, nor powers, nor
Eph. 1:21, Far above all **p**, and power
Titus 3:1, mind to be subject to **p**-s
Prison—*place of confinement*
Judg. 16:21, did grind in the **p** house
1 Kin. 22:27, Put this fellow in the **p**
Ps. 142:7, Bring my soul out of **p**
Matt. 4:12, John was cast into **p**
14:10, beheaded John in the **p**

Acts 5:19, Lord . . . opened the **p** doors
16:27, keeper of the **p** awaking
Prisoner—*a captive*
Ps. 102:20, groaning of the **p**
146:7, The Lord looseth the **p**-s
Matt. 27:15, release unto the people a **p**
Eph. 3:1, Paul, the **p** of Jesus Christ
2 Tim. 1:8, Lord, nor of me his **p**
Proceed—*move, pass, advance*
Deut. 8:3, word that **p**-eth out of the
Jer. 9:3, **p** from evil to evil
Matt. 4:4, that **p**-eth out of the mouth
Mark 7:21, heart of man, **p** evil thoughts
John 15:26, which **p**-eth from the Father
Proclaim—*announce publicly*
Ex. 33:19, **p** the name of the Lord
Is. 61:1, **p** liberty to the captives
2, **p** the acceptable year of
Jer. 34:15, **p**-ing liberty every man
Luke 12:3, **p**-ed upon the housetops
Profane—*impure, unholy, to desecrate*
Lev. 20:3, to **p** my holy name
21:7, take a wife that is . . . **p**
23, **p** not my sanctuaries
Ezek. 22:8, hast **p**-d my sabbaths
Matt. 12:5, priests . . . **p** the sabbath
1 Tim. 4:7, **p** and old wives' fables
2 Tim. 2:16, **p** and vain babblings
Profess—*acknowledge openly*
Rom. 1:22, **P**-ing themselves to be wise
1 Tim. 6:12, **p**-ed a good profession
Titus 1:16, **p** that they know God
Heb. 10:23, hold fast the **p**-ion of our
Profit—*gain, benefit*
Gen. 37:26, What **p** is it if we slay
Prov. 14:23, In all labour there is **p**
Eccles. 1:3, What **p** hath a man of all
Is. 48:17, God . . . teacheth thee to **p**
Jer. 7:8, lying words, that cannot **p**
16:19, things . . . there is no **p**
Matt. 16:26, For what is a man **p**-ed
Mark 7:11, thou mightest be **p**-ed by me
John 6:63, the flesh **p**-eth nothing
1 Cor. 13:3, not charity, it **p**-eth me
1 Tim. 4:8, bodily exercise **p**-eth little
2 Tim. 3:16, **p**-able for doctrine
Prolong—*lengthen*
Deut. 4:26, shall not **p** your days upon
Job 6:11, that I should **p** my life
Prov. 10:27, fear of the Lord **p**-eth
Promise—*declaration, engage to do*
Num. 14:34, know my breach of **p**
Acts 2:33, **p** of the Holy Ghost
26:6, the hope of the **p**

133

Promise (*Continued*)
Rom. 4:14, **p** made of none effect
    9:8, children of the **p**
Gal. 3:14, might receive the **p**
Eph. 6:2, first commandment with **p**
2 Tim. 1:1, **p** of life . . . in Christ
Titus 1:2, **p**-d before the world began
Heb. 10:23, he is faithful that **p**-d
2 Pet. 1:4, great and precious **p**-s
Proof—*evidence*
2 Cor. 8:24, **p** of your love
    13:3, **p** of Christ speaking in me
2 Tim. 4:5, full **p** of thy ministry
Prophecy—*a foretelling*
Dan. 9:24, seal up the vision and **p**
1 Cor. 13:2, I have the gift of **p**
2 Pet. 1:19, a more sure word of **p**
    21, **p** came not in old time by
Rev. 19:10, testimony . . . spirit of **p**
Prophesy—*to expound, to foretell*
1 Sam. 10:11, **p**-ed among the prophets
1 Chr. 25:3, who **p**-ed with a harp
Is. 30:10, **P** not unto us right things
Jer. 14:14, prophets **p** lies
Ezek. 37:4, **P** upon these bones
Joel 2:28, sons . . . daughters . . . **p**
Matt. 7:22, we not **p**-ed in thy name
    26:68 **P** unto us, thou Christ
1 Cor. 13:9, part, and we **p** in part
1 Thess. 5:20, Despise not **p**-ings
Prophet—*a preacher, a foreteller*
Gen. 20:7, for he is a **p**
Deut. 13:1, arise among you a **p**
    18:18, I will raise them up a **p**
Judg. 4:4, Deborah, a **p**-ess
1 Sam. 9:9, **P** was . . . called a seer
1 Kin. 20:35, of the sons of the **p**-s
Is. 9:15, the **p** that teacheth lies
Jer. 23:11, **p** and priest are profane
Ezek. 13:3, Woe unto the foolish **p**-s
Amos 7:14, neither was I a **p**'s son
Matt. 1:22, was spoken . . . by the **p**
    5:12, persecuted they the **p**-s
    10:41, **p** . . . receive a **p**'s reward
    11:9, out for to see? A **p**
    13:57, **p** is not without honour
    21:11, Jesus the **p** of Nazareth
Luke 4:24, No **p** is accepted in his own
    6:23, their fathers unto the **p**-s
    7:28, greater **p** than John the
John 1:21, Art thou that **p**
    4:19, perceive that thou art a **p**
    7:52, out of Galilee ariseth no **p**

Acts 13:6, sorcerer, a false **p**
    15, reading of the law and the **p**
1 Cor. 14:37, any man think himself . . . **p**
Eph. 4:11, some, apostles; and some **p**-s
Heb. 1:1, unto the fathers by the **p**-s
Proselyte—*a convert*
Matt. 23:15, to make one **p**
Acts 2:10, Jews and **p**-s
    13:43, religious **p**-s followed Paul
Prosper—*to favor, to succeed*
Gen. 39:3, all that he did to **p**
Prov. 28:13, covereth his sins . . . not **p**
1 Cor. 16:2, as God hath **p**-ed him
Prosperity—*good fortune*
Job 15:21, **p** the destroyer shall come
Ps. 73:3, saw the **p** of the wicked
Prov. 1:32, **p** of fools . . . destroy them
Proud—*haughty, lordly*
Ps. 12:3, tongue that speaketh **p**
    94:2, a reward to the **p**
Prov. 6:17, A **p** look, a lying tongue
Is. 13:11, arrogancy of the **p** to cease
Jer. 50:32, **p** shall stumble and fall
Luke 1:51, **p** in the imagination
Rom. 1:30, despiteful, **p**, boasters
1 Tim. 6:4, is **p**, knowing nothing
James 4:6, God resisteth the **p**
Prove—*try, test*
Ex. 20:20, God is come to **p** you
1 Kin. 10:1, **p** him with hard questions
Luke 14:19, oxen, and I go to **p** them
Rom. 12:2, **p** what is that good
2 Cor. 8:8, **p** the sincerity of your
    13:5, **p** your own selves
Proverb—*old saying, maxim*
Deut. 28:37, an astonishment, a **p**
1 Kin. 4:32, he spake three thousand **p**-s
    9:7, a **p** and a byword
Jer. 24:9, reproach and a **p**, a taunt
John 16:29, and speakest no **p**
2 Pet. 2:22, according to the true **p**
Provide—*secure in advance*
Gen. 22:8, God will **p** himself a lamb
1 Sam. 16:17, **P** me now a man that can
Matt. 10:9, **P** neither gold, nor silver
Luke 12:33, **p** yourselves bags which
1 Tim. 5:8, if any **p** not for his own
Provision—*victuals, preparations*
Josh. 9:5, their **p** was dry and mouldy
Ps. 132:15, abundantly bless her **p**
Dan. 1:5, daily **p** of the king's meat
Rom. 13:14, make not **p** for the flesh

Provoke—*awake anger*
Ex. 23:21, obey his voice, **p** him not
Num. 14:11, long will this people **p** me
Job 12:6, they that **p** God are secure
Prov. 20:2, **p**-th him to anger sinneth
Rom. 10:19, I will **p** you to jealousy
1 Cor. 13:5, is not easily **p**-d
Eph. 6:4, **p** not your children to wrath
Prudent—*cautious, careful*
Prov. 12:16, **p** man covereth shame
16:21, wise in heart . . . called **p**
19:14, **p** wife is from the Lord
Jer. 49:7, counsel perished from the **p**
Matt. 11:25, hid . . . from the wise and **p**
1 Cor. 1:19, understanding of the **p**
Psalms—*songs of praise*
1 Chr. 16:9, sing **p** unto him
Ps. 95:2, joyful noise . . . with **p**
Luke 20:42, saith in the book of **P**
24:44, in the **p**, concerning me
Eph. 5:19, Speaking to yourselves in **p**
James 5:13, Is any merry? let him sing **p**
Publican—*collector of taxes*
Matt. 5:46, even the **p**-s the same
10:3, and Matthew the **p**
11:19, friend of **p**-s and sinners
Luke 18:13, the **p**, standing afar off
Publish—*make widely known*
Deut. 32:3, **p** the name of the Lord
Is. 52:7, **p**-eth peace . . . **p**-eth salvation
Mark 13:10, be **p**-ed among all nations
Pull—*to draw forcibly*
Gen. 8:9, **p**-ed her in unto him in the ark
Ps. 31:4, **P** me out of the net
Jer. 12:3, **p** them out like sheep
Matt. 7:4, **p** out the mote out of thine
Luke 12:18, I will **p** down my barns
14:5, **p** him out on the Sabbath
Jude 23, **p**-ing them out of the fire
Punish—*impose a penalty upon*
Lev. 26:18, **p** you seven times more
Prov. 22:3, simple passion, and are **p**-ed
Is. 13:11, **p** the world for their evil
Acts 26:11, And I **p**-ed them oft
2 Thess. 1:9, be **p**-ed with everlasting
Punishment—*inflicted suffering*
Gen. 4:13, **p** is greater than I can bear
Job 19:29, the **p**-s of the sword
Matt. 25:46, go . . . into everlasting **p**
2 Cor. 2:6, Sufficient . . . is this **p**
Purchase—*a sale, to buy*
Gen. 49:32, The **p** of the field
Ruth 4:10, have I **p**-d to be my wife

Acts 8:20, gift of God . . . **p** with money
20:28, **p**-d with his own blood
Pure—*clean, clear, unmixed*
Deut. 32:14, the **p** blood of the grape
2 Sam. 22:27, the **p** . . . shew thyself **p**
Job 4:17, be more **p** than his Maker
11:4, My doctrine is **p**
Ps. 12:6, words of the Lord are **p**
19:8, commandment of the Lord is **p**
24:4, clean hands . . . **p** heart
Prov. 30:5, Every word of God is **p**
Is. 1:25, **p**-ly purge away thy dross
Dan. 7:9, hair . . . like the **p** wool
Matt. 5:8, Blessed are the **p** in heart
Phil. 4:8, whatsoever things are **p**
1 Tim. 1:5, charity out of a **p** heart
Titus 1:15, **p** all things are **p**
James 1:27, **P** religion and undefiled
Purge—*cleanse, wash away*
Ps. 51:7, **P** me with hyssop
79:9, **p** away our sins
Is. 1:25, **p** away thy dross
Matt. 3:12, throughly **p** his floor
1 Cor. 5:7, **P** out . . . the old leaven
2 Pet. 1:9, **p**-d from his old sins
Purify—*make pure or clean*
Ps. 12:6, earth, **p**-ed seven times
Dan. 12:10, Many shall be **p**-ed
Acts 15:9, **p**-ing their hearts by faith
James 4:8, **p** your hearts
1 Pet. 1:22, **p**-ed your souls in obeying
Purpose—*end or aim, to resolve*
Ezra 4:5, to frustrate their **p**
Job 33:17, withdraw man from his **p**
Prov. 15:22, **p**-s are disappointed
Jer. 49:20, **p**-s, that he hath **p**-d
Acts 26:16, appeared unto thee for this **p**
Rom. 8:28, according to his **p**
Eph. 3:11, eternal **p** which he **p**-d
Pursue—*to follow, to chase*
Gen. 31:36, so hotly **p**-d after me
Lev. 26:17, flee when none **p**-th you
Job 30:15, **p** my soul as the wind
Ps. 34:14, seek peace, and **p** it
Jer. 48:2, the sword shall **p** thee
Put—*place, lay, set*
Gen. 3:15, **p** enmity between thee and
Ex. 3:5, **p** off thy shoes from off thy
23:1, **p** not thine hand with the
Josh. 1:18, he shall be **p** to death
2 Chr. 18:22, **p** a lying spirit in the
Job 18:6, his candle shall be **p** out
38:36, **p** wisdom in the inward parts

Put (*Continued*)
Ps. 40:3, **p** a new song in my mouth
Is. 52:1, **p** on thy beautiful garments
Matt. 1:19, **p** her away privily
    5:31, shall **p** away his wife
    12:18, **p** my spirit upon him
    19:6, let not man **p** asunder
    26:52, **P** up against thy sword
Mark 4:21, **p** under a bushel
Luke 9:62, **p** his hand to the plough
John 19:2, **p** on him a purple robe
Rom. 13:14, **p** ye on the Lord Jesus
1 Cor. 13:11, **p** away childish things
    15:53, **p** on immortality
Eph. 4:24, **p** on the new man
    6:11, **P** on the whole armour

Q

Queen—*wife of a king, highest of her kind*
1 Kin. 10:1, the **q** of Sheba
Esther 1:9, Vashti the **q** made a feast
Jer. 7:18, cakes to the **q** of heaven
Matt. 12:42, The **q** of the south shall
Acts 8:27, Candace **q** of the Ethiopians
Quench—*extinguish, stifle, check*
Ps. 104:11, wild asses **q** their thirst
Song 8:7, Many waters cannot **q** love
Is. 42:3, smoking flax shall he not **q**
Mark 9:43, fire that never shall be **q**-ed
1 Thess. 5:19, **Q** not the Spirit
Question—*act of asking, to inquire*
1 Kin. 10:1, prove·him with hard **q**-s
Matt. 22:35, lawyer, asked him a **q**
Mark 8:11, began to **q** with him
    11:29, ask of you one **q**
Acts 18:15, **q** of words and names
1 Cor. 10:25, no **q** for conscience sake
1 Tim. 6:4, **q**-s and strifes of words
2 Tim. 2:23, foolish and unlearned **q**-s
Quick—*rapidly, alive*
Ps. 55:15, go down **q** into hell
Is. 11:3, of **q** understanding
Acts 10:42, Judge of **q** and dead
Heb. 4:12, word of God is **q**
Quicken—*revive, stimulate*
Ps. 119:88, **Q** me . . . thy loving kindness
John 5:21, Son **q**-eth whom he will
Rom. 8:11, **q** your mortal bodies
Eph. 2:5, **q**-ed us together with Christ
1 Pet. 3:18, **q**-ed by the Spirit

Quickly—*with haste, speedily*
Gen. 18:6, Make ready **q** three measures
Eccles. 4:12, cord is not **q** broken
Matt. 5:25, Agree with thine adversary **q**
John 13:27, That thou doest, do **q**
Rev. 3:11, Behold, I come **q**
Quiet—*at rest, meek*
2 Chr. 14:1, land was **q** ten years
Job 21:23, wholly at ease and **q**
Eccles. 9:17, men are heard in **q** more
Is. 7:4, be **q**; fear not
Acts 19:36, ye ought to be **q**, and to do
1 Thess. 4:11, study to be **q**
1 Tim. 2:2, lead a **q** and peaceable life
Quietness—*tranquility*
Judg. 8:28, country was in **q** forty years
Job 20:20, not feel **q** in his belly
Prov. 17:1, dry morsel, and **q** therewith
Eccles. 4:6, an handful with **q**
Acts 24:2, by thee we enjoy great **q**
Quit—*freed, to behave*
Ex. 21:19, he that smote him be **q**
Josh. 2:20, be **q** of thine oath
1 Sam. 4:9, **q** yourselves like men
1 Cor. 16:13, **q** you like men, be strong

R

Race—*a contest of speed*
Ps. 19:5, strong man to run a **r**
Eccles. 9:11, **r** is not to the swift
1 Cor. 9:24, which run in a **r** run all
Rage—*anger, to be violent*
Ps. 2:1, Why do the heathen **r**
Prov. 6:34, jealousy is the **r** of a man
    20:1, strong drink is **r**-ing
Nah. 2:4, chariots . . . **r** in the streets
Raiment—*clothing*
Deut. 8:4, Thy **r** waxed not old
Is. 63:3, I will stain all my **r**
Matt. 3:4, his **r** of camel's hair
    6:25, meat, and the body than **r**
    28:3, his **r** white as snow
Luke 23:34, they parted his **r**
1 Tim. 6:8, having food and **r** let us
Rain—*water falling from the clouds*
Gen. 7:12, **r** was upon the earth forty
Ex. 16:4, **r** bread from heaven for
Lev. 26:4, give you **r** in due season
Deut. 32:2, as the **r** . . . the small **r**
1 Kin. 18:41, sound of abundance of **r**

Prov. 25:14, clouds and wind without **r**
23, wind driveth away **r**
Song 2:11, winter is past . . . **r** is over
Matt. 5:45, **r** on the just . . . unjust
7:25, And the **r** descended
Heb. 6:7, earth . . . drinketh in the **r**
Raise—*lift or build up*
Ex. 23:1, not **r** a false report
Deut. 18:18, **r** them up a Prophet
Judg. 2:16, Lord **r**-d up judges
Job 14:12, be **r**-d out of their sleep
Hos. 6:2, third day he will **r** us up
Luke 3:8, **r** up children unto Abraham
John 2:19, three days will I **r** it up
6:39, 40, **r** it . . . at the last day
1 Cor. 15:35, How are the dead **r**-d
42, **r**-d in incorruption
44, **r**-d a spiritual body
Eph. 2:6, **r**-d us up together
Heb. 11:19, God was able to **r** him up
Ransom—*price of redemption*
Ex. 30:12, man a **r** for his soul
Prov. 6:35, will not regard any **r**
Matt. 20:28, give his life a **r**
Tim. 2:6, gave himself a **r** for all
Read—*utter what is written, comprehend*
Ex. 24:7, **r** in the audience of the
Is. 34:16, the book of the Lord, and **r**
Dan. 5:8, could not **r** the writing
Hab. 2:2, he may run that **r**-eth
Matt. 24:15, whoso **r**-eth . . . understand
Luke 4:16, stood up for to **r**
Acts 8:28, chariot **r** Easias
2 Cor. 3:14, **r**-ing of the old testament
1 Tim. 4:13, give attendance to **r**-ing
Rev. 1:3, Blessed is he that **r**-eth
Ready—*prepared, willing*
Gen. 18:6, Make **r** . . . three measures
Neh. 9:17, a God **r** to pardon
Job 12:5, **r** to slip with his feet
32:19, **r** to burst like new bottles
Ps. 86:5, good, and **r** to forgive
Eccles. 5:1, be more **r** to hear, than to
Is. 32:4, **r** to speak plainly
Matt. 22:8, The wedding is **r**
Mark 14:38, The spirit truly is **r**
Rom. 1:15, **r** to preach the gospel
1 Tim. 6:18, good works, **r** to distribute
Titus 3:1, **r** to every good work
Reap—*gather as a harvest*
Lev. 19:9, not wholly **r** the corners
Job 4:8, sow wickedness, **r** the same
Ps. 126:5, sow in tears . . . **r** in joy
Prov. 22:8, iniquity shall **r** vanity

Hos. 8:7, shall **r** the whirlwind
Matt. 6:26, neither do they **r**, nor
25:26, **r** where I sowed not
Luke 12:24, ravens . . . neither sow nor **r**
2 Cor. 9:6, shall **r** also sparingly
Gal. 6:7, that shall he also **r**
8, flesh **r** corruption
9, in due season we shall **r**
Rev. 14:16, and the earth was **r**-ed
Reason—*motive, purpose, to argue*
1 Sam. 12:7, **r** with you before the Lord
Job 17:7, eye . . . dim by **r** of sorrow
Prov. 20:4, not plow by **r** of the cold
Is. 1:18, let us **r** together
41:21, bring forth your strong **r**-s
Matt. 16:7, **r**-ed among themselves
Luke 5:22, What **r** ye in your hearts
Acts 28:29, great **r**-ing among
Rebel—*renounce, resist*
Num. 14:9, **r** not ye against the Lord
1 Sam. 12:15, **r** against . . . commandment
Ps. 107:11, **r**-ed against the words of
Is. 63:10, **r**-ed . . . vexed his holy Spirit
Ezek. 20:21, children **r**-ed against me
Rebellious—*resisting authority*
Deut. 9:7, **r** against the Lord
Ps. 66:7, let not the **r** exalt
78:8, stubborn and **r** generation
Jer. 5:23, revolting and a **r** heart
Rebuke—*a reprimand, to reprove*
Lev. 19:17, in anywise **r** thy neighbour
Ps. 38:1, **r** me not in thy wrath
Prov. 9:8, **r** a wise man, and he will
27:5, Open **r** is better than
Mic. 4:3, **r** strong nations afar off
Zech. 3:2, Lord **r** thee, O Satan
Matt. 8:26, **r**-d the winds and the sea
17:18, Jesus **r**-d the devil
Mark 9:25, **r**-d the foul spirit
Luke 4:39, **r**-d the fever; and it left
1 Tim. 5:1, **R** not an elder, but intreat
Rev. 3:19, I love, I **r** and chasten
Receive—*obtain, admit, take in*
Job 2:10, **r** good at the hand of God
Prov. 1:3, **r** the instruction of wisdom
Is. 40:2, **r**-d . . . Lord's hand double
Jer. 2:30, they **r**-d no correction
Ezek. 18:17, **r**-d usury nor increase
Matt. 10:8, freely ye have **r**-d
40, **r**-th you, **r**-th me
11:5, blind **r** their sight
18:5, **r** one such little child
25:27, **r**-d mine own with usury

Receive (*Continued*)
Mark 4:20, hear the word, and **r** it
  16:19, **r**-d up into heaven
Luke 15:2, This man **r**-th sinners
  20:47, **r** greater damnation
John 1:11, his one **r**-d him not
  5:44, **r** honour one of another
  14:3, **r** you unto myself
  20:22, **R** ye the Holy Ghost
Acts 20:35, blessed to give than to **r**
Rom. 5:17, **r** abundance of grace
  8:15, **r**-d the Spirit of adoption
  15:7, **r** ye one another
1 Cor. 3:8, shall **r** his own reward
  9:24, one **r**-th the prize
Gal. 4:5, **r** the adoption of sons
1 Thess. 1:6, **r**-d the word in much
2 Thess. 2:10, **r**-d not the love of the
Heb. 2:2, **r**-d a just recompence
James 1:12, **r** the crown of life
Reckon—*compute, estimate*
Matt. 25:19, cometh, and **r**-eth with
Luke 22:37, **r**-ed among . . . transgressors
Rom. 4:4, reward not **r**-ed of grace
Recompence—*reward, repayment*
Job 15:31, vanity shall be his **r**
Jer. 51:6, render unto her a **r**
Hos. 9:7, days of **r** are come
Rom. 11:9, stumbling block . . . a **r**
Heb. 2:2, just **r** of reward
Recompense—*to repay*
Ruth 2:12, The Lord **r** thy work
Prov. 11:31, righteous . . . **r**-d in the
Jer. 18:20, evil be **r**-d for good
Luke 14:14, **r**-d at the resurrection
Rom. 12:17, **R** to no man evil for evil
Heb. 10:30, I will **r**, saith the Lord
Reconcile—*to reunite*
Matt. 5:24, be **r**-d to thy brother
1 Cor. 7:11, be **r**-d to her husband
2 Cor. 5:20, by ye **r**-d to God
Col. 1:20, **r** all things unto himself
Record—*a register, make a note of*
Job 16:19, my **r** is on high
John 1:32, John bear **r**, saying, I saw
  8:14, **r** of myself . . . my **r** is true
2 Cor. 1:23, God for a **r** upon my soul
Phil. 1:8, For God is my **r**
1 John 5:7, three that bear **r**
Red—*of the color of blood*
Gen. 25:25, first came out **r**, all over
  49:12, eyes shall be **r** with wine
Ex. 10:19, cast them into the **R** sea
Esther 1:2, pavement of **r**, and blue

Prov. 23:31, upon the wine when it is **r**
Is. 1:18, they be **r** like crimson
Zech. 1:8, man riding upon a **r** horse
Matt. 16:2, fair weather . . . sky is **r**
Rev. 6:4, another horse that was **r**
Redeem—*buy back, free from sin*
Ex. 6:6, **r** you . . . stretched out arm
Ruth 4:4, wilt **r** it, **r** it
2 Sam. 4:9, who hath **r**-ed my soul
Ps. 26:11, **r** me, and be merciful
  49:15, God will **r** my soul
Gal. 3:13, **r**-ed us from the curse
Titus 2:14, **r** us from all iniquity
Rev. 5:9, **r**-ed us to God by thy blood
Redeemer—*one who frees from bondage*
Job 19:25, know that my **r** liveth
Ps. 19:14, my strength, and my **r**
Is. 63:16, art our father, our **r**
Jer. 50:34, Their **R** is strong
Redemption—*the ransom of sinners*
Ps. 130:7, with him is plenteous **r**
Luke 21:28, your **r** draweth nigh
Rom. 3:24, **r** that is in Christ Jesus
Eph. 1:7, **r** through his blood
  4:30, sealed unto the day of **r**
Reed—*a coarse stalk, a measure*
Is. 19:7, paper **r**-s by the brooks
  36:6, staff of this broken **r**
  42:3, bruised **r** shall he not break
Ezek. 40:5, measuring **r** of six cubits
  41:8, **r** of six great cubits
Matt. 11:7, **r** shaken with the wind
  27:30, **r**, and smote him on the
  48, vinegar, and put it on a **r**
Refrain—*hold back, forebear*
Job 7:11, I will not **r** my mouth
Prov. 1:15, **r** thy foot from their
Prov. 10:19, **r**-eth his lips is wise
Eccles. 3:5, time to **r** from embracing
Jer. 31:16, **R** thy voice from weeping
1 Pet. 3:10, **r** his tongue from evil
Refreshed—*renewed, enlivened*
Ex. 23:12, and the stranger, may be **r**
  31:17, he rested, and was **r**
Job 32:20, speak, that I may be **r**
Rom. 15:32, may with you be **r**
1 Cor. 16:18, **r** my spirit and yours
Refuge—*shelter from danger or distress*
Deut. 33:27, eternal God is thy **r**
Ps. 9:9, a **r** in times of trouble
  46:1, God is our **r** and strength
Is. 28:17, sweep away the **r** of lies
Jer. 16:19, **r** in the day of affliction

Refuse—*decline to do or grant*
Ps. 118:22, stone . . . the builders r
Prov. 21:25, his hands r to labour
Jer. 13:10, r to hear my words
1 Tim. 4:7, r profane and old wives'
Heb. 12:25, r not him that speaketh
Regard—*keep in view, esteem*
Ex. 5:9, let them r not vain words
Job 36:21, r not iniquity
Prov. 5:2, thou mayest r discretion
   15:5, r-eth reproof is prudent
Is. 5:12, r not the work of the Lord
Matt. 22:16, r-est not the person of
Luke 18:2, not God, neither r-ed man
Rom. 14:6, r-eth the day, r-eth it
Reign—*exercise sovereign power*
Ex. 15:18, Lord . . . r for ever and ever
Judg. 9:8, olive tree, R thou over us
Job 34:30, the hyprocrite r not, lest
Prov. 8:15, By me kings r
Is. 32:1, king shall r in righteousness
Luke 19:14, not have this man to r over
Rom. 15:12, to r over the Gentiles
1 Cor. 15:25, must r, till he hath put
2 Tim. 2:12, we shall also r with him
Rev. 20:6, r with him a thousand years
Reins—*the loins, affections, passions*
Job 16:13, cleaveth my r asunder
Ps. 7:9, trieth the hearts and r
   139:13, thou hast possessed my r
Jer. 17:10, the heart, I try the r
Reject—*throw away, discard*
Is. 53:3, despised and r-ed of men
Hos. 4:6, I will also r thee
Matt. 21:42, stone . . . builders r-ed
Luke 17:25, r-ed of this generation
John 12:48, He that r-eth me
Rejoice—*to feel joy*
Job 21:12, r at the sound of the organ
Ps. 65:12, the little hills r
Prov. 5:18, r with the wife of thy youth
Eccles. 11:9, R, O young man
Matt. 5:12, R, and be exceeding glad
Luke 6:23, R ye in that day, and leap
   10:21, Jesus r-d in spirit
John 14:28, loved me, ye would r
Rom. 12:15, R with them that do r
1 Cor. 13:6, R-th not in iniquity
Phil. 3:1, brethren, r in the Lord
   4:4, R in the Lord alway . . . R
1 Thess. 5:16, R evermore
James 1:9, brother of low degree r
1 Pet. 1:8, r with joy unspeakable

Rejoicing—*feeling joy*
Ps. 19:8, Lord are right, r the heart
Acts 5:41, r that they were counted
   8:39, went on his way r
Rom. 12:12, R in hope; patient in
2 Cor. 1:12, For our r is this
   6:10, sorrowful, yet always r
Phil. 1:26, r may be more abundant
1 Thess. 2:19, or joy, or crown of r
James 4:16, all such r is evil
Release—*to let loose, set free*
Matt. 27:26, Then r-d he Barabbas
Mark 15:9, r unto you the King of the
Luke 23:20, Pilate . . . willing to r Jesus
John 19:12, Pilate sought to r him
Remain—*continue, stay, abide*
Gen. 8:22, While the earth r-eth
Deut. 21:23, body shall not r all
1 Sam. 16:11, r-eth yet the youngest
Job. 19:4, mine error r-eth with
   21:34, answers there r-eth falsehood
   41:22, neck r-eth strength
Is. 66:22, seed and your name r
Matt. 14:20, fragments that r-ed twelve
John 15:11, my joy might r in you
   19:31, not r upon the cross
1 Cor. 7:11, let her r unmarried
1 Thess. 4:15, r unto the coming of
Rev. 3:2, strengthen the things which r
Remember—*bring to mind again*
Gen. 9:15, I will r my covenant
Ex. 20:8, R the sabbath day, to keep
Deut. 5:15, r that thou wast a servant
   32:7, R the days of old
1 Chr. 16:12, R his marvellous works
Job 7:7, r that my life is wind
   11:16, r it as waters that pass
Ps. 25:7, R not the sins of my youth
   63:6, r thee upon my bed
   105:42, r-ed his holy promise
Eccles. 12:1, R now thy Creator
Is. 46:8, R . . . shew yourselves men
Jer. 15:15, r me, and visit me
   31:34, I will r their sin no more
Ezek. 21:32, shalt be no more r-ed
Matt. 26:75, Peter r the word of Jesus
   27:63, r that that deceiver said
Luke 17:32, R Lot's wife
   23:42, r me when thou comest into
John 15:20, R the word that I said
Acts 20:35, r the words of the Lord
Gal. 2:10, we should r the poor

Remember (*Continued*)
Heb. 13:3, **R** them that are in bonds
    7, **R** them . . . have the rule over
Rev. 2:5, **R** . . . whence thou art fallen
Remembrance—*something held in mind*
2 Sam. 18:18, son to keep my name in **r**
Job 18:17, his **r** shall perish from
Eccles. 1:11, no **r** of former things
Is. 43:26, Put me in **r**; let us plead
Lam. 3:20, soul hath them still in **r**
Mal. 3:16, a book of **r** was written
Luke 22:19, this do in **r** of me
Acts 10:31, thine alms are had in **r**
1 Cor. 11:25, drink it, in **r** of me
2 Pet. 1:15, these things always in **r**
Remission—*pardon of a transgression*
Matt. 26:28, for the **r** of sins
Mark 1:4, repentance for the **r** of sins
Luke 24:47, **r** of sins . . . be preached
Acts 10:43, shall receive **r** of sins
Heb. 9:22, shedding of blood is no **r**
Remnant—*small portion remaining*
Deut. 3:11, of the **r** of giants
Jer. 6:9, glean the **r** . . . as a vine
    23:3, gather the **r** of my flock
Matt. 22:6, the **r** took his servants
Rom. 11:5, **r** according to the election
Rev. 19:21, **r** were slain with the
Remove—*move away, change place*
Gen. 8:13, **r-d** . . . covering of the ark
Deut. 19:14, not **r** . . . landmark
1 Kin. 15:12, **r-d** all the idols
2 Kin. 17:23, Lord **r-d** Israel out of his
    18:4, He **r-d** the high places
Job 19:10, hope . . . **r-d** like a tree
    24:2, Some **r** the landmarks
Ps. 46:2, earth be **r-d**
    103:12, **r-d** our transgressions
Prov. 10:30, righteous . . . never be **r-d**
Is. 13:13, earth . . . **r** out of her place
    24:20, be **r-d** like a cottage
    29:13, **r-d** their heart far from
Matt. 21:21, Be thou **r-d**
Luke 22:42, **r** this cup from me
1 Cor. 13:2, I could **r** mountains
Rend—*to tear apart*
Lev. 10:6, neither **r** your clothes
Eccles. 3:7, time to **r** . . . time to sew
Is. 64:1, wouldest **r** the heavens
Ezek. 13:11, stormy wind shall **r** it
Joel 2:13, And **r** your heart
Matt. 7:6, turn again and **r** you
John 19:24, Let us not **r** it, but cast

Render—*inflict, yield, contribute*
Deut. 32:41, will **r** vengeance to mine
Ps. 94:2, **r** a reward to the proud
Prov. 24:12, **r** to every man according
    26:16, seven men . . . **r** a reason
Matt. 22:21, **R** . . . unto Caesar the
Rom. 13:7, **R** . . . to all their dues
1 Cor. 7:3, husband **r** unto the wife
1 Thess. 5:15, none **r** evil for evil
1 Pet. 3:9, not **r**-ing evil for evil
Renew—*make new, restore*
Ps. 51:10, **r** a right spirit within
    103:5, youth is **r**-ed like the
Lam. 5:21, **r** our days as of old
Rom. 12:2, **r**-ing of your mind
2 Cor. 4:16, inward man is **r**-ed day by
Col. 3:10, which is **r**-ed in knowledge
Titus 3:5, **r**-ing of the Holy Ghost
Rent—*torn asunder or into pieces*
Gen. 37:33, without doubt **r** in pieces
Josh. 9:4, bottles, old, and **r**
2 Sam. 13:19, **r** her garment of divers
1 Kin. 11:30, **r** it in twelve pieces
    19:11, wind **r** the mountains
Job 1:20, Job arose, and **r** his mantle
Is. 3:24, instead of a girdle a **r**
Matt. 26:65, high priest **r** his clothes
    27:51, vail of the temple was **r**
Repay—*refund, restore, compensate*
Deut. 7:10, **r** him to his face
Luke 10:35, come again, I will **r** thee
Rom. 12:19, I will **r**, saith the Lord
Philem. 19, own hand, I will **r** it
Repent—*feel regret or sorrow*
Gen. 6:6, **r**-ed the Lord . . . made man
Ex. 13:17, people **r** when they see war
Num. 23:19, son of man . . . he should **r**
1 Sam. 15:35, and the Lord **r**-ed
Job 42:6, **r** in dust and ashes
Ezek. 18:30, **R**, and turn yourselves
Matt. 3:2, **R** ye: for the kingdom of
Mark 1:15, **r** ye, and believe the gospel
    6:12, preached that men should **r**
Luke 13:3, except ye **r**, ye shall all
    15:7, one sinner that **r**-eth
Acts 2:38, **R**, and be baptized
    3:19, **R** . . . and be converted
    26:20, should **r** and turn to God
2 Cor. 7:10, not to be **r**-ed of
Repentance—*being sorry for sin*
Matt. 3:8, fruits meet for **r**
    11, with water unto **r**
Mark 1:4, the baptism of **r**
    2:17, but sinners to **r**

Luke 24:47, **r** and remission of sins
Acts 26:20, do works meet for **r**
2 Cor. 7:10, godly sorrow worketh **r**
Heb. 6:1, laying . . . foundation of **r**
2 Pet. 3:9, all should come to **r**
Report—*account, description, to tell*
Ex. 23:1, not raise a false **r**
Prov. 15:30, good **r** maketh the bones
Is. 53:1, Who hath believed our **r**
John 12:38, who hath believed our **r**
Acts 6:3, seven men of honest **r**
    16:2, well **r**-ed of by the brethren
Phil. 4:8, things are of good **r**
1 Tim. 5:10, Well **r**-ed of for good works
Heb. 11:39, obtained a good **r**
Reproach—*disrepute, to condemn*
Gen. 30:23, God hath taken away my **r**
Job 19:3, ten times have ye **r**-ed me
    27:6, my heart shall not **r** me
Ps. 15:3, **r** against his neighbour
    44:13, makest us a **r** to our
    74:10, long shall the adversary **r**
    119:39, Turn away my **r**
Prov. 14:34, sin is a **r** to any people
Is. 51:7, fear ye not the **r** of men
Jer. 24:9, be a **r** and a proverb
    29:18, a hissing, and a **r**
Ezek. 5:14, a **r** among the nations
Hos. 12:14, his **r** shall his Lord return
Luke 6:22, **r** you, and cast out your
Rom. 15:3, **r**-es of them that **r**-ed
1 Tim. 3:7, fall into **r** . . . and snare of
    4:10, both labour and suffer **r**
Heb. 11:26, Esteeming the **r** of Christ
1 Pet. 4:14, **r**-ed for the name of Christ
Reprobate—*condemned, abandoned*
Jer. 6:30, **R** silver shall men call
Rom. 1:28, gave them over to a **r** mind
2 Cor. 13:5-7, be **r**-s . . . not **r**-s . . . as **r**-s
2 Tim. 3:8, **r** concerning the faith
Titus 1:16, unto every good work **r**
Reproof—*correction*
Job 26:11, astonished at his **r**
Ps. 38:14, whose mouth are no **r**-s
Prov. 1:30, despised all my **r**
    10:17, he that refuseth **r** erreth
    15:5, regardeth **r** is prudent
    10, hateth **r** shall die
    29:15, rod and **r** give wisdom
2 Tim. 3:16, for doctrine, for **r**, for
Reprove—*scold, blame, censure*
Gen. 20:16, Sarah . . . thus she was **r**-d
Job 13:10, He will surely **r** you
    40:2, he that **r**-th God, let him

Prov. 9:8, **R** not a scorner, lest he
    29:1, often **r**-d hardeneth his
Jer. 2:19, backslidings shall **r** thee
John 16:8, **r** the world of sin
Eph. 5:11, but rather **r** them
2 Tim. 4:2, **r**, rebuke, exhort with all
Request—*a favor, to ask a favor*
Judg. 8:24, would desire a **r** of you
Neh. 2:4, what dost thou make **r**
Job 6:8, that I might have my **r**
Rom. 1:10, Making **r**, if by any means
Phil. 4:6, let your **r**-s be made known
Require—*demand*
Gen. 9:5, blood of your lives will I **r**
Deut. 10:12, what doth . . . God **r** of thee
Ruth 3:11, do to thee all that thou **r**-st
Ezra 3:4, the duty of every day **r**-d
Ps. 10:13, Thou wilt not **r** it
Prov. 30:7, things have I **r**-d of thee
Is. 1:12, hath **r**-d this at your hand
Mic. 6:8, doth the Lord **r** of thee
Luke 12:20, thy soul shall be **r**-d of
    19:23, **r**-d mine own with usury
1 Cor. 1:22, Jews **r** a sign
    4:2, it is **r** in stewards
Requite—*to repay, satisfy*
Gen. 50:15, certainly **r** us all the evil
Deut. 32:6, Do ye thus **r** the Lord
1 Sam. 25:21, **r**-d me evil for good
Jer. 51:56, God shall surely **r**
1 Tim. 5:4, to **r** their parents
Reserved—*kept, set aside*
Gen. 27:36, not **r** a blessing for me
Judg. 21:22, **r** not to each man his wife
Job 21:30, **r** to the day of destruction
1 Pet. 1:4, **r** in heaven for you
2 Pet. 3:7, **r** unto fire against the day
Jude 6, **r** in everlasting chains
Residue—*that which is left over*
Ex. 10:5, eat the **r** . . . which is escaped
Is. 38:10, deprived . . . **r** of my years
Mal. 2:15, had he the **r** of the spirit
Mark 16:13, and told it unto the **r**
Resist—*oppose, withstand*
Matt. 5:39, That ye **r** not evil
Luke 21:15, able to gainsay nor **r**
Acts 6:10, not able to **r** the wisdom
    7:51, ye do always **r** the Holy
Rom. 13:2, **r**-eth the power, **r**-eth
Heb. 12:4, not yet **r**-ed unto blood
James 4:6, God **r**-eth the proud
    7, **R** the devil, and he will
Respect—*to esteem, regard, estimation*
Gen. 4:4, Lord had **r** unto Abel

RESPECT

Respect (*Continued*)
Lev. 19:15, r the person of the poor
Deut. 1:17, not r persons in judgment
Prov. 28:21, have r of persons is not
Is. 17:7, have r to the Holy One of
Acts 10:34, God is no r-er of persons
Rom. 2:11, no r of persons with God
Heb. 11:26, r unto the recompence
Rest—*repose, remainder, be quiet*
Gen. 2:2, he r-ed on the seventh day
8:9, dove found no r for the sole
49:15, he saw that r was good
Ex. 23:12, seventh day thou shalt r
Josh. 1:13, Lord . . . hath given you r
14:15, land had r from war
Ruth 1:9, grant you that ye may find r
Job 3:17, there the weary be at r
11:18, shalt take thy r in safety
Ps. 37:7, R in the Lord, and wait
116:7, Return . . . thy r, O my soul
Prov. 14:33, Wisdom r-eth in the heart
29:17, son . . . shall give thee r
Eccles. 7:9, anger r-eth in the bosom
Song 1:7, thy flock to r at noon
Is. 11:2, spirit of the Lord . . . r upon
10, his r shall be glorious
14:3, give thee r from thy sorrow
57:2, shall r in their beds
Jer. 6:16, find r for your souls
Lam. 5:5, we labour, and have no r
Hab. 3:16, r in the day of trouble
Matt. 11:28, and I will give you r
26:45, sleep on . . . take you r
Luke 11:24, dry places, seeking r
2 Cor. 2:13, I had no r in my spirit
Heb. 3:11, not enter into my r
1 Pet. 4:2, live the r of his time in
Restore—*replace, rebuild, cure*
Gen. 20:7, r the man his wife
Lev. 6:5, r it in the principal
2 Sam. 12:6, r the lamb fourfold
Ps. 23:3, he r-th my soul: he leadeth
Jer. 30:17, will r health unto thee
Matt. 17:11, first come, and r all
Mark 3:5, his hand was r-d whole
Luke 19:8, I r him fourfold
Restrain—*hold back, check, limit*
Gen. 8:2, rain from heaven was r-ed
Job 15:8, dost thou r wisdom
Ezek. 31:15, I r-ed the floods
Acts 14:18, scarce r-ed they the people
Resurrection—*risen from the dead*
Matt. 22:23, which say . . . there is no r
30, r they neither marry

Luke 14:14, at the r of the just
20:27, deny that there is any r
36, the children of the r
John 5:29, r of life . . . r of damnation
11:25, the r, and the life
Acts 24:15, shall be a r of the dead
21, Touching the r of the dead
1 Cor. 15:13, if there be no r
Phil. 3:11, attain unto the r
Heb. 11:35, might obtain a better r
1 Pet. 1:3, lively hope by the r
Rev. 20:5, This is the first r
Retain—*to keep, hold*
Job 2:9, still r thine integrity
Prov. 4:4, thine heart r my words
John 20:23, sins ye r, they are r-ed
Rom. 1:28, r God in their knowledge
Return—*go back, restore, report*
Gen. 3:19, thou r unto the ground
8:3, waters r-ed from off the
32:9, R unto thy country, and
43:18, money . . . r-ed in our sacks
Ex. 14:28, waters r-ed, and covered
Deut. 30:2, r unto the Lord thy God
Ruth 1:16, r from following after thee
2 Sam. 1:22, sword of Saul r-ed not empty
1 Kin. 20:26, at the r of the year
22:17, r every man . . . in peace
2 Kin. 20:10, shadow r backward
Job 1:21, naked shall I r thither
10:21, go whence I shall not r
33:25, r to the days of his youth
Ps. 80:14, R, we beseech thee, O God
Prov. 26:27, stone, it will r upon him
Eccles. 12:2, clouds r after the rain
7, dust r to the earth
Is. 10:21, The remnant shall r
38:8, sun r-ed ten degrees
55:11, not r unto me void
Jer. 3:22, R, ye backsliding children
4:1, Lord, r unto me
23:20, anger of the Lord shall not r
Ezek. 16:55, r to their former estate
Dan. 4:36, my reason r-ed unto me
Hos. 2:7, r to my first husband
Joel 2:14, if he will r and repent
Mal. 3:7, R unto me, and I will r unto
Matt. 10:13, let your peace r to you
12:44, I will r into my house
Luke 2:39, they r-ed into Galilee
4:14, r-ed in the power of the
10:17, the seventy r-ed again
24:9, r-ed from the sepulchre

142

Acts 13:34, no more to **r** to corruption
1 Pet. 2:25, now **r**-ed unto the Shepherd
Reveal—*disclose, make known*
Job 20:27, heaven shall **r** his iniquity
Prov. 11:13, talebearer **r**-eth secrets
Is. 40:5, glory of the Lord . . . be **r**-ed
53:1, arm of the Lord **r**-ed
Dan. 2:47, couldest **r** this secret
Matt. 11:25, **r**-ed them unto babes
16:17, blood hath not **r**-ed it
Luke 17:30, when the Son of man is **r**-ed
Rom. 8:18, glory . . . be **r**-ed in us
1 Cor. 3:13, shall be **r**-ed by fire
Gal. 1:16, To **r** his Son in me
Eph. 3:5, **r**-ed unto his holy apostles
2 Thess. 2:3, that man of sin be **r**-ed
8, shall that Wicked be **r**-ed
1 Pet. 1:5, be **r**-ed in the last time
Revelation—*disclosing of truth*
Rom. 16:25, the **r** of the mystery
1 Cor. 14:6, speak to you . . . by **r**
Gal. 1:12, by the **r** of Jesus Christ
2:2, And I went up by **r**
Eph. 1:17, spirit of wisdom and **r**
Rev. 1:1, the **R** of Jesus Christ
Revenge—*to inflict harm, retaliation*
Jer. 15:15, **r** me of my persecutors
20:10, take our **r** on him
Nah. 1:2, the Lord **r**-th
2 Cor. 7:11, what zeal, yea, what **r**
10:6, to **r** all disobedience
Reverence—*awe, adoration, to venerate*
Lev. 19:30, and **r** my sanctuary
2 Sam. 9:6, fell on his face, and did **r**
Ps. 89:7, to be had in **r**
Matt. 21:37, They will **r** my son
Eph. 5:33, wife . . . **r** her husband
Heb. 12:28, **r** and godly fear
Revile—*to speak ill of, reproach*
Ex. 22:28, shalt not **r** the gods
Matt. 5:11, when men shall **r** you
27:39, passed by **r**-d him
Mark 15:32, crucified with him **r**-d him
Acts 23:4, **R**-st thou God's high priest
1 Cor. 4:12, being **r**-d, we bless
1 Pet. 2:23, Who, when he was **r**-d
Reward—*to give in return, recompense*
Gen. 15:1, thy exceeding great **r**
44:4, **r**-ed evil for good
Deut. 10:17, not persons, nor taketh **r**
27:25, **r** to slay an innocent
2 Sam. 3:39, Lord . . . **r** the door of evil

Job 7:2, hireling . . . **r** of his work
Ps. 58:11, a **r** for the righteous
94:2, render a **r** to the proud
Prov. 11:18, righteousness . . . a sure **r**
24:20, no **r** to the evil man
Eccles. 4:9, good **r** for their labour
Is. 1:23, followeth after **r**-s
5:23, justify the wicked for **r**
45:13, not for price nor **r**
62:11, his **r** is with him
Mic. 7:3, judge asketh for a **r**
Matt. 5:12, great is your **r** in heaven
6:2, They have their **r**
18, **r** thee openly
10:42, no wise lose his **r**
Acts 1:18, field with the **r** of iniquity
1 Cor. 3:8, shall receive his own **r**
Col. 2:18, no man beguile you of your **r**
1 Tim. 5:18, is worthy of his **r**
2 Pet. 2:13, **r** of unrighteousness
2 John 8, we receive a full **r**
Rev. 22:12, my **r** is with me
Rich—*wealthy, plentiful*
Gen. 13:2, Abram was very **r** in cattle
Ex. 30:15, **r** shall not give more
1 Sam. 2:7, Lord maketh poor, and . . . **r**
Ps. 49:2, low and high, **r** and poor
Prov. 10:4, hand . . . diligent maketh **r**
18:23, the **r** answereth roughly
23:4, Labour not to be **r**
Eccles. 10:20, curse not the **r**
Jer. 9:23, **r** man glory in his riches
Matt. 19:23, **r** man shall hardly enter
Luke 1:53, **r** he hath sent empty away
6:24, woe unto you that are **r**
16:1, There was a certain **r** man
21, fell from the **r** man's table
18:23, for he was very **r**
Rom. 10:12, **r** unto all that call upon
1 Cor. 4:8, full, now ye are **r**
Eph. 2:4, God, who is **r** in mercy
Col. 3:16, word . . . dwell in you **r**-ly
1 Tim. 6:18, be **r** in good works
James 1:11, the **r** man fade away
2:6, Do not **r** men oppress you
Rev. 13:16, **r** and poor, free and bond
Riches—*wealth, plenty, abundance*
1 Kin. 3:11, neither . . . asked **r** for
Job 20:15, swallowed down **r**
36:19, esteem thy **r**? no, not gold
Ps. 61:20, if **r** increase, set not your
104:24, earth is full of thy **r**

Riches (*Continued*)
Prov. 3:16, left hand **r** and honour
11:4, **R** profit not in the day of
13:7, poor, yet hath great **r**
22:1, to be chosen than great **r**
23:5, **r** . . . make themselves wings
30:8, neither poverty nor **r**
Is. 45:3, hidden **r** of secret places
Jer. 9:23, rich man glory in his **r**
Matt. 13:22, deceitfulness of **r**
Mark 10:24, trust in **r** to enter
Luke 8:14, choked with cares and **r**
2 Cor. 8:2, **r** of their liberality
Eph. 1:7, the **r** of his grace
3:8, unsearchable **r** of Christ
1 Tim. 6:17, nor trust in uncertain **r**
James 5:2, Your **r** are corrupted
Ride—*to be carried or borne*
1 Kin. 1:33, Solomon my son to **r** upon
Is. 19:1, Lord **r**-th upon a swift cloud
Ezek. 23:12, horsemen **r**-ing upon horses
Zech. 9:9, lowly, and **r**-ing upon an ass
Right—*correct, true*
Gen. 24:48, led me in the **r** way
Deut. 12:25, **r** the sight of the Lord
21:17, **r** of the firstborn is
32:4, God . . . just and **r** is he
Judg. 17:6, man did that which was **r**
2 Kin. 10:15, Is thine heart **r**, as my
Job 34:6, Should I lie against my **r**
23, not lay upon man more than **r**
36:6, giveth **r** to the poor
Ps. 17:1, Hear the **r**, O Lord
19:8, statutes of the Lord are **r**
51:10, renew a **r** spirit within me
119:75, thy judgments are **r**
Prov. 3:16, length of days . . . **r** hand
4:11, led thee in **r** paths
14:12, a way which seemeth **r**
24:26, lips that giveth a **r**
Is. 41:13, God will hold thy **r** hand
Jer. 17:11, getteth riches . . . not by **r**
Ezek. 18:5, which is lawful and **r**
Hos. 14:9, ways of the Lord are **r**
Matt. 5:29, **r** eye offend thee
22:44, Sit thou on my **r** hand
26:64, on the **r** hand of power
Mark 5:15, and in his **r** mind
16:19, sat on the **r** hand of God
Luke 22:50, cut off his **r** ear
John 21:6, the **r** side of the ship
Acts 8:21, thy heart is not **r**

Gal. 2:9, **r** hands of fellowship
2 Pet. 2:15, forsaken the **r** way
Rev. 22:14, **r** to the tree of life
Righteous—*upright, just, holy*
Gen. 18:23, Wilt thou . . . destroy the **r**
Ex. 9:27, Lord is **r**, and I and my
23:7, innocent and **r** slay thou not
Num. 23:10, die the death of the **r**
1 Sam. 24:17, Thou art more **r** than I
Job 4:7, where were the **r** cut off
Ps. 1:5, the congregation of the **r**
11:5, The Lord trieth the **r**
33:1, Rejoice in the Lord, O ye **r**
37:16, little that a **r** man hath
55:22, suffer the **r** to be moved
119:137, **R** art thou, O Lord
Prov. 2:20, keep the paths of the **r**
10:30, **r** shall never be removed
11:28, **r** shall flourish as a
13:5, **r** man hateth lying
16:13, **R** lips are the delight of
28:1, the **r** are bold as a lion
Eccles. 3:17, God shall judge the **r**
7:16, Be not **r** over much
Is. 53:11, my **r** servant justify many
Jer. 23:5, unto David a **r** Branch
Ezek. 13:22, made the heart of the **r** sad
Dan. 9:14, God is **r** in all his works
Amos 2:6, sold the **r** for silver
Matt. 9:13, not come to call the **r**
10:41, a **r** man's reward
13:43, shall the **r** shine forth
25:46, **r** into life eternal
Luke 23:47, Certainly this was a **r** man
John 7:24, judge **r** judgment
Rom. 3:10, none **r**, no, not one
1 Tim. 1:9, law is not made for a **r** man
James 5:16, prayer of a **r** man availeth
1 Pet. 4:18, **r** scarcely be saved
1 John 2:1, Jesus Christ the **r**
Righteousness—*being right with God*
Gen. 15:6, counted to him for **r**
1 Sam. 26:23, render to every man his **r**
Job 27:6, My **r** I hold fast
29:14, I put on **r**, and it clothed
36:3, ascribe **r** to my Maker
Ps. 17:15, behold thy face in **r**
23:3, leadeth me in the paths of **r**
48:10, right hand is full **r**
96:13, judge the world with **r**
97:6, heavens declare his **r**
111:3, his **r** endureth for ever

Prov. 10:2, r delivereth from death
11:19, r tendeth to life
14:34, **R** exalteth a nation
16:8, Better is a little with r
Is. 32:1, a king shall reign in r
45:8, skies pour down r
48:18, r as the waves of the sea
51:5, My r is near; my salvation
59:17, put on r as a breastplate
Jer. 23:6, called, THE LORD OUR **R**
33:15, Branch of r to grow up
Ezek. 33:13, trust to his own r
Dan. 12:3, turn many to r
Hos. 10:12, Sow to yourselves in r
Mal. 4:2, Sun of r arise
Matt. 5:6, hunger and thirt after r
10, persecuted for r-s' sake
Matt. 5:20, I shall exceed the r
6:33, kingdom of God, and his r
Luke 1:75, In holiness and r before
Acts 13:10, devil, thou enemy of all r
Rom. 4:3, counted unto him for r
22, imputed to him for r
5:18, by the r of one the free
8:10, Spirit is life because of r
1 Cor. 15:34, Awake to r, and sin not
2 Cor. 6:14, fellowship hath r with
Gal. 2:21, if r come by the law
3:6, accounted to him for r
Eph. 4:24, created in r and true
6:14, the breastplate of r
1 Tim. 6:11, follow after r, godliness
2 Tim. 4:8, laid up for me a crown of r
Heb. 7:2, interpretation King of r
12:11, the peaceable fruit of r
James 1:20, wrath . . . worketh not the r
1 Pet. 3:14, ye suffer for r-s' sake
1 John 3:10, doeth not r is not of God
Riot—*confusion, disturbance*
Prov. 23:20, r-ous eaters of flesh
Luke 15:13, substance with r-ous living
Rom. 13:13, not in r-ing and drunkenness
Titus 1:6, not accused of r
2 Pet. 2:13, pleasure to r in the day
Ripe—*mature, ready for gathering*
Gen. 40:10, brought forth r grapes
Ex. 22:29, first of thy r fruits
Jer. 24:2, figs that are first r
Joel 3:13, for the harvest is r
Rev. 14:15, harvest of the earth is r
18, her grapes are fully r
Rise—*to arise, ascend*
Gen. 19:2, ye shall r up early
Lev. 19:32, r up before the hoary head

Num. 24:17, Sceptre shall r . . . Israel
Josh. 12:1, the r-ing of the sun
Job 9:7, the sun, and it r-th not
31:14, shall I do when God r-th up
Ps. 27:3, war should r against me
35:11, False witnesses did r up
86:14, proud are r-n against me
113:3, r-ing of the sun unto the
Prov. 31:15, r-th . . . while it is yet
Is. 32:9, **R** up, ye women . . . at ease
60:1, glory of the Lord is r-n
Jer. 47:2, waters r up out of the
Ezek. 7:11, Violence is r-n up into
Matt. 11:11, not r-n a greater than
14:2, Baptist . . . r-n from the
20:19, third day he shall r
24:7, nation . . . r against nation
11, many false prophets . . . r
27:63, three days I will r again
Mark 12:25, shall r from the dead
13:12, r up against their parents
16:6, he is r-n; he is not here
Luke 5:23, **R** up and walk
11:31, queen of the south shall r
12:54, cloud r out of the west
22:46, r and pray, lest ye
24:34, The Lord is r-n indeed
Acts 10:13, **R**, Peter; kill, and eat
1 Cor. 15:13, then is Christ not r-n
14, if Christ be not r-n
Col. 3:1, ye then be r-n with Christ
1 Thess. 4:16, dead in Christ shall r
River—*stream of water, abundance*
Gen. 2:10, a r went out of Eden
Ex. 2:3, flags by the r-'s brink
Josh. 1:4, great r, the r Euphrates
Job 28:10, cutteth out r-s among the
Job 40:23, drinketh up a r
Ps. 1:3, planted by the r-s of water
46:4, a r, the streams whereof
137:1, By the r-s of Babylon
Eccles. 1:7, All the r-s run into the
Is. 11:15, shake his hand over the r
32:2, r-s of water in a dry place
Jer. 2:18, drink the waters of the r
Lam. 2:18, tears run down like a r
Ezek. 47:5, r . . . not be passed over
Mark 1:5, baptized in the r of Jordan
John 7:38, flow r-s of living water
Rev. 22:1, pure r of water of life
Roar—*deep, loud cry, to cry loudly*
1 Chr. 16:32, Let the sea r
Job 4:10, r-ing of the lion
37:4, After it a voice r-eth

145

Roar (*Continued*)
Ps. 96:11, let the sea **r**
Is. 59:11, We **r** all like bears
Jer. 25:30, The Lord shall **r** from
1 Pet. 5:8, devil, as a **r**-ing lion
Rob—*steal, plunder*
Lev. 26:22, **r** you of your children
Judg. 9:25, **r**-ed all that came along
Prov. 17:12, bear **r**-ed of her whelps
22:22, **R** not the poor
28:24, Whoso **r**-eth his father
Is. 10:2, they may **r** the fatherless
42:22, a people **r** and spoiled
Mal. 3:8, Will a man **r** God?
2 Cor. 11:8, I **r**-ed other churches
Robber—*a thief*
Job 5:5, **r** swalloweth . . . substance
12:6, tabernacles of **r**-s prosper
Jer. 7:11, become a den of **r**-s
John 10:1, same is a thief and a **r**
18:40, Barabbas was a **r**
Acts 19:37, **r**-s of churches
Robbery—*theft, spoilation*
Ps. 62:10, become not vain in **r**
Nah. 3:1, city . . . full of lies and **r**
Phil. 2:6, **r** to be equal with God
Robe—*an outer garment*
1 Sam. 24:4, off the skirt of Saul's **r**
Job 29:14, judgment was as a **r**
Is. 61:10, the **r** of righteousness
Matt. 27:28, put on him a scarlet **r**
Luke 15:22, Bring forth the best **r**
20:46, desire to walk in long **r**-s
John 19:2, put on him a purple **r**
Rev. 7:14, have washed their **r**-s
Rock—*mass of stone, a refuge*
Ex. 17:6, thou shalt smite the **r**
33:22, thee in a clift of the **r**
Num. 20:11, rod he smote the **r** twice
Deut. 32:4, He is the **R**
13, oil out of the flinty **r**
1 Sam. 2:2, any **r** like our God
2 Sam. 22:2, The Lord is my **r**
Job. 19:24, graven . . . in the **r** for ever
29:6, **r** poured me out rivers of oil
Ps. 27:5, shall set me up upon a **r**
31:3, art my **r** and my fortress
Prov. 30:19, way of a serpent upon a **r**
Is. 8:14, for a **r** of offence
51:1, **r** whence ye are hewn
Jer. 5:3, faces harder than a **r**
Matt. 7:24, built his house upon a **r**
16:18, upon this **r** . . . build my

Mark 15:46, sepulchre . . . hewn out
of a **r**
Luke 8:6, some fell upon a **r**
Rom. 9:33, **r** of offence
1 Cor. 10:4, drink of that spiritual **R**
Rod—*slender, round piece of wood*
Gen. 30:37, **r**-s of green poplar
Ex. 4:4, became a **r** in his hand
7:12, Aaron's **r** swallowed up
Num. 17:8, **r** or Aaron . . . budded
2 Sam. 7:14, chasten him with the **r**
Ps. 2:9, break them with a **r** of iron
23:4, **r** and thy staff they comfort
Prov. 13:24, spareth his **r** hateth his
26:3, a **r** for the fool's back
Is. 10:5, the **r** of mine anger
11:1, **r** out of the stem of Jesse
Ezek. 20:37, to pass under the **r**
2 Cor. 11:25, Thrice . . . beaten with **r**-s
Heb. 9:4, Aaron's rod that budded
Rev. 19:15, rule them with a **r** of iron
Roll—*move, turn over, ancient book*
Is. 8:1, Take thee a great **r** . . . write
34:4, heavens . . . **r**-ed together as
Jer. 36:2, Take thee a **r** of a book
Ezek. 3:1, eat this **r**, and go speak
Zech. 5:1, and behold a flying **r**
Matt. 27:60, **r**-ed a great stone to the
28:2, **r**-ed back the stone from
Mark 16:3, shall **r** us away the stone
Roof—*cover of a building*
Gen. 19:8, under the shadow of my **r**
Josh. 2:6, up to the **r** . . . and hid them
2 Sam. 11:2, from the **r** he saw a woman
Job 29:10, to the **r** of their mouth
Matt. 8:8, shouldest come under my **r**
Mark 2:4, uncovered the **r** where he
Room—*space, section of a building*
Gen. 6:14, **r**-s shalt thou make . . . ark
Ps. 31:8, set my feet in a large **r**
Prov. 18:16, man's gift maketh **r** for
Matt. 23:6, uppermost **r**-s at feasts
Mark 14:15, large upper **r** furnished
Luke 2:7, no **r** for them in the inn
14:8, sit not down . . . highest **r**
Acts 1:13, went up into an upper **r**
1 Cor. 14:16, **r** of the unlearned
Root—*source of nourishment, dig out*
Deut. 29:18, a **r** that beareth gall
Job 5:3, the foolish taking **r**
18:14, confidence shall be **r**-ed out
19:28, the **r** of the matter
Ps. 80:9, cause it to take deep **r**

Is. 5:24, r shall be as rottenness
53:2, r out of a dry ground
Jer. 12:2, they have taken r
Matt. 3:10, axe is laid unto the r
Mark 4:6, had no r, it withered
Luke 17:6, plucked up by the r
Rom. 11:16, if the r be holy
Eph. 3:17, r-ed and grounded in love
1 Tim. 6:10, money is the r of all evil

Rose—*a flower*
Song 2:1, I am the r of Sharon
Is. 35:1, desert . . . blossom as the r

Rose—*mounted, sprung up or into action*
Deut. 33:2, Lord . . . r up from Seir
Josh. 3:16, waters . . . r up upon an heap
Luke 16:31, though one r from the dead
Rom. 14:9, Christ both died, and r

Rough—*not smooth, violent*
1 Sam. 20:10, father answer thee r-ly
Prov. 18:23, the rich answereth r-ly
Is. 40:4, and the r places plain
Zech. 13:4, a r garment to deceive

Round—*circular, on all sides*
Lev. 19:27, r the corners of your
Jos. 6:3, go r about the city once
2 Sam. 5:9, built r about from Millo
Is. 3:18, r tires like the moon
Rev. 4:3, rainbow r about the throne

Rubies—*jewels, precious stones*
Job 28:18, price of wisdom is above r
Prov. 3:15, She is more precious than r
31:10, her price is far above r

Ruin—*destruction*
Prov. 26:28, flattering mouth worketh r
Is. 23:13, he brought it to r
Ezek. 18:30, iniquity . . . not be your r
Luke 6:49, r of that house was great
Acts 15:16, will build again the r-s

Rule—*direction, to control*
Gen. 1:16, r the day . . . r the night
Judg. 8:22, R thou over us
Prov. 8:16, By me princes r
16:32, he that r-th his spirit
25:28, no r over his own spirit
Is. 3:12, women r over them
Matt. 2:6, r my people Israel
Mark 10:42, r over the Gentiles
Gal. 6:16, walk according to this r
Col. 3:15, peace of God r in your
1 Tim. 3:5, not how to r his own house
Rev. 2:27, r them with a rod of iron

Ruler—*one having authority*
Ex. 22:28, curse the r of thy people
Deut. 1:13, make them r-s over you

Ps. 2:2, r-s take counsel together
Prov. 6:7, no guide, overseer, or r
29:12, If a r harken to lies
Is. 22:3, All thy r-s are fled together
Matt. 9:18, came a certain r
24:45, r over his household
John 3:1, Nicodemus, a r of the Jews
Acts 7:27, made thee a r and a judge
Eph. 6:12, the r-s of the darkness of

Rumour—*common talk, a current story*
Jer. 49:14, heard a r from the Lord
Ezek. 7:26, r shall be upon r
Matt. 24:6, wars and r-s of wars
Luke 7:17, r of him went forth

Run—*move quickly, contend in a race*
Gen. 49:22, branches r over the wall
Lev. 15:13, bathe his flesh in r-ing
Judg. 18:25, angry fellows r upon thee
2 Kin. 4:22, may r to the man of God
2 Chr. 16:9, eyes of the Lord r to and
Ps. 19:5, strong man to r a race
23:5, my cup r-eth over
Prov. 1:16, their feet r to evil
5:15, r-ing waters . . . own well
6:18, feet . . . r-ing to mischief
Is. 40:31, r, and not be weary
Ezek. 32:14, rivers to r like oil
Nah. 2:4, r like the lightnings
Matt. 9:17, the wine r-eth out
1 Cor. 9:24, r in a race r all
Gal. 2:2, r, or had r, in vain
5:7, Ye did r well
Heb. 12:1, r with patience the race
Rev. 9:9, many horses r-ing to battle

Rust—*corrosion*
Matt. 6:19, moth and r doth corrupt
James 5:3, the r . . . shall be a witness

S

Sabbath—*the day of rest and worship*
Ex. 16:26, seventh day, which is the s
20:8, Remember the s day, to keep
11, Lord blessed the s day
31:15, seventh is the s of rest
35:3, kindle no fire . . . upon the s
Lev. 25:8, number seven s-s of years
26:2, Ye shall keep my s-s
Num. 15:32, gathered sticks upon s
Deut. 5:12, Keep the s day to sanctify
2 Kin. 4:23, neither new moon, nor s

Sabbath (*Continued*)
Matt. 12:8, Lord even of the s day
28:1, In the end of the s
Mark 2:27, s was made for man
3:4, do good on the s days
John 19:31, s day was an high day
Acts 1:12, a s day's journey
Sackcloth—*garment worn in mourning*
Esther 4:1, put on s with ashes
Job 16:15, sewed s upon my skin
Dan. 9:3, fasting, and s, and ashes
Matt. 11:21, repented . . . in s and ashes
Rev. 6:12, sun . . . black as s of hair
Sacrifice—*an offering made to God*
Gen. 31:54, Jacob offered s upon the
Ex. 12:27, s of the Lord's passover
Ps. 51:17, s-s of God are a broken
Prov. 15:8, s of wicked is an
Is. 43:23, honoured me with thy s-s
Jer. 46:10, God of hosts hath a s
Dan. 11:31, take away the daily s
Hos. 6:6, desired mercy, and not s
Matt. 9:13, have mercy, and not s
Acts 7:41, offered s unto the idol
Rom. 12:1, your bodies a living s
1 Cor. 10:20, they s to devils
Phil. 4:18, s acceptable, wellpleasing
Heb. 9:26, put away sin by the s of
11:4, a more excellent s than Cain
13:16, such s-s God is well pleased
Sad—*sorrowful, gloomy*
1 Kin. 21:5, Why is thy spirit so s
Neh. 2:2, Why is thy countenance s
Mark 10:22, was s at that saying
Luke 24:17, as ye walk, and are s
Safe—*secure, free from harm*
2 Sam. 18:29, Is the young man . . . s
Job 21:9, houses are s from fear
Ezek. 34:27, shall be s in their land
Luke 15:27, received him s and sound
Phil. 3:1, but for you it is s
Safely—*without danger*
Lev. 26:5, dwell in your land s
Prov. 3:23, walk in thy way s
31:11, husband doth s trust in her
Mark 14:44, lead him away s
Acts 16:23, jailor to keep them s
Saints—*holy and godly persons*
Deut. 33:2, with ten thousands of s
1 Sam. 2:9, keep the feet of his s
Job 15:15, putteth no trust in his s
Ps. 37:28, forsaketh not his s
89:5, congregation of the s
Matt. 27:52, bodies of the s . . . arose

Acts 26:10, s did I shut up in prison
Rom. 1:7, called to be s
8:27, intercession for the s
1 Cor. 6:2, s shall judge the world
Eph. 2:19, fellowcitizens with the s
Phil. 1:1, all the s in Christ Jesus
1 Thess. 3:13, Christ with all his s
Rev. 14:12, patience of the s
20:9, the camp of the s
Sake—*cause, motive, reason*
Gen. 8:21, curse the ground . . . man's s
1 Sam. 12:22, for his great name's s
Neh. 9:31, thy great mercies' s
Ps. 23:3, for his name's s
44:22, for thy s are we killed
115:1, for thy truth's s
Is. 42:21, righteousness' s
Matt. 5:11, evil . . . falsely, for my s
16:25, lose his life for my s
Mark 13:20, for the elect's s
Luke 6:22, Son of man's s
18:29, kingdom of God's s
John 13:37, lay down my life for thy s
Rom. 8:36, thy s we are killed all the
13:5, for conscience s
1 Cor. 9:23, do for the gospel's s
2 Cor. 8:9, for your s-s he became poor
1 Tim. 5:23, wine for thy stomach's s
Titus 1:11, for filthy lucre's s
2 John 2, For the truth's s
Salt—*a seasoning and preservative*
Gen.19:26, became a pillar of s
Judg. 9:45, city, and sowed it with s
Job 6:6, be eaten without s
Matt. 5:13, the s of the earth
Mark 9:50, S is good
Col. 4:6, seasoned with s
James 3:12, yield s water and fresh
Salvation—*deliverance from destruction*
Gen. 49:18, waited for thy s, O Lord
Ex. 15:2, he is become my s
Deut. 32:15, the Rock of his s
Job 13:16, He also shall be my s
Ps. 3:8, S belongeth unto the Lord
27:1, my light and my s
62:1, from him cometh my s
68:20, our God is the God of s
85:9, s is nigh them that fear him
98:3, seen the s of our God
116:13, take the cup of s
119:155, S is far from the wicked

Is. 12:3, water out of the wells of s
33:2, our s . . . time of trouble
49:6, s unto the end of the earth
51:6, s shall be for ever
52:7, that publisheth s
56:1, s is near to come
59:17, helmet of s upon his head
Jonah 2:9, S is of the Lord
Zech. 9:9, he is just, and having s
Luke 2:30, eyes have seen thy s
3:6, flesh shall see the s of God
19:9, is s come to this house
Acts 4:12, Neither . . . s in any other
13:26, the word of this s sent
16:17, shew unto us the way of s
Rom. 1:16, power of God unto s
11:11, s is come unto the Gentiles
2 Cor. 6:2, in the day of s
7:10, worketh repentance to s
Eph. 6:17, helmet of s
Phil. 2:12, work out your own s
1 Thess. 5:9, obtain s by our Lord
2 Tim. 3:15, make thee wise unto s
Titus 2:11, grace of God . . . bringeth s
Heb. 1:14, who shall be heirs of s
2:3, we neglect so great s
9:28, without sin unto s
1 Pet. 1:5, through faith unto s
2 Pet. 3:15, longsuffering . . . Lord is s
Rev. 7:10, S to our God which sitteth
12:10, Now is come s, and strength
Same—*not different*
2 Sam. 5:7, s is the city of David
Job 4:8, sow wickedness, reap the s
Ps. 102:27, But thou art the s, and
Is. 7:20, s day shall the Lord shave
Matt. 5:46, even the publicans the s
12:50, s is my brother, and
Luke 2:8, in the s country shepherds
Luke 6:38, s measure that ye mete
23:40, the s condemnation
John 1:2, s was in the beginning
Rom. 10:12, s Lord over all is rich
1 Cor. 7:20, abide in the s calling
12:4, of gifts, but the s Spirit
Heb. 13:8, s yesterday . . . to day . . . for
Sanctify—*make sacred, set apart, purify*
Gen. 2:3, seventh day, and s-ied it
Ex. 13:2, S unto me all the firstborn
Lev. 11:44, s yourselves
Deut. 5:12, Keep the sabbath day to s it
Is. 29:23, they shall s my name
John 10:36, whom the Father hath s-ied
17:17, S them through thy truth

Rom. 15:16, s-ied by the Holy Ghost
1 Cor. 6:11, washed, but ye are s-ied
7:14, wife is s by the husband
1 Thess. 5:23, God of peace s you wholly
Heb. 2:11, s-eth and they who are s-ied
Jude 1, s-ed by God the Father
Sanctuary—*sacred place, place of refuge*
Ex. 25:8, let them make me a s
Lev. 19:30, and reverence my s
Ps. 73:17, I went into the s of God
150:1, Praise God in his s
Is. 60:13, beautify the place of my s
Jer. 51:51, s-s of the Lord's house
Dan. 8:14, shall the s be cleansed
Heb. 8:2, A minister of the s
Sand—*finely crushed stone*
Gen. 32:12, seed as the s of the sea
Deut. 33:19, treasures hid in the s
Job 29:18, multiply my days as the s
Prov. 27:3, stone is heavy . . . s weighty
Matt. 7:26, built his house upon the s
Heb. 11:12, s . . . by the sea shore
Sapphire—*a jewel*
Ex. 28:18, an emerald, a s
Song 5:14, ivory overlaid with s-s
Ezek. 28:13, jasper, the s, the emerald
Rev. 21:19, jasper; the second, s
Sat—*was sitting*
Gen. 18:1, s in the tent door in the
Ex. 2:15, he s down by a well
16:3, s by the flesh pots
Job 2:8, s down among the ashes
Ps. 26:4, not s with vain persons
Jonah 4:5, booth, and s under it
Matt. 4:16, which s in darkness
9:10, Jesus s at meat
26:20, s down with the twelve
Mark 11:2, whereon never man s
16:19, s on the right hand of
Luke 7:15, he that was dead s up
10:39, Mary . . . s at Jesus' feet
Acts 2:3, and it s upon each of them
Satan—*man's grand adversary*
Job 1:6, S came also among them
Zech. 3:2, Lord rebuke thee, O S
Matt. 4:10, Get thee hence, S
12:26, S cast out S
16:23, Get thee behind me, S
Mark 1:13, forty days, tempted of S
Luke 10:18, beheld S . . . fall from heaven
22:3, entered S into Judas
Acts 5:3, why hath S filled thine heart
Rom. 16:20, bruise S under your feet
2 Cor. 2:11, S should get an advantage

Satan (*Continued*)
1 Thess. 2:18, but S hindered us
1 Tim. 1:20, have delivered unto S
Rev. 3:9, of the synagogue of S
  12:9, called the Devil, and S
  20:7, S . . . loosed out of his prison
Satisfied—*gratified to the full*
Lev. 26:26, eat, and not be s
Job 27:14, shall not be s with bread
Ps. 22:26, meek shall eat and be s
Prov. 12:11, tilleth his land . . . be s
  27:20, eyes of man are never s
Joel 2:26, eat in plenty, and be s
Satisfy—*to gratify*
Job 38:27, s the desolate and waste
Ps. 91:16, long life will I s him
Prov. 6:30, steal to s his soul
Mark 8:4, man s these men with bread
Save—*except*
Gen. 14:24, S only that which the young
Ex. 22:20, any god, s unto the Lord
Ps. 18:31, s the Lord . . . s our God
Matt. 11:27, man the Father, s the Son
Luke 18:19, none is good, s one . . . God
2 Cor. 11:24, forty stripes s one
Save—*preserve, deliver from sin*
Deut. 28:29, no man shall s thee
1 Sam. 10:27, How shall this man s us
  14:6, to s by many or by few
Job 22:29, shall s the humble person
Ps. 6:4, s me for thy mercies' sake
  28:9, S thy people, and bless
  60:5, s with thy right hand
  86:2, s thy servant that trusteth
Prov. 20:22, and he shall s thee
Is. 35:4, your God . . . will come and s
  63:1, mighty to s
Jer. 30:10, will s thee from afar
  42:11, with you to s you
Ezek. 18:27, s his soul alive
Matt. 1:21, s his people from their
  16:25, s his life shall lose it
  18:11, s that which was lost
Mark 3:4, to s life, or to kill
Luke 23:35, s himself, if he be Christ
John 12:27, Father, s me from this hour
Acts 27:43, centurion, willing to s Paul
1 Cor. 7:16, s thy husband . . . s thy wife
1 Tim. 1:15, world to s sinners
James 1:21, able to s your souls
  4:12, to s and to destroy
  5:15, prayer of faith . . . s the sick
Saved—*preserved, delivered from sin*
Deut. 33:29, s by the Lord, the shield

Judg. 7:2, own hand hath s me
Ps. 44:7, s us from our enemies
Is. 45:22, unto me, and be ye s
Jer. 8:20, ended, and we are not s
Matt. 19:25, Who then can be s
Mark 13:13, end, the same shall be s
  16:16, is baptized shall be s
Luke 1:71, s from our enemies
  7:50, faith hath s thee; go in
John 3:17, world through him . . . be s
  10:9, enter in, he shall be s
Acts 4:12, whereby we must be s
  16:30, what must I do to be s
Rom. 5:10, we shall be s by his life
  8:24, For we are s by hope
Eph. 2:5, by grace ye are s
2 Tim. 1:9, hath s us, and called us
1 Pet. 4:18, righteous scarcely be s
Saviour—*one who saves, Jesus Christ*
2 Sam. 22:3, my refuge, my s
Ps. 106:21, forgat God their s
Is. 19:20, he shall send them a s
  43:11, beside me there is no s
  45:21, a just God and a s
  49:26, I the Lord am thy S
Luke 2:11, a S, which is Christ the
John 4:42, Christ, the S of the world
Acts 5:31, be a Prince and a S
Eph. 5:23, he is the s of the body
1 Tim. 4:10, God . . . S of all men
2 Tim. 1:10, our S Jesus Christ
Titus 2:13, God and our S Jesus Christ
2 Pet. 1:11, our Lord and S Jesus
1 John 4:14, sent the Son to be the S
Savour—*taste, flavor, odor*
Gen. 8:21, Lord smelled a sweet s
Song 1:3, s of thy goodly ointments
Joel 2:20, his ills shall come up
Matt. 5:13, salt have lost his s
2 Cor. 2:15, a sweet s of Christ
  16, s of death . . . s of life
Saw—*had seen*
Gen. 1:4, God s the light, that it was
Ex. 10:23, They s not one another
Num. 22:23, ass s the angel
Job 29:11, when the eye s me, it gave
Ps. 114:3, The sea s it, and fled
Eccles. 2:13, s that wisdom excelleth
Is. 59:16, s that there was no man
Dan. 4:5, I s a dream
Matt. 2:11, s the young child
Mark 1:10, s the heavens opened
John 1:48, fig tree, I s thee

Say—*speak, express in words*
Gen. 20:13, s of me, He is my brother
Ex. 3:13, what shall I s unto them
Job 33:32, If thou hast anything to s
37:19, Teach us what we shall s
Ps. 27:14, wait, I s, on the Lord
106:48, let all the people s, Amen
Prov. 3:28, S not unto thy neighbour
30:15, four things s not
Is. 58:9, he shall s, Here I am
Matt. 7:22, will s to me in that day
16:13, Whom do men s that I
Luke 7:40, somewhat to s unto thee
17:21, Neither shall they s, Lo
2 Cor. 12:6, for I will s the truth
1 John 1:8, s that ye have no sin
Rev. 22:17, Spirit . . . bride s, Come

Saying—*a proverb*
Gen. 37:11, his father observed the s
1 Chr. 21:19, went up at the s of Gad
Ps. 49:13, posterity approve their s-s
78:2, utter dark s-s of old
Matt. 7:14, whosoever heareth these s-s
Luke 18:34, this s was hid from them
John 6:60, This is an hard s
8:51, If a man keep my s
1 Tim. 1:15, This is a faithful s

Scarlet—*a vivid, bright red*
Gen. 38:28, upon his hand a s thread
Ex. 25:4, blue, and purple, and s
Josh 2:18, bind this line of s thread
Song 4:3, Thy lips are like . . . s
Is. 1:18, your sins be as s
Nah. 2:3, valiant men are in s
Matt. 27:28, put on him a s robe
Rev. 17:3, upon a s coloured beast

Scatter—*disperse, spread about*
Lev. 26:33, s you among the heathen
Job 18:15, brimstone . . . s-ed upon his
38:24, s-eth the east wind upon
Ps. 92:9, workers of iniquity . . . s-ed
141:7, bones are s-ed at the grave's
Prov. 11:24, There is that s-eth, and
Is. 18:7, a people s-ed and peeled
41:16, whirlwind shall s them
Jer. 23:1, destroy and s the sheep
Matt. 26:31, the flock shall be s-ed

Scourge—*a whip, to whip severely*
Job 5:21, the s of the tongue
Matt. 10:17, s you in their synagogues
20:19, mock . . . s, and to crucify
27:26, when he had s-ed Jesus
John 2:15, made a s of small cords
Heb. 12:6, s-eth every son . . . receiveth

Scribe—*recorder, one learned in the Law*
Neh. 8:4, Ezra the s stood upon a
Jer. 8:8, the pen of the s-s is in
Matt. 2:4, chief priests and s-s
23:13, woe . . . s-s and Pharisees
Mark 1:22, authority, and not as the s-s
12:38, Beware of the s-s
1 Cor. 1:20, wise? where is the s

Scripture(s)—*a writing, the Bible*
Dan. 10:21, noted in the s of truth
Matt. 21:42, ye never read in the s-s
22:29, err, not knowing the s-s
Mark 14:49, the s-s must be fulfilled
Luke 4:21, day is this s fulfilled
24:32, he opened to us the s-s
John 5:39, Search the s-s; for in them
10:35, s cannot be broken
20:9, For . . . they knew not the s
Acts 18:24, mighty in the s-s
Rom. 4:3, For what saith the s
15:4, patience and comfort . . . s-s
2 Tim. 3:15, hast known the holy s-s
16, s is given by inspiration

Sea—*a body of water*
Gen. 1:10, waters called he S-s
26, dominion . . . fish of the s
Ex. 10:19, cast them into the Red s
2 Sam. 17:11, sand that is by the s
Job 7:12, Am I a s, or a whale
38:3, shut up the s with doors
Ps. 24:2, founded it upon the s-s
65:5, are afar off upon the s
107:23, down to the s in ships
146:6, s, and all that therein is
Is. 11:9, as the waters cover the s
57:20, are like the troubled s
Jer. 25:22, isles . . . beyond the s
Nah. 1:4, He rebuketh the s
Matt. 8:26, rebuked the winds and the s
14:26, saw him walking on the s
2 Cor. 11:26, in perils in the s
Rev. 4:6, was a s of glass
21:1, there was no more s

Seal—*a stamp, to mark, make fast*
1 Kin. 21:8, s-ed them with his s
Job 14:17, transgression is s-ed up
Song 8:6, as a s upon thine heart
Is. 29:11, a book that is s-ed
Jer. 32:10, evidence, and s-ed it
Dan. 9:24, s up the vision
12:4, words, and s the book
Rom. 4:11, s of the righteousness
2 Cor. 1:22, Who hath also s-ed us
Eph. 1:13, s-ed with that holy Spirit

SEAL

Seal (*Continued*)
Rev. 5:1, s-ed with seven s-s
9:4, s of God in their foreheads
Search—*look or seek diligently*
Judg. 5:16, great s-ings of heart
1 Chr. 28:9, Lord s-eth all hearts
Job 11:7, by s-ing find out God
28:3, and s-eth out all perfection
Ps. 139:23, S me . . . know my heart
Prov. 20:27, s-ing all the inward
Jer. 17:10, I the Lord s the heart
John 5:29, S the scriptures; for in
7:52, S, and look
Acts 17:11, s-ed the scriptures daily
Season—*division of the year, to savour*
Gen. 1:14, be for signs, and for s-s
Lev. 26:4, give you rain in due s
Job 5:26, corn cometh in his s
Ps. 1:3, forth his fruit in his s
104:27, their meat in due s
Eccles. 3:1, every thing there is a s
Is. 50:4, how to speak a word in s
Dan. 2:21, changeth the times . . . s-s
Matt. 24:45, give them meat in due s
Luke 14:34, wherewith shall it be s-ed
John 5:25, willing for a s to rejoice
Acts 1:7, to know the times of the s-s
13:11, seeing the sun for a s
24:25, when I have a convenient s
Gal. 6:9, in due s we shall reap
Col. 4:6 with grace, s-ed with salt
2 Tim. 4:2, instant in s, out of s
Heb. 11:25, pleasures of sin for a s
Seat—*chair, bench or stool*
Ex. 25:17, a mercy s of pure gold
1 Sam. 4:18, from off the s backward
Ps. 1:1, in the s of the scornful
Ezek. 28:2, I sit in the s of God
Matt. 23:6, chief s-s in the synagogues
27:19, on the judgment s
Rom. 14:10, the judgment s of Christ
Second—*next to the first*
Gen. 1:8, were the s day
Eccles. 4:8, and there is not a s
Ezek. 10:14, the s face was the face
Matt. 22:39, s is like unto it
1 Cor. 15:47, s man is the Lord
Rev. 2:11, hurt of the s death
Secret—*hidden, something concealed*
Deut. 25:11, taketh him by the s-s
27:15, putteth it in a s place
Job 11:6, shew thee the s-s of wisdom
15:8, heard the s of God
40:13, bind their faces in s

Ps. 19:12, cleanse . . . me from s faults
44:21, knoweth the s-s of the heart
91:1, s place of the most high
Prov. 9:17, bread eaten in s
21:14, A gift in s pacifieth
27:5, rebuke is better than S love
Song 2:14, s places of the stairs
Is. 45:3, hidden riches of s places
19, I have not spoken in s
Dan. 2:22, the deep and s things
4:9, no s troubleth thee
Matt. 6:4, thine alms may be in s
Luke 8:17, For nothing is s
Rom. 2:16, God shall judge the s-s
16:25, kept s since the world
Secretly—*in a secret manner*
Deut. 13:6, entice thee s, saying
Josh. 2:1, two men to spy s
Job 13:10, do s accept persons
31:27, heart hath been s enticed
Hab. 3:14, to devour the poor s
John 11:28, called Mary her sister s
See—*observe, meet with, visit*
Ex. 33:20, no man s me, and live
Num. 24:17, s him, but not now
Job 9:11, by me, and I s him not
19:26, my flesh shall I s God
24:15, No eye shall s me
34:32, I s not teach thou me
Ps. 16:10, Holy One to s corruption
34:8, s that the Lord is good
36:9, thy light shall we s light
49:19, They shall never s light
66:5, and s the works of God
Ps. 115:5, eyes . . . but they s not
Song 7:12, us s if the vine flourish
Is. 29:18, the blind shall s
35:2, s the glory of the Lord
62:2, Gentiles s thy righteousness
Jer. 2:31, s ye the word of the Lord
Ezek. 12:2, eyes to s, and s not
Joel 2:28, young men shall s visions
Matt. 5:16, may s your good works
11:8, went ye out for to s
16:28, s the Son of man coming
Luke 2:26, he should not s death
8:10, s-ing the night not s
17:23, S here; or, s there
John 4:29, and s a man, which told me
16:16, little while . . . not s me
1 Cor. 13:12, s through a glass, darkly
Heb. 12:14, no man shall s the Lord
1 John 3:2, we shall s him as he is

152

Seed—*fruit, offspring*
Gen. 1:11, herb yielding s
    8:22, s-time and harvest
Lev. 19:19, not sow . . . mingled s
    26:16, sow your s in
Ps. 37:28, s of the wicked . . . cut off
Eccles. 11:6, morning sow thy s
Is. 55:10, give s to the sower
    65:9, bring forth a s out of Jacob
Hag. 2:19, Is the s yet in the barn
Matt. 13:22, s among the thorns
    31, like to a grain of mustard s
Luke 8:5, sower went out to sow his s
    11, s is the word of God
Rom. 4:18, So shall thy s be
1 Pet. 1:23, not of corruptible s
Seek—*look or ask for, strive after*
Num. 15:39, s not . . . your own heart
Deut. 4:29, s the Lord thy God
1 Sam. 26:20, come out to s a flea
2 Chr. 7:14, pray, and s my face
Job 7:21, shalt s me in the morning
Ps. 24:6, generation of them that s him
    34:14, s peace, and pursue it
    63:1, early will I s thee
    119:2, s him with the whole heart
Prov. 8:17, s me early shall find me
Eccles. 7:25, to s out wisdom
Is. 34:16, S ye out of the book of
    55:6, S ye the Lord while he may
Jer. 29:13, shall s me, and find me
Ezek. 7:25, they shall s peace
    34:12, will I s out my sheep
    16, s that which was lost
Dan. 9:3, s by prayer and supplications
Hos. 10:12, it is time to s the Lord
Amos 5:4, S ye me . . . and ye shall live
    14, s good, and not evil
Matt. 6:33, s ye first the kingdom
    7:7, s, and ye shall find
Mark 8:12, generation s after a sign
Luke 11:10, he that s-eth findeth
John 1:38, What s ye
    5:30, I s not mine own will
    8:50, one that s-eth and judgeth
Acts 10:21, I am he whom ye s
1 Cor. 10:24, Let no man s his own
    13:5, s-eth not her own
Gal. 1:10, do I s to please men
Col. 3:1, s those things . . . above
Seem—*appear, look, to be taken as*
Gen. 19:14, s-ed as one that mocked
    29:20, s-ed . . . but a few days

1 Sam. 8:23, S-eth it to you a light
Prov. 14:12, s-eth right unto a man
Nah. 2:4 they shall s like torches
Matt. 11:26, s-ed good in thy sight
1 Cor. 3:18, s-eth to be wise in this
James 1:26, s to be religious
Seen—*was visible*
Gen. 9:14, bow shall be s in the cloud
    32:30, s God face to face
2 Sam. 22:11, s upon the wings of the
Job 5:3, s the foolish taking root
    38:22, s the treasures of the hail
Is. 6:5, eyes have s the King
Matt. 2:2, s his star in the east
Luke 2:30, eyes have s thy salvation
John 1:18, No man hath s God at any
Rom. 8:24, hope . . . s is not hope
1 Cor. 2:9, Eye hath not s
Heb. 11:1, evidence of things not s
Sell—*exchange for something of value*
Gen. 25:31, S me . . . thy birthright
Lev. 25:29, s a dwelling house
Deut. 2:28, s me meat for money
2 Kin. 4:7, Go, s the oil, and pay thy
Prov. 23:23, Buy the truth, and s it
Matt. 19:21, go and s that thou hast
James 4:13, buy and s and get gain
Send—*cause to go, dispatch*
Gen. 24:7, S his angel before thee
Num. 13:2, S thou men, that they may
Job 5:10, s-eth waters upon the fields
    38:25, Canst thou s lightnings
Is. 6:8, Here I am; s me
Matt. 5:45, s-eth rain on the just and
    9:38, s forth labourers into
Luke 12:49, s fire on the earth
2 Thess. 2:11, s them strong delusion
Sent—*caused to go, dispatched*
Gen. 8:7, 8, s forth a raven . . . a dove
Is. 48:16, God, and his Spirit, hath s
    61:1, s me to bind . . . brokenhearted
Matt. 10:5, These twelve Jesus s forth
Luke 4:18, s me to heal . . .
    brokenhearted
Acts 13:4, s forth by the Holy Ghost
Gal. 4:4, God s forth his Son
1 Pet. 1:12, Holy Ghost s down from
1 John 4:9, s his only begotten Son
Separate—*to disunite, disconnected*
Gen. 13:9, s thyself, I pray thee
Lev. 20:24, s-d you from other people
Num. 6:3, s himself from wine
Prov. 16:28, whisperer s-th . . . friends

153

Separate (*Continued*)
Acts 13:2, S me Barnabas and Saul
Rom. 8:35, s us from the love of
Sepulchre—*a grave, a tomb*
Deut. 34:6, no man knoweth of his s
Ps. 5:9, throat is an open s
Is. 22:16, hewed thee out a s
Matt. 23:27, like unto whited s-s
John 19:41, garden a new s, wherein
20:11, Mary stood without at the s
Serpent—*a snake*
Gen. 3:1, s was more subtil
Ex. 7:12, rod, and they became s-s
Num. 21:9, made a s of brass
Ps. 58:4, like the poison of a s
Prov. 23:32, it biteth like a s
Is. 30:6, viper and fiery flying s
Matt. 7:10, will he give him a s
Mark 16:18, they shall take up s-s
John 3:14, Moses lifted up the s
2 Cor. 11:3, s beguiled Eve
Rev. 12:9, old s, called the Devil
Servant—*one who works for another*
Gen. 9:25, a s of s-s shall he be
Ex. 14:31, Lord, and his s Moses
1 Sam. 3:9, Speak, Lord . . . s heareth
Job 1:8, considered my s Job
4:18, put no trust in his s-s
Ps. 31:16, face to shine upon thy s
Prov. 11:29, fool . . . s to the wise
22:7, borrower is s to the lender
Matt. 25:21, good and faithful s
Luke 2:29, thy s depart in peace
1 Cor. 7:21, Art thou called being a s
Gal. 4:7, no more a s, but a son
Col. 3:22, S-s, obey in all things your
Serve—*to work for, to obey or worship*
Deut. 6:13, fear the Lord . . . and s him
Josh. 22:5, s him with all your heart
Ps. 2:11, S the Lord with fear
100:2, S the Lord with gladness
Jer. 5:19, so shall ye s strangers
Matt. 4:10, him only shalt thou s
6:24, No man can s two masters
Luke 10:40, cumbered about much s-ing
John 12:26, If any man s me
Rom. 7:6, s in newness of spirit
12:11, in spirit; s-ing the Lord
Gal. 5:13, by love s one another
Titus 3:3, s-ing divers lusts and
Heb. 12:28, may s God acceptably
Service—*labor performed for another*
Jer. 22:13, useth his neighbour's s
Rom. 12:1, is your reasonable s

Phil. 2:30, supply your lack of s
Heb. 9:6, accomplishing the s of God
Set—*place, put, fix*
Gen. 4:15, s a mark upon Cain
9:13, s my bow in the cloud
Lev. 17:10, s my face against
Deut. 30:19, s before you life and death
Ps. 8:1, s thy glory above the heavens
40:2, s my feet upon a rock
Eccles. 10:6, folly is s in great
Song 8:6, S me as a seal upon thine
Is. 3:24, instead of well s hair
11:12, s up an ensign . . . nations
38:1, S thine house in order
Jer. 5:26, s a trap, they catch men
Ezek. 2:2, s me upon my feet
Matt. 5:14, city . . . s-on an hill
Acts 13:47, s thee to be a light
Rom. 14:10, s at nought thy brother
Col. 3:2, S your affection on things
James 3:6, is s on fire of hell
Seven—*one more than six*
Gen. 21:29, mean these s ewe lambs
29:20, Jacob served s years for
Ps. 119:164, S times a day do I praise
Prov. 9:1, Wisdom . . . her s pillars
Eccles. 11:2, Give a portion to s
Is. 4:1, s women shall take hold of
Dan. 9:25, Prince shall be s weeks
Zech. 4:2, s pipes . . . s lamps
Matt. 12:45, s other spirits more
18:21, forgive him? till s times
Acts 6:3, s men of honest report
Rev. 1:4, John to the s churches
12, s golden candlesticks
3:1, s Spirits of God
15:1, s angels . . . s last plagues
Shadow—*shade, obscurity, faint image*
Gen. 19:8, under the s of my roof
2 Kin. 20:11, s ten degrees backward
1 Chr. 20:15, our days . . . are as a s
Job 3:5, s of death stain it
Ps. 17:8, under the s of thy wings
23:4, valley of the s of death
Ps. 91:9, s of the almighty
Song 2:17, day break . . . s-s flee away
Is. 9:2, land of the s of death
Col. 2:17, a s of things to come
Heb. 8:5, s of heavenly things
James 1:17, neither s of turning
Shake—*quiver, tremble*
Lev. 26:36, sound of a s-n leaf
Job 4:14, made all my bones to s
16:4, s mine head at you

Is. 13:13, s the heavens . . . earth
Zech. 2:9, s mine hand upon them
Matt. 10:14, s off the dust of your
    11:7, a reed s-n with the wind
Luke 6:38, pressed down . . . s-n together
Shame—*dishonor, disgrace*
Ex. 32:25, naked unto their s
Ps. 4:2, turn my glory into s
    83:16, Fill their faces with s
Prov. 12:16, a prudent man covereth s
    19:26, a son that causeth s
Is. 54:4, forget the s of thy youth
Zeph. 3:5, unjust knoweth no s
Acts 5:41, worthy to suffer s
1 Cor. 11:6, s for a woman to be shorn
    14:35, s for women to speak in
Phil. 3:19, glory is in their s
Sharp—*not dull*
Ex. 4:25, Zipporah took a s stone
Ps. 57:4, tongue a s sword
Prov. 5:4, s as a twoedged sword
    27:17, Iron s-eneth iron
Heb. 4:12, s-er . . . any twoedged sword
Shave—*cut close, remove with a razor*
Gen. 41:14, he s-d himself
Judg. 16:19, s off the seven locks
2 Sam. 10:4, s-d . . . half of their beards
Is. 7:20, Lord s with a razor that
1 Cor. 11:6, woman to be shorn or s-n
Shed—*part with, as blood*
Gen. 9:6, man shall his blood be s
Prov. 1:16, make haste to s blood
Matt. 26:28, my blood . . . s for many
Luke 22:20, blood, which is s for you
Rom. 3:15, feet are swift to s blood
    5:5, love of God is s abroad
Sheep—*an animal, God's people*
Gen. 4:2, Abel was a keeper of s
    29:9, Rachel . . . with her father's s
Num. 27:17, s which have no shepherd
1 Sam. 15:14, this bleating of the s
    16:19, David . . . is with the s
Job 31:20, warmed . . . fleece of my s
Ps. 44:22, as s for the slaughter
    100:3, the s of his pasture
    119:176, astray like a lost s
Is. 53:6, All we like s . . . gone astray
    7, s before her shearers
Jer. 12:3, s for the slaughter
    50:6, My people hath been lost s
Matt. 9:36, s having no shepherd
    15:24, lost s of the house of
    25:32, divideth his s from the
    26:31, s of the flock . . . scattered

Luke 15:6, I have found my s . . . lost
John 10:3, calleth his own s by name
    7, I am the door of the s
    27, My s hear my voice
    21:16, Feed my s
Heb. 13:20, great shepherd of the s
1 Pet. 2:25, were as s going astray
Shepherd—*a sheep herder*
Gen. 46:34, every s is an abomination
Num. 27:17, as sheep which have no s
1 Sam. 17:40, put them in a s's bag
Ps. 23:1, The Lord is my s
Is. 40:11, feed his flock like a s
Ezek. 34:5, because there is no s
    12, s seeketh out his flock
    37:24, all shall have one s
Zeph. 2:6, dwellings and cottages for s-s
Zech. 11:16, I will raise up a s
Matt. 9:36, as sheep having no s
    26:31, I will smite the s
Luke 2:8, s-s abiding in the field
John 10:11, I am the good s
Heb. 13:20, that great s of the sheep
1 Pet. 2:25, unto the S and Bishop
    5:4, the chief S shall appear
Shew—*exhibit, reveal (See also Show)*
Gen. 12:1, a land that I will s thee
Ex. 33:18, s me thy glory
Deut. 5:10, s-ing mercy unto thousands
Esther 1:11, s the people . . . her beauty
Job 11:6, s thee the secrets of wisdom
Ps. 25:4, S me thy ways, O Lord
Prov. 18:24, must s himself friendly
Dan. 2:2, s the king his dream
Matt. 22:19, S me the tribute money
John 14:8, s us the Father
Acts 26:23, s light unto the people
Rom. 9:22, willing to s his wrath
Gal. 6:12, make a fair s in the flesh
1 Tim. 5:4, s piety at home
2 Tim. 2:15, s thyself approved
Shield—*a piece of armor, a defense*
Gen. 15:1, Abram: I am thy s
2 Sam. 22:3, he is my s, and the horn
Ps. 28:7, my strength and my s
Eph. 6:16, taking the s of faith
Shine—*give off light, radiate*
Num. 6:25, make his face s upon thee
2 Sam. 23:4, clear s-ing after rain
Job 41:32, path to s after him
Ps. 104:15, oil to make his face to s

Shine *(Continued)*
Prov. 4:18, s-th more and more unto
Is. 60:1, Arise, s; for thy light is
Matt. 5:16, Let your light so s
    13:43, righteous s forth
Luke 24:4, men . . . in s-ing garments
John 1:5, light s-th in darkness
2 Cor. 4:4, gospel should s unto them
2 Pet. 1:19, light that s-th in a dark
1 John 2:8, true light now s-th
Shoe—*a foot covering*
Ex. 12:11, your s-s on your feet
Deut. 29:5, s is not waxen old
    33:25, s-s shall be iron and brass
Amos 2:6, poor for a pair of s-s
Mark 1:7, latchet of whose s-s I am
Acts 7:33, Put off thy s-s from thy
Shone—*gave off light*
Ex. 34:29, the skin of his face s
2 Kin. 3:22, sun s upon the water
Luke 2:9, glory of the Lord s round
Acts 22:6, s from heaven a great light
Shook—*moved violently*
2 Sam. 6:6, for the oxen s it
Neh. 5:13, Also I s my lap
Ps. 68:8, The earth s
Acts 28:5, he s off the beast into
Heb. 12:26, voice then s the earth
Shoot—*to discharge a weapon*
1 Sam. 20:20, I will s three arrows
Ps. 11:2, privily s at the upright
    22:7, they s out the lip
    64:4, s in secret at the perfect
Mark 4:32, s-eth out great branches
Shore—*edge of a body of water*
Matt. 13:2, multitude stood on the s
John 21:4, Jesus stood on the s
Acts 21:5, kneeled down on the s
Short—*not full or complete*
Num. 11:23, the Lord's hand waxed s
Job 17:12, the light is s because of
Ps. 89:47, how s my time is
Rom. 3:23, come s of the glory
    9:28, s work will the Lord make
1 Cor. 7:29, brethren, the time is s
Heb. 13:23, if he come s-ly
Shot—*discharged a weapon*
Gen. 40:10, her blossoms s forth
1 Sam. 20:20, as though I s at a mark
Jer. 9:8, tongue is as an arrow s out
Shout—*utter a sudden loud cry*
Ex. 32:18, them that s for mastery
Josh. 6:16, Joshua said . . . S

Ps. 5:11, let them ever s for joy
    47:5, God is gone up with a s
    78:65, s-eth by reason of wine
1 Thess. 4:16, descend . . . with a s
Shower—*short, light rain*
Deut. 32:2, the s-s upon the grass
Job 24:8, wet with the s-s
Ps. 65:10, makest it soft with s-s
Jer. 14:22, can the heavens give s-s
Luke 12:54, ye say, There cometh a s
Shut—*to close, to confine*
Gen. 7:16, the Lord s him in
Job 38:8, who s up the sea with doors
Song 4:12, a spring s up, a fountain
Jer. 36:5, I am s up; I cannot go
Dan. 6:22, hath s the lions' mouths
    12:4, Daniel, s up the words
Matt. 23:13, s up the kingdom of
Acts 5:23, prison truly found we s
Gal. 3:23, s up unto the faith
1 John 3:17, s-eth up his bowels of
Rev. 21:25, gates of it shall not be s
Sick—*ill, not in health*
Prov. 13:12, Hope. . . maketh the heart s
Song 2:5, for I am s of love
Matt. 25:36, I was s, and ye visited
Mark 2:17, physician . . . they that are s
Luke 7:2, was s, and ready to die
John 11:2, brother Lazarus was s
James 5:14, Is any s among you
    15, prayer of faith . . . save the s
Sickle—*a reaping tool*
Deut. 16:9, to put the s to the corn
Joel 3:13, Put ye in the s, for the
Rev. 14:15, Thrust in thy s, and reap
Sickness—*ill health*
Deut. 7:15, take away from thee all s
Ps. 41:3, make all his bed in his s
Matt. 4:23, healing all manner of s
Mark 3:15, have power to heal s-es
John 11:4, This s is not unto death
Side—*margin, edge, or border*
Ex. 32:26, Who is on the Lord's s
Ps. 118:6, Lord is on my s
Is. 60:4, daughters . . . nursed at thy s
Ezek. 36:3, swallowed you up on every s
Matt. 13:4, seeds fell by the way s
John 19:34, a spear pierced his s
    20:20, his hands and his s
2 Cor. 4:8, troubled on every s
Sight—*act of seeing, a spectacle*
Gen. 2:9, tree . . . pleasant to the s
    18:3, have found favour in thy s
Ruth 2:13, Let me find favour in thy s

Job 19:15, I am an alien in their s
Ps. 19:14, acceptable in thy s, O Lord
  90:4, thousand years in thy s
Eccles. 6:9, Better is the s of the eyes
Matt. 11:5, blind receive their s
  20:34, their eyes received s
Luke 4:18, recovering of s to the blind
  21:11, fearful s-s and great signs
Acts 9:9, three days without s
  22:13, Saul, receive thy s
2 Cor. 5:7, walk by faith, not by s
Rev. 4:3, in s like unto an emerald

Sign—*mark, token, miracle, wonder*
Ex. 31:13, a s between me and you
Is. 7:11, Ask thee a s of the Lord
  14, Lord . . . shall give you a s
  55:13, for an everlasting s
Ezek. 14:8, make him a s and a proverb
Matt. 12:38, we would see a s from thee
  16:3, not discern the s-s
  24:3, be the s of thy coming
Mark 13:22, shew s-s and wonders
  16:20, confirming . . . with s-s
Luke 21:25, shall be s-s in the sun
1 Cor. 1:22, the Jews require a s
2 Thess. 2:9, with all power and s-s
Rev. 15:1, saw another s in heaven

Silence—*absence of sound*
Ps. 31:18, lying lips be put to s
Eccles. 3:7, a time to keep s
Jer. 8:14, God hath put us to s
Amos 5:13, prudent shall keep s
Acts 21:40, there was made a great s
1 Cor. 14:28, keep s in the church
  34, your women keep s
Rev. 8:1, there was s in heaven

Silver—*a precious metal*
Gen. 13:2, rich in cattle, in s
Job 27:16, heap up s as the dust
Prov. 16:16, to be chosen than s
  25:11, of gold in pictures of s
Eccles. 5:10, loveth s shall not be
Is. 1:22, Thy s is become dross
  39:2, s . . . gold . . . spices
Jer. 6:30, Reprobate s shall men call
Amos 2:6, sold the righteous for s
Zech. 11:12, price thirty pieces of s
Matt. 26:15, for thirty pieces of s
Acts 3:6, S and gold have I none
  20:33, coveted no man's s
James 5:3, gold and s is cankered

Simple—*plain, artless, foolish*
Ps. 19:7, making wise the s
  116:6, Lord preserveth the s

Prov. 14:15, s believeth every word
Rom. 16:18, deceive the hearts of the s

Sin—*an offense in the sight of God*
Gen. 4:7, s lieth at the door
  18:20, their s is very grievous
Ex. 10:17, forgive . . . my s . . . this once
  32:30, Ye have s-ed a great s
Job 2:10, did not Job s with his lips
Ps. 25:7, Remember not the s-s of my
  51:2, cleanse me from my s
  3, my s is ever before me
  79:9, purge away our s-s
Prov. 10:12, love covereth all s-s
  14:9, Fools make a mock at s
Is. 1:18, s-s be as scarlet
  30:1, they may add s to s
Jer. 51:5, s against the Holy One
Mic. 6:7, body for the s of my soul
Matt. 1:21, save his people from . . . s-s
  12:31, All manner of s . . . forgiven
  18:21, brother s against me
Matt. 26:28, for the remission of s-s
Mark 2:7, forgive s-s but God only
Luke 11:4, forgive us our s-s
John 1:29, taketh away the s of the
  8:7, He that is without s
  11, go and s no more
  15:22, have no cloak for their s
  16:8, will reprove the world of s
Acts 22:16, wash away thy s-s
  26:18, receive forgiveness of s-s
Rom. 5:12, s entered into the world
  6:23, wages of s is death
  14:23, not of faith is s
1 Cor. 15:3, Christ died for our s-s
  56, sting of death is s
2 Cor. 5:21, s for us, who knew no s
Heb. 11:25, enjoy the pleasures of s
James 5:20, hide a multitude of s-s
1 Pet. 2:22, Who did no s, neither was
1 John 1:8, we say that we have no s
  9, If we confess our s-s
  2:1, any man s, we have an
  3:4, s in the transgression of
  5:16, There is a s unto death
  17, All unrighteousness is s
Rev. 1:5, washed us from our s-s

Sinful—*wicked, unholy*
Num. 32:14, an increase of s men
Is. 1:4, Ah s nation, a people laden
Mark 8:38, s generation
Luke 5:8, for I am a s man, O Lord
Rom. 8:3, the likeness of s flesh

157

Sing—*make musical sounds with the voice*
Ex. 15:1, I will s unto the Lord
2 Sam. 22:50, s praises unto thy name
1 Chr. 16:33, trees of the wood s out
2 Chr. 23:13, such as taught to s praise
Job 29:13, widow's heart to s for joy
Ps. 33:3, S unto him a new song
    100:2, his presence with s-ing
Prov. 29:6, righteous doth s and
Song 2:12, time of the s-ing of birds
Is. 5:1, s to my well beloved a song
1 Cor. 14:15, I will s with the spirit
Col. 3:16, s-ing with grace in your
James 5:13, merry? let him s psalms
Rev. 5:9, they **sung** a new song
Sinned—*did wickedly*
Ex. 32:30, Ye have s a great sin
Deut. 1:41, have s against the Lord
Job 1:22, In all this Job s not
Ps. 41:4, I have s against thee
    51:4, thee only, have I s
Dan. 9:15, s . . . done wickedly
Luke 15:18, s against heaven
Rom. 3:23, s, and come short of the
    5:12, for that all have s
1 John 1:10, say that we have not s
Sinner—*one who has committed sin*
Ps. 1:1, standeth in the way of s-s
Prov. 1:10, if s-s entice thee
    13:21, Evil pursueth s-s
    23:17, not thine heart envy s-s
Eccles. 9:18, one s destroyeth . . . good
Matt. 9:10, publicans and s-s
    13, but s-s to repentance
Mark 14:41 into the hands of s-s
Luke 6:34, s-s also lend to s-s
    15:7, one s that repenteth
    18:13, be merciful to me a s
John 9:31, God heareth not s-s
Rom. 5:8, while we were yet s-s
1 Tim. 1:15, Jesus came . . . to save s-s
James 4:8, Cleanse your hands, ye s-s
Sister—*female relative or associate*
Gen. 12:13, Say . . . thou art my s
Job 17:14, art my mother, and my s
Prov. 7:4, wisdom, Thou art my s
Song 8:8, We have a little s
Matt. 12:50, is my brother, and my s
Luke 10:39, had a s called Mary
Rom. 16:1, unto you Phebe our s
Sit—*rest upon the haunches, rest*
Ruth 3:18, S still, my daughter

1 Kin. 22:19, Lord s-ing on his throne
Ps. 1:1, s-teth in the seat . . . scornful
    107:10, Such as s in darkness
    110:1, S thou at my right hand
    127:2, to s up late
Jer. 17:11, partridge s-teth on eggs
Ezek. 28:2, I s in the seat of God
Matt. 9:9, s-ing at receipt of custom
    21:5, meek, and s-ing upon an
    26:36, S ye here, while I go
    27:61, s-ing over against the
Luke 2:46, s-ing . . . midst . . . doctors
    8:35, s-ing at the feet of Jesus
John 12:15, s-ing on an ass's colt
Acts 8:28, s-ing in his chariot
Skin—*outer covering*
Ex. 34:29, the s of his face shone
Job 2:4, S for s, yea, all that a
    10:11, clothed me with s and
    19:20, My bone cleaveth to my s
    30:30, My s is black upon me
Jer. 13:23, Ethiopian change his s
Mark 1:6, a girdle of a s about his
Skull—*the head bones*
Judg. 9:53, and all to brake his s
Matt. 27:33, to say, a place of a s
Sky—*the vault of heaven*
Job 37:18, spread out the s
Matt. 16:2, 3, for the s is red
Luke 12:56, discern the face of the s
Heb. 11:12, as the stars of the s
Slack—*weak, backward, loose*
Deut. 23:21, shalt not s to pay it
Josh. 10:6, S not thy hand from
Prov. 10:4, dealeth with a s hand
2 Pet. 3:9, The Lord is not s
Slain—*killed*
Gen. 4:23, s a man to my wounding
1 Sam. 18:7, Saul hath s his thousands
Prov. 24:11, those . . . ready to be s
Luke 9:22, s . . . raised the third day
Rev. 5:12, Worthy . . . Lamb that was s
Slaughter—*wanton killing, butchering*
Ps. 44:22, as sheep for the s
Prov. 7:22, an ox goeth to the s
Is. 53:7, as a lamb to the s
Rom. 8:36, as sheep for the s
James 5:5, as in a day of s
Slay—*kill*
Gen. 4:14, findeth me shall s me
Ex. 21:14, s him with guile
Job 13:15, Though he s me, yet will I
Ps. 34:21, Evil shall s the wicked

John 5:16, Jesus, and sought to s him
Acts 11:7, Arise, Peter; s and eat
Sleep—*slumber, repose, death*
Gen. 2:21, deep s to fall upon Adam
Deut. 31:16, s with thy fathers
Job 7:21, now shall I s in the dust
Ps. 13:3, s the s of death
76:6, cast into a dead s
Prov. 3:24, thy s shall be sweet
6:10, Yet a little s, a little
20:13, Love not s, lest thou
Eccles. 5:12, s of a labouring man
Jer. 31:26, my s was sweet
Matt. 9:24, not dead, but s-eth
26:45, S on now, and take your
Mark 13:36, coming . . . he find you s-ing
John 11:11, Our friend Lazarus s-eth
Acts 20:9, fallen into a deep s
1 Cor. 15:51, We shall not all s
1 Thess. 4:14, also which s in Jesus
5:7, that s s in the night
10, whether we wake or s
Slew—*violently killed*
Gen. 4:8, Abel his brother, and s him
Ex. 13:15, Lord s all the firstborn
Num. 31:8, they s the kings of Midian
1 Sam. 17:50, Phillistine, and s him
29:5, Saul s his thousands
Matt. 2:16, s all the children
Acts 10:39, s and hanged on a tree
Sling—*a stone thrower, to throw*
Judg. 20:16, s stones at an hair breadth
1 Sam. 17:40, his s was in his hand
25:29, them shall he s out
Slothful—*slow, lazy*
Prov. 12:27, s man roasteth not
18:9, that is s in his work
Matt. 25:26, wicked and s servant
Rom. 12:11, Not s in business
Heb. 6:12, That ye be not s
Slow—*not swift or hasty*
Ex. 4:10, s of speech . . . s tongue
Ps. 103:8, s to anger, and plenteous
Prov. 16:32, He that is s to anger
Luke 24:25, O fools, and s of heart
Titus 1:12, evil beasts, s bellies
James 1:19, s to speak, s to wrath
Slumber—*sleep*
Job 33:15, in s-ings upon the bed
Ps. 121:3, keepeth thee will not s
132:4, or s to mine eyelids
Prov. 6:10, a little sleep, a little s

Is. 5:27, none shall s nor sleep
56:10, lying down, loving to s
Matt. 25:5, they all s-ed and slept
Rom. 11:8, given them the spirit of s
Small—*little, not large or great*
Ex. 16:14, s as the hoar frost
Deut. 25:13, weights, a great and a s
2 Sam. 7:19, s thing in thy sight
22:43, best them as s as the dust
Job 8:7, thy beginning was s
Eccles. 2:7, great and s cattle
Mark 8:7, they had a few s fishes
John 2:15, Made a scourge of s cords
James 3:4, with a very s helm
Smell—*an odor, obtain the scent of*
Gen. 27:27, s of my son is as the s
Deut. 4:28, nor hear, nor eat, nor s
Job 39:25, s-eth the battle afar off
Ps. 115:6, noses . . . but they s not
Song 2:13, grape give a good s
Is. 3:24, instead of sweet s
Smite—*strike, with the fist or a weapon*
Ex. 7:17, I will s with the rod
12:12, s all the firstborn
Deut. 28:27, s thee with the botch
Ps. 121:6, sun . . . not s thee by day
Prov. 19:25, S a scorner, and the
Jer. 18:18, s him with the tongue
Nah. 2:10, the knees together
Matt. 5:39, s thee on thy right cheek
26:31, I will s the shepherd
Acts 23:3, God shall s thee, thou
2 Cor. 11:20, if a man s you
Smitten—*struck, as with a heavy blow*
Ex. 9:31, flax . . . barley was s
Job 16:10, s me upon the cheek
Jer. 14:19, why hast thou s us
Rev. 8:12, third part of the sun was s
Smoke—*vapor from a fire, to be kindled*
Gen. 15:17, behold a s-ing furnace
Job 41:20, Out of his nostrils goeth s
Ps. 102:3, days are consumed like s
Prov. 10:26, as s to the eyes
Is. 6:4, house was filled with s
42:3, s-ing flax shall he not
Matt. 12:20, s-ing flax shall he not
Smooth—*even surfaced, not rough*
Gen. 27:11, and I am a s man
16, upon the s of his neck
1 Sam. 17:40, chose him five s stones
Ps. 55:21, words . . . s-er than butter
Prov. 5:3, her mouth is s-er than oil
Is. 30:10, speak unto us s things
Luke 3:5, rough ways . . . made s

Smote—*struck*
Ex. 7:20, s the waters . . . in the river
Num. 20:11, he s the rock twice
    22:23, Balaam s the ass
Matt. 26:51, and s off his ear
Luke 18:13, s upon his breast
Acts 12:23, angel of the Lord s him
Snare—*a trap, to trap*
Ex. 10:7, this man be a s unto us
Job 18:8, he walketh upon a s
    40:24, nose pierceth through s-s
Ps. 91:3, from the s of the fowler
Prov. 7:23, bird hasteth to the s
Eccles. 7:26, heart is s-s and nets
Rom. 11:9, their table be made a s
2 Tim. 2:26, out of the s of the devil
Snow—*frozen moisture*
Num. 12:10, leprous, white as s
Job 9:30, wash myself with s water
    38:22, the treasures of the s
Ps. 51:7, I shall be whiter than s
Prov. 25:13, cold of s in the time of
    26:1, As s in summer
Is. 1:18, scarlet . . . be as white as s
Matt. 28:3, his raiment white as s
Rev. 1:14, like wool, as white as s
Sober—*grave, temperate, steady*
Acts 26:25, words of truth and s-ness
Rom. 12:3, to think s-ly
1 Thess. 5:6, watch and be s
Titus 2:2, aged men be s, grave
    4, the young women to be s
1 Pet. 5:8, Be s, be vigilant
Soft—*yielding, smooth, gentle*
Judg. 4:21, went s-ly unto him
Job 23:16, God maketh my heart s
Ps. 65:10, makest it s with showers
Prov. 15:1, s answer . . . away wrath
    25:15, s tongue breaketh the bone
Acts 27:13, south wind blew s-ly
Sojourn—*dwell for a time*
Gen. 26:3, S in this land, and I will
Ex. 12:48, stranger shall s with thee
Is. 23:7, carry her afar off to s
Acts 7:6, s in a strange land
1 Pet. 1:17, time of your s-ing here
Sold—*exchanged for something of value*
Gen. 25:33, s his birthright
    45:4, brother, whom ye s into
Lev. 25:23, land . . . not be s for ever
1 Kin. 21:20, s thyself to work evil
Joel 3:3, s a girl for wine
Matt. 10:29, sparrows s for a farthing

Matt. 13:46, went and s all that he had
Acts 5:1, his wife, s a possession
Rom. 7:14, carnal, s under sin
Soldier—*a warrior*
Mark 15:16, s-s led him away into the
Luke 23:36, the s-s also mocked him
John 19:23, parts, to every s a part
Acts 28:16, with a s that kept him
2 Tim. 2:3, as a good s of Jesus Christ
Somebody—*one unknown, one of importance*
Luke 8:46, S hath touched me
Acts 5:36, boasting himself to be s
Somewhat—*more or less*
1 Kin. 2:14, s to say unto thee
Luke 7:40, I have s to say unto thee
Acts 25:26, might have s to write
Rev. 2:4, I have s against thee
Son—*a male child*
Gen. 6:2, s-s of God saw the daughters
    22:2, Take now thy s, thine only s
    37:33, It is my s's coat
Ex. 20:10, any work, thou, nor thy s
Deut. 8:5, as a man chasteneth his s
2 Sam. 13:37, David mourned for his s
2 Kin. 2:3, the s-s of the prophets
Ps. 2:7, Thou art my S
    8:4, s of man, that thou visitest
Prov. 10:1, wise s maketh a glad
    17:25, A foolish s is a grief
Is. 7:14, virgin shall . . . bear a s
    14:12, Lucifer, s of the morning
    60:4, thy s-s shall come from far
Ezek. 2:1, S of man, stand upon thy
Dan. 7:13, one like the S of man
Hos. 11:1, called my s out of Egypt
Mal. 3:17, man spareth his own s
Matt. 2:15, Out of Egypt . . . called my s
    3:17, This is my beloved S
    11:27, no man knoweth the S
    13:55, not this the carpenter's s
    16:16, S of the living God
    22:42, Christ? whose s is he
    26:33, the Christ, the S of God
    27:43, I am the S of God
Mark 5:7, S of the most high God
    14:61, the S of the Blessed
Luke 1:31, bring forth a s, and shalt
    2:7, her firstborn s
    4:22, Is not this Joseph's s
    15:11, certain man had two s-s
    24, this my s was dead

John 1:18, only begotten S
    4:50, Go thy way; thy s liveth
    5:21, the S quickeneth whom he
    6:42, this Jesus, the s of Joseph
    14:13, be glorified in the S
    19:26, Woman, behold thy s
Acts 4:36, The s of consolation
Rom. 8:32, spared not his own S
Gal. 4:7, but a s; and if a s
2 Thess. 2:3, the s of perdition
Heb. 6:6, crucify . . . S of God afresh
1 John 2:22, denieth the Father and the S
Rev. 21:7, be his God . . . be my s

Song—*musical composition, a byword*
Ex. 15:2, The Lord is my strength and s
Judg. 5:12, awake, awake, utter a s
Job 30:9, now am I their s
    35:10, giveth s-s in the night
Ps. 33:3, Sing unto him a new s
    137:4, How . . . sing the Lord's s
Prov. 25:20, singeth s-s . . . heavy heart
Song 1:1, The s of s-s
Is. 5:1, sing to my well beloved a s
    23:16, sweet melody, sing many s-s
    24:9, not drink wine with a s
Ezek. 33:32, as a very lovely s
Eph. 5:19, hymns and spiritual s-s

Soon—*quickly, presently*
Ex. 2:18, ye are come so s
Job 32:22, maker would s take me away
Ps. 37:2, s be cut down like the
Prov. 14:17, s angry dealeth foolishly
Matt. 21:20, s is the fig tree withered
2 Thess. 2:2, be not s shaken in mind
Titus 1:7, not s angry, not given to

Sore—*sensitive, severely*
Gen. 20:8, men were s afraid
Ex. 14:10, and they were s afraid
Job 5:18, maketh s, and bindeth up
Is. 59:11, and mourn s like doves
Matt. 17:15, lunatick, and s vexed
Mark 9:26, the spirit . . . rent him s
Luke 16:21, came and licked his s-s

Sorrow—*grief, distress, to mourn*
Gen. 3:16, greatly multiply thy s
    42:38, with s to the grave
Deut. 28:65, of eyes, and s of mind
1 Sam. 1:15, woman of a s-ful spirit
2 Sam. 22:6, s-s of hell compassed me
1 Chr. 4:9, I bare him with s
Job 6:7, are as my s-ful meat
    10, harden myself in s
    21:17, God distributeth s-s
    41:22, s is turned into joy

Ps. 18:4, s-s of death compassed me
    127:2, eat the bread of s-s
Prov. 10:10, winketh . . . causeth s
    15:13, by s of the heart the
Eccles. 1:18, knowledge increaseth s
    7:3, S is better than laughter
Is. 14:3, give thee rest from thy s
    35:10, s and sighing shall flee away
    53:3, a man of s-s
Jer. 8:18, comfort myself against s
    30:15, s is incurable
    49:23, there is s on the sea
Lam. 1:12, s like unto my s
Matt. 26:38, My soul is exceeding s-ful
Mark 13:8, the beginnings of s-s
Luke 22:45, sleeping for s
John 16:20, be s-ful, but your s
2 Cor. 2:7, swallowed . . . overmuch s
    7:10, s worketh repentance

Sorry—*feeling regret*
Neh. 8:10, neither be ye s
Ps. 38:18, I will be s for my sin
2 Cor. 2:2, For if I make you s
    7:9, s after a godly manner

Sort—*kind*
Gen. 6:19, two of every s shalt thou
Deut. 22:11, garment of divers s-s
2 Kin. 24:14, poorest s of the people
Acts 17:5, lewd fellows of the baser s

Sought—*looked for*
Ex. 2:15, he s to slay Moses
    33:7, every one which s the Lord
1 Kin. 1:3, they s for a fair damsel
2 Chr. 16:12, he s not to the Lord
Eccles. 2:3, I s in mine heart to give
    7:29, s out many inventions
Matt. 2:20, s the young child's life
    21:46, s to lay hands on him
Luke 2:44, s him among their kinsfolk
    19:3, he s to see Jesus
Rom. 9:32, s it not by faith
2 Tim. 1:17, s me out very diligently

Soul—*the immortal part of man*
Gen. 2:7, man became a living s
    12:13, my s shall live because of
Lev. 4:2, if a s shall sin
Num. 11:6, our s is dried away
Deut. 4:9, keep thy s diligently
    29, with all thy heart and . . . s
Judg. 16:16, s was vexed unto death
1 Sam. 1:26, as thy s liveth
    18:1, knit with the s of David

Soul (*Continued*)
Job 3:20, life unto the bitter in s
 10:1, My s is weary of my life
 19:2, long will ye vex my s
 27:8, God taketh away his s
 33:30, back his s from the pit
Ps. 16:10, not leave my s in hell
 19:7, perfect, converting the s
 23:3, He restoreth my s
 24:4, lifted up his s unto vanity
 42:1, panteth my s after thee
 62:1, my s waiteth upon God
 63:1, my s thirsteth for thee
 103:1, Bless the Lord, O my s
 107:9, satisfieth the longing s
Prov. 11:25, liberal s shall be made fat
 24:12, he that keepeth thy s
 25:25, cold waters to a thirsty s
Is. 32:6, empty the s of the hungry
 55:3, hear, and your s shall live
Jer. 31:12, s . . . as a watered garden
 38:16, Lord . . . that made us this s
 17, then thy s shall live
Ezek. 18:4, s that sinneth, it shall die
 27, shall save his s alive
Matt. 10:28, not able to kill the s
 11:29, find rest unto your s-s
 16:26, world, and lose his own s
 26:38, s is exceeding sorrowful
Luke 1:46, s doth magnify the Lord
 12:19, say to my s, S, thou hast
John 12:27, Now is my s troubled
Acts 4:32, one heart and of one s
Rom. 13:1, Let every s be subject
1 Thess. 5:23, spirit and s and body
Heb. 4:12, dividing . . . of s and spirit
 6:19, as an anchor of the s
 10:39, to the saving of the s
James 1:21, is able to save your s-s
 5:20, save a s from death
1 Pet. 2:11, which war against the s
2 Pet. 2:14, beguiling unstable s-s
Rev. 16:3, every living s died in

Sound—*a noise, to make a noise, firm*
Lev. 26:36, s of a shaken leaf
1 Kin. 18:41, s of abundance of rain
Job 15:21, dreadful s is in his ears
Ps. 119:80, let my heart be s
Prov. 2:7, layeth up s wisdom
 3:21, Keep s wisdom
Eccles. 12:4, s of the grinding is low
Jer. 25:10, s of the millstones
 50:22, s of battle is in the land
Joel 2:1, s an alarm in my holy

Luke 15:27, received him safe and s
Acts 2:2, came a s from heaven
Rom. 10:18, s went into all the earth
1 Cor. 13:1, become as s-ing brass
1 Tim. 1:10, contrary to s doctrine
2 Tim. 1:13, the form of s words
Titus 1:13, may be s in the faith
Rev. 1:15, s of many waters
 8:7, The first angel s-ed

Sour—*acid, puckery*
Is. 18:5, the s grape is ripening
Jer. 31:29, fathers . . . eaten a s grape
Hos. 4:18, Their drink is s

South—*to the right when facing east*
Gen. 12:9, going on still toward the s
 24:62, dwelt in the s country
Num. 13:17, Get you up this way s-ward
Job 37:9, Out of the s . . . whirlwind
 17, quieteth . . . by the s wind
Eccles. 11:3, tree fall toward the s
Matt. 12:42, queen of the s
Luke 12:55, see the s wind blow
Acts 27:13, the s wind blew softly

Sow—*to scatter, as seed*
Gen. 47:23, Ye shall s the land
Lev. 26:16, s your seed in vain
Deut. 22:9, not s . . . with divers seed
Job 4:8, iniquity, and s wickedness
 31:8, Then let me s
Ps. 126:5, s in tears . . . reap in joy
Prov. 22:8, s iniquity shall reap vanity
Eccles. 11:4, the wind shall not s
 6, In the morning s thy seed
Is. 32:20, that s beside all waters
 55:10, may give seed to the s-er
Jer. 4:3, s not among thorns
Hos. 8:7, they have s-n the wind
Matt. 6:26, fowls . . . for they s not
 13:3, s-er went forth to s
Luke 12:24, neither s nor reap
 19:21, reapest that . . . didst not s
John 4:36, both he that s-eth and he
1 Cor. 9:11, s-n unto you spiritual
 15:42, s-n in corruption
 44, s-n a natural body
2 Cor. 9:6, He which s-eth sparingly
Gal. 6:7, whatsoever a man s-eth
James 3:18, is s-n in peace

Space—*place, room, quantity of time*
Gen. 29:14, abode . . . the s of a month
Lev. 25:30, the s of a full year
Luke 22:59, about the s of one hour
Acts 5:34, apostles forth a little s
Rev. 2:21, I gave her s to repent

162

Spake—*uttered in words by mouth*
Gen. 8:15, God s unto Noah
Job 2:13, none s a word unto him
Ps. 33:9, he s, and it was done
    78:19, Yea, they s against God
Jonah 2:10, Lord s unto the fish
Mal. 3:16, Lord s often one to another
Matt. 13:34, s Jesus . . . in parables
Mark 3:9, he s to his disciples
John 7:46, Never man s like this man
Acts 19:6, and s with tongues
1 Cor. 13:11, I s as a child
    14:5, that ye all s with tongues
2 Pet. 1:21, s as they were moved
Spare—*keep unused, retain, show mercy*
Job 30:10, s not to spit in my face
Ps. 72:13, s the poor and needy
    78:50, s-d not their soul from
Prov. 13:24, s-th his rod hateth his
Is. 9:19, no man shall s his brother
Jer. 13:14, I will not pity, nor s
    50:14, shoot . . . s no arrows
Mal. 3:17, s them as a man s-th his
Luke 15:17, bread enough and to s
Acts 20:29, not s-ing the flock
Rom. 8:32, s-d not his own Son
    11:21, s not the natural branches
2 Cor. 9:6, which soweth s-ingly
    13:2, I come again, I will not s
2 Pet. 2:4, God s-d not the angels
Speak—*utter words, convey thoughts*
Gen. 18:32, s yet but this once
Ex. 4:14, I know that he can s well
    23:2, s in a cause to decline
Lev. 1:2, S unto the children
Num. 22:35, s unto thee . . . thou shalt s
Deut. 9:4, S not thou in thine heart
1 Kin. 12:7, s good words to them
Job 11:5, oh that God would s
    17:5, s-eth flattery to his friends
    33:14, God s-eth once, yea twice
    41:3, s soft words unto thee
Ps. 28:3, which s peace to their
    41:5, Mine enemies s evil of me
    135:16, mouths, but they s not
Prov. 23:9, S not in the ears of a fool
Eccles. 3:7, silence, and a time to s
Is. 29:4, s out of the ground
    32:4, stammerers . . . ready to s
    40:2, S ye comfortably
Zeph. 3:13, do iniquity, nor s lies
Matt. 10:19, how or what ye shall s
Mark 13:11, not ye that s, but the
    16:17, shall s with new tongues

Luke 1:20, dumb, and not able to s
    6:26, men shall s well of you
John 3:11, We s that we do know
    16:13, shall not s of himself
Acts 2:4, began to s with other tongues
    18:9, Be not afraid, but s
Rom. 3:5, (I s as a man)
1 Cor. 2:7, we s the wisdom of God
    13:1, I s with the tongues of men
Eph. 4:31, evil s-ing, be put away
    6:20, boldly, as I ought to s
Titus 3:2, s evil of no man
James 1:19, slow to s, slow to wrath
    2:12, So s ye, and so do
    4:11, S not evil one of another
1 Pet. 4:11, If any man s, let him s
2 Pet. 2:18, s great swelling words
Spear—*a weapon*
Josh. 8:18, Stretch out the s that is
1 Sam. 26:7, his s stuck in the ground
2 Sam. 1:6, Saul leaned upon his s
Job 41:29, at the shaking of a s
Ps. 46:9, cutteth the s in sunder
Is. 2:4, their s-s into pruninghooks
Joel 3:10, pruninghooks into s-s
John 19:34, with a s pierced his side
Speech—*spoken words*
Gen. 11:1, one language . . . one s
Ex. 4:10, but I am slow of s
Deut. 32:2, my s shall distil . . . dew
Job 13:17, Hear diligently my s
    37:19, we cannot order our s
Prov. 17:7, s becometh not a fool
Song 4:3, thy s is comely
Is. 33:19, people of a deeper s
Mark 7:32, an impediment in his s
Acts 20:7, his s until midnight
Rom. 16:18, good words, and fair s-s
2 Cor. 11:6, though I be rude in s
Col. 4:6, s be always with grace
Speed—*swiftness, favorable issue*
Gen. 24:12, send me good s this day
1 Sam. 20:38, Make s, haste, stay not
Ezra 6:12, let it be done with s
Ps. 31:2, deliver me s-ily
Is. 5:19, Let him make s
Luke 18:8, he will avenge them s-ily
Spend—*lay out, pass, as time*
Deut. 32:23, I will s mine arrows
Job 21:13, s their days in wealth
Ps. 90:9, s our years as a tale
Is. 55:2, do ye s money
2 Cor. 12:15, I will very gladly s and

Spent—*exhausted, time passed*
Gen. 21:15, water was s in the bottle
Judg. 19:11, day was far s
Ps. 31:10, my life is s with grief
Mark 5:26, s all that she had
Luke 24:29, the day is far s
Rom. 13:12, The night is far s
Spice—*a seasoning, to season*
Ex. 35:28, s, and oil for the light
Song 8:2, to drink of s-d wine
Ezek. 24:10, flesh, and s it well
John 19:40, linen clothes with the s-s
Spies—*scouts, informers*
Gen. 42:9, Ye are s
Josh. 6:23, young men that were s
Luke 20:20, sent forth s
Heb. 11:31, she had received the s
Spirit—*the immortal part of man*
Gen. 1:2, the S of God moved upon
Ex. 31:3, filled him with the s of God
Lev. 20:27, that hath a familiar s
Num. 5:14, the s of jealousy
16:22, s-s of all flesh
Judg. 9:23, God sent an evil s
1 Sam. 1:15, woman of a sorrowful s
1 Kin. 22:22, I will be a lying s in
2 Kin. 2:9, double portion of thy s
Job 6:4, poison . . . drinketh up my s
27:3, s of God is in my nostrils
Ps. 31:5, Into thine . . . I commit my s
51:10, renew a right s within me
Prov. 16:18, haughty s before a fall
Eccles. 3:21, s of man . . . goeth upward
7:8, patient in s . . . proud in s
12:7, s shall return unto God
Is. 11:2, s of wisdom . . . knowledge
32:15, s be poured upon us
42:1, put my s upon him
57:15, contrite and humble s
61:1, S of the Lord God is upon me
Ezek. 3:12, s took me up
11:19, put a new s within you
Joel 2:28, pour out my s . . . all flesh
Mic. 3:8, full of power by the s
Zech. 6:5, four s-s of the heavens
Matt. 3:16, S of God descending
5:3, Blessed are the poor in s
10:1, power against unclean s-s
12:18, put my s upon him
45, seven other s-s more
Mark 1:10, S like a dove descending
14:38, s truly is ready, but the

Luke 4:18, S of the Lord is upon me
11:13, give the Holy S to them
24:37, supposed . . . had seen a s
39, s hath not flesh and bones
John 3:5, born of water and of the s
4:24, God is a S
14:17, Even the S of truth
Acts 2:17, I will pour out my s
18:25, being fervent in the s
Rom. 2:29, in the s, and not in the
7:6, serve in newness of s
8:1, walk . . . after the s
15:19, by the power of the S of
1 Cor. 2:10, S searcheth all things
3:16, S of God dwelleth in you
5:3, absent in body . . . present in s
12:4, gifts, but the same s
14:15, I will pray with the s
2 Cor. 3:6, of the letter, but of the s
Gal. 4:6, sent forth the S of his Son
5:16, Walk in the S
22, fruit of the S is love, joy
Eph. 1:13, that holy S of promise
2:18, access by one S unto the
4:4, one body, and one S
30, grieve not the holy S of
Phil. 1:27, stand fast in one s
Col. 2:5, am I with you in the s
1 Thess. 5:19, Quench not the S
1 Tim. 4:12, charity, in s, in faith
Heb. 1:7, maketh his angels s-s
4:12, dividing . . . of soul and s
James 2:26, body without the s is dead
1 Pet. 4:6, according to God in the s
1 John 4:1, believe not every s
5:6, S that beareth witness
8, s, and the water . . . blood
Rev. 1:10, I was in the S on the Lord's
3:1, that hath the seven s of God
22:17, The S and the Bride say
Spiritual—*of the spirit*
Hos. 9:7, the s man is mad
Rom. 8:6, to be s-ly minded is life
15:27, partakers of their s things
1 Cor. 10:3, eat the same s meat
14:1, desire s gifts
15:44, raised a s body
Eph. 1:3, blessed us . . . s blessings
5:19, hymns and s songs
1 Pet. 2:5, are built up a s house
Spit—*eject from the mouth*
Job 30:10, spare not to s in my face
Matt. 26:67, they s in his face
27:30, and they s upon him

Mark 8:23, when he had s on his eyes
  14:65, some began to s on him
John 9:6, made clay of the s-tle
Spoil—*booty, plunder, to rob, pillage*
Gen. 49:27, he shall divide the s
Ex. 3:22, Ye shall s the Egyptians
Job 12:17, leadeth counsellors . . . s-ed
Ps. 76:5, stouthearted are s-ed
Prov. 16:19, divide the s with the
Song 2:15, foxes, that s the vines
Ezek. 25:7, will deliver thee for a s
Matt. 12:29, s his goods . . . his house
Col. 2:8, Beware lest any man s you
Spoken—*said, declared*
Ps. 62:11, God hath s once; twice
  87:3, Glorious things are s
Prov. 25:11, word fitly is like
Matt. 26:65, He hath s blasphemy
Mark 14:9, be s of for a memorial
John 12:49, I have not s of myself
Rom. 14:16, your good be evil s of
Heb. 1:2, s unto us by his Son
Spot—*blemish, mark, stain, fault*
Gen. 30:32, speckled and s-ed cattle
Num. 19:2, red heifer without s
Job 11:15, lift up thy face without s
Song 4:7, there is no s in thee
Jer. 13:23, skin, or the Leopard his s-s
Eph. 5:27, not having s, or wrinkle
1 Tim. 6:14, This commandment . . . s
Heb. 9:14, offered . . . without s to God
1 Pet. 1:19, blemish and without s
2 Pet. 2:13, S-s they are and blemishes
Jude 12, are s-s in your feasts
  23, garment s-ed by the flesh
Spread—*expanded, opened, divulged*
Gen. 33:19, where he had s his tent
Ex. 9:29, I will s abroad my hands
Job 29:19, root was s out by the
Job 37:18, s out the sky
Prov. 29:5, s-eth a net for his feet
Is. 19:8, s nets upon the waters
  33:23, could not s the sail
Ezek. 16:8, s my skirt over thee
Joel 2:2, morning s upon the mountains
Matt. 21:8, s their garments in the
Mark 1:28, his fame s abroad
Luke 19:36, S their clothes in the way
Spring—*beginning, flowing water, leap up*
Judg. 19:25, the day began to s
1 Sam. 9:26, about the s of the day
Job 38:16, into the s-s of the sea
Ps. 85:11, Truth . . . s out of the earth
  92:7, wicked s as the grass

Prov. 25:26, fountain, and a corrupt s
Song 4:12, s shut up, a fountain
Is. 45:8, let righteousness s up
  58:11, like a s of water
John 4:14, of water s-ing up into
Heb. 12:15, root of bitterness s-ing
Stablish—*to make firm*
Ps. 119:38, S thy word unto thy servant
Rom. 16:25, s you according . . . gospel
1 Thess. 3:13, he may s your hearts
2 Thess. 2:17, s you in every good word
James 5:8, s your hearts
Staff—*a pole or stick*
Gen. 38:18, thy s that is in thine hand
Num. 13:23, between two upon a s
  22:27, he smote the ass with a s
Judg. 6:21, angel . . . end of the s
2 Kin. 4:29, s upon the face of the
Ps. 23:4, thy rod and thy s they
Is. 14:5, broken the s of the wicked
Ezek. 4:16, break the s of bread
Zech. 11:10, my s, even Beauty
Mark 6:8, save a s only
Stand—*be in an upright position*
Ex. 14:13, Fear ye not, s still
Josh. 10:12, Sun, s thou still
Job 8:15, house, but it shall not s
Ps. 1:5, ungodly shall not s in the
  130:3, O Lord, who shall s
Prov. 22:29, he shall s before kings
  27:4, able to s before envy
Is. 40:8, word of our God shall s
  50:8, let us s together
Jer. 6:16, S ye in the ways, and see
  35:19, man to s before me for ever
Ezek. 2:1, Son of man, s upon thy feet
  13:5, s in the battle in the day of
Dan. 11:2, s up yet three kings
Nah. 1:6, s before his indignation
Matt. 12:25, house divided . . . shall not s
  20:3, s-ing idle . . . marketplace
Mark 11:25, ye s praying, forgive
John 1:26, s-eth one among you
Acts 1:11, why s ye gazing up into
  7:33, where thou s-est is holy
Rom. 5:2, this grace wherein we s
  14:4, God is able to make him s
1 Cor. 2:5, s in the wisdom of men
  16:13, s fast in the faith
2 Cor. 1:24, for by faith ye s
Eph. 6:14, S . . . having your loins girt
2 Tim. 2:19, foundation of God s-eth
2 Pet. 3:5, earth s-eth out of the

Stand (*Continued*)
Rev. 3:20, Behold, I s at the door
    20:12, dead . . . s before God
Star—*a heavenly body, a luminary*
Gen. 1:16, he made the s-s also
Num. 24:17, a S out of Jacob
Job 22:12, behold the height of the s-s
    38:7, morning s-s sang together
Ps. 136:9, moon and s-s to rule by
    147:4, telleth the number of the s-s
Jer. 31:35, s-s for a light by night
Matt. 2:2, seen his s in the east
    24:29, s-s shall fall from heaven
1 Cor. 15:41, one s differeth from
2 Pet. 1:19, the day s arise in your
Jude 13, wandering s-s, to whom is
Rev. 1:16, right hand seven s-s
    8:10, fell a great s from
    11, s is called Wormwood
    22:16, bright and morning s
Stature—*height of a person*
Num. 13:32, are men of a great s
1 Sam. 16:7, the height of his s
Matt. 6:27, one cubit unto his s
Luke 2:52, increased in wisdom and s
    19:3, he was little of s
Statute—*law, ordinance, edict*
Gen. 26:5, my commandments, my s-s
Ex. 29:9, for a perpetual s
Lev. 18:5, Ye shall keep my s-s
Num. 35:29, be for a s of judgment
Ps. 19:8, s-s of the Lord are right
    119:12, teach me thy s-s
Ezek. 5:7, have not walked in my s-s
Stay—*to stop, to remain, a support*
Gen. 19:17, s thou in all the plain
Ex. 17:12, Aaron and Hur s-ed up his
1 Sam. 20:38, Make speed, haste, s not
Job 38:37, can s the bottles of heaven
Ps. 18:18, the Lord was my s
Song 2:5, S me with flagons
Is. 3:1, s of bread . . . s of water
Dan. 4:35, none can s his hand
Hag. 1:10, heaven . . . is s-ed from dew
Stead—*place of another*
Gen. 30:2, Am I in God's s
Num. 32:14, risen up in your father's s
Deut. 2:23, and dwelt in their s
Job 16:4, your soul . . . in my soul-s s
2 Cor. 5:20, we pray you in Christ's s
Steal—*take by theft*
Gen. 31:27, and s away from me
Ex. 20:15, Thou shalt not s
    21:16, he that s-eth a man

Lev. 19:11, Ye shall not s
Deut. 5:19, Neither shalt thou s
    24:7, If a man be found s-ing
2 Sam. 19:3, being ashamed s away
Prov. 30:9, I be poor, and s
Matt. 6:19, break through and s
    19:18, Thou shalt not s
Mark 10:19, Do not kill, Do not s
Eph. 4:28, that stole s no more
Stedfast—*firmly fixed, unwavering*
Job 11:15, thou shalt be s
Luke 9:51, s-ly set his face to go
Acts 1:10, looked s-ly toward heaven
1 Cor. 7:37, standeth s in his heart
    15:58, be ye s
Col. 2:5, s-ness of your faith
1 Pet. 5:9, resist s in the faith
Steel—*a hard metal*
2 Sam. 22:35, bow of s is broken
Jer. 15:12, northern iron and the s
Steps—*stairs, paces*
1 Kin. 10:19, The throne had six s
Job 14:16, thou numberest my s
    29:6, washed my s with butter
Prov. 5:5, her s take hold on hell
Rom. 4:12, walk in the s of that faith
1 Pet. 2:21, ye should follow his s
Steward—*a responsible agent*
Gen. 43:19, s of Joseph's house
Luke 12:42, faithful and wise s
    16:2, an account of thy s-ship
1 Cor. 4:1, s-s of the mysteries of God
    2, it is required of s-s
Stick—*piece of wood, adhere, protrude*
2 Kin. 6:6, he cut down a s, and cast
Job 33:21, bones . . . s out
    41:17, they s together
Ps. 38:2, arrows s fast in me
Ezek. 37:16, take thee one s
    16, the s of Ephraim
    19, the s of Joseph . . . Judah
Prov. 18:24, s-eth closer than s
Still—*quiet, at rest*
Gen. 41:21, they were s ill favoured
Ex. 15:16, be as s as a stone
Josh. 10:12, Sun, stand thou s upon
1 Kin. 19:12, fire a s small voice
2 Kin. 7:4, if we sit s here, we die
Ps. 23:2, beside the s waters
    65:7, s-eth the noise of the seas
Jer. 8:14, Why do we sit s
Hab. 3:11, sun and moon stood s
Mark 4:39, Peace, be s

Sting—*poisonous bite*
Prov. 23:32, s-eth like an adder
1 Cor. 15:55, death, where is thy s
    56, s of death is sin
Rev. 9:10, s-s in their tails
Stir—*to move, disturb, commotion*
Deut. 32:11, eagle s-reth up her nest
Ps. 35:23, S up thyself, and awake
Prov. 10:12, Hatred s-reth up strifes
    15:1, words s up anger
    28:25, proud heart s-reth up
    29:22, angry man s-reth up
Is. 22:2, Thou that art full of s-s
    42:13, he shall s up jealousy
Acts 14:2, Jews s-ed up the Gentiles
2 Pet. 3:1, s up your pure minds
Stocks—*an instrument of punishment*
Job 13:27, my feet also in the s
Prov. 7:22, correction of the s
Acts 16:24, feet fast in the s
Stole—*robbed*
Gen. 31:19, Rachel had s-en the images
2 Sam. 15:6, Absalom s the hearts of
Prov. 9:17, S-en waters are sweet
Eph. 4:28, him that s steal no more
Stone—*rock, to throw rocks at*
Gen. 11:3, they had brick for s
    29:3, s from the well's mouth
Ex. 4:25, Zipporah took a sharp s
    15:16, as still as a s
    20:25, not build it of hewn s
    34:1, hew thee two tables of s
Lev. 20:2, shall s him with s-s
Num. 15:35, s him with s-s
Deut. 8:9, land whose s-s are iron
    9:9, to receive the tables of s
1 Sam. 17:49, took . . . a s, and slang it
2 Sam. 17:13, not one small s found
1 Kin. 6:18, there was no s seen
2 Kin. 12:12, masons, and hewers of s
2 Chr. 34:11, buy hewn s, and timber
Job 14:19, waters wear the s-s
    28:2, brass is molten out of the s
    41:24, heart is as firm as a s
Ps. 18:12, hail s-s and coals of fire
    91:12, dash thy foot against a s
    118:22, s . . . builders refused
Prov. 26:27, he that rolleth a s
    27:3, A s is heavy
Is. 8:14, for a s of stumbling
    28:16, a precious corner s, a sure
    54:11, s-s with fair colours
    57:6, smooth s-s of the stream

Ezek. 11:19, take the s-y heart out of
    20:32, to serve wood and s
Dan. 2:34, s was cut out without hands
Amos 5:11, built houses of hewn s
Hab. 2:11, s shall cry out of the wall
Zech. 7:12, hearts as an adamant s
Matt. 4:3, these s-s be made bread
    6, dash thy foot against a s
    7:9, bread . . . give him a s
    13:5, Some fell upon s-y places
    21:42, s . . . builders rejected
    27:60, a great s to the door
    28:2, rolled back the s
Mark 12:4, at him they cast s-s
Luke 19:44, one s upon another
    22:41, about a s's cast
John 1:42, by interpretation, A s
    2:6, six waterpots of s
    8:7, first cast a s at her
    11:39, Jesus said, Take ye . . . the s
Acts 7:59, they s-ed Stephen
2 Cor. 3:3, not in tables of s
Eph. 2:20, the chief corner s
1 Pet. 2:5, Ye also, as lively s-s
    8, s of stumbling
Rev. 2:17, will give him a white s
Stood—*rested in an upright position*
Gen. 18:2, three men s by him
    37:7, sheaves s round about
Num. 22:22, angel . . . s in the way
Deut. 31:15, pillar of the cloud s over
Josh. 10:13, the sun s still
Job 4:15, hair of my flesh s up
Amos 7:7, Lord s upon a wall
Matt. 2:9, s over where the young
Luke 4:16, s up for to read
    24:36, Jesus . . . s in the midst
John 19:25, s by the cross of Jesus
    20:11, Mary s without
    21:4, Jesus s on the shore
Acts 21:40, Paul s on the stairs
2 Tim. 4:16, no man s with me
Rev. 5:6, s a Lamb as it had been
    13:1, s upon the sand of the sea
Stop—*to cease, halt, close*
Gen. 8:2, windows of heaven were s-ped
1 Kin. 18:44, the rain s thee not
Job 5:16, iniquity s-peth her mouth
Ps. 63:11, that speak lies shall be s-ped
Prov. 21:13, Whoso s-peth his ears
Rom. 3:19, every mouth may be s-ped
2 Cor. 11:10, s me of this boasting

Store—*fund, supply, abundance*
  Gen. 26:14, great s of servants
  Deut. 28:5, thy basket and thy s
  Amos 3:10, s up violence and robbery
  1 Cor. 16:2, lay by him in s
  1 Tim. 6:19, Laying up in s for
Storm—*disturbance in the atmosphere*
  Job 21:18, chaff . . . s carrieth away
  Ps. 55:8, escape from the windy s
    107:25, raiseth the s-y wind
  Is. 25:4, a refuge from the s
  Ezek. 38:9, ascend and come like a s
  Mark 4:37, arose a great s of wind
Straight—*not crooked or turning*
  1 Sam. 6:12, kine took the s way
  Ps. 5:8, make thy way s before
  Eccles. 1:15, crooked cannot be made s
  Is. 40:3, make s . . . a highway
    4, crooked shall be made s
  Matt. 3:3, make his paths s
  Luke 3:5, crooked shall be made s
  John 1:23, Make s the way of the Lord
  Acts 9:11, street which is called S
  Heb. 12:13, s paths for your feet
Straightway—*immediately, without delay*
  1 Sam. 9:13, ye shall s find him
  Matt. 3:16, went up s out of the water
    4:20, s left their nets
    21:2, s ye shall find an ass tied
  Luke 12:54, s ye say, there cometh a
    14:5, s pull him out . . . sabbath
  Acts 9:20, s he preached Christ
Strait—*narrow, strict, impasse*
  1 Sam. 13:6, they were in a s
  2 Sam. 24:14, I am in a great s
  Is. 49:20, place is too s for me
  Matt. 7:13, enter ye in at the s gate
  Acts 26:5, the most s-est sect of our
  2 Cor. 6:12, Ye are not s-ened in us
Strange—*foreign, not one's own*
  Gen. 35:2, Put away the s gods
  Ex. 2:22, stranger in a s land
  Judg. 11:2, son of a s woman
  1 Kin. 11:1, Solomon . . . many s women
  Ezra 10:2, have taken s wives
  Job 19:17, breath is s to my wife
  Ps. 137:4, Lord's song in a s land
  Prov. 22:14, mouth of s women is a deep
  Ezek. 3:5, people of a s speech
  Luke 5:26, seen s things today
  Heb. 13:9, divers and s doctrines
  1 Pet. 4:12, think it not s concerning
  Jude 7, going after s flesh

Stranger—*foreigner, not a native*
  Gen. 15:13, a s in a land that is
    23:4, I am a s
  Ex. 2:22, s in a strange land
    20:10, s that is within thy gates
    22:21, neither vex a s
  Deut. 10:19, Love ye therefore the s
  Ruth 2:10, seeing I am a s
  2 Sam. 1:13, I am the son of a s
  Prov. 5:20, embrace the bosom of a s
  Is. 1:7, s-s devour it in your presence
  Jer. 22:3, do no violence to the s
  Matt. 25:35, I was a s, and ye took
    27:7, potter's field, to bury s-s
  John 10:5, know not the voice of s-s
  Eph. 2:19, ye are no more s-s
  Heb. 13:2, to entertain s-s
Straw—*stalks, stubble*
  Gen. 24:25, both s and provender
  Ex. 5:7, s to make bricks
  1 Kin. 4:28, and s for the horses
  Job 41:27, esteemeth iron as s
  Is. 11:7, lion . . . eat s like the ox
Street—*public way in a town or village*
  Gen. 19:2, abide in the s all night
  Judg. 19:20, lodge not in the s
  2 Sam. 1:20, publish it not in the s-s
    22:43, as the mire of the s
  Is. 59:14, truth is fallen in the s
  Jer. 37:21, bread out of the baker's s
  Nah. 2:4, chariots shall rage in the s-s
  Matt. 6:5, in the corners of the s-s
  Mark 6:56, laid the sick in the s-s
  Acts 9:11, s which is called Straight
  Rev. 21:21, s of the city was pure gold
Strength—*power, security*
  Gen. 4:12, not . . . yield . . . thee her s
  Ex. 15:2, The Lord is my s and song
  Deut. 33:25, days, so shall thy s be
  Judg. 8:21, man is, so is his s
    16:6, wherein thy great s lieth
  1 Sam. 28:20, was no s in him
  2 Sam. 22:33, God is my s and power
  Job 6:12, Is my s the s of stones
    21:23, one dieth in his full s
    39:19, given the horse s
  Ps. 18:2, my God, my s
    19:14, Lord, my s, and my redeemer
    28:7, Lord is my s and my shield
    46:1, God is our refuge and s
    84:7, They go from s to s
  Prov. 10:29, way of the Lord is s
    20:29, glory of young men . . . s
    31:3, not thy s unto women

Eccles. 9:16, Wisdom is better than s
Is. 17:10, rock of thy s
   26:4, Jehovah is everlasting s
   30:7, Their s is to sit still
   41:1, people renew their s
   51:9, awake, put on s
Hab. 3:19, The Lord God is my s
Mark 12:30, mind, and with all thy s
1 Cor. 15:56, s of sin is the law
2 Cor. 12:9, s is made perfect in
Rev. 1:16, sun shineth in his s
Strengthen—*add strength to, encourage*
Deut. 3:28, encourage him, and s
Judg. 16:28, s me, I pray . . . this once
1 Sam. 23:16, s-ed his hand in God
Ezra 6:22, s their hands in the work
Job 4:3, s-ed the weak hands
Is. 35:3, S ye the weak hands
Ezek. 34:16, s that which was sick
Luke 22:32, s thy brethren
Col. 1:11, S with all might
1 Pet. 5:10, stablish, s settle you
Stretch—*to reach out, extend*
Ex. 9:15, now I will s out my hand
Job 30:24, s out his hand to the grave
   38:5, s-ed the line upon it
Ps. 68:31, s out her hands unto God
   104:2, s-est out the heavens like
Is. 3:16, walk with s-ed forth necks
   28:20, than that a man can s
   44:13, carpenter s-eth out his rule
Jer. 10:12, s-ed out the heavens
Matt. 12:13, S forth thine hand
2 Cor. 10:14, we s not ourselves
Stricken—*advanced, struck*
Gen. 24:1, Abraham . . . old, and well s
Judg. 5:26, s through his temples
Is. 1:5, Why should ye be s any more
   53:4, did esteem his s, smitten
Luke 1:7, both . . . well s in years
Strife—*violent contention*
Gen. 13:7, a s between the herdmen
Ps. 106:32, at the waters of s
Prov. 10:12, Hatred stirreth up s-s
   16:28, froward man soweth s
   20:3, a man to cease from s
Is. 58:4, ye fast for s and debate
Rom. 13:13, not in s and envying
1 Cor. 3:3, s, and divisions
Gal. 5:20, wrath, s, seditions
Phil. 2:3, nothing be done through s
James 3:16, where envying and s is

Strike—*hit, punish, make*
Ex. 12:22, s the lintel and the two
Job 17:3, will s hands with me
Prov. 17:26, s princess for equity
   22:26, one of them that s hands
1 Tim. 3:3, to wine, no s-r, not greedy
String—*small cord or line*
Ps. 11:2, their arrow upon the s
   33:2, an instrument of ten s-s
Hab. 3:19, singer . . . s-ed instruments
Mark 7:35, s of his tongue was loosed
Stripes—*blows*
Deut. 25:3, Forty s he may give him
Prov. 19:29, s for the back of fools
Luke 12:47, be beaten with many s
2 Cor. 11:23, in s above measure
   24, forty s save one
1 Pet. 2:24, by whose s ye are healed
Strive—*struggle, contend*
Gen. 6:3, spirit shall not always s
Ex. 21:18, if men s together
Prov. 3:30, S not with a man without
   25:8, forth hastily to s
Luke 13:24, S to enter in at the
1 Cor. 9:25, s-th for the mastery
2 Tim. 2:5, also s for masteries
   14, s not about words to no
Strong—*having great power, violent*
Gen. 49:14, Issachar is a s ass
Ex. 10:19, mighty s west wind
   14:21, go back by a s east wind
Lev. 10:9, wine nor s drink
Deut. 31:6, Be s and of good courage
Judg. 14:18, what is s-er than a lion
1 Sam. 4:9, Be s, and quit yourselves
Job 17:9, clean hands shall be s-er
Ps. 19:5, s man to run a race
   24:8, The Lord s and mighty
Prov. 11:16, s men retain riches
   20:1, s drink is raging
   31:6, s drink unto him that is
Eccles. 9:11, nor the battle to the s
Song. 8:6, love is s as death
Is. 5:11, they may follow s drink
Jer. 20:7, thou are s-er than I
   48:17, How is the s staff broken
   50:34, Their Redeemer is s
Ezek. 30:21, s to hold the sword
Joel 3:10, weak say, I am s
Mic. 4:3, rebuke s nations afar off
Luke 2:40, child . . . waxed s in spirit
1 Cor. 4:10, we are weak, but ye are s
2 Cor. 12:10, am weak, then am I s

Strong (*Continued*)
Eph. 6:10, be s in the Lord
Heb. 11:34, out of weakness were made s
Study—*earnest endeavor, deep thought*
Eccles. 12:12, much s is a weariness
1 Thess. 4:11, ye s to be quiet
2 Tim. 2:15, S to shew thyself approved
Stumble—*to trip, fall into error*
Prov. 3:23, thy foot shall not s
Is. 28:7, they s in judgment
Jer. 50:32, most proud shall s
Dan. 11:19, shall s and fall
1 Pet. 2:8, which s at the word
Subject—*under control of another*
Luke 2:51, and was s unto them
Rom. 8:20, was made s to vanity
1 Cor. 9:27, body, and bring it into s-ion
2 Cor. 9:13, s-ion unto the gospel
Eph. 5:24, church is s unto Christ
1 Tim. 2:11, in silence with all s-ion
Heb. 2:8, all things in s-ion under
12:9, in s-ion unto the Father
1 Pet. 2:18, be s to your masters
3:1, s-ion to your own husbands
22, being made s unto him
5:5, s one to another
Substance—*material possessions, wealth*
Gen. 7:23, every living s was destroyed
Deut. 33:11, Bless, Lord, his s
Job 5:5, robber swalloweth up their s
Prov. 3:9, Honour the Lord with thy s
Hos. 12:8, I have found me out s
Luke 15:13, wasted his s with riotous
Heb. 11:1, faith in the s of things
Subvert—*corrupt, turn from the truth*
Lam. 3:36, s a man in his cause
Acts 15:24, s-ing your souls
Titus 1:11, s whole houses
Such—*of a certain or like kind*
Gen. 4:20, of s as dwell in tents
Ex. 10:14, no s locusts as they
2 Sam. 12:8, given unto thee s and s
Ps. 107:10, S as sit in darkness
139:6, S knowledge is too
Prov. 11:20, s as are upright in their way
Matt. 19:14, s is the kingdom of
Mark 4:18, s as hear the word
Acts 3:6, s as I have given I thee
2 Cor. 3:12, we have s hope
2 Tim. 3:5, from s turn away
Heb. 13:16, s sacrifices God is well
Suddenly—*quickly*
Deut. 7:4, and destroy thee s
Is. 29:5, be at an instant s

Mark 13:36, coming s he find you
Acts 2:2, s there came a sound
1 Tim. 5:22, Lay hands s on no man
Suffer—*permit, endure*
Ex. 12:23, s the destroyer to come
Job 24:11, and s thirst
Ps. 16:10, s thine Holy One to see
34:10, do lack, and s hunger
Matt. 3:15, S it to be so now
19:14, S little children, and
Mark 8:31, Son of man must s many
Luke 24:46, it behoved Christ to s
Acts 2:27, s thine Holy One to see
1 Cor. 9:12, but s all things
10:13, s you to be tempted
13:4, Charity s-eth long, and
1 Tim. 2:12, s not a woman to teach
2 Tim. 2:12, If we s, we shall also
1 Pet. 2:21, Christ also s-ed for us
4:13, partakers of Christ's s-ings
Sufficient—*equal to, ample, enough*
Ex. 36:7, stuff they had was s
Prov. 25:16, eat so much as is s
Matt. 6:34, S unto the day is the evil
John 6:7, pennyworth of bread is not s
2 Cor. 12:9, My grace is s for thee
Summer—*warmest season of the year*
Gen. 8:22, heat, and s and winter
Judg. 3:20, sitting in a s parlour
Ps. 74:17, hast made s and winter
Prov. 26:1, As snow in s, and as rain
Jer. 8:20, past, the s is ended
Zech. 14:8, s and in winter shall it be
Matt. 24:32, ye know that s is nigh
Sun—*heavenly orb, source of light*
Gen. 15:12, the s was going down
Ex. 16:21, the s waxed hot
Lev. 22:7, And when the s is down
Josh. 10:12, S, stand thou still
Ps. 72:5, as the s and moon endure
84:11, God is a s and shield
104:19, s knoweth his going down
121:6, s shall not smite thee by
Eccles. 1:9, no new thing under the s
Song 6:10, moon, clear as the s
Is. 38:8, s returned ten degrees
60:19, s shall be no more thy light
Ezek. 32:7, cover the s with a cloud
Amos 8:9, s to go down at noon
Matt. 5:45, maketh his s to rise
13:43, righteous shine . . . as the s
Luke 21:25, shall be signs in the s
1 Cor. 15:41, is one glory of the s

Eph. 4:26, s go down upon your wrath
Rev. 12:1, woman clothed with the s
    22:5, neither light of the s
Supper—*the evening meal*
Mark 6:21, birthday made a s to his
Luke 14:16, certain man made a great s
John 13:4, He riseth from s, and laid
1 Cor. 11:20, not to eat the Lord's s
Rev. 19:9, marriage s of the Lamb
Supplications—*plea, entreaty*
1 Sam. 13:12, not made s unto the Lord
Job 8:5, make thy s to the Almighty
Ps. 28:2, Hear the voice of my s-s
Dan. 9:3, seek by prayer and s-s
Acts 1:14, one accord in prayer and s
1 Tim. 2:1, first of all, s-s, prayers
Sure—*certain*
Num. 32:23, s your sin will find you
Job 24:22, no man is s of life
Ps. 19:7, testimony of the Lord is s
Prov. 11:18, righteousness . . . s reward
Is. 22:23, as a nail in a s place
Matt. 27:66, made the sepulchre s
John 6:69, s that thou art the Christ
2 Tim. 2:19, foundation . . . standeth s
2 Pet. 1:10, calling and election s
    19, s word of prophecy
Surely—*without doubt, securely*
Gen. 2:17, eatest . . . thou shalt s die
    28:16, S the Lord is in this place
Ex. 4:25, S a bloody husband art thou
Num. 14:23, S they shall not see
Job 35:13, S God will not hear vanity
Ps. 23:6, S goodness and mercy
Is. 53:4, S he hath borne our griefs
Mark 14:70, S thou art one of them
Luke 1:1, things . . . most s believed
Heb. 6:14, S blessing I will bless
Rev. 22:20, S I come quickly
Swallow—*consume, draw into, a bird*
Num. 16:34, Lest the earth s us up
Job 6:3, my words are s-ed up
    20:15, He hath s-ed down riches
Ps. 84:3, the s a nest for herself
Prov. 26:2, as the s by flying
Is. 25:8, s up death in victory
Jer. 8:7, s observe the time of . . . coming
Jonah 1:17, great fish to s up Jonah
Matt. 23:24, gnat, and s a camel
1 Cor. 15:54, Death is s-ed up in
Swear—*declare under oath to God*
Gen. 50:5, father made me s
Lev. 19:12, not s by my name falsely

Num. 30:2, s an oath to bind
Is. 45:23, every tongue shall s
Zech. 5:3, one that s-eth . . . be cut off
Matt. 5:34, S not at all; neither by
    23:18, whosoever s-eth by the gift
    26:74, began he to curse and to s
Mark 14:71, began to curse and to s
James 5:12, all things . . . s not
Sweet—*pleasing*
Gen. 8:21, Lord smelled a s savour
2 Sam. 23:1, the s psalmist of Israel
Ps. 55:14, took s counsel together
Prov. 3:24, thy sleep shall be s
    9:17, Stolen waters are s
Eccles. 5:12, sleep . . . is s
Is. 5:20, bitter for s, and s for bitter
    43:24, bought me no s cane
Jer. 6:20, s cane from a far country
2 Cor. 2:15, a s savour of Christ
James 3:11, s water and bitter
Swell—*enlarge*
Num. 5:21, and thy belly to s
    22, make thy belly to s
Deut. 8:4, neither did thy foot s
Is. 30:12, s-ing out in a high wall
2 Pet. 2:18, great s-ing words of vanity
Swift—*quick*
Deut. 28:49, s as the eagle flieth
Job 7:6, My days are s-er than a
Prov. 6:18, s in running to mischief
Eccles. 9:11, race is not to the s
Rom. 3:15, s to shed blood
James 1:19, man be s to hear
Swine—*pigs*
Prov. 11:22, gold in a s's snout
Matt. 7:6, cast ye . . . pearls before s
Mark 5:11, great herd of s feeding
Luke 15:15, into his fields to feed s
Sword—*a weapon, and destruction by it*
Gen. 3:24, a flaming s which turned
    27:40, by thy s shalt thou live
Ex. 5:3, pestilence, or with the s
Deut. 32:25, s without, and terror within
Judg. 7:18, s of the Lord, and of
2 Sam. 2:26, Shall the s devour for ever
Ps. 57:4, their tongue a sharp s
    64:3, whet their tongue like a s
Prov. 5:4, sharp as a two-edged s
    30:14, whose teeth are as s-s
Is. 2:4, beat their s-s into plowshares
    4, not lift up s against nation
Jer. 15:2, as are for the s, to the s
Hos. 1:7, save them by bow, nor by s
    2:18, break the bow and the s

Sword (*Continued*)
Mic. 4:3, beat . . . s-s into plowshares
Matt. 10:34, not . . . peace, but a s
26:51, drew his s, and struck
52, take the s . . . perish with
Eph. 6:17, s of the Spirit
Rev. 1:16, sharp two-edged s
Synagogue—*assembly of Jews for worship*
Matt. 12:9, he went into their s
13:54, taught them in their s
John 16:2, put you out of the s-s
18:20, I ever taught in the s
Acts 9:20, preached Christ in the s-s
Rev. 2:9, but are the s of Satan

T

Tabernacle—*place of worship*
Ex. 26:1, t with ten curtains
Job 12:6, t-s of robbers prosper
Ps. 15:1, who shall abide in thy t
61:4, I will abide in thy t
Jer. 10:20, My t is spoiled
Matt. 17:4, make here three t-s
2 Pet. 1:14, I must put off this my t
Rev. 21:3, t of God is with men
Table —*piece of furniture, a slab*
Ex. 24:12, give thee t-s of stone
31:18, t-s of testimony
Lev. 24:6, upon the pure t
Judge. 1:7, their meat under my t
2 Kin. 4:10, for him . . . a bed, and a t
Ps. 23:5, preparest a t before me
Jer. 17:1, graven . . . t of their heart
Matt. 21:12, t-s of the moneychangers
Mark 7:28, dogs under the t eat of
Luke 1:63, asked for a writing t
John 2:15, and overthrew the t-s
Acts 6:2, word of God, and serve t-s
1 Cor. 10:21, partakers of the Lord's t
2 Cor. 3:3, fleshy t-s of the heart
Take—*grasp, carry away, engage, bear*
Gen. 3:22, t also of the tree of life
12:19, behold thy wife, t her
22:2, T now thy son
Ex. 20:7, not t the name of the Lord
34:9, t us for thine inheritance
Num. 16:7, t too much upon you
Deut. 1:13, T you wise men
Job 5:13, t-th the wise in . . . craftiness
9:18, suffer me to t my breath

Ps. 116:13, t the cup of salvation
Prov. 4:13, T fast hold of instruction
6:25, t thee with her eyelids
7:18, t our fill of love
Song 2:15, T us the foxes
Is. 4:1, seven women . . . t hold of one
Ezek. 36:26, t away the stony heart
37:19, t the stick of Joseph
Hos. 1:2, Go t unto thee a wife
Mic. 2:4, t up a parable against you
Matt. 5:40, t away thy coat
6:25, T no thought for your life
11:29, T my yoke upon you
26:26, T, eat; this is my body
Mark 2:9, Arise, t up thy bed
10:21, t up the cross and follow
13:33, T ye heed, watch and pray
16:18, shall t up serpents
Luke 9:3, T nothing for your journey
John 1:29, t-th away the sin of the
7:30, they sought to t him
11:39, T ye away the stone
20:2, have t-n away the Lord
Acts 1:9, he was t-n up
20, bishoprick let another t
1 Cor. 11:24, T, eat: this is my body
Eph. 6:16, t-ing the shield of faith
Rev. 10:9, T it, and eat it up
Tale—*a count, a story*
Ex. 5:18, deliver the t of bricks
Ps. 90:9, years as a t that is told
Ezek. 22:9, carry t-s to shed blood
Luke 24:11, words seemed . . . as idle t-s
Talk—*to utter words, conversation*
Deut. 5:24, God doth t with man
1 Sam. 2:3, T no more so . . . proudly
Job 11:2, should a man full of t
15:3, with unprofitable t
Prov. 24:2, their lips t of mischief
Matt. 22:15, entangle him in his t
Eph. 5:4, nor foolish t-ing, nor jesting
Titus 1:10, vain t-ers and deceivers
Tarry—*stay, wait, delay*
Gen. 19:2, t all night, and wash
Prov. 23:30, that t long at wine
Matt. 26:38, t ye here, and watch
John 21:22, that he t till I come
1 Tim. 3:15, But if I t long
Taste—*to test the flavor, flavor*
Ex. 16:31, t of it was like wafers
Job 6:6, t in the white of an egg
Job 34:3, as the mouth t-th meat
Ps. 34:8, t and see that the Lord is

Prov. 24:13, honeycomb . . . sweet to thy t
Matt. 16:28, shall not t of death
Heb. 2:9, t death for every man
    6:4, t-d of the heavenly gift
Taught—*impart knowledge, guide*
2 Chr. 23:13, such as t to sing praise
Ps. 71:17, hast t me from my youth
Is. 54:13, children . . . t of the Lord
Matt. 7:29, t them as one having
Mark 4:2, he t them . . . by parables
Luke 19:47, t daily in the temple
John 8:28, as my Father hath t me
Gal. 1:12, neither was I t it
1 Thess. 4:9, t of God to love one
Tax—*a levy of money*
2 Kin. 23:35, he t-ed the land
Dan. 11:20, a raiser of t-es
Luke 2:1, all the world should be t-ed
Acts 5:37, in the days of the t-ing
Teach—*to impart instruction, to guide*
Ex. 4:12, t thee what thou shalt say
Deut. 4:9, t them thy sons
1 Kin. 8:36, t them the good way
Job 21:22, Shall any t God
    37:19, T us what we shall say
Ps. 25:4, t me thy paths
    27:11, T me thy way, O Lord
    143:10, T me to do thy will
Is. 28:9, Whom shall he t knowledge
Matt. 11:1, to t and to preach
    15:9, t-ing for doctrines
    28:19, Go . . . and t all nations
Luke 11:1, Lord, t us to pray
    12:12, Holy Ghost shall t you
John 14:26, shall t you all things
Acts 1:1, began both to do and t
    15:35, t-ing and preaching the
Rom. 2:21, t-est another . . . t-est thou
1 Cor. 11:14, nature itself t you
Col. 3:16, t-ing and admonishing
1 Tim. 1:3, t no other doctrine
    2:12, suffer not a woman to t
Heb. 8:11, t every man his neighbour
Rev. 2:20, t and to seduce my servants
Teacher—*an instructor*
1 Chr. 25:8, the t as the scholar
Prov. 5:13, obeyed the voice of my t-s
John 3:2, art a t come from God
Rom. 2:20, a t of babes
1 Cor. 12:29, all prophets? are all t-s
Eph. 4:11, some, pastors and t-s
1 Tim. 2:7, t of the Gentiles
2 Tim. 4:3, heap to themselves t-s

Titus 2:3, t-s of good things
2 Pet. 2:1, be false t-s among you
Tear—*rip, pull apart, move violently*
Judg. 8:7, t your flesh . . . thorns
Job 18:4, t-eth himself in his anger
Ps. 7:2, t my soul like a lion
Jer. 15:3, sword to slay . . . dogs to t
Ezek. 13:20, t them from your arms
Luke 9:39, t-eth him that me foameth
Tears—*excessive moisture from the eyes*
2 Kin. 20:5, I have seen thy t
Job 16:20, mine eye poureth out t
Ps. 56:8, put . . . my t into thy bottle
    80:5, t to drink in great measure
    126:5, sow in t shall reap in joy
Eccles. 4:1, t of such as were oppressed
Is. 16:9, water thee with my t
    25:8, God will wipe away t
Jer. 9:1, mine eyes a fountain of t
Lam. 1:2, her t are on her cheeks
    2:18, t run down like a river
Luke 7:38, wash his feet with t
2 Tim. 1:4, being mindful of thy t
Rev. 7:17, God shall wipe away all t
Teeth—*bony appendages on the jaws*
Gen. 49:12, t white with milk
1 Sam. 2:13, fleshhook of three t
Job 13:14, take my flesh in my t
    19:20, escaped . . . the skin of my t
    41:14, his t are terrible
Ps. 57:4, t are spears and arrows
Prov. 10:26, as vinegar to the t
Jer. 31:29, t are set on edge
Amos 4:6, given you cleanness of t
Matt. 8:12, weeping and gnashing of t
Tell—*relate, recount, to count*
Gen. 15:5, and t the stars
Ex. 19:3, t the children of Israel
Judg. 7:15, Gideon heard the t-ing of
Ps. 101:7, he that t-eth lies shall
Eccles. 10:14, man cannot t what
Dan. 2:36, will t the interpretation
Joel 1:3, T ye your children of it
Matt. 8:4, See thou t no man
    26:63, t us . . . thou be the Christ
Luke 13:32, Go ye, and t that fox
John 4:25, he will t us all things
    8:45, I t you the truth
    18:34, others t it thee
2 Cor. 12:2, in the body, I cannot t
Temperance—*moderation*
Acts 24:25, righteousness, t
Gal. 5:23, Meekness, t

Tempest—*a violent storm*
Job 9:17, breaketh me with a **t**
Ps. 55:8, the windy storm and **t**
Is. 28:2, **t** of hail
Amos 1:14, **t** in the day of the whirlwind
Jonah 1:4, a mighty **t** in the sea
    12, great **t** is upon you
Acts 27:18, tossed with a **t**
Heb. 12:18, darkness, and **t**
2 Pet. 2:17, clouds . . . carried with a **t**
Temple—*place of worship, God's residence*
1 Sam. 1:9, seat by a post of the **t**
2 Sam. 22:7, my voice out of his **t**
Neh. 6:11, go into the **t** to save his life
Ps. 11:4, Lord is in his holy **t**
Jer. 7:4, **t** of the Lord, The **t** of the
Matt. 4:5, pinnacle of the **t**
    12:6, one greater than the **t**
Mark 14:58, **t** . . . made with hands
Luke 23:45, vail of the **t** was rent
John 2:19, Destroy this **t**
    21, the **t** of his body
Acts 7:48, dwelleth not in **t**-s
1 Cor. 3:17, is holy, which **t** ye are
2 Cor. 6:16, ye are the **t** of . . . God
2 Thess. 2:4, God sitteth in the **t**
Rev. 21:22, God . . . the Lamb are the **t**
Tempt—*put to trial, test, seduce*
Gen. 22:1, God did **t** Abraham
Ex. 17:2, wherefore ye **t** the Lord
Deut. 6:16, Ye shall not **t** the Lord
Matt. 22:18, Why **t** ye me
Luke 4:2, forty days **t**-ed of the devil
Acts 5:9, **t** the Spirit of the Lord
1 Cor. 10:13, not suffer you to be **t**-ed
1 Thess. 3:5, the tempter have **t**-ed you
Heb. 4:15, **t**-ed like as we are
James 1:13, God cannot be **t**-ed with evil
Temptations—*trials, seductions*
Deut. 7:19, The great **t**-s which thine
Ps. 95:8, in the day of **t**
Matt. 6:13, lead us not into **t**
    26:41, enter not into **t**
Luke 8:13, time of **t** fall away
1 Cor. 10:13, hath no **t** taken you
Gal. 4:14, **t** which was in my flesh
James 1:12, man that endureth **t**
2 Pet. 2:9, deliver the godly out of **t**
Ten—*nine and one, twice five*
Gen. 31:7, changed my wages **t** times
Num. 14:22, tempted me . . . **t** times
Deut. 10:4, the **t** commandments
Job 19:3, **t** time have ye reproached

Ps. 33:2, an instrument of **t** strings
    91:7, **t** thousand at thy right
Song 5:10, chiefest among **t** thousand
Is. 38:8, **t** degrees backward
Ezek. 45:14, **t** baths are an homer
Dan. 1:14, proved them **t** days
    7:7, and it had **t** horns
Matt. 25:1, likened unto **t** virgins
Luke 15:8, having **t** pieces of silver
    17:17, Were there not **t** cleansed
Heb. 7:2, Abraham gave a **t**-th part
Jude 14, **t** thousands of his saints
Rom. 5:11, **t** thousand times **t** thousand
Tender—*not firm, delicate*
Gen. 18:7, fetcht a calf **t** and good
Deut. 32:2, small rain upon the **t** herb
2 Sam. 23:4, **t** grass springing out
2 Kin. 22:19, thine heart was **t**
1 Chr. 22:5, my son is young and **t**
Ps. 25:6, Remember . . . thy **t** mercies
Prov. 27:25, **t** grass sheweth itself
Song 2:15, our vines have **t** grapes
Is. 53:2, grow up . . . as a **t** plant
Matt. 24:32, When his branch is yet **t**
Luke 1:78, **t** mercy of our God
Eph. 4:32, **t**-hearted, forgiving one
Tent—*a portable dwelling*
Gen. 4:20, of such as dwell in **t**-s
    18:1, he sat in the **t** door
    24:67, his mother Sarah's **t**
    25:27, dwelling in **t**-s
Num. 24:5, How goodly are thy **t**-s, O
1 Kin. 12:16, to your **t**-s, O Israel
Ps. 84:10, in the **t**-s of wickedness
Song 1:8, kids beside the shepherds' **t**-s
Is. 38:12, removed . . . as a shepherds' **t**
Terrible—*awful, dreadful*
Deut. 8:15, great and **t** wilderness
Judg. 13:6, angel of God, very **t**
Neh. 1:5, the great and **t** God
Job 37:22, with God is **t** majesty
    41:14, his teeth are **t**
Song 6:4, **t** as an army with banners
Is. 21:1, desert, from a **t** land
Ezek. 28:7, the **t** of the nations
Joel 2:31, great and the **t** day of the
Terror—*alarm, fright, dread*
Lev. 26:16, appoint over you **t**
Deut. 32:25, sword without . . . **t** within
Job 24:17, **t**-s of the shadow of death
Ps. 91:5, afraid for the **t** by night
Is. 33:18, heart shall meditate **t**
Rom. 13:3, not a **t** to good works
2 Cor. 5:11, the **t** of the Lord

Testament—*a covenant, an agreement*
Matt. 26:28, my blood of the new t
Luke 22:20, This cup is the new t
2 Cor. 3:6, ministers of the new t
14, reading of the old t
Heb. 7:22, Jesus . . . surety of a better t
Rev. 11:19, the ark of his t
Testify—*bear witness*
Num. 35:30, witness shall not t
Deut. 19:18, t-ied falsely against his
2 Sam. 1:16, mouth hath t-ied against
Job 15:6, own lips t against thee
Is. 59:12, our sins t against us
John 3:11, t that we have seen
5:39, they which t of me
Acts 2:40, many other words did he t
20:24, to t the gospel
Gal. 5:3, t again to every man
1 Pet. 5:12, t-ing that this the true
Testimony—*evidence, proof, the law*
Ex. 16:34, laid it up before the T
25:16, put into the ark the t
31:18, two tables of t
Lev. 16:13, seat that is upon the t
Ps. 19:7, t of the Lord is sure
119:46, I will speak of thy t-ies
Is. 8:16, Bind up the t, seal the law
Matt. 8:4, the gift . . . for a t
John 8:17, the t of two men is true
21:24, his t is true
1 Cor. 1:6, t of Christ was confirmed
2 Tim. 1:8, ashamed of the t of our
Rev. 19:10, t of Jesus is the spirit
Thank—*express gratitude*
1 Chr. 16:7, this psalm to t the Lord
Ps. 100:4, be t-ful unto him
Matt. 11:25, I t thee, O Father
Luke 6:32, what t have ye
18:11, God, I t thee, that I am not
Rom. 6:17, But, God be t-ed
2 Thess. 1:3, bound to t God always
Thanks—*expressed gratitude*
1 Chr. 16:34, O give t unto the Lord
Ps. 92:1, good thing to give t
Matt. 15:36, gave t, and brake
26:27, took the cup, and gave t
Luke 22:19, took bread, and gave t
Rom. 14:6, for he giveth God t
1 Cor. 14:6, Amen at thy giving of t
15:57, But t be to God, which
Eph. 1:16, Cease not to give t
5:20, Giving t always

1 Thess. 3:9, what t can we render to
5:18, In every thing give t
Thanksgiving—*expression of gratitude*
Lev. 7:12, If he offer it for a t
Neh. 11:17, begin the t in prayer
Ps. 26:7, with the voice of t
95:2, before his presence with t
100:4, Enter into his gates with t
Phil. 4:6, supplication with t
1 Tim. 4:3, to be received with t
Rev. 7:12, and t, and honour
Theirs—*possessed by them*
Gen. 15:13, a land that is not t
Ex. 29:9, priest's office shall be t
2 Chr. 18:12, be like one of t
Matt. 5:3, t is the kingdom of heaven
1 Cor. 1:2, Christ . . . both t and ours
Then—*at that time*
Gen. 4:26, t began men to call upon
Ex. 15:1, T sang Moses and the
Matt. 24:14, t shall the end come
Mark 4:28, first the blade, t the ear
13:26, t shall they see the Son
Rom. 3:9, What t? are we better
1 Cor. 13:12, t face to face
2 Cor. 12:10, t am I strong
1 John 1:5, This t is the message
There—*in or at that place*
Gen. 1:3, Let t be light: and t was
Lev. 7:7, t is one law for them
Matt. 2:13, be thou t until I bring
24:23, Lo, here is Christ, or t
Luke 8:32, t an herd of many swine
Rev. 21:25, shall be no night t
Therefore—*because of this*
Gen. 2:24, t shall a man leave his
Ex. 1:20, t God dealt well with
Matt. 6:9, this manner t pray ye
Mark 1:38, for t came I forth
Luke 20:25, Render t unto Caesar
1 Cor. 5:7, Purge out t the old leaven
1 Pet. 4:7, be ye t sober
Thick—*compact, crowded*
Ex. 10:22, a t darkness in all the
Lev. 23:40, boughs of t trees
Deut. 32:15, fat, thou art grown t
Joel 2:2, and of t darkness
Luke 11:29, gathered t together
Thief—*a robber*
Deut. 24:7, then that t shall die
Job 24:14, in the night is as a t
Ps. 50:18, When thou sawest a t
Prov. 29:24, is partner with a t

175

Thief (*Continued*)
Is. 1:23, and companions of t-s
Joel 2:9, enter . . . windows like a t
Matt. 6:19, t-s break through and
21:13, made it a den of t-s
Mark 15:27, him they crucify two t-s
Luke 10:30, and fell among t-s
22:52, come out, as against a t
John 10:10, t cometh not, but for to
1 Cor. 6:10, Nor t-s, nor covetous
1 Thess. 5:2, as a t in the night
Thine—*yours, your*
Gen. 22:2, thy son, t only son Isaac
Ex. 4:4, Put forth t hand, and take
1 Kin. 20:4, I am t
Matt. 6:13, t is the kingdom
Luke 15:31, all that I have is t
22:42, not my will, but t, be done
John 17:10 mine are t . . . t are mine
Thing—*any object, thought or deed*
Gen. 15:1, After these t-s the word of
Ex. 20:17 any t that is thy neighbour's
Num. 16:9, Seemeth it but a small t
Job 42:2, thou canst do every t
Ps. 2:1, people imagine a vain t
8:6, all t-s under his feet
92:1, good t to give thanks
Eccles. 1:9, no new t under the sun
3:1, every t there is a season
9:5, dead know not any t
Is. 7:13, Is it a small t
12:5, hath done excellent t-s
Ezek. 8:17, Is it a light t
Matt. 19:26, God all t-s are possible
21:24, will ask you one t
Mark 9:23, all t-s are possible
10:21, One t thou lackest
16:18, drink any deadly t
Luke 2:19, Mary kept all these t-s
10:42, But one t is needful
John 14:14, ask any t in my name
Acts 2:44, had all t-s common
Phil. 3:13, this one t I do
4:8, think on these t-s
1 Tim. 4:15, Meditate upon these t-s
James 3:10, t-s ought not so to be
Think—*conceive, imagine, meditate*
Gen. 40:14, t on me when it shall
Job 31:1, should I t upon a maid
Prov. 23:7, as he t-eth in his heart
Matt. 5:17, t not that I am come
22:42, What t ye of Christ
John 5:39, ye t ye have eternal life
Rom. 12:3, but to t soberly

1 Cor. 13:5, t-eth no evil
2 Cor. 11:16, no man t me a fool
Gal. 6:3, t himself to be something
Phil. 4:8, t on these things
Third—*next beyond the second*
Ex. 20:5, t and fourth generation
Matt. 16:21, raised again the t day
Luke 24:21, to day is the t day since
John 21:17, saith unto him the t time
1 Cor. 15:4, he rose again the t day
2 Cor. 12:2, caught up to the t heaven
Thirst—*craving for liquids, want*
Ex. 17:3, people t-ed there for water
Deut. 29:19, add drunkenness to t
Judg. 15:18, now shall I die for t
Ps. 42:2, My soul t-eth for God
69:21, t they gave me vinegar
104:11, wild asses quench their t
Prov. 25:25, cold waters to a t-y soul
Is. 29:8, when a t-y man dreameth
41:17, their tongue faileth for t
49:10, shall not hunger nor t
65:13, drink, but ye shall be t-y
Lam. 4:4, roof of his mouth for t
Matt. 5:6, t after righteousness
25:35, I was t-y, and ye gave
John 4:13, drinketh . . . shall t again
6:35, believeth . . . shall never t
19:28, Jesus . . . saith, I t
Rom. 12:20, if he t, give him drink
2 Cor. 11:27, in hunger and t
Thirty—*three times ten*
Ex. 21:32, t shekels of silver
Num. 20:29, mourned for Aaron t days
Judg. 10:4, t sons that rode on t
12:9, t sons, and t daughters
14:12, t change of garments
Zech. 11:12, price t pieces of silver
Matt. 26:15, for t pieces of silver
Luke 3:23, began to be about t years
Thorn—*sharp spine, worry, annoyance*
Gen. 3:18, T-s also and thistles
Num. 33:55, and t-s in your sides
Judg. 8:7, tear your flesh with the t-s
Job 41:2, bore . . . through with a t
Prov. 15:19, as an hedge of t-s
26:9, t goeth up into the hand
Eccles. 7:6, crackling of t-s under a
Song 2:2, a lily among t-s
Is. 55:13, t shall come up the fir tree
Jer. 4:3, sow not among t-s
12:13, sown wheat . . . reap t-s

Matt. 7:16, gather grapes of t-s
13:7, some fell among t-s
27:29, platted a crown of t-s
John 19:5, wearing the crown of t-s
2 Cor. 12:7, a t in the flesh
Thought—*conceived, imagined, an idea*
Gen., 6:5, t-s of his heart was only
48:11, not t to see thy face
50:20, t evil against me
1 Chr. 28:9, imaginations of the t-s
Job 21:27, I know your t, and the
Ps. 94:11, knoweth the t-s of man
Prov. 30:32, or if thou hast t evil
Is. 55:8, my t-s are not your t-s
Matt. 6:25, Take no t for your life
27, by taking t can add one
34, no t for the morrow
9:4, Jesus knowing their t-s
15:19, heart proceed evil t-s
Luke 24:38, t-s arise in your hearts
1 Cor. 3:20, knoweth the t-s of the wise
13:11, child, I t as a child
James 2:4, become judges of evil t-s
Thousand—*ten times one hundred*
Lev. 26:8, put ten t to flight
1 Sam. 18:7, slain his t-s . . . his ten t-s
Job 9:3, answer him one of a t
Ps. 84:10, a day . . . is better than a t
91:7, t shall fall . . . ten t at thy
Eccles. 6:6, live a t years twice told
7:28, one man among a t have
Song 5:10, chiefest among ten t
Is. 30:17, One t shall flee at the
60:22, little one shall become a t
Jer. 32:18, lovingkindness unto t-s
Dan. 7:10, ten t times ten t stood
Mark 6:44, were about five t men
8:9, were about four t
1 Cor. 4:15, ten t instructors in Christ
14:19, ten t words . . . unknown
2 Pet. 3:8, t years as one day
Jude 14, with ten t-s of his saints
Three—*one more than two*
Gen. 6:10, Noah begat t sons, Shem
Job 2:11, Job's t friends
Ps. 90:10, are t-score years and ten
Prov. 30:15, t things . . . never satisfied
18, t things . . . too wonderful
21, t things . . . disquieted
29, t things which go well
Eccles. 4:12, and a t-fold cord
Dan. 6;10, his knees t times a day
Jonah 1:17, fish t days and t nights

Matt. 12:40, t days . . . nights in the
17:4, make here t tabernacles
18:20, two or t are gathered
27:63, After t days I will rise
Luke 2:46, after t days they found him
10:36, Which now of these t
12:52, t against two, and two
John 2:19, t days I will raise it up
Acts 2:41, about t thousand souls
9:9, t days without sight
1 Cor. 13:13, hope, charity, these t
1 John 5:7, are t that bear record
8, these t agree in one
Thresh—*beat grain out of the ear*
Judg. 6:11, Gideon t-ed wheat
2 Sam. 24:21, To buy the t-ingfloor of
1 Chr. 21:20, Ornan was t-ing wheat
Is. 21:10, O my t-ing, and the corn
Hab. 3:12, t the heathen in anger
Threw—*tossed, hurled*
2 Sam. 16:13, t stones at him, and cast
2 Kin. 9:33, So they t her down
Mark 12:42, widow . . . t in two mites
Luke 9:42, devil t him down
Acts 22:23, t dust into the air
Thrice—*three times*
Ex. 34:23, T in the year shall
Matt. 26:34, shalt deny me t
2 Cor. 11:25, T was I beaten . . . t I
12:8, besought the Lord t
Throat—*front part of the neck*
Ps. 5:9, t is an open sepulchre
69:3, crying: my t is dried
115:7, speak . . . through their t
Prov., 23:2, put a knife to thy t
Matt. 18:28, and took him by the t
Rom. 3:13, t is an open sepulchre
Throne—*a seat of great honor*
Gen. 41:40, in the t will I be greater
Ex. 11:5, that sitteth upon his t
1 Kin. 22:19, Lord sitting on his t
Ps. 11:4, Lord's t is in heaven
93:2, t is established of old
Is. 66:1, The heaven is my t
Matt. 5:34, for it is God's t
19:28, sit upon twelve t-s
Acts 7:49, Heaven is my t
Heb. 1:8, Thy t . . . is for ever and ever
4:16, boldly unto the t of grace
Rev. 4:2, a t was set in heaven
20:11, I saw a great white t
Through—*from end to end, because of*
Gen. 12:6, Abraham passed t the land
Ex. 14:16, t the midst of the sea

Through (*Continued*)
Num. 15:27, soul sin t ignorance
Ps. 18:29, have run t a troop
Prov. 24:3, t wisdom is an house
Eccles. 10:18, t idleness of the hands
Is. 43:2, t the waters . . . t the fire
   62:10, Go t, go t the gates
Matt. 6:19, thieves break t and
   19:24, camel . . . t the eye of a
Luke 6:1, went t the corn fields
John 3:17, world t him might be saved
Acts 10:43, t his name whosoever
Rom. 1:8, thank my God t Jesus Christ
1 Cor. 13:12, see t a glass, darkly
Gal. 4:7, heir of God t Christ
Eph. 2:8, are ye saved t faith
Phil. 4:13, do all things t Christ
1 John 4:9, we might live t him

Thrust—*push, drive, stab*
Ps. 118:13, hast t sore at me
Luke 4:29, t him out of the city
   10:15, be t down to hell
John 20:27, hand, and t it into my side
Rev. 14:15, T in thy sickle

Thunder—*a loud noise, to roar*
Ex. 9:23, Lord sent t and hail
1 Sam. 2:10, shall he t upon them
2 Sam. 22:14, Lord t-ed from heaven
Job 39:19, thou clothed his neck with t
Ps. 81:7, in the secret place of t
Is. 29:6, Lord of hosts with t
Mark 3:17, Boanerges . . . The sons of t
John 12:29, heard it, said that it t-ed
Rev. 14:2, as the voice of a great t

Tidings—*news, information*
Gen. 29:13, heard the t of Jacob
1 Kin. 14:6, sent to thee with heavy t
2 Kin. 7:9, day is a day of good t
Ps. 112:7, not be afraid of evil t
Is. 52:7, feet that bringeth good t
Luke 2:10, good t of great joy
Rom. 10:15, glad t of good things
1 Thess. 3:6, good t of your faith

Till—*to dig in the earth, to cultivate*
Gen. 2:5, not a man to t the ground
2 Sam. 9:10, shall t the land for him
Jer. 27:11, and they shall t it, and
Ezek. 36:9, ye shall be t-ed and sown

Time—*duration, a season, certain period*
Gen. 4:3, in process of t it came
Judg. 15:1, t of wheat harvest
Job 7:1, appointed t to man upon earth
   22:16, were cut down out of t

Ps. 41:1, deliver him in t of trouble
   89:47, how short my t is
Prov. 25:13, snow in t of harvest
Eccles. 3:1-8, t to every purpose
   7:17, die before thy t
   9:12, man also knoweth not his t
Song 2:12, t of the singing of birds
Dan. 12:7, t, times, and a half
Hos. 10:12, it is t to seek the Lord
Amos 5:13, for it is an evil t
Hag. 1:2, The t is not come
Zech. 14:7, at evening t it shall be
Matt. 26:18, My t is at hand
Luke 4:11, lest at any t thou dash
John 7:6, My t is not yet come
Rom. 13:11, it is high t to awake
1 Cor. 7:29, the t is short
Gal. 4:2, t appointed of the Father
1 Tim. 2:6, be testified in due t
Jude 18, mockers in the last t
Rev. 1:3, the t is at hand
   10:6, there should be t no longer

Times—*distinct ages or periods*
Lev. 19:26, nor observe t
1 Chr. 12:32, had understanding of the t
Job 24:1, t are not hidden from the
Ps. 9:9, refuge in t of trouble
   31:15, My t are in thy hand
Matt. 16:3, discern the signs of the t
Acts 1:7, know the t or the seasons
Gal. 4:10, observe days . . . and t
Rev. 12:14, time, and t, and half a

Tingle—*thrilling sensation*
1 Sam. 3:11, heareth it shall t
2 Kin. 21:12, both his ears shall t
Jer. 19:3, heareth, his ears shall t

Tithe—*a levy of, to give, a tenth part*
Gen. 14:20, he gave him t-s of all
Lev. 27:30, all the t of the land
Num. 18:26, a tenth part of the t
   28, offering . . . of all your t-s
Deut. 12:17, the t of thy corn
   14:22, t all the increase
Matt. 23:23, pay t of mint and anise
Luke 18:12, t-s of all that I possess
Heb. 7:5, take t-s of the people
   8, men that die receive t-s

Toil—*work, labor*
Gen. 5:29, work and t of our hands
   41:51, made me forget all my t
Matt. 6:28, t not, neither do they
Luke 5:5, we have t-ed all the night

Token—*a sign or symbol*
Gen. 9:12, the t of the covenant

Ex. 3:12, be a t unto thee
    12:13, blood shall be . . . for a t
Job 21:29, do ye not know their t-s
Ps. 86:17, Show me a t for good
Mark 14:44, had given them a t
Phil. 1:28, evident t of perdition
2 Thess. 3:17, the t in every epistle
Told—*related to*
Ps. 90:9, as a tale that is t
Matt. 24:25, I have t you before
Luke 2:18, t them by the shepherds
John 4:39, t me all that ever I did
    14:2, not so, I would have t you
Tongue—*an organ in the mouth, language*
Gen. 10:5, every one after his t
Ex. 4:10, and of a slow t
    11:7, not a dog move his t
Esther 7:4, I had held my t
Job 5:21, hid from the scourge of the t
    6:30, is there iniquity in my t
    20:12, hide it under his t
    29:10, t cleaved to the roof of
Ps. 5:9, they flatter with their t
    34:13, Keep thy t from evil
    57:4, their t a sharp sword
    64:3, whet their t like a sword
    140:3, sharpened their t-s . . . serpent
Prov. 6:17, proud look, a lying t
    12:18, t of the wise is health
    15:4, Wholesome t is a tree of
    25:15, soft t breaketh the bone
Is. 30:27, t as a devouring fire
    50:4, me the t of the learned
Jer. 9:8, Their t is as an arrow
Amos 6:10, shall he say, Hold thy t
Mark 16:17, shall speak with new t-s
Luke 16:24, water, and cool my t
Acts 2:4, to speak with other t-s
Rom. 14:11, every t shall confess
1 Cor. 13:1, with the t-s of men and of
    14:4, speaketh . . . unknown t
    5, that ye all spake with t-s
    14, pray in an unknown t
    39, forbid not to speak with t-s
Phil. 2:11, every t . . . confess . . . Jesus
James 3:5, t is a little member
    8, t can no man tame
1 Pet. 3:10, refrain his t from evil
Rev. 5:9, every kindred, and t
Tooth—*bony appendage on the jaw*
Ex. 21:24, Eye for eye, t for t
Lev. 24:20, eye for eye, t for t
Deut. 19:21, t for t, hand for hand

Prov. 25:19, like a broken t
Matt. 5:38, t for a t
Top—*highest part*
Gen. 28:12, t of it reached to heaven
Ex. 19:20, t of the mount
2 Kin. 19:26, grass on the house t-s
Matt. 27:51, t to the bottom
Heb. 11:21, leaning upon the t
Torment—*extreme pain, anguish, torture*
Matt. 8:6, palsy, grievously t-ed
Luke 8:28, beseech thee, t me not
    16:23, hell . . . being in t-s
    28, into this place of t
1 John 4:18, because fear hath t
Rev. 9:5, was as the t of a scorpion
Toss—*throw upward, to roll and tumble*
Job 7:4, I am full of t-ings to and fro
Ps. 109:23, I am t-ed up and down
Is. 22:18, t thee like a ball
    54:11, t-ed with tempest
Eph. 4:14, t-ed to and fro, and carried
James 1:6, driven with the wind and t-ed
Touch—*come in contact with*
Gen. 3:3, neither shall ye t it
Ex. 19:12, or t the border of it
Lev. 5:2, t any unclean thing
Job 5:19, there shall no evil t thee
    19:21, hand of God hath t-ed me
Ps. 105:15, T not mine anointed
Matt. 9:21, but t his garment
Mark 5:30, Who t-ed my clothes
John 20:17, T me not
1 Cor. 7:1, not to t a woman
Col. 2:21, (T not, taste not . . .)
Tower—*high, narrow structure, a defense*
Gen. 11:4, build us a city and a t
2 Sam. 22:3, my high t, and my refuge
Ps. 48:12, tell the t-s thereof
Prov. 18:10, name . . . Lord is a strong t
Mic. 4:8, thou, O t of the flock
Matt. 21:33, and built a t
Transgress—*to sin*
Num. 14:41, t the commandment
Josh. 7:11, t-ed my covenant
1 Sam. 2:24, Lord's people to t
Ps. 25:3, which t without cause
Jer. 2:8, pastors also t-ed against
Luke 15:29, neither t-ed I at any
Transgression—*a sin*
Ex. 34:7, forgiving iniquity and t
Num. 14:18, forgiving iniquity and t
Josh. 24:19, not forgive your t-s
1 Sam. 24:11, neither evil nor t

Transgression (*Continued*)
Job 13:23, make me to know my **t**
   14:17, My **t** is sealed up in a bag
   33:9, I am clean without **t**
Ps. 32:1, he whose **t** is forgiven
   39:8, Deliver me from all my **t-s**
   51:3, I acknowledge my **t**
   103:12, removed our **t-s** from us
Prov. 29:6, **t** of an evil man there is
Is. 53:5, he was wounded for our **t-s**
Ezek. 18:30, turn . . . from all your **t-s**
Rom. 4:15, no law is, there is no **t**
1 John 3:4, sin is the **t** of the law
Transgressor—*the sinner*
Ps. 37:38, the **t-s** shall be destroyed
   51:13, teach **t-s** thy ways
Prov. 2:22, **t-s** shall be rooted out
   13:15, way of **t-s** is hard
   22:12, the words of the **t**
Is. 53:12, numbered with the **t-s**
Mark 15:28, numbered with the **t-s**
James 2:11, art become a **t** of the law
Travail—*labor with pain*
Gen. 38:27, in the time of her **t**
Job 15:20, wicked man **t-eth** with pain
Ps. 48:6, as of a woman in **t**
Eccles. 2:26, the sinner he giveth **t**
Is. 42:14, cry like a **t-ing** woman
Rom. 8:22, **t-eth** in pain together
Gal. 4:19, **t** in birth again until
2 Thess 3:8, wrought with labour and **t**
Rev. 12:2, being with child cried, **t-ing**
Treacherous—*faithless, false*
Is. 21:2, **t** dealer dealeth **t-ly**
   24:16, **t** dealers have dealt
Jer. 3:20, as a wife **t-ly** departeth
Lam. 1:2, her friends have dealt **t-ly**
Hos. 5:7, dealt **t-ly** against the Lord
Mal. 2:10, why do we deal **t-ly** every
Tread—*to step or walk on*
Deut. 25:4, ox . . . **t-eth** out the corn
Job 9:8, **t-eth** upon the waves
   24:11, **t** their winepresses
Is. 16:10, **t-ers** shall **t** out no wine
   41:25, as the potter **t-eth** clay
Jer. 25:30, they that **t** the grapes
Amos 5:11, **t-ing** is upon the poor
Luke 10:19, power to **t** on serpents
1 Tim. 5:18, muzzle the ox that **t-eth**
Rev. 19:15, **t-eth** the winepress
Treasure—*wealth, plenty*
Gen. 43:23, given you **t** in your sacks
Ex. 19:5, be a peculiar **t** unto me

Deut. 28:12, open unto thee his good **t**
   33:19, **t-s** hid in the sand
Prov. 10:2, **T-s** of wickedness profit
   21:20, There is **t** to be desired
Job 3:21, dig for . . . hid **t-s**
   38:22, the **t-s** of the snow . . . hail
Is. 33:6, fear of the Lord is his **t**
Matt. 6:21, where your **t** is, there will
   12:35, good **t** of the heart
   13:44, **t** hid in a field
   19:21, thou shalt have **t** in heaven
Col. 2:3, hid all the **t-s** of wisdom
James 5:3, heaped **t** together
Tree—*large, single stemmed plant*
Gen. 1:11, fruit **t** yielding fruit
   2:9, the **t** of life . . . knowledge
   3:8, God amongst the **t-s**
   18:4, rest yourselves under the **t**
Deut. 20:19, **t** of the field is man's life
   21:22, thou hang him on a **t**
Judg. 9:8, **t-s** went forth . . . to anoint
Job 40:21, lieth under the shady **t-s**
Ps. 1:3, **t** planted by the rivers
   37:35, like a green bay **t**
Ps. 104:16, **t-s** . . . are full of sap
Prov. 3:18, She is a **t** of life
   27:18, keepeth the fig **t** shall
Song 8:5, under the apple **t**
Is. 40:20, a **t** that will not rot
   55:12, **t-s** . . . shall clap their hands
Mic. 4:4, vine and under his fig **t**
Matt. 7:17, good **t** . . . corrupt **t**
   12:33, **t** is known by his fruit
Mark 8:24, I see men as **t-s**
Luke 19:4, climbed . . . a sycamore
John 1:50, saw thee under the fig **t**
Acts 5:30, slew and hanged on a **t**
Rev. 2:7, eat of the **t** of life
Tremble—*shiver, quiver, quake*
Deut. 20:3, fear not, and do not **t**
Judg. 5:4, earth **t-d**, and the heavens
Job 26:11, pillars of heaven **t**
Ps. 2:11, rejoice with **t-ing**
Is. 51:17, the cup of **t-ing**
Mark 5:33, woman fearing and **t-ing**
Phil. 2:12, with fear and **t-ing**
James 2:19, devils also believe, and **t**
Trespass—*commit an offense, to sin*
Gen. 31:36, What is my **t**? what is my
Ex. 22:9, For all manner of **t**
Ezra 9:6, **t** is grown up into the
   10:2, **t-ed** against our God
Matt. 6:14, forgive men their **t-es**
   18:15, brother . . . **t** against thee

Eph. 2:1, dead in t-es and sins
Col. 2:13, forgiven you all t-es
Tribe—*a division of people*
Gen. 49:28, these are the twelve t-s
Num. 1:4, be a man of every t
Ps. 122:4, the t-s of the Lord
Matt. 24:30, all the t-s of earth
Luke 22:30, judging the twelve t-es
Tribulation—*trouble, affliction*
Deut. 4:30, When thou art in t
1 Sam. 26:24, deliver me out of all t
Matt. 24:21, then shall be great t
John 16:33, world ye shall have t
Rom. 5:3, t worketh patience
12:12, in hope; patient in t
Eph. 3:13, faint not at my t-s
2 Thess. 1:6, t to them that trouble
Tribute—*tax*
Gen. 49:15, a servant unto t
Num. 31:28, levy a t unto the Lord
1 Kin. 9:21, a t of bondservice
Ezra 7:24, to impose toll, t, or custom
Prov. 12:24, slothful shall be under t
Matt. 17:24, not your master pay t
22:19, Shew me the t money
Luke 20:22, give t to Caesar
Rom. 13:7, t to whom t is due
Tried—*examined, proved*
Deut. 21:5, every stroke be t
2 Sam. 22:31, word of the Lord is t
Ps. 12:6, as silver t in a furnace
Is. 28:16, a t stone, a . . . corner stone
Zech. 13:9, try them as gold is t
1 Pet. 1:7, be t with fire
Rev. 3:18, gold t in the fire
Trouble—*distress, to disturb*
2 Kin. 19:3, This day is a day of t
Job 5:6, t spring out of the ground
7, Yet man is born unto t
Ps. 9:9, a refuge in times of t
27:5, time of t he shall hide me
41:1, deliver him in time of t
77:4, so t-d that I cannot speak
138:7, I walk in the midst of t
Prov. 15:16, treasure and t therewith
Is. 22:5, For it is a day of t
33:2, salvation . . . in the time of t
65:16, former t-s are forgotten
Matt. 26:10, Why t ye the woman
Mark 13:8, be famines and t-s
Luke 24:38, Why are ye t-d
John 5:4, t-ing of the water
12:27, Now is my soul t-d

2 Cor. 4:8, We are t-d on every side
1 Pet. 3:14, neither be t-d
True—*pure, real*
Gen. 42:11, we are t men
1 Kin. 22:16, nothing but that which is t
Ps. 119:160, Thy word is t
Matt. 22:16, know that thou art t
Luke 16:11, trust the t riches
John 1:9, That was the t Light
6:32, giveth you the t bread
7:28, he that sent me is t
8:17, testimony of two men is t
Rom. 3:4, let God be t
Phil. 4:8, whatsoever things are t
1 Tim. 3:1, This is a t saying
Titus 1:13, This witness is t
1 Pet. 5:12, The t grace of God
Rev. 3:14, faithful and t witness
Truly—*certainly, surely*
Gen. 24:49, deal kindly and t
Num. 14:21, But as t as I live
Deut. 14:22, t tithe all the increase
Ps. 62:1, T my soul waiteth upon God
Prov. 12:22, They that deal t are his
Eccles. 11:7, T the light is sweet
Matt. 9:37, harvest t is plenteous
Mark 14:38, spirit t is ready
Acts 1:5, John t baptized with water
Trumpet—*a wind instrument, a horn*
Ex. 19:16, the voice of the t
Lev. 25:9, make the t sound
Judg. 7:16, t in every man's hand
Is. 27:13, great t shall be blown
Matt. 6:2, alms, do not sound a t
1 Cor. 14:8, t give an uncertain sound
Trust—*belief, faith, to believe*
Judg. 9:15, put your t in my shadow
2 Sam. 22:3, in him will I t
Job 8:14, t shall be a spider's web
Ps. 4:5, put your t in the Lord
Prov. 11:28, t-eth in his riches shall fall
Is. 26:4, T ye in the Lord for ever
Jer. 7:4, T ye not in lying words
Mic. 7:5, T ye not in a friend
Mark 10:24, them that t in riches
2 Cor. 1:9, should not t in ourselves
1 Tim. 4:10, t in the living God
Heb. 2:13, put my t in him
13:18, t we have a good
conscience
Truth—*verity, that proven, righteousness*
Gen. 42:16, there be any t in you
Deut. 32:4, a God of t

181

Truth (*Continued*)
1 Kin. 2:4, walk before me in **t**
Ps. 15:2, speaketh the **t** in his heart
Prov. 3:3, not mercy and **t** forsake
    23:23, Buy the **t**, and sell it
Is. 39:8, peace and **t** in my days
Zech. 8:16, Speak ye every man the **t**
Matt. 15:27, **T**, Lord, yet the dogs
Luke 4:25, I tell you of a **t**
John 1:14, full of grace and **t**
    8:32, **t** shall make you free
    14:6, way, the **t**, and the life
Rom. 1:25, **t** of God into a lie
Gal. 2:5, the **t** of the gospel might
Phil. 1:18, in pretence, or in **t**
1 Tim. 3:15, pillar and ground of the **t**
2 Tim. 2:15, dividing the word of **t**
1 John 1:8, the **t** is not in us

Try—*to prove*
Job 12:11, Doth not the ear **t** words
Ps. 26:2, **t** my reins and my heart
1 Cor. 3:13, fire shall **t** every man's
James 1:3, **t**-ing of your faith
1 Pet. 4:12, fiery trial . . . to **t** you
1 John 4:1, **t** the spirits whether

Turn—*take a new direction*
Ruth 1:12, **T** again, my daughters
2 Kin. 17:13, **T** ye from your evil ways
Job 23:13, who can **t** him
Ps. 80:3, **T** us again, O God
Is. 53:6, **t**-ed every one to his own
Jer. 26:3, **t** every man from his evil
Joel 2:31, sun . . . **t**-ed into darkness
Matt. 5:39, cheek, **t** to him the other
Acts 17:6, **t**-ed the world upside down
2 Tim. 3:5, from such **t** away
1 Tim. 5:15, **t**-ed aside after Satan
James 1:17, neither shadow of **t**-ing

Twain—*two*
Matt. 5:41, mile, go with him **t**
    19:5, **t** shall be one flesh
Eph. 2:15, make . . . of **t** one new man

Twelve—*twice six*
Gen. 17:20, **t** princes shall he beget
    35:22, the sons of Jacob were **t**
Matt. 10:1, called . . . his **t** disciples
Mark 3:14, he ordained **t**
Luke 2:42, when he was **t** years old
John 11:9, **t** hours in the day
Rev. 12:1, crown of **t** stars

Twice—*two times*
Gen. 41:32, doubled unto Pharaoh **t**
Num. 20:11, he smote the rock **t**
1 Sam. 18:11, out of his presence **t**

Mark 14:30, before the cock crow **t**
Luke 18:12, I fast **t** in the week
Jude 12, without fruit, **t** dead

Two—*one plus one*
Gen. 1:16, God made **t** great lights
Ex. 31:18, **t** tables of testimony
Lev. 8:2, **t** rams, and a basket
Eccles. 4:9, **T** are better than one
Matt 6:24, No man can serve **t** masters
    18:19, **t** of you shall agree on
Luke 17:35, **T** women shall be grinding
1 Cor. 6:16, **t** . . . shall be one flesh
Gal. 4:24, these are the **t** covenants
Phil. 1:23, in a strait betwixt **t**

U

Unawares—*without knowing or realizing*
Gen. 31:20, Jacob stole away **u**
Luke 21:34, day come upon you **u**
Heb. 13:2, entertained angels **u**
Jude 4, certain men crept in **u**

Unbelief—*withholding belief, doubt*
Matt. 17:20, Because of your **u**
Mark 9:24, help thou mine **u**
Rom. 11:23, abide not still in **u**
Heb. 3:12, evil heart of **u**

Unbelievers—*doubters*
Luke 12:46, portion with the **u**
1 Cor. 14:23, unlearned, or **u**
2 Cor. 6:14, yoked together with **u**

Unclean—*dirty, impure*
Lev. 5:2, soul touch any **u** thing
Job 14:4, clean thing out of an **u**
Is. 6:5, a man of **u** lips
Matt. 10:1, power against **u** spirits
Mark 5:13, **u** spirits went out
Luke 9:42, rebuked the **u** spirit
Acts 10:14, that is common or **u**
Rom. 14:14, nothing **u** of itself
1 Thess. 4:7, not called us unto **u**-ness
Rev. 16:13, three **u** spirits like frogs

Undefiled—*pure, not contaminated*
Ps. 119:1, Blessed are the **u** in the
Heb. 7:26, holy, harmless, **u**
    13:4, and the bed **u**
James 1:27, Pure religion and **u**

Under—*beneath*
Gen. 1:9, waters **u** the heaven
Ex. 23:5, lying **u** his burden
Matt. 5:15, put it **u** a bushel

John 1:50, saw thee **u** the fig tree
Rom. 3:9, they are all **u** sin
Eph. 1:22, all things **u** his feet
1 Pet. 5:6, **u** the mighty hand of God
Understand—*know about, comprehend*
Gen. 11:7, not **u** one another's speech
1 Chr. 28:19, made me **u** in writing
Prov. 8:5, O ye simple, **u** wisdom
Is. 6:9, Hear ye . . . but **u** not
Dan. 8:17, U, O son of man
Matt. 15:10, Hear, and **u**
Luke 24:45, might **u** the scriptures
John 8:43, Why do ye not **u** my speech
1 Cor. 13:2, and **u** all mysteries
Understanding—*knowledge, perception*
Ex. 36:1, Lord put wisdom and **u**
Deut. 1:13, Take you wise men, and **u**
1 Kin. 3:12, a wise and an **u** heart
Job 17:4, hid their heart from **u**
Ps. 32:9, mule, which have no **u**
Prov. 2:2, apply thine heart to **u**
Is. 27:11, a people of no **u**
Matt. 15:16, Are ye also yet without **u**
Luke 24:45, opened he their **u**
1 Cor. 14:20, be not children in **u**
Eph. 4:18, Having the **u** darkened
Phil. 4:7, peace . . . passeth all **u**
2 Tim. 2:7, Lord give thee **u** in all
Understood—*knew about, comprehended*
Ps. 81:5, language that I **u** not
1 Cor. 13:11, I **u** as a child
2 Pet. 3:16, some things hard to be **u**
Unfruitful—*unproductive, barren of good*
Matt. 13:22, and he becometh **u**
Mark 4:19, word, and it becometh **u**
1 Cor. 14:14, my understanding is **u**
Eph. 5:11, **u** works of darkness
2 Pet. 1:8, **u** in the knowledge
Ungodly—*wicked, sinful*
Ps. 1:1, not in the counsel of the **u**
Prov. 16:27, **u** man diggeth up evil
Rom. 5:6, Christ died for the **u**
Titus 2:12, denying **u**-iness
Jude, 18, after their own **u** lusts
Unjust—*false, not acting justly*
Prov. 29:27, **u** man is an abomination
Matt. 5:45, on the just and on the **u**
Luke 16:10, **u** in the least is **u** also
Acts 24:15, both of the just and the **u**
1 Pet. 3:18, the just for the **u**
2 Pet. 2:9, reserve the **u** unto the day
Rev. 22:11, He that is **u**, let him be **u**
Unknown—*not known*
Acts 17:23, To The U God

1 Cor. 14:2, 4, 14, 19, **u** tongue
2 Cor. 6:9, As **u**, and yet well known
Gal. 1:22, was **u** by face
Unlearned—*without knowledge*
Acts 4:13, were **u** and ignorant men
1 Cor. 14:16, the **u** say Amen at thy
2 Tim. 2:23, foolish and **u** questions
2 Pet. 3:16, that are **u** and unstable
Unprofitable—*worthless*
Job 15:3, reason with **u** talk
Matt. 25:30, cast ye the **u** servant
Luke 17:10, We are **u** servants
Rom. 3:12, are together become **u**
Titus 3:9, they are **u** and vain
Heb. 13:17, for that is **u** for you
Unrighteous—*evil, sinful, wicked*
Ex. 23:1, to be an **u** witness
Lev. 19:15, Ye shall do no **u**-ness
Ps. 71:4, the **u** and cruel man
Is. 55:7, **u** man his thoughts
Jer. 22:13, buildeth his house by **u**-ness
Luke 16:11, faithful in the **u** mammon
Rom. 3:5, Is God **u**
1 Cor. 6:9, **u** shall not inherit the
2 Cor. 6:14, righteousness with **u**-ness
Heb. 6:10, God is not **u** to forget
2 Pet. 2:13, receive the reward of **u**-ness
1 John 5:17, all **u** is sin
Unwise—*foolish, indiscreet*
Deut. 32:6, O foolish people and **u**
Hos. 13:13, He is an **u** son
Rom. 1:14, the wise, and to the **u**
Eph. 5:17, be ye not **u**
Upper—*topmost*
Ex. 12:7, **u** door post of the houses
Matt. 23:6, love the **u**-most rooms
Luke 22:12, large **u** room furnished
Acts 1:13, went into an **u** room
19:1, passed through the **u** coasts
Upright—*vertical, honest, just*
Gen. 37:7, sheaf arose . . . stood **u**
Ex. 15:8, floods stood **u** as an heap
2 Sam. 22:26, wilt shew thyself **u**
Job 1:8, perfect and an **u** man
Ps. 15:2, He that walketh **u**-ly
Prov. 10:9, walketh **u**-ly walketh surely
Eccles. 7:29, God hath made man **u**
Jer. 10:5, **u** as the palm tree
Mic. 7:2, is none **u** among men
Acts 14:10, Stand **u** on thy feet
Gal. 2:14, they walked not **u**-ly
Use—*employment, to employ*
1 Chr. 12:2, **u** both the right hand and

Use (*Continued*)
Matt. 5:44, which despitefully **u** you
2 Cor. 3:12, **u** great plainness of speech
Gal. 5:13, **u** not liberty for an
1 Tim. 5:23, **u** a little wine for thy
1 Pet. 4:9, **U** hospitality one to
Usury—*interest on a loan*
Ex. 22:25, thou lay upon him **u**
Lev. 25:36, Take thou no **u** of him
Deut. 23:20, thou mayest lend upon **u**
Neh. 5:10, let us leave off this **u**
Ps. 15:5, putteth not out . . . to **u**
Prov. 28:8, **u** and unjust gain
Is. 24:2, with the taker of **u**
Matt. 25:27, mine own with **u**
Utter—*speak, give forth, complete*
Lev. 5:1, if he do not **u** it
Judg. 5:12, awake, awake, **u** a song
1 Kin. 20:42, appointed to **u** destruction
Job 15:5, mouth **u**-eth thine iniquity
Ps. 119:171, lips shall **u** praise
Prov. 14:5, false witness will **u** lies
Jer. 1:16, I will **u** my judgments
Zech. 14:11, no more **u** destruction
Rom. 8:26, groanings . . . cannot be **u**-ed
1 Cor. 14:9, **u** by the tongue words
2 Cor. 12:4, not lawful for a man to **u**
Utterance—-*speech*
Acts 2:4, as the Spirit gave them **u**
2 Cor. 8:7, faith, and, **u**, and knowledge
Eph. 6:19, **u** may be given unto me
Col. 4:3, open unto us a door of **u**
Utterly—*completely, fully*
Num. 15:31, soul shall be **u** cut off
Is. 2:18, idols he shall **u** abolish
Jer. 23:39, even I, will **u** forget you
1 Cor. 6:7, is **u** a fault among you
2 Pet. 2:12, shall **u** perish in their
Rev. 18:8, be **u** burned with fire
Uttermost—*extreme, in greatest degree*
Neh. 1:9, **u** part of the heaven
Ps. 2:8, **u** parts of the earth
Matt. 5:26, paid the **u** farthing
Mark 13:27, **u** part of the earth
1 Thess. 2:16, wrath is come . . . to the **u**
Heb. 7:25, to save them to the **u**

V

Vail—*a cover* (*See also:* Veil)
Gen. 24:65, therefore she took a **v**
Ex. 34:33, he put a **v** on his face

Lev. 4:6, the **v** of the sanctuary
Ruth 3:15, Bring the **v** that thou hast
Is. 25:7, **v** . . . spread over all nations
2 Cor. 3:13, put a **v** over his face
Vain—*empty, void, petty, fruitlessly*
Ex. 5:9, not regard **v** words
Lev. 26:16, sow your seed in **v**
Judg. 9:4, hired **v** and light persons
1 Sam. 12:21, **v** things . . . for they are **v**
2 Kin. 18:20, but they are but **v** words
Job 16:3, Shall **v** words have an end
Ps. 2:1, people imagine a **v** thing
33:17, horse is a **v** thing for safety
Prov. 12:11, he that followeth **v** persons
Is. 45:18, he created it not in **v**
Jer. 8:8, pen of the scribes is in **v**
Lam. 2:14, seen **v** and foolish things
Matt. 6:7, use not **v** repetitions
Acts 4:25, people imagine **v** things
Rom. 1:21, **v** in their imaginations
1 Cor. 15:14, then is our preaching **v**
Col. 2:18, **v**-ly puffed up
Gal. 2:21, Christ is dead in **v**
Eph. 5:6, deceive you with **v** words
Phil. 2:3, through strife or **v**-glory
1 Tim. 6:20, profane and **v** babblings
James 1:26, this man's religion is **v**
Valley—*depression between higher lands*
Josh. 10:12, Moon, in the **v** of Ajalon
1 Kin. 20:28, is not God of the **v**-s
2 Kin. 3:16, Make this **v** full of ditches
Ps. 23:4, the **v** of the shadow
Song 2:1, and the lily of the **v**-s
Jer. 31:40, the whole **v** of the dead bodies
Ezek. 37:1, **v** which was full of bones
Joel 3:14, the **v** of decision
Luke 3:5, Every **v** shall be filled
Vanity—*pride, emptiness, worthlessness*
Job 7:16, my days are **v**
Ps. 10:7, under his tongue is . . . **v**
24:4, lifted up his soul unto **v**
Prov. 22:8, soweth iniquity . . . reap **v**
Eccles. 1:2, **V** of **v**-s . . . all is **v**
Jer. 2:5, have walked after **v**
Rom. 8:20, made subject to **v**
Eph. 4:17, walk, in the **v** of their mind
2 Pet. 2:18, great swelling words of **v**
Veil—*a covering* (*See also:* Vail)
Song 5:7 took away my **v**
Matt. 27:51, **v** of the temple was rent
Heb. 6:19, that within the **v**
9:3, after the second **v**

Vengeance—*revenge, harm*
Gen. 4:15, v shall be taken on him
Deut. 32:35, To me belongeth v
Ps. 94:1, God, to whom v belongeth
Is. 34:8, The day of the Lord's v
Rom. 3:5, unrighteous who taketh v
Heb. 10:30, V belongeth unto me
Jude 7, v of eternal fire
Verily—*so be it, in fact, in very truth*
Ex. 31:13, V my sabbaths ye shall keep
Ps. 37:3, v thou shalt be fed
Is. 45:15, V thou art a God that
Matt. 5:18, for v I say unto you
John 1:51, V, v I say unto you
Acts 19:4, John v baptized
Rom. 15:27, hath pleased them v
Very—*exceedingly, true, actual*
Gen. 1:31, behold, it was v good
Num. 12:3, Moses was v meek
Deut. 28:43, v high . . . v low
Judg. 3:17, a v fat man
1 Sam. 5:11, hand of God was v heavy
2 Chr. 6:18, God in v deed
Ps. 46:1, v present help in trouble
Prov. 17:9, separateth v friends
Is. 16:6, he is v proud
Jer. 4:19, pained at my v heart
Ezek. 33:32, a v lovely song
Matt. 15:28, whole from that v hour
Mark 16:2, v early in the morning
Luke 12:7, the v hairs of your head
Acts 9:22, that this is v Christ
2 Cor. 11:5, v chiefest apostles
1 Thess. 5:23, the v God of peace
James 5:11, the Lord is v pitiful
Vessel—*a hollow utensil, a person*
Ex. 7:19, v-s of wood . . . v-s of stone
Num. 5:17, holy water in an earthen v
1 Kin. 17:10, a little water in a v
2 Kin. 4:3, borrow thee v-s abroad
Ps. 31:12, I am like a broken v
Jer. 48:11, emptied from v to v
Matt. 25:4, wise took oil in their v-s
John 19:29, set a v full of vinegar
Acts 9:15, he is a chosen v
Rom. 9:22, v-s of wrath
2 Cor. 4:7, treasure in earthen v-s
2 Tim. 2:21, be a v unto honour
1 Pet. 3:7, as unto the weaker v
Rev. 2:27, as the v-s of a potter
Vesture—*clothing*
Gen. 41:42, in v-s of fine linen
Ps. 22:18, cast lots upon my v

Matt. 27:35, my v did they cast lots
Heb. 1:12, as a v shalt thou fold
Rev. 19:16, on his v and on his thigh
Vex—*make angry, trouble*
Ex. 22:21, neither v a stranger
Job 19:2, long will ye v my soul
Is. 63:10, v-ed his holy Spirit
Ezek. 32:9, v the hearts of many
Matt. 15:22, v-ed with a devil
Luke 6:18, v-ed with unclean spirits
Acts 12:1, v certain of the church
2 Pet. 2:8, v-ed his righteous soul
Victory—*defeat of an enemy, conquest*
2 Sam. 23:10, Lord wrought a great v
1 Chr. 29:11, the glory, and the v
Ps. 98:1, holy arm . . . gotten him the v
Is. 25:8, swallow up death in v
Matt. 12:20, judgment unto v
1 Cor. 15:54, Death is swallowed up in v
55, grave, where is thy v
1 John 5:4, v that overcometh the world
Rev. 15:2, the v over the beast
Vile—*low, base, worthless, impure*
1 Sam. 3:13, his sons made themselves v
Job 40:4, I am v; what shall I
Ps 15:4, a v person is contemned
Jer. 29:17, make them like v figs
Rom. 1:26, unto v affections
Phil. 3:21, change our v body
James 2:2, poor man in v raiment
Vine—*a climbing plant*
Gen. 40:9, a v was before me
Judg. 9:12, said the trees unto the v
1 Kin. 4:25, every man under his v
Ps. 128:3, wife shall be as a fruitful v
Song 2:13, v-s with the tender grape
Is. 36:16, eat ye every one of his v
Jer. 2:21, planted thee a noble v
Ezek. 19:10, mother is like a v in thy
Joel 1:12, The v is dried up
Mal. 3:11, your v cast her fruit
Matt. 26:29, drink . . . fruit of the v
John 15:1, I am the true v
Vinegar—*soured fruit juices*
Ruth 2:14, dip thy morsel in the v
Ps. 69:21, gave me v to drink
Prov. 10:26, As v to the teeth
Matt. 27:48, spunge . . . filled it with v
John 19:29, set a vessel full of v
Vineyard—*a planting of grape vines*
Gen. 9:20, and he planted a v
Lev. 19:10, shalt not glean thy v
1 Kin. 21:1, Naboth . . . had a v

VINEYARD

Vineyard (*Continued*)
Song 1:6, own v have I not kept
Is. 1:8, as a cottage in a v
Jer. 12:10, pastors have destroyed my v
Matt. 20:4, Go ye also into the v
1 Cor. 9:7, planteth a v, and eateth
Violence—*fierceness, outrage, assault*
Gen. 6:11, earth was filled with v
Ps. 55:9, v and strife in the city
Prov. 4:17, drink the wine of v
Is. 53:9, he had done no v
Jer. 22:3, do no v to the stranger
Mic. 2:2, covet fields . . . take them by v
Luke 3:14, Do v to no man
Heb. 11:34, Quenched the v of fire
Violent—*fierce, passionate*
Ps. 18:48, delivered me from the v man
Prov. 16:29, v man enticeth . . . neighbour
Is. 22:18, v-ly turn and toss thee
Matt. 8:32, swine ran v down a steep
Viper—*a poisonous snake*
Job 20:16, v's tongue shall slay him
Is. 30:6, v and fiery flying serpent
Matt. 3:7, O generation of v-s
Acts 28:3, came a v out of the heat
Virgin—*a chaste maid*
Gen. 24:16, fair to look upon, a v
Ex. 22:17, the dowry of v-s
Jer. 31:13, v rejoice in the dance
Matt. 1:23, v shall be with child
25:1, likened unto ten v-s
Luke 1:27, the v's name was Mary
1 Cor. 7:28, if a v marry
2 Cor. 11:2, a chaste v to Christ
Virtue—*power, moral excellence, chastity*
Ruth 3:11, thou art a v-ous woman
Prov. 12:4, v-ous woman is a crown to
Mark 5:30, v had gone out of him
Phil. 4:8, if there be any v
2 Pet. 1:5, to your faith v . . . v knowledge
Vision—*supernatural sight, a dream*
Gen. 15:1, came to Abram in a v
1 Sam. 3:1, there was no open v
Job 20:8, as a v of the night
Prov. 29:18, Where there is no v
Is. 22:1, burden of the valley of v
Lam. 2:9, find no v from the Lord
Dan. 2:19, revealed . . . in a night v
Joel 2:28, young men shall see v-s
Hab. 2:2, Write the v, and make it plain
Matt. 17:9, Tell the v to no man
Acts 2:17, young men shall see v-s
2 Cor. 12:1, come to v-s and revelations

Visit—*call upon, go to see*
Gen. 50:24, God will surely v you
Ex. 20:5, v-ing the iniquity of the
Job 7:18, v him every morning
Ps. 8:4, that thou v-est him
Is. 26:16, trouble have they v-ed thee
Jer. 15:15, remember me, and v me
Lam. 4:22, he will v thine iniquity
Matt. 25:36, sick, and ye v-ed me
Luke 1:68, v-ed and redeemed his people
James 1:27, v the fatherless and
Voice—*sound uttered by the mouth*
Gen. 3:8, heard the v of the Lord
Ex. 4:8, v of the latter sign
Deut. 4:30, be obedient unto his v
Josh. 6:10, make any noise with your v
2 Sam., 19:35, V of singing men
1 Kin. 19:12, the fire a still small v
Job 4:10, the v of the fierce lion
Ps. 19:3, where their v is not heard
Prov. 5:13, the v of my teachers
Eccles. 5:3, a fool's v is known
Song 2:12, the v of the turtle
Is. 28:23, Give ye ear, and hear my v
40:3, v of him that crieth in the
Jer. 7:34, v of mirth . . . v of gladness
9:10, v of the cattle
Dan. 4:31, fell a v from heaven
Matt. 2:18, Rama was there a v heard
3:17, lo a v from heaven
Mark 9:7, v came out of the cloud
Luke 3:4, v of one crying . . . wilderness
John 5:25, v of the Son of God
Acts 10:13, came a v to him, Rise, Peter
1 Cor. 14:10, many kinds of v-s
Gal. 4:20, and to change my v
1 Thess. 4:16, the v of the archangel
Heb. 12:26, v then shook the earth
2 Pet. 2:16, dumb ass . . . with a man's v
Rev. 3:20, if any man hear my v
5:11, heard the v of many angels
Void—*containing nothing, empty*
Gen. 1:2, without form, and v
Deut. 32:28, a nation v of counsel
Ps. 119:126, have made v thy law
Prov. 7:7, man v of understanding
Is. 55:11, not return unto me v
Jer. 19:7, make v the counsel
Acts 24:16, conscience v of offense
Rom. 4:14, faith is made v
Vomit—*throw up, matter thrown up*
Job 20:15, shall v them up again
Prov. 26:11, dog returneth to his v
Is. 19:14, staggereth in his v

186

Jonah 2:10, it v-ed out Jonah
2 Pet. 2:22, dog is turned to his own **v**
Vow—*a solemn promise, make a promise*
Gen. 28:20, Jacob v-ed a **v**
Lev. 7:16, sacrifice . . . be a **v**
Deut. 23:22, if thou shalt forbear to **v**
Judg. 11:30, Jephthah v-ed a **v**
2 Sam. 15:7, let me go and pay my **v**
Ps. 22:25, I will pay my v-s before
Eccles. 5:5, not **v** . . . **v** and not pay
Acts 18:18, for he had a **v**

W

Wages—*pay for services rendered*
Gen. 29:15, what shall thy **w** be
Ex. 2:9, I will give thee thy **w**
Lev. 19:13, **w** of him that is hired
Jer. 22:13, service without **w**
Hag. 1:6, earneth **w** to put it into a
Mal 3:5, oppress the hireling in his **w**
Luke 3:14, be content with your **w**
John 4:36, that reapeth receiveth **w**
2 Pet. 2:15, **w** of unrighteousness
Wail—*weep or cry loudly*
Esther 4:3, and weeping, and w-ing
Jer. 9:19, a voice of w-ing is heard
Mic. 1:8, I will **w** and howl
Matt. 13:42, w-ing and gnashing of
Mark 5:38, wept and w-ed greatly
Rev. 1:7, kindreds of the earth shall **w**
Wait—*to stop or remain, to attend upon*
Gen. 49:18, w-ed for thy salvation
Josh. 8:4, ye shall lie in **w**
2 Kin. 5:2, she w-ed on Naaman's wife
Job 14:14, appointed time will I **w**
17:13, If I **w**, the grave is mine
Ps. 25:5, on thee do I **w** all the day
27:14, **W** on the Lord . . . **w**, I say, on
37:34, **W** on the Lord, and keep his
Prov. 1:18, lay **w** for their own blood
7:12, lieth in **w** at every corner
Is. 26:8, Lord, have we w-ed for thee
30:18, will the Lord **w**
Lam. 3:10, as a bear lying in **w**
Dan. 12:12, Blessed is he that w-eth
Hos. 6:9, as . . . robbers **w** for a man
Mic. 7:2, all lie in **w** for blood
Hab. 2:3, though it tarry, **w** for it
Zech. 11:11, poor of the flock that **w**
Mark 15:43, w-ed for the kingdom

Luke 12:36, men that **w** for their
John 5:3, w-ing for the moving of the
Acts 10:7, that w-ed on him continually
Rom. 8:23, w-ing for the adoption
1 Cor. 1:7, w-ing for the coming of our
Gal. 5:5, **w** for the hope of
Eph. 4:14, they lie in **w** to deceive
Walk—*move by steps, conduct one's self*
Gen. 3:8, God w-ing in the garden
5:24, Enoch w-ed with God
Ex. 14:29, w-ed upon dry land
Lev. 26:3, If ye **w** in my statutes
Josh. 18:8, Go and **w** through the land
1 Sam. 2:30, **w** before me for ever
1 Kin. 2:4, **w** before me in truth
Job 1:17, w-ing up and down in it
18:8, he w-eth upon a snare
22:14, w-eth in the circuit of
Ps. 1:1, w-eth not in the counsel of
15:2, He that w-eth uprightly
23:4, **w** through the valley of the
26:3, have w-ed in thy truth
39:6, w-eth in a vain shew
Prov. 10:9, w-eth uprightly w-eth surely
28:10, w-eth uprightly . . . be saved
Eccles. 2:14, fool w-eth in darkness
10:7, princes w-ing as servants
Is. 2:3, we will **w** in his paths
Is. 2:5, **w** in the light of the Lord
3:16, w-ing and mincing as they go
9:2, people that w-ed in darkness
20:2, w-ing naked and barefoot
Jer. 2:5, have w-ed after vanity
9:14, w-ed after the imagination
Ezek. 36:12, cause men to **w** upon you
Hos. 11:10, They shall **w** after the Lord
Joel 2:8, **w** every one in his path
Amos 3:3, Can two **w** together, except
Mic. 6:8, to **w** humbly with thy God
Nah. 2:5, shall stumble in their **w**
Zeph. 1:17, shall **w** like blind men
Mal. 2:6, w-ed with me in peace
Matt. 9:5, Arise, and **w**
14:29, he w-ed on the water
Mark 1:16, he w-ed by the sea of Galilee
Luke 13:33, **w** to day, and to morrow
John 6:19, Jesus w-ing on the sea
7:1, would not **w** in Jewry
Acts 3:6, name of Jesus . . . rise up and **w**
14:8, cripple . . . never had w-ed
Rom. 6:4, **w** in newness of life
8:1, **w** not after the flesh
1 Cor. 3:3, carnal, and **w** as men

Walk (*Continued*)
2 Cor. 4:2, w-ing in craftiness
    5:7, w by faith, not by sight
Gal. 5:16, W in the Spirit
    6:16, w according to this rule
Eph. 4:1, w worthy of the vocation
    5:2, w in love, as Christ also
    8, w as children of light
Col. 2:6, so w ye in him
    4:5, W in wisdom
1 Thess. 2:12, w worthy of God
1 Pet. 5:8, devil . . . w-eth about, seeking
1 John 2:6, so to w, even as he w-ed
Jude 16, w-ing after their own lusts
Rev. 3:4, shall w with me in white
    21:24, saved shall w in the light
Wall—*a barrier, a defense*
Gen. 49:22, branches run over the w
Ex. 14:22, waters were a w into them
Josh. 2:15, she dwelt upon the w
1 Kin. 20:30, w fell upon twenty and
2 Kin. 20:2, turned his face to the w
Neh. 4:6, So built we the w
Job 24:11, oil within their w-s
Ps. 18:29, have I leaped over a w
Prov. 18:11, high w in his own conceit
Is. 25:4, as a storm against the w
Ezek. 8:7, behold a hole in the w
    12:5, Dig thou through the w
Joel 2:9, shall run upon the w
Amos 7:7, w made by a plumbline
Hab. 2:11, stone shall cry out of the w
Acts 9:25, down by the w in a basket
    23:3, smite thee, thou whited w
Eph. 2:14, middle w of partition
Heb. 11:30, the w-s of Jericho fell
Rev. 21:12, had a w great and high
Wander—*to roam, to stray, to go astray*
Gen. 21:14, w-ed in the wilderness
Deut. 27:18, maketh the blind to w
Job 15:23, w-eth abroad for bread
Ps. 55:7, then would I w far off
Prov. 27:8, bird . . . w-eth from her nest
Eccles. 6:9, the w-ing of the desire
Is. 16:2, as a w-ing bird cast out
Lam 4:14, have w-ed as blind men
Hos. 9:17, w-ers among the nations
1 Tim. 5:13, w-ing . . . house to house
Jude 13, w-ing stars, to whom is
Want—*need, have need of, desire*
Deut. 28:48, in w of all things
Judg. 18:10, place where there is no w
Job 30:3, For w and famine they were
Ps. 23:1, shepherd; I shall not w

Prov. 10:21, fools die for w of wisdom
Is. 34:16, none shall w her mate
Ezek. 4:17, may w bread and water
Dan. 5:27, and art found w-ing
Luke 15:14, he began to be in w
John 2:3, when they w-ed wine
Titus 1:5, in order the things . . . w-ing
James 1:4, w-ing nothing
War—*contest between large groups*
Gen. 14:2, made w with Bera
Ex. 13:17, repent when they see w
Num. 21:14, book of the w-s of . . . Lord
Deut. 24:5, new wife . . . not go out to w
Josh. 11:23, the land rested from w
2 Sam. 17:8, thy father is a man of w
Ps. 46:9, maketh w-s to cease
    55:21, w was in his heart
Prov. 20:18, with good advice make w
Eccles. 3:8, a time of w . . . of peace
Is. 2:4, neither . . . learn w any more
    21:15, the grievousness of w
Ezek. 26:9, shall set engines of w
Dan. 9:26, the w of desolations
Mic. 2:8, as men averse from w
Matt. 24:6, hear of w-s . . . rumours of w-s
Luke 14:31, what king, going to make w
Rom. 7:23, w-ring against the law of my
1 Cor. 9:7, Who goeth a w-fare any time
2 Cor. 10:3, do not w after the flesh
    4, weapons of our w-fare are
1 Tim. 1:18 mightest w a good w-fare
James 4:1, whence come w-s
    1, that w in your members
1 Pet. 2:11, which w against the soul
Rev. 12:7, there was w in heaven
    19:11, he doth judge and make w
Warm—*having heat or ardor*
2 Kin. 4:34, flesh of the child waxed w
Job 31:20, w-ed with the fleece of my
Eccles. 4:11, how can one be w alone
Is. 47:14, not be a coal to w at
Hag. 1:6, but there is none w
Mark 14:54, w-ed himself at the fire
John 18:25, Peter stood and w-ed
James 2:16, be ye w-ed and filled
Warn—*to notify, to admonish*
2 Kin. 6:10, God told him and w-ed him
Ezek. 33:8, speak to w the wicked
Acts 20:31, ceased not to w every one
1 Cor. 4:14, beloved sons I w you
Col. 1:28, w-ing every man
1 Thess. 5:14, w them that are unruly
Heb. 11:7, being w-ed of God

Wash—*cleanse with water, to take away*
Gen. 18:4, w your feet, and rest
Ex. 19:10, let them w their clothes
2 Sam. 11:2, saw a woman w-ing herself
1 Kin. 22:38, one w-ed the chariot in
2 Kin. 5:10, Go and w in Jordan seven
Job 9:30, w myself with snow water
Ps. 26:6, w mine hands in innocency
    51:2, W me . . . from mine iniquity
Song 5:12, eyes . . . w-ed with milk
Is. 1:16, W you, make you clean
Jer. 4:14, w thine heart
Ezek. 16:9, w-ed away thy blood
Matt. 6:17, w thy face
    15:2, w not their hands when
Mark 7:4, except they w, they eat not
Luke 7:44, w-ed my feet with tears
    11:38, first w-ed before dinner
John 9:7, Go, w in the pool of Siloam
Acts 22:16, and w away thy sins
1 Cor. 6:11, ye are w-ed . . . sanctified
1 Tim. 5:10, she have w-ed the saints'
Heb. 9:10, drinks, and divers w-ings
    10:22, bodies w-ed with pure
Rev. 1:5, w-ed us from our sins

Waste—*desolate, stripped bare*
Lev. 26:31, will make your cities w
1 Kin. 17:14, barrel of meal shall not w
Job 14:10, man dieth, and w-th away
Ps. 79:7, laid w his dwelling place
Is. 5:6, I will lay it w
    23:14, your strength is laid w
Joel 1:7, hath laid my vine w
Nah. 3:7, Nineveh is laid w
Matt. 26:8, To what purpose is this w
Luke 15:13, there w-d his substance
Gal. 1:13, church of God, and w-d it

Watch—*be awake, to observe, a guard*
Gen. 31:49, Lord w between me and thee
Ex. 14:24, in the morning w
2 Kin. 11:5, keepers of the w
2 Chr. 23:6, keep the w of the Lord
Job 7:12, settest a w over me
Ps. 63:6, in the night w-es
Prov. 8:34, w-ing daily at my gates
Is. 21:5, w in the w-tower
Matt. 24:42, W wherefore: for ye know
    26:42, W wherefore: for ye know
    26:40, could ye not w with me
Mark 13:37, unto you . . . unto all, W
Luke 2:8, keeping w over their flock
Acts 20:31, Therefore W, and remember
1 Cor. 16:13, W ye, stand fast in the
2 Cor. 11:27, in w-ings often

1 Thess. 5:6, let us w and be sober
2 Tim. 4:5, w thou in all things
Heb. 13:17, they w for your souls
1 Pet. 4:7, and w unto prayer
Rev. 16:15, Blessed is he that w-eth

Watchman, Watchmen—*guards, sentinels*
2 Kin. 9:17, stood a w on the tower
Song 3:3, w that go about the city
Is. 21:11, W, what of the night
Hos. 9:8, w of Ephraim

Water—*fluid which falls as rain*
Gen. 1:2, upon the face of the w-s
    24:43, virgin cometh . . . to draw w
Ex. 2:10, drew him out of the w
    20:4, the w under the earth
Deut. 8:7, land of brooks of w
Josh. 7:5, melted, and became as w
Judg. 5:4, clouds also dropped w
    6:38, fleece, a bowl full of w
2 Sam. 14:14, as w split on the ground
1 Kin. 13:22, Eat no bread . . . drink no w
2 Kin. 3:11, w on the hands of Elijah
Neh. 9:11, a stone into the mighty w-s
Job 8:11, flag grow without w
    9:30, wash myself with snow w
    11:16, as w-s that pass away
    14:19, The w-s wear the stones
Ps. 1:3, planted by the rivers of w
    6:6, w my couch with my tears
    22:14, poured out like w
    23:2, beside the still w-s
    46:3, w-s . . . roar and be troubled
Prov. 5:15, w-s out of thine own cistern
    9:17, stolen w-s are sweet
    20:5, heart . . . is like deep w
Eccles. 11:1, thy bread upon the w-s
Song 5:12, eyes of doves . . . rivers of w-s
Is. 1:30, garden that hath no w
    11:9, as the w-s cover the sea
    19:5, w-s shall fail from the sea
    32:2, rivers of w in a dry place
Jer. 2:13, the fountain of living w-s
    8:14, w of gall to drink
Lam. 1:16, eye runneth down with w
Ezek. 4:11, drink also w by measure
Dan. 1:12, pulse to eat, and w to drink
Matt. 3:11, baptize you with w
    10:42, little ones a cup of cold w
Mark 14:13, man bearing a pitcher of w
Luke 7:44, gavest me no w for my feet
John 3:5, man be born of w and of
    4:10, given thee living w
Acts 1:5, John . . . baptized with w
    8:36, See, here is w; what doth

Water (*Continued*)
1 Cor. 3:6, have planted, Appolos w-ed
2 Cor. 11:26, in perils of w-s
Eph. 5:26, washing of w by the word
1 Tim. 5:23, Drink no longer w
James 3:11, sweet w and bitter
1 Pet. 3:20, eight souls were saved by w
2 Pet. 3:5, out of the w and in the w
1 John 5:6, that came by w and blood
Rev. 22:17, take the w of life freely
Waves—*swells on the surface of a liquid*
2 Sam. 22:5, w of death compassed me
Job 9:8, treadeth . . . w of the sea
Ps. 42:7, w and thy billows are gone
Is. 48:18, righteousness as the w
Matt. 8:24, covered with the w
Mark 4:37, w beat into the ship
Jude 13, Raging w of the sea
Wax—*grow bigger, a fatty solid*
Gen. 26:13, And the man w-ed great
Ex. 16:21, when the sun w-ed hot
Lev. 25:47, stranger w rich
Num. 11:23, Lord's hand w-ed short
Deut. 8:4, Thy raiment w-ed not old
1 Sam. 3:2, eyes began to w dim
Job 6:17, time they w warm
Ps. 22:14, my heart is like w
Is. 50:9, w old as a garment
Matt. 24:12, love of many shall w cold
Luke 2:40, child grew, and w-ed strong
1 Tim. 5:11, w wanton against Christ
2 Tim. 3:13, seducers shall w worse
Heb. 11:34, w-ed valiant in fight
Way—*direction, path*
Gen. 3:24, w of the tree of life
Num. 20:17, go by the king's high w
Deut. 8:6, to walk in his w-s
Josh. 23:14, the w of all the earth
1 Sam. 12:23, teach . . . good . . . right w
2 Sam. 22:33, he maketh my w perfect
2 Kin. 17:13, Turn ye from your evil w-s
2 Chr. 18:23, Which w went the Spirit
Ezra 8:21, seek of him a right w
Neh. 9:19, w wherein they should go
Job 3:23, a man whose w is hid
12:24, wilderness where there is no w
Ps. 1:6, the w of the righteous
18:30, God, his w is perfect
25:8, teach sinners in the w
Prov. 3:17, w-s are w-s of pleasantness
6:6, ant . . . consider her w-s
7:27, Her house is the w to hell
12:15, w of a fool is right in

Eccles. 11:15 the w of the spirit
Is. 2:3, he will teach us of his w-s
26:7, w of the just is uprightness
30:21, This is the w, walk ye in it
35:8, w . . . called The w of holiness
Is. 40:3, Prepare ye the w of the Lord
Jer. 2:36, about so much to change thy w
6:16, where is the good w
12:1, w of the wicked prosper
Lam. 3:40, searched and try our w-s
Ezek. 3:18, wicked from his wicked w
7:3, judge . . . according to thy w-s
Joel 2:7, march every one on his w-s
Nah. 1:3, his w in the whirlwind
Hab. 3:6, his w-s are everlasting
Mal. 3:1, prepare the w before me
Matt. 7:13, broad is the w
15:32, lest they faint in the w
Mark 1:3, Prepare ye the w of the Lord
9:33, ye disputed . . . by the w
Luke 1:79, into the w of peace
19:36, spread their clothes in the w
John 1:23, straight the w of the Lord
14:6, I am the w, the truth, and
Acts 9:2, found any of this w
27, had seen the Lord in the w
Rom. 3:17, w of peace . . . not known
1 Cor. 4:17, w-s which be in Christ
12:31, a more excellent w
Heb. 5:2, them that are out of the w
10:20, By a new and living w
James 1:8, unstable in all his w-s
5:20, from the error of his w
2 Pet. 2:2, follow their pernicious w-s
15, forsaken the right w
Jude 11, gone in the w of Cain
Weak—*lacking strength, feeble*
Num. 13:18, they be strong or w
Judg. 16:17, I shall become w
2 Chr. 15:7, let not your hands be w
Is. 14:10, also become w as we
Ezek. 7:17, knees . . . w as water
Joel 3:10, w say, I am strong
Matt. 26:41, but the flesh is w
Mark 14:38, but the flesh is w
Acts 20:35, ought to support the w
Rom. 4:19, being not w in faith
1 Cor. 1:27, w things of the world
4:10, we are w, but ye are
2 Cor. 10:10, his bodily presence is w
1 Thess. 5:14, support the w

Weakness—*lack of strength*
1 Cor. 1:25, **w** of God is stronger than
2:3, with you in **w**, and in fear
15:43, it is sown in **w**
2 Cor. 12:9, strength is . . . perfect in **w**
13:4, crucified through **w**
Heb. 11:34, out of **w** were made strong
Wealth—*riches, possessions*
Deut. 8:18, giveth thee power to get **w**
Ruth 2:1, a mighty man of **w**
2 Chr. 1:11, not asked riches, **w**
Ezra 9:12, nor seek their . . . **w**
Esther 10:3, seeking the **w**
Job. 21:13, spend their days in **w**
Ps. 49:6, that trust in their **w**
Prov. 13:11, **W** gotten by vanity
Eccles. 5:19, given riches and **w**
Acts 19:25, by this craft . . . our **w**
1 Cor. 10:24, every man another's **w**
Weapon—*implement of offense or defense*
Deut. 1:41, every man his **w**-s of war
2 Chr. 23:10, his **w** in his hand
Neh. 4:17, other hand held a **w**
Job 20:24, flee from the iron **w**
Eccles. 9:18, Wisdom is better than **w**-s
Jer. 21:4, turn back the **w**-s of war
Ezek. 32:27, down to hell with their **w**-s
2 Cor. 10:4, **w**-s of our warfare
Wear—*to have on, to waste away*
Ex. 18:18, Thou wilt surely **w** away
Deut 22:5, woman shall not **w** that
1 Sam. 2:28, to **w** an ephod
Job 14:19, The waters **w** the stones
Dan. 7:25, **w** out the saints of the
Matt. 11:8, that **w** soft clothing
Luke 9:12, day began to **w** away
John 19:5, Jesus . . . **w**-ing the crown of
James 2:3, that **w**-eth the gay clothing
1 Pet. 3:3, and of **w**-ing of gold
Weary—*tired, fatigued, irked*
Gen. 27:46, I am **w** of my life
Judg. 4:21, I fast asleep and **w**
2 Sam. 17:2, while he is **w** and weak
Job 3:17, there the **w** be at rest
Ps. 69:3, I am **w** of my crying
Prov. 25:17, lest he be **w** of thee
Eccles. 12:12, a **w**-ness of the flesh
Is. 5:27, None shall be **w** nor stumble
Jer. 6:11, **w** with holding in
Hab. 2:13, **w** themselves for very vanity
John 4:6, **w**-ed with his journey
2 Cor. 11:27, In **w**-ness and painfulness
Gal. 6;9, not be **w** in well doing

Weather—*state of the atmosphere*
Job. 37:22, Fair **w** . . . out of the north
Prov. 25:20, a garment in cold **w**
Matt. 16:2, will be fair **w**
3, It will be foul **w**
Week—*period of seven days*
Gen. 29:27, Fulfil her **w**, and we will
Ex. 34:22, observe the feast of **w**-s
Dan. 9:24, Seventy **w**-s are determined
Matt. 28:1, first day of the **w**
Luke 18:12, fast twice in the **w**
Weep—*shed tears*
Gen. 43:30, he sought where to **w**
Num. 11:13, for they **w** unto me
Deut. 34:8, days of **w**-ing and mourning
1 Sam. 1:8, why **w**-est thou
Neh. 8:9, mourn not, nor **w**
Job 16:16, face is foul with **w**-ing
Ps. 6:8, heard the voice of my **w**-ing
Eccles. 3:4, A time to **w**, and a time to
Is. 22:4, I will **w** bitterly
Jer. 9:1, might **w** day and night
Joel 1:5, Awake, ye drunkards, and **w**
Matt. 2:18, Rachel **w**-ing for her
Mark 5:39, this ado, and **w**
Luke 6:21, Blessed are ye that **w** now
John 11:31, unto the grave to **w**
Acts 9:39, widows stood by him **w**-ing
Rom. 12:15, do rejoice, and **w**
James 4:9, afflicted, and mourn, and **w**
Rev. 5:5, **W** not: behold, the Lion of
Weigh—*determine the heft of, ascertain*
Gen. 23:16, Abraham **w**-ed . . . the silver
1 Sam. 2:3, by him actions are **w**-ed
Job 6:2, Oh that my grief were . . . **w**-ed
Ps. 58:2, **w** the violence of your hands
Prov. 16:2, the Lord **w**-eth the spirits
Is. 26:7, **w** the path of the just
Dan. 5:27, Thou art **w**-ed in the
Weight—*relative heaviness, heavy mass*
Gen. 24:22, of half a shekel **w**
Lev. 19:36, Just balances, just **w**-s
Deut. 25:15, a perfect and just **w**
Job 28:25, make the **w** for the winds
Prov. 11:1, just **w** is his delight
Ezek. 4:16, shall eat bread by **w**
Mic. 6:11, bag of deceitful **w**-s
2 Cor. 4:17, eternal **w** of glory
Heb. 12:1, let us lay aside every **w**
Well—*source of water, in health, rightly*
Gen. 4:7, doest **w** . . . doest not **w**
Ex. 4:14, I know that he can speak **w**
Lev. 24:16, as **w** the stranger
Deut. 4:40, that it may go **w** with thee

Well (*Continued*)
1 Sam. 9:10, W said
2 Sam. 17:21, they came up out of the w
2 Kin. 3:19, stop all w-s of water
1 Chr. 11:17, of the w of Bethlehem
Job 33:31, Mark w, O Job
Ps. 48:13, Mark ye w her bulwarks
Prov. 5:15, out of thine own w
Eccles. 8:13, not be w with the wicked
Song 4:15, a w of living waters
Is. 1:17, Learn to do w
Jonah 4:4, Doest thou w to be angry
Matt., 3:17, in whom I am w pleased
Mark 7:37, hath done all things w
Luke 6:26, men shall speak w of you
John 4:6, Jacob's w was there
Acts 15:29, shall do w. Fare ye w
Rom. 2:7, continuance in w doing
Gal. 5:7, Ye did run w
1 Tim. 3:4, ruleth w his own house
Heb. 13:16, sacrifices God is w pleased
2 Pet. 2:17, w-s without water

Wept—*cried*
Gen. 50:17, Joseph w when they
Ex. 2:6, behold, the babe w
Matt. 26:75, went out, and w
Luke 7:32, ye have not w
    19:41, beheld the city, and w over
John 11:35, Jesus w
Rev. 5:4, And I w much

West—*opposite the sunrise*
Gen. 12:8, having Beth-el on the w
Ex. 10:19, mighty strong w wind
Ps. 107:3, east, and from the w
Dan. 8:4, saw the ram pushing w-ward

Wet—*damp or soaked with water*
Job 24:8, w with the showers
Dan. 4:15, w with the dew of heaven

Whale—*a great sea animal*
Gen. 1:21, God created great w-s
Job. 7:12, Am I a sea, or a w
Ezek. 32:2, as a w in the seas
Matt. 12:40, three nights in the w's

Whatsoever—*no matter what*
Gen. 31:16, W God hath said unto thee
Job 37:12, do w he commandeth
Ps. 1:3, w he doeth shall prosper
Eccles. 9:10, W thy hand findeth to do
Jer. 1:7, w I command thee
Matt. 7:12, w ye would that men should
Luke 12:3, w ye have spoken
John 11:22, w thou wilt ask of God
Rom. 14:23, w is not of faith
1 Cor. 10:31, w ye do, do all to the

Gal. 6:7, w a man soweth
Eph. 6:8, w good thing any man
Phil. 4:8, w things are true . . . honest
Col. 3:17, w ye do in word or deed

Wheat—*a cereal grain*
Gen. 30:14, in the days of w harvest
Ex. 34:22, firstfruits of w harvest
Deut. 8:8, A land of w, and barley
Judg. 6:11, son Gideon threshed w
1 Sam. 12:17, Is it not w harvest to day
Job 31:40, thistles grow instead of w
Jer. 23:28, What is the chaff to the w
Matt. 3:12, gather his w into the
Luke 22:31, he may sift you as w
John 12:24, corn of w fall into the
Rev. 6:6, measure of w for a penny

Wheel—*a circular frame or disk*
1 Kin. 7:33, work of a chariot w
Ps. 83:13, God, make them like a w
Prov. 20:26, bringeth the w over
Eccles. 12:6, w broken at the cistern
Is. 5:28, w-s like a whirlwind
Ezek. 1:16, w in the middle of a w
Dan. 7:9, his w-s as burning fire
Nah. 3:2, the rattling of the w-s

Whelp—*young of beasts of prey*
Gen. 49:9, Judah is a lion's w
Deut. 33:22, Dan is a lion's w
2 Sam. 17:8, a bear robbed of her w-s
Jer. 51:38, shall yell as lion's w-s
Nah. 2:11, the lion's w

Where—*at or in what place*
Gen. 3:9, W art thou
Ruth 1:17, W thou diest, will I die
Job 28:12, w shall wisdom be found
Ps. 42:3, W is thy God
Prov. 29:18, W there is no vision
Is. 19:12, w are thy wise men
Matt. 2:2, W is he that is born
Luke 8:25, W is your faith
John 8:19, W is thy Father
    11:34, W have ye laid him
Rom. 4:15, w no law is
1 Cor. 1:20, W is the wise

Whet—*to sharpen*
Deut. 32:41, w my glittering sword
Ps. 64:3, Who w their tongue
Eccles. 10:10, do not w the edge

Whip—*a lash*
1 Kin. 12:11, chastised you with w-s
Prov. 26:3, A w for the horse
Nah. 3:2, The noise of a w

Whirlwind—*a violent, destructive wind*
2 Kin. 2:1, into heaven by a w

192

Job 37:9, Out of the south cometh . . . w
Ps. 58:9, away as with a w
Prov. 1:27, destruction cometh as a w
Is. 17:13, rolling thing before the w
Jer. 4:13, chariots shall be as a w
Hos. 8:7, they shall reap the w
Whisper—*low speech*
Ps. 41:7, hate me w together
Prov. 16:28, w-er separateth . . . friends
Rom. 1:29, deceit, malignity; w-ers
2 Cor. 12:20, w-ings, swellings, tumults
White—*like snow, pure, uncolored*
Gen. 49:12, teeth w with milk
Num. 12:10, leprous, w as snow
Job 6:6, taste in the w of an egg
Ps. 51:7, shall be w-r than snow
Song 5:10, My beloved is w
Is. 1:18, they shall be as w as snow
Dan. 7:9, garment was w as snow
Matt. 5:36, one hair w or black
Luke 9:29, raiment was w and glistening
John 4:35, w already to harvest
Acts 23:3, thou w-d wall
Rev. 6:2, behold a w horse
Whither—*to what place*
Gen. 28:15, all places w thou goest
Ex. 21:13, place w he shall flee
Ruth 1:16, w thou goest, I will go
1 Sam. 27:10, W have ye made a road
Ps. 139:7, W shall I go from thy
John 8:21, w I go, ye cannot come
Whole—*entire, complete, vigorous*
Gen. 2:6, watered the w face
2 Sam. 1:9, my life is yet w in me
Job 5:18, his hands make w
Eccles. 12:13, the w duty of man
Matt. 6:22, w body . . . full of light
Luke 5:31, w need not a physician
John 5:6, Wilt thou be made w
Acts 9:34, Jesus Christ maketh thee w
1 Cor. 5:6, leaveneth the w lump
Eph. 6:11, the w armour of God
1 John 2:2, sins of the w world
Whomsoever—*any person*
Gen. 44:9, w of thy servants
Matt. 26:48, W I shall kiss, that same
Luke 12:48, unto w much is given
Acts 8:19, on w I lay hands
1 Cor. 16:3, w ye shall approve
Wicked—*evil, sinful*
Gen. 38:7, w in the sight of the Lord
Ex. 23:1, put not thine hand with the w

Lev. 20:17, it is a w thing
Deut. 23:9, keep thee from every w
2 Sam. 24:17, I have done w-ly
Job 8:22, w shall come to nought
10:15, If I be w, woe unto me
11:20, eyes of the w shall fail
Ps. 7:11, God is angry with the w
10:13, doth the w contemn God
12:8, w walk on every side
17:13, deliver my soul from the w
Prov. 4:19, way of the w is as darkness
10:30, w shall not inhabit the
11:7, When a w man dieth
13:9, lamp of the w . . . put out
Eccles. 7:17, Be not over much w
Is. 53:9, made his grave with the w
Ezek. 3:18, warn the w from his w way
Dan. 12:10, w shall do w-ly
Matt. 12:45, this w generation
Acts 2:23, w hands have crucified
2 Thess. 2:8, shall that W be revealed
1 John 2:13, overcome the w one
Wickedness—*sin, evil*
Gen. 6:5, the w of man was great
Judg. 20:3, Tell us, how was this w
1 Kin. 21:25, sell himself to work w
Job 4:8, plow iniquity, and sow w
Ps. 5:9, their inward part is very w
Prov. 4:17, they eat the bread of w
Is. 9:18, w burneth as the fire
Jer. 14:20, We acknowledge . . . our w
Ezek. 3:19, turn not from his w
Hos. 10:13, Ye have plowed w
Matt. 22:18, Jesus perceived their w
Acts 8:22, Repent . . . of this thy w
Eph. 6:12, spiritual w in high places
1 John 5:19, whole world lieth in w
Wide—*broad, having great extent*
Deut. 15:8, open thine hand w
1 Chr. 4:40, land was w
Job 29:23, opened their mouth w
Ps. 104:25, this great and w sea
Prov. 21:9, woman in a w house
Jer. 22:14, build me a w house
Nah. 3:13, shall be set w open
Matt. 7:13, for w is the gate
Widow—*woman who has lost her husband*
Gen. 38:11, Remain a w at thy father's
Ex. 22:22, Ye shall not afflict any w
Lev. 21:14, A w, or a divorced woman
2 Sam. 14:5, I am indeed a w woman
Job 22:9, sent w-s away empty
Ps. 68:5, and a judge of the w-s

Widow (*Continued*)
Is. 1:17, plead for the **w**
Matt. 23:14, ye devour **w-s'** houses
Mark 12:43, **w** hath cast more in
Luke 18:5, this **w** troubleth me
1 Tim. 5:3, Honour **w-s** that are **w-s**
Wife—*a married woman*
Gen. 2:24, and shall cleave unto his **w**
Ex. 20:17, not covet thy neighbour's **w**
Lev. 18:15, she is thy son's **w**
Job 31:10, let my **w** grind unto another
Ps. 128:3, Thy **w** . . . as a fruitful vine
Prov. 18:22, findeth a **w** findeth a
Eccles. 9:9, Live joyfully with the **w**
Matt. 5:31, Whosoever . . . away his **w**
Mark 1:30, Simon's **w's** mother
Luke 17:32, Remember Lot's **w**
1 Cor. 7:2, every man have his own **w**
Eph. 5:23, husband . . . head of the **w**
1 Tim. 3:2, the husband of one **w**
1 Pet. 3:7, giving honour unto the **w**
Wild—*savage, rude*
Gen. 16:12, he will be a **w** man
Lev. 26:22, send **w** beasts
Job 11:12, born like a **w** ass's colt
Ps. 104:11, **w** asses quench their thirst
Is. 5:2, brought forth **w** grapes
Jer. 50:39, **w** beasts of the desert
Mark 1:6, did eat locusts and **w** honey
Acts 10:12, **w** beasts, and creeping
Wilderness—*desert or waste land*
Gen. 16:7, fountain of water in the **w**
Ex. 14:11, away to die in the **w**
Lev. 7:38, in the **w** of Sinai
Deut. 29:5, forty years in the **w**
Ps. 65:12, the pastures of the **w**
Prov. 21:19, better to dwell in the **w**
Is. 40:3, voice . . . that crieth in the **w**
Matt. 3:3, voice . . . crying in the **w**
Mark 1:13, there in the **w** forty days
1 Cor. 10:5, overthrown in the **w**
Heb. 3:8, day of temptation in the **w**
Rev. 12:6, woman fled into the **w**
Will—*determine to, inclination, desire*
Ps. 40:8, delight to do thy **w**
Matt. 6:10, Thy **w** be done
    7:21, doeth the **w** of my Father
Mark 3:35, shall do the **w** of God
Luke 2:14, peace, good **w** toward men
    22:42, not my **w**, but thine
John 1:13, **w** of the flesh . . . **w** of man
    4:34, **w** of him that sent me
Acts 21:14, **w** of the Lord be done
Rom. 12:2, and perfect, **w** of God

1 Cor. 4:19, if the Lord **w**
Eph. 5:17, what the **w** of the Lord is
Phil. 2:13, both to **w** and to do
Heb. 10:9, I come to do thy **w**, O God
James 4:15, If the Lord **w**, we shall
Willing—*ready, desirous to do or be*
Gen. 24:5, will not be **w** to follow
Ex. 35:5, is of a **w** heart
1 Chr. 28:9, and with a **w** mind
Ps. 110:3, shall be **w** in the day
Is. 1:19, If ye be **w** and obedient
Matt. 26:41, spirit indeed is **w**
Luke 22:42, Father, if thou be **w**
1 Cor. 9:17, if I do this thing **w-ly**
2 Cor. 8:12, be first a **w-mind**
2 Pet. 3:9, not **w** that any . . . perish
Win—*gain by skill or effort*
2 Chr. 32:1, to **w** them for himself
Prov. 11:30, he that **w-neth** souls is
Phil. 3:8, that I may **w** Christ
Wind—*air in motion*
Gen. 8:1, God made a **w** to pass over
1 Kin. 19:11, **w** rent the mountains
2 Kin. 3:17, Ye shall not see **w**
Job 7:7, my life is **w**
Ps. 1:4, chaff which the **w** driveth
Prov. 11:29, shall inherit the **w**
Eccles. 5:16, laboured for the **w**
Song 4:16, Awake, O north **w**
Is. 7:2, trees . . . moved with the **w**
Jer. 22:22, **w** . . . eat up all thy pastors
Ezek. 37:9, Come from the four **w-s**
Hos. 8:7, they have sown the **w**
Matt. 7:25, floods came . . . **w-s** blew
Mark 4:41, **w** and the sea obey him
Luke 8:24, rebuked the **w**
John 3:8, **w** bloweth where it listeth
Acts 2:2, as of a rushing mighty **w**
Eph. 4:14, every **w** of doctrine
James 3:4, driven of fierce **w-s**
Jude 12, carried about of **w-s**
Rev. 6:13, shaken of a mighty **w**
Window—*opening in a wall*
Gen. 7:11, **w-s** of heaven were opened
Josh. 2:15, by a cord through the **w**
Judg., 5:28, Sisera looked out at a **w**
2 Kin. 7:12, make **w-s** in heaven
Is. 60:8, as the doves to their **w-s**
Jer. 9:21, death is come up into our **w-s**
Joel 2:9, enter in at the **w-s** like a
Acts 20:9, sat in a **w** a certain
2 Cor. 11:33, through a **w** in a basket
Wine—*liquor obtained from fruits*
Gen. 9:24, Noah awoke from his **w**

Ex. 29:40, part of an hin of w
Lev. 10:9, Do not drink w
1 Sam. 11:4, put away thy w from thee
2 Sam. 13:28, heart is merry with w
Ps. 60:3, the w of astonishment
Prov. 3:10, burst out with new w
Eccles. 9:7, drink thy w with a merry
Song 1:2, thy love is better than w
Is. 5:22, mighty to drink w
Jer. 35:6, We will drink no w
Matt. 9:17, new w into old bottles
Mark 15:23, w mingled with myrrh
Luke 10:34, pouring in oil and w
John 2:9, water that was made w
Acts 2:13, men are full of new w
Eph. 5:18, be not drunk with w
1 Tim. 3:3, Not given to w
Rev. 6:6, hurt not the oil and the w
Wings—*organs used for flying*
Ex. 19:4, bare you on eagles' w
Lev. 1:17, cleave it with the w
Deut. 32:11, beareth them on her w
Ruth 2:12, under whose w thou are
2 Sam. 22:11, upon the w of the wind
Job 39:13, goodly w unto the peacocks
Ps. 17:8, under the shadow of thy w
Prov. 23:5, riches . . . make themselves w
Is. 6:2, each one had six w
Jer. 48:9, Give w unto Moab
Ezek. 1:6, every one had four w
Zech 5:9, wind was in their w
Mal. 4:2, with healing in his w
Matt. 23:37, chickens under her w
Luke 13:34, her brood under her w
Wink—*open and shut the eye lids*
Job 15:12, what do thy eyes w at
Ps. 35:19, w with the eye
Prov. 6:13, He w-eth with his eyes
Acts 17:30, ignorance God w-ed at
Winter—*season of the coldest months*
Gen. 8:22, summer and w . . . not cease
Song 2:11, w is past, the rain is over
1 Cor. 16:6, I will . . . w with you
Wipe—*clean or dry by rubbing*
2 Kin. 21:13, as a man w-th a dish
Prov. 6:33, reproach . . . not be w-d away
Is. 25:8, God will w away tears
John 11:2, w-d his feet with her hair
Rev. 21:4, shall w away all tears
Wisdom—*prudence, discretion*
Ex. 28:3, filled with the spirit of w

1 Kin. 2:6, Do . . . according to thy w
1 Chr. 22:12, the Lord give thee w
2 Chr. 1:10, Give me now w
Job 12:2, and w shall die with you
Ps. 51:6, make me to know w
Prov. 1:7, fools despise w
    4:5, Get w, get understanding
Eccles. 1:18, in much w is much grief
    7:12, w giveth life
Jer. 9:23, wise man glory in his w
Mic. 6:9, man of w shall see thy name
Matt. 11:19, w is justified of her
Luke 2:52, increased in w and stature
    21:15, give you a mouth and w
1 Cor. 1:17, not with w of words
2 Cor. 1:12, not with fleshly w
James 1:5, If any of you lack w
Rev. 13:18, Here is w
Wise—*sensible, sage, manner or mode*
Gen. 3:6, tree . . . to make one w
Ex. 23:8, gift blindeth the w
Num. 6:23, On this w ye shall bless
Job 17:10, cannot find one w man
Ps. 19:7, making w the simple
Prov. 3:7, not w in thine own eyes
Is. 19:12, where are thy w men
Matt. 2:1, came w men from the east
    10:16, w as serpents
Luke 10:21, hid these things from the w
Acts 7:6, God spake on this w
Rom. 1:14, w, and to the unwise
1 Cor. 1:19, destroy the wisdom of the w
    3:18, that he may be w
Eph. 5:15, not as fools, but as w
2 Tim. 3:15, w unto salvation
James 3:13, Who is a w man
Jude 25, only w God our Saviour
Withdraw—*draw or take back or away*
1 Sam. 14:19, W thine hand
Job 9:13, God will not w his anger
Prov. 25:17, W thy foot from thy
Joel 2:10, stars . . . w their shining
2 Thess. 3:6, w yourselves
1 Tim. 6:5, from such w thyself
Wither—*dry up*
Ps. 1:3, leaf also shall not w
    37:2, and w as the green herb
Is. 19:6, reeds and flags shall w
Joel 1:12, joy is w-ed away
Matt. 13:6, no root, they w-ed away
Mark 3:1, man . . . had a w-ed hand
Jude 12, trees whose fruit w-eth
Withhold—*keep back, hoard*
Gen. 23:6, shall w from thee

Withhold (*Continued*)
Job 22:7, w-en bread from the hungry
Prov. 11:24, w-eth more than is meet
    26, He that w-eth corn
Within—*on the inner side*
Gen. 9:21, uncovered w his tent
Ps. 51:10, renew a right spirit w me
Prov. 22:18, keep them w thee
Ezek. 11:19, a new spirit w you
Matt. 23:26, that which is w the cup
Mark 7:23, evil things come from w
Luke 17:21, kingdom of God is w you
Acts 5:23, we found no man w
1 Cor. 5:12, Judge them that are w
2 Cor. 7:5, fightings, w were fears
Rev. 5:1, throne a book written w
Without—*on the outside of, lacking*
Gen. 1:2, earth was w form, and void
Deut. 32:25, sword w, and terror
2 Chr. 15:3, been w the true God
Job 5:9, things w number
    8:11, rush grow up w mire
Prov. 1:20, Wisdom crieth w
Is. 10:4, W me they shall bow down
    52:3, redeemed w money
Ezek. 2:10, written within and w
Hos. 7:11, like a silly dove w heart
Matt. 10:29, w your Father
    13:57, prophet is not w honour
Mark 14:58, made w hands
John 1:3, w him was not any thing made
    8:7, He that is w sin
Rom. 3:28, faith w the deeds
    12:9, love be w dissimulation
1 Cor. 11:11, man w the woman
2 Cor. 7:5, w were fightings
Eph. 2:12, time ye were w Christ
Col. 2:11, made w hands
1 Thess. 5:17, Pray w ceasing
1 Tim. 6:14, commandment w spot
Heb. 7:3, W father, w mother, w descent
James 2:20, faith w works is dead
1 Pet. 1:19, w blemish and w spot
2 Pet. 2:17, are wells w water
Jude 12, w fear . . . w water . . . w fruit
Rev. 22:15, For w are dogs
Witness—*one who gives evidence, to attest*
Gen. 31:48, w between me and thee
Ex. 20:16, shalt not bear false w
Deut. 4:26, call heaven and earth to w
Judge. 11:10, Lord be w between us
Job 16:19, my w is in heaven
Ps. 89:37, faithful w in heaven

Prov. 6:19, false w that speaketh
Is. 19:20, for a sign and for a w
Matt. 19:18, not bear false w
Mark 10:19, Do not bear false w
Luke 22:71, need we any further w
John 1:7, to bear w of the Light
Acts 26:22, w-ing both to small and
Rom. 1:9, For God is my w
1 Cor. 15:15, we are found false w-s
Titus 1:13, This w is true
Heb. 10:15, Holy Ghost also is a w
1 John 5:9, receive the w of men
Rev. 1:5, Christ . . . the faithful w
Wives—*married women*
Deut. 17:17, Neither shall he multiply w
Ezra 10:2, have taken strange w
Eph. 5:22, W, submit yourselves unto
1 Tim. 4:7, old w' fables
1 Pet. 3:1, w, be in subjection
Woe—*grief, sorrow, affliction*
Num. 21:29, W to thee, Moab
Job 10:15, If I be wicked, w unto me
Ps. 120:5, W is me, that I sojourn
Prov. 23:29, Who hath w? who hath
Is. 6:5, said I, W is me
Jer. 4:13, W unto us! for we are
Matt. 11:21, W unto thee, Chorazin
Mark 14:21, w to that man by whom
Rev. 8:13, W, w, w, to the inhabiters
Wolf—*a wild animal*
Gen. 49:27, shall ravin as a w
Is. 65:25, w and the lamb shall feed
Jer. 5:6, w of the evenings
Matt. 7:15, they are ravening w-ves
Woman—*an adult female person*
Gen. 2:23, she shall be called W
Ex. 2:9, w took the child
Deut. 22:5, man put on a w's garment
Ruth 3:11, thou art a virtuous w
1 Sam. 1:15, a w of a sorrowful spirit
Job 14:1, Man that is born of a w
Prov. 11:16, gracious w retaineth
    12:4, virtuous w is a crown
Is. 49:15, w forget her sucking child
Matt. 5:28, looketh on a w to lust
    15:28, O w, great is thy faith
Luke 7:44, Simon, Seest thou this w
    10:38, certain w named Martha
John 4:7, w of Samaria to draw water
    8:4, w was taken in adultery
Acts 9:36, w was full of good works
1 Cor. 7:1, a man not to touch a w
    2, w have her own husband

Gal. 4:4, his Son, made of a **w**
1 Tim. 2:11, Let the **w** learn in silence
Rev. 12:1, **w** clothed with the sun
Womb—*uterus, any place of generation*
Gen. 25:23, Two nations are in thy **w**
Ex. 13:2, whatsoever openeth the **w**
Num. 12:12, out of his mother's **w**
Deut. 7:13, bless the fruit of thy **w**
Ruth 1:11, more sons in my **w**
Job 1:21, Naked . . . out of my
  mother's **w**
Ps. 110:3, from the **w** of the morning
Prov. 30:16, the barren **w**
Is. 44:2, formed thee from the **w**
Luke 1:41, babe leaped in her **w**
John 3:4, enter . . . into his mother's **w**
Acts 3:2, from his mother's **w**
Women—*adult females*
Gen. 31:35, custom of **w** is upon me
Judg. 5:24, Blessed above **w** shall
2 Sam. 1:26, passing the love of **w**
1 Kin. 11:1, loved many strange **w**
Prov. 31:3, not thy strength unto **w**
Song 1:8, O thou fairest among **w**
Is. 4:1, seven **w** . . . take hold of one
Jer. 50:37, they shall become as **w**
Matt. 24:41, Two **w** shall be grinding
Mark 15:40, also **w** looking on afar off
Luke 1:28, blessed art thou among **w**
1 Cor. 14:35, **w** to speak in the church
1 Tim. 2:9, **w** adorn themselves in
2 Tim. 3:6, silly **w** laden with sins
Titus 2:4, young **w** to be sober
1 Pet. 3:5, the holy **w** also
Wonder—*something strange, be surprised*
Deut. 4:34, by signs, and by **w**-s
Job 9:10, **w**-s without number
Ps. 71:7, I am as a **w** unto many
Is. 9:6, his name shall be called **W**-ful
Jer. 4:9, the prophets shall **w**
Dan. 6:27, signs and **w**-s in heaven
Joel 2:30, shew **w**-s in the heavens
Matt. 15:31, the multitude **w**-ed
Acts 2:11, the **w**-ful works of God
Rom. 15:19, mighty signs and **w**-s
2 Thess. 2:9, and signs and lying **w**-s
Rev. 12:1, a great **w** in heaven
  13:3, and all the world **w**
Wondrous—*strange, marvelous*
1 Chr. 16:9, of all his **w** works
Job 37:14, the **w** works of God
Ps. 71:17, I declared thy **w** works
  72:18, who only doeth **w** things
Joel 2:26, dealt **w**-ly with you

Wood—*timber, a collection of trees*
Gen. 6:14, an ark of gopher **w**
Deut. 19:5, into the **w** . . . to hew **w**
2 Sam. 18:8, **w** devoured more people
2 Kin. 2:24, she bears out of the **w**
1 Chr. 16:33, trees of the **w** sing out
2 Chr. 2:16, we will cut **w** out of
Neh. 8:4, stood upon a pulpit of **w**
Job 41:27, and brass as rotten **w**
Ps. 83:14, As the fire burneth a **w**
Prov. 26:20, Where no **w** is . . . the fire
Eccles. 10:9, he that cleaveth **w**
Jer. 7:18, The children gather **w**
Lam. 5:4, our **w** is sold unto us
Ezek. 24:10, Heap on **w**, kindle the fire
1 Cor. 3:12, stones, **w**, hay, stubble
Rev. 18:12, of most precious **w**
Wool—*the fleece of sheep*
Deut. 22:11, **w**-len and linen together
Judg. 6:37, a fleece of **w** in the floor
Ps. 147:16, He giveth snow like **w**
Is. 1:18, they shall be as **w**
Ezek. 44:17, no **w** . . . come upon them
Dan. 7:9, hair . . . like the pure **w**
Heb. 9:19, scarlet **w**, and hyssop
Rev. 1:14, his hairs were white like **w**
Word—*a part of speech, scripture*
Gen. 15:1, **w** of the Lord . . . unto Abram
  30:34, according to thy **w**
Ex. 20:1, God spake all these **w**-s
Lev. 10:7, according to the **w** of Moses
Num. 30:2, he shall not break his **w**
Deut. 5:5, shew you the **w** of the Lord
Josh. 24:26, wrote these **w**-s in the book
Judg. 13:12, Now let thy **w**-s . . . to pass
1 Sam. 3:1, **w** of the Lord was precious
2 Kin. 18:36, answered him not a **w**
2 Chr. 6:17, Let thy **w** be verified
Ezra 6:11, whosoever shall alter this **w**
Job 2:13, none spake a **w** unto him
  6:25, how forcible are right **w**-s
  12:11, Doth not the ear try **w**-s
Ps. 12:6, **w**-s of the Lord are pure **w**-s
  19:14, Let the **w**-s of my mouth
Prov. 15:1, grievous **w**-s stir up anger
  23, **w** spoken in due season
Eccles. 5:2, Let thy **w**-s be few
Is. 5:24, despised the **w** of the Holy
  29:11, **w**-s of a book that is sealed
Jer. 5:13, the **w** is not in them
Mal. 1:1, The burden of the **w**

Word (*Continued*)
Matt. 4:4, every w that proceedeth
    8:8, speak the w only
    12:36, every idle w that men
Mark 4:14, sower soweth the w
    7:13, w of God of none effect
Luke 1:2, ministers of the w
    4:4, but by every w of God
    32, his w was with power
    36, What a w is this
John 1:1, beginning was the W
    14, W was made flesh
    6:68, the w-s of eternal life
Acts 2:41, his w were baptized
    6:7, the w of God increased
Rom. 10:8, w is nigh thee . . . w of faith
1 Cor. 1:17, not with wisdom of w-s
    4:20, kingdom of God is not in w
2 Cor. 4:2, w of God deceitfully
Gal. 5:14, law is fulfilled in one w
Eph. 5:6, deceive you with vain w-s
Phil. 2:16, Holding forth the w of life
Col. 3:16, Let the w of Christ dwell
1 Thess. 1:5, gospel came not . . . in w
  only
2 Thess. 2:17, you in every good w
1 Tim. 4:5, sanctified by the w of God
    5:17, who labour in the w
2 Tim. 2:15, dividing the w of truth
Titus 1:9, Holding fast the . . . w
Heb. 2:2, w spoken by angels
    4:12, w of God is quick
James 1:21, the engrafted w
    22, be ye doers of the w
1 Pet. 1:23, w of God, which liveth
2 Pet. 1:19, sure w of prophecy
1 John 1:1, handled, of the w of life
Jude 16, great swelling w-s
Rev. 19:13, is called The w of God
Work—*effort, to employ effort*
Gen. 2:2, God ended his w
Ex. 20:9, Six days . . . do all thy w
Lev. 23:3, Six days shall w be done
Deut. 4:28, the w of men's hands
1 Sam. 14:6, the Lord will w for us
1 Chr. 23:4, w of the house of the Lord
2 Chr. 15:7, your w shall be rewarded
Neh. 4:6, the people had a mind to w
Job 7:2, for the reward of his w
Ps. 9:1, shew . . . thy marvelous w-s
    14:1, done abominable w-s
    62:12, man according to his w
Prov. 11:18, wicked w-eth a deceitful w
    16:3, Commit thy w-s . . . the Lord

Eccles. 7:13, Consider the w of God
    11:5, knowest not the w-s of God
Is. 5:19, make speed, and hasten his w
    10:12, Lord . . . performed his whole w
Jer. 22:13, giveth him not for his w
Hab. 1:5, I will w a w in your days
Matt. 5:16, see your good w-s
Mark 6:5, there do no mighty w
Luke 13:14, men ought to w
John 5:17, w-eth hitherto, and I w
    6:28, might w the w-s of God
    9:4, w the w-s of him that sent
Acts 5:38, or this w be of men
Rom. 2:15, shew the w of the law
    8:28, things w together for good
1 Cor. 3:13, man's w . . . made manifest
    14, If any man's w abide
Gal. 5:19, w-s of the flesh are
Eph. 2:9, Not of w-s, lest any man
    4:12, for the w of the ministry
Phil. 2:12, w out your own salvation
Col. 1:10, fruitful in every good w
2 Thess. 3:10, if any would not w
1 Tim. 6:18, be rich in good w-s
2 Tim. 4:5, w of an evangelist
Titus 3:1, ready to every good w
Heb. 6:1, repentance from dead w-s
James 1:4, patience have her perfect w
    2:18, my faith by my w-s
1 John 3:8, destroy the w-s of the devil
Rev. 2:2, I know thy w-s, and thy
    14:13, their w-s do follow them
Workers—*those who put forth effort*
2 Kin. 23:24, w with familiar spirits
Ps. 5:5, hatest all w of iniquity
Prov. 10:29, w of iniquity
Luke 13:27, me, all ye w of iniquity
1 Cor. 12:29, w of miracles
2 Cor. 6:1, We then, as w together
Phil. 3:2, beware of evil w
Working—*doing work*
Ps. 52:2, like a sharp razor, w
Ezek. 46:1, shut the six w days
Mark 16:20, the Lord w with them
1 Cor. 4:12, w with our own hands
2 Thess. 2:9, after the w of Satan
Workman—*laborer, artisan*
Ex. 38:23, engraver, and a cunning w
Matt. 10:10, w is worthy of his meat
Eph. 2:10, For we are his w-ship
World—*all creation*
2 Sam. 22:16, the foundations of the w
1 Chr. 16:30, w also shall be stable
Job 34:13, disposed the whole w

Ps. 17:14, from men of the **w**
Prov. 8:26, of the dust of the **w**
Eccles. 3:11, set the **w** in their heart
Is. 14:21, fill . . . the **w** with cities
Matt. 5:14, Ye are the light of the **w**
    12:32, this **w** . . . **w** to come
    13:38, The field is the **w**
Mark 10:30, **w** to come eternal life
Luke 16:8, the children of this **w**
John 1:10, He was in the **w** . . . **w** was
    made by him . . . **w** knew him
    3:16, God so loved the **w**
    4:42, Saviour of the **w**
    6:33, giveth light unto the **w**
    7:7, **w** cannot hate you
    8:12, I am the light of the **w**
Acts 17:6, turned the **w** upside down
Rom. 5:12, sin entered into the **w**
1 Cor. 1:28, base things of the **w**
    2:12, not the spirit of the **w**
2 Cor. 7:10, sorrow of the **w** worketh
Eph. 3:21, all ages, **w** without end
1 Tim. 6:17, that are rich in this **w**
2 Tim. 4:10, loved this present **w**
Heb. 6:5, powers of the **w** to come
James 1:27, unspotted from the **w**
2 Pet. 2:5, spared not the old **w**
1 John 2:15, Love not the **w**
    17, the **w** passeth away
Worm—*small creeping animal*
Ex. 16:20, it bred **w**-s, and stank
Job 7:5, My flesh is clothed with **w**-s
    24:20, **w** shall feed sweetly on him
Ps. 22:6, But I am a **w**
Is. 14:11, and the **w**-s cover thee
Jon. 4:7, God prepared a **w**
Mark 9:44, Where their **w** dieth not
Acts 12:23, he was eaten of **w**-s
Wormwood—*a bitter plant*
Deut. 29:18, that beareth gall and **w**
Prov. 5:4, her end is bitter as **w**
Jer. 23:15, feed them with **w**
Amos 5:7, who turn judgment to **w**
Rev. 8:11, the star is called **W**
Worse—*more bad or evil*
Jer. 7:26, did **w** than their fathers
Matt. 9:16, the rent is made **w**
John 5:14, lest a **w** thing come unto
1 Cor. 11:17, better, but for the **w**
2 Tim. 3:13, shall wax **w** and **w**
Worship—*showing respect and reverence*
Gen. 22:5, go yonder and **w**
Ex. 34:14, shalt **w** no other god

2 Chr. 29:28, all the congregation **w**-ed
Ps. 29:2, **w** the Lord in the beauty of
Is. 66:23, all flesh come to **w**
Mic. 5:13, **w** the work of thine hands
Matt. 2:2, and are come to **w** him
    4:10, shalt **w** the Lord thy God
John 4:20, place where men ought to **w**
    22, Ye **w** ye know not what
Acts 24:14, **w** I the God of my fathers
Phil. 3:3, **w** God in the spirit
Rev. 4:10, **w** him that liveth for ever
Worthy—*deserving, worth consideration*
Gen. 32:10, I am not **w** of the least
Deut. 17:6, **w** of death
1 Sam. 26:16, ye are **w** to die
1 Kin. 1:52, will shew himself a **w** man
Matt. 3:11, shoes I am not **w** to bear
Matt. 10:10, workmen is **w** of his meat
Luke 3:8, fruits **w** of repentance
    10:7, labourer is **w** of his hire
Acts 24:2, very **w** deeds are done
Eph. 4:1, walk **w** of the vocation
1 Thess. 2:12, ye would walk **w** of God
1 Tim. 1:15, **w** of all acceptation
Heb. 11:38, the world was not **w**
Rev. 5:2, Who is **w** to open the book
Wound—*a cut or stab, to hurt violently*
Gen. 4:23, slain a man to my **w**-ing
Ex. 21:25, **w** for **w**, stripe for stripe
Deut. 32:39, I **w**, and I heal
Job 34:6, my **w** is incurable
Ps. 147:3, bindeth up their **w**-s
Prov. 23:29, hath **w**-s without cause
Is. 53:5, **w**-ed for our transgressions
Jer. 30:17, heal thee of thy **w**-s
Luke 10:34, and bound up his **w**-s
Acts 19:16, fled . . . naked and **w**-ed
Wrapped—*enclosed by winding or folding*
Gen. 38:14, a vail, and **w** herself
1 Kin. 19:13, **w** his face in his mantle
Ezek. 21:15, **w** up for the slaughter
Matt. 27:59, **w** it in a clean linen
Mark 15:46, **w** him in the linen
Luke 2:7, **w** him in swaddling clothes
John 20:7, napkin . . . **w** together in a
Wrath—*fury, violent anger*
Gen. 39:19, his **w** was kindled
Ex. 22:24, my **w** shall wax hot
Job 5:2, **w** killeth the foolish man
Ps. 37:8, forsake **w**
Prov. 12:16, fool's **w** is presently known
    14:29, He that is slow to **w**
Eccles. 5:17, much sorrow and **w**

Wrath (*Continued*)
Is. 54:8, a little **w** I hid my face
Matt. 3:7, flee from the **w** to come
John 3:36, the **w** of God abideth
Rom. 2:5, **w** against the day of **w**
Gal. 5:20, emulations, **w**
Eph. 2:3, the children of **w**
    4:26, sun go down upon your **w**
Col. 3:6, **w** of God cometh
1 Thess. 5:9, not appointed us to **w**
Heb. 3:11, I sware in my **w**
James 1:19, slow to speak, slow to **w**
Rev. 6:16, from the **w** of the Lamb
Write—*set down in letters*
Ex. 17:14, **W** this for a memorial
Judg. 5:14, handle the pen of the **w-r**
Prov. 3:3, **w** them upon the table of
Is. 8:1, **w** in it with a man's pen
Hab. 2:2, **W** the vision, and make it
Mark 10:4, **w** a bill of divorcement
John 19:21, **W** not, The King of the Jews
1 Tim. 3:14, things **w** I unto thee
Heb. 10:16, minds will I **w** them
1 John 2:8, new commandment I **w** unto
2 John 12, not **w** with paper and ink
Rev. 14:13, **W**, Blessed are the dead
Writing—*any thing written down*
Ex. 32:16, **w** was the **w** of God
1 Chr. 28:19, made me understand in **w**
2 Chr. 2:11, king . . . answered in **w**
Dan. 5:8, could not read the **w**
Matt. 5:31, a **w** of divorcement
Luke 1:63, asked for a **w** table
John 5:47, ye believe not his **w-s**
Written—*set down in letters*
Ex. 31:18, **w** with the finger of God
Num. 11:26, them that were **w**
Job 19:23, my words were now **w**
Mal. 3:16, book of remembrance was **w**
Matt. 2:5, it is **w** by the prophet
John 19:22, What I have **w** I have **w**
Acts 1:20, **w** in the book of Psalms
Rom. 2:15, law **w** in their hearts
2 Cor. 3:7, **w** and engraven in stones
Philem. 19, **w** it with mine own hand
Rev. 13:8, not **w** in the book of life
    17:5, forehead was a name **w**
Wrong—*not right, an injustice, to harm*
Gen. 16:5, My **w** be upon thee
Ex. 2:13, him that did the **w**
1 Chr. 12:17, no **w** in mine hands
Esther 1:16, queen hath not done **w**
Jer. 22:3, do no **w**, do no violence
Matt. 20:13, Friend, I do thee no **w**

Acts 7:26, ye do **w** one to another
1 Cor. 6:7, ye not rather take **w**
2 Cor. 7:2, we have **w-ed** no man
Wrote—*set down in letters*
Ex. 24:4, Moses **w** all the words
Jer. 36:18, **w** them with ink in the
Mark 12:19, Master, Moses **w**
John 8:6, finger **w** on the ground
Rom. 16:22, Teritus, who **w** this epistle
2 John 5, I **w** a new commandment
3 John 9, I **w** unto the church
Wroth—*angry, indignant*
Gen. 4:6, Why art thou **w**
Esther 1:12, was the king very **w**
Ps. 89:38, thou hast been **w** with
Is. 64:9, Be not **w** very sore
Matt. 2:16, Herod . . . was exceeding **w**
Wrought—*worked*
Gen. 34:7, he had **w** folly in Israel
Lev. 20:12, they have **w** confusion
1 Sam. 14:45, hath **w** with God this day
Neh. 6:16, work was **w** of our God
Eccles. 2:11, that my hands had **w**
Is. 26:12, **w** all our works in us
Jer. 18:3, **w** a work on the wheels
Matt. 20:12, last have **w** but one hour
Mark 14:6, **w** a good work on me
John 3:21, they are **w** in God
Acts 18:3, he abode with them, and **w**
Rom. 15:18, Christ hath not **w** by me
Gal. 2:8, **w** effectually in Peter
2 Thess. 3:8, **w** with labour and travail
1 Pet. 4:3, **w** the will of the Gentiles

Y

Yea—*yes*
Gen. 3:1, **Y**, hath God said, Ye shall
Lev. 35:35, **y**, though he be a
Ps. 23:4, **Y**, though I walk through
Prov. 8:19, gold, **y** than fine gold
Matt. 5:37, communication be, **Y**, **y**
Luke 12:5, **y**, I say unto you
John 11:27, **Y**, Lord: I believe
2 Cor. 1:17, there should be **y y**
Heb. 11:36, **y**, moreover of bonds
James 5:12, but let your **y** be **y**
1 Pet. 5:5, **Y**, all of you be
Rev. 14:13, **Y**, saith the Spirit
Year—*period of the earth's revolution*
Gen. 1:14, for seasons . . . days . . . **y-s**
    7:11, six hundredth **y** of Noah's

Ex. 13:10, in his season from y to y
Lev. 16:34, an atonement . . . once a y
Num. 14:34, each day for a y, shall ye
1 Sam. 7:16, went from y to y in circuit
2 Sam. 14:26, every y's end that he polled
1 Kin. 17:1, dew nor rain these y-s
2 Chr. 14:6, no war in those y-s
Job 10:5, are thy y-s as man's days
Ps. 90:4, thousand y-s in thy sight
Prov. 4:10, y-s of thy life . . . be many
Is. 61:2, acceptable y of the Lord
Jer. 11:23, y of their visitation
Joel 2:25, y-s that the locust . . . eaten
Matt. 2:16, two y-s old and under
Luke 3:23, to be about thirty y-s of age
Gal. 4:10, months, and times, and y-s
Rev. 9:15, day . . . month . . . y
Yesterday—*the day before*
Ex. 5:14, making brick both y
Job 8:9, for we are but of y
Ps. 90:4, in thy sight are but as y
Acts 7:28, the Egyptian y
Heb. 13:8, the same y, and to day
Yet—*nevertheless, in addition*
Gen. 7:4, For y seven days
Ex. 9:34, he sinned y more
Lev. 5:17, y is he guilty
Deut. 9:29, Y they are thy people
Judg. 7:4, people are y too many
Job 13:15, y will I trust in him
Ps. 37:10, For y a little while
Prov. 6:10, Y a little sleep
Is. 28:4, it is y in his hand
Dan. 11:35, y for a time appointed
Jonah 3:4, Y forty days, and Nineveh
Matt. 15:17, not ye y understand
19:20, what lack I y
Mark 12:6, y therefore one son
Luke 24:44, while I was y with you
John 2:4, mine hour is not y come
Rom. 5:6, y without strength
1 Cor. 7:10, y not I, but the Lord
2 Cor. 4:8, y not distressed
Heb. 11:7, things not seen as y
1 John 3:2, y appear what we shall be
Yield—*produce, give up*
Gen. 1:11, the herb y-ing seed
Num. 17:8, blossoms, and y-ed almonds
Ps. 67:6, earth y her increase
Eccles. 10:4, y-ing pacifeth great
Mark 4:8, y fruit that sprang us
Rom. 6:13, Neither y ye your members

Heb. 12:11, y-eth the peaceable fruit
James 3:12, both y salt water and
Yoke—*a draw bar for oxen*
Gen. 27:40, break his y from off thy
Lev. 26:13, the bands of your y
Deut. 28:48, y of iron upon thy neck
1 Sam. 14:14, y of oxen might plow
1 Kin. 12:4, made our y grievous
Is. 9:4, broken the y of his burden
Jer. 27:2, Make thee bonds and y-s
Lam. 1:14, y of my transgressions
Matt. 11:29, Take my y upon you
2 Cor. 6:14, unequally y-ed together
Gal. 5:1, with the y of bondage
1 Tim. 6:1, servants as are under the y
Young—*not old, offspring of animals*
Gen. 4:23, y man to my hurt
Ex. 23:26, shall nothing cast their y
Lev. 4:3, y bullock without blemish
Deut. 32:11, fluttereth over her y
Ruth 2:9, not charged the y men
1 Sam. 8:16, your goodliest y men
Job 19:18, y children despised me
Ps. 37:25, been y, and now am old
Prov. 20:29, glory of y men is their
Eccles. 11:9, Rejoice, O y man, in thy
Is. 11:7, y ones . . . lie down together
Ezek. 17:4, top of his y twigs
Matt. 2:9, where the y child was
John 21:18, When thou wast y, thou
Acts 2:17, y men shall see visions
Titus 2:4, y women to be sober
1 John 2:13, I write . . . y men
Younger—*less old*
Gen. 25:23, elder shall serve the y
Judg. 15:2, not her y sister fairer
Luke 15:13, y son gathered all together
1 Tim. 5:11, But the y widows refuse
1 Pet. 5:5, ye y, submit yourselves
Yours—*that or those belonging to you*
Gen. 45:20, good . . . of Egypt is y
Josh. 2:14, Our life for y, if ye utter
2 Chr. 20:15, battle is not y, but God's
Jer. 5:19, a land that is not y
Luke 6:20, y is the kingdom of God
John 15:20, they will keep y also
1 Cor. 3:21, for all things are y
2 Cor. 12:14, for I seek not y, but you
Yourselves—*you, not others*
Gen. 18:4, rest y under the tree
Ex. 19:12, Take heed to y
Lev. 11:44, sanctify y
Deut. 4:16, Lest ye corrupt y

Yourselves (*Continued*)
Josh. 24:22, witnesses against **y**
2 Chr. 29:31, consecrated **y**
Jer. 37:9, Deceive not **y**
Hos. 10:12, Sow to **y** in righteousness
Matt. 6:19, lay not up for **y** treasures
Mark 9:50, Have salt in **y**
Luke 12:33, provide **y** bags
Acts 20:10, Trouble not **y**
Rom. 6:13, yield **y** unto God
2 Cor. 13:5, Examine **y**
Eph. 5:19, Speaking to **y** in psalms
1 Thess. 5:13, be at peace among **y**
1 John 5:21, keep **y** from idols
Jude 21, Keep **y** in the love of God
Youth—*state of being young*
Gen. 8:21, heart is evil from his **y**
Num. 30:16, yet in her **y**
Judg. 8:20, because he was yet a **y**
Job 33:25, return to the days of his **y**
Ps. 25:7, not the sins of my **y**
Prov. 5:18, with the wife of thy **y**
Eccles. 11:9, Rejoice . . . in thy **y**
Is. 40:30, Even the **y**-s shall faint
Jer. 3:4, art the guide of my **y**
    31:19, bear the reproach of my **y**

Matt. 19:20, kept from my **y** up
Acts 26:4, life from my **y**
1 Tim. 4:12, Let no man despise thy **y**
2 Tim. 2:22, Flee also **y**-ful lusts

Z

Zeal—*earnestness, passionate ardor*
2 Sam. 21:2, slay them in his **z**
2 Kin. 10:16, see my **z** for the Lord
Ps. 119:139, My **z** hath consumed me
Is. 59:17, clad with **z** as a cloak
John 2:17, **z** of thine house hath
Rom. 10:2, have a **z** of God
2 Cor. 7:11, yea, what **z**
Phil. 3:6, Concerning **z**
Col. 4:13, he hath a great **z** for you
Zealous—*fervent, eager, earnest*
Num. 25:11, he was **z** for my sake
Acts 21:20, all **z** of the law
1 Cor. 14:12, **z** of spiritual gifts
Gal. 4:17, They **z**-ly affect you
Titus 2:14, **z** of good works
Rev. 3:19, be **z** therefore, and repent

BIBLE STUDY NOTES

BIBLE STUDY NOTES

BIBLE STUDY NOTES

BIBLE STUDY NOTES

BIBLE STUDY NOTES

BIBLE STUDY NOTES

BIBLE STUDY NOTES

BIBLE STUDY NOTES